LINCOLN CHRISTIAN UNIV

W9-BUT-306

LINCOLN CHRISTIAN UNIVERSITY

THE AMERICAN
CIVIL WAR

THE AMERICAN
CIVIL WAR

AN ANTHOLOGY OF ESSENTIAL WRITINGS

IAN FREDERICK FINSETH

Routledge
Taylor & Francis Group
New York   London

Routledge is an imprint of the
Taylor & Francis Group, an informa business

Published in 2006 by
Routledge
Taylor & Francis Group
270 Madison Avenue
New York, NY 10016

Published in Great Britain by
Routledge
Taylor & Francis Group
2 Park Square
Milton Park, Abingdon
Oxon OX14 4RN

© 2006 by Taylor & Francis Group, LLC
Routledge is an imprint of Taylor & Francis Group

Printed in the United States of America on acid-free paper
10 9 8 7 6 5 4 3 2 1

International Standard Book Number-10: 0-415-97743-6 (Hardcover) 0-415-97744-4 (Softcover)
International Standard Book Number-13: 978-0-415-97743-2 (Hardcover) 978-0-415-97744-9 (Softcover)
Library of Congress Card Number 2006007644

No part of this book may be reprinted, reproduced, transmitted, or utilized in any form by any electronic, mechanical, or other means, now known or hereafter invented, including photocopying, microfilming, and recording, or in any information storage or retrieval system, without written permission from the publishers.

Trademark Notice: Product or corporate names may be trademarks or registered trademarks, and are used only for identification and explanation without intent to infringe.

Library of Congress Cataloging-in-Publication Data

The American Civil War : an anthology of essential writings / edited by Ian Frederick Finseth.
    p. cm.
  Includes bibliographical references and index.
  ISBN 0-415-97743-6 (hardback : alk. paper) -- ISBN 0-415-97744-4 (paperback : alk. paper)
  1. American literature--19th century--History and criticism. 2. United States--History--Civil War, 1861 1865--Literature and the war. 3. War and literature--United States--History--19th century. 4. American literature--19th century--History and criticism. 5. War in literature. I. Finseth, Ian Frederick.

PS217.C58A43 2006
810.9'358--dc22
                                                  2006007644

Taylor & Francis Group
is the Academic Division of Informa plc.

Visit the Taylor & Francis Web site at
http://www.taylorandfrancis.com

and the Routledge Web site at
http://www.routledge-ny.com

CONTENTS

3803

121373

LIST OF ILLUSTRATIONS

Cover: Battle of Chickamauga. Wash drawing by Alfred R. Waud, 1863.

Figure page 1: Alfred R. Waud, artist of *Harper's Weekly*, sketching on battlefield, Gettysburg, Pa., July 1863. Photograph by Timothy H. O'Sullivan.

Figure page 17: The last moments of John Brown. Etching by Thomas Hovenden, 1885.

Figure page 61: Antietam, Md. Bodies of Confederate dead gathered for burial, September 1862. Photograph by Alexander Gardner.

Figure page 187: Co. E, 4th U.S. Colored Infantry, Ft. Lincoln, defenses of Washington.

Figure page 329: Portrait of a musician, 2d Regulars, U.S. Cavalry.

Figure page 377: "Home again." Lithograph by Endicott & Co., 1866.

Figure page 481: Bull Run, Va. Dedication of the battle monument, June 10, 1865. Photograph by William Morris Smith.

Figure page 607: Signifcant Battles, Forts, and Cities.

Figure page 608: Demographic Information: 1860.

Figure page 609: The Election of 1860.

ACKNOWLEDGMENTS

This book would not have come into existence without the generous assistance of my editor at Routledge, Kimberly Guinta; the project editor, Julie Spadaro; Lynn Goeller at EvS Communications; and the anonymous readers who provided astute feedback on the original proposal. I am also deeply grateful to Stephanie Hawkins, whose scholarly insights made the book much better than it otherwise would have been, and whose love and encouragement sustained me during the whole process.

Thanks are due to the following for permission to republish copyrighted or privately owned material: Harvard University Press (Oliver Wendell Holmes, "The Soldier's Faith"; selected poems of Emily Dickinson); Simon & Schuster (selections from Sam Watkins, *Co. Aytch: A Confederate Memoir of the Civil War*); University of Virginia Press (Stephen Crane, "The Battle Hymn"); and Marius B. Péladeau (Portrait of a Musician, 2nd Regulars, U.S. Cavalry). The writings of John Wilkes Booth are in the public domain, but the selection from his diary is reprinted courtesy of Ford's Theatre National Historic Site, National Park Service, and his letter to Mary Ann Holmes Booth is reprinted courtesy of the U.S. National Archives and Records Administration.

INTRODUCTION

Alfred R. Waud, artist of *Harper's Weekly*, sketching on battlefield, Gettysburg, Pa., July 1863. Photograph by Timothy H. O'Sullivan.

INTRODUCTION:
THE WRITTEN WAR

The Rationale and Design of this Book

The purpose of this anthology is to encourage attention to the most significant or compelling writings produced both during the Civil War and in the decades after. By gathering together a generous variety of these works, I have tried to provide readers with an original and dynamic arrangement of writings illustrating the war's influence on the literary imagination and cultural politics of nineteenth-century America.

Surprising though it may be—given the rate at which university and trade presses continue to publish historical and critical studies on the Civil War—there has not yet appeared a single volume devoted to the wide range of primary materials dealing with the war. Single-genre and single-author collections exist, along with scholarly editions of correspondence, memoirs, and documentary material, but thus far one could search in vain for an anthology presenting, in one place, Lincoln's Gettysburg Address and Ambrose Bierce's fiction, Herman Melville's war poetry and Mary Chesnut's diary entries, Louisa May Alcott's short stories and Ulysses S. Grant's memoirs, Frederick Douglass's speeches and Julia Ward Howe's song lyrics.

Taken singly, these writings do not always, or even frequently, convey the full measure of the Civil War's psychic and social impact. Taken together, however, they attain something of the effect of a symphony, in which all the instruments contribute to the musical experience. It is a central argument of this book that Civil War writings, including those of canonical authors such as Walt Whitman or Stephen Crane, are best understood in relation to one another, and in the context of the full range of literary expression that the war stimulated. The piccolo or the tuba when unaccompanied is a lonely voice; in concert with other instruments, they are indispensable.

Deciding what to include, however, and what to leave out, proved a remarkably difficult undertaking. Some choices were obvious, such as Lincoln's second inaugural address or Whitman's "The Real War Will Never Get in the Books." But many more decisions could have gone either way, and for each text that made the cut, several others could not. The sheer volume of available material meant that many early selections had to be borne from the field, casualties of the editorial process, and the ones left standing are the survivors of that process. In the end, this anthology represents just one possible configuration of Civil War writings; ten other editors would have produced ten different collections.

The result is far from random, however. A number of active principles guided the selection of texts. First, priority has been given to literature in which the meanings of the war are not simplified, but explored in their fuller psychological and cultural complexity. Daniel Aaron may be correct in arguing that the Civil War produced no undisputed masterpiece of fiction, and that American writers had trouble assimilating it, but his conclusion that the war was "not so much unfelt as unfaced" does an injustice to the literary record.[1] Certainly the war prompted a good deal of essentially propagandistic writing, along with a slew of indigestible novels and a scattering of literary scraps and shards. Yet it also called forth an impressive number of free-spirited works that took seriously the job of exploring different aspects of the war and its aftermath: the experience of combat, the complexities of race, the implications of violence, and peace, for relationships and families. Epic they are not. But, each in its own way, these more focused writings are passionate, conflicted, amazed, humorous, brooding, and tragic.

Chronologically, the texts range from 1859 (Daniel Emmett's "Dixie") to 1903 (W. E. B. Du Bois's *The Souls of Black Folk*). They include some material only tangentially related to the war itself, but directly related to the war's aftermath and the difficulties of national reconciliation. Throughout the late nineteenth century and into the twentieth, the Civil War made itself felt, both directly and indirectly, not only in the country's literature but in a variety of professional disciplines: philosophy, medical science, psychology, journalism. Here, I have emphasized short stories, poetry, essays, and oratory which reflect a committed imaginative engagement with the Civil War, and which illustrate how the conflict could be soberly interpreted, and creatively reinterpreted, for a variety of audiences. These works represent a range of social perspectives: Southern and Northern, African American and European American, male and female, patrician and plebeian.

In the spirit of inclusiveness and the interest of breadth, this collection includes both canonical works and many less familiar writings by authors whose renown grows dim. There is a double benefit to this approach. The more famous pieces, such as Walt Whitman's "When Lilacs Last in the Dooryard Bloom'd," are brought into sharper relief when restored to the full context of Civil War literary interpretation and remembrance. At the same time, the great variety of noncanonical works help to provide a rich sense of the war's impact on American culture, and a fresh perspective on the development of American literature during the crucial decades before World War I.

To the degree possible, the selection process has been ideologically neutral, valuing literary quality more than literary correctness, but I am also aware that any anthology represents an implicit thesis about its subject matter—in this case, an implicit narrative of American history. To lay the cards on the table, then, it is worth observing up front that this book gives weighty emphasis to the conflicts of race and slavery that lay at the heart of the Civil War and that hardly abated in its echoing aftermath. That is actually not a very eccentric or controversial statement, but it might shed light on certain editorial decisions—on why, for instance, "African American Experience" forms the collection's largest section. More importantly, however, I have tried to design the architecture of this anthology such that there are both resonances among the texts and a built-in tension among different viewpoints. The goal has been a dynamic balance of harmony and discord. The anthology will have succeeded, in part, if rather than simply reproducing the familiar polemics, it conveys a sense of the various meanings the Civil War quickly acquired, and of how thoughtful observers both shaped and navigated those meanings.

As for the many necessary exclusions, several considerations prevailed. With a few exceptions of notable merit or cultural importance, such as Ulysses S. Grant and Mary

Chesnut, I have avoided memoirs, autobiographies, and diaries, preferring to include works in their entirety whenever possible. Novels, for the same reason, do not appear here, although at a number of interesting ones did emerge from the Civil War—notably Rebecca Harding Davis's *Waiting for the Verdict* (1867), John W. De Forest's *Miss Ravenel's Conversion from Secession to Loyalty* (1867), Elizabeth Phelps's *The Gates Ajar* (1868), S. Weir Mitchell's *In War Time* (1885), Paul Laurence Dunbar's *The Fanatics* (1901), and, of course, Stephen Crane's *The Red Badge of Courage* (1896). Other kinds of writing, finally, have been excluded for reasons of space and originality: soldiers' correspondence; antebellum antislavery or proslavery literature; documentary narratives, such as *Battles and Leaders of the Civil War*; and works that are commonly anthologized elsewhere, such as Ambrose Bierce's "Chickamauga."

Organizationally, the anthology is divided into six broad categories meant to give clear definition to a large body of literature by highlighting certain natural connections among the writings. Within each section—"Origins," "Battlefields," "African American Experience," "The Civil War in Song" "The Home Front," and "Remembrance and Forgetting." The texts appear for the most part chronologically, although some writings belonged next to one another regardless of their date of publication. Despite its advantages, the drawbacks of a thematic approach are worth acknowledging. Primarily, it entails a certain pigeon-holing of works and authors. Many works could plausibly fit into more than one category, and some are simply hard to categorize, such as John Wilkes Booth's correspondence or Harriet Beecher Stowe's "The Chimney-Corner." Complex works operate on multiple levels, and the particular organizational decisions here by no means foreclose on alternative ways of conceptualizing the material. In that spirit, the anthology does not segregate African American writers into their own category, even as it is important to highlight African American participation in and perceptions of the war and reconstruction. Accordingly, the section "African American Experience" includes some works by white writers, such as Louisa May Alcott and Thomas Wentworth Higginson, while some works by black writers are included in other groupings, such as George Moses Horton's war poems (in "Battlefields") or Frederick Douglass's "Address on the Unknown Dead" (in "Remembrance and Forgetting").

What this anthology offers, then, is a portrait of war in its broad dimensions. It represents just a fraction of the totality of Civil War literature, but in their psychological, ideological, and stylistic diversity, the writings here should convey something of the scope of the war's influence on American literature and culture.

War and Language

Writing about war—about the organized killing of people, the complex forces that go into that killing, and the profound consequences that flow from it—is almost as old as war itself. War fascinates, appalls, and defies those who would put words to it. It stretches the language we have, and demands that we come up with new language to describe the ever-startling face it shows us.

The essential material of writing is language, and the essential material of war is violence, or what Whitman called "the red business," and these materials, language and violence, intertwine in complex ways. On the one hand, writing seems the apex of civilization, the triumph of culture over nature, while war seems to confirm the survival of a primal, even animalistic, savagery. Social theorists and philosophers of violence have taught us that physical violence, in its overwhelming literalness, can warp and constrain language, which depends on abstraction and metaphor. The suffering of extreme violence so radically departs from ordinary individual experience that it thwarts the human impulse to give voice to that suffering, whether as participant or observer. And violence thrives on the breakdown of language, erupting at the moment when dialogue, negotiation, and self-expression stumble and fail. As long as people are talking, to put it simply, they are not fighting. At the same time, words and war have a long and intimate history, and that history has much to do with how language is used in the furtherance of violence. Elementally, the destructive power of language—in war or in daily life—involves the use of dehumanizing epithets that remove a person from the circle of human empathy, and makes them, so to speak, fair game. In a more general sense, language establishes the full conceptual framework within which a conflict proceeds. It sets the terms by which people understand the violence (including, frequently, the contractual terms governing the conduct of participants); it promotes ideological coherence amidst the chaos of violence; and, in a very practical sense, it enables the planning and coordination necessary for organized violence.[2]

For all that, however, the violence of war is one of the most powerful of stimuli to the creative imagination. Even as violence stymies language, it requires that we use language to represent it—and thus is born the literature of war.

Generalizations about war literature are perilous, but we might hazard a few. To write about war is to write about a human experience that is horrific and yet all too routine. It is to try to communicate something of the moral ambiguity of deliberate killing; of the feelings of soldiers and civilians; of the unexpected artistry of war. Writing about war is to heroize a nation or an ethnic group; to absolve oneself of cowardice or incompetence; or to anatomize a socio-historical moment. It means evaluating the social relations between the men (and women) who fight, their changed relations to those left at home, and the transformation of personality that can take place in combat. It means weighing the pain and the horror against the visceral thrill and sense of glory that war can invoke, and making room for the random absurdities that cling to all wars. And above all, to write about war is to offer some interpretation, implicit or explicit, of what the conflict means for the present.

We can approach these issues as they apply to the Civil War by considering two other defining wars in American history. In her study of King Philip's War, a brutal conflict involving English colonists and Algonquian tribes in 1675–1676, Jill Lepore has explained the impulse to build language out of the destruction of war:

> At first, the pain and violence of war are so extraordinary that language fails us: we cannot name our suffering and, without words to describe it, reality itself becomes confused, even unreal. But we do not remain at a loss for words for long. Out of the chaos we soon make new meanings of our world, finding words to make reality real again.... War twice cultivates language: it requires justification, it demands description.[3]

This "cultivation" of language often leads in the direction of propaganda, toward a restricted and manipulative interpretation of what the war entailed. For the Puritans, in this case, writing about King Philip's War became a means of securing their own English identity over and against both the Native Americans and other European societies. Yet the literary response to war can also lead in more creative, open-ended directions—if a writer chooses to explore the deeper, uncertain meanings of the conflict.

Some three centuries after King Philip's War, Tim O'Brien looked back on his experience in Vietnam and described both the need to articulate that experience and the difficulty in doing so:

> Partly catharsis, partly communication, [telling stories] was a way of grabbing people by the shirt and explaining exactly what had happened to me, how I'd allowed myself to get dragged into a wrong war, all the mistakes I'd made, all the terrible things I had seen and done....By telling stories, you objectify your own experience. You separate it from yourself. You pin down certain truths. You make up others. You start sometimes with an incident that truly happened...and you carry it forward by inventing incidents that did not in fact occur but that nonetheless help to clarify and explain.[4]

This blending of imagination and reportage—even when the goal is "objectivity"—has been a universal feature of the literature of war. From the *Iliad* to *Catch-22* to *Safe Area Gorazde*, communicating the truths of war has required more than the objective transcription of events and details, if such a thing were even possible. It has required many different voices, and a willingness to bend language and to enlist the imagination in order to get at the deeper nerve centers of human experience.

And yet, it is precisely this imaginative dimension of war literature that raises difficult moral questions. Can we rely on the imagination to find the "real story" behind the cold hard facts of war? What do we make of a subjective response to war masquerading as general human truth? Do the aesthetic qualities of literature help to bring home the horrors of war, or make them more remote? Is figurative language a path to understanding or a glorified form of escapism?

Literature of the Civil War

In his second inaugural address, given about a month before the peace settlement at Appomattox, Lincoln observed that neither North nor South had expected the Civil War to become the kind of conflict it grew into: "Each looked for an easier triumph, and a result less fundamental and astounding." The war had stunned and transformed the nation, with a force that the imagination found hard to reckon, and at a cost difficult to fathom. In the literature of the Civil War—even the literature produced during the war itself—one can sense the feeling of staggered awe with which American authors contemplated the wreckage of the conflict. Yet one can also hear other notes: humor, outrage, perplexity, denial, forgiveness, guilt, revenge.

The war evoked a spectrum of writerly responses in the decades that followed. Some authors retreated into fantasies of a Southern golden age; others imagined the reunion of North and South as a romance culminating in marriage. A few writers handled it analytically, even sociologically; many more treated it obliquely, folding it into works whose principal focus lay elsewhere. A number of authors approached the war in its fragments rather than its totality. Some concentrated on its gothic qualities, while others thought its truths were best reported straight, in realistic accounts of battles and episodes. What late nineteenth-century writers found hard to do was to avoid the war altogether.

Literature was a mode of both psychological and social reconstruction. As James Dawes has suggested, the Civil War fundamentally "challenged the communicative and deliberative procedures of the republic," so writing about the war represented a means of repairing and reinforcing those traditions. "The struggle to talk during and after violence," Dawes writes, "is language's struggle to regain mastery over violence, whether manifest in the individual's attempt to speak her trauma or a culture's attempt to produce a literary record."[5] For authors whom the war had affected most directly, such as Ambrose Bierce or Oliver Wendell Holmes, Jr., putting language to their experiences could serve as a probing or a closing of personal wounds. For authors too young to fight in or remember the war, as were many of those represented here, turning to the war enabled them to write about the society the war had created: increasingly consolidated, more economically and politically powerful than ever before, yet still riven by the faultlines of social class and race. The challenge was to discern in the Civil War a source of meaning for the post-bellum period, a pattern of cause and effect, right and wrong, that would serve as philosophical and emotional ballast for Americans who lived in its turbulent wake.

This does not mean that writing about the Civil War or its aftermath was simply an exercise in social healing or a good-faith effort to reinvigorate the traditions of American public discourse. In some cases, war literature became a second front on which the festering conflicts could be fought anew, or on which old scores could be settled. The military phase of the conflict had concluded, but the struggle to define American culture had by no means waned—even when it appeared to be submerged under an outpouring of nostalgia and reconciliationist sentiment. The old adage that history is written by the victors was not entirely borne out by the late nineteenth-century American literary scene. Magazines, novels, newspapers, public speeches, autobiographies—all formed an interpretive arena in which the meanings of the war, and of the racial, political, and economic conflicts that gave rise to the war, were up for grabs. The stakes were high, for what kind of country the United States would become depended in large measure on what kind of war Americans imagined they had fought.

In wars fought between different nations or cultures, with different languages and histories, the process of post-war interpretation does not have the same closed, impacted quality as it does after a civil war. In this case, the veterans, partisans, and commentators inhabit the same political territory, speak the same language, share the same cultural reference points, and look back to the same past, all of which are nonetheless fought over. After King Philip's War, the English colonists did not have to compete with or accommodate Native American interpretations of the conflict; they had only to work out amongst themselves how the war would be remembered. After the Civil War, by contrast, writers from a more or less reintegrated North and South drew from the same bag of cultural tropes and icons and narratives (the martyrdom of Lincoln, the beckoning frontier, the plantation fallen into disrepair), even if they had very different purposes in doing so—and they had to negotiate the expectations of the same publishing industry and of overlapping, increasingly self-aware reading publics.

The production and consumption of Civil War literature between the 1860s and the early 1900s did not take place in a vacuum, but rather in a kind of literary ecosystem involving writers, editors, publishers, distribution syndicates, critics, and readers. It thrived, indeed, in a burgeoning periodical culture in which the number of American newspapers rose from about 4,000 in 1860 to almost 19,000 in 1899, while the number of other periodicals rose from about 700 in 1865 to more than 3,000 in 1885.[6] Newspapers, illustrated weeklies, and monthly magazines regularly published fiction, poetry, commentary, and, in serial form, novels dealing with the war and its legacies—including the work of such major authors as Mark Twain, Kate Chopin, Henry James, and many others. Significantly, not only the newspapers but the big literary magazines represented a far-reaching geographic diversity: the *Atlantic Monthly* (Boston), *Putnam's Monthly Magazine*, *Harper's Monthly*, the *Century*, and the *Galaxy* (all New York); the *Southern Magazine* (Baltimore), the *Overland Monthly* (San Francisco), and the *Lakeside Monthly* (Chicago), to name just a few of the most prominent. Kathleen Diffley has estimated that between 1861 and 1876, some sixteen literary magazines, representing the Northeast, the South, and the West, printed more than 300 pieces of short fiction about the Civil War.[7] Given the large circulations of many of these periodicals, and given the relatively high rate of American literacy in the late nineteenth century, writings about the Civil War worked down into the capillary level of American culture, reaching millions of readers, in scores of towns and cities, representing a wide range of social backgrounds.

By the same token, Civil War writings had to be responsive to the pressures of the literary marketplace. Social values and expectations became business considerations, and business considerations in turn weighed on editorial and authorial decisions. For this reason, the ideological diversity of Civil War literature was to a certain degree constrained by a subtle yet pervasive cultural desire to avoid the most difficult subjects, such as race, or war guilt. All writings on the war communicated, perforce, a particular vision of the nation's past and future, whether implicitly or explicitly. They engaged in a titanic, slow-motion struggle with each other to determine how the nation would understand regionalism, civil rights, economic growth, and moral responsibility for the war and its aftermath. Yet even when it broke into acrimony, this struggle went forward on the basis of a shared national identity, against the backdrop of a reconciliationist national mood, and within the same national system of commerce.[8]

At one end of this relatively narrow spectrum, some Civil War writings were openly reconciliationist. The best example of this may be *Battles and Leaders of the Civil War*, a compendium of generals' and veterans' accounts, representing both Northern and Southern perspectives, published serially in the *Century* magazine between 1884 and 1887, and issued in book form in 1887–1888. At the other end of the spectrum, some literature was aggressively vindicationist, such as the publications of the Southern Historical Society, the brainchild of Gen. Jubal Early dedicated to keeping the Confederate point of view alive and in the public consciousness.

In the midst of the histories and the memoirs, other American authors turned to a variety of literary modes or genres in an effort to get at the lingering mysteries of the conflict. Frequently they had to navigate the crosscurrents of the literary marketplace in order to find a publisher, let alone a receptive audience, and Civil War literature often reveals how a writer could work both within and against the conventions of any particular form or tradition. Hence we see Charles Chesnutt, for instance, in response to the popular plantation and dialect fiction of Thomas Nelson Page and Joel Chandler Harris, submitting to magazines short stories that invoke the antebellum plantation not romantically, but for the purpose of representing slavery's unique fusion of economics and cruelty. In like fashion, Sarah Morgan Bryan Piatt turned to the well-worn conventions of sentimental poetry not as a retreat from emotional candor but in order to reimagine the feelings of women whose experiences and loyalties resisted easy classification. In short, much Civil War literature can be read against the grain of dominant literary tastes and cultural values. We should read it with an eye toward the recurrent fissures and omissions in its treatment of national identity, toward the unacknowledged or imperfectly suppressed African American presence in its picture of American life, toward the psychological tics and conflicts that belie the notion of a hale postwar culture. Much American literature reduced the war to its simplicities—and, it might be noted, some of this literature did so in a perversely illuminating way—but many other writings struggled against themselves, and against the cultural tide, in order to come to terms with some piece of the war or with its aftermath. The Civil War became many civil wars when refracted through the prism of literary style. The war can look very different depending on whether we approach it through William T. Sherman's factualism, Oliver Wendell Holmes's heroic romanticism, Lucy Larcom's ironic sentimentalism, or Hamlin Garland's regionalism. Each of these styles brings to the fore different meanings and perspectives; each renders just an aspect of the war, however sweeping a writer's ambition may be; and our impression of the war will vary from one to the next. Local color, humor, naturalism: all will imply certain attitudes toward or perceptions of the war's impact on people. At issue is not only subject matter (military tactics vs. domestic tribulation) but the worldview, the moral sense, and the epistemology embodied in different ways of using the language. What distinguishes a tabulation of regimental losses, for instance, from an elegiac poem goes beyond genre to embrace a fundamentally different view of human mortality.

The ascendancy of "realism" in late nineteenth-century American culture is of particular significance for the development of Civil War literature. While there were (and are) competing theories of realism, and as many practitioners as there were ideas of what constituted "reality" in the first place, signal patterns emerge across the era's fiction, nonfiction, and visual art. Realism of the nineteenth-century variety is generally oriented less toward the heroic individual than toward the representative type. It concerns itself with the details and material conditions of everyday life—with how people look, sound, interact, entertain themselves, earn a living, face the day—in a carefully wrought social context. The realist novel, painting, or photograph often has political overtones, reflecting a progressive concern with the plight of the "common man." Particularly in its early years, realism retained a belief in a universal moral order that transcended and compensated for the brutalities of the economic and social order. In its local color or regionalist varieties, realism focused on the lives of unusual people in the less familiar areas of the country—coastal Maine, New Orleans, rural Wisconsin—and on the cultural adhesives that held together a geographically diverse nation. In the strain of realism that evolved into naturalism, we find a concern with the forces working in an individual life, from within and without, as biology or culture. Realism, broadly conceived, was an effort to apprehend the textures and operating principles of a world whose startling complexity both the social scientists and the natural scientists made more evident every day.[9]

Realism in the arts and literature was nurtured by a heightened demand for and an increased supply of information, and the Civil War contributed to both. In 1860, the United

States was well on its way to becoming an information culture, and the war accelerated that process by stimulating the public's appetite for reliable knowledge about military and political matters, and by encouraging the improvement of communication networks. It quickly became the most visible, accessible war in American history, with photographers and print journalists recording almost every imaginable fact and facet of the conflict, and distributing their findings to a knowledge-hungry public.

The rise of reproducible images and syndicated news reports as dominant modes of public knowledge had profound implications for how nineteenth-century Americans understood the world. Along with the proliferation of news outlets and the increasing professionalization of journalism, improvements in photographic and lithographic technology made the representation of "reality" a matter of course. The photograph, seemingly, could not lie, and it set a standard for reliability that the canons of professional journalism echoed by emphasizing "objectivity" as a core principle of the reporter's craft. More than ever before, information became a commodity, and quick, seemingly accurate knowledge of the world could be had for a penny. Yet both the photograph and the news story have the strange effect of making the world at once more available and more remote. Photographs, in John Berger's words, "offer appearances—with all the credibility and gravity we normally lend to appearances—prised away from their meaning." The photographic image "offers information, but information severed from all lived experience."[10] In strikingly similar terms, Alan Trachtenberg has made the same point about newspapers in the Gilded Age: "the dailies dramatized a paradox of metropolitan life itself: the more knowable the world came to seem as information, the more remote and opaque it came to seem as experience."[11]

Writings about the Civil War, "literary" or otherwise, can be read partly for how they respond to these problems of realism and the culture of information. On the one hand, both fiction and nonfiction bear the imprint of the era's photographic and journalistic norms in their concern with detail, panorama, visual impact, and the detached point of view. It is not coincidental that many of the major authors of the late nineteenth century—Crane, Bierce, Frank Norris, Mark Twain, and Harold Frederic, among others—were also professional journalists. This was an age, by and large, when the brooding romances of Hawthorne, the elaborate idealism of Emerson, and the stylistic excesses of Melville seemed less in keeping with the hard-nosed, no-nonsense culture the United States imagined itself becoming. Imaginative symbolism, flights of fancy, and other forms of authorial self-indulgence did not always seem well-suited to communicating the difficult truths and social nuances of an increasingly complex culture.

On the other hand, postbellum American literature—both fiction and nonfiction—often reveals an uncertainty about the adequacy of realism, about the capacity of writing to get at the deeper truths of the war, or of society more broadly. The conventions of linear narrative, expository description, character development, conflict resolution, and so forth, gave literary texts their form and coherence, but at what cost? The sober factuality of military memoirs, orthodox histories, and occasional speeches was indispensable to capturing the war's meaning, but was it sufficient? These questions hung in the air, and they help to explain why much of the salient literature of the period—from S. Weir Mitchell's medical fiction to Bierce's gothic gems—extravagantly violates the norms of "realistic" representation, even as it borrows freely from the realist palette. If imagination had to supplement or trump reportorial objectivity, so be it.

For realism's confounding challenge was violent death. The central reality of the Civil War that Americans had to assimilate was the unprecedented level of trauma and bereavement: more than 620,000 dead and more than one million wounded. The numbers have become somewhat numbing in their familiarity, but we need to remember that civil war brought death on a scale, and with a ferocity, wholly new to Americans. It is true, as Lewis Saum writes, that in the antebellum era "death was an ever present fact of life," and that Americans had "an immediate, not a derivative or vicarious, awareness" of it.[12] But the Civil War marked a quantum shift, not only in the numbers of dead (about 2 percent of the population, or the equivalent of about six million Americans today), but in its spectacular disbursement of agony and disfigurement. How does one put words to such suffering without either trivializing, heroizing, or otherwise falsifying the experience? Memorial Day tributes to the fallen? Elegiac verse? Earnest personal testimony? Stories of battles, triumphs, hospitals, widows, and reunions? Where the carnage lies raw, unburied and unforgotten, the most effective realism may be one that embodies the failure of words, a realism akin to what Mitchell Breitwieser has discerned in Mary Rowlandson's narrative, which "is a realistic work, not because it faithfully reports real events, but because it is an account of experience that breaks through or outdistances her own and her culture's dominant means of representation, and because it is itself a continuation of that breakthrough rather than a fully composed and tranquilized recollection."[13]

Americans are good at burial; thus Saum sees in nineteenth-century American thought "a seeming insouciance, a capacity to register without questioning."[14] This ability to hold death at a remove would have helped both soldiers and civilians get through the scenes they encountered, and the war had the paradoxical effect of rendering death both shockingly present and increasingly impersonal, through the statistical banality of the body count and through the accumulation of the "unknown dead." From this perspective, the power and the obligation of realism might be to startle its audience out of that unquestioning insouciance. "Realism," Philip Fisher writes in connection to Baudelaire, "surprises us into unwanted moments or necessary moments of confronted sight. We face [the] carrion, and by means of the object, face what lies behind it, decay and death, the fate of the body in its relation to beauty."[15] It takes a rare art to accomplish that, however. How far does graphic description—"The greater part of the forehead was torn away, and from the jagged hole the brain protruded"—take us? Do the symmetries of verse—"Two white roses upon his cheeks, / And one, just over his heart, blood red!"—take us any further? Perhaps the desperation of the living is the most vivid mark of the fearsomeness of mortality: "A hundred ghastly fears and fancies strutted a moment, pecking at the young girl's naked heart, like sandpipers on the weltering beach."[16] The dilemma can be sensed even in these brief passages, and it was essentially this: Even for writers who wanted to confront mortality honestly, writing about death is like chasing one's own shadow, the experience itself always flitting away before the net of words.

Those who wrote about the Civil War wrote about a social earthquake whose aftershocks reverberated through American culture, politics, psychology, and literature. In its technical innovations and its violent reorganization of American society, the war marked the advent of a new age and audaciously challenged Americans' sensibilities and moral certainties. The nation's economic and political life was forever altered, and emancipation hardly solved the grinding conflicts of race in the United States. It is not surprising, perhaps, that many Americans and many writers lapsed into platitudes or silence. Yet others made the effort to rise to the occasion—made the effort, that is, to overcome the shock in order to reach and represent the deeper experiences of war, to find the soft tissue and the hard feelings beneath the banalities of press reportage and gauzy reminiscence. They did so even as American society had much to occupy itself with between the 1860s and the 1910s: class antagonism and labor strikes; the final push against the Native Americans in the West; a steady influx of European immigrants; the radical expansion of American geopolitical power during the Spanish-American War; an ongoing effort to reconcile religious orthodoxy with new forms of science.

In the midst of such upheaval, Americans did what came naturally: they embraced both tradition and the modern world. Michael D. Clark has written that tradition, especially for the elite, "could be a psychological anodyne offering a sense of stability in the midst of unsettling change and the feeling of time-hallowed certainty in the face of religious or metaphysical doubt." At the same time, "[s]ome Americans came to view tradition as extending rather than merely limiting the possibilities of individual and collective life," and it was therefore "the problem of tradition to find the middle ground, or the linkages, which would plausibly bind immediate to transcendent, past to present, local to imperial."[17] Anne C. Rose, stressing the importance of religious change, has also found in Victorian American culture a capacity for preserving or updating the old ways and the old beliefs in the face of widespread social transformation:

> The Victorians were not unaware of the trials and horrors of war. They felt keen disappointment at the failure of the founder's republicanism and saw clearly the suffering of soldiers and civilians alike. But the war's prospects of personal glory and shared idealism contested their soberer judgment, drew them powerfully toward the conflict, and came to dominate their recollections of war. To the extent that the Victorians' relentless search for meaning in secular activities finally achieved resolution, it was the Civil War, conceived as a struggle over profound issues, that convinced them that human effort even without clear supernatural references still had value.[18]

The literature of the American Civil War did not always reach that same conclusion. But as much as anything else, these writings represented part of the wider cultural effort to come to terms with the changes the United States underwent during the late nineteenth century. That was actually inevitable, for these changes depended, to no small degree, on the conduct and the outcome of the war.

If language and literature are forms of social and personal reconstruction, what they were able to accomplish in the fifty years after the Civil War was precarious, imperfect, and incomplete. Indeed, it is a sign of that precariousness that Americans are still coming to terms with the Civil War. The war settled the defining constitutional crisis of the country's history, and yet in other respects it seems to have resolved so little. The political tensions involving race and region, federal power and states' rights, modernity and tradition, continue to make themselves felt across the cultural landscape, from presidential campaigns to landscape conservation to civil rights. In its continuing hold on the national psyche, the Civil War has become a touchstone for understanding modern American culture, but it means very different things to different people. An essential part of coming to terms with its unresolved status in the American imagination is to explore how earlier generations came to terms with it—and that is best done through an exploration of the writings they left us.

NOTES

1. Daniel Aaron, *The Unwritten War*, p. 328.
2. These issues are treated at much greater length in a number of classic works, including: Elaine Scarry, *The Body in Pain: The Making and Unmaking of the World* (New York: Oxford University Press, 1985); Hannah Arendt, *On Violence* (New York: Harvest, 1970); and Jürgen Habermas, *Moral Consciousness and Communicative Action* (Cambridge: MIT Press, 1990). More recently, see James Dawes, *The Language of War: Literature and Culture in the U.S. from the Civil War through World War II* (Cambridge: Harvard University Press, 2002); and Judith Butler, *Excitable Speech: A Politics of the Performative* (New York: Routledge, 1997).
3. Jill Lepore, *The Name of War: King Philip's War and the Origins of American Identity* (Vintage, 1999), p. x.
4. Tim O'Brien, *The Things They Carried* (Broadway Books, 1998), pp. 157–58.
5. Dawes, *The Language of War*, p. 4, p. 11.
6. Charles Johanningsmeier, *Fiction and the American Literary Marketplace: The Role of Newspaper Syndicates, 1860–1900* (Cambridge: Cambridge University Press, 1997), pp. 2–3; Patricia Okker, *Social Stories: The Magazine Novel in Nineteenth-Century America* (Charlottesville: University of Virginia Press, 2003), ch. 1, ch. 5.
7. Kathleen Diffley, "Home from the Theatre of War: The *Southern Magazine* and Recollections of the Civil War," in Kenneth M. Price and Susan Belasco Smith, eds., *Periodical Literature in Nineteenth-Century America* (University of Virginia Press, 1995), pp. 183–201, p. 184.
8. See Lawrence Buell, "American Civil War Poetry and the Meaning of Literary Commodification: Whitman, Melville, and Others" in Steven Fink and Susan S. Williams, eds., *Reciprocal Influences: Literary Production, Distribution, and Consumption in America* (Columbus: Ohio State University Press, 1999).
9. Recent relevant studies of realism include Phillip Barrish, *American Literary Realism, Critical Theory, and Intellectual Prestige, 1880–1995* (Cambridge: Cambridge University Press, 2001); Augusta Rohrbach, *Truth Stranger than Fiction: Race, Realism, and the U.S. Literary Marketplace* (New York: Palgrave, 2002); Philip Fisher, *Still the New World: American Literature in a Culture of Creative Destruction* (Cambridge: Harvard University Press, 1999), esp. Part IV.
10. John Berger, "Uses of Photography," in *About Looking* (New York: Pantheon, 1980; New York: Vintage, 1991), pp. 55–56.
11. Alan Trachtenberg, *The Incorporation of America: Culture and Society in the Gilded Age* (New York: Hill and Wang, 1982), p. 125.
12. Lewis O. Saum, "Death in the Popular Mind of Pre-Civil War America," in David E. Stannard, ed., *Death in America* (Philadelphia: University of Pennsylvania Press, 1975), p. 32.
13. Mitchell Breitwieser, *American Puritanism and the Defense of Mourning: Religion, Grief, and Ethnology in Mary White Rowlandson's Captivity Narrative* (Madison: University of Wisconsin Press, 1990), p. 10.
14. Saum, p. 35.
15. Fisher, *Still the New World*, p. 199.
16. Ambrose Bierce, "Chickamauga"; Henry Wadsworth Longfellow, "Killed at the Ford"; Henry James, "The Story of a Year."
17. Michael D. Clark, *The American Discovery of Tradition, 1865–1942* (Baton Rouge: Louisiana State University Press, 2005), p. 16, p. 17, p. 20.
18. Anne C. Rose, *Victorian America and the Civil War* (New York: Cambridge University Press, 1992), p. 5.

SUGGESTED READING

Aaron, Daniel. *The Unwritten War: American Writers and the Civil War.* New York: Alfred A. Knopf, 1973.

Blanton, De Anne and Lauren M. Cook. *They Fought Like Demons: Women Soldiers in the Civil War.* New York: Vintage, 2003.

Cullen, Jim. *The Civil War in Popular Culture: A Reusable Past.* Washington, DC: Smithsonian Institution Press, 1995.

Dawes, James. *The Language of War: Literature and Culture in the U.S. from the Civil War through World War II.* Cambridge: Harvard University Press, 2002.

Diffley, Kathleen. *Where My Heart Is Turning Ever: Civil War Stories and Constitutional Reform.* Athens: University of Georgia Press, 1992.

Eiselein, Gregory. *Literature and Humanitarian Reform in the Civil War Era*. Bloomington: Indiana University Press, 1996.

Fahs, Alice. *The Imagined Civil War: Popular Literature of the North and South, 1861–1865*. Chapel Hill: University of North Carolina Press, 2001.

Fahs, Alice and Joan Waugh, eds. *The Memory of The Civil War in American Culture*. Chapel Hill: University of North Carolina Press, 2004.

Frederickson, George. *The Inner Civil War: Northern Intellectuals and the Crisis of the Union*. New York: Harper and Row, 1965.

Gardner, Sarah E. *Blood and Irony: Southern White Women's Narratives of the Civil War, 1861–1937*. Chapel Hill: University of North Carolina Press, 2004.

Jimerson, Randall C. *The Private Civil War: Popular Thought during the Sectional Conflict*. Baton Rouge: Louisiana State University Press, 1988.

Madden, David. *Beyond the Battlefield: The Ordinary Life and Extraordinary Times of the Civil War Soldier*. New York: Simon & Schuster, 2000.

Lively, Robert A. *Fiction Fights the Civil War*. Chapel Hill: University of North Carolina Press, 1957.

Long, Lisa A. *Rehabilitating Bodies: Health, History, and the American Civil War*. Philadelphia: University of Pennsylvania Press, 2004.

Rose, Anne C. *Victorian America and the Civil War*. New York: Cambridge University Press, 1992.

Samuels, Shirley. *Facing America: Iconography and the Civil War*. New York: Oxford University Press, 2003.

Sizer, Lyde Cullen. *The Political Work of Northern Women Writers and the Civil War, 1850–1872*. Chapel Hill: University of North Carolina Press, 2000.

Sweet, Timothy. *Traces of War: Poetry, Photography, and the Crisis of the Union*. Baltimore: Johns Hopkins University Press, 1990.

Wilson, Edmund. *Patriotic Gore: Studies in the Literature of the American Civil War*. New York: W.W. Norton, 1994; Farrar, Straus and Giroux, 1962.

Woodworth, Steven E. *While God Is Marching On: The Religious World of Civil War Soldiers*. Lawrence: University Press of Kansas, 2001.

I
ORIGINS

The last moments of John Brown. Etching by Thomas Hovenden, 1885.

1

INTRODUCTION

The Civil War was caused by the national fight over Southern slavery. We might say that it represented the most cataclysmically violent phase of that fight. The conflict often manifested itself as a constitutional debate over states' rights and federal power, or as a philosophical debate over race and freedom, but the central driving force was the uncertain future of slave-based economics as the country expanded geographically. By the 1840s, slavery was generating both tremendous profits (for a few) and moral outrage (among a growing minority), and although most white Americans would have preferred not to have to think about it, the polarization of aggressive proslavery and aggressive antislavery ideologies steadily eroded the cultural middle ground on which the nation had stood since 1787. The problem refused to go away because the undetermined status of new states and territories—slave or free?—kept the controversy always front and center. As the center crumbled during the 1850s, then, every political compromise only seemed to polarize the country further, until all compromise evaporated with the firing on Fort Sumter in 1861.

Needless to say, this thumbnail sketch only hints at the complexity of the Civil War's origins, and of the questions involved. As a general matter, what leads two societies—or two halves of the same society—to commit themselves to war? In the American case, what interests were so compelling that the escalation to total war seemed a worthwhile price to pay? At which historical junctures were the crucial decisions made, and how were they made? During the war itself, what motivated people to fight and die? How, and to what degree, did the thinking of ordinary civilians and soldiers differ from that of their political and military leaders, and what is the historical significance of that difference? How best to understand the kaleidoscope of American opinion when it came to matters of slavery, economics, and the union?

Two major considerations press forward. First, the Civil War resulted from both proximate and root causes, both immediate events that spurred the conflict forward and underlying forces operating behind the scenes. In the former category stand forth such vivid moments as the Dred Scott decision of 1856, John Brown's 1859 raid on Harper's Ferry, and the election of Lincoln in 1860. In the latter we might reckon such trends or patterns as the gradual divergence of Northern and Southern attitudes toward the family, and the intensifying literary, philosophical, and anthropological debate about what constituted a human being. Second, while these "causative factors" are certainly important, history is not the same thing as fate, and although the war can seem to have emerged inexorably and inevitably from its historical background, an irreducible contingency—of psychology, of accident and random chance, of unintended consequences—hovers around it. The Civil War had causes, but it did not absolutely *have* to happen, or turn out the way it did.

Debate about the origins of the war simmers on, and different accounts emphasize different forces, processes, and events: the growing incompatibility of "free-labor" and slave-based economics; the Northern bourgeoisie's increasing distaste for slavery; the South's fear that containing slavery geographically meant destroying a way of life; the pressure exerted on political elites by slave rebellions and slave narratives; the histrionics of the American press; the competing visions of "modernity" in both North and South; structural changes in antebellum electoral politics; the social force of group-think or camaraderie; a long-in-the-making clash of property interests; conflicting definitions of liberty and racial identity; the emergence of higher law philosophy and its connection to transcendentalism and literary romanticism. We can rightfully consider all of these as contributing factors, and all of them revolved in relation to each other, and in relation to the great question of human bondage.

Given that complexity, a responsible view of history obliges us not to reduce these issues to simplistic equations pitting abolitionism against greed, industrialism against agrarianism, or political philosophy against apolitical self-interest. In both the North and South, the cultural and intellectual landscape was crossed and recrossed by unpredictable differences of opinion and commonalities of interest. Political and ethical alignments shifted in response to events, and even as the rhetoric about slavery became more feverish, it is worth remembering that the alignment which held in 1860 was just one possible configuration. As Edward L. Ayers has written in a recent essay:

> The war came through misunderstanding, confusion, miscalculation. Both sides underestimated the location of fundamental loyalty in the other. Both received incorrect images of the other in the partisan press. Political belief distorted each side's view of the other's economy and class relations. . . . By the time people made up their minds to fight, slavery itself had become obscured. Southern white men did not fight for slavery; they fought for a new nation built on slavery. White Northerners did not fight to end slavery; they fought to defend the integrity of their nation. Yet slavery, as Abraham Lincoln later put it, 'somehow' drove everything.[1]

Despite the almost haphazard way it came about, and despite the "obscuring" of the central issue of slavery, once launched the war quickly escalated, taking on both military momentum and the character of a war of beliefs. "The Civil War," Randall Jimerson observes, "became a total war involving the entire population precisely because both sides fought for ideological principles. Compromise and surrender were unthinkable when so much was at stake."[2]

That the "root" cause of slavery was not always or primarily what partisans and participants invoked as a reason for war raises an interesting possibility: that what people *thought* they fought for, politically or militarily, might not have corresponded fully to what they *actually* fought for. This is the problem of false consciousness, and it puts the historian in the unenviable position of questioning or clarifying dead people's stated reasons for acting as they did. And yet ideological principles such as "states' rights" or "preserving the union" only motivate people to kill and die when there are more tangible, immediate considerations at work. People do fight for abstractions, but they *really* fight for the deeply personal interests those abstractions articulate: family and social group; self-respect, self-protection, and self-promotion; resources and access to resources; investment in a place and a way of life. In nineteenth-century America, these matters increasingly turned, for both Northerners and Southerners, on the question of whether and in what form slavery would exist in the United States. This question had been building for decades, and the Civil War, at once necessary and astounding, went a good distance toward resolving it.

NOTES

1. Edward L. Ayers, *What Caused the Civil War? Reflections on the South and Southern History* (New York: W.W. Norton, 2005), p. 134.
2. Jimerson, Randall C. *The Private Civil War: Popular Thought during the Sectional Conflict* (Baton Rouge: Louisiana State University Press, 1988), p. 11.

SUGGESTED READING

Ashworth, John. *Slavery, Capitalism and Politics in the Antebellum Republic: Volume I, Commerce and Compromise, 1820–1850.* Cambridge: Cambridge University Press, 1996.

Boritt, Gabor S., ed. *Why the Civil War Came.* New York: Oxford University Press, 1996.

Dew, Charles B. *Apostles of Disunion: Southern Secession Commissioners and the Causes of the Civil War.* Charlottesville: University Press of Virginia, 2001.

Faust, Drew Gilpin. *The Creation of Confederate Nationalism: Ideology and Identity in the Civil War South.* Baton Rouge: Louisiana State University Press, 1989.

Freehling, William W. *The Road to Disunion: The Secessionists at Bay.* New York: Oxford University Press, 1990.

Freehling, William W. *The South vs. the South: How Anti-Confederate Southerners Shaped the Course of the Civil War.* New York: Oxford University Press, 2001.

Huston, James. *Calculating the Value of the Union: Slavery, Property Rights, and the Economic Origins of the Civil War.* Chapel Hill: University of North Carolina Press, 2003.

McPherson, James M. *For Cause and Comrades: Why Men Fought in the Civil War.* New York: Oxford University Press, 1997.

McPherson, James M. *What They Fought For, 1861–1865.* Baton Rouge: Louisiana State University Press, 1994.

Nudelman, Franny. *John Brown's Body: Slavery, Violence, and the Culture of War.* Chapel Hill: University of North Carolina Press, 2004.

Potter, David M. *The Impending Crisis, 1848–1861.* New York: Harper & Row, 1976.

Ratner, Lorman A., and Dwight L. Teeter, Jr. *Fanatics and Fire-Eaters: Newspapers and the Coming of the Civil War.* Urbana: University of Illinois Press, 2003.

Reid, Brian Holden. *The Origins of the American Civil War.* London: Longman, 1996.

Herman Melville

from *Battle-Pieces and Aspects of the War* (1866)

THE PORTENT

Hanging from the beam,
    Slowly swaying (such the law),
Gaunt the shadow on your green,
    Shenandoah!
The cut is on the crown
(Lo, John Brown),
And the stabs shall heal no more.

Hidden in the cap
    Is the anguish none can draw;
So your future veils its face,
    Shenandoah!
But the streaming beard is shown
(Weird John Brown),
The meteor of the war.

Herman Melville

from *Battle-Pieces and Aspects of the War* (1866)

MISGIVINGS

When ocean-clouds over inland hills
    Sweep storming in late autumn brown,
And horror the sodden valley fills,
    And the spire falls crashing in the town,
I muse upon my country's ills—
The tempest bursting from the waste of Time
On the world's fairest hope linked with man's foulest crime.

Nature's dark side is heeded now
    (Ah! optimist-cheer disheartened flown)—
A child may read the moody brow
    Of yon black mountain lone.
With shouts the torrents down the gorges go,
    And storms are formed behind the storm we feel:
The hemlock shakes in the rafter, the oak in the driving keel.

Walt Whitman

from *Collect* (1882)

ORIGINS OF ATTEMPTED SECESSION

Not the whole matter, but some side facts worth conning to-day and any day.

I consider the war of attempted secession, 1860-65, not as a struggle of two distinct and separate peoples, but a conflict (often happening, and very fierce) between the passions and paradoxes of one and the same identity—perhaps the only terms on which that identity could really become fused, homogeneous and lasting. The origin and conditions out of which it arose, are full of lessons, full of warnings yet to the Republic—and always will be. The underlying and principal of those origins are yet singularly ignored. The Northern States were really just as responsible for that war, (in its precedents, foundations, instigations,) as the South. Let me try to give my view. From the age of 21 to 40, (1840–'60,) I was interested in the political movements of the land, not so much as a participant, but as an observer, and a regular voter at the elections. I think I was conversant with the springs of action, and their workings, not only in New York city [sic] and Brooklyn, but understood them in the whole country, as I had made leisurely tours through all the middle States, and partially through the western and southern, and down to New Orleans, in which city I resided for some time. (I was there at the close of the Mexican war—saw and talk'd with General Taylor,[1] and the other generals and officers, who were fêted and detain'd several days on their return victorious from that expedition.)

Of course many and very contradictory things, specialties, developments, constitutional views, &c., went to make up the origin of the war—but the most significant general fact can be best indicated and stated as follows: For twenty-five years previous to the outbreak, the controling [sic] "Democratic" nominating conventions of our Republic—starting from their primaries in wards or districts, and so expanding to counties, powerful cities, States, and to the great Presidential nominating conventions—were getting to represent and be composed of more and more putrid and dangerous materials. Let me give a schedule, or list, of one of these representative conventions for a long time before, and inclusive of, that which nominated Buchanan. (Remember they had come to be the fountains and tissues of the American body politic, forming, as it were, the whole blood, legislation, office-holding, &c.) One of these conventions, from 1840 to '60, exhibited a spectacle such as could never be seen except in our own age and in these States. The members who composed it were, seven-eighths of them, the meanest kind of bawling and blowing office-holders, office-seekers, pimps, malignants, conspirators, murderers, fancy-men, custom-house clerks, contractors, kept-editors, spaniels well-train'd to carry and fetch jobbers, infidels, disunionists, terrorists, mail-riflers, slave-catchers, pushers of slavery, creatures of the President, creatures of would-be Presidents, spies, bribers, compromisers, lobbyers, sponges, ruin'd sports, expell'd gamblers, policy-backers, monte-dealers, duellists, carriers of conceal'd weapons, deaf men, pimpled men, scarr'd inside with vile disease, gaudy outside with gold chains made from the people's money and harlots' money twisted together; crawling, serpentine men, the lousy combings and born freedom-sellers of the earth. And whence came they? From back-yards and bar-rooms; from out of the custom-houses, marshals' offices, post-offices, and gambling-hells; from the President's house, the jail, the station-house; from unnamed by-places, where devilish disunion was hatch'd at midnight; from political hearses, and from the coffins inside, and from the shrouds inside of the coffins; from the tumors and abscesses of the land; from the skeletons and skulls in the vaults of the federal alms-houses; and from the running sores of the great cities. Such, I say, form'd, or absolutely control'd the forming of, the entire personnel, the atmosphere, nutriment and chyle; of our municipal, State, and National politics—substantially permeating, handling, deciding, and wielding everything—legislation, nominations, elections, "public sentiment," &c.—while the great masses of the people, farmers, mechanics, and traders, were helpless in their gripe. These conditions were mostly prevalent in the north and west, and especially in New York and Philadelphia cities; and the southern leaders, (bad enough, but of a far higher order,) struck hands and affiliated with, and used them. Is it strange that a thunder-storm follow'd such morbid and stifling cloud-strata?

I say then, that what, as just outlined, heralded, and made the ground ready for secession revolt, ought to be held up, through all the future, as the most instructive lesson in American political history—the most significant warning and beacon-light to coming generations. I say that the sixteenth, seventeenth and eighteenth terms of the American Presidency[2] have shown that the villainy and shallowness of rulers (back'd by the machinery of great parties) are just as eligible to these States as to any foreign despotism, kingdom, or empire—there is not a bit of difference. History is to record those three Presidentiads, and especially the administrations of Fillmore and Buchanan, as so far our topmost warning and shame. Never were publicly display'd more deform'd, mediocre, snivelling, unreliable, false-hearted men. Never were these States so insulted, and attempted to be betray'd. All the main purposes for which the government was establish'd were openly denied. The perfect equality of slavery with freedom was flauntingly preach'd in the north—nay, the superiority of slavery. The slave trade was proposed to be renew'd. Everywhere frowns and misunderstandings—everywhere exasperations and humiliations. (The slavery contest is settled—and the war is long over—yet do not those putrid conditions, too many of them, still exist? still result in diseases, fevers, wounds—not of war and army hospitals—but the wounds and diseases of peace?)

Out of those generic influences, mainly in New York, Pennsylvania, Ohio, &c., arose the attempt at disunion. To philosophical examination, the malignant fever of that war shows its embryonic sources, and the original nourishment of its life and growth, in the north. I say secession, below the surface, originated and was brought to maturity in the free States. I allude to the score of years preceding 1860. My deliberate opinion is now, that if at the opening of the contest the abstract duality-question of *slavery and quiet* could have been submitted to a direct popular vote, as against their opposite, they would have triumphantly carried the day in a majority of the northern States—in the large cities, leading off with New York and Philadelphia, by tremendous majorities. The events of '61 amazed everybody north and south, and burst all prophecies and calculations like bubbles. But even then, and during the whole war, the stern fact remains that (not only did the north put it down, but) the secession cause had numerically just as many sympathizers in the free as in the rebel States.[3]

As to slavery, abstractly and practically, (its idea, and the determination to establish and expand it, especially in the new territories, the future America,) it is too common, I repeat, to identify it exclusively with the south. In fact down to the opening of the war, the whole country had about an equal hand in it. The north had at least been just as guilty, if not more guilty; and the east and west had. The former Presidents and Congresses had been guilty—the governors and legislatures of every northern State had been guilty, and the majors of New York and other northern cities had all been guilty—their hands were all stain'd. And as the conflict took decided shape, it is hard to tell which class, the leading southern or northern disunionists, was more stunn'd and disappointed at the non-action of the free-state secession element, so largely existing and counted on by those leaders, both sections.

So much for that point, and for the north. As to the inception and direct instigation of the war, in the south itself, I shall not attempt interiors or complications. Behind all, the idea that it was from a resolute and arrogant determination on the part of the extreme slaveholders, the Calhounites,[4] to carry the states rights' portion of the constitutional compact to its farthest verge, and nationalize slavery, or else disrupt the Union, and found a new empire, with slavery for its corner-stone, was and is undoubtedly the true theory. (If successful, this attempt might—I am not sure, but it might—have destroy'd not only our American republic, in anything like first-class proportions, in itself and its prestige, but for ages at least, the cause of Liberty and Equality everywhere—and would have been the greatest triumph of reaction, and the severest blow to political and every other freedom, possible to conceive. Its worst result would have inured to the southern States themselves.) That our national democratic experiment, principle, and machinery, could triumphantly sustain such a shock, and that the Constitution could weather it, like a ship a storm, and come out of it as sound and whole as before, is by far the most signal proof yet of the stability of that experiment, Democracy, and of those principles, and that Constitution.

Of the war itself, we know in the ostent what has been done. The numbers of the dead and wounded can be told or approximated, the debt posted and put on record, the material events narrated, &c. Meantime, elections go on, laws are pass'd, political parties struggle, issue their platforms, &c., just the same as before. But immensest result, not only in politics, but in literature, poems, and sociology, are doubtless waiting yet unform'd in the future. How long they will wait I cannot tell. The pageant of history's retrospect shows us, ages since, all Europe marching on the crusades, those arm'd uprisings of the people, stirr'd by a mere idea, to grandest attempt—and, when once baffled in it, returning, at intervals, twice, thrice, and again. An unsurpass'd series of revolutionary events, influences. Yet it took over two hundred years for the seeds of the crusades to germinate, before beginning even to sprout. Two hundred years they lay, sleeping, not dead, but dormant in the ground. Then, out of them, unerringly, arts, travel, navigation, politics, literature, freedom, the spirit of adventure, inquiry, all arose, grew, and steadily sped on to what we see at present. far back there, that huge agitation-struggle of the crusades stands, as undoubtedly the embryo, the start, of the high preëminence of experiment, civilization and enterprise which the European nations have since sustain'd, and of which these States are the heirs.

Another illustration—(history is full of them, although the war itself, the victory of the Union, and the relations of our equal States, present features of which there are no precedents in the past.) The conquest of England eight centuries ago, by the Franco-

Normans—the obliteration of the old, (in many respects so needing obliteration)—the Domesday Book,[5] and the repartition of the land—the old impedimenta removed, even by blood and ruthless violence, and a new, progressive genesis establish'd, new seeds sown— time has proved plain enough that, bitter as they were, all these were the most salutary series of revolutions that could possibly have happen'd. Out of them, and by them mainly, have come, out of Albic, Roman and Saxon England—and without them could not have come—not only England of the 500 years down to the present, and of the present—but these States. Nor, except for that terrible dislocation and overturn, would these States, as they are, exist to-day.

It is certain to me that the United States, by virtue of that war and its results, and through that and them only, are now ready to enter, and must certainly enter, upon their genuine career in history, as no more torn and divided in their spinal requisites, but a great homogeneous Nation—free states all—a moral and political unity in variety, such as Nature shows in her grandest physical works, and as much greater than any mere work of Nature, as the moral and political, the work of man, his mind, his soul, are, in their loftiest sense, greater than the merely physical. Out of that war not only has the nationality of the States escaped from being strangled, but more than any of the rest, and, in my opinion, more than the north itself, the vital heart and breath of the south have escaped as from the pressure of a general nightmare, and are henceforth to enter on a life, development, and active freedom, whose realities are certain in the future, notwithstanding all the southern vexations of the hour—a development which could not possibly have been achiev'd on any less terms, or by any other means than that grim lesson, or something equivalent to it. And I predict that the south is yet to outstrip the north.

Ulysses S. Grant

from *Personal Memoirs of U. S. Grant* (1885–86)

CHAPTER XVI – RESIGNATION – PRIVATE LIFE –
LIFE AT GALENA – THE COMING CRISIS

My family, all this while,[6] was at the East. It consisted now of a wife and two children. I saw no chance of supporting them on the Pacific coast out of my pay as an army officer. I concluded, therefore, to resign, and in March applied for a leave of absence until the end of the July following, tendering my resignation to take effect at the end of that time. I left the Pacific coast very much attached to it, and with the full expectation of making it my future home. That expectation and that hope remained uppermost in my mind until the Lieutenant-Generalcy bill was introduced into Congress in the winter of 1863–4. The passage of that bill, and my promotion, blasted my last hope of ever becoming a citizen of the further West.[7]

In the late summer of 1854 I rejoined my family, to find in it a son whom I had never seen, born while I was on the Isthmus of Panama.[8] I was now to commence, at the age of thirty-two, a new struggle for our support. My wife had a farm near St. Louis, to which we went, but I had no means to stock it. A house had to be built also. I worked very hard, never losing a day because of bad weather, and accomplished the object in a moderate way. If nothing else could be done I would load a cord of wood on a wagon and take it to the city for sale. I managed to keep along very well until 1858, when I was attacked by fever and ague. I had suffered very severely and for a long time from this disease, while a boy in Ohio. It lasted now over a year, and, while it did not keep me in the house, it did interfere greatly with the amount of work I was able to perform. In the fall of 1858 I sold out my stock, crops and farming utensils at auction, and gave up farming.

In the winter I established a partnership with Harry Boggs, a cousin of Mrs. Grant, in the real estate agency business. I spent that winter at St. Louis myself, but did not take my family into town until the spring. Our business might have become prosperous if I had been able to wait for it to grow. As it was, there was no more than one person could attend to, and not enough to support two families. While a citizen of St. Louis and engaged in the real estate agency business, I was a candidate for the office of county engineer, an office of respectability and emolument which would have been very acceptable to me at that time. The incumbent was appointed by the county court, which consisted of five members. My opponent had the advantage of birth over me (he was a citizen by adoption) and carried off the prize. I now withdrew from the co-partnership with Boggs, and, in May, 1860, removed to Galena, Illinois, and took a clerkship in my father's store.

While a citizen of Missouri, my first opportunity for casting a vote at a Presidential election occurred. I had been in the army from before attaining my majority and had thought but little about politics, although I was a Whig by education and a great admirer of Mr. Clay.[9] But the Whig party had ceased to exist before I had an opportunity of exercising the privilege of casting a ballot; the Know-Nothing party had taken its place, but was on the wane; and the Republican party was in a chaotic state and had not yet received a name. It had no existence in the Slave States except at points on the borders next to Free States. In St. Louis City and County, what afterwards became the Republican party was known as the Free-Soil Democracy, led by the Honorable Frank P. Blair.[10] Most of my neighbors had known me as an officer of the army with Whig proclivities. They had been on the same side, and, on the death of their party, many had become Know-Nothings, or members of the American party. There was a lodge near my new home, and I was invited to join it. I accepted the invitation; was initiated; attended a meeting just one week later, and never went to another afterwards.

I have no apologies to make for having been one week a member of the American party; for I still think native-born citizens of the United States should have as much protection, as many privileges in their native country, as those who voluntarily select it for a home. But all secret, oath-bound political parties are dangerous to any nation, no matter how pure or how patriotic the motives and principles which first bring them together. No political party can or ought to exist when one of its corner-stones is opposition to freedom of thought and to the right to worship God "according to the dictate of one's own conscience,"[11] or according to the creed of any religious denomination whatever. Nevertheless, if a sect sets up its laws as binding above the State laws, wherever the two come in conflict this claim must be resisted and suppressed at whatever cost.

Up to the Mexican war there were a few out and out abolitionists, men who carried their hostility to slavery into all elections, from those for a justice of the peace up to the Presidency of the United States. They were noisy but not numerous. But the great majority of people at the North, where slavery did not exist, were opposed to the institution, and looked upon its existence in any part of the country as unfortunate. They did not hold the States where slavery existed responsible for it; and believed that protection should be given to the right of property in slaves until some satisfactory way could be reached to be rid of the institution. Opposition to slavery was not a creed of either political party. In some sections more anti-slavery men belonged to the Democratic party, and in others to the Whigs. But with the inauguration of the Mexican war, in fact with the annexation of Texas, "the inevitable conflict" commenced.

As the time for the Presidential election of 1856—the first at which I had the opportunity of voting—approached, party feeling began to run high. The Republican party was regarded in the South and the border States not only as opposed to the extension of slavery, but as favoring the compulsory abolition of the institution without compensation to the owners. The most horrible visions seemed to present themselves to the minds of people who, one would suppose, ought to have known better. Many educated and, otherwise, sensible persons appeared to believe that emancipation meant social equality. Treason to the Government was openly advocated and was not rebuked. It was evident to my mind that the election of a Republican President in 1856 meant the secession of all the Slave States, and rebellion. Under these circumstances I preferred the success of a candidate whose election would prevent or postpone secession, to seeing the country plunged into a war the end of which no man could foretell. With a Democrat elected by the unanimous vote of the Slave States, there could be no pretext for secession for four years. I very much hoped that the passions of the people would subside in that time, and the catastrophe be averted altogether; if it was not, I believed the country would be better prepared to receive the shock and to resist it. I therefore voted for James Buchanan for President. Four years later the Republican party was successful in electing its candidate to the Presidency. The civilized world has learned the consequence. Four millions of human beings held as chattels have been liberated; the ballot has been given to them; the free schools of the country have been opened to their children. The nation still lives, and the people are just as free to avoid social intimacy with the blacks as ever they were, or as they are with white people.

While living in Galena I was nominally only a clerk supporting myself and family on a stipulated salary. In reality my position was different. My father had never lived in Galena himself, but had established my two brothers there, the one next younger than myself in charge of the business, assisted by the youngest. When I went there it was my father's intention to give up all connection with the business himself, and to establish his three sons in it: but the brother who had really built up the business was sinking with consumption, and it was not thought best to make any change while he was in this condition. He lived until September, 1861, when he succumbed to that insidious disease which always flatters its victims into the belief that they are growing better up to the close of life. A more honorable man never transacted business. In September, 1861, I was engaged in an employment which required all my attention elsewhere.

During the eleven months that I lived in Galena prior to the first call for volunteers, I had been strictly attentive to my business, and had made but few acquaintances other than customers and people engaged in the same line with myself. When the election took place in November, 1860, I had not been a resident of Illinois long enough to gain citizenship and could not, therefore, vote. I was really glad of this at the time, for my pledges would have compelled me to vote for Stephen A. Douglas, who had no possible chance of election. The contest was really between Mr. Breckinridge[12] and Mr. Lincoln; between minority rule and rule by the majority. I wanted, as between these candidates, to see Mr. Lincoln elected. Excitement ran high during the canvass, and torch-light processions enlivened the scene in the generally quiet streets of Galena many nights during the campaign. I did not parade with either party, but occasionally met with the "wide awakes"—Republicans—in their rooms, and superintended their drill. It was evident, from the time of the Chicago nomination to the close of the canvass, that the election of the Republican candidate would be the signal for some of the Southern States to secede. I still had hopes that the four years which had elapsed since the first nomination of a Presidential candidate by a party distinctly opposed to slavery extension, had given time for the extreme pro-slavery sentiment to cool down; for the Southerners to think well before they took the awful leap which they had so vehemently threatened. But I was mistaken.

The Republican candidate was elected, and solid substantial people of the North-west, and I presume the same order of people throughout the entire North, felt very serious, but determined, after this event. It was very much discussed whether the South would carry out its threat to secede and set up a separate government, the corner-stone of which should be, protection to the "Divine" institution of slavery. For there were people who believed in the "divinity" of human slavery, as there are now people who believe Mormonism and Polygamy to be ordained by the Most High. We forgive them for entertaining such notions, but forbid their practice. It was generally believed that there would be a flurry; that some of the extreme Southern States would go so far as to pass ordinances of secession. But the common impression was that this step was so plainly suicidal for the South, that the movement would not spread over much of the territory and would not last long.

Doubtless the founders of our government, the majority of them at least, regarded the confederation of the colonies as an experiment. Each colony considered itself a separate government; that the confederation was for mutual protection against a foreign foe, and the prevention of strife and war among themselves. If there had been a desire on the part of any single State to withdraw from the compact at any time while the number of States was limited to the original thirteen, I do not suppose there would have been any to contest the right, no matter how much the determination might have been regretted. The problem changed on the ratification of the Constitution by all the colonies; it changed still more when amendments were added; and if the right of any one State to withdraw continued to exist at all after the ratification of the Constitution, it certainly ceased on the formation of new States, at least so far as the new States themselves were concerned. It was never possessed at all by Florida or the States west of the Mississippi, all of which were purchased by the treasury of the entire nation. Texas and the territory brought into the Union in consequence of annexation, were purchased with both blood and treasure; and Texas, with a domain greater than that of any European state except Russia, was permitted to retain as state property all the public lands within its borders. It would have been ingratitude and injustice of the most flagrant sort for this State to withdraw from the Union after all that had been spent and done to introduce her; yet, if separation had actually occurred, Texas must necessarily have gone with the South, both on account of her institutions and her geographical position. Secession was illogical as well as impracticable; it was revolution.

Now, the right of revolution is an inherent one. When people are oppressed by their government, it is a natural right they enjoy to relieve themselves of the oppression, if they are strong enough, either by withdrawal from it, or by over-throwing it and substituting a government more acceptable. But any people or part of a people who resort to this remedy, stake their lives, their property, and every claim for protection given by citizenship—on the issue. Victory, or the conditions imposed by the conqueror—must be the result.

In the case of the war between the States it would have been the exact truth if the South had said,—"We do not want to live with you Northern people any longer; we know our institution of slavery is obnoxious to you, and, as you are growing numerically stronger than we, it may at some time in the future be endangered. So long as you permitted us to control the government, and with the aid of a few friends at the North to enact laws constituting your section a guard against the escape of our property, we were willing to live with you. You have been submissive to our rule heretofore; but it looks now as if you did not intend to continue so, and we will remain in the Union no longer." Instead of this the seceding States cried lustily,—"Let us alone; you have no constitutional power to interfere with us." Newspapers and people at the North reiterated the cry. Individuals might ignore the constitution; but the Nation itself must not only obey it, but must enforce the strictest construction of that instrument; the construction put upon it by the Southerners themselves. The fact is the constitution did not apply to any such contingency as the one existing from 1861 to 1865. Its framers never dreamed of such a contingency occurring. If they had foreseen it, the probabilities are they would have sanctioned the right of a State or States to withdraw rather than that there should be war between brothers.

The framers were wise in their generation and wanted to do the very best possible to secure their own liberty and independence, and that also of their descendants to the latest days. It is preposterous to suppose that the people of one generation can lay down the best and only rules of government for all who are to come after them, and under unforeseen contingencies. At the time of the framing of our constitution the only physical forces that had been subdued and made to serve man and do his labor, were the currents in the streams and in the air we breathe. Rude machinery, propelled by water power, had been invented; sails to propel ships upon the waters had been set to catch the passing breeze—but the application of steam to propel vessels against both wind and current, and machinery to do all manner of work had not been thought of. The instantaneous transmission of messages around the world by means of electricity would probably at that day have been attributed to witchcraft or a league with the Devil. Immaterial circumstances had changed as greatly as material ones. We could not and ought not to be rigidly bound by the rules laid down under circumstances so different for emergencies so utterly unanticipated. The fathers themselves would have been the first to declare that their prerogatives were not irrevocable. They would surely have resisted secession could they have lived to see the shape it assumed.

I travelled through the Northwest considerably during the winter of 1860–1. We had customers in all the little towns in south-west Wisconsin, south-east Minnesota and north-east Iowa. These generally knew I had been a captain in the regular army and had served through the Mexican war. Consequently wherever I stopped at night, some of the people would come to the public-house where I was, and sit till a late hour discussing the probabilities of the future. My own views at that time were like those officially expressed by Mr. Seward at a later day, that "the war would be over in ninety days." I continued to entertain these views until after the battle of Shiloh. I believe now that there would have been no more battles at the West after the capture of Fort Donelson if all the troops in that region had been under a single commander who would have followed up that victory.[13]

There is little doubt in my mind now that the prevailing sentiment of the South would have been opposed to secession in 1860 and 1861, if there had been a fair and calm expression of opinion, unbiased by threats, and if the ballot of one legal voter had counted for as much as that of any other. But there was no calm discussion of the question. Demagogues who were too old to enter the army if there should be a war, others who entertained so high an opinion of their own ability that they did not believe they could be spared from the direction of the affairs of state in such an event, declaimed vehemently and unceasingly against the North; against its aggressions upon the South; its interference with Southern rights, etc., etc. They denounced the Northerners as cowards, poltroons, negro-worshippers; claimed that one Southern man was equal to five Northern men in battle; that if the South would stand up for its rights the North would back down. Mr. Jefferson Davis said in a speech, delivered at La Grange, Mississippi, before the secession of that State, that he would agree to drink all the blood spilled south of Mason and Dixon's line if there should be a war. The young men who would have the fighting to do in case of war, believed all these statements, both in regard to the aggressiveness of the North and its cowardice. They, too, cried out for a separation from such people. The great bulk of the legal voters of the South were men who owned no slaves; their homes were generally in the hills and poor country; their facilities for educating their children, even up to the point of reading and writing, were very limited; their interest in the contest was very meagre—what there was, if they had been capable of seeing it, was with the North; they too needed emancipation. Under the old regime they were looked down upon by those who controlled all the affairs in the interest of slave-owners, as poor white trash who were allowed the ballot so long as they cast it according to direction.[14]

I am aware that this last statement may be disputed and individual testimony perhaps adduced to show that in antebellum days the ballot was as untrammelled in the South as in any section of the country; but in the face of any such contradiction I reassert the statement. The shot-gun was not resorted to. Masked men did not ride over the country at night intimidating voters; but there was a firm feeling that a class existed in every State with a sort of divine right to control public affairs. If they could not get this control by one means they must by another. The end justified the means. The coercion, if mild, was complete.

There were two political parties, it is true, in all the States, both strong in numbers and respectability, but both equally loyal to the institution which stood paramount in Southern eyes to all other institutions in state or nation. The slave-owners were the minority, but governed both parties. Had politics ever divided the slave-holders and the non-slave-holders, the majority would have been obliged to yield, or internecine war would have been the consequence. I do not know that the Southern people were to blame for this condition of affairs. There was a time when slavery was not profitable, and the discussion of the merits of the institution was confined almost exclusively to the territory where it existed. The States of Virginia and Kentucky came near abolishing slavery by their own acts, one State defeating the measure by a tie vote and the other only lacking one. But when the institution became profitable, all talk of its abolition ceased where it existed; and naturally, as human nature is constituted, arguments were adduced in its support. The cotton-gin probably had much to do with the justification of slavery.

The winter of 1860–1 will be remembered by middle-aged people of to-day as one of great excitement. South Carolina promptly seceded after the result of the Presidential election was known.[15] Other Southern States proposed to follow. In some of them the Union sentiment was so strong that it had to be suppressed by force. Maryland, Delaware, Kentucky and Missouri, all Slave States, failed to pass ordinances of secession; but they were all represented in the so-called congress of the so-called Confederate States. The Governor and Lieutenant-Governor of Missouri, in 1861, Jackson and Reynolds, were both supporters of the rebellion and took refuge with the enemy.[16] The governor soon died, and the lieutenant-governor assumed his office; issued proclamations as governor of the State; was recognized as such by the Confederate Government, and continued his pretensions until the collapse of the rebellion. The South claimed the sovereignty of States, but claimed the right to coerce into their confederation such States as they wanted, that is, all the States where slavery existed. They did not seem to think this course inconsistent. The fact is, the Southern slave-owners believed that, in some way, the ownership of slaves conferred a sort of patent of nobility—a right to govern independent of the interest or wishes of those who did not hold such property. They convinced themselves, first, of the divine origin of the institution and, next, that that particular institution was not safe in the hands of any body of legislators but themselves.

Meanwhile the Administration of President Buchanan looked helplessly on and proclaimed that the general government had no power to interfere; that the Nation had no power to save its own life. Mr. Buchanan had in his cabinet two members at least, who were as earnest—to use a mild term—in the cause of secession as Mr. Davis or any Southern statesman. One of them, Floyd, the Secretary of War, scattered the army so that much of it could be captured when hostilities should commence, and distributed the cannon and small arms from Northern arsenals throughout the South so as to be on hand when treason wanted them.[17] The navy was scattered in like manner. The President did not prevent his cabinet preparing for war upon their government, either by destroying its resources or storing them in the South until a de facto government was established with Jefferson Davis as its President, and Montgomery, Alabama, as the Capital.[18] The secessionists had then to leave the cabinet. In their own estimation they were aliens in the country which had given them birth. Loyal men were put into their places. Treason in the executive branch of the government was estopped. But the harm had already been done. The stable door was locked after the horse had been stolen.

During all of the trying winter of 1860–1, when the Southerners were so defiant that they would not allow within their borders the expression of a sentiment hostile to their views, it was a brave man indeed who could stand up and proclaim his loyalty to the Union. On the other hand men at the North—prominent men—proclaimed that the government had no power to coerce the South into submission to the laws of the land; that if the North undertook to raise armies to go south, these armies would have to march over the dead bodies of the speakers. A portion of the press of the North was constantly proclaiming similar views. When the time arrived for the President-elect to go to the capital of the Nation to be sworn into office, it was deemed unsafe for him to travel, not only as a President-elect, but as any private citizen should be allowed to do. Instead of going in a special car, receiving the good wishes of his constituents at all the stations along the road, he was obliged to stop on the way and to be smuggled into the capital. He disappeared from public view on his journey, and the next the country knew, his arrival was announced at the capital. There is little doubt that he would have been assassinated if he had attempted to travel openly throughout his journey.

Jefferson Davis

SPEECH IN U.S. SENATE (FAREWELL ADDRESS)
(January 21, 1861)

I rise, Mr. President, for the purpose of announcing to the Senate that I have satisfactory evidence that the State of Mississippi, by a solemn ordinance of her people in convention assembled, has declared her separation from the United States.[19] Under these circumstances, of course, my functions are terminated here. It has seemed to me proper, however, that I should appear in the Senate to announce that fact to my associates, and I will say but very little more. The occasion does not invite me to go into argument; and my physical condition would not permit me to do so if it were otherwise; and yet it seems to become me to say something on the part of the State I here represent, on an occasion so solemn as this.

It is known to Senators who have served with me here, that I have for many years advocated, as an essential attribute of State sovereignty, the right of a State to secede from the Union. Therefore, if I had not believed there was justifiable cause; if I had thought that Mississippi was acting without sufficient provocation, or without an existing necessity, I should still, under my theory of the Government, because of my allegiance to the State of which I am a citizen, have been bound by her action. I, however, may be permitted to say that I do think she has justifiable cause, and I approve of her act. I conferred with her people before that act was taken, counseled them then that if the state of things which they apprehended should exist when the convention met, they should take the action which they have now adopted.

I hope none who hear me will confound this expression of mine with the advocacy of the right of a State to remain in the Union, and to disregard its constitutional obligations by the nullification of the law. Such is not my theory. Nullification and secession, so often confounded, are indeed antagonistic principles. Nullification is a remedy which it is sought to apply within the Union, and against the agent of the States. It is only to be justified when the agent has violated his constitutional obligation, and a State, assuming to judge for itself, denies the right of the agent thus to act, and appeals to the other States of the Union for a decision; but when the States themselves, and when the people of the States, have so acted as to convince us that they will not regard our constitutional rights, then, and then for the first time, arises the doctrine of secession in its practical application.

A great man who now reposes with his fathers, and who has been often arraigned for a want of fealty to the Union, advocated the doctrine of nullification, because it preserved the Union. It was because of his deep-seated attachment to the Union, his determination to find some remedy for existing ills short of a severance of the ties which bound South Carolina to the other States, that Mr. Calhoun advocated the doctrine of nullification, which he proclaimed to be peaceful, to be within the limits of State power, not to disturb the Union, but only to be a means of bringing the agent before the tribunal of the States for their judgment.

Secession belongs to a different class of remedies. It is to be justified upon the basis that the States are sovereign. There was a time when none denied it. I hope the time may come again, when a better comprehension of the theory of our Government, and the inalienable rights of the people of the States, will prevent any one from denying that each State is a sovereign, and thus may reclaim the grants which it has made to any agent whomsoever.

I therefore say I concur in the action of the people of Mississippi, believing it to be necessary and proper, and should have been bound by their action if my belief had been otherwise; and this brings me to the important point which I wish on this last occasion to present to the Senate. It is by this confounding of nullification and secession that the name of a great man, whose ashes now mingle with his mother earth, has been invoked to justify coercion against a seceded State. The phrase "to execute the laws," was an expression which General Jackson[20] applied to the case of a State refusing to obey the laws while yet a member of the Union. That is not the case which is now presented. The laws are to be executed over the United States, and upon the people of the United States. They have no relation to any foreign country. It is a perversion of terms, at least it is a great misapprehension of the case, which cites that expression for application to a State which has withdrawn from the Union. You may make war on a foreign State. If it be the purpose of gentlemen, they may make war against a State which has withdrawn from the Union; but there are no laws of the United States to be executed within the limits of a seceded State. A State finding herself in the condition in which Mississippi has judged she is, in which her safety requires that she should provide for the maintenance of her rights out of the Union, surrenders all the benefits, (and they are known to be many,) deprives herself of the advantages, (they are known to be great,) severs all the ties of affection, (and they are close and enduring,) which have bound her to the Union; and thus divesting herself of every benefit, taking upon herself every burden, she claims to be exempt from any power to execute the laws of the United States within her limits.

I well remember an occasion when Massachusetts was arraigned before the bar of the Senate, and when then the doctrine of coercion was rife and to be applied against her because of the rescue of a fugitive slave in Boston.[21] My opinion then was the same that it is now. Not in a spirit of egotism, but to show that I am not influenced in my opinion because the case is my own, I refer to that time and that occasion as containing the opinion which I then entertained, and on which my present conduct is based. I then said, if Massachusetts, following her through a stated line of conduct, chooses to take the last step which separates her from the Union, it is her right to go, and I will neither vote one dollar nor one man to coerce her back; but will say to her, God speed, in memory of the kind associations which once existed between her and the other States.

It has been a conviction of pressing necessity, it has been a belief that we are to be deprived in the Union of the rights which our fathers bequeathed to us, which has brought Mississippi into her present decision. She has heard proclaimed the theory that all men are created free and equal, and this made the basis of an attack upon her social institutions; and the sacred Declaration of Independence has been invoked to maintain the position of the equality of the races. That Declaration of Independence is to be construed by the circumstances and purposes for which it was made. The communities were declaring their independence; the people of those communities were asserting that no man was born—to use the language of Mr. Jefferson—booted and spurred to ride over the rest of mankind; that men were created equal—meaning the men of the political community; that there was no divine right to rule; that no man inherited the right to govern; that there were no classes by which power and place descended to families, but that all stations were equally within the grasp of each member of the body-politic. These were the great principles they announced; these were the purposes for which they made their declaration; these were the ends to which their enunciation was directed. They have no reference to the slave; else, how happened it that among the items of arraignment made against George III was that he endeavored to do just what the North has been endeavoring of late to do—to stir up insurrection among our slaves?[22] Had the Declaration announced that the negroes were free and equal, how was the Prince to be arraigned for stirring up insurrection among them? And how was this to be enumerated among the high crimes which caused the colonies to sever their connection with the mother country? When our Constitution was formed, the same idea was rendered more palpable, for there we find provision made for that very class of persons as property; they were not put upon the footing of equality with white men—not even upon that of paupers and convicts; but, so far as representation was concerned, were discriminated against as a lower caste, only to be represented in the numerical proportion of three fifths.[23]

Then, Senators, we recur to the compact which binds us together; we recur to the principles upon which our Government was founded; and when you deny them, and when you deny to us the right to withdraw from a Government which thus perverted threatens to be destructive of our rights, we but tread in the path of our fathers when we proclaim our independence, and take the hazard. This is done not in hostility to others, not to injure any section of the country, not even for our own pecuniary benefit; but from the high and solemn motive of defending and protecting the rights we inherited, and which it is our sacred duty to transmit unshorn to our children.

I find in myself, perhaps, a type of the general feeling of my constituents towards yours. I am sure I feel no hostility to you, Senators from the North. I am sure there is not one of you, whatever sharp discussion there may have been between us, to whom I cannot now say, in the presence of my God, I wish you well; and such, I am sure, is the feeling of the people whom I represent towards those whom you represent. I therefore feel that I but express their desire when I say I hope, and they hope, for peaceful relations with you, though we must part. They may be mutually beneficial to us in the future, as they have been in the past, if you so will it. The reverse may bring disaster on every portion of the country; and if you will have it thus, we will invoke the God of our fathers, who delivered them from the power of the lion, to protect us from the ravages of the bear; and thus, putting our trust in God and in our own firm hearts and strong arms, we will vindicate the right as best we may.

In the course of my service here, associated at different times with a great variety of Senators, I see now around me some with whom I have served long; there have been points of collision; but whatever of offense there has been to me, I leave here; I carry with me no hostile remembrance. Whatever offense I have given which has not been redressed, or for which satisfaction has not been demanded, I have, Senators, in this hour of our parting, to offer you my apology for any pain which, in heat of discussion, I have inflicted. I go hence unencumbered of the remembrance of any injury received, and having discharged the duty of making the only reparation in my power for any injury offered.

Mr. President, and Senators, having made the announcement which the occasion seemed to me to require, it only remains to me to bid you a final adieu.

Henry Timrod

ETHNOGENESIS* (February 1861)

I.

Hath not the morning dawned with added light?
And shall not evening call another star
Out of the infinite regions of the night,
To mark this day in Heaven? At last, we are
A nation among nations; and the world
Shall soon behold in many a distant port
       Another flag unfurled!
Now, come what may, whose favor need we court?
And, under God, whose thunder need we fear?
       Thank Him who placed us here
Beneath so kind a sky—the very sun
Takes part with us; and on our errands run
All breezes of the ocean; dew and rain
Do noiseless battle for us; and the Year,
And all the gentle daughters in her train,
March in our ranks, and in our service wield
       Long spears of golden grain!
A yellow blossom as her fairy shield,
June flings her azure banner to the wind,
       While in the order of their birth
Her sisters pass; and many an ample field
Grows white beneath their steps, till now, behold
       Its endless sheets unfold
THE SNOW OF SOUTHERN SUMMERS! Let the earth
Rejoice! beneath those fleeces soft and warm
       Our happy land shall sleep
       In a repose as deep
       As if we lay intrenched behind
Whole leagues of Russian ice and Arctic storm!

II.

And what if, mad with wrongs themselves have wrought,
       In their own treachery caught,
       By their own fears made bold,
       And leagued with him of old,
Who long since, in the limits of the North,

---

*Written during the meeting of the first Southern Congress, at Montgomery, February, 1861.

Set up his evil throne, and warred with God—
What if, both mad and blinded in their rage,
Our foes should fling us down their mortal gage,
And with a hostile step profane our sod!
We shall not shrink, my brothers, but go forth
To meet them, marshalled by the Lord of Hosts,
And overshadowed by the might ghosts
Of Moultrie and of Eutaw[24]—who shall foil
Auxiliars such as these? Nor these alone,
        But every stock and stone
        Shall help us; but the very soil,
And all the generous wealth it gives to toil,
And all for which we love our noble land,
Shall fight beside, and through us, sea and strand,
        The heart of woman, and her hand,
Tree, fruit, and flower, and every influence,
        Gentle, or grave, or grand;
        The winds in our defence
Shall seem to blow; to us the hills shall lend
        Their firmness and their calm;
And in our stiffened sinews we shall blend
        The strength of pine and palm!

III.
Nor would we shun the battle-ground,
        Though weak as we are strong;
Call up the clashing elements around,
        And test the right and wrong!
On one side, creeds that dare to teach
What Christ and Paul refrained to preach;[25]
Codes built upon a broken pledge,
And charity that whets a poniard's edge;
Fair schemes that leave the neighboring poor
To starve and shiver at the schemer's door,
While in the world's most liberal ranks enrolled,
He turns some vast philanthropy to gold;
Religion taking every mortal form
But that a pure and Christian faith makes warm,
Where not to vile fanatic passion urged,
Or not in vague philosophies submerged,
Repulsive with all Pharisaic leaven,
And making laws to stay the laws of Heaven!
And on the other, scorn of sordid gain,
Unblemished honor, truth without a stain,
Faith, justice, reverence, charitable wealth,
And, for the poor and humble, laws which give,

Not the mean right to buy the right to live,
  But life, and home, and health!
To doubt the end were want of trust in God,
  Who, if he has decreed
 That we must pass a redder sea
Than that which rang to Miriam's holy glee,
  Will surely raise at need
  A Moses with his rod!

IV.
But let our fears—if fears we have—be still,
And turn us to the future! Could we climb
Some mighty Alp, and view the coming time,
 The rapturous sight would fill
  Our eyes with happy tears!
Not only for the glories which the years
Shall bring us; not for lands from sea to sea,
And wealth, and power, and peace, though these shall be;
But for the distant peoples we shall bless,
And the hushed murmurs of a world's distress:
For, to give labor to the poor,
  The whole sad planet o'er,
And save from want and crime the humblest door,
Is one among the many ends for which
  God makes us great and rich!
The hour perchance is not yet wholly ripe
When all shall own it, but the type
Whereby we shall be known in every land
Is that vast gulf which laves our Southern strand,
And through the cold, untempered ocean pours
Its genial streams, that far-off Arctic shores
May sometimes catch upon the softened breeze
Strange tropic warmth and hints of summer seas.

Abraham Lincoln

FIRST INAUGURAL ADDRESS
(March 4, 1861)

Fellow-citizens of the United States:

In compliance with a custom as old as the government itself, I appear before you to address you briefly, and to take, in your presence, the oath prescribed by the Constitution of the United States, to be taken by the President "before he enters on the execution of his office."

I do not consider it necessary, at present, for me to discuss those matters of administration about which there is no special anxiety, or excitement.

Apprehension seems to exist among the people of the Southern States, that by the accession of a Republican Administration, their property, and their peace, and personal security, are to be endangered. There has never been any reasonable cause for such apprehension. Indeed, the most ample evidence to the contrary has all the while existed, and been open to their inspection. It is found in nearly all the published speeches of him who now addresses you. I do but quote from one of those speeches when I declare that "I have no purpose, directly or indirectly, to interfere with the institution of slavery in the States where it exists. I believe I have no lawful right to do so, and I have no inclination to do so." Those who nominated and elected me did so with full knowledge that I had made this, and many similar declarations, and had never recanted them. And more than this, they placed in the platform, for my acceptance, and as a law to themselves, and to me, the clear and emphatic resolution which I now read:

> *Resolved,* That the maintenance inviolate of the rights of the States, and especially the right of each State to order and control its own domestic institutions according to its own judgment exclusively, is essential to that balance of power on which the perfection and endurance of our political fabric depend; and we denounce the lawless invasion by armed force of the soil of any State or Territory, no matter under what pretext, as among the gravest of crimes.

I now reiterate these sentiments: and in doing so, I only press upon the public attention the most conclusive evidence of which the case is susceptible, that the property, peace and security of no section are to be in anywise endangered by the now incoming Administration. I add too, that all the protection which, consistently with the Constitution and the laws, can be given, will be cheerfully given to all the States when lawfully demanded, for whatever cause—as cheerfully to one section, as to another.

There is much controversy about the delivering up of fugitives from service or labor. The clause I now read is as plainly written in the Constitution as any other of its provisions:

No person held to service or labor in one State, under the laws thereof, escaping into another, shall, in consequence of any law or regulation therein, be discharged from such service or labor, but shall be delivered up on claim of the party to whom such service or labor may be due.

It is scarcely questioned that this provision was intended by those who made it, for the reclaiming of what we call fugitive slaves; and the intention of the law-giver is the law. All members of Congress swear their support to the whole Constitution-to this provision as much as to any other. To the proposition, then, that slaves whose cases come within the terms of this clause, "shall be delivered up," their oaths are unanimous. Now, if they would make the effort in good temper, could they not, with nearly equal unanimity, frame and pass a law, by means of which to keep good that unanimous oath?

There is some difference of opinion whether this clause should be enforced by national or by state authority; but surely that difference is not a very material one. If the slave is to be surrendered, it can be of but little consequence to him, or to others, by which authority it is done. And should any one, in any case, be content that his oath shall go unkept, on a merely unsubstantial controversy as to how it shall be kept?

Again, in any law upon this subject, ought not all the safeguards of liberty known in civilized and humane jurisprudence to be introduced, so that a free man be not, in any case, surrendered as a slave? And might it not be well, at the same time, to provide by law for the enforcement of that clause, in the Constitution which guaranties that "The citizens of each State shall be entitled to all privileges and immunities of citizens in the several States?"

I take the official oath to-day, with no mental reservations, and with no purpose to construe the Constitution or laws, by any hyper-critical rules. And while I do not choose now to specify particular acts of Congress as proper to be enforced, I do suggest, that it will be much safer for all, both in official and private stations, to conform to, and abide by, all those acts which stand unrepealed, than to violate any of them, trusting to find impunity in having them held to be unconstitutional.

It is seventy-two years since the first inauguration of a President under our National Constitution. During that period fifteen different and greatly distinguished citizens, have, in succession, administered the executive branch of the government. They have conducted it through many perils; and, generally, with great success. Yet, with all this scope for precedent, I now enter upon the same task for the brief constitutional term of four years, under great and peculiar difficulty. A disruption of the Federal Union, heretofore only menaced, is now formidably attempted.

I hold, that in contemplation of universal law, and of the Constitution, the Union of these States is perpetual. Perpetuity is implied, if not expressed, in the fundamental law of all national governments. It is safe to assert that no government proper, ever had a provision in its organic law for its own termination. Continue to execute all the express provisions of our National Constitution, and the Union will endure forever—it being impossible to destroy it except by some action not provided for in the instrument itself.

Again, if the United States be not a government proper, but an association of States in the nature of contract merely, can it, as a contract, be peaceably unmade, by less than all the parties who made it? One party to a contract may violate it—break it, so to speak; but does it not require all to lawfully rescind it?

Descending from these general principles, we find the proposition that, in legal contemplation, the Union is perpetual, confirmed by the history of the Union itself. The Union is much older than the Constitution. It was formed in fact, by the Articles of Association in 1774. It was matured and continued by the Declaration of Independence in 1776. It was further matured and the faith of all the then thirteen States expressly plighted and engaged that it should be perpetual, by the Articles of Confederation in 1778. And finally, in 1787, one of the declared objects for ordaining and establishing the Constitution, was "to form a more perfect Union."

But if destruction of the Union, by one, or by a part only, of the States, be lawfully possible, the Union is less perfect than before the Constitution, having lost the vital element of perpetuity.

It follows from these views that no State, upon its own mere motion, can lawfully get out of the Union; that resolves and ordinances to that effect are legally void; and that acts of violence, within any State or States, against the authority of the United States, are insurrectionary or revolutionary, according to circumstances.

I therefore consider that, in view of the Constitution and the laws, the Union is unbroken; and, to the extent of my ability, I shall take care, as the Constitution itself expressly enjoins upon me, that the laws of the Union be faithfully executed in all the States. Doing this I deem to be only a simple duty on my part; and I shall perform it, so far as practicable, unless my rightful masters, the American people, shall withhold the requisite means, or, in some authoritative manner, direct the contrary. I trust this will not be regarded as a menace, but only as the declared purpose of the Union that it will constitutionally defend, and maintain itself.

In doing this there needs to be no bloodshed or violence; and there shall be none, unless it be forced upon the national authority. The power confided to me, will be used to hold, occupy, and possess the property, and places belonging to the government, and to collect the duties and imposts; but beyond what may be necessary for these objects, there will be no invasion, no using of force against or among the people anywhere. Where hostility to the United States, in any interior locality, shall be so great and so universal, as to prevent competent resident citizens from holding the Federal offices, there will be no attempt to force obnoxious strangers among the people for that object. While the strict legal right may exist in the government to enforce the exercise of these offices, the attempt to do so would be so irritating, and so nearly impracticable with all, that I deem it better to forego, for the time, the uses of such offices.

The mails, unless repelled, will continue to be furnished in all parts of the Union. So far as possible, the people everywhere shall have that sense of perfect security which is most favorable to calm thought and reflection. The course here indicated will be followed, unless current events, and experience, shall show a modification, or change, to be proper; and in every case and exigency, my best discretion will be exercised, according to circumstances actually existing, and with a view and a hope of a peaceful solution of the national troubles, and the restoration of fraternal sympathies and affections.

That there are persons in one section, or another who seek to destroy the Union at all events, and are glad of any pretext to do it, I will neither affirm or deny; but if there be such, I need address no word to them. To those, however, who really love the Union may I not speak?

Before entering upon so grave a matter as the destruction of our national fabric, with all its benefits, its memories, and its hopes, would it not be wise to ascertain precisely why we do it? Will you hazard so desperate a step, while there is any possibility that any portion of the ills you fly from, have no real existence? Will you, while the certain ills you fly to, are greater than all the real ones you fly from—will you risk the commission of so fearful a mistake?

All profess to be content in the Union, if all constitutional rights can be maintained. Is it true, then, that any right, plainly written in the Constitution, has been denied? I think not. Happily the human mind is so constituted, that no party can reach to the audacity of doing this. Think, if you can, of a single instance in which a plainly written provision of the Constitution has ever been denied. If, by the mere force of numbers, a majority should deprive a minority of any clearly written constitutional right, it might, in a moral point of view, justify revolution—certainly would, if such right were a vital one. But such is not our case. All the vital rights of minorities, and of individuals, are so plainly assured to them, by affirmations and negations, guarranties and prohibitions, in the Constitution, that controversies never arise concerning them. But no organic law can ever be framed with a provision specifically applicable to every question which may occur in practical administration. No foresight can anticipate, nor any document of reasonable length contain express provisions for all possible questions. Shall fugitives from labor be surrendered by national or by State authority? The Constitution does not expressly say. *May* Congress prohibit slavery in the territories? The Constitution does not, expressly say. *Must* Congress protect slavery in the territories? The Constitution does not expressly say.

From questions of this class spring all our constitutional controversies, and we divide upon them into majorities and minorities. If the minority will not acquiesce, the majority must, or the government must cease. There is no other alternative; for continuing the government, is acquiescence on one side or the other.

If a minority, in such case, will secede rather than acquiesce, they make a precedent which, in turn, will divide and ruin them; for a minority of their own will secede from them, whenever a majority refuses to be controlled by such minority. For instance, why may not any portion of a new confederacy, a year or two hence, arbitrarily secede again, precisely as portions of the present Union now claim to secede from it? All who cherish disunion sentiments, are now being educated to the exact temper of doing this.

Is there such perfect identity of interests among the States to compose a new Union, as to produce harmony only, and prevent renewed secession?

Plainly, the central idea of secession, is the essence of anarchy. A majority, held in restraint by constitutional checks, and limitations, and always changing easily, with deliberate changes of popular opinions and sentiments, is the only true sovereign of a free people. Whoever rejects it, does, of necessity, fly to anarchy or to despotism. Unanimity is impossible; the rule of a minority, as a permanent arrangement, is wholly inadmissible; so that, rejecting the majority principle, anarchy, or despotism in some form, is all that is left.

I do not forget the position assumed by some, that constitutional questions are to be decided by the Supreme Court; nor do I deny that such decisions must be binding in any case, upon the parties to a suit, as to the object of that suit, while they are also entitled to very high respect and consideration, in all parallel cases, by all other departments of the government. And while it is obviously possible that such decision may be erroneous in any given case, still the evil effect following it, being limited to that particular case, with the chance that it may be over-ruled, and never become a precedent for other cases, can better be borne than could the evils of a different practice. At the same time, the candid citizen must confess that if the policy of the government, upon vital questions affecting the whole people, is to be irrevocably fixed by decisions of the Supreme Court, the instant they are made, in ordinary litigation between parties, in personal actions, the people will have ceased, to be their own rulers, having, to that extent, practically resigned their government, into the hands of that eminent tribunal. Nor is there, in this view, any assault upon the court, or the judges. It is a duty from which they may not shrink to decide cases properly brought before them, and it is no fault of theirs if others seek to turn their decisions to political purposes.

One section of our country believes slavery is right, and ought to be extended, while the other believes it is wrong, and ought not to be extended. This is the only substantial dispute. The fugitive-slave clause of the Constitution, and the law for the suppression of the foreign slave trade, are each as well enforced, perhaps, as any law can ever be in a community where the moral sense of the people imperfectly supports the law itself. The great body of the people abide by the dry legal obligation in both cases, and a few break over in each. This, I think, cannot be perfectly cured; and it would be worse in both cases after the separation of the sections, than before. The foreign slave trade, now imperfectly suppressed, would be ultimately revived, without restriction, in one section; while fugitive slaves, now only partially surrendered, would not be surrendered at all by the other.

Physically speaking, we cannot separate. We cannot remove our respective sections from each other, nor build an impassable wall between them. A husband and wife may be divorced, and go out of the presence, and beyond the reach of each other; but the different parts of our country cannot do this. They cannot but remain face to face; and intercourse, either amicable or hostile, must continue between them. Is it possible then to make that intercourse more advantageous or more satisfactory after separation than before? Can aliens make treaties easier than friends can make laws? Can treaties be more faithfully enforced between aliens than laws can among friends? Suppose you go to war, you cannot fight always; and when, after much loss on both sides, and no gain on either, you cease fighting, the identical old questions as to terms of intercourse are again upon you.

This country, with its institutions, belongs to the people who inhabit it. Whenever they shall grow weary of the existing government, they can exercise their constitutional right of amending it, or their revolutionary right to dismember or overthrow it. I can not be ignorant of the fact that many worthy and patriotic citizens are desirous of having the National Constitution amended. While I make no recommendation of amendments, I fully recognize the rightful authority of the people over the whole subject, to be exercised in either of the modes prescribed in the instrument itself; and I should, under existing circumstances, favor rather than oppose a fair opportunity being afforded the people to act upon it. I will venture to add that to me the convention mode seems preferable, in that it allows amendments to originate with the people themselves, instead of only permitting them to take or reject propositions originated by others not especially chosen for the purpose, and which might not be precisely such as they would wish to either accept or refuse. I understand a proposed amendment to the Constitution—which amendment, however, I have not seen—has passed Congress, to the effect that the federal government shall never interfere with the domestic institutions of the States, including that of persons held to service. To avoid misconstruction of what I have said, I depart from my purpose not to speak of particular amendments so far as to say that, holding such a provision to now be implied constitutional law, I have no objection to its being made express and irrevocable.

The chief magistrate derives all his authority from the people, and they have conferred none upon him to fix terms for the separation of the States. The people themselves can do this also if they choose; but the executive, as such, has nothing to do with it. His duty is to administer the present government, as it came to his hands, and to transmit it, unimpaired by him, to his successor.

Why should there not be a patient confidence in the ultimate justice of the people? Is there any better or equal hope in the world? In our present differences is either party without faith of being in the right? If the Almighty Ruler of nations, with his eternal truth and justice, be on your side of the North, or on yours of the South, that truth and that justice will surely prevail by the judgment of this great tribunal of the American people.

By the frame of the government under which we live, this same people have wisely given their public servants but little power for mischief; and have, with equal wisdom, provided for the return of that little to their own hands at very short intervals. While the people retain their virtue and vigilance, no administration, by any extreme of wickedness or folly, can very seriously injure the government in the short space of four years.

My countrymen, one and all, think calmly and well upon this whole subject. Nothing valuable can be lost by taking time. If there be an object to hurry any of you in hot haste to a step which you would never take deliberately, that object will be frustrated by taking time; but no good object can be frustrated by it. Such of you as are now dissatisfied, still have the old Constitution unimpaired, and, on the sensitive point, the laws of your own framing under it; while the new administration will have no immediate power, if it would, to change either. If it were admitted that you who are dissatisfied hold the right side in the dispute, there still is no single good reason for precipitate action. Intelligence, patriotism, Christianity, and a firm reliance on Him who has never yet forsaken this favored land, are still competent to adjust in the best way all our present difficulty.

In your hands, my dissatisfied fellow countrymen, and not in mine, is the momentous issue of civil war. The government will not assail you. You can have no conflict without being yourselves the aggressors. You have no oath registered in Heaven to destroy the government, while I shall have the most solemn one to "preserve, protect, and defend" it.

I am loath to close. We are not enemies, but friends. We must not be enemies. Though passion may have strained, it must not break our bonds of affection. The mystic chords of memory, stretching from every battle-field and patriot grave to every living heart and hearthstone all over this broad land, will yet swell the chorus of the Union when again touched, as surely they will be, by the better angels of our nature.

Mary Chesnut

from *A Diary from Dixie* (1905)

CHAPTER 2

Montgomery, Ala., *February 19*, 1861 — The brand-new Confederacy is making or remodeling its Constitution. Everybody wants Mr. Davis to be General-in-Chief or President. Keitt and Boyce and a party preferred Howell Cobb* for President. And the fire-eaters per se wanted Barnwell Rhett.[26]

My brother Stephen brought the officers of the "Montgomery Blues" to dinner. "Very soiled Blues," they said, apologizing for their rough condition. Poor fellows! they had been a month before Fort Pickens and not allowed to attack it. They said Colonel Chase built it, and so were sure it was impregnable. Colonel Lomax telegraphed to Governor Moore[†] if he might try to take it, "Chase or no Chase," and got for his answer, "No." "And now," say the Blues, "we have worked like niggers, and when the fun and fighting begin, they send us home and put regulars there." They have an immense amount of powder. The wheel of the car in which it was carried took fire. There was an escape for you! We are packing a hamper of eatables for them.

I am despondent once more. If I thought them in earnest because at first they put their best in front, what now? We have to meet tremendous odds by pluck, activity, zeal, dash, endurance of the toughest, military instinct. We have had to choose born leaders of men who could attract love and secure trust. Everywhere political intrigue is as rife as in Washington.

Cecil's saying of Sir Walter Raleigh that he could "toil terribly" was an electric touch. Above all, let the men who are to save South Carolina be young and vigorous. While I was reflecting on what kind of men we ought to choose, I fell on Clarendon, and it was easy to construct my man out of his portraits. What has been may be again, so the men need not be purely ideal types.

Mr. Toombs[‡] told us a story of General Scott and himself. He said he was dining in Washington with Scott, who seasoned every dish and every glass of wine with the eternal refrain, "Save the Union; the Union must be preserved." Toombs remarked that he knew why the Union was so dear to the General, and illustrated his point by a steamboat anec-

---

* A native of Georgia, Howell Cobb had long served in Congress, and in 1849 was elected Speaker. In 1851 he was elected Governor of Georgia, and in 1857 became Secretary of the Treasury in Buchanan's Administration. In 1861 he was a delegate from Georgia to the Provisional Congress which adoped the Constitution of the Confederacy, and presided over each of its four sessions.

† Andrew Bary Moore, elected Governor of Alabama in 1859. In 1861, before Alabama seceded, he directed the seisure of United States forts and arsenals and was active afterwards in the equipment of State troops.

‡ Robert Toombs, a native of Georgia, who early acquired fame as a lawyer, served in the Creek War under General Scott, became known in 1842 as a "State Rights Whig," being elected to Congress, where he was active in the Compromise measures of 1850. He served in the United States Senate from 1853 to 1861, where he was a pronounced advocate of the sovereignty of States, the extension of slavery, and secession. He was a member of the Confederate Congress at its first session and, by a single vote, failed of election as President of the Confederacy. After the war, he was conspicuous for his hostility to the Union.

dote, an explosion, of course. While the passengers were struggling in the water a woman ran up and down the bank crying, "Oh, save the red-headed man!" The red-headed man was saved, and his preserver, after landing him noticed with surprise how little interest in him the woman who had made such moving appeals seemed to feel. He asked her "Why did you make that pathetic outcry?" She answered, "Oh, he owes me ten thousand dollars." "Now General," said Toombs, "the Union owes you seventeen thousand dollars a year!" I can imagine the scorn on old Scott's face.

February 25th — Find every one working very hard here. As I dozed on the sofa last night, could hear the scratch, scratch of my husband's pen as he wrote at the table until midnight.

After church to-day, Captain Ingraham[27] called. He left me so uncomfortable. He dared to express regrets that he had to leave the United States Navy. He had been stationed in the Mediterranean, where he liked to be, and expected to be these two years, and to take those lovely daughters of his to Florence. Then came Abraham Lincoln, and rampant black Republicanism, and he must lay down his life for South Carolina. He, however, does not make any moan. He says we lack everything necessary in naval gear to retake Fort Sumter. Of course, he only expects the navy to take it. He is a fish out of water here. He is one of the finest sea-captains; so I suppose they will soon give him a ship and send him back to his own element.

At dinner Judge—was loudly abusive of Congress.[28] He said: "They have trampled the Constitution underfoot. They have provided President Davis with a house." He was disgusted with the folly of parading the President at the inauguration in a coach drawn by four white horses. Then some one said Mrs. Fitzpatrick was the only lady who sat with the Congress. After the inaugural she poked Jeff Davis in the back with her parasol that he might turn and speak to her. "I am sure that was democratic enough," said some one.

Governor Moore came in with the latest news—a telegram from Governor Pickens[29] to the President, "that a war steamer is lying off the Charleston bar laden with reenforcements for Fort Sumter, and what must we do?" Answer: "Use your own discretion!" There is faith for you, after all is said and done. It is believed there is still some discretion left in South Carolina fit for use.

Everybody who comes here wants an office, and the many who, of course, are disappointed raise a cry of corruption against the few who are successful. I thought we had left all that in Washington. Nobody is willing to be out of sight, and all will take office.

"Constitution" Browne[30] says he is going to Washington for twenty-four hours. I mean to send by him to Mary Garnett for a bonnet ribbon. If they take him up as a traitor, he may cause a civil war. War is now our dread. Mr. Chesnut told him not to make himself a bone of contention.

Everybody means to go into the army. If Sumter is attacked, then Jeff Davis's troubles will begin. The Judge says a military despotism would be best for us—anything to prevent a triumph of the Yankees. All right, but every man objects to any despot but himself.

Mr. Chesnut, in high spirits, dines to-day with the Louisiana delegation. Breakfasted with "Constitution" Browne, who is appointed Assistant Secretary of State, and so does not go to Washington. There was at table the man who advertised for a wife, with the wife so obtained. She was not pretty. We dine at Mr. Pollard's and go to a ball afterward at Judge Bibb's. The New York *Herald* says Lincoln stood before Washington's picture at his inauguration, which was taken by the country as a good sign. We are always frantic for a good sign. Let us pray that a Cæsar or a Napoleon may be sent us. That would be our best sign of success. But they still say, "No war." Peace let it be, kind Heaven!

Dr. De Leon[31] called, fresh from Washington, and says General Scott is using all his power and influence to prevent officers from the South resigning their commissions, among other things promising that they shall never be sent against us in case of war. Captain Ingraham, in his short, curt way, said: "That will never do. If they take their government's pay they must do its fighting."

A brilliant dinner at the Pollards's. Mr. Barnwell* took me down. Came home and found the Judge and Governor Moore waiting to go with me to the Bibbs's. And they say it is dull in Montgomery! Clayton,[32] fresh from Washington, was at the party and told us "there was to be peace."

February 28th — In the drawing-room a literary lady began a violent attack upon this mischief-making South Carolina. She told me she was a successful writer in the magazines of the day, but when I found she used "incredible" for "incredulous," I said not a word in defense of my native land. I left her "incredible." Another person came in, while she was pouring upon me her home troubles, and asked if she did not know I was a Carolinian. Then she gracefully reversed her engine, and took the other tack, sounding our praise, but I left her incredible and I remained incredulous, too.

Brewster[33] says the war specks are growing in size. Nobody at the North, or in Virginia, believes we are in earnest. They think we are sulking and that Jeff Davis and Stephens† are getting up a very pretty little comedy. The Virginia delegates were insulted at the peace conference; Brewster said, "kicked out."

The Judge thought Jefferson Davis rude to him when the latter was Secretary of War. Mr. Chesnut persuaded the Judge to forego his private wrong for the public good, and so he voted for him, but now his old grudge has come back with an increased venomousness. What a pity to bring the spites of the old Union into this new one! It seems to me already men are willing to risk an injury to our cause, if they may in so doing hurt Jeff Davis.

March 1st — Dined to-day with Mr. Hill‡ from Georgia, and his wife. After he left us she told me he was the celebrated individual who, for Christian scruples, refused to fight a duel with Stephens.§ She seemed very proud of him for his conduct in the affair. Ignoramus that I am, I had not heard of it. I am having all kinds of experiences. Drove to-day with a lady who fervently wished her husband would go down to Pensacola and be shot. I

---

* Robert Woodward Barnwell, of South Carolina, a graduate of Harvard, twice a member of Congress and afterward United States Senator. In 1860, after the passage of the Ordinance of Secession, he was one of the Commissioners who went to Washington to treat with the National Government for its property within the State. He was a member of the Convention at Montgomery and gave the casting vote which made Jefferson Davis President of the Confederacy.

† Alexander H. Stephens, the eminent statesman of Georgia, who before the war had been conspicuous in all the political movements of his time and in 1861 became Vice-President of the Confederacy. After the war he again became conspicuous in Congress and wrote a history entitled "The War between the States."

‡ Benjamin H. Hill, who had already been active in State and National affairs when the Secession movement was carried through. He had been an earnest advocate of the Union until in Georgia the resolution was passed declaring that the State ought to secede. He then became a prominent supporter of secession. He was a member of the Confederate Congress, which met in Montgomery in 1861, and served in the Confederate Senate until the end of the war. After the war, he was elected to Congress and opposed the Reconstruction policy of that body. In 1877 he was elected United States Senator from Georgia.

§ Governor Herschel V. Johnson also declined, and doubtless for similar reasons, to accept a challenge from Alexander H. Stephens, who, though endowed with the courage of a gladiator, was very small and frail.

was dumb with amazement, of course. Telling my story to one who knew the parties, was informed, "Don't you know he beats her?" So I have seen a man "who lifts his hand against a woman in aught save kindness."

Brewster says Lincoln passed through Baltimore disguised, and at night, and that he did well, for just now Baltimore is dangerous ground. He says that he hears from all quarters that the vulgarity of Lincoln, his wife, and his son is beyond credence, a thing you must see before you can believe it. Senator Stephen A. Douglas told Mr. Chesnut that "Lincoln is awfully clever, and that he had found him a heavy handful."

Went to pay my respects to Mrs. Jefferson Davis. She met me with open arms. We did not allude to anything by which we are surrounded. We eschewed politics and our changed relations.

March 3rd — Everybody in fine spirits in my world. They have one and all spoken in the Congress* to their own perfect satisfaction. To my amazement the Judge took me aside, and, after delivering a panegyric upon himself (but here, later, comes in the amazement), he praised my husband to the skies, and said he was the fittest man of all for a foreign mission. Aye; and the farther away they send us from this Congress the better I will like it.

Saw Jere Clemens and Nick Davis, social curiosities. They are Anti-Secession leaders; then George Sanders and George Deas.[34] The Georges are of opinion that it is folly to try to take back Fort Sumter from Anderson and the United States; that is, before we are ready. They saw in Charleston the devoted band prepared for the sacrifice; I mean, ready to run their heads against a stone wall. Dare devils they are. They have dash and courage enough, but science only could take that fort. They shook their heads.

March 4th — The Washington Congress has passed peace measures. Glory be to God (as my Irish Margaret used to preface every remark, both great and small).

At last, according to his wish, I was able to introduce Mr. Hill, of Georgia, to Mr. Mallory,[†] and also Governor Moore and Brewster, the latter the only man without a title of some sort that I know in this democratic subdivided republic.

I have seen a negro woman sold on the block at auction. She overtopped the crowd. I was walking and felt faint, seasick. The creature looked so like my good little Nancy, a bright mulatto with a pleasant face. She was magnificently gotten up in silks and satins. She seemed delighted with it all, sometimes ogling the bidders, sometimes looking quiet, coy, and modest, but her mouth never relaxed from its expanded grin of excitement. I dare say the poor thing knew who would buy her. I sat down on a stool in a shop and disciplined my wild thoughts. I tried it Sterne fashion. You know how women sell themselves and are sold in marriage from queens downward, eh? You know what the Bible says about slavery and marriage; poor women! poor slaves! Sterne, with his starling—what did he know? He only thought, he did not feel.

---

* It was at this Congress that Jefferson Davis, on February 9, 1861, was elected President, and Alexander H. Stephens Vice-President of the Confederacy. The Congress continued to meet in Montgomery until its removal to Richmond, in July, 1861.

† Stephen R. Mallory was the son of a shipmaster of Connecticut, who had settled in Key West in 1820. From 1851 to 1861 Mr. Mallory was United States Senator from Florida, and after the formation of the Confederacy, became its Secretary of the Navy.

In *Evan Harrington* I read: "Like a true English female, she believed in her own inflexible virtue, but never trusted her husband out of sight."[35]

The New York *Herald* says: "Lincoln's carriage is not bomb-proof; so he does not drive out." Two flags and a bundle of sticks have been sent him as gentle reminders. The sticks are to break our heads with. The English are gushingly unhappy as to our family quarrel. Magnanimous of them, for it is their opportunity.

March 5th — We stood on the balcony to see our Confederate flag go up. Roars of cannon, etc., etc. Miss Sanders complained (so said Captain Ingraham) of the deadness of the mob. "It was utterly spiritless," she said; "no cheering, or so little, and no enthusiasm." Captain Ingraham suggested that gentlemen "are apt to be quiet," and this was "a thoughtful crowd, the true mob element with us just -now is hoeing corn." And yet! It is uncomfortable that the idea has gone abroad that we have no joy, no pride, in this thing. The band was playing "Massa in the cold, cold ground." Miss Tyler, daughter of the former President of the United States, ran up the flag.

Captain Ingraham pulled out of his pocket some verses sent to him by a Boston girl. They were well rhymed and amounted to this: she held a rope ready to hang him, though she shed tears when she remembered his heroic rescue of Koszta. Koszta, the rebel![36] She calls us rebels, too. So it depends upon whom one rebels against—whether to save or not shall be heroic.

I must read Lincoln's inaugural. Oh, "comes he in peace, or comes he in war, or to tread but one measure as Young Lochinvar?" Lincoln's aim is to seduce the border States.

The people, the natives, I mean, are astounded that I calmly affirm, in all truth and candor, that if there were awful things in society in Washington, I did not see or hear of them. One must have been hard to please who did not like the people I knew in Washington.

Mr. Chesnut has gone with a list of names to the President—de Treville, Kershaw, Baker, and Robert Rutledge. They are taking a walk, I see. I hope there will be good places in the army for our list.

March 8th — Judge Campbell,* of the United States Supreme Court, has resigned. Lord! how he must have hated to do it. How other men who are resigning high positions must hate to do it.

Now we may be sure the bridge is broken. And yet in the Alabama Convention they say Reconstructionists abound and are busy.

Met a distinguished gentleman that I knew when he was in more affluent circumstances. I was willing enough to speak to him, but when he saw me advancing for that purpose, to avoid me, he suddenly dodged around a corner—William, Mrs. de Saussure's former coachman. I remember him on his box, driving a handsome pair of bays, dressed sumptuously in blue broadcloth and brass buttons; a stout, respectable, fine-looking, middle-aged mulatto. He was very high and mighty.

Night after night we used to meet him as fiddler-in-chief of all our parties. He sat in solemn dignity, making faces over his bow, and patting his foot with an emphasis that

---

* John Archibald Campbell, who had settled in Montgomery and was appointed Associate Justice of the United States Supreme Court by President Pierce in 1853. Before he resigned, he exerted all his influence to prevent Civil War and opposed secession, although he believed that States had a right to secede.

shook the floor. We gave him five dollars a night; that was his price. His mistress never refused to let him play for any party. He had stable-boys in abundance. He was far above any physical fear for his sleek and well-fed person. How majestically he scraped his foot as a sign that he was tuned up and ready to begin!

Now he is a shabby creature indeed. He must have felt his fallen fortunes when he met me—one who knew him in his prosperity. He ran away, this stately yellow gentleman, from wife and children, home and comfort. My Molly asked him "Why? Miss Liza was good to you, I know." I wonder who owns him now; he looked forlorn.

Governor Moore brought in, to be presented to me, the President of the Alabama Convention. It seems I had known him before he had danced with me at a dancing-school ball when I was in short frocks, with sash, flounces, and a wreath of roses. He was one of those clever boys of our neighborhood, in whom my father* saw promise of better things, and so helped him in every way to rise, with books, counsel, sympathy. I was enjoying his conversation immensely, for he was praising my father I without stint, when the Judge came in, breathing fire and fury. Congress has incurred his displeasure. We are abusing one another as fiercely as ever we have abased Yankees. It is disheartening.

March 10th — Mrs. Childs was here to-night (Mary Anderson, from Statesburg), with several children. She is lovely. Her hair is piled up on the top of her head oddly. Fashions from France still creep into Texas across Mexican borders. Mrs. Childs is fresh from Texas. Her husband is an artillery officer, or was. They will be glad to promote him here. Mrs. Childs had the sweetest Southern voice, absolute music. But then, she has all of the high spirit of those sweet-voiced Carolina women, too.

Then Mr. Browne came in with his fine English accent, so pleasant to the ear. He tells us that Washington society is not reconciled to the Yankee régime. Mrs. Lincoln means to economize. She at once informed the majordomo that they were poor and hoped to save twelve thousand dollars every year from their salary of twenty thousand. Mr. Browne said Mr. Buchanan's farewell was far more imposing than Lincoln's inauguration.

The people were so amusing, so full of Western stories. Dr. Boykin behaved strangely. All day he had been gaily driving about with us, and never was man in finer spirits. To-night, in this brilliant company, he sat dead still as if in a trance. Once, he waked somewhat—when a high public functionary came in with a present for me, a miniature gondola, "A perfect Venetian specimen," he assured me again and again. In an undertone Dr. Boykin muttered: "That fellow has been drinking." "Why do you think so?" "Because he has told you exactly the same thing four times." Wonderful! Some of these great statesmen always tell me the same thing—and have been telling me the same thing ever since we came here.

A man came in and some one said in an undertone, "The age of chivalry is not past, O ye Americans!" "What do you mean?" "That man was once nominated by President Buchanan for a foreign mission, but some Senator stood up and read a paper printed by this man abusive of a woman, and signed by his name in full. After that the Senate would have none of him; his chance was gone forever."

---

* Mrs. Chesnut's father was Stephen Decatur Miller, who was born in South Carolina in 1787, and died in Mississippi in 1838. He was elected to Congress in 1816, as an Anti-Calhoun Democrat, and from 1828 to 1830 was Governor of South Carolina. He favored Nullification, and in 1830 was elected United States Senator from South Carolina, but resigned three years afterward in consequence of ill health. In 1835 he removed to Mississippi and engaged in cotton growing.

March 11th — In full conclave to-night, the drawing-room crowded with Judges, Governors, Senators, Generals, Congressmen. They were exalting John C. Calhoun's hospitality. He allowed everybody to stay all night who chose to stop at his house. An ill-mannered person, on one occasion, refused to attend family prayers. Mr. Calhoun said to the servant, "Saddle that man's horse and let him go." From the traveler Calhoun would take no excuse for the "Deity offended." I believe in Mr. Calhoun's hospitality, but not in his family prayers. Mr. Calhoun's piety was of the most philosophical type, from all accounts.*

The latest news is counted good news; that is, the last man who left Washington tells us that Seward is in the ascendancy. He is thought to be the friend of peace. The man did say, however that "that serpent Seward is in the ascendancy just now."

Harriet Lane has eleven suitors. One is described as likely to win, or he would be likely to win, except that he is too heavily weighted. He has been married before and goes about with children and two mothers. There are limits beyond which! Two mothers-in-law!

Mr. Ledyard spoke to Mrs. Lincoln in behalf of a doorkeeper who almost felt he had a vested right, having been there since Jackson's time; but met with the same answer; she had brought her own girl and must economize. Mr. Ledyard thought the twenty thousand (and little enough it is) was given to the President of these United States to enable him to live in proper style, and to maintain an establishment of such dignity as befits the head of a great nation. It is an infamy to economize with the public money and to put it into one's private purse. Mrs. Browne was walking with me when we were airing our indignation against Mrs. Lincoln and her shabby economy. The Herald says three only of the élite Washington families attended the Inauguration Ball.

The Judge has just come in and said: "Last night, after Dr. Boykin left on the cars, there came a telegram that his little daughter, Amanda, had died suddenly." In some way he must have known it beforehand. He changed so suddenly yesterday, and seemed so careworn and unhappy. He believes in clairvoyance, magnetism, and all that. Certainly, there was some terrible foreboding of this kind on his part.

Tuesday — Now this, they say, is positive: "Fort Sumter is to be released and we are to have no war." After all, far too good to be true. Mr. Browne told us that, at one of the peace intervals (I mean intervals in the interest of peace), Lincoln flew through Baltimore, locked up in an express car. He wore a Scotch cap.

We went to the Congress. Governor Cobb, who presides over that august body, put James Chesnut in the chair, and came down to talk to us. He told us why the pay of Congressmen was fixed in secret session, and why the amount of it was never divulged—to prevent the lodginghouse and hotel people from making their bills of a size to cover it all. "The bill would be sure to correspond with the pay," he said.

In the hotel parlor we had a scene. Mrs. Scott was describing Lincoln, who is of the cleverest Yankee type. She said: "Awfully ugly, even grotesque in appearance, the kind who are always at the corner stores, sitting on boxes, whittling sticks, and telling stories as funny as they are vulgar." Here I interposed: "But Stephen A. Douglas said one day to Mr. Chesnut, 'Lincoln is the hardest fellow to handle I have ever encountered yet.' " Mr. Scott is from California, and said Lincoln is "an utter American specimen, coarse, rouge, and strong; a good-natured, kind creature; as pleasant-tempered as he is clever, and if this

---

* John C. Calhoun had died in March, 1850.

country can be joked and laughed out of its rights he is the kind-hearted fellow to do it. Now if there is a war and it pinches the Yankee pocket instead of filling it—"

Here a shrill voice came from the next room (which opened upon the one we were in by folding doors thrown wide open) and said: "Yankees are no more mean and stingy than you are. People at the North are just as good as people at the South." The speaker advanced upon us in great wrath.

Mrs. Scott apologized and made some smooth, polite remark, though evidently much embarrassed. But the vinegar face and curly pate refused to receive any concessions, and replied: "That comes with a very bad grace after what you were saying," and she harangued us loudly for several minutes. Some one in the other room giggled outright, but we were quiet as mice. Nobody wanted to hurt her feelings. She was one against so many. If I were at the North, I should expect them to belabor us, and should hold my tongue. We separated North from South because of incompatibility of temper. We are divorced because we have hated each other so. If we could only separate, a "separation à l'agréable," as the French say it, and not have a horrid fight for divorce.

The poor exile had already been insulted, she said. She was playing "Yankee Doodle" on the piano before breakfast to soothe her wounded spirit, and the Judge came in and calmly requested her to "leave out the Yankee while she played the Doodle." The Yankee end of it did not suit our climate, he said; was totally out of place and had got out of its latitude.

A man said aloud: "This war talk is nothing. It will soon blow over. Only a fuss gotten up by that Charleston clique." Mr. Toombs asked him to show his passports, for a man who uses such language is a suspicious character.

Walt Whitman

from *Drum-Taps* (1865)

DRUM-TAPS

First, O songs, for a prelude,
Lightly strike on the stretch'd tympanum, pride and joy in my city,
How she led the rest to arms—how she gave the cue,
How at once with lithe limbs, unwaiting a moment, she sprang;
(O superb! O Manhattan, my own, my peerless!
O strongest you in the hour of danger, in crisis! O truer than steel!
How you sprang! how you threw off the costumes of peace with indifferent hand;
How your soft opera-music changed, and the drum and fife were heard in their
        stead;
How you led to the war, (that shall serve for our prelude, songs of soldiers,)
How Manhattan drum-taps led.

Forty years had I in my city seen soldiers parading;
Forty years as a pageant—till unawares, the Lady of this teeming and turbulent city,
Sleepless, amid her ships, her houses, her incalculable wealth,
With her million children around her—suddenly,
At dead of night, at news from the south,
Incens'd, struck with clench'd hand the pavement.

A shock electric—the night sustain'd it;
Till with ominous hum, our hive at day-break, pour'd out its myriads.

From the houses then, and the workshops, and through all the doorways,
Leapt they tumultuous—and lo! Manhattan arming.

To the drum-taps prompt,
The young men falling in and arming;
The mechanics arming, (the trowel, the jack-plane, the blacksmith's hammer,
        tost aside with precipitation;)
The lawyer leaving his office, and arming—the judge leaving the court;
The driver deserting his wagon in the street, jumping down, throwing the reins
        abruptly down on the horses' backs;
The salesman leaving the store—the boss, book-keeper, porter, all leaving;
Squads gathering everywhere by common consent, and arming;
The new recruits, even boys—the old men show them how to wear their
        accoutrements—they buckle the straps carefully;
Outdoors arming—indoors arming—the flash of the musket-barrels;

The white tents cluster in camps—the arm'd sentries around—the sunrise cannon,
 and again at sunset;
Arm'd regiments arrive every day, pass through the city, and embark from
 the wharves;
(How good they look as they tramp down to the river, sweaty, with their guns on
 their shoulders!
How I love them! how I could hug them, with their brown faces, and their clothes
 and knapsacks cover'd with dust!)
The blood of the city up—arm'd! arm'd! the cry everywhere;
The flags flung out from the steeples of churches, and from all the public buildings
 and stores;
The fearful parting—the mother kisses her son—the son kisses his mother;
(Loth is the mother to part—yet not a word does she speak to detain him;)
The tumultuous escort—the ranks of policemen preceding, clearing the way;
The unpent enthusiasm—the wild cheers of the crowd for their favorites;
The artillery—the silent cannons, bright as gold, drawn along, rumble lightly over
 the stones;
(Silent cannons—soon to cease your silence!
Soon, unlimber'd, to begin the red business;)
All the mutter of preparation—all the determin'd arming;
The hospital service—the lint, bandages, and medicines;
The women volunteering for nurses—the work begun for, in earnest—no mere
 parade now;
War! an arm'd race is advancing!—the welcome for battle—no turning away;
War! be it weeks, months, or years—an arm'd race is advancing to welcome it.

Mannahatta a-march!—and it's O to sing it well!
It's O for a manly life in the camp!

And the sturdy artillery!
The guns, bright as gold—the work for giants—to serve well the guns;
Unlimber them! no more, as the past forty years, for salutes for courtesies merely;
Put in something else now besides powder and wadding.

And you, Lady of Ships! you Mannahatta!
Old matron of the city! this proud, friendly, turbulent city!
Often in peace and wealth you were pensive, or covertly frown'd amid all your
 children;
But now you smile with joy, exulting old Mannahatta!

Emily Dickinson

A Day! Help! Help!
Another Day!
Your prayers — Oh Passer by!
From such a common ball as this
Might date a Victory!
From mashallings as simple
The flags of nations swang.
Steady — my soul! What issues
Opon thine arrow hang!

—1859

Success is counted sweetest
By those who ne'er succeed.
To comprehend a nectar
Requires sorest need.

Not one of all the purple Host
Who took the Flag today
Can tell the definition
So clear of Victory

As he defeated — dying —
On whose forbidden ear
The distant strains of triumph
Burst agonized and clear!

—1859

THE TEXTS

Herman Melville, "The Portent" and "Misgivings." Source: *The Works of Herman Melville*. Vol. 16 (London: Constable and Company Ltd., 1924). Originally published in *Battle-Pieces and Aspects of the War* (New York: Harper & Bros., 1866).

Walt Whitman, "Origins of Attempted Secession." Source: *Specimen Days & Collect* (Philadelphia: D. McKay, 1882–83).

Ulysses S. Grant, from *Personal Memoirs*. Source: *Personal Memoirs of U. S. Grant*. Vol. 1 (New York: C. L. Webster & Co., 1885–86).

Jefferson Davis, "Speech in U.S. Senate." Source: *Jefferson Davis: The Essential Writings*, ed. William J. Cooper, Jr. (New York: The Modern Library, 2003).

Henry Timrod, "Ethnogenesis." Source: *War Poetry of the South*, ed. William Gilmore Simms (New York: Richardson & Company, 1866).

Abraham Lincoln, Inaugural Address. Source: *Complete Works of Abraham Lincoln, Comprising his Speeches, Letters, State Papers, and Miscellaneous Writings*, ed. John G. Nicolay and John Hay. Vol. 2 (New York: The Century Company, 1920).

Mary Chesnut, from *A Diary from Dixie*. Source: *A Diary from Dixie, as written by Mary Boykin Chesnut, wife of James Chesnut, Jr., United States Senator from South Carolina, 1859–1861, and afterward an Aide to Jefferson Davis and a Brigadier-General in the Confederate Army*, ed. Isabella D. Martin and Myrta Lockett Avary (New York: D. Appleton and Company, 1905). *A Diary from Dixie* represents a redacted version of the text that Chesnut wrote between 1881 and 1884, based primarily on the journal she kept between 1861 and 1865. According to C. Vann Woodward, the 1905 title was originally chosen by *The Saturday Evening Post*, which serialized five installments of the book in 1905, and retained by Appleton. Also, despite the volume's editorial credits, Woodward notes, most of the editorial work, including footnotes, was undertaken by Appleton editor Francis W. Halsey (C. Vann Woodward, ed., *Mary Chesnut's Civil War*. New Haven: Yale University Press, 1981, p. xxviii).

Walt Whitman, "Drum-Taps." Source: *Walt Whitman's Drum-Taps* (New York: s.n., 1865). Retitled "First O Songs for a Prelude," but not significantly revised, when later included in *Leaves of Grass*.

Emily Dickinson, poems #58 and #112. Source: *The Poems of Emily Dickinson*, ed. R. W. Franklin (Cambridge: The Belknap Press of Harvard University Press, 1999).

NOTES

1. Along with Winfield Scott, Zachary Taylor (1784–1850) helped lead American troops to victory in the Mexican War of 1846–48, a controversial conflict that intensified the domestic debate over the expansion of slavery. After returning to the U.S. in triumph, Taylor won the Presidency in 1848 as a Whig, revealing himself to be both a staunch unionist and, in James McPherson's words, "a free-soil wolf in the clothing of a state's rights sheep" (*Battle Cry of Freedom*, 66). Taylor's death of gastroenteritis, about 16 months after taking office, brought to the Oval Office Millard Fillmore, also a Whig, who would soon sign into law the five bills making up the fateful Compromise of 1850.

2. I.e., the Presidencies of Millard Fillmore (Whig, 1850–53), Franklin Pierce (Democrat, 1853–57), and James Buchanan (Democrat, 1857–1861).

3. A highly doubtful claim, but certainly there were many Northerners and Midwesterners who would have welcomed a separation of the states – some, such as radical abolitionists, who wanted nothing to do with slavery, and others out of the simple pragmatic desire to let the Southern states do as they would. Moreover, even if Whitman's claim were true in absolute terms, it would still be the case that the South, proportionately, had a much greater number of secessionists.

4. Adherents of the ideas, and/or supporters of the various candidacies, of John C. Calhoun (1782–1850), the politician from South Carolina, best known for articulating the doctrine of nullification, who spent vast amounts of energy on promoting states' rights, defending the South against antislavery agitation, and seeking ways of preventing the sectional controversy from spinning out of control.

5. The Domesday Book, commissioned by William the Conqueror in 1085, was a comprehensive hand-written survey of English land ownership and usage, intended as an assessment of resources and taxable property.

6. From mid-1852 to mid-1854, while Grant served in California.

7. In February, 1864, in order to clarify the Federal army's top command structure, Congress resurrected the post of lieutenant general, previously held by George Washington, and President Lincoln named Grant to the post, with the title of general in chief.

8. In the summer of 1852, the 4th Infantry, including Grant, was redeployed to the Pacific Coast. Sailing from New York, the regiment passed through Panama on its way to San Francisco.

9. Henry Clay (1777–1852), Kentucky's most famous statesman, was, along with John C. Calhoun and Daniel Webster, one of the primary architects of the Compromise of 1850.

10. Francis Preston Blair (1791–1876) had one of the more colorful careers in American history, editing the Jacksonian newspaper *The Globe*, helping to organize both the Democratic and Republican parties, becoming a trusted friend and adviser to President Lincoln, and ultimately advocating a gentle policy of Southern reconstruction.

11. The Virginia Declaration of Rights (1776) held that "all men are equally entitled to the free exercise of religion, according to the dictates of conscience."

12. John C. Breckinridge of Kentucky ran as a Democrat with the support of states'-right forces in the South, winning about 45 percent of the region's popular vote.

13. Grant led the successful attack on Fort Donelson, Tennessee, in February 1862. After the surrender of this outpost on the Cumberland River, however, which gave the Union a crucial foothold, Gen. Henry Halleck, who had overall command in the West, pursued a cautious strategy rather than moving aggressively southward.

14. Consider William L. Barney's discussion of "cooperationist" sentiment among rural whites in Alabama and Mississippi in 1860: "The mountain whites, deeply resentful of the planters' wealth and privileges, did not hate slavery so much as they did the second-class citizenship to which it relegated them" (*The Secessionist Impulse: Alabama and Mississippi in 1860* [Princeton: Princeton University Press, 1974], p. 271).

15. The South Carolina legislature voted unanimously to secede on 20 December 1860.

16. Clairborne Fox Jackson (1806–1862) led the secessionist faction in a sharply divided state, taking military steps against federal government after Missouri rejected secession in February, 1861, and prompting unionists to convene a rival state government. After a series of clashes across Missouri in the summer and early fall of 1861, Confederate progress spurred the pro-Southern Missouri legislature to secede, and the state was inducted into the Confederacy in November. Jackson died of pneumonia in December, 1862, as vicious guerrilla warfare raged across the state; he was succeeded by Thomas Reynolds in February, 1863.

17. In 1860, Virginia-born John Buchanan Floyd (1806–1863) ordered the transfer of 125,000 federal firearms to Southern arsenals, ostensibly to make room for new inventory; he was investigated for this order, and on suspicion of graft, but to no result. After resigning in December 1860, Floyd became a Confederate general, but served without distinction, and died of ill health in 1863.

18. The first Confederate Cabinet was formed in Montogomery in February, 1861. The Confederacy voted to relocate its capital to Richmond, Virginia, on 20 May 1861.

19. Mississippi's legislature passed an Ordinance of Secession on January 9, 1861, making the state the second to secede.

20. I.e., President Andrew Jackson, who through threat of force secured the repeal of South Carolina's 1832 "Ordinance of Nullification," passed in response to the federal tariffs of 1828 and 1832.

21. Davis is apparently referring to the 1851 arrest of Shadrach Minkins, a fugitive slave who had escaped to Boston from Norfolk, Virginia, and his subsequent rescue, from a courtroom, by a group of black activists. Three days after this incident, with national attention focused on Massachusetts, then-Senator Davis argued that "if the people of Massachusetts uniformly resisted, then 'the law is dead' and there was no point in using federal force" (Gary Collison, *Shadrach Minkins: From Fugitive Slave to Citizen* [Cambridge: Harvard Unviersity Press, 1997], p. 139).

22. Jefferson's original draft of the Declaration of Independence included among its catalogue of complaints against King George III the following: "[H]e has waged cruel war against human nature itself, violating it's [sic] most sacred rights of life and liberty in the persons of a distant people who never offended him, captivating & carrying them into slavery in another hemisphere . . . [A]nd that this assemblage of horrors might want no fact of distinguished die, he is now exciting those very people to rise in arms among us, and to purchase that liberty of which he has deprived them, by murdering the people on whom he also obtruded them." The Continental Congress struck out this clause in preparing the final version of the Declaration.

23. U.S. Constitution Article 1, Section 2, Paragraph 3, subsequently superseded by the Fourteenth Amendment.

24. The battles of Fort Moultrie and Eutaw Springs, in South Carolina, were Continental victories in the American Revolution.

25. I.e., antislavery. Timrod is referring to those Biblical passages, such as Ephesians 6:5, Colossians 3:22, and Paul's letter to Philemon, which were construed by proslavery writers as sanctioning slavery.

26. Lawrence Masillon Keitt (1824–1864) was a South Carolina "fire-eater" who resigned his Congressional seat after the 1860 election. William Waters Boyce (1818–1890) was Keitt's less rabid fellow Representative from South Carolina. Robert Barnwell Rhett, Sr. (1800–1876), was an extreme secessionist who helped shaped the Confederate Constitution, but spent much of the war complaining about the leadership of Jefferson Davis.

27. "Duncan Nathaniel Ingraham of Charleston resigned as a U.S. Navy commander in Jan. 1861 and was commissioned captain in the Confederate States Navy (C.S.N.) in March" (C. Vann Woodward, *Mary Chesnut's Civil War*, p. 8, n. 2).

28. "Common-law judge Thomas Jefferson Withers of Camden, a delegate to the S.C. secession convention and a member of the Provisional Congress, was M.B.C.'s uncle and former guardian" (Woodward, p. 8, n. 3).

29. South Carolina Gov. Francis Wilkinson Pickens (1805–1869).

30. "William Montague Browne of Washington, D.C., was the Irish-born editor of the Buchanan administration newspaper, the Washington Constitution. His commission as colonel in the C.S.A. and his title, assistant secretary of state, were the result of his friendship with Howell Cobb and Jefferson Davis" (Woodward, p. 9, n. 9).

31. "David Camden DeLeon, a native of Camden, resigned as a U.S. Army surgeon on Feb. 19 and soon became the first surgeon general of the Confederacy" (Woodward, p. 11, n. 4).

32. "Phillip Clayton of Ga. had resigned as assistant secretary of the U.S. Treasury. He held the same post in the Confederate government" (Woodward, p. 11, n. 5).

33. "Born in S.C., Henry Percy Brewster became secretary of war of the Texas Republic and a prominent lawyer in Tex. and Washington, D.C." (Woodward, p. 11, n. 6).

34. Clemens was a former U.S. Senator; Davis was an Alabama planter; Sanders "became a Confederate agent in Canada and Europe"; Deas was "acting adjutant general of the Confederacy" (Woodward, p. 14).

35. The idea, but not the direct quote, is from George Meredith's *Evan Harrington* (1860).

36. "Martin Koszta took part in the Hungarian revolution against Austria in 1848 and fled to the U.S. in 1850. Traveling to Turkey three years later, he was kidnapped and held prisoner aboard an Austrian man-of-war off Smyrna. Duncan Ingraham, commander of the U.S.S. St. Louis, forced Koszta's release with an ultimatum on July 2, 1853. This exploit, occurring at a high point of American sympathy for the revolutionaries of 1848 and dislike for Austria, made Ingraham a national hero" (Woodward, p. 16, n. 6).

II
BATTLEFIELDS

Antietam, Md. Bodies of Confederate dead gathered for burial, September 1862. Photograph by Alexander Gardner

2

INTRODUCTION

The Civil War was fought in eighteen states (counting West Virginia), in ten territories (not counting "Indian Territory"), on hundreds of battlefields. It was fought amidst heavy forest, on mountainsides and bayous, across open plains, on waves and beaches, in rural hamlets and in major cities. The war left its mark on all these places: left it so firmly that the history can still be imagined in the turn of a road or the crest of a hill. Some Civil War battlefields—Antietam, Shiloh, Gettysburg—have taken on a mythic quality that seems only to deepen with time, like Troy or Agincourt. The very word "battlefield" grows archaic, more akin to the Anglo Saxon *waelstow* (field of slaughter) than to today's more cryptic, decentralized sites of mass killing.

Yet the Civil War marked a period of rapid advance, if we can call it that, in the history of armed conflict. The changes in military strategy and technology it ushered in greatly increased the number of combat casualties, and as the bodies accumulated on each American *waelstow* the dead seemed to bear collective witness to the sudden arrival of the furious modern world.

In characteristically American fashion, Civil War commanders, engineers, and innovators placed greater emphasis on the practical than on the theoretical when it came to waging war. Military advances occurred in a rather ad hoc fashion, even haphazardly, as the Union and Confederate war machines tried to adapt to evolving needs and contingencies. Technological, organizational, and strategic adaptations all worked together, and they were all responsive to the particularities of American culture and geography.

First, the pressures of war stimulated the invention of a large number of new military technologies, hundreds of which received patents during the 1860s. Not all of these innovations—such as the submarine or the telescopic sight—were widely adopted at the time, but they set the stage for later refinement. The development of the minié ball, a conical, high-impact bullet; the mass manufacture of the rifled musket, which could shoot much farther and more accurately than traditional smoothbore muskets; and the introduction of the Spencer repeating rifle and the Henry repeater, had the greatest impact on battlefield casualties and, eventually, tactics. In naval warfare, the key breakthrough involved the armoring of ships with metal plates, which spelled the end for traditional wooden ships. Above all, perhaps, the Civil War highlighted the importance of industrial mass production to the creation of a modern war machine, for a central factor in the North's ultimate victory was its greater manufacturing capacity.

Organizationally, the Civil War required the military—whose last conflict had been the comparatively straightforward Mexican War of 1846–48—to upgrade, across the board, its logistical and command procedures. The necessity, particularly for the North, of waging sustained operations in distant theaters of war called for better coordination up and down the military hierarchy, and for improvements in transportation methods and supply line security. Again, many of these lessons of the Civil War would not be applied until America's next major conflict, the Spanish-American War.

Finally, in strategy and tactics the Civil War marked a decisive turn away from the Napoleonic style of conflict, characterized by marching lines, formal assaults, and occupation of territory. New thinking and new weaponry had rendered that style obsolete, and what emerged, haltingly, was something more familiar to us today. The rifle, in particular, shifted the combat advantage to defensive positions, and in digging and protecting their fortified lines, Civil War units saw some of the world's first trench warfare. At the same time, some Civil War commanders—notably Grant in Mississippi, Lee in Pennsylvania, and Sherman in Georgia and South Carolina—came to see the possibilities in an army living off the land and, in effect, terrorizing the locals. The policy of total war, in which a society's entire infrastructure is deemed fair game, and in which an "enemy" civilian population can be made to feel the bite of war, represents the Civil War's most enduring, and most troubling, military legacy.

These changes in technology, organization, and strategy generated a startling variety of combat experience. The Civil War battlefield could be a place of grinding routine or primal hand-to-hand combat; formal infantry charges or improvised cavalry raids; artillery bombardments or amphibious landings; of scouting, spying, digging, looting, burning, fleeing, and chasing.

The emerging forms of warfare also changed the experience of combat for American soldiers, who found themselves in battle environments for which they were necessarily ill prepared. The fluidity and intensity of Civil War combat, with its acoustic and visual uncertainties, and unpredictable yet pervasive lethality, is a recurrent theme in soldiers' letters and memoirs. What many soldiers also described, often in graphic detail, was the spectacle of death: the piles of dead, the look of death, the wounds, and the decomposing.

Combatants adapt and harden, of course, because they have to. Simple repetition could dull the horrors of war, as one soldier observed: "The work of removing and burying the dead has become so common and tame that the lifeless body of a man was looked upon as nothing more than that of a brute."[1] Other inner resources also helped to buttress the men psychologically: camaraderie; feelings of excitement, and determination; a sense of honor and valor; the conviction of fighting for a good cause. Nonetheless, we should not underestimate the level of psychological stress and trauma that Civil War combat produced.

What heightened that psychological impact was the very personal nature of Civil War battlefield experience. These soldiers faced and killed adversaries who, for the most part, were very much like themselves, culturally, physically, and linguistically. They fought on farms and roads, in woods and towns, that they knew, in terrain charged with personal memories, nationalist and family feeling, even future plans. The Civil War was an intimate war, and its battlefields were close and personal crucibles.

NOTE

1.   Yacovone, Donala, ed. *A Voice of Thunder: The Civil War Letters of George E. Stephens*. Urbana: University of Illinois Press, 1997, p. 214.

SUGGESTED READING

Bacon, Benjamin W. *Sinews of War: How Technology, Industry, and Transportation Won the Civil War*. Novato, CA: Presidio Press, 1997.

Daniel, Larry J. *Shiloh: The Battle that Changed the Civil War*. New York: Simon & Schuster, 1997.

Griffith, Paddy. *Battle Tactics of the Civil War*. New Haven: Yale University Press, 1989.

Hagerman, Edward. *The American Civil War and the Origins of Modern Warfare: Ideas, Organization, and Field Command*. Bloomington: Indiana University Press, 1988.

Hess, Earl J. *The Union Soldier in Battle: Enduring the Ordeal of Combat*. Lawrence: University of Kansas Press, 1997.

Linderman, Gerald F. *Embattled Courage: The Experience of Combat in the American Civil War*. New York: Free Press; London: Collier Macmillan, 1987.

Mindell, David A. *War, Technology, and Experience aboard the USS Monitor*. Baltimore: The Johns Hopkins University Press, 2000.

Nosworthy, Brent. *The Bloody Crucible of Courage: Fighting Methods and Combat Experience of the Civil War*. New York: Carroll & Graf, 2003.

Herman Melville

from *Battle-Pieces and Aspects of the War* (1866)

THE MARCH INTO VIRGINIA
ENDING IN THE FIRST MANASSAS (JULY 1861)

Did all the lets and bars appear
    To every just or larger end
Whence should come the trust and cheer?
    Youth must its ignorant impulse lend—
Age finds place in the rear.
    All wars are boyish, and are fought by boys,
The champions and enthusiasts of the state:
    Turbid ardors and vain joins
        Not barrenly abate—
    Stimulants to the power mature,
        Preparatives of fate.

Who here forecasteth the event?
What heart but spurns at precedent
And warnings of the wise,
Contemned foreclosures of surprise?
The banners play, the bugles call,
The air is blue and prodigal.
    No berrying party, pleasure-wooed,
No picnic party in the May,
Ever went less loth than they
    Into that leafy neighborhood.
In Bacchic glee they file toward Fate,
Moloch's uninitiate;
Expectancy, and glad surmise
Of battle's unknown mysteries.
All they feel is this: 'tis glory,
A rapture sharp, though transitory,
Yet lasting in belaureled story.
So they gayly go to fight,
Chatting left and laughing right.

But some who this blithe mood present,
    As on in lightsome files they fare,
Shall die experienced ere three days are spent—
    Perish, enlightened by the vollied glare;
Or shame survive, and, like to adamant,
    The throe of Second Manassas share.

Herman Melville

from *Battle-Pieces and Aspects of the War* (1866)

A UTILITARIAN VIEW OF THE MONITOR'S FIGHT WITH THE MERRIMAC

Plain be the phrase, yet apt the verse,
    More ponderous than nimble;
For since grimed War here laid aside
His Orient pomp, 'twould ill befit
        Overmuch to ply
    The rhyme's barbaric cymbal.

Hail to victory without the gaud
    Of glory; zeal that needs no fans
Of banners; plain mechanic power
Plied cogently in War now placed—
        Where War belongs—
    Among the trades and artisans.

Yet this was battle, and intense—
    Beyond the strife of fleets heroic;
Deadlier, closer, calm 'mid storm;
No passion; all went on by crank,
        Pivot, and screw,
    And calculations of caloric.

Needless to dwell; the story's known.
    The ringing of those plates on plates
Still ringeth round the world—
The clangor of that blacksmith's fray.
        The anvil-din
    Resounds this message from the Fates:

War shall yet be, and to the end;
    But war-paint shows the streaks of weather;
War yet shall be, but warriors
Are now but operatives; War's made
        Less grand than Peace,
    And a singe runs through lace and feather.

Herman Melville

from *Battle-Pieces and Aspects of the War* (1866)

SHILOH: A REQUIEM (APRIL 1862)

Skimming lightly, wheeling still,
    The swallows fly low
Over the field in clouded days,
    The forest-field of Shiloh—
Over the field where April rain
Solaced the parched ones stretched in pain
Through the pause of night
That followed the Sunday fight
    Around the church of Shiloh—
The church so lone, the log-built one,
That echoed to many a parting groan
    And natural prayer
    Of dying foemen mingled there—
Foemen at morn, but friends at eve—
    Fame or country least their care:
(What like a bullet can undeceive!)
    But now they lie low,
While over them the swallows skim,
    And all is hushed at Shiloh.

Herman Melville

from *Battle-Pieces and Aspects of the War* (1866)

MALVERN HILL (JULY 1862)

Ye elms that wave on Malvern Hill
    In prime of morn and May,
Recall ye how McClellan's men
      Here stood at bay?
While deep within yon forest dim
    Our rigid comrades lay—
Some with the cartridge in their mouth,
Others with fixed arms lifted South—
      Invoking so
The cypress glades? Ah wilds of woe!

The spires of Richmond, late beheld
    Through rifts in musket-haze,
Were closed from view in clouds of dust
    On leaf-walled ways,
Where streamed our wagons in caravan;
    And the Seven Nights and Days
Of march and fast, retreat and fight,
Pinched our grimed faces to ghastly plight—
    Does the elm wood
Recall the haggard beards of blood?

The battle-smoked flag, with stars eclipsed,
    We followed (it never fell!)—
Its silence husbanded our strength—
    Received their yell;
Till on this slope we patient turned
    With cannon ordered well;
Reverse we proved was not defeat;
But ah, the sod what thousands meet!—
    Does Malvern Wood
Bethink itself, and muse and brood?

    We elms of Malvern Hill
      Remember every thing;
    But sap the twig will fill;
    Wag the world how it will,
      Leaves must be green in Spring.

Herman Melville

from *Battle-Pieces and Aspects of the War* (1866)

THE SWAMP ANGEL[1]

There is a coal-black Angel
    With a thick Afric lip,
And he dwells (like the hunted and harried)
    In a swamp where the green frogs dip.
But his face is against a City
    Which is over a bay of the sea,
And he breathes with a breath that is blastment,
    And dooms by a far decree.

By night there is fear in the City,
    Through the darkness a star soareth on;
There's a scream that screams up to the zenith,
    Then the poise of a meteor lone—
Lighting far the pale fright of the faces,
    And downward the coming is seen;
Then the rush, and the burst, and the havoc,
    And wails and shrieks between.

It comes like a thief in the gloaming;
    It comes, and none may foretell
The place of the coming—the glaring;
    They live in a sleepless spell
That wizens, and withers, and whitens;
    It ages the young, and the bloom
Of the maiden is ashes of roses—
    The Swamp Angel broods in his gloom.

Swift in his messengers' going,
    But slowly he saps their halls,
As if by delay deluding.
    They move from their crumbling walls
Farther and farther away;
    But the Angel sends after and after,
By night with the flame of his ray—
    By night with the voice of his screaming—
Sends after them, stone by stone,
    And farther walls fall, farther portals,
And weed follows weed through the Town.

Is this the proud City? the scorner
    Which never would yield the ground?
Which mocked at the coal-black Angel?
    The cup of despair goes round.
Vainly she calls upon Michael
    (The white man's seraph was he),
For Michael has fled from his tower
    To the Angel over the sea.

Who weeps for the woeful City
    Let him weep for our guilty kind;
Who joys at her wild despairing—
    Christ, the Forgiver, convert his mind.

George Moses Horton

from *Naked Genius* (1865)

THE DYING SOLDIER'S MESSAGE

Weep, mother, weep, it must be so,
    A tear when parting must be shed,
    The falling tribute is due the dead,
Which leaves the world in gloom below.
    Go flitting bird that splits the sky,
Where sits my mother sighing,
    And should she rise and ask you why,
O, tell her I am dying.

Weep, Father, I shall soon be gone;
    I travel to return no more,
    But sorrow cannot life restore,
I leave the whole to God alone.
    Go, gentle zephyrs, bear the tale,
While sweet the dove is sighing;
    Tell mother never long bewail,
However, I am dying.

Weep, brother, for fraternal love,
    Death is about to close the scene—
    Short is the space that lies between
My soul and better worlds above.
    Let thunder storms my fate betray,
Ye sable vapors flying,
    Sound that my life has past away,
Tell mother I am dying.

Weep, sister, love was born to grieve
    For one thus passing out of time;
    From this to other worlds sublime,
I shut my eyes and take my leave.
    The favorite bird will soon have fled;
The fate there's no denying,
    I soon shall lodge among the dead,
For I am surely dying.

George Moses Horton

from *Naked Genius* (1865)

"EXECUTION OF PRIVATE HENRY ANDERSON" CO. D., 9TH MICH. CAV. VOLS., AT LEXINGTON, NORTH CAROLINA, MAY 13TH, 1865

This verse is plain, that all may understand,
The scene is solemn and expressly grand;
The must'ring concourse form'd in grand array,
Betrayed the fate of the expiring day;
Gazing spectators seemed completely dumb,
Beneath the sound of bugle and the drum.
The fun'ral march attracted every eye,
To see the trembling malefactor die;
O, memorable eve, not soon forgot,
'Tis written on a tablet ne'er to blot;
We never can the scene portray,
The ghastly aspect of the fatal day.

We've heard of martyrs at the cruel stake,
From which an adamantine heart would break;
We've heard of victims on the fun'ral pyre,
Containing sacrifice and set on fire,
When victims died beneath the ruthless flame,
The brutal torture of eternal shame.

This case seems to bear the mark, tho' justly done,
A case that every sober man may shun;
'Twas for the deed of open homicide,
This guilty malefactor fell and died.
See well arrayed the attentive squadrons stand,
Thus to discharge their guns at one command;
'Till pointing at one mark the shaft of death,
He breaths at once his last decisive breath.

It is, indeed, a sad infernal crime
To one's own self, thus hurried out of time;
He introduces first the murderous strife,
By his own hand he spurns away his life!
How many creatures thus have fell,
Imbibing nectar from the bowls of hell!

Inspiring depredations all the night,
And thus betrayed the death at morning light;
Thus flies the deadly shaft without control—
He fell upon his coffin, O, my soul!
Let all that live the scene appall—
He dies! no more to live at all, at all!

George Moses Horton

from *Naked Genius* (1865)

THE SPECTATOR OF THE BATTLE OF BELMONT, NOVEMBER 6, 1863[2]

O brother spectators, I long shall remember,
    The blood-crimson veil which spreads over the field,
When battle commenc'd on the sixth of November,
    With war-beaming aspect, the sword and the shield.

The sound of destruction breaks loud from the mortars,
    The watchman is tolling the death-tuning knell,
The heroes are clustering from quarter to quarter;
    What mortal, the fate of this combat shall tell?

Blood breaks from its vein like a stream from its fountain;
    Spectators the pain of the conflict explore;
The fugitives fly to the cave on the mountain,
    Betray'd by the vestige of blood in their gore.

The conflict begins from the twang of the drummer,
    And ends with the peal of a tragical tale;
O yes, it subsides like a storm into summer,
    No less for the dead shall the living bewail.

I've heard of the battles of many foreign nations;
    I've heard of the wonderful conflict of Troy,
And battles, with bloodshed, thro' all generations,
    But nothing like this could my feelings annoy.

The dark dirge of destiny, sung by a spirit,
    Alone can the scene of the combat display,
For surely no dull earthly mortal can merit
    A wonder to equal this tragical lay.

George Moses Horton

from *Naked Genius* (1865)

THE TERRORS OF WAR

He bids the comet play,
    And empires tremble at his burning tail;
Commanding troops without delay,
The distant land his calls obey,
Ye proud imperial powers give way,
    And at the cause bewail.

Along the common tide,
    Pallid he floated with a hideous yell;
Napoleon bellowed at his side,
And saw compassion all denied;
Beneath his stroke, ten thousand died,
    And wounded millions fell.

Ye breathe a doleful strain,
    Pursued at once by heavy rending peals;
He heaved his thunders from the main,
In purple gore he dyed the plain,
Then boasted his legions slain,
    Beneath the ruthless wheel.

Pregnant with every ill,
    He breathed his stenched diseases from afar;
A quiet world no more was still,
And terrors broke from hill to hill,
Whose bloody thirst was all to kill,
    Which stood before his car.

Sarah Morgan Bryan Piatt

from *The Nests at Washington and Other Poems* (1864)

HEARING THE BATTLE—JULY 21, 1861

One day in the dreamy summer,
    On the Sabbath hills, from afar
We heard the solemn echoes
    Of the first fierce words of war.

Ah, tell me, thou veilèd Watcher
    Of the storm and the calm to come,
How long by the sun or shadow
    Till these noises again are dumb.

And soon in a hush and glimmer
    We thought of the dark, strange fight,
Whose close in a ghastly quiet
    Lay dim the beautiful night.

Then we talk'd of coldness and pallor,
    And of things with blinded eyes
That stared at the golden stillness
    Of the moon in those lighted skies;

And of souls, at morning wrestling
    In the dust with passion and moan,
So far away at evening
   · In the silence of worlds unknown.

But a delicate wind beside us
    Was rustling the dusky hours,
As it gather'd the dewy odors
    Of the snowy jessamine-flowers.

And I gave you a spray of blossoms,
    And said: "I shall never know
How the hearts in the land are breaking,
    My dearest, unless you go."

Henry Wadsworth Longfellow

THE CUMBERLAND (DECEMBER 1862)

At anchor in Hampton Roads we lay,
    On board of the Cumberland, sloop-of-war;
And at times from the fortress across the bay
      The alarum of drums swept past,
      Or a bugle blast
    From the camp on the shore.

Then far away to the south uprose
    A little feather of snow-white smoke,
And we knew that the iron ship of our foes
      Was steadily steering its course
      To try the force
    Of our ribs of oak.

Down upon us heavily runs,
    Silent and sullen, the floating fort;
Then comes a puff of smoke from her guns,
      And leaps the terrible death,
      With fiery breath,
    From each open port.

We are not idle, but send her straight
    Defiance back in a full broadside!
As hail rebounds from a roof of slate,
      Rebounds our heavier hail
      From each iron scale
    Of the monster's hide.

"Strike your flag!" the rebel cries,
    In his arrogant old plantation strain.
"Never!" our gallant Morris replies;
      "It is better to sink than to yield!"
      And the whole air pealed
    With the cheers of our men.

Then, like a kraken huge and black,
    She crushed our ribs in her iron grasp!
Down went the Cumberland all a wrack,
      With a sudden shudder of death,
      And the cannon's breath
    For her dying gasp.

Next morn, as the sun rose over the bay,
    Still floated our flag at the mainmast head.
Lord, how beautiful was Thy day!
      Every waft of the air
      Was a whisper of prayer,
    Or a dirge for the dead.

Ho! brave hearts that went down in the seas!
    Ye are at peace in the troubled stream;
Ho! brave land! with hearts like these,
      Thy flag, that is rent in twain,
      Shall be one again,
    And without a seam!

Henry Wadsworth Longfellow

KILLED AT THE FORD (APRIL 1866)

He is dead, the beautiful youth,
The heart of honor, the tongue of truth,
He, the life and light of us all,
Whose voice was blithe as a bugle-call,
Whom all eyes followed with one consent,
The cheer of whose laugh, and whose pleasant word,
Hushed all murmurs of discontent.

Only last night, as we rode along,
Down the dark of the mountain gap,
To visit the picket-guard at the ford,
Little dreaming of any mishap,
He was humming the words of some old song:
"Two red roses he had on his cap
And another he bore at the point of his sword."

Sudden and swift a whistling ball
Came out of a wood, and the voice was still;
Something I heard in the darkness fall,
And for a moment my blood grew chill;
I spake in a whisper, as he who speaks
In a room where some one is lying dead;
But he made no answer to what I said.

We lifted him up to his saddle again,
And through the mire and the mist and the rain
Carried him back to the silent camp,
And laid him as if asleep on his bed;
And I saw by the light of the surgeon's lamp
Two white roses upon his cheeks,
And one, just over his heart, blood-red!

And I saw in a vision how far and fleet
That fatal bullet went speeding forth,
Till it reached a town in the distant North,
Till it reached a house in a sunny street,
Till it reached a heart that ceased to beat,
Without a murmur, without a cry;
And a bell was tolled, in that far-off town,
For one who had passed from cross to crown
And the neighbors wondered that she should die.

Lucy Larcom

from *Songs for War Time* (1863)

THE SINKING OF THE MERRIMACK
MAY, 1862

Gone down in the flood, and gone out in the flame!
What else could she do, with her fair Northern name?
Her font was a river whose last drop is free:
That river ran boiling with wrath to the sea,
To hear of her baptismal blessing profaned:
A name that was Freedom's, by treachery stained.

'T was the voice of our free Northern mountains that broke
In the sound of her guns, from her stout ribs of oak:
'T was the might of the free Northern hand you could feel
In her sweep and her moulding, from topmast to keel:
When they made her speak treason, (does Hell know of worse?)
How her strong timbers shook with the shame of her curse!

Let her go! Should a deck so polluted again
Ever ring to the tread of our true Northern men?
Let the suicide-ship thunder forth, to the air
And the sea she has blotted, her groan of despair!
Let her last heat of anguish throb out into flame!
Then sink them together,—the ship and the name!

Walt Whitman

from *Specimen Days* (1882)

A NIGHT BATTLE, OVER A WEEK SINCE

May 12. — There was part of the late battle at Chancellorsville, (second Fredericksburgh,) a little over a week ago, Saturday, Saturday night and Sunday, under Gen. Joe Hooker, I would like to give just a glimpse of—(a moment's look in a terrible storm at sea—of which a few suggestions are enough, and full details impossible.) The fighting had been very hot during the day, and after an intermission the latter part, was resumed at night, and kept up with furious energy till 3 o'clock in the morning. That afternoon (Saturday) an attack sudden and strong by Stonewall Jackson had gain'd a great advantage to the southern army, and broken our lines, entering us like a wedge, and leaving things in that position at dark. But Hooker at 11 at night made a desperate push, drove the secesh forces back, restored his original lines, and resumed his plans. This night scrimmage was very exciting, and afforded countless strange and fearful pictures. The fighting had been general both at Chancellorsville and northeast at Fredericksburgh. (We heard of some poor fighting, episodes, skedaddling on our part. I think not of it. I think of the fierce bravery, the general rule.) One corps, the 6th, Sedgewick's,[3] fights four dashing and bloody battles in thirty-six hours, retreating in great jeopardy, losing largely but maintaining itself, fighting with the sternest desperation under all circumstances, getting over the Rappahannock only by the skin of its teeth, yet getting over. It lost many, many brave men, yet it took vengeance, ample vengeance.

But it was the tug of Saturday evening, and through the night and Sunday morning, I wanted to make a special note of. It was largely in the woods, and quite a general engagement. The night was very pleasant, at times the moon shining out full and clear, all Nature so calm in itself, the early summer grass so rich, and foliage of the trees—yet there the battle raging, and many good fellows lying helpless, with new accessions to them, and every minute amid the rattle of muskets and crash of cannon, (for there was an artillery contest too,) the red life-blood oozing out from heads or trunks or limbs upon that green and dew-cool grass. Patches of the woods take fire, and several of the wounded, unable to move, are consumed—quite large spaces are swept over, burning the dead also—some of the men have their hair and beards singed—some, burns on their faces and hands—others holes burnt in their clothing. The flashes of fire from the cannon, the quick flaring flames and smoke, and the immense roar—the musketry so general, the light nearly bright enough for each side to see the other—the crashing, tramping of men—the yelling—close quarters—we hear the secesh yells—our men cheer loudly back, especially if Hooker is in sight—hand to hand conflicts, each side stands up to it, brave, determin'd as demons, they often charge upon us—a thousand deeds are done worth to write newer greater poems on—and still the woods on fire—still many are not only scorch'd—too many, unable to move, are burn'd to death.

Then the camps of the wounded—O heavens, what scene is this?—is this indeed *hu-manity*—these butchers' shambles? There are several of them. There they lie, in the largest, in an open space in the woods, from 200 to 300 poor fellows—the groans and screams—the odor of blood, mixed with the fresh scent of the night, the grass, the trees—that slaugh-ter—house! O well is it their mothers, their sisters cannot see them—cannot conceive, and never conceiv'd, these things. One man is shot by a shell, both in the arm and leg—both are amputated—there lie the rejected members. Some have their legs blown off—some bullets through the breast—some indescribably horrid wounds in the face or head, all mutilated, sickening, torn, gouged out—some in the abdomen—some mere boys—many rebels, badly hurt—they take their regular turns with the rest, just the same as any—the surgeons use them just the same. Such is the camp of the wounded—such a fragment, a reflection afar off of the bloody scene—while over all the clear, large moon comes out at times softly, quietly shining. Amid the woods, that scene of flitting souls—amid the crack and crash and yelling sounds—the impalpable perfume of the woods—and yet the pun-gent, stifling smoke—the radiance of the moon, looking from heaven at intervals so plac-id—the sky so heavenly—the clear—obscure up there, those buoyant upper oceans—a few large placid stars beyond, coming silently and languidly out, and then disappearing—the melancholy, draperied night above, around. And there, upon the roads, the fields, and in those woods, that contest, never one more desperate in any age or land—both parties now in force—masses—no fancy battle, no semi–play, but fierce and savage demons fighting there—courage and scorn of death the rule, exceptions almost none.

What history, I say, can ever give—for who can know—the mad, determin'd tussle of the armies, in all their separate large and little squads—as this—each steep'd from crown to toe in desperate, mortal purports? Who know the conflict, hand-to-hand—the many conflicts in the dark, those shadowy-tangled, flashing moonbeam'd woods—the writing groups and squads—the cries, the din, the cracking guns and pistols—the distant can-non—the cheers and calls and threats and awful music of the oaths—the indescribable mix—the officers' orders, persuasions, encouragements—the devils fully rous'd in human hearts—the strong shout, *Charge, men, charge*—the flash of the naked sword, and rolling flame and smoke? And still the broken, clear and clouded heaven—and still again the moonlight pouring silvery soft its radiant patches over all. Who paint the scene, the sud-den partial panic of the afternoon, at dusk? Who paint the irrepressible advance of the second division of the Third corps, under Hooker himself, suddenly order'd up—those rapid-filing phantoms through the woods? Who show what moves there in the shadows, fluid and firm—to save, (and it did save,) the army's name, perhaps the nation? as there the veterans hold the field. (Brave Berry falls not yet—but death has mark'd him—soon he falls.)[4]

Walt Whitman

from *Specimen Days* (1882)

A GLIMPSE OF WAR'S HELL-SCENES

In one of the late movements of our troops in the valley, (near Upperville, I think,) a strong force of Moseby's mounted guerillas attack'd a train of wounded, and the guard of cavalry convoying them.[5] The ambulances contain'd about 60 wounded, quite a number of them officers of rank. The rebels were in strength, and the capture of the train and its partial guard after a short snap was effectually accomplish'd. No sooner had our men surrender'd, the rebels instantly commenced robbing the train and murdering their prisoners, even the wounded. Here is the scene or a sample of it, ten minutes after. Among the wounded officers in the ambulances were one, a lieutenant of regulars, and another of higher rank. These two were dragg'd out on the ground on their backs, and were now surrounded by the guerillas, a demoniac crowd, each member of which was stabbing them in different parts of their bodies. One of the officers had his feet pinn'd firmly to the ground by bayonets stuck through them and thrust into the ground. These two officers, as afterwards found on examination, had receiv'd about twenty such thrusts, some of them through the mouth, face, &c. The wounded had all been dragg'd (to give a better chance also for plunder,) out of their wagons; some had been effectually dispatch'd, and their bodies were lying there lifeless and bloody. Others, not yet dead, but horribly mutilated, were moaning or groaning. Of our men who surrender'd, most had been thus maim'd or slaughter'd.

At this instant a force of our cavalry, who had been following the train at some interval, charge suddenly upon the secesh captors, who proceeded at once to make the best escape they could. Most of them got away, but we gobbled two officers and seventeen men, in the very acts just described. The sight was one which admitted of little discussion, as may be imagined. The seventeen captur'd men and two officers were put under guard for the night, but it was decided there and then that they should die. The next morning the two officers were taken in the town, separate places, put in the centre of the street, and shot. The seventeen men were taken to an open ground, a little one side. They were placed in a hollow square, half-encompass'd by two of our cavalry regiments, one of which regiments had three days before found the bloody corpses of three of their men hamstrung and hung up by the heels to limbs of trees by Moseby's guerillas, and the other had not long before had twelve men, after surrendering, shot and then hung by the neck to limbs of trees, and jeering inscriptions pinn'd to the breast of one of the corpses, who had been a sergeant. Those three, and those twelve, had been found, I say, by these environing regiments. Now, with revolvers, they form'd the grim cordon of the seventeen prisoners. The latter were placed in the midst of the hollow square, unfasten'd, and the ironical remark made to them that they were now to be given "a chance for themselves." A few ran for it. But what use? From every side the deadly pills came. In a few minutes the seventeen corpses strew'd the hollow square. I was curious to know whether some of the Union soldiers, some few, (some one or two at least of the youngsters,) did not abstain from shooting on the helpless men. Not one. There was no exultation, very little said, almost nothing, yet every man there contributed his shot.

Multiply the above by scores, aye hundreds—verify it in all the forms that different circumstances, individuals, places, could afford—light it with every lurid passion, the wolf's, the lion's lapping thirst for blood—the passionate, boiling volcanoes of human revenge for comrades, brothers slain—with the light of burning farms, and heaps of smutting, smouldering black embers—and in the human heart everywhere black, worse embers—and you have an inkling of this war.

Walt Whitman

from *Specimen Days* (1882)

THE WEATHER.—DOES IT SYMPATHIZE WITH THESE TIMES?

Whether the rains, the heat and cold, and what underlies them all, are affected with what affects man in masses, and follow his play of passionate action, strain'd stronger than usual, and on a larger scale than usual—whether this, or no, it is certain that there is now, and has been for twenty months or more, on this American continent north, many a remarkable, many an unprecedented expression of the subtile world of air above us and around us. There, since this war, and the wide and deep national agitation, strange analogies, different combinations, a different sunlight, or absence of it; different products even out of the ground. After every great battle, a great storm. Even civic events the same. On Saturday last, a forenoon like whirling demons, dark, with slanting rain, full of rage; and then the afternoon, so calm, so bathed with flooding splendor from heaven's most excellent sun, with atmosphere of sweetness; so clear, it show'd the stars, long, long before they were due. As the President came out on the capitol portico, a curious little white cloud, the only one in that part of the sky, appear'd like a hovering bird, right over him.

Indeed, the heavens, the elements, all the meteorological influences, have run riot for weeks past. Such caprices, abruptest alternation of frowns and beauty, I never knew. It is a common remark that (as last summer was different in its spells of intense heat from any preceding it,) the winter just completed has been without parallel. It has remain'd so down to the hour I am writing. Much of the daytime of the past month was sulky, with leaden heaviness, fog, interstices of bitter cold, and some insane storms. But there have been samples of another description. Nor earth nor sky ever knew spectacles of superber beauty than some of the nights lately here. The western star, Venus, in the earlier hours of evening, has never been so large, so clear; it seems as if it told something, as if it held rapport indulgent with humanity, with us Americans. Five or six nights since, it hung close by the moon, then a little past its first quarter. The star was wonderful, the moon like a young mother. The sky, dark blue, the transparent night, the planets, the moderate west wind, the elastic temperature, the miracle of that great star, and the young and swelling moon swimming in the west, suffused the soul. Then I heard, slow and clear, the deliberate notes of a bugle come up out of the silence, sounding so good through the night's mystery, no hurry, but firm and faithful, floating along, rising, falling leisurely, with here and there a long-drawn note; the bugle, well-play'd, sounding tattoo, in one of the army hospitals near here, where the wounded (some of them personally so dear to me,) are lying in their cots, and many a sick boy come down to the war from Illinois, Michigan, Wisconsin, Iowa, and the rest.

Walt Whitman

from *Specimen Days* (1882)

TWO BROTHERS, ONE SOUTH, ONE NORTH

May 28-9. — I staid to-night a long time by the bedside of a new patient, a young Baltimorean, aged about 19 years, W. S. P., (2d Maryland, southern,)[6] very feeble, right leg amputated, can't sleep hardly at all—has taken a great deal of morphine, which, as usual, is costing more than it comes to. Evidently very intelligent and well bred—very affectionate—held on to my hand, and put it by his face, not willing to let me leave. As I was lingering, soothing him in his pain, he says to me suddenly, "I hardly think you know who I am—I don't wish to impose upon you—I am a rebel soldier." I said I did not know that, but it made no difference. Visiting him daily for about two weeks after that, while he lived, (death had mark'd him, and he was quite alone,) I loved him much, always kiss'd him, and he did me. In an adjoining ward I found his brother, an officer of rank, a Union soldier, a brave and religious man, (Col. Clifton K. Prentiss, sixth Maryland infantry, Sixth corps, wounded in one of the engagements at Petersburgh, April 2—linger'd, suffer'd much, died in Brooklyn, Aug. 20, '65.)[7] It was in the same battle both were hit. One was a strong Unionist, the other Secesh; both fought on their respective sides, both badly wounded, and both brought together here after a separation of four years. Each died for his cause.

Walt Whitman

from *Drum-Taps* (1865)

BY THE BIVOUAC'S FITFUL FLAME

By the bivouac's fitful flame,
A procession winding around me, solemn and sweet and slow;—but first I note,
The tents of the sleeping army, the fields' and woods' dim outline,
The darkness lit by spots of kindled fire—the silence;
Like a phantom far or near an occasional figure moving;
The shrubs and trees, (as I lift my eyes they seem to be stealthily watching me;)
While wind in procession thoughts, O tender and wond'rous thoughts,
Of life and death—of home and the past and loved, and of those that are far away;
A solemn and slow procession there as I sit on the ground,
By the bivouac's fitful flame.

Walt Whitman

from *Drum-Taps* (1865)

THE DRESSER

An old man bending, I come, among new faces,
Years looking backward, resuming, in answer to children,
Come tell us old man, as from young men and maidens that love me;
Years hence of these scenes, of these furious passions, these chances,
Of unsurpass'd heroes, (was one side so brave? the other was equally brave;)
Now be witness again—paint the mightiest armies of earth;
Of those armies so rapid so wondrous what saw you to tell us?
What stays with you latest and deepest? of curious panics,
Of hard-fought engagements, or sieges tremendous, what deepest remains?

O maidens and young men I love, and that love me,
What you ask of my days, those the strangest and sudden your talking recals; [sic]
Soldier alert I arrive, after a long march, cover'd with sweat and dust;
In the nick of time I come, plunge in the fight, loudly shout in the rush of successful
    charge;
Enter the captur'd works…yet lo! like a swift-running river, they fade;
Pass and are gone, they fade—I dwell not on soldiers' perils or soldiers' joys;
(Both I remember well—many the hardships, few the joys, yet I was content.)

But in silence, in dreams' projections,
While the world of gain and appearance and mirth goes on,
So soon what is over forgotten, and waves wash the imprints off the sand,
In nature's reverie sad, with hinged knees returning, I enter the doors—(while for
    you up there,
Whoever you are, follow without noise, and be of strong heart.)

Bearing the bandages, water and sponge,
Straight and swift to my wounded I go,
Where they lie on the ground after the battle brought in;
Where their priceless blood reddens the grass, the ground;
Or to the rows of the hospital tent, or under the roof'd hospital;
To the long rows of cots, up and down, each side, I return;
To each and all, one after another, I draw near—not one do I miss;
An attendant follows, holding a tray—he carries a refuse pail,
Soon to be fill'd with clotted rags and blood, emptied, and fill'd again.

I onward go, I stop,
With hinged knees and steady hand, to dress wounds;
I am firm with each—the pangs are sharp, yet unavoidable;
One turns to me his appealing eyes—(poor boy! I never knew you,
Yet I think I could not refuse this moment to die for you, if that would save you.)

On, on I go—(open, doors of time! open, hospital doors!)
The crush'd head I dress, (poor crazed hand, tear not the bandage away;)
The neck of the cavalry-man with the bullet through and through, I examine;
Hard the breathing rattles, quite glazed already the eye, yet life struggles hard;
(Come sweet death! be persuaded, O beautiful death!
In mercy come quickly.)

From the stump of the arm, the amputated hand,
I undo the clotted lint, remove the slough, wash off the matter and blood;
Back on his pillow the soldier bends, with curv'd neck, and side-falling head;
His eyes are closed, his face is pale, he dares not look on the bloody stump,
And has not yet look'd on it.

I dress a wound in the side, deep, deep;
But a day or two more—for see, the frame all wasted and sinking,
And the yellow-blue countenance see.

I dress the perforated shoulder, the foot with the bullet-wound,
Cleanse the one with a gnawing and putrid gangrene, so sickening, so offensive,
While the attendant stands behind aside me, holding the tray and pail.

I am faithful, I do not give out;
The fractur'd thigh, the knee, the wound in the abdomen,
These and more I dress with impassive hand—(yet deep in my breast a fire,
    a burning flame.)

Thus in silence, in dreams' projections,
Returning, resuming, I thread my way through the hospitals;
The hurt and the wounded I pacify with soothing hand,
I sit by the restless all the dark night—some are so young;
Some suffer so much—I recall the experience sweet and sad;
(Many a soldier's loving arms about this neck have cross'd and rested,
Many a soldier's kiss dwells on these bearded lips.)

Walt Whitman

from *Drum-Taps* (1865)

VIGIL STRANGE I KEPT ON THE FIELD ONE NIGHT

Vigil strange I kept on the field one night,
When you, my son and my comrade, dropt at my side that day,
One look I but gave, which your dear eyes return'd, with a look I shall never forget;
One touch of your hand to mine, O boy, reach'd up as you lay on the ground;
Then onward I sped in the battle, the even-contested battle;
Till late in the night reliev'd, to the place at last again I made my way;
Found you in death so cold, dear comrade—found your body, son of responding
      kisses, (never again on earth responding;)
Bared your face in the starlight—curious the scene—cool blew the moderate
      night-wind;
Long there and then in vigil I stood, dimly around me the battle-field spreading;
Vigil wondrous and vigil sweet, there in the fragrant silent night;
But not a tear fell, not even a long-drawn sigh—Long, long I gazed;
Then on the earth partially reclining, sat by your side, leaning my chin in my hands;
Passing sweet hours, immortal and mystic hours with you, dearest comrade—
      Not a tear, not a word;
Vigil of silence, love and death—vigil for you, my son and my soldier,
As onward silently stars aloft, eastward new ones upward stole;
Vigil final for you, brave boy, (I could not save you, swift was your death,
I faithfully loved you and cared for you living—I think we shall surely meet again;)
Till at latest lingering of the night, indeed just as the dawn appear'd,
My comrade I wrapt in his blanket, envelop'd well his form,
Folded the blanket well, tucking it carefully over head, and carefully under feet;
And there and then, and bathed by the rising sun, my son in his grave, in his
      rude-dug grave I deposited;
Ending my vigil strange with that—vigil of night and battle-field dim;
Vigil for boy of responding kisses, (never again on earth responding;)
Vigil for comrade swiftly slain—vigil I never forget, how as day brighten'd,
I rose from the chill ground, and folded my soldier well in his blanket,
And buried him where he fell.

Walt Whitman

from *Drum-Taps* (1865)

CAMPS OF GREEN

Not alone our camps of white, O soldiers,
When, as order'd forward, after a long march,
Footsore and weary, soon as the light lessens, we halt for the night;
Some of us so fatigued, carrying the gun and knapsack, dropping asleep in
     our tracks;
Others pitching the little tents, and the fires lit up begin to sparkle;
Outposts of pickets posted, surrounding, alert through the dark,
And a word provided for countersign, careful for safety;
Till to the call of the drummers at daybreak loudly beating the drums,
We rise up refresh'd, the night and sleep pass'd over, and resume our journey,
Or proceed to battle.

Lo! the camps of the tents of green,
Which the days of peace keep filling, and the days of war keep filling,
With a mystic army, (is it too order'd forward? is it too only halting awhile,
Till night and sleep pass over?)

Now in those camps of green—in their tents dotting the world;
In the parents, children, husbands, wives, in them—in the old and young,
Sleeping under the sunlight, sleeping under the moonlight, content and silent
     there at last,
Behold the mighty bivouac-field, and waiting-camp of us and ours and all,
Of our corps and generals all, and the President over the corps and generals all,
And of each of us, O soldiers, and of each and all in the ranks we fight,
(There without hatred we shall all meet.)

For presently, O soldiers, we too camp in our place in the bivouac-camps of green;
But we need not provide for outposts, nor word for the countersign,
Nor drummer to beat the morning drum.

S. Weir Mitchell

THE CASE OF GEORGE DEDLOW
(1866)

The following notes of my own case have been declined on various pretexts by every medical journal to which I have offered them. There was, perhaps, some reason in this, because many of the medical facts which they record are not altogether new, and because the psychical deductions to which they have led me are not in themselves of medical interest. I ought to add that a great deal of what is here related is not of any scientific value whatsoever; but as one or two people on whose judgment I rely have advised me to print my narrative with all the personal details, rather than in the dry shape in which, as a psychological statement, I shall publish it elsewhere, I have yielded to their views. I suspect, however, that the very character of my record will, in the eyes of some of my readers, tend to lessen the value of the metaphysical discoveries which it sets forth.

I am the son of a physician, still in large practice, in the village of Abington, Scofield County, Indiana. Expecting to act as his future partner, I studied medicine in his office, and in 1859 and 1860 attended lectures at the Jefferson Medical College in Philadelphia. My second course should have been in the following year, but the outbreak of the Rebellion so crippled my father's means that I was forced to abandon my intention. The demand for army surgeons at this time became very great; and although not a graduate, I found no difficulty in getting the place of assistant surgeon to the Tenth Indiana Volunteers. In the subsequent Western campaigns this organization suffered so severely that before the term of its service was over it was merged in the Twenty-first Indiana Volunteers; and I, as an extra surgeon, ranked by the medical officers of the latter regiment, was transferred to the Fifteenth Indiana Cavalry. Like many physicians, I had contracted a strong taste for army life, and, disliking cavalry service, sought and obtained the position of first lieutenant in the Seventy-ninth Indiana Volunteers, an infantry regiment of excellent character.[8]

On the day after I assumed command of my company, which had no captain, we were sent to garrison a part of a line of blockhouses stretching along the Cumberland River below Nashville, then occupied by a portion of the command of General Rosecrans.

The life we led while on this duty was tedious and at the same time dangerous in the extreme. Food was scarce and bad, the water horrible, and we had no cavalry to forage for us. If, as infantry, we attempted to levy supplies upon the scattered farms around us, the population seemed suddenly to double, and in the shape of guerrillas "potted" us industriously from behind distant trees, rocks, or fences. Under these various and unpleasant influences, combined with a fair infusion of malaria, our men rapidly lost health and spirits.[9] Unfortunately, no proper medical supplies had been forwarded with our small force (two companies), and, as the fall advanced, the want of quinine and stimulants became a serious annoyance. Moreover, our rations were running low; we had been three weeks without a new supply; and our commanding officer, Major Henry L. Terrill, began to be uneasy as to the safety of his men. About this time it was supposed that a train with rations would be due from the post twenty miles to the north of us; yet it was quite possible that it would bring us food, but no medicines, which were what we most needed. The command was too small to detach any part of it, and the major therefore resolved to send an officer alone to the post above us, where the rest of the Seventy-ninth lay, and whence they could easily forward quinine and stimulants by the train, if it had not left, or, if it had, by a small cavalry escort.

It so happened, to my cost, as it turned out, that I was the only officer fit to make the journey, and I was accordingly ordered to proceed to Blockhouse No. 3 and make the required arrangements. I started alone just after dusk the next night, and during the darkness succeeded in getting within three miles of my destination. At this time I found that I had lost my way, and, although aware of the danger of my act, was forced to turn aside and ask at a log cabin for directions. The house contained a dried-up old woman and four white-headed, half-naked children. The woman was either stone-deaf or pretended to be so; but, at all events, she gave me no satisfaction, and I remounted and rode away. On coming to the end of a lane, into which I had turned to seek the cabin, I found to my surprise that the bars had been put up during my brief parley. They were too high to leap, and I therefore dismounted to pull them down. As I touched the top rail, I heard a rifle, and at the same instant felt a blow on both arms, which fell helpless. I staggered to my horse and tried to mount; but, as I could use neither arm, the effort was vain, and I therefore stood still, awaiting my fate. I am only conscious that I saw about me several graybacks, for I must have fallen fainting almost immediately.

When I awoke I was lying in the cabin near by, upon a pile of rubbish. Ten or twelve guerrillas were gathered about the fire, apparently drawing lots for my watch, boots, hat, etc. I now made an effort to find out how far I was hurt. I discovered that I could use the left forearm and hand pretty well, and with this hand I felt the right limb all over until I touched the wound. The ball had passed from left to right through the left biceps, and directly through the right arm just below the shoulder, emerging behind. The right arm and forearm were cold and perfectly insensible. I pinched them as well as I could, to test the amount of sensation remaining; but the hand might as well have been that of a dead man. I began to understand that the nerves had been wounded, and that the part was utterly powerless. By this time my friends had pretty well divided the spoils, and, rising together, went out. The old woman then came to me, and said: "Reckon you'd best git up. They-'uns is a-goin' to take you away." To this I only answered, "Water, water." I had a grim sense of amusement on finding that the old woman was not deaf, for she went out, and presently came back with a gourdful, which I eagerly drank. An hour later the graybacks returned, and finding that I was too weak to walk, carried me out and laid me on the bottom of a common cart, with which they set off on a trot. The jolting was horrible, but within an hour I began to have in my dead right hand a strange burning, which was rather a relief to me. It increased as the sun rose and the day grew warm, until I felt as if the hand was caught and pinched in a red-hot vise. Then in my agony I begged my guard for water to wet it with, but for some reason they desired silence, and at every noise threatened me with a revolver. At length the pain became absolutely unendurable, and I grew what it is the fashion to call demoralized. I screamed, cried, and yelled in my torture, until, as I suppose, my captors became alarmed, and, stopping, gave me a handkerchief,—my own, I fancy,—and a canteen of water, with which I wetted the hand, to my unspeakable relief.

It is unnecessary to detail the events by which, finally, I found myself in one of the rebel hospitals near Atlanta. Here, for the first time, my wounds were properly cleansed and dressed by a Dr. Oliver T. Wilson, who treated me throughout with great kindness. I told him I had been a doctor, which, perhaps, may have been in part the cause of the unusual tenderness with which I was managed. The left arm was now quite easy, although, as will be seen, it never entirely healed. The right arm was worse than ever—the humerus broken, the nerves wounded, and the hand alive only to pain. I use this phrase because it is connected in my mind with a visit from a local visitor,—I am not sure he was a preacher,— who used to go daily through the wards, and talk to us or write our letters. One morning he stopped at my bed, when this little talk occurred:

"How are you, lieutenant?"

"Oh," said I, "as usual. All right but this hand, which is dead except to pain."

"Ah," said he, "such and thus will the wicked be—such will you be if you die in your sins: you will go where only pain can be felt. For all eternity, all of you will be just like that hand—knowing pain only."

I suppose I was very weak, but somehow I felt a sudden and chilling horror of possible universal pain, and suddenly fainted. When I awoke the hand was worse, if that could be. It was red, shining, aching, burning, and, as it seemed to me, perpetually rasped with hot files. When the doctor came I begged for morphia. He said gravely: "We have none. You know you don't allow it to pass the lines." It was sadly true.

I turned to the wall, and wetted the hand again, my sole relief. In about an hour Dr. Wilson came back with two aids, and explained to me that the bone was so crushed as to make it hopeless to save it, and that, besides, amputation offered some chance of arresting the pain. I had thought of this before, and the anguish I felt—I cannot say endured—was so awful that I made no more of losing the limb than of parting with a tooth on account of toothache. Accordingly, brief preparations were made, which I watched with a sort of eagerness such as must forever be inexplicable to any one who has not passed six weeks of torture like that which I had suffered.

I had but one pang before the operation. As I arranged myself on the left side, so as to make it convenient for the operator to use the knife, I asked: "Who is to give me the ether?" "We have none," said the person questioned. I set my teeth, and said no more.

I need not describe the operation. The pain felt was severe, but it was insignificant as compared with that of any other minute of the past six weeks. The limb was removed very near to the shoulder-joint. As the second incision was made, I felt a strange flash of pain play through the limb, as if it were in every minutest fibril of nerve. This was followed by instant, unspeakable relief, and before the flaps were brought together I was sound asleep. I dimly remember saying, as I pointed to the arm which lay on the floor: "There is the pain, and here am I. How queer!" Then I slept—slept the sleep of the just, or, better, of the painless. From this time forward I was free from neuralgia. At a subsequent period I saw a number of cases similar to mine in a hospital in Philadelphia.

It is no part of my plan to detail my weary months of monotonous prison life in the South. In the early part of April, 1863, I was exchanged, and after the usual thirty days' furlough returned to my regiment a captain.[10]

On the 19th of September, 1863, occurred the battle of Chickamauga, in which my regiment took a conspicuous part.[11] The close of our own share in this contest is, as it were,

burned into my memory with every least detail. It was about 6 P.M., when we found ourselves in line, under cover of a long, thin row of scrubby trees, beyond which lay a gentle
slope, from which, again, rose a hill rather more abrupt, and crowned with an earthwork.
We received orders to cross this space and take the fort in front, while a brigade on our
right was to make a like movement on its flank.

Just before we emerged into the open ground, we noticed what, I think, was common
in many fights—that the enemy had begun to bowl round shot at us, probably from failure
of shell. We passed across the valley in good order, although the men fell rapidly all along
the line. As we climbed the hill, our pace slackened, and the fire grew heavier. At this moment a battery opened on our left, the shots crossing our heads obliquely. It is this moment
which is so printed on my recollection. I can see now, as if through a window, the gray
smoke, lit with red flashes, the long, wavering line, the sky blue above, the trodden furrows, blotted with blue blouses. Then it was as if the window closed, and I knew and saw
no more. No other scene in my life is thus scarred, if I may say so, into my memory. I have
a fancy that the horrible shock which suddenly fell upon me must have had something to
do with thus intensifying the momentary image then before my eyes.

When I awakened, I was lying under a tree somewhere at the rear. The ground was
covered with wounded, and the doctors were busy at an operating-table, improvised from
two barrels and a plank. At length two of them who were examining the wounded about
me came up to where I lay. A hospital steward raised my head and poured down some
brandy and water, while another cut loose my pantaloons. The doctors exchanged looks
and walked away. I asked the steward where I was hit.

"Both thighs," said he; "the doctors won't do nothing."

"No use?" said I.

"Not much," said he.

"Not much means none at all," I answered.

When he had gone I set myself to thinking about a good many things I had better
have thought of before, but which in no way concern the history of my case. A half-hour
went by. I had no pain, and did not get weaker. At last, I cannot explain why, I began to
look about me. At first things appeared a little hazy. I remember one thing which thrilled
me a little, even then.

A tall, blond-bearded major walked up to a doctor near me, saying, "When you 've a
little leisure, just take a look at my side."

"Do it now," said the doctor.

The officer exposed his wound. "Ball went in here, and out there."

The doctor looked up at him—half pity, half amazement. "If you 've got any message,
you 'd best send it by me."

"Why, you don't say it 's serious?" was the reply.

"Serious! Why, you 're shot through the stomach. You won't live over the day."

Then the man did what struck me as a very odd thing. He said, "Anybody got a pipe?"
Some one gave him a pipe. He filled it deliberately, struck a light with a flint, and sat down
against a tree near to me. Presently the doctor came to him again, and asked him what he
could do for him.

"Send me a drink of Bourbon."

"Anything else?"

"No."

As the doctor left him, he called him back. "It's a little rough, doc, is n't it?"

No more passed, and I saw this man no longer. Another set of doctors were handling my legs, for the first time causing pain. A moment after, a steward put a towel over my mouth, and I smelled the familiar odor of chloroform, which I was glad enough to breathe. In a moment the trees began to move around from left to right, faster and faster; then a universal grayness came before me, and I recall nothing further until I awoke to consciousness in a hospital-tent. I got hold of my own identity in a moment or two, and was suddenly aware of a sharp cramp in my left leg. I tried to get at it to rub it with my single arm, but, finding myself too weak, hailed an attendant. "Just rub my left calf," said I, "if you please."

"Calf?" said he. "You ain't none. It 's took off."

"I know better," said I. " I have pain in both legs."

"Wall, [sic] I never!" said he. "You ain't got nary leg." [sic]

As I did not believe him, he threw off the covers, and, to my horror, showed me that I had suffered amputation of both thighs, very high up.

"That will do," said I, faintly.

A month later, to the amazement of every one, I was so well as to be moved from the crowded hospital at Chattanooga to Nashville, where I filled one of the ten thousand beds of that vast metropolis of hospitals.[12] Of the sufferings which then began I shall presently speak. It will be best just now to detail the final misfortune which here fell upon me. Hospital No. 2, in which I lay, was inconveniently crowded with severely wounded officers. After my third week an epidemic of hospital gangrene broke out in my ward. In three days it attacked twenty persons. Then an inspector came, and we were transferred at once to the open air, and placed in tents. Strangely enough, the wound in my remaining arm, which still suppurated, was seized with gangrene. The usual remedy, bromine, was used locally, but the main artery opened, was tied, bled again and again, and at last, as a final resort, the remaining arm was amputated at the shoulder-joint. Against all chances I recovered, to find myself a useless torso, more like some strange larval creature than anything of human shape. Of my anguish and horror of myself I dare not speak. I have dictated these pages, not to shock my readers, but to possess them with facts in regard to the relation of the mind to the body; and I hasten, therefore, to such portions of my case as best illustrate these views.

In January, 1864, I was forwarded to Philadelphia, in order to enter what was known as the Stump Hospital, South Street, then in charge of Dr. Hopkinson. This favor was obtained through the influence of my father's friend, the late Governor Anderson, who had always manifested an interest in my case, for which I am deeply grateful. It was thought, at the time, that Mr. Palmer, the leg-maker,[13] might be able to adapt some form of arm to my left shoulder, as on that side there remained five inches of the arm-bone, which I could move to a moderate extent. The hope proved illusory, as the stump was always too tender to bear any pressure. The hospital referred to was in charge of several surgeons while I was an inmate, and was at all times a clean and pleasant home. It was filled with men who had lost one arm or leg, or one of each, as happened now and then. I saw one man who had lost both legs, and one who had parted with both arms; but none, like myself, stripped of every limb. There were collected in this place hundreds of these cases, which gave to it, with reason enough, the not very pleasing title of Stump Hospital.

I spent here three and a half months, before my transfer to the United States Army Hospital for Injuries and Diseases of the Nervous System.[14] Every morning I was carried out in an arm-chair and placed in the library, where some one was always ready to write or read for me, or to fill my pipe. The doctors lent me medical books; the ladies brought me luxuries and fed me; and, save that I was helpless to a degree which was humiliating, I was as comfortable as kindness could make me.

I amused myself at this time by noting in my mind all that I could learn from other limbless folk, and from myself, as to the peculiar feelings which were noticed in regard to lost members. I found that the great mass of men who had undergone amputations for many months felt the usual consciousness that they still had the lost limb. It itched or pained, or was cramped, but never felt hot or cold. If they had painful sensations referred to it, the conviction of its existence continued unaltered for long periods; but where no pain was felt in it, then by degrees the sense of having that limb faded away entirely. I think we may to some extent explain this. The knowledge we possess of any part is made up of the numberless impressions from without which affect its sensitive surfaces, and which are transmitted through its nerves to the spinal nerve-cells, and through them, again, to the brain. We are thus kept endlessly informed as to the existence of parts, because the impressions which reach the brain are, by a law of our being, referred by us to the part from which they come. Now, when the part is cut off, the nerve-trunks which led to it and from it, remaining capable of being impressed by irritations, are made to convey to the brain from the stump impressions which are, as usual, referred by the brain to the lost parts to which these nerve-threads belonged. In other words, the nerve is like a bell-wire. You may pull it at any part of its course, and thus ring the bell as well as if you pulled at the end of the wire; but, in any case, the intelligent servant will refer the pull to the front door, and obey it accordingly. The impressions made on the severed ends of the nerve are due often to changes in the stump during healing, and consequently cease when it has healed, so that finally, in a very healthy stump, no such impressions arise; the brain ceases to correspond with the lost leg, and, as *les absents ont toujours tort,*[15] it is no longer remembered or recognized. But in some cases, such as mine proved at last to my sorrow, the ends of the nerves undergo a curious alteration, and get to be enlarged and altered. This change, as I have seen in my practice of medicine, sometimes passes up the nerves toward the centers, and occasions a more or less constant irritation of the nerve-fibers, producing neuralgia, which is usually referred by the brain to that part of the lost limb to which the affected nerve belonged. This pain keeps the brain ever mindful of the missing part, and, imperfectly at least, preserves to the man a consciousness of possessing that which he has not.

Where the pains come and go, as they do in certain cases, the subjective sensations thus occasioned are very curious, since in such cases the man loses and gains, and loses and regains, the consciousness of the presence of the lost parts, so that he will tell you, "Now I feel my thumb, now I feel my little finger." I should also add that nearly every person who has lost an arm above the elbow feels as though the lost member were bent at the elbow, and at times is vividly impressed with the notion that his fingers are strongly flexed.

Other persons present a peculiarity which I am at a loss to account for. Where the leg, for instance, has been lost, they feel as if the foot were present, but as though the leg were shortened. Thus, if the thigh has been taken off, there seems to them to be a foot at the knee; if the arm, a hand seems to be at the elbow, or attached to the stump itself.

Before leaving Nashville I had begun to suffer the most acute pain in my left hand, especially the little finger; and so perfect was the idea which was thus kept up of the real presence of these missing parts that I found it hard at times to believe them absent. Often at night I would try with one lost hand to grope for the other. As, however, I had no pain in the right arm, the sense of the existence of that limb gradually disappeared, as did that of my legs also.

Everything was done for my neuralgia which the doctors could think of; and at length, at my suggestion, I was removed, as I have said, from the Stump Hospital to the United States Army Hospital for Injuries and Diseases of the Nervous System. It was a pleasant, suburban, old-fashioned country-seat, its gardens surrounded by a circle of wooden, one-story wards, shaded by fine trees. There were some three hundred cases of epilepsy, paralysis, St. Vitus's dance, and wounds of nerves. On one side of me lay a poor fellow, a Dane, who had the same burning neuralgia with which I once suffered, and which I now learned was only too common. This man had become hysterical from pain. He carried a sponge in his pocket, and a bottle of water in one hand, with which he constantly wetted the burning hand. Every sound increased his torture, and he even poured water into his boots to keep himself from feeling too sensibly the rough friction of his soles when walking. Like him, I was greatly eased by having small doses of morphia injected under the skin of my shoulder with a hollow needle fitted to a syringe.

As I improved under the morphia treatment, I began to be disturbed by the horrible variety of suffering about me. One man walked sideways; there was one who could not smell; another was dumb from an explosion. In fact, every one had his own abnormal peculiarity. Near me was a strange case of palsy of the muscles called rhomboids, whose office it is to hold down the shoulder-blades flat on the back during the motions of the arms, which, in themselves, were strong enough. When, however, he lifted these members, the shoulder-blades stood out from the back like wings, and got him the sobriquet of the "Angel." In my ward were also the cases of fits, which very much annoyed me, as upon any great change in the weather it was common to have a dozen convulsions in view at once. Dr. Neek, one of our physicians, told me that on one occasion a hundred and fifty fits took place within thirty-six hours. On my complaining of these sights, whence I alone could not fly, I was placed in the paralytic and wound ward, which I found much more pleasant.

A month of skilful treatment eased me entirely of my aches, and I then began to experience certain curious feelings, upon which, having nothing to do and nothing to do anything with, I reflected a good deal. It was a good while before I could correctly explain to my own satisfaction the phenomena which at this time I was called upon to observe. By the various operations already described I had lost about four fifths of my weight. As a consequence of this I ate much less than usual, and could scarcely have consumed the ration of a soldier. I slept also but little; for, as sleep is the repose of the brain, made necessary by the waste of its tissues during thought and voluntary movement, and as this latter did not exist in my case, I needed only that rest which was necessary to repair such exhaustion of the nerve-centers as was induced by thinking and the automatic movements of the viscera.

I observed at this time also that my heart, in place of beating, as it once did, seventy-eight in the minute, pulsated only forty-five times in this interval—a fact to be easily explained by the perfect quiescence to which I was reduced, and the consequent absence of that healthy and constant stimulus to the muscles of the heart which exercise occasions.

Notwithstanding these drawbacks, my physical health was good, which, I confess, surprised me, for this among other reasons: It is said that a burn of two thirds of the surface destroys life, because then all the excretory matters which this portion of the glands of the skin evolved are thrown upon the blood, and poison the man, just as happens in an animal whose skin the physiologist has varnished, so as in this way to destroy its function. Yet here was I, having lost at least a third of my skin, and apparently none the worse for it.

Still more remarkable, however, were the psychical changes which I now began to perceive. I found to my horror that at times I was less conscious of myself, of my own existence, than used to be the case. This sensation was so novel that at first it quite bewildered me. I felt like asking some one constantly if I were really George Dedlow or not; but, well aware how absurd I should seem after such a question, I refrained from speaking of my case, and strove more keenly to analyze my feelings. At times the conviction of my want of being myself was overwhelming and most painful. It was, as well as I can describe it, a deficiency in the egoistic sentiment of individuality. About one half of the sensitive surface of my skin was gone, and thus much of relation to the outer world destroyed. As a consequence, a large part of the receptive central organs must be out of employ, and, like other idle things, degenerating rapidly. Moreover, all the great central ganglia, which give rise to movements in the limbs, were also eternally at rest. Thus one half of me was absent or functionally dead. This set me to thinking how much a man might lose and yet live. If I were unhappy enough to survive, I might part with my spleen at least, as many a dog has done, and grow fat afterwards. The other organs with which we breathe and circulate the blood would be essential; so also would the liver; but at least half of the intestines might be dispensed with, and of course all of the limbs. And as to the nervous system, the only parts really necessary to life are a few small ganglia. Were the rest absent or inactive, we should have a man reduced, as it were, to the lowest terms, and leading an almost vegetative existence. Would such a being, I asked myself, possess the sense of individuality in its usual completeness, even if his organs of sensation remained, and he were capable of consciousness? Of course, without them, he could not have it any more than a dahlia or a tulip. But with them—how then? I concluded that it would be at a minimum, and that, if utter loss of relation to the outer world were capable of destroying a man's consciousness of himself, the destruction of half of his sensitive surfaces might well occasion, in a less degree, a like result, and so diminish his sense of individual existence.

I thus reached the conclusion that a man is not his brain, or any one part of it, but all of his economy, and that to lose any part must lessen this sense of his own existence. I found but one person who properly appreciated this great truth. She was a New England lady, from Hartford—an agent, I think, for some commission, perhaps the Sanitary. After I had told her my views and feelings, she said: "Yes, I comprehend. The fractional entities of vitality are embraced in the oneness of the unitary Ego. Life," she added, "is the garnered condensation of objective impressions; and as the objective is the remote father of the subjective, so must individuality, which is but focused subjectivity, suffer and fade when the sensation lenses, by which the rays of impression are condensed, become destroyed." I am not quite clear that I fully understood her, but I think she appreciated my ideas, and I felt grateful for her kindly interest.

The strange want I have spoken of now haunted and perplexed me so constantly that I became moody and wretched. While in this state, a man from a neighboring ward fell one morning into conversation with the chaplain, within ear-shot of my chair. Some of their words arrested my attention, and I turned my head to see and listen. The speaker, who wore a sergeant's chevron and carried one arm in a sling, was a tall, loosely made person, with a pale face, light eyes of a washed-out blue tint, and very sparse yellow whiskers. His mouth was weak, both lips being almost alike, so that the organ might have been turned upside down without affecting its expression. His forehead, however, was high and thinly covered with sandy hair. I should have said, as a phrenologist, will feeble; emotional, but not passionate; likely to be an enthusiast or a weakly bigot.

I caught enough of what passed to make me call to the sergeant when the chaplain left him.

"Good morning," said he. "How do you get on?"

"Not at all," I replied. "Where were you hit?"

"Oh, at Chancellorsville. I was shot in the shoulder. I have what the doctors call paralysis of the median nerve, but I guess Dr. Neek and the lightnin' battery will fix it. When my time 's out I 'll go back to Kearsarge and try on the school-teaching again. I 've done my share."

"Well," said I, "you 're better off than I."

"Yes," he answered, "in more ways than one. I belong to the New Church. It 's a great comfort for a plain man like me, when he 's weary and sick, to be able to turn away from earthly things and hold converse daily with the great and good who have left this here world. We have a circle in Coates Street. If it wa'n't for the consoling I get there, I 'd of wished myself dead many a time. I ain't got kith or kin on earth; but this matters little, when one can just talk to them daily and know that they are in the spheres above us."

"It must be a great comfort," I replied, "if only one could believe it."

"Believe!" he repeated. "How can you help it? Do you suppose anything dies?"

"No," I said. "The soul does not, I am sure; and as to matter, it merely changes form."

"But why, then," said he, "should not the dead soul talk to the living? In space, no doubt, exist all forms of matter, merely in finer, more ethereal being. You can't suppose a naked soul moving about without a bodily garment—no creed teaches that; and if its new clothing be of like substance to ours, only of ethereal fineness,—a more delicate re-crystallization about the eternal spiritual nucleus, must it not then possess powers as much more delicate and refined as is the new material in which it is reclad?"

"Not very clear," I answered; "but, after all, the thing should be susceptible of some form of proof to our present senses."

"And so it is," said he. "Come to-morrow with me, and you shall see and hear for yourself."

"I will," said I, "if the doctor will lend me the ambulance."

It was so arranged, as the surgeon in charge was kind enough, as usual, to oblige me with the loan of his wagon, and two orderlies to lift my useless trunk.

On the day following I found myself, with my new comrade, in a house in Coates Street, where a "circle" was in the daily habit of meeting. So soon as I had been comfortably deposited in an armchair, beside a large pine table, the rest of those assembled seated themselves, and for some time preserved an unbroken silence. During this pause I scrutinized the persons present. Next to me, on my right, sat a flabby man, with ill-marked, baggy features and injected eyes. He was, as I learned afterwards, an eclectic doctor, who had tried his hand at medicine and several of its quackish variations, finally settling down on eclecticism, which I believe professes to be to scientific medicine what vegetarianism is to common-sense, every-day dietetics. Next to him sat a female—authoress, I think, of two somewhat feeble novels, and much pleasanter to look at than her books. She was, I thought, a good deal excited at the prospect of spiritual revelations. Her neighbor was a pallid, care-worn young woman, with very red lips, and large brown eyes of great beauty. She was, as I learned afterwards, a magnetic patient of the doctor, and had deserted her husband, a master mechanic, to follow this new light. The others were, like myself, strangers brought hither by mere curiosity. One of them was a lady in deep black, closely veiled. Beyond her, and opposite to me, sat the sergeant, and next to him the medium, a man named Brink. He wore a good deal of jewelry, and had large black side-whiskers—a shrewd-visaged, large-nosed, full-lipped man, formed by nature to appreciate the pleasant things of sensual existence.

Before I had ended my survey, he turned to the lady in black, and asked if she wished to see any one in the spirit-world.

She said, "Yes," rather feebly.

"Is the spirit present?" he asked. Upon which two knocks were heard in affirmation. "Ah!" said the medium, "the name is—it is the name of a child. It is a male child. It is—"

"Alfred!" she cried. "Great Heaven! My child! My boy!"

On this the medium arose, and became strangely convulsed. "I see," he said — "I see—a fair-haired boy. I see blue eyes—I see above you, beyond you—" at the same time pointing fixedly over her head.

She turned with a wild start. "Where—whereabouts?"

"A blue-eyed boy," he continued, "over your head. He cries—he says, 'Mama, mama!'"

The effect of this on the woman was unpleasant. She stared about her for a moment, and exclaiming, "I come—I am coming, Alfy!" fell in hysterics on the floor.

Two or three persons raised her, and aided her into an adjoining room; but the rest remained at the table, as though well accustomed to like scenes.

After this several of the strangers were called upon to write the names of the dead with whom they wished to communicate. The names were spelled out by the agency of affirmative knocks when the correct letters were touched by the applicant, who was furnished with an alphabet-card upon which he tapped the letters in turn, the medium, meanwhile, scanning his face very keenly. With some, the names were readily made out. With one, a stolid personage of disbelieving type, every attempt failed, until at last the spirits signified by knocks that he was a disturbing agency, and that while he remained all our efforts would fail. Upon this some of the company proposed that he should leave, of which invitation he took advantage, with a skeptical sneer at the whole performance.

As he left us, the sergeant leaned over and whispered to the medium, who next addressed himself to me. "Sister Euphemia," he said, indicating the lady with large eyes, "will act as your medium. I am unable to do more. These things exhaust my nervous system."

"Sister Euphemia," said the doctor, "will aid us. Think, if you please, sir, of a spirit, and she will endeavor to summon it to our circle."

Upon this a wild idea came into my head. I answered: "I am thinking as you directed me to do."

The medium sat with her arms folded, looking steadily at the center of the table. For a few moments there was silence. Then a series of irregular knocks began. "Are you present?" said the medium.

The affirmative raps were twice given.

"I should think," said the doctor, "that there were two spirits present."

His words sent a thrill through my heart. "Are there two?" he questioned.

A double rap.

"Yes, two," said the medium. "Will it please the spirits to make us conscious of their names in this world?"

A single knock. " No."

"Will it please them to say how they are called in the world of spirits?"

Again came the irregular raps—3, 4, 8, 6; then a pause, and 3, 4, 8, 7.

"I think," said the authoress, "they must be numbers. Will the spirits," she said, "be good enough to aid us? Shall we use the alphabet?"

"Yes," was rapped very quickly.

"Are these numbers?"

"Yes," again.

"I will write them," she added, and, doing so, took up the card and tapped the letters. The spelling was pretty rapid, and ran thus as she tapped, in turn, first the letters, and last the numbers she had already set down:

"UNITED STATES ARMY MEDICAL MUSEUM, Nos. 3486, 3487."[16]

The medium looked up with a puzzled expression.

"Good gracious!" said I, "they are *my legs—my legs!*"

What followed, I ask no one to believe except those who, like myself, have communed with the things of another sphere. Suddenly I felt a strange return of my self-consciousness. I was reindividualized, so to speak. A strange wonder filled me, and, to the amazement of every one, I arose, and, staggering a little, walked across the room on limbs invisible to them or me. It was no wonder I staggered, for, as I briefly reflected, my legs had been nine months in the strongest alcohol. At this instant all my new friends crowded around me in astonishment. Presently, however, I felt myself sinking slowly. My legs were going, and in a moment I was resting feebly on my two stumps upon the floor. It was too much. All that was left of me fainted and rolled over senseless.

I have little to add. I am now at home in the West, surrounded by every form of kindness and every possible comfort; but alas! I have so little surety of being myself that I doubt my own honesty in drawing my pension, and feel absolved from gratitude to those who are kind to a being who is uncertain of being enough of himself to be conscientiously responsible. It is needless to add that I am not a happy fraction of a man, and that I am eager for the day when I shall rejoin the lost members of my corporeal family in another and a happier world.

Helen Hunt Jackson

from *Sonnets and Lyrics* (1886)

SONGS OF BATTLE

Old as the world—no other things so old;
Nay, older than the world, else, how had sprung
Such lusty strength in them when earth was young?—
Stand valor and its passion hot and bold,
Insatiate of battle. How, else, told
Blind men, born blind, that red was fitting tongue
Mute, eloquent, to show how trumpets rung
When armies charged and battle-flags unfurled?
Who sings of valor speaks for life, for death,
Beyond all death, and long as life is life,
In rippled waves the eternal air his breath
Eternal bears to stir all noble strife.
Dead Homer from his lost and vanished grave
Keeps battle glorious still and soldiers brave.

Louisa May Alcott

from *Hospital Sketches* (1863)

CHAPTER III: A DAY

"They've come! they've come! hurry up, ladies—you're wanted."

"Who have come? the rebels?"

This sudden summons in the gray dawn was somewhat startling to a three days' nurse like myself, and, as the thundering knock came at our door, I sprang up in my bed, prepared

"To gird my woman's form,
And on the ramparts die,"

if necessary; but my room-mate took it more coolly, and, as she began a rapid toilet, answered my bewildered question,—

"Bless you, no child; it's the wounded from Fredericksburg; forty ambulances are at the door, and we shall have our hands full in fifteen minutes."

"What shall we have to do?"

"Wash, dress, feed, warm and nurse them for the next three months, I dare say. Eighty beds are ready, and we were getting impatient for the men to come. Now you will begin to see hospital life in earnest, for you won't probably find time to sit down all day, and may think yourself fortunate if you get to bed by midnight. Come to me in the ball-room when you are ready; the worst cases are always carried there, and I shall need your help."

So saying, the energetic little woman twirled her hair into a button at the back of her head, in a "cleared for action" sort of style, and vanished, wrestling her way into a feminine kind of pea-jacket as she went.

I am free to confess that I had a realizing sense of the fact that my hospital bed was not a bed of roses just then, or the prospect before me one of unmingled rapture. My three days' experiences had begun with a death, and, owing to the defalcation of another nurse, a somewhat abrupt plunge into the superintendence of a ward containing forty beds, where I spent my shining hours washing faces, serving rations, giving medicine, and sitting in a very hard chair, with pneumonia on one side, diptheria on the other, five typhoids on the opposite, and a dozen dilapidated patriots, hopping, lying, and lounging about, all staring more or less at the new "nuss," who suffered untold agonies, but concealed them under as matronly an aspect as a spinster could assume, and blundered through her trying labors with a Spartan firmness, which I hope they appreciated, but am afraid they didn't. Having a taste for "ghastliness," I had rather longed for the wounded to arrive, for rheumatism wasn't heroic, neither was liver complaint, or measles; even fever had lost its charms since "bathing burning brows" had been used up in romances, real and ideal; but when I peeped into the dusky street lined with what I at first had innocently called market carts, now unloading their sad freight at our door, I recalled sundry reminiscences I had heard from nurses of longer standing, my ardor experienced a sudden chill, and I indulged in a most unpatriotic wish that I was safe at home again, with a quiet day before me, and no necessity for being hustled up, as if I were a hen and had only to hop off my roost, give my plumage a peck, and be ready for action. A second bang at the door sent this recreant desire to the right about, as a little woolly head popped in, and Joey, (a six years' old contraband,) announced—

"Miss Blank is jes' wild fer ye, and says fly round right away. They's comin' in, I tell yer, heaps on 'em—one was took out dead, and I see him,—hi! warn't he a goner!"

With which cheerful intelligence the imp scuttled away, singing like a blackbird, and I followed, feeling that Richard was *not* himself again, and wouldn't be for a long time to come.[17]

The first thing I met was a regiment of the vilest odors that ever assaulted the human nose, and took it by storm. Cologne, with its seven and seventy evil savors, was a posy-bed to it; and the worst of this affliction was, every one had assured me that it was a chronic weakness of all hospitals, and I must bear it. I did, armed with lavender water, with which I so besprinkled myself and premises, that, like my friend Sairy,[18] I was soon known among my patients as "the nurse with the bottle." Having been run over by three excited surgeons, bumped against by migratory coal-hods, water-pails, and small boys, nearly scalded by an avalanche of newly-filled tea-pots, and hopelessly entangled in a knot of colored sisters coming to wash, I progressed by slow stages up stairs and down, till the main hall was reached, and I paused to take breath and a survey. There they were! "our brave boys," as the papers justly call them, for cowards could hardly have been so riddled with shot and shell, so torn and shattered, nor have borne suffering for which we have no name, with an uncomplaining fortitude, which made one glad to cherish each as a brother. In they came, some on stretchers, some in men's arms, some feebly staggering along propped on rude crutches, and one lay stark and still with covered face, as a comrade gave his name to be re-corded before they carried him away to the dead house. All was hurry and confusion; the hall was full of these wrecks of humanity, for the most exhausted could not reach a bed till duly ticketed and registered; the walls were lined with rows of such as could sit, the floor covered with the more disabled, the steps and doorways filled with helpers and lookers on; the sound of many feet and voices made that usually quiet hour as noisy as noon; and, in the midst of it all, the matron's motherly face brought more comfort to many a poor soul, than the cordial draughts she administered, or the cheery words that welcomed all, mak-ing of the hospital a home.

The sight of several stretchers, each with its legless, armless, or desperately wounded occupant, entering my ward, admonished me that I was there to work, not to wonder or weep; so I corked up my feelings, and returned to the path of duty, which was rather "a hard road to travel" just then. The house had been a hotel before hospitals were needed, and many of the doors still bore their old names; some not so inappropriate as might be imagined, for my ward was in truth a *ball-room*, if gun-shot wounds could christen it. For-ty beds were prepared, many already tenanted by tired men who fell down anywhere, and drowsed till the smell of food roused them. Round the great stove was gathered the drear-iest group I ever saw—ragged, gaunt and pale, mud to the knees, with bloody bandages untouched since put on days before; many bundled up in blankets, coats being lost or useless; and all wearing that disheartened look which proclaimed defeat, more plainly than any telegram of the Burnside blunder. I pitied them so much, I dared not speak to them, though, remembering all they had been through since the route at Fredericksburg, I yearned to serve the dreariest of them all. Presently, Miss Blank tore me from my refuge behind piles of one-sleeved shirts, odd socks, bandages and lint; put basin, sponge, towels, and a block of brown soap into my hands, with these appalling directions:

"Come, my dear, begin to wash as fast as you can. Tell them to take off socks, coats and shirts, scrub them well, put on clean shirts, and the attendants will finish them off, and lay them in bed."

If she had requested me to shave them all, or dance a hornpipe on the stove funnel, I should have been less staggered; but to scrub some dozen lords of creation at a moment's notice, was really—really—. However, there was no time for nonsense, and, having resolved when I came to do everything I was bid, I drowned my scruples in my wash-bowl, clutched my soap manfully, and, assuming a business-like air, made a dab at the first dirty specimen I saw, bent on performing my task *vi et armis*[19] if necessary. I chanced to light on a withered old Irishman, wounded in the head, which caused that portion of his frame to be tastefully laid out like a garden, the bandages being the walks, his hair the shrubbery. He was so overpowered by the honor of having a lady wash him, as he expressed it, that he did nothing but roll up his eyes, and bless me, in an irresistible style which was too much for my sense of the ludicrous; so we laughed together, and when I knelt down to take off his shoes, he "flopped" also, and wouldn't hear of my touching "them dirty craters. May your bed above be aisy darlin', for the day's work ye ar doon!—Whoosh! there ye are, and bedad, it's hard tellin' which is the dirtiest, the fut or the shoe." It was; and if he hadn't been to the fore, I should have gone on pulling, under the impression that the "fut" was a boot, for trousers, socks, shoes and legs were a mass of mud. This comical tableau produced a general grin, at which propitious beginning I took heart and scrubbed away like any tidy parent on a Saturday night. Some of them took the performance like sleepy children, leaning their tired heads against me as I worked, others looked grimly scandalized, and several of the roughest colored like bashful girls. One wore a soiled little bag about his neck, and, as I moved it, to bathe his wounded breast, I said,

"Your talisman didn't save you, did it?"

"Well, I reckon it did, marm, for that shot would a gone a couple a inches deeper but for my old mammy's camphor bag," answered the cheerful philosopher.

Another, with a gun-shot wound through the cheek, asked for a looking-glass, and when I brought one, regarded his swollen face with a dolorous expression, as he muttered—

"I vow to gosh, that's too bad! I warn't a bad looking chap before, and now I'm done for; won't there be a thunderin' scar? and what on earth will Josephine Skinner say?"

He looked up at me with his one eye so appealingly, that I controlled my risibles, and assured him that if Josephine was a girl of sense, she would admire the honorable scar, as a lasting proof that he had faced the enemy, for all women thought a wound the best decoration a brave soldier could wear. I hope Miss Skinner verified the good opinion I so rashly expressed of her, but I shall never know.

The next scrubbee was a nice looking lad, with a curly brown mane, and a budding trace of gingerbread over the lip, which he called his beard, and defended stoutly, when the barber jocosely suggested its immolation. He lay on a bed, with one leg gone, and the right arm so shattered that it must evidently follow: yet the little Sergeant was as merry as if his afflictions were not worth lamenting over; and when a drop or two of salt water

mingled with my suds at the sight of this strong young body, so marred and maimed, the
boy looked up, with a brave smile, though there was a little quiver of the lips, as he said,

"Now don't you fret yourself about me, miss; I'm first rate here, for it's nuts to lie still
on this bed, after knocking about in those confounded ambulances, that shake what there
is left of a fellow to jelly. I never was in one of these places before, and think this cleaning
up a jolly thing for us, though I'm afraid it isn't for you ladies."

"Is this your first battle, Sergeant?"

"No, miss; I've been in six scrimmages, and never got a scratch till this last one; but it's
done the business pretty thoroughly for me, I should say. Lord! what a scramble there'll be
for arms and legs, when we old boys come out of our graves, on the Judgment Day: wonder if we shall get our own again? If we do, my leg will have to tramp from Fredericksburg,
my arm from here, I suppose, and meet my body, wherever it may be."

The fancy seemed to tickle him mightily, for he laughed blithely, and so did I; which,
no doubt, caused the new nurse to be regarded as a light-minded sinner by the Chaplain,
who roamed vaguely about, informing the men that they were all worms, corrupt of heart,
with perishable bodies, and souls only to be saved by a diligent perusal of certain tracts,
and other equally cheering bits of spiritual consolation, when spirituous ditto would have
been preferred.

"I say, Mrs.!" called a voice behind me; and, turning, I saw a rough Michigander, with
an arm blown off at the shoulder, and two or three bullets still in him—as he afterwards
mentioned, as carelessly as if gentlemen were in the habit of carrying such trifles about
with them. I went to him, and, while administering a dose of soap and water, he whispered, irefully:

"That red-headed devil, over yonder, is a reb, damn him! You'll agree to that, I'll bet?
He's got shet of a foot, or he'd a cut like the rest of the lot. Don't you wash him, nor feed
him, but jest let him holler till he's tired. It's a blasted shame to fetch them fellers in here,
along side of us; and so I'll tell the chap that bosses this concern; cuss me if I don't."

I regret to say that I did not deliver a moral sermon upon the duty of forgiving our
enemies, and the sin of profanity, then and there; but, being a red-hot Abolitionist, stared
fixedly at the tall rebel, who was a copperhead, in every sense of the word, and privately
resolved to put soap in his eyes, rub his nose the wrong way, and excoriate his cuticle generally, if I had the washing of him.

My amiable intentions, however, were frustrated; for, when I approached, with as
Christian an expression as my principles would allow, and asked the question—"Shall I
try to make you more comfortable, sir?" all I got for my pains was a gruff—

"No; I'll do it myself."

"Here's your Southern chivalry, with a witness," thought I, dumping the basin down
before him, thereby quenching a strong desire to give him a summary baptism, in return
for his ungraciousness; for my angry passions rose, at this rebuff, in a way that would have
scandalized good Dr. Watts. He was a disappointment in all respects, (the rebel, not the
blessed Doctor,) for he was neither fiendish, romantic, pathetic, or anything interesting;
but a long, fat man, with a head like a burning bush, and a perfectly expressionless face:
so I could dislike him without the slightest drawback, and ignored his existence from that
day forth. One redeeming trait he certainly did possess, as the floor speedily testified; for
his ablutions were so vigorously performed, that his bed soon stood like an isolated island,
in a sea of soap-suds, and he resembled a dripping merman, suffering from the loss of a

fin. If cleanliness is a near neighbor to godliness, then was the big rebel the godliest man in my ward that day.

Having done up our human wash, and laid it out to dry, the second syllable of our version of the word war-fare [sic] was enacted with much success. Great trays of bread, meat, soup and coffee appeared; and both nurses and attendants turned waiters, serving bountiful rations to all who could eat. I can call my pinafore to testify to my good will in the work, for in ten minutes it was reduced to a perambulating bill of fare, presenting samples of all the refreshments going or gone. It was a lively scene; the long room lined with rows of beds, each filled by an occupant, whom water, shears, and clean raiment, had transformed from a dismal ragamuffin into a recumbent hero, with a cropped head. To and fro rushed matrons, maids, and convalescent "boys," skirmishing with knives and forks; retreating with empty plates; marching and counter-marching, with unvaried success, while the clash of busy spoons made most inspiring music for the charge of our Light Brigade:[20]

"Beds to the front of them,
Beds to the right of them,
Beds to the left of them,
    Nobody blundered.
Beamed at by hungry souls,
Screamed at with brimming bowls,
Steamed at by army rolls,
    Buttered and sundered.
With coffee not cannon plied,
Each must be satisfied,
Whether they lived or died;
    All the men wondered."

Very welcome seemed the generous meal, after a week of suffering, exposure, and short commons; soon the brown faces began to smile, as food, warmth, and rest, did their pleasant work; and the grateful "Thankee's" were followed by more graphic accounts of the battle and retreat, than any paid reporter could have given us. Curious contrasts of the tragic and comic met one everywhere; and some touching as well as ludicrous episodes, might have been recorded that day. A six foot New Hampshire man, with a leg broken and perforated by a piece of shell, so large that, had I not seen the wound, I should have regarded the story as a Munchausenism,[21] beckoned me to come and help him, as he could not sit up, and both his bed and beard were getting plentifully anointed with soup. As I fed my big nestling with corresponding mouthfuls, I asked him how he felt during the battle.

"Well, 'twas my fust, you see, so I aint ashamed to say I was a trifle flustered in the beginnin', there was such an allfired racket; for ef there's anything I do spleen agin, it's noise. But when my mate, Eph Sylvester, caved, with a bullet through his head, I got mad, and pitched in, licketty cut. Our part of the fight didn't last long; so a lot of us larked round Fredericksburg, and give some of them houses a pretty consid'able of a rummage, till we was ordered out of the mess. Some of our fellows cut like time; but I warn't a-goin' to run for nobody; and, fust thing I knew, a shell bust, right in front of us, and I keeled over, feelin' as if I was blowed higher'n a kite. I sung out, and the boys come back for me, double quick; but the way they chucked me over them fences was a caution, I tell you. Next day I was most as black as that darkey yonder, lickin' plates on the sly. This is bully coffee, ain't it? Give us another pull at it, and I'll be obleeged to you."

I did; and, as the last gulp subsided, he said, with a rub of his old handkerchief over eyes as well as mouth:

"Look a here; I've got a pair a earbobs and a handkercher pin I'm a goin' to give you, if you'll have them; for you're the very moral o' Lizy Sylvester, poor Eph's wife: that's why I signalled you to come over here. They aint much, I guess, but they'll do to memorize the rebs by."

Burrowing under his pillow, he produced a little bundle of what he called "truck," and gallantly presented me with a pair of earrings, each representing a cluster of corpulent grapes, and the pin a basket of astonishing fruit, the whole large and coppery enough for a small warming-pan. Feeling delicate about depriving him of such valuable relics, I accepted the earrings alone, and was obliged to depart, somewhat abruptly, when my friend stuck the warming-pan in the bosom of his night-gown, viewing it with much complacency, and, perhaps, some tender memory, in that rough heart of his, for the comrade he had lost.

Observing that the man next him had left his meal untouched, I offered the same service I had performed for his neighbor, but he shook his head.

"Thank you, ma'am; I don't think I'll ever eat again, for I'm shot in the stomach. But I'd like a drink of water, if you aint too busy."

I rushed away, but the water-pails were gone to be refilled, and it was some time before they reappeared. I did not forget my patient patient, meanwhile, and, with the first mugful, hurried back to him. He seemed asleep; but something in the tired white face caused me to listen at his lips for a breath. None came. I touched his forehead; it was cold: and then I knew that, while he waited, a better nurse than I had given him a cooler draught, and healed him with a touch. I laid the sheet over the quiet sleeper, whom no noise could now disturb; and, half an hour later, the bed was empty. It seemed a poor requital for all he had sacrificed and suffered,—that hospital bed, lonely even in a crowd; for there was no familiar face for him to look his last upon; no friendly voice to say, Good bye; no hand to lead him gently down into the Valley of the Shadow; and he vanished, like a drop in that red sea upon whose shores so many women stand lamenting. For a moment I felt bitterly indignant at this seeming carelessness of the value of life, the sanctity of death; then consoled myself with the thought that, when the great muster roll was called, these nameless men might be promoted above many whose tall monuments record the barren honors they have won.

All having eaten, drank, and rested, the surgeons began their rounds; and I took my first lesson in the art of dressing wounds. It wasn't a festive scene, by any means; for Dr. P., whose Aid I constituted myself, fell to work with a vigor which soon convinced me that I was a weaker vessel, though nothing would have induced me to confess it then. He had served in the Crimea, and seemed to regard a dilapidated body very much as I should have regarded a damaged garment; and, turning up his cuffs, whipped out a very unpleasant looking housewife, cutting, sawing, patching and piecing, with the enthusiasm of an accomplished surgical seamstress; explaining the process, in scientific terms, to the patient, meantime; which, of course, was immensely cheering and comfortable. There was an uncanny sort of fascination in watching him, as he peered and probed into the mechanism of those wonderful bodies, whose mysteries he understood so well. The more intricate the wound, the better he liked it. A poor private, with both legs off, and shot through the lungs, possessed more attractions for him than a dozen generals, slightly scratched in some "masterly retreat;" and had any one appeared in small pieces, requesting to be put together again, he would have considered it a special dispensation.

The amputations were reserved till the morrow, and the merciful magic of ether was not thought necessary that day, so the poor souls had to bear their pains as best they might. It is all very well to talk of the patience of woman; and far be it from me to pluck that feather from her cap, for, heaven knows, she isn't allowed to wear many; but the patient endurance of these men, under trials of the flesh, was truly wonderful. Their fortitude seemed contagious, and scarcely a cry escaped them, though I often longed to groan for them, when pride kept their white lips shut, while great drops stood upon their foreheads, and the bed shook with the irrepressible tremor of their tortured bodies. One or two Irishmen anathematized the doctors with the frankness of their nation, and ordered the Virgin to stand by them, as if she had been the wedded Biddy[22] to whom they could administer the poker, if she didn't; but, as a general thing, the work went on in silence, broken only by some quiet request for roller, instruments, or plaster, a sigh from the patient, or a sympathizing murmur from the nurse.

It was long past noon before these repairs were even partially made; and, having got the bodies of my boys into something like order, the next task was to minister to their minds, by writing letters to the anxious souls at home; answering questions, reading papers, taking possession of money and valuables; for the eighth commandment was reduced to a very fragmentary condition, both by the blacks and whites, who ornamented our hospital with their presence. Pocket books, purses, miniatures, and watches, were sealed up, labelled, and handed over to the matron, till such times as the owners thereof were ready to depart homeward or campward again. The letters dictated to me, and revised by me, that afternoon, would have made an excellent chapter for some future history of the war; for, like that which Thackeray's "Ensign Spooney" wrote his mother just before Waterloo, they were "full of affection, pluck, and bad spelling;"[23] nearly all giving lively accounts of the battle, and ending with a somewhat sudden plunge from patriotism to provender, desiring "Marm," "Mary Ann," or "Aunt Peters," to send along some pies, pickles, sweet stuff, and apples, "to yourn in haste," Joe, Sam, or Ned, as the case might be.

My little Sergeant insisted on trying to scribble something with his left hand, and patiently accomplished some half dozen lines of hieroglyphics, which he gave me to fold and direct, with a boyish blush, that rendered a glimpse of "My Dearest Jane," unnecessary, to assure me that the heroic lad had been more successful in the service of Commander-in-Chief Cupid than that of Gen. Mars; and a charming little romance blossomed instanter in Nurse Periwinkle's romantic fancy, though no further confidences were made that day, for Sergeant fell asleep, and, judging from his tranquil face, visited his absent sweetheart in the pleasant land of dreams.

At five o'clock a great bell rang, and the attendants flew, not to arms, but to their trays, to bring up supper, when a second uproar announced that it was ready. The new comers woke at the sound; and I presently discovered that it took a very bad wound to incapacitate the defenders of the faith for the consumption of their rations; the amount that some of them sequestered was amazing; but when I suggested the probability of a famine hereafter, to the matron, that motherly lady cried out: "Bless their hearts, why shouldn't they eat? It's their only amusement; so fill every one, and, if there's not enough ready to-night, I'll lend my share to the Lord by giving it to the boys." And, whipping up her coffee-pot and plate of toast, she gladdened the eyes and stomachs of two or three dissatisfied heroes, by serving them with a liberal hand; and I haven't the slightest doubt that, having cast her bread upon the waters, it came back buttered, as another large-hearted old lady was wont to say.

Then came the doctor's evening visit; the administration of medicines; washing feverish faces; smoothing tumbled beds; wetting wounds; singing lullabies; and preparations for the night. By twelve, the last labor of love was done; the last "good night" spoken; and, if any needed a reward for that day's work, they surely received it, in the silent eloquence of those long lines of faces, showing pale and peaceful in the shaded rooms, as we quitted them, followed by grateful glances that lighted us to bed, where rest, the sweetest, made our pillows soft, while Night and Nature took our places, filling that great house of pain with the healing miracles of Sleep, and his diviner brother, Death.

Abraham Lincoln

ADDRESS AT THE DEDICATION OF THE GETTYSBURG NATIONAL CEMETERY
November 19, 1863

Fourscore and seven years ago our fathers brought forth on this continent a new nation, conceived in liberty, and dedicated to the proposition that all men are created equal.

Now we are engaged in a great civil war, testing whether that nation, or any nation so conceived and so dedicated, can long endure. We are met on a great battle-field of that war. We have come to dedicate a portion of that field as a final resting place for those who here gave their lives that that nation might live. It is altogether fitting and proper that we should do this.

But, in a larger sense, we can not dedicate—we can not consecrate—we can not hallow—this ground. The brave men, living and dead, who struggled here, have consecrated it far above our poor power to add or detract. The world will little note nor long remember what we say here, but it can never forget what they did here. It is for us, the living, rather, to be dedicated here to the unfinished work which they who fought here have thus far so nobly advanced. It is rather for us to be here dedicated to the great task remaining before us—that from these honored dead we take increased devotion to that cause for which they gave the last full measure of devotion; that we here highly resolve that these dead shall not have died in vain; that this nation, under God, shall have a new birth of freedom; and that government of the people, by the people, for the people, shall not perish from the earth.

Emily Dickinson

To fight aloud, is very brave —
But *gallanter*, I know
Who charge within the bosom
The Cavalry of Wo —

Who win, and nations do not see —
Who fall — and none observe —
Whose dying eyes, no Country
Regards with patriot love —

We trust, in plumed procession
For such, the Angels go —
Rank and Rank, with even feet —
And Uniforms of snow.

—1860

The name — of it — is "Autumn" —
The hue — of it — is Blood —
An Artery — opon the Hill —
A Vein — along the Road —

Great Globules — in the Alleys —
And Oh, the Shower of Stain —
When Winds — upset the Basin —
And spill the Scarlet Rain —

It sprinkles Bonnets — far below —
It gathers ruddy Pools —
Then — eddies like a Rose — away —
Opon Vermilion Wheels —

—1862

Whole Gulfs — of Red, and Fleets — of Red —
And Crews — of solid Blood —
Did place about the West — Tonight —
As 'twere specific Ground —

And They — appointed Creatures —
In Authorized Arrays —
Due — promptly — as a Drama —
That bows — and disappears —

—1862

They dropped like Flakes —
They dropped like stars —
Like Petals from a Rose —
When suddenly across the June
A Wind with fingers — goes —

They perished in the seamless Grass —
No eye could find the place —
But God can summon every face
On his Repealless — List.

—1863

If any sink, assure that this, now standing —
Failed like Themselves — and conscious that it rose —
Grew by the Fact, and not the Understanding
How Weakness passed — or Force — arose —

Tell that the Worst, is easy in a Moment —
Dread, but the Whizzing, before the Ball —
When the Ball enters, enters Silence —
Dying — annuls the power to kill.

—1863

The Battle fought between the Soul
And No Man — is the One
Of all the Battles prevalent —
By far the Greater One —

No News of it is had abroad —
Its Bodiless Campaign
Establishes, and terminates —
Invisible — Unknown —

Nor History — record it —
As Legions of a Night
The Sunrise scatters — These endure —
Enact — and terminate —

—1863

My Portion is Defeat — today —
A paler luck than Victory —
Less Paeans — fewer Bells —
The Drums dont follow Me — with tunes —
Defeat — a somewhat slower — means —
More Arduous than Balls —

'Tis populous with Bone and stain —
And Men too straight to stoop again,
And Piles of solid Moan —
And Chips of Blank — in Boyish Eyes —
And scraps of Prayer —
And Death's surprise,
Stamped visible — in Stone —

There's somewhat prouder, Over there —
The Trumpets tell it to the Air —
How different Victory
To Him who has it — and the One
Who to have had it, would have been
Contenteder — to die —

—1863

The hallowing of Pain
Like hallowing of Heaven,
Obtains at a corporeal cost —
The Summit is not given —

To Him who strives severe
At middle of the Hill —
But He who has achieved the Top —
All — is the price of All —

—1864

Ambrose Bierce

from *Bits of Autobiography* (1909)

ON A MOUNTAIN

They say that the lumberman has looked upon the Cheat Mountain country[24] and seen that it is good, and I hear that some wealthy gentlemen have been there and made a game preserve. There must be lumber and, I suppose, sport, but some things one could wish were ordered otherwise. Looking back upon it through the haze of near half a century, I see that region as a veritable realm of enchantment; the Alleghanies as the Delectable Mountains. I note again their dim, blue billows, ridge after ridge interminable, beyond purple valleys full of sleep, "in which it seemed always afternoon."[25] Miles and miles away, where the lift of earth meets the stoop of sky, I discern an imperfection in the tint, a faint graying of the blue above the main range—the smoke of an enemy's camp.

It was in the autumn of that "most immemorial year,"[26] the 1861st of our Lord, and of our Heroic Age the first, that a small brigade of raw troops—troops were all raw in those days—had been pushed in across the Ohio border and after various vicissitudes of fortune and mismanagement found itself, greatly to its own surprise, at Cheat Mountain Pass, holding a road that ran from Nowhere to the southeast. Some of us had served through the summer in the "three-months' regiments,"[27] which responded to the President's first call for troops. We were regarded by the others with profound respect as "old soldiers." (Our ages, if equalized, would, I fancy, have given about twenty years to each man.) We gave ourselves, this aristocracy of service, no end of military airs; some of us even going to the extreme of keeping our jackets buttoned and our hair combed. We had been in action, too; had shot off a Confederate leg at Philippi, "the first battle of the war,"[28] and had lost as many as a dozen men at Laurel Hill and Carrick's Ford,[29] whither the enemy had fled in trying, Heaven knows why, to get away from us. We now "brought to the task" of subduing the Rebellion a patriotism which never for a moment doubted that a rebel was a fiend accursed of God and the angels—one for whose extirpation by force and arms each youth of us considered himself specially "raised up."

It was a strange country. Nine in ten of us had never seen a mountain, nor a hill as high as a church spire, until we had crossed the Ohio River. In power upon the emotions nothing, I think, is comparable to a first sight of mountains. To a member of a plains-tribe, born and reared on the flats of Ohio or Indiana, a mountain region was a perpetual miracle. Space seemed to have taken on a new dimension; areas to have not only length and breadth, but thickness.

Modern literature is full of evidence that our great grandfathers looked upon mountains with aversion and horror. The poets of even the seventeenth century never tire of damning them in good, set terms. If they had had the unhappiness to read the opening lines of "The Pleasures of Hope," they would assuredly have thought Master Campbell had gone funny and should be shut up lest he do himself an injury.[30]

The flatlanders who invaded the Cheat Mountain country had been suckled in another creed, and to them western Virginia—there was, as yet, no West Virginia—was an enchanted land.[31] How we reveled in its savage beauties! With what pure delight we inhaled its fragrances of spruce and pine! How we stared with something like awe at its clumps of laurel!—real laurel, as we understood the matter, whose foliage had been once accounted excellent for the heads of illustrious Romans and such—mayhap to reduce the swelling. We carved its roots into finger-rings and pipes. We gathered spruce-gum and sent it to our sweethearts in letters. We ascended every hill within our picket-lines and called it a "peak."

And, by the way, during those halcyon days (the halcyon was there, too, chattering above every creek, as he is all over the world) we fought another battle. It has not got into history, but it had a real objective existence, although by a felicitous afterthought called by us who were defeated a "reconnaissance in force." Its short and simple annals are that we marched a long way and lay down before a fortified camp of the enemy at the farther edge of a valley. Our commander had the forethought to see that we lay well out of range of the small-arms of the period. A disadvantage of this arrangement was that the enemy was out of reach of us as well, for our rifles were no better than his. Unfortunately—one might almost say unfairly—he had a few pieces of artillery very well protected, and with those he mauled us to the eminent satisfaction of his mind and heart. So we parted from him in anger and returned to our own place, leaving our dead—not many.

Among them was a chap belonging to my company, named Abbott; it is not odd that I recollect it, for there was something unusual in the manner of Abbott's taking off. He was lying flat upon his stomach and was killed by being struck in the side by a nearly spent cannon-shot that came rolling in among us. The shot remained in him until removed. It was a solid round-shot, evidently cast in some private foundry, whose proprietor, setting the laws of thrift above those of ballistics, had put his "imprint" upon it: it bore, in slightly sunken letters, the name "Abbott." That is what I was told—I was not present.

It was after this, when the nights had acquired a trick of biting and the morning sun appeared to shiver with cold, that we moved up to the summit of Cheat Mountain to guard the pass through which nobody wanted to go. Here we slew the forest and builded us giant habitations (astride the road from Nowhere to the southeast) commodious to lodge an army and fitly loopholed for discomfiture of the adversary. The long logs that it was our pride to cut and carry! The accuracy with which we laid them one upon another, hewn to the line and bullet-proof! The Cyclopean doors that we hung, with sliding bolts fit to be "the mast of some great admiral"![32] And when we had "made the pile complete" some marplot of the Regular Army[33] came that way and chatted a few moments with our commander, and we made an earthwork away off on one side of the road (leaving the other side to take care of itself) and camped outside it in tents! But the Regular Army fellow had not the heart to suggest the demolition of our Towers of Babel, and the foundations remain to this day to attest the genius of the American volunteer soldiery.

We were the original game-preservers of the Cheat Mountain region, for although we hunted in season and out of season over as wide an area as we dared to cover we took less game, probably, than would have been taken by a certain single hunter of disloyal views whom we scared away. There were bear galore and deer in quantity, and many a winter day, in snow up to his knees, did the writer of this pass in tracking bruin to his den, where, I am bound to say, I commonly left him. I agreed with my lamented friend, the late Robert Weeks, poet:

Pursuit may be, it seems to me,
Perfect without possession.[34]

There can be no doubt that the wealthy sportsmen who have made a preserve of the Cheat Mountain region will find plenty of game if it has not died since 1861. We left it there.

Yet hunting and idling were not the whole of life's programme up there on that wild ridge with its shaggy pelt of spruce and firs, and in the riparian lowlands that it parted. We had a bit of war now and again. There was an occasional "affair of outposts"; sometimes a hazardous scout into the enemy's country, ordered, I fear, more to keep up the appearance of doing something than with a hope of accomplishing a military result. But one day it was bruited about that a movement in force was to be made on the enemy's position miles away, at the summit of the main ridge of the Alleghanies—the camp whose faint blue smoke we had watched for weary days. The movement was made, as was the fashion in those 'prentice days of warfare, in two columns, which were to pounce upon the foeman from opposite sides at the same moment. Led over unknown roads by untrusty guides, encountering obstacles not foreseen—miles apart and without communication, the two columns invariably failed to execute the movement with requisite secrecy and precision. The enemy, in enjoyment of that inestimable military advantage known in civilian speech as being "surrounded," always beat the attacking columns one at a time or, turning red-handed from the wreck of the first, frightened the other away.

All one bright wintry day we marched down from our eyrie; all one bright wintry night we climbed the great wooded ridge opposite. How romantic it all was; the sunset valleys full of visible sleep; the glades suffused and interpenetrated with moonlight; the long valley of the Greenbrier stretching away to we knew not what silent cities; the river itself unseen under its "astral body" of mist! Then there was the "spice of danger."

Once we heard shots in front; then there was a long wait. As we trudged on we passed something—some things—lying by the wayside. During another wait we examined them, curiously lifting the blankets from their yellow-clay faces. How repulsive they looked with their blood-smears, their blank, staring eyes, their teeth uncovered by contraction of the lips! The frost had begun already to whiten their deranged clothing. We were as patriotic as ever, but we did not wish to be that way. For an hour afterward the injunction of silence in the ranks was needless.

❧

Repassing the spot the next day, a beaten, dispirited and exhausted force, feeble from fatigue and savage from defeat, some of us had life enough left, such as it was, to observe that these bodies had altered their position. They appeared also to have thrown off some of their clothing, which lay near by, in disorder. Their expression, too, had an added blankness—they had no faces.

As soon as the head of our straggling column had reached the spot a desultory firing had begun. One might have thought the living paid honors to the dead. No; the firing was a military execution; the condemned, a herd of galloping swine. They had eaten our fallen, but—touching magnanimity!—we did not eat theirs.

The shooting of several kinds was very good in the Cheat Mountain country, even in 1861.

Ambrose Bierce

from *Tales of Soldiers and Civilians* (1891)

A HORSEMAN IN THE SKY

I

One sunny afternoon in the autumn of the year 1861 a soldier lay in a clump of laurel by the side of a road in western Virginia. He lay at full length upon his stomach, his feet resting upon the toes, his head upon the left forearm. His extended right hand loosely grasped his rifle. But for the somewhat methodical disposition of his limbs and a slight rhythmic movement of the cartridge-box at the back of his belt he might have been thought to be dead. He was asleep at his post of duty. But if detected he would be dead shortly afterward, death being the just and legal penalty of his crime.

The clump of laurel in which the criminal lay was in the angle of a road which after ascending southward a steep acclivity to that point turned sharply to the west, running along the summit for perhaps one hundred yards. There it turned southward again and went zigzagging downward through the forest. At the salient of that second angle was a large flat rock, jutting out northward, overlooking the deep valley from which the road ascended. The rock capped a high cliff; a stone dropped from its outer edge would have fallen sheer downward one thousand feet to the tops of the pines. The angle where the soldier lay was on another spur of the same cliff. Had he been awake he would have commanded a view, not only of the short arm of the road and the jutting rock, but of the entire profile of the cliff below it. It might well have made him giddy to look.

The country was wooded everywhere except at the bottom of the valley to the northward, where there was a small natural meadow, through which flowed a stream scarcely visible from the valley's rim. This open ground looked hardly larger than an ordinary door-yard, but was really several acres in extent. Its green was more vivid than that of the inclosing forest. Away beyond it rose a line of giant cliffs similar to those upon which we are supposed to stand in our survey of the savage scene, and through which the road had somehow made its climb to the summit. The configuration of the valley, indeed, was such that from this point of observation it seemed entirely shut in, and one could but have wondered how the road which found a way out of it had found a way into it, and whence came and whither went the waters of the stream that parted the meadow more than a thousand feet below.

No country is so wild and difficult but men will make it a theatre of war; concealed in the forest at the bottom of that military rat-trap, in which half a hundred men in possession of the exits might have starved an army to submission, lay five regiments of Federal infantry. They had marched all the previous day and night and were resting. At nightfall they would take to the road again, climb to the place where their unfaithful sentinel now slept, and descending the other slope of the ridge fall upon a camp of the enemy at about midnight. Their hope was to surprise it, for the road led to the rear of it. In case of failure, their position would be perilous in the extreme; and fail they surely would should accident or vigilance apprise the enemy of the movement.

II

The sleeping sentinel in the clump of laurel was a young Virginian named Carter Druse. He was the son of wealthy parents, an only child, and had known such ease and cultivation and high living as wealth and taste were able to command in the mountain country of western Virginia. His home was but a few miles from where he now lay. One morning he had risen from the breakfast-table and said, quietly but gravely: "Father, a Union regiment has arrived at Grafton. I am going to join it."

The father lifted his leonine head, looked at the son a moment in silence, and replied "Well, go, sir, and whatever may occur do what you conceive to be your duty. Virginia, to which you are a traitor, must get on without you. Should we both live to the end of the war, we will speak further of the matter. Your mother, as the physician has informed you, is in a most critical condition; at the best she cannot be with us longer than a few weeks, but that time is precious. It would be better not to disturb her."

So Carter Druse, bowing reverently to his father, who returned the salute with a stately courtesy that masked a breaking heart, left the home of his childhood to go soldiering. By conscience and courage, by deeds of devotion and daring, he soon commended himself to his fellows and his officers; and it was to these qualities and to some knowledge of the country that he owed his selection for his present perilous duty at the extreme outpost. Nevertheless, fatigue had been stronger than resolution and he had fallen asleep. What good or bad angel came in a dream to rouse him from his state of crime, who shall say? Without a movement, without a sound, in the profound silence and the languor of the late afternoon, some invisible messenger of fate touched with unsealing finger the eyes of his consciousness—whispered into the ear of his spirit the mysterious awakening word which no human lips ever have spoken, no human memory ever has recalled. He quietly raised his forehead from his arm and looked between the masking stems of the laurels, instinctively closing his right hand about the stock of his rifle.

His first feeling was a keen artistic delight. On a colossal pedestal, the cliff,—motionless at the extreme edge of the capping rock and sharply outlined against the sky,—was an equestrian statue of impressive dignity. The figure of the man sat the figure of the horse, straight and soldierly, but with the repose of a Grecian god carved in the marble which limits the suggestion of activity. The gray costume harmonized with its aërial background; the metal of accoutrement and caparison was softened and subdued by the shadow; the animal's skin had no points of high light. A carbine strikingly foreshortened lay across the pommel of the saddle, kept in place by the right hand grasping it at the "grip"; the left hand, holding the bridle rein, was invisible. In silhouette against the sky the profile of the horse was cut with the sharpness of a cameo; it looked across the heights of air to the confronting cliffs beyond. The face of the rider, turned slightly away, showed only an outline of temple and beard; he was looking downward to the bottom of the valley. Magnified by its lift against the sky and by the soldier's testifying sense of the formidableness of a near enemy the group appeared of heroic, almost colossal, size.

For an instant Druse had a strange, half-defined feeling that he had slept to the end of the war and was looking upon a noble work of art reared upon that eminence to commemorate the deeds of an heroic past of which he had been an inglorious part. The feeling was dispelled by a slight movement of the group: the horse, without moving its feet, had drawn its body slightly backward from the verge; the man remained immobile as before. Broad awake and keenly alive to the significance of the situation, Druse now brought the butt of his rifle against his cheek by cautiously pushing the barrel forward through the bushes, cocked the piece, and glancing through the sights covered a vital spot of the horseman's breast. A touch upon the trigger and all would have been well with Carter Druse. At that instant the horseman turned his head and looked in the direction of his concealed foeman—seemed to look into his very face, into his eyes, into his brave, compassionate heart.

Is it then so terrible to kill an enemy in war—an enemy who has surprised a secret vital to the safety of one's self and comrades—an enemy more formidable for his knowledge than all his army for its numbers? Carter Druse grew pale; he shook in every limb, turned faint, and saw the statuesque group before him as black figures, rising, falling, moving unsteadily in arcs of circles in a fiery sky. His hand fell away from his weapon, his head slowly dropped until his face rested on the leaves in which he lay. This courageous gentleman and hardy soldier was near swooning from intensity of emotion.

It was not for long; in another moment his face was raised from earth, his hands resumed their places on the rifle, his forefinger sought the trigger; mind, heart, and eyes were clear, conscience and reason sound. He could not hope to capture that enemy; to alarm him would but send him dashing to his camp with his fatal news. The duty of the soldier was plain: the man must be shot dead from ambush—without warning, without a moment's spiritual preparation, with never so much as an unspoken prayer, he must be sent to his account. But no—there is a hope; he may have discovered nothing—perhaps he is but admiring the sublimity of the landscape. If permitted, he may turn and ride carelessly away in the direction whence he came. Surely it will be possible to judge at the instant of his withdrawing whether he knows. It may well be that his fixity of attention—Druse turned his head and looked through the deeps of air downward, as from the surface to the bottom of a translucent sea. He saw creeping across the green meadow a sinuous line of figures of men and horses—some foolish commander was permitting the soldiers of his escort to water their beasts in the open, in plain view from a dozen summits!

Druse withdrew his eyes from the valley and fixed them again upon the group of man and horse in the sky, and again it was through the sights of his rifle. But this time his aim was at the horse. In his memory, as if they were a divine mandate, rang the words of his father at their parting: "Whatever may occur, do what you conceive to be your duty." He was calm now. His teeth were firmly but not rigidly closed; his nerves were as tranquil as a sleeping babe's—not a tremor affected any muscle of his body; his breathing, until suspended in the act of taking aim, was regular and slow. Duty had conquered; the spirit had said to the body: "Peace, be still." He fired.

III

An officer of the Federal force, who in a spirit of adventure or in quest of knowledge had left the hidden *bivouac* in the valley, and with aimless feet had made his way to the lower edge of a small open space near the foot of the cliff, was considering what he had to gain by pushing his exploration further. At a distance of a quarter-mile before him, but apparently at a stone's throw, rose from its fringe of pines the gigantic face of rock, towering to so great a height above him that it made him giddy to look up to where its edge cut a sharp, rugged line against the sky. It presented a clean, vertical profile against a background of blue sky to a point half the way down, and of distant hills, hardly less blue, thence to the tops of the trees at its base. Lifting his eyes to the dizzy altitude of its summit the officer saw an astonishing sight—a man on horseback riding down into the valley through the air!

Straight upright sat the rider, in military fashion, with a firm seat in the saddle, a strong clutch upon the rein to hold his charger from too impetuous a plunge. From his bare head his long hair streamed upward, waving like a plume. His hands were concealed in the cloud of the horse's lifted mane. The animal's body was as level as if every hoofstroke encountered the resistant earth. Its motions were those of a wild gallop, but even as the officer looked they ceased, with all the legs thrown sharply forward as in the act of alighting from a leap. But this was a flight!

Filled with amazement and terror by this apparition of a horseman in the sky—half believing himself the chosen scribe of some new Apocalypse, the officer was overcome by the intensity of his emotions; his legs failed him and he fell. Almost at the same instant he heard a crashing sound in the trees—a sound that died without an echo—and all was still.

The officer rose to his feet, trembling. The familiar sensation of an abraded shin recalled his dazed faculties. Pulling himself together he ran rapidly obliquely away from the cliff to a point distant from its foot; thereabout he expected to find his man; and thereabout he naturally failed. In the fleeting instant of his vision his imagination had been so wrought upon by the apparent grace and ease and intention of the marvelous performance that it did not occur to him that the line of march of aërial cavalry is directly downward, and that he could find the objects of his search at the very foot of the cliff. A half-hour later he returned to camp.

This officer was a wise man; he knew better than to tell an incredible truth. He said nothing of what he had seen. But when the commander asked him if in his scout he had learned anything of advantage to the expedition he answered

"Yes, sir; there is no road leading down into this valley from the southward."

The commander, knowing better, smiled.

IV

After firing his shot, Private Carter Druse reloaded his rifle and resumed his watch. Ten minutes had hardly passed when a Federal sergeant crept cautiously to him on hands and knees. Druse neither turned his head nor looked at him, but lay without motion or sign of recognition.

"Did you fire?" the sergeant whispered.

"Yes."

"At what?"

"A horse. It was standing on yonder rock—pretty far out. You see it is no longer there. It went over the cliff."

The man's face was white, but he showed no other sign of emotion. Having answered, he turned away his eyes and said no more. The sergeant did not understand.

"See here, Druse," he said, after a moment's silence, "it's no use making a mystery. I order you to report. Was there anybody on the horse?"

"Yes."

"Well?"

"My father."

The sergeant rose to his feet and walked away. "Good God!" he said.

Ambrose Bierce

from *Tales of Soldiers and Civilians* (1891)

A SON OF THE GODS: A STUDY IN THE PRESENT TENSE

A breezy day and a sunny landscape. An open country to right and left and forward; behind, a wood. In the edge of this wood, facing the open but not venturing into it, long lines of troops, halted. The wood is alive with them, and full of confused noises—the occasional rattle of wheels as a battery of artillery goes into position to cover the advance; the hum and murmur of the soldiers talking; a sound of innumerable feet in the dry leaves that strew the interspaces among the trees; hoarse commands of officers. Detached groups of horsemen are well in front—not altogether exposed—many of them intently regarding the crest of a hill a mile away in the direction of the interrupted advance. For this powerful army, moving in battle order through a forest, has met with a formidable obstacle—the open country. The crest of that gentle hill a mile away has a sinister look; it says, Beware! Along it runs a stone wall extending to left and right a great distance. Behind the wall is a hedge; behind the hedge are seen the tops of trees in rather straggling order. Among the trees—what? It is necessary to know.

Yesterday, and for many days and nights previously, we were fighting somewhere; always there was cannonading, with occasional keen rattlings of musketry, mingled with cheers, our own or the enemy's, we seldom knew, attesting some temporary advantage. This morning at daybreak the enemy was gone. We have moved forward across his earthworks, across which we have so often vainly attempted to move before, through the débris of his abandoned camps, among the graves of his fallen, into the woods beyond.

How curiously we had regarded everything! how odd it all had seemed! Nothing had appeared quite familiar; the most commonplace objects—an old saddle, a splintered wheel, a forgotten canteen—everything had related something of the mysterious personality of those strange men who had been killing us. The soldier never becomes wholly familiar with the conception of his foes as men like himself; he cannot divest himself of the feeling that they are another order of beings, differently conditioned, in an environment not altogether of the earth. The smallest vestiges of them rivet his attention and engage his interest. He thinks of them as inaccessible; and, catching an unexpected glimpse of them, they appear farther away, and therefore larger, than they really are—like objects in a fog. He is somewhat in awe of them.

From the edge of the wood leading up the acclivity are the tracks of horses and wheels—the wheels of cannon. The yellow grass is beaten down by the feet of infantry. Clearly they have passed this way in thousands; they have not withdrawn by the country roads. This is significant—it is the difference between retiring and retreating.

That group of horsemen is our commander, his staff and escort. He is facing the distant crest, holding his field-glass against his eyes with both hands, his elbows needlessly elevated. It is a fashion; it seems to dignify the act; we are all addicted to it. Suddenly he lowers the glass and says a few words to those about him. Two or three aides detach them-selves from the group and canter away into the woods, along the lines in each direction. We did not hear his words, but we know them: "Tell General X. to send forward the skir-mish line." Those of us who have been out of place resume our positions; the men resting at ease straighten themselves and the ranks are re-formed without a command. Some of us staff officers dismount and look at our saddle girths; those already on the ground remount.

Galloping rapidly along in the edge of the open ground comes a young officer on a snow-white horse. His saddle blanket is scarlet. What a fool! No one who has ever been in action but remembers how naturally every rifle turns toward the man on a white horse; no one but has observed how a bit of red enrages the bull of battle. That such colors are fashionable in military life must be accepted as the most astonishing of all the phenomena of human vanity. They would seem to have been devised to increase the death-rate.

This young officer is in full uniform, as if on parade. He is all agleam with bullion—a blue-and-gold edition of the Poetry of War. A wave of derisive laughter runs abreast of him all along the line. But how handsome he is!—with what careless grace he sits his horse!

He reins up within a respectful distance of the corps commander and salutes. The old soldier nods familiarly; he evidently knows him. A brief colloquy between them is going on; the young man seems to be preferring some request which the elder one is indisposed to grant. Let us ride a little nearer. Ah! too late—it is ended. The young officer salutes again, wheels his horse, and rides straight toward the crest of the hill!

A thin line of skirmishers, the men deployed at six paces or so apart, now pushes from the wood into the open. The commander speaks to his bugler, who claps his instrument to his lips. *Tra-la-la! Tra-la-la!* The skirmishers halt in their tracks.

Meantime the young horseman has advanced a hundred yards. He is riding at a walk, straight up the long slope, with never a turn of the head. How glorious! Gods! what would we not give to be in his place—with his soul! He does not draw his sabre; his right hand hangs easily at his side. The breeze catches the plume in his hat and flutters it smartly. The sunshine rests upon his shoulder-straps, lovingly, like a visible benediction. Straight on he rides. Ten thousand pairs of eyes are fixed upon him with an intensity that he can hardly fail to feel; ten thousand hearts keep quick time to the inaudible hoof-beats of his snowy steed. He is not alone—he draws all souls after him. But we remember that we laughed! On and on, straight for the hedge-lined wall, he rides. Not a look backward. O, if he would but turn—if he could but see the love, the adoration, the atonement!

Not a word is spoken; the populous depths of the forest still murmur with their un-seen and unseeing swarm, but all along the fringe is silence. The burly commander is an equestrian statue of himself. The mounted staff officers, their field glasses up, are motion-less all. The line of battle in the edge of the wood stands at a new kind of "attention," each man in the attitude in which he was caught by the consciousness of what is going on. All these hardened and impenitent man-killers, to whom death in its awfulest forms is a fact familiar to their every-day observation; who sleep on hills trembling with the thunder of great guns, dine in the midst of streaming missiles, and play at cards among the dead faces of their dearest friends—all are watching with suspended breath and beating hearts the outcome of an act involving the life of one man. Such is the magnetism of courage and devotion.

If now you should turn your head you would see a simultaneous movement among the spectators—a start, as if they had received an electric shock—and looking forward again to the now distant horseman you would see that he has in that instant altered his direction and is riding at an angle to his former course. The spectators suppose the sudden deflection to be caused by a shot, perhaps a wound; but take this field-glass and you will observe that he is riding toward a break in the wall and hedge. He means, if not killed, to ride through and overlook the country beyond.

You are not to forget the nature of this man's act; it is not permitted to you to think of it as an instance of bravado, nor, on the other hand, a needless sacrifice of self. If the enemy has not retreated he is in force on that ridge. The investigator will encounter nothing less than a line-of-battle; there is no need of pickets, videttes, skirmishers, to give warning of our approach; our attacking lines will be visible, conspicuous, exposed to an artillery fire that will shave the ground the moment they break from cover, and for half the distance to a sheet of rifle bullets in which nothing can live. In short, if the enemy is there, it would be madness to attack him in front; he must be manœuvred out by the immemorial plan of threatening his line of communication, as necessary to his existence as to the diver at the bottom of the sea his air tube. But how ascertain if the enemy is there? There is but one way,—somebody must go and see. The natural and customary thing to do is to send forward a line of skirmishers. But in this case they will answer in the affirmative with all their lives; the enemy, crouching in double ranks behind the stone wall and in cover of the hedge, will wait until it is possible to count each assailant's teeth. At the first volley a half of the questioning line will fall, the other half before it can accomplish the predestined retreat. What a price to pay for gratified curiosity! At what a dear rate an army must sometimes purchase knowledge! "Let me pay all," says this gallant man—this military Christ!

There is no hope except the hope against hope that the crest is clear. True, he might prefer capture to death. So long as he advances, the line will not fire—why should it? He can safely ride into the hostile ranks and become a prisoner of war. But this would defeat his object. It would not answer our question; it is necessary either that he return unharmed or be shot to death before our eyes. Only so shall we know how to act. If captured—why, that might have been done by a half-dozen stragglers.

Now begins an extraordinary contest of intellect between a man and an army. Our horseman, now within a quarter of a mile of the crest, suddenly wheels to the left and gallops in a direction parallel to it. He has caught sight of his antagonist; he knows all. Some slight advantage of ground has enabled him to overlook a part of the line. If he were here he could tell us in words. But that is now hopeless; he must make the best use of the few minutes of life remaining to him, by compelling the enemy himself to tell us as much and as plainly as possible—which, naturally, that discreet power is reluctant to do. Not a rifleman in those crouching ranks, not a cannoneer at those masked and shotted guns, but knows the needs of the situation, the imperative duty of forbearance. Besides, there has been time enough to forbid them all to fire. True, a single rifle-shot might drop him and be no great disclosure. But firing is infectious—and see how rapidly he moves, with never a pause except as he whirls his horse about to take a new direction, never directly backward toward us, never directly forward toward his executioners. All this is visible through the glass; it seems occurring within pistol-shot; we see all but the enemy, whose presence, whose thoughts, whose motives we infer. To the unaided eye there is nothing but a black figure on a white horse, tracing slow zigzags against the slope of a distant hill—so slowly they seem almost to creep.

Now—the glass again—he has tired of his failure, or sees his error, or has gone mad; he is dashing directly forward at the wall, as if to take it at a leap, hedge and all! One moment only and he wheels right about and is speeding like the wind straight down the slope—toward his friends, toward his death! Instantly the wall is topped with a fierce roll of smoke for a distance of hundreds of yards to right and left. This is as instantly dissipated by the wind, and before the rattle of the rifles reaches us he is down. No, he recovers his seat; he has but pulled his horse upon its haunches. They are up and away! A tremendous cheer bursts from our ranks, relieving the insupportable tension of our feelings. And the horse and its rider? Yes, they are up and away. Away, indeed—they are making directly to our left, parallel to the now steadily blazing and smoking wall. The rattle of the musketry is continuous, and every bullet's target is that courageous heart.

Suddenly a great bank of white smoke pushes upward from behind the wall. Another and another—a dozen roll up before the thunder of the explosions and the humming of the missiles reach our ears and the missiles themselves come bounding through clouds of dust into our covert, knocking over here and there a man and causing a temporary distraction, a passing thought of self.

The dust drifts away. Incredible!—that enchanted horse and rider have passed a ravine and are climbing another slope to unveil another conspiracy of silence, to thwart the will of another armed host. Another moment and that crest too is in eruption. The horse rears and strikes the air with its forefeet. They are down at last. But look again—the man has detached himself from the dead animal. He stands erect, motionless, holding his sabre in his right hand straight above his head. His face is toward us. Now he lowers his hand to a level with his face and moves it outward, the blade of the sabre describing a downward curve. It is a sign to us, to the world, to posterity. It is a hero's salute to death and history.

Again the spell is broken; our men attempt to cheer; they are choking with emotion; they utter hoarse, discordant cries; they clutch their weapons and press tumultuously forward into the open. The skirmishers, without orders, against orders, are going forward at a keen run, like hounds unleashed. Our cannon speak and the enemy's now open in full chorus; to right and left as far as we can see, the distant crest, seeming now so near, erects its towers of cloud and the great shot pitch roaring down among our moving masses. Flag after flag of ours emerges from the wood, line after line sweeps forth, catching the sunlight on its burnished arms. The rear battalions alone are in obedience; they preserve their proper distance from the insurgent front.

The commander has not moved. He now removes his field-glass from his eyes and glances to the right and left. He sees the human current flowing on either side of him and his huddled escort, like tide waves parted by a rock. Not a sign of feeling in his face; he is thinking. Again he directs his eyes forward; they slowly traverse that malign and awful crest. He addresses a calm word to his bugler. *Tra-la-la! Tra-la-la!* The injunction has an imperiousness which enforces it. It is repeated by all the bugles of all the subordinate commanders; the sharp metallic notes assert themselves above the hum of the advance and penetrate the sound of the cannon. To halt is to withdraw. The colors move slowly back; the lines face about and sullenly follow, bearing their wounded; the skirmishers return, gathering up the dead.

Ah, those many, many needless dead! That great soul whose beautiful body is lying over yonder, so conspicuous against the sere hillside—could it not have been spared the bitter consciousness of a vain devotion? Would one exception have marred too much the pitiless perfection of the divine, eternal plan?

Ambrose Bierce

from *Tales of Soldiers and Civilians* (1891)

ONE OF THE MISSING

Jerome Searing, a private soldier of General Sherman's army, then confronting the enemy at and about Kennesaw Mountain, Georgia, turned his back upon a small group of officers with whom he had been talking in low tones, stepped across a light line of earthworks, and disappeared in a forest. None of the men in line behind the works had said a word to him, nor had he so much as nodded to them in passing, but all who saw understood that this brave man had been intrusted with some perilous duty. Jerome Searing, though a private, did not serve in the ranks; he was detailed for service at division headquarters, being borne upon the rolls as an orderly. "Orderly" is a word covering a multitude of duties. An orderly may be a messenger, a clerk, an officer's servant—anything. He may perform services for which no provision is made in orders and army regulations. Their nature may depend upon his aptitude, upon favor, upon accident. Private Searing, an incomparable marksman, young, hardy, intelligent and insensible to fear, was a scout. The general commanding his division[35] was not content to obey orders blindly without knowing what was in his front, even when his command was not on detached service, but formed a fraction of the line of the army; nor was he satisfied to receive his knowledge of his *vis-à-vis* through the customary channels; he wanted to know more than he was apprised of by the corps commander and the collisions of pickets and skirmishers. Hence Jerome Searing, with his extraordinary daring, his woodcraft, his sharp eyes, and truthful tongue. On this occasion his instructions were simple: to get as near the enemy's lines as possible and learn all that he could.

In a few moments he had arrived at the picket-line, the men on duty there lying in groups of two and four behind little banks of earth scooped out of the slight depression in which they lay, their rifles protruding from the green boughs with which they had masked their small defenses. The forest extended without a break toward the front, so solemn and silent that only by an effort of the imagination could it be conceived as populous with armed men, alert and vigilant—a forest formidable with possibilities of battle. Pausing a moment in one of these rifle-pits to apprise the men of his intention Searing crept stealthily forward on his hands and knees and was soon lost to view in a dense thicket of underbrush.

"That is the last of him," said one of the men; "I wish I had his rifle; those fellows will hurt some of us with it."

Searing crept on, taking advantage of every accident of ground and growth to give himself better cover. His eyes penetrated everywhere, his ears took note of every sound. He stilled his breathing, and at the cracking of a twig beneath his knee stopped his progress and hugged the earth. It was slow work, but not tedious; the danger made it exciting, but by no physical signs was the excitement manifest. His pulse was as regular, his nerves were as steady as if he were trying to trap a sparrow.

"It seems a long time," he thought, "but I cannot have come very far; I am still alive."

He smiled at his own method of estimating distance, and crept forward. A moment later he suddenly flattened himself upon the earth and lay motionless, minute after minute. Through a narrow opening in the bushes he had caught sight of a small mound of yellow clay—one of the enemy's rifle-pits. After some little time he cautiously raised his head, inch by inch, then his body upon his hands, spread out on each side of him, all the while intently regarding the hillock of clay. In another moment he was upon his feet, rifle in hand, striding rapidly forward with little attempt at concealment. He had rightly interpreted the signs, whatever they were; the enemy was gone.

To assure himself beyond a doubt before going back to report upon so important a matter, Searing pushed forward across the line of abandoned pits, running from cover to cover in the more open forest, his eyes vigilant to discover possible stragglers. He came to the edge of a plantation—one of those forlorn, deserted homesteads of the last years of the war, upgrown with brambles, ugly with broken fences and desolate with vacant buildings having blank apertures in place of doors and windows. After a keen reconnoissance from the safe seclusion of a clump of young pines Searing ran lightly across a field and through an orchard to a small structure which stood apart from the other farm buildings, on a slight elevation. This he thought would enable him to overlook a large scope of country in the direction that he supposed the enemy to have taken in withdrawing. This building, which had originally consisted of a single room elevated upon four posts about ten feet high, was now little more than a roof; the floor had fallen away, the joists and planks loosely piled on the ground below or resting on end at various angles, not wholly torn from their fastenings above. The supporting posts were themselves no longer vertical. It looked as if the whole edifice would go down at the touch of a finger.

Concealing himself in the debris of joists and flooring Searing looked across the open ground between his point of view and a spur of Kennesaw Mountain, a half-mile away. A road leading up and across this spur was crowded with troops—the rear-guard of the retiring enemy, their gun-barrels gleaming in the morning sunlight.

Searing had now learned all that he could hope to know. It was his duty to return to his own command with all possible speed and report his discovery. But the gray column of Confederates toiling up the mountain road was singularly tempting. His rifle—an ordinary "Springfield," but fitted with a globe sight and hair-trigger—would easily send its ounce and a quarter of lead hissing into their midst. That would probably not affect the duration and result of the war, but it is the business of a soldier to kill. It is also his habit if he is a good soldier. Searing cocked his rifle and "set" the trigger.

But it was decreed from the beginning of time that Private Searing was not to murder anybody that bright summer morning, nor was the Confederate retreat to be announced by him. For countless ages events had been so matching themselves together in that wondrous mosaic to some parts of which, dimly discernible, we give the name of history, that the acts which he had in will would have marred the harmony of the pattern. Some twenty-five years previously the Power charged with the execution of the work according to the design had provided against that mischance by causing the birth of a certain male child in a little village at the foot of the Carpathian Mountains, had carefully reared it, supervised its education, directed its desires into a military channel, and in due time made it an officer of artillery. By the concurrence of an infinite number of favoring influences and their preponderance over an infinite number of opposing ones, this officer of artillery had been made to commit a breach of discipline and flee from his native country to avoid punishment. He had been directed to New Orleans (instead of New York), where a recruiting officer awaited him on the wharf. He was enlisted and promoted, and things were so ordered that he now commanded a Confederate battery some two miles along the line from where Jerome Searing, the Federal scout, stood cocking his rifle. Nothing had been neglected—at every step in the progress of both these men's lives, and in the lives of their contemporaries and ancestors, and in the lives of the contemporaries of their ancestors, the right thing had been done to bring about the desired result. Had anything in all this vast concatenation been overlooked Private Searing might have fired on the retreating Confederates that morning, and would perhaps have missed. As it fell out, a Confederate captain of artillery, having nothing better to do while awaiting his turn to pull out and be off, amused himself by sighting a field-piece obliquely to his right at what he mistook for some Federal officers on the crest of a hill, and discharged it. The shot flew high of its mark.

As Jerome Searing drew back the hammer of his rifle and with his eyes upon the distant Confederates considered where he could plant his shot with the best hope of making a widow or an orphan or a childless mother,—perhaps all three, for Private Searing, although he had repeatedly refused promotion, was not without a certain kind of ambition,—he heard a rushing sound in the air, like that made by the wings of a great bird swooping down upon its prey. More quickly than he could apprehend the gradation, it increased to a hoarse and horrible roar, as the missile that made it sprang at him out of the sky, striking with a deafening impact one of the posts supporting the confusion of timbers above him, smashing it into matchwood, and bringing down the crazy edifice with a loud clatter, in clouds of blinding dust!

When Jerome Searing recovered consciousness he did not at once understand what had occurred. It was, indeed, some time before he opened his eyes. For a while he believed that he had died and been buried, and he tried to recall some portions of the burial service. He thought that his wife was kneeling upon his grave, adding her weight to that of the earth upon his breast. The two of them, widow and earth, had crushed his coffin. Unless the children should persuade her to go home he would not much longer be able to breathe. He felt a sense of wrong. "I cannot speak to her," he thought; "the dead have no voice; and if I open my eyes I shall get them full of earth."

He opened his eyes. A great expanse of blue sky, rising from a fringe of the tops of trees. In the foreground, shutting out some of the trees, a high, dun mound, angular in outline and crossed by an intricate, patternless system of straight lines; the whole an immeasurable distance away—a distance so inconceivably great that it fatigued him, and he closed his eyes. The moment that he did so he was conscious of an insufferable light. A sound was in his ears like the low, rhythmic thunder of a distant sea breaking in successive waves upon the beach, and out of this noise, seeming a part of it, or possibly coming from beyond it, and intermingled with its ceaseless undertone, came the articulate words: "Jerome Searing, you are caught like a rat in a trap—in a trap, trap, trap."

Suddenly there fell a great silence, a black darkness, an infinite tranquillity, and Jerome Searing, perfectly conscious of his rathood, and well assured of the trap that he was in, remembering all and nowise alarmed, again opened his eyes to reconnoitre, to note the strength of his enemy, to plan his defense.

He was caught in a reclining posture, his back firmly supported by a solid beam. Another lay across his breast, but he had been able to shrink a little away from it so that it no longer oppressed him, though it was immovable. A brace joining it at an angle had wedged him against a pile of boards on his left, fastening the arm on that side. His legs, slightly parted and straight along the ground, were covered upward to the knees with a mass of débris which towered above his narrow horizon. His head was as rigidly fixed as in a vise; he could move his eyes, his chin—no more. Only his right arm was partly free. "You must help us out of this," he said to it. But he could not get it from under the heavy timber athwart his chest, nor move it outward more than six inches at the elbow.

Searing was not seriously injured, nor did he suffer pain. A smart rap on the head from a flying fragment of the splintered post, incurred simultaneously with the frightfully sudden shock to the nervous system, had momentarily dazed him. His term of unconsciousness, including the period of recovery, during which he had had the strange fancies, had probably not exceeded a few seconds, for the dust of the wreck had not wholly cleared away as he began an intelligent survey of the situation.

With his partly free right hand he now tried to get hold of the beam that lay across, but not quite against, his breast. In no way could he do so. He was unable to depress the shoulder so as to push the elbow beyond that edge of the timber which was nearest his knees; failing in that, he could not raise the forearm and hand to grasp the beam. The brace that made an angle with it downward and backward prevented him from doing anything in that direction, and between it and his body the space was not half so wide as the length of his forearm. Obviously he could not get his hand under the beam nor over it; the hand could not, in fact, touch it at all. Having demonstrated his inability, he desisted, and began to think whether he could reach any of the débris piled upon his legs.

In surveying the mass with a view to determining that point, his attention was arrested by what seemed to be a ring of shining metal immediately in front of his eyes. It appeared to him at first to surround some perfectly black substance, and it was somewhat more than a half-inch in diameter. It suddenly occurred to his mind that the blackness was simply shadow and that the ring was in fact the muzzle of his rifle protruding from the pile of débris. He was not long in satisfying himself that this was so—if it was a satisfaction. By closing either eye he could look a little way along the barrel—to the point where it was hidden by the rubbish that held it. He could see the one side, with the corresponding eye, at apparently the same angle as the other side with the other eye. Looking with the right eye, the weapon seemed to be directed at a point to the left of his head, and *vice versa.* He was unable to see the upper surface of the barrel, but could see the under surface of the stock at a slight angle. The piece was, in fact, aimed at the exact centre of his forehead.

In the perception of this circumstance, in the recollection that just previously to the mischance of which this uncomfortable situation was the result he had cocked the rifle and set the trigger so that a touch would discharge it, Private Searing was affected with a feeling of uneasiness. But that was as far as possible from fear; he was a brave man, somewhat familiar with the aspect of rifles from that point of view, and of cannon too. And now he recalled, with something like amusement, an incident of his experience at the storming of Missionary Ridge, where, walking up to one of the enemy's embrasures from which he had seen a heavy gun throw charge after charge of grape among the assailants he had thought for a moment that the piece had been withdrawn; he could see nothing in the opening but a brazen circle. What that was he had understood just in time to step aside as it pitched another peck of iron down that swarming slope. To face firearms is one of the commonest incidents in a soldier's life—firearms, too, with malevolent eyes blazing behind them. That is what a soldier is for. Still, Private Searing did not altogether relish the situation, and turned away his eyes.

After groping, aimless, with his right hand for a time he made an ineffectual attempt to release his left. Then he tried to disengage his head, the fixity of which was the more annoying from his ignorance of what held it. Next he tried to free his feet, but while exerting the powerful muscles of his legs for that purpose it occurred to him that a disturbance of the rubbish which held them might discharge the rifle; how it could have endured what had already befallen it he could not understand, although memory assisted him with several instances in point. One in particular he recalled, in which in a moment of mental abstraction he had clubbed his rifle and beaten out another gentleman's brains, observing afterward that the weapon which he had been diligently swinging by the muzzle was loaded, capped, and at full cock—knowledge of which circumstance would doubtless have cheered his antagonist to longer endurance. He had always smiled in recalling that blunder of his "green and salad days" as a soldier, but now he did not smile. He turned his eyes again to the muzzle of the rifle and for a moment fancied that it had moved; it seemed somewhat nearer.

Again he looked away. The tops of the distant trees beyond the bounds of the plantation interested him: he had not before observed how light and feathery they were, nor how darkly blue the sky was, even among their branches, where they somewhat paled it with their green; above him it appeared almost black. "It will be uncomfortably hot here," he thought, "as the day advances. I wonder which way I am looking."

Judging by such shadows as he could see, he decided that his face was due north; he would at least not have the sun in his eyes, and north—well, that was toward his wife and children.

"Bah!" he exclaimed aloud, "what have they to do with it?"

He closed his eyes. "As I can't get out I may as well go to sleep. The rebels are gone and some of our fellows are sure to stray out here foraging. They'll find me."

But he did not sleep. Gradually he became sensible of a pain in his forehead—a dull ache, hardly perceptible at first, but growing more and more uncomfortable. He opened his eyes and it was gone—closed them and it returned. "The devil!" he said, irrelevantly, and stared again at the sky. He heard the singing of birds, the strange metallic note of the meadow lark, suggesting the clash of vibrant blades. He fell into pleasant memories of his childhood, played again with his brother and sister, raced across the fields, shouting to alarm the sedentary larks, entered the sombre forest beyond and with timid steps followed the faint path to Ghost Rock, standing at last with audible heart-throbs before the Dead Man's Cave and seeking to penetrate its awful mystery. For the first time he observed that the opening of the haunted cavern was encircled by a ring of metal. Then all else vanished and left him gazing into the barrel of his rifle as before. But whereas before it had seemed nearer, it now seemed an inconceivable distance away, and all the more sinister for that. He cried out and, startled by something in his own voice—the note of fea—lied to himself in denial: "If I don't sing out I may stay here till I die."

He now made no further attempt to evade the menacing stare of the gun barrel. If he turned away his eyes an instant it was to look for assistance (although he could not see the ground on either side the ruin), and he permitted them to return, obedient to the imperative fascination. If he closed them it was from weariness, and instantly the poignant pain in his forehead—the prophecy and menace of the bullet—forced him to reopen them.

The tension of nerve and brain was too severe; nature came to his relief with intervals of unconsciousness. Reviving from one of these he became sensible of a sharp, smarting pain in his right hand, and when he worked his fingers together, or rubbed his palm with them, he could feel that they were wet and slippery. He could not see the hand, but he knew the sensation; it was running blood. In his delirium he had beaten it against the jagged fragments of the wreck, had clutched it full of splinters. He resolved that he would meet his fate more manly. He was a plain, common soldier, had no religion and not much philosophy; he could not die like a hero, with great and wise last words, even if there had been some one to hear them, but he could die "game," and he would. But if he could only know when to expect the shot!

Some rats which had probably inhabited the shed came sneaking and scampering about. One of them mounted the pile of débris that held the rifle; another followed and another. Searing regarded them at first with indifference, then with friendly interest; then, as the thought flashed into his bewildered mind that they might touch the trigger of his rifle, he cursed them and ordered them to go away. "It is no business of yours," he cried.

The creatures went away; they would return later, attack his face, gnaw away his nose, cut his throat—he knew that, but he hoped by that time to be dead.

Nothing could now unfix his gaze from the little ring of metal with its black interior. The pain in his forehead was fierce and incessant. He felt it gradually penetrating the brain more and more deeply, until at last its progress was arrested by the wood at the back of his head. It grew momentarily more insufferable: he began wantonly beating his lacerated hand against the splinters again to counteract that horrible ache. It seemed to throb with a slow, regular recurrence, each pulsation sharper than the preceding, and sometimes he cried out, thinking he felt the fatal bullet. No thoughts of home, of wife and children, of country, of glory. The whole record of memory was effaced. The world had passed away—not a vestige remained. Here in this confusion of timbers and boards is the sole universe. Here is immortality in time—each pain an everlasting life. The throbs tick off eternities.

Jerome Searing, the man of courage, the formidable enemy, the strong, resolute warrior, was as pale as a ghost. His jaw was fallen; his eyes protruded; he trembled in every fibre; a cold sweat bathed his entire body; he screamed with fear. He was not insane—he was terrified.

In groping about with his torn and bleeding hand he seized at last a strip of board, and, pulling, felt it give way. It lay parallel with his body, and by bending his elbow as much as the contracted space would permit, he could draw it a few inches at a time. Finally it was altogether loosened from the wreckage covering his legs; he could lift it clear of the ground its whole length. A great hope came into his mind: perhaps he could work it upward, that is to say backward, far enough to lift the end and push aside the rifle; or, if that were too tightly wedged, so place the strip of board as to deflect the bullet. With this object he passed it backward inch by inch, hardly daring to breathe lest that act somehow defeat his intent, and more than ever unable to remove his eyes from the rifle, which might perhaps now hasten to improve its waning opportunity. Something at least had been gained: in the occupation of his mind in this attempt at self-defense he was less sensible of the pain in his head and had ceased to wince. But he was still dreadfully frightened and his teeth rattled like castanets.

The strip of board ceased to move to the suasion of his hand. He tugged at it with all his strength, changed the direction of its length all he could, but it had met some extended obstruction behind him and the end in front was still too far away to clear the pile of débris and reach the muzzle of the gun. It extended, indeed, nearly as far as the trigger guard, which, uncovered by the rubbish, he could imperfectly see with his right eye. He tried to break the strip with his hand, but had no leverage. In his defeat, all his terror returned, augmented tenfold. The black aperture of the rifle appeared to threaten a sharper and more imminent death in punishment of his rebellion. The track of the bullet through his head ached with an intenser anguish. He began to tremble again.

Suddenly he became composed. His tremor subsided. He clenched his teeth and drew down his eyebrows. He had not exhausted his means of defense; a new design had shaped itself in his mind—another plan of battle. Raising the front end of the strip of board, he carefully pushed it forward through the wreckage at the side of the rifle until it pressed against the trigger guard. Then he moved the end slowly outward until he could feel that it had cleared it, then, closing his eyes, thrust it against the trigger with all his strength! There was no explosion; the rifle had been discharged as it dropped from his hand when the building fell. But it did its work.

Lieutenant Adrian Searing, in command of the picket-guard on that part of the line through which his brother Jerome had passed on his mission, sat with attentive ears in his breastwork behind the line. Not the faintest sound escaped him; the cry of a bird, the barking of a squirrel, the noise of the wind among the pines—all were anxiously noted by his overstrained sense. Suddenly, directly in front of his line, he heard a faint, confused rumble, like the clatter of a falling building translated by distance. The lieutenant mechanically looked at his watch. Six o'clock and eighteen minutes. At the same moment an officer approached him on foot from the rear and saluted.

"Lieutenant," said the officer, "the colonel directs you to move forward your line and feel the enemy if you find him. If not, continue the advance until directed to halt. There is reason to think that the enemy has retreated."

The lieutenant nodded and said nothing; the other officer retired. In a moment the men, apprised of their duty by the non-commissioned officers in low tones, had deployed from their rifle-pits and were moving forward in skirmishing order, with set teeth and beating hearts.

This line of skirmishers sweeps across the plantation toward the mountain. They pass on both sides of the wrecked building, observing nothing. At a short distance in their rear their commander comes. He casts his eyes curiously upon the ruin and sees a dead body half buried in boards and timbers. It is so covered with dust that its clothing is Confederate gray. Its face is yellowish white; the cheeks are fallen in, the temples sunken, too, with sharp ridges about them, making the forehead forbiddingly narrow; the upper lip, slightly lifted, shows the white teeth, rigidly clenched. The hair is heavy with moisture, the face as wet as the dewy grass all about. From his point of view the officer does not observe the rifle; the man was apparently killed by the fall of the building.

"Dead a week," said the officer curtly, moving on and absently pulling out his watch as if to verify his estimate of time. Six o'clock and forty minutes.

Ambrose Bierce

from *Can Such Things Be?* (1893)

A TOUGH TUSSLE

One night in the autumn of 1861 a man sat alone in the heart of a forest in western Virginia. The region was one of the wildest on the continent—the Cheat Mountain country. There was no lack of people close at hand, however; within a mile of where the man sat was the now silent camp of a whole Federal brigade. Somewhere about—it might be still nearer—was a force of the enemy, the numbers unknown. It was this uncertainty as to its numbers and position that accounted for the man's presence in that lonely spot; he was a young officer of a Federal infantry regiment and his business there was to guard his sleeping comrades in the camp against a surprise. He was in command of a detachment of men constituting a picket-guard. These men he had stationed just at nightfall in an irregular line, determined by the nature of the ground, several hundred yards in front of where he now sat. The line ran through the forest, among the rocks and laurel thickets, the men fifteen or twenty paces apart, all in concealment and under injunction of strict silence and unremitting vigilance. In four hours, if nothing occurred, they would be relieved by a fresh detachment from the reserve now resting in care of its captain some distance away to the left and rear. Before stationing his men the young officer of whom we are writing had pointed out to his two sergeants the spot at which he would be found if it should be necessary to consult him, or if his presence at the front line should be required.

It was a quiet enough spot—the fork of an old wood-road, on the two branches of which, prolonging themselves deviously forward in the dim moonlight, the sergeants were themselves stationed, a few paces in rear of the line. If driven sharply back by a sudden onset of the enemy—and pickets are not expected to make a stand after firing—the men would come into the converging roads and naturally following them to their point of intersection could be rallied and "formed." In his small way the author of these dispositions was something of a strategist; if Napoleon had planned as intelligently at Waterloo he would have won that memorable battle and been overthrown later.

Second-Lieutenant Brainerd Byring was a brave and efficient officer, young and comparatively inexperienced as he was in the business of killing his fellow-men. He had enlisted in the very first days of the war as a private, with no military knowledge whatever, had been made first-sergeant of his company on account of his education and engaging manner, and had been lucky enough to lose his captain by a Confederate bullet; in the resulting promotions he had gained a commission. He had been in several engagements, such as they were—at Philippi, Rich Mountain, Carrick's Ford and Greenbrier[36]—and had borne himself with such gallantry as not to attract the attention of his superior officers. The exhilaration of battle was agreeable to him, but the sight of the dead, with their clay faces, blank eyes and stiff bodies, which when not unnaturally shrunken were unnaturally swollen, had always intolerably affected him. He felt toward them a kind of reasonless antipathy that was something more than the physical and spiritual repugnance common to us all. Doubtless this feeling was due to his unusually acute sensibilities—his keen sense of the beautiful, which these hideous things outraged. Whatever may have been the cause, he could not look upon a dead body without a loathing which had in it an element of resentment. What others have respected as the dignity of death had to him no existence—was altogether unthinkable. Death was a thing to be hated. It was not picturesque, it had no tender and solemn side—a dismal thing, hideous in all its manifestations and suggestions. Lieutenant Byring was a braver man than anybody knew, for nobody knew his horror of that which he was ever ready to incur.

Having posted his men, instructed his sergeants and retired to his station, he seated himself on a log, and with senses all alert began his vigil. For greater ease he loosened his sword-belt and taking his heavy revolver from his holster laid it on the log beside him. He felt very comfortable, though he hardly gave the fact a thought, so intently did he listen for any sound from the front which might have a menacing significance—a shout, a shot, or the footfall of one of his sergeants coming to apprise him of something worth knowing. From the vast, invisible ocean of moonlight overhead fell, here and there, a slender, broken stream that seemed to plash against the intercepting branches and trickle to earth, forming small white pools among the clumps of laurel. But these leaks were few and served only to accentuate the blackness of his environment, which his imagination found it easy to people with all manner of unfamiliar shapes, menacing, uncanny, or merely grotesque.

He to whom the portentous conspiracy of night and solitude and silence in the heart of a great forest is not an unknown experience needs not to be told what another world it all is—how even the most commonplace and familiar objects take on another character. The trees group themselves differently; they draw closer together, as if in fear. The very silence has another quality than the silence of the day. And it is full of half-heard whispers—whispers that startle—ghosts of sounds long dead. There are living sounds, too, such as are never heard under other conditions: notes of strange night-birds, the cries of small animals in sudden encounters with stealthy foes or in their dreams, a rustling in the dead leaves—it may be the leap of a wood-rat, it may be the footfall of a panther. What caused the breaking of that twig? what the low, alarmed twittering in that bushful of birds? There are sounds without a name, forms without substance, translations in space of objects which have not been seen to move, movements wherein nothing is observed to change its place. Ah, children of the sunlight and the gaslight, how little you know of the world in which you live!

Surrounded at a little distance by armed and watchful friends, Byring felt utterly alone. Yielding himself to the solemn and mysterious spirit of the time and place, he had forgotten the nature of his connection with the visible and audible aspects and phases of the night. The forest was boundless; men and the habitations of men did not exist. The universe was one primeval mystery of darkness, without form and void, himself the sole, dumb questioner of its eternal secret. Absorbed in thoughts born of this mood, he suffered the time to slip away unnoted. Meantime the infrequent patches of white light lying amongst the tree-trunks had undergone changes of size, form and place. In one of them near by, just at the roadside, his eye fell upon an object that he had not previously observed. It was almost before his face as he sat; he could have sworn that it had not before been there. It was partly covered in shadow, but he could see that it was a human figure. Instinctively he adjusted the clasp of his sword-belt and laid hold of his pistol—again he was in a world of war, by occupation an assassin.

The figure did not move. Rising, pistol in hand, he approached. The figure lay upon its back, its upper part in shadow, but standing above it and looking down upon the face, he saw that it was a dead body. He shuddered and turned from it with a feeling of sickness and disgust, resumed his seat upon the log, and forgetting military prudence struck a match and lit a cigar. In the sudden blackness that followed the extinction of the flame he felt a sense of relief; he could no longer see the object of his aversion. Nevertheless, he kept his eyes set in that direction until it appeared again with growing distinctness. It seemed to have moved a trifle nearer.

"Damn the thing!" he muttered. "What does it want?"

It did not appear to be in need of anything but a soul.

Byring turned away his eyes and began humming a tune, but he broke off in the middle of a bar and looked at the dead body. Its presence annoyed him, though he could hardly have had a quieter neighbor. He was conscious, too, of a vague, indefinable feeling that was new to him. It was not fear, but rather a sense of the supernatural—in which he did not at all believe.

"I have inherited it," he said to himself. "I suppose it will require a thousand ages—perhaps ten thousand—for humanity to outgrow this feeling. Where and when did it originate? Away back, probably, in what is called the cradle of the human race—the plains of Central Asia. What we inherit as a superstition our barbarous ancestors must have held as a reasonable conviction. Doubtless they believed themselves justified by facts whose nature we cannot even conjecture in thinking a dead body a malign thing endowed with some strange power of mischief, with perhaps a will and a purpose to exert it. Possibly they had some awful form of religion of which that was one of the chief doctrines, sedulously taught by their priesthood, as ours teach the immortality of the soul. As the Aryans moved slowly on, to and through the Caucasus passes, and spread over Europe, new conditions of life must have resulted in the formulation of new religions. The old belief in the malevolence of the dead body was lost from the creeds and even perished from tradition, but it left its heritage of terror, which is transmitted from generation to generation—is as much a part of us as are our blood and bones."

In following out his thought he had forgotten that which suggested it; but now his eye fell again upon the corpse. The shadow had now altogether uncovered it. He saw the sharp profile, the chin in the air, the whole face, ghastly white in the moonlight. The clothing was gray, the uniform of a Confederate soldier. The coat and waistcoat, unbuttoned, had fallen away on each side, exposing the white shirt. The chest seemed unnaturally prominent, but the abdomen had sunk in, leaving a sharp projection at the line of the lower ribs. The arms were extended, the left knee was thrust upward. The whole posture impressed Byring as having been studied with a view to the horrible.

"Bah!" he exclaimed; "he was an actor—he knows how to be dead."

He drew away his eyes, directing them resolutely along one of the roads leading to the front, and resumed his philosophizing where he had left off.

"It may be that our Central Asian ancestors had not the custom of burial. In that case it is easy to understand their fear of the dead, who really were a menace and an evil. They bred pestilences. Children were taught to avoid the places where they lay, and to run away if by inadvertence they came near a corpse. I think, indeed, I'd better go away from this chap."

He half rose to do so, then remembered that he had told his men in front and the officer in the rear who was to relieve him that he could at any time be found at that spot. It was a matter of pride, too. If he abandoned his post he feared they would think he feared the corpse. He was no coward and he was unwilling to incur anybody's ridicule. So he again seated himself, and to prove his courage looked boldly at the body. The right arm—the one farthest from him—was now in shadow. He could barely see the hand which, he had before observed, lay at the root of a clump of laurel. There had been no change, a fact which gave him a certain comfort, he could not have said why. He did not at once remove his eyes; that which we do not wish to see has a strange fascination, sometimes irresistible. Of the woman who covers her eyes with her hands and looks between the fingers let it be said that the wits have dealt with her not altogether justly.

Byring suddenly became conscious of a pain in his right hand. He withdrew his eyes from his enemy and looked at it. He was grasping the hilt of his drawn sword so tightly that it hurt him. He observed, too, that he was leaning forward in a strained attitude—crouching like a gladiator ready to spring at the throat of an antagonist. His teeth were clenched and he was breathing hard. This matter was soon set right, and as his muscles relaxed and he drew a long breath he felt keenly enough the ludicrousness of the incident. It affected him to laughter. Heavens! what sound was that? what mindless devil was uttering an unholy glee in mockery of human merriment? He sprang to his feet and looked about him, not recognizing his own laugh.

He could no longer conceal from himself the horrible fact of his cowardice; he was thoroughly frightened! He would have run from the spot, but his legs refused their office; they gave way beneath him and he sat again upon the log, violently trembling. His face was wet, his whole body bathed in a chill perspiration. He could not even cry out. Distinctly he heard behind him a stealthy tread, as of some wild animal, and dared not look over his shoulder. Had the soulless living joined forces with the soulless dead?—was it an animal? Ah, if he could but be assured of that! But by no effort of will could he now unfix his gaze from the face of the dead man.

I repeat that Lieutenant Byring was a brave and intelligent man. But what would you have? Shall a man cope, single-handed, with so monstrous an alliance as that of night and solitude and silence and the dead,—while an incalculable host of his own ancestors shriek into the ear of his spirit their coward counsel, sing their doleful death-songs in his heart, and disarm his very blood of all its iron? The odds are too great—courage was not made for so rough use as that.

One sole conviction now had the man in possession: that the body had moved. It lay nearer to the edge of its plot of light—there could be no doubt of it. It had also moved its arms, for, look, they are both in the shadow! A breath of cold air struck Byring full in the face; the boughs of trees above him stirred and moaned. A strongly defined shadow passed across the face of the dead, left it luminous, passed back upon it and left it half obscured. The horrible thing was visibly moving! At that moment a single shot rang out upon the picket-line—a lonelier and louder, though more distant, shot than ever had been heard by mortal ear! It broke the spell of that enchanted man; it slew the silence and the solitude, dispersed the hindering host from Central Asia and released his modern manhood. With a cry like that of some great bird pouncing upon its prey he sprang forward, hot-hearted for action!

Shot after shot now came from the front. There were shoutings and confusion, hoof-beats and desultory cheers. Away to the rear, in the sleeping camp, were a singing of bugles and grumble of drums. Pushing through the thickets on either side the roads came the

Federal pickets, in full retreat, firing backward at random as they ran. A straggling group that had followed back one of the roads, as instructed, suddenly sprang away into the bushes as half a hundred horsemen thundered by them, striking wildly with their sabres as they passed. At headlong speed these mounted madmen shot past the spot where Byring had sat, and vanished round an angle of the road, shouting and firing their pistols. A moment later there was a roar of musketry, followed by dropping shots—they had encountered the reserve-guard in line; and back they came in dire confusion, with here and there an empty saddle and many a maddened horse, bullet-stung, snorting and plunging with pain. It was all over—"an affair of out-posts."

The line was reëstablished with fresh men, the roll called, the stragglers were re-formed. The Federal commander with a part of his staff, imperfectly clad, appeared upon the scene, asked a few questions, looked exceedingly wise and retired. After standing at arms for an hour the brigade in camp "swore a prayer or two" and went to bed.

Early the next morning a fatigue-party, commanded by a captain and accompanied by a surgeon, searched the ground for dead and wounded. At the fork of the road, a little to one side, they found two bodies lying close together—that of a Federal officer and that of a Confederate private. The officer had died of a sword-thrust through the heart, but not, apparently, until he had inflicted upon his enemy no fewer than five dreadful wounds. The dead officer lay on his face in a pool of blood, the weapon still in his breast. They turned him on his back and the surgeon removed it.

"Gad!" said the captain—"It is Byring!"—adding, with a glance at the other, "They had a tough tussle."

The surgeon was examining the sword. It was that of a line officer of Federal infantry—exactly like the one worn by the captain. It was, in fact, Byring's own. The only other weapon discovered was an undischarged revolver in the dead officer's belt.

The surgeon laid down the sword and approached the other body. It was frightfully gashed and stabbed, but there was no blood. He took hold of the left foot and tried to straighten the leg. In the effort the body was displaced. The dead do not wish to be moved—it protested with a faint, sickening odor. Where it had lain were a few maggots, manifesting an imbecile activity.

The surgeon looked at the captain. The captain looked at the surgeon.

Stephen Crane

from *The Little Regiment, and Other Episodes of the American Civil War* (1896)

A GRAY SLEEVE

I

"It looks as if it might rain this afternoon," remarked the lieutenant of artillery.

"So it does," the infantry captain assented. He glanced casually at the sky. When his eyes had lowered to the green-shadowed landscape before him, he said fretfully: "I wish those fellows out yonder would quit pelting at us. They've been at it since noon."

At the edge of a grove of maples, across wide fields, there occasionally appeared little puffs of smoke of a dull hue in this gloom of sky which expressed an impending rain. The long wave of blue and steel in the field moved uneasily at the eternal barking of the far-away sharpshooters, and the men, leaning upon their rifles, stared at the grove of maples. Once a private turned to borrow some tobacco from a comrade in the rear rank, but, with his hand still stretched out, he continued to twist his head and glance at the distant trees. He was afraid the enemy would shoot him at a time when he was not looking.

Suddenly the artillery officer said: "See what's coming!"

Along the rear of the brigade of infantry a column of cavalry was sweeping at a hard gallop. A lieutenant riding some yards to the right of the column bawled furiously at the four troopers just at the rear of the colors. They had lost distance and made a little gap, but at the shouts of the lieutenant they urged their horses forward. The bugler, careering along behind the captain of the troop, fought and tugged like a wrestler to keep his frantic animal from bolting far ahead of the column.

On the springy turf the innumerable hoofs thundered in a swift storm of sound. In the brown faces of the troopers their eyes were set like bits of flashing steel.

The long line of the infantry regiments standing at ease underwent a sudden movement at the rush of the passing squadron. The foot soldiers turned their heads to gaze at the torrent of horses and men.

The yellow folds of the flag fluttered back in silken shuddering waves as if it were a reluctant thing. Occasionally a giant spring of a charger would rear the firm and steady figure of a soldier suddenly head and shoulders above his comrades. Over the noise of the scudding hoofs could be heard the creaking of leather trappings, the jingle and clank of steel, and the tense, low-toned commands or appeals of the men to their horses. And the horses were mad with the headlong sweep of this movement. Powerful under jaws bent back and straightened so that the bits were clamped as rigidly as vices [sic] upon the teeth, and glistening necks arched in desperate resistance to the hands at the bridles. Swinging their heads in rage at the granite laws of their lives, which compelled even their angers and their ardors to chosen directions and chosen paces, their flight was as a flight of harnessed demons.

The captain's bay kept its pace at the head of the squadron with the lithe bounds of a thoroughbred, and this horse was proud as a chief at the roaring trample of his fellows behind him. The captain's glance was calmly upon the grove of maples from whence the sharpshooters of the enemy had been picking at the blue line. He seemed to be reflecting. He stolidly rose and fell with the plunges of his horse in all the indifference of a deacon's figure seated plumply in church. And it occurred to many of the watching infantry to wonder why this officer could remain imperturbable and reflective when his squadron was thundering and swarming behind him like the rushing of a flood.

The column swung in a saber-curve toward a break in a fence and dashed into a road-way. Once a little plank bridge was encountered, and the sound of the hoofs upon it was like the long roll of many drums. An old captain in the infantry turned to his first lieu-tenant and made a remark which was a compound of bitter disparagement of cavalry in general and soldierly admiration of this particular troop.

Suddenly the bugle sounded and the column halted with a jolting upheaval amid sharp, brief cries. A moment later the men had tumbled from their horses and carbines in hand were running in a swarm toward the grove of maples. In the road, one of every four of the troopers was standing with braced legs, and pulling and hauling at the bridles of four frenzied horses.

The captain was running awkwardly in his boots. He held his saber low so that the point often threatened to catch in the turf. His yellow hair ruffled out from under his faded cap. "Go in hard now!" he roared in a voice of hoarse fury. His face was violently red.

The troopers threw themselves upon the grove like wolves upon a great animal. Along the whole front of the wood there was the dry, crackling of musketry, with bitter, swift flashes and smoke that writhed like stung phantoms. The troopers yelled shrilly and spanged bullets low into the foliage.

For a moment, when near the woods, the line almost halted. The men struggled and fought for a time like swimmers encountering a powerful current. Then with a supreme effort they went on again. They dashed madly at the grove, whose foliage from the high light of the field was as inscrutable as a wall.

Then suddenly each detail of the calm trees became apparent, and with a few more frantic leaps the men were in the cool gloom of the woods. There was a heavy odor as from burned paper. Wisps of gray smoke wound upward. The men halted and, grimy, perspir-ing and puffing, they searched the recesses of the woods with eager, fierce glances. Figures could be seen flitting afar off. A dozen carbines rattled at them in an angry volley.

During this pause the captain strode along the line, his face lit with a broad smile of contentment. "When he sends this crowd to do anything, I guess he'll find we do it pretty sharp," he said to the grinning lieutenant.

"Say, they didn't stand that rush a minute, did they?" said the subaltern. Both officers were profoundly dusty in their uniforms, and their faces were soiled like those of two ur-chins.

Out in the grass behind them were three tumbled and silent forms.

Presently the line moved forward again. The men went from tree to tree like hunters stalking game. Some at the left of the line fired occasionally and those at the right gazed curiously in that direction. The men still breathed heavily from their scramble across the field.

Of a sudden a trooper halted and said: "Hello! there's a house!" Everyone paused. The men turned to look at their leader.

The captain stretched his neck and swung his head from side to side. "By George, it is a house!" he said.

Through the wealth of leaves there vaguely loomed the form of a large, white house. These troopers, brown-faced from many days of campaigning, each feature of them telling of their placid confidence and courage, were stopped abruptly by the appearance of this house. There was some subtle suggestion—some tale of an unknown thing—which watched them from they knew not what part of it.

A rail fence girted a wide lawn of tangled grass. Seven pines stood along a driveway which led from two distant posts of a vanished gate. The blue-clothed troopers moved forward until they stood at the fence peering over it.

The captain put one hand on the top rail and seemed to be about to climb the fence when suddenly he hesitated, and said in a low voice: "Watson, what do you think of it?"

The lieutenant stared at the house. "Derned if I know!" he replied.

The captain pondered. It happened that the whole company had turned a gaze of profound awe and doubt upon this edifice which confronted them. The men were very silent.

At last the captain swore and said: "We are certainly a pack of fools. Derned old deserted house halting a company of Union cavalry and making us gape like babies!"

"Yes, but there's something—something—" insisted the subaltern in a half stammer.

"Well, if there's 'something—something' in there, I'll get it out," said the captain. "Send Sharpe clean around to the other side with about twelve men, so we will sure bag your 'something—something,' and I'll take a few of the boys and find out what's in the d——d old thing."

He chose the nearest eight men for his "storming party," as the lieutenant called it. After he had waited some minutes for the others to get into position, he said "Come ahead" to his eight men, and climbed the fence.

The brighter light of the tangled lawn made him suddenly feel tremendously apparent, and he wondered if there could be some mystic thing in the house which was regarding this approach. His men trudged silently at his back. They stared at the windows and lost themselves in deep speculations as to the probability of there being, perhaps, eyes behind the blinds—malignant eyes, piercing eyes.

Suddenly a corporal in the party gave vent to a startled exclamation, and half threw his carbine into position. The captain turned quickly and the corporal said: "I saw an arm move the blinds. An arm with a gray sleeve!"

"Don't be a fool, Jones, now," said the captain sharply.

"I swear t'—" began the corporal, but the captain silenced him.

When they arrived at the front of the house the troopers paused, while the captain went softly up the front steps. He stood before the large front door and studied it. Some crickets chirped in the long grass and the nearest pine could be heard in its endless sighs. One of the privates moved uneasily and his foot crunched the gravel. Suddenly the captain swore angrily and kicked the door with a loud crash. It flew open.

II

The bright lights of the day flashed into the old house when the captain angrily kicked open the door. He was aware of a wide hallway carpeted with matting and extending deep into the dwelling. There was also an old walnut hat rack and a little marble-topped table with a vase and two books upon it. Further back was a great, venerable fireplace containing dreary ashes.

But directly in front of the captain was a young girl. The flying open of the door had obviously been an utter astonishment to her and she remained transfixed there in the middle of the floor, staring at the captain with wide eyes.

She was like a child caught at the time of a raid upon the cake. She wavered to and fro upon her feet and held her hands behind her. There were two little points of terror in her eyes as she gazed up at the young captain in dusty blue, with his reddish, bronze complexion, his yellow hair, his bright saber held threateningly.

These two remained motionless and silent, simply staring at each other for some moments.

The captain felt his rage fade out of him and leave his mind limp. He had been violently angry, because this house had made him feel hesitant, wary. He did not like to be wary. He liked to feel confident, sure. So he had kicked the door open, and had been prepared to march in like a soldier of wrath.

But now he began, for one thing, to wonder if his uniform was so dusty and old in appearance. Moreover, he had a feeling that his face was covered with a compound of dust, grime, and perspiration. He took a step forward and said, "I didn't mean to frighten you." But his voice was coarse from his battle-howling. It seemed to him to have hempen fibers in it.

The girl's breath came in little, quick gasps, and she looked at him as she would have looked at a serpent.

"I didn't mean to frighten you," he said again.

The girl, still with her hands behind her, began to back away.

"Is there anyone else in the house?" he went on, while slowly following her. "I don't wish to disturb you, but we had a fight with some rebel skirmishers in the woods, and I thought maybe some of them might have come in here. In fact, I was pretty sure of it. Are there any of them here?"

The girl looked at him and said: "No!" He wondered why extreme agitation made the eyes of some women so limpid and bright.

"Who is here besides yourself?"

By this time his pursuit had driven her to the end of the hall, and she remained there with her back to the wall and her hands still behind her. When she answered this question she did not look at him, but down at the floor. She cleared her voice and then said, "There is no one here."

"No one?"

She lifted her eyes to him in that appeal that the human being must make even to falling trees, crashing bowlders, the sea in a storm, and said, "No, no, there is no one here." He could plainly see her tremble.

Of a sudden he bethought him that she had always kept her hands behind her. As he recalled her air when first discovered, he remembered she appeared precisely as a child detected at one of the crimes of childhood. Moreover, she had always backed away from him. He thought now that she was concealing something which was an evidence of the presence of the enemy in the house.

"What are you holding behind you?" he said suddenly.

She gave a little quick moan, as if some grim hand had throttled her.

"What are you holding behind you?"

"Oh, nothing—please. I am not holding anything behind me; indeed I'm not."

"Very well. Hold your hands out in front of you, then."

"Oh, indeed, I'm not holding anything behind me. Indeed, I'm not."

"Well," he began. Then he paused, and remained for a moment dubious. Finally, he laughed. "Well, I shall have my men search the house, anyhow. I'm sorry to trouble you, but I feel sure that there is some one here whom we want." He turned to the corporal, who, with the other men, was gaping quietly in at the door, and said: "Jones, go through the house."

As for himself, he remained planted in front of the girl, for she evidently did not dare to move and allow him to see what she held so carefully behind her back. So she was his prisoner.

The men rummaged around on the ground floor of the house. Sometimes the captain called to them, "Try that closet," "Is there any cellar?" But they found no one, and at last they went trooping toward the stairs which led to the second floor.

But at this movement on the part of the men the girl uttered a cry—a cry of such fright and appeal that the men paused. "Oh, don't go up there! Please don't go up there!—ple-ease! There is no one there! Indeed—indeed there is not! Oh, ple-ease!"

"Go on, Jones," said the captain, calmly.

The obedient corporal made a preliminary step, and the girl bounded toward the stairs with another cry.

As she passed him, the captain caught sight of that which she had concealed behind her back, and which she had forgotten in this supreme moment. It was a pistol.

She ran to the first step, and standing there, faced the men, one hand extended with perpendicular palm, and the other holding the pistol at her side. "Oh, please, don't go up there! Nobody is there—indeed, there is not! P-l-e-a-s-e!" Then suddenly she sank swiftly down upon the step, and, huddling forlornly, began to weep in the agony and with the convulsive tremors of an infant. The pistol fell from her fingers and rattled down to the floor.

The astonished troopers looked at their astonished captain. There was a short silence.

Finally, the captain stooped and picked up the pistol. It was a heavy weapon of the army pattern. He ascertained that it was empty.

He leaned toward the shaking girl, and said gently, "Will you tell me what you were going to do with this pistol?"

He had to repeat the question a number of times, but at last a muffled voice said, "Nothing."

"Nothing!" He insisted quietly upon a further answer. At the tender tones of the captain's voice, the phlegmatic corporal turned and winked gravely at the man next to him.

"Won't you tell me?"

The girl shook her head.

"Please tell me!"

The silent privates were moving their feet uneasily and wondering how long they were to wait.

The captain said, "Please won't you tell me?"

Then this girl's voice began in stricken tones half coherent, and amid violent sobbing: "It was grandpa's. He—he—he said he was going to shoot anybody who came in here—he didn't care if there were thousands of 'em. And—and I know he would, and I was afraid they'd kill him. And so—and—so I stole away his pistol—and I was going to hide it when you—you—you kicked open the door."

The men straightened up and looked at each other. The girl began to weep again.

The captain mopped his brow. He peered down at the girl. He mopped his brow again. Suddenly he said, "Ah, don't cry like that."

He moved restlessly and looked down at his boots. He mopped his brow again.

Then he gripped the corporal by the arm and dragged him some yards back from the others. "Jones," he said, in an intensely earnest voice, "will you tell me what in the devil I am going to do?"

The corporal's countenance became illuminated with satisfaction at being thus requested to advise his superior officer. He adopted an air of great thought, and finally said: "Well, of course, the feller with the gray sleeve must be upstairs, and we must get past the girl and up there somehow. Suppose I take her by the arm and lead her—"

"What!" interrupted the captain from between his clinched teeth. As he turned away from the corporal, he said fiercely over his shoulder: "You touch that girl and I'll split your skull!"

III

The corporal looked after his captain with an expression of mingled amazement, grief, and philosophy. He seemed to be saying to himself that there unfortunately were times, after all, when one could not rely upon the most reliable of men. When he returned to the group he found the captain bending over the girl and saying, "Why is it that you don't want us to search upstairs?"

The girl's head was buried in her crossed arms. Locks of her hair had escaped from their fastenings and these fell upon her shoulder.

"Won't you tell me?"

The corporal here winked again at the man next to him.

"Because," the girl moaned—"because—there isn't any-body up there."

The captain at last said timidly: "Well, I'm afraid—I'm afraid we'll have to—".

The girl sprang to her feet again, and implored him with her hands. She looked deep into his eyes with her glance, which was at this time like that of the fawn when it says to the hunter, "Have mercy upon me!"

These two stood regarding each other. The captain's foot was on the bottom step, but he seemed to be shrinking. He wore an air of being deeply wretched and ashamed. There was a silence.

Suddenly the corporal said in a quick, low tone, "Look out, captain!"

All turned their eyes swiftly toward the head of the stairs. There had appeared there a youth in a gray uniform. He stood looking coolly down at them. No word was said by the troopers. The girl gave vent to a little wail of desolation, "O Harry!"

He began slowly to descend the stairs. His right arm was in a white sling and there were some fresh blood stains upon the cloth. His face was rigid and deathly pale, but his eyes flashed like lights. The girl was again moaning in an utterly dreary fashion, as the youth came slowly down toward the silent men in blue.

Six steps from the bottom of the flight he halted and said, "I reckon it's me you're looking for."

The troopers had crowded forward a trifle and, posed in lithe, nervous attitudes, were watching him like cats. The captain remained unmoved. At the youth's question he merely nodded his head and said, "Yes."

The young man in gray looked down at the girl and then, in the same even tone which now, however, seemed to vibrate with suppressed fury, he said, "And is that any reason why you should insult my sister?"

At this sentence, the girl intervened, desperately, between the young man in gray and the officer in blue. "Oh, don't, Harry, don't! He was good to me! He was good to me, Harry—indeed he was."

The youth came on in his quiet, erect fashion until the girl could have touched either of the men with her hand, for the captain still remained with his foot upon the first step. She continually repeated: "O Harry! O Harry!"

The youth in gray manœuvered to glare into the captain's face, first over one shoulder of the girl and then over the other. In a voice that rang like metal, he said: "You are armed and unwounded, while I have no weapons and am wounded; but—"

The captain had stepped back and sheathed his saber. The eyes of these two men were gleaming fire, but otherwise the captain's countenance was imperturbable. He said: "You are mistaken. You have no reason to—"

"You lie!"

All save the captain and the youth in gray started in an electric movement. These two words crackled in the air like shattered glass. There was a breathless silence.

The captain cleared his throat. His look at the youth contained a quality of singular and terrible ferocity, but he said in his stolid tone, "I don't suppose you mean what you say now."

Upon his arm he had felt the pressure of some unconscious little fingers. The girl was leaning against the wall as if she no longer knew how to keep her balance, but those fingers—he held his arm very still. She murmured: "O Harry, don't! He was good to me—indeed he was!"

The corporal had come forward until he in a measure confronted the youth in gray, for he saw those fingers upon the captain's arm, and he knew that sometimes very strong men were not able to move hand nor foot under such conditions.

The youth had suddenly seemed to become weak. He breathed heavily and hung to the railing. He was glaring at the captain, and apparently summoning all his will power [sic] to combat his weakness. The corporal addressed him with profound straightforwardness, "Don't you be a derned fool!" The youth turned toward him so fiercely that the corporal threw up a knee and an elbow like a boy who expects to be cuffed.

The girl pleaded with the captain. "You won't hurt him, will you? He don't know what he's saying. He's wounded, you know. Please don't mind him!"

"I won't touch him," said the captain, with rather extraordinary earnestness; "don't you worry about it at all. I won't touch him!"

Then he looked at her, and the girl suddenly withdrew her fingers from his arm.

The corporal contemplated the top of the stairs, and remarked without surprise, "There's another of 'em coming!"

An old man was clambering down the stairs with much speed. He waved a cane wildly. "Get out of my house, you thieves! Get out! I won't have you cross my threshold! Get out!" He mumbled and wagged his head in an old man's fury. It was plainly his intention to assault them.

And so it occurred that a young girl became engaged in protecting a stalwart captain, fully armed, and with eight grim troopers at his back, from the attack of an old man with a walking-stick!

A blush passed over the temples and brow of the captain, and he looked particularly savage and weary. Despite the girl's efforts, he suddenly faced the old man.

"Look here," he said distinctly, "we came in because we had been fighting in the woods yonder, and we concluded that some of the enemy were in this house, especially when we saw a gray sleeve at the window. But this young man is wounded, and I have nothing to say to him. I will even take it for granted that there are no others like him upstairs. We will go away, leaving your d——d old house just as we found it! And we are no more thieves and rascals than you are!"

The old man simply roared: "I haven't got a cow nor a pig nor a chicken on the place! Your soldiers have stolen everything they could carry away. They have torn down half my fences for firewood. This afternoon some of your accursed bullets even broke my window panes!"

The girl had been faltering: "Grandpa! O grandpa!"

The captain looked at the girl. She returned his glance from the shadow of the old man's shoulder. After studying her face a moment, he said, "Well, we will go now." He strode toward the door and his men clanked docilely after him.

At this time there was the sound of harsh cries and rushing footsteps from without. The door flew open, and a whirlwind composed of blue-coated troopers came in with a swoop. It was headed by the lieutenant. "Oh, here you are!" he cried, catching his breath. "We thought—Oh, look at the girl!"

The captain said intensely, "Shut up, you fool!"

The men settled to a halt with a clash and bang. There could be heard the dulled sound of many hoofs outside of the house.

"Did you order up the horses?" inquired the captain.

"Yes, we thought—"

"Well, then, let's get out of here," interrupted the captain, morosely.

The men began to filter out into the open air. The youth in gray had been hanging dismally to the railing of the stairway. He now was climbing slowly up to the second floor. The old man was addressing himself directly to the serene corporal.

"Not a chicken on the place!" he cried.

"Well, I didn't take your chickens, did I?"

"No, maybe you didn't, but—"

The captain crossed the hall and stood before the girl in rather a culprit's fashion. "You are not angry at me, are you?" he asked timidly.

"No," she said. She hesitated a moment and then suddenly held out her hand. "You were good to me—and I'm—much obliged."

The captain took her hand, and then he blushed, for he found himself unable to formulate a sentence that applied in any way to the situation.

She did not seem to need that hand for a time.

He loosened his grasp presently, for he was ashamed to hold it so long without saying anything clever. At last, with an air of charging an intrenched brigade, he contrived to say, "I would rather do anything than frighten you or trouble you."

His brow was warmly perspiring. He had a sense of being hideous in his dusty uniform and with his grimy face.

She said: "Oh, I'm so glad it was you instead of somebody who might have—might have hurt brother Harry and grandpa!"

He told her, "I wouldn't have hurt 'em for anything!"

There was a little silence.

"Well, good-bye!" he said at last.

"Good-bye!"

He walked toward the door past the old man, who was scolding at the vanishing figure of the corporal. The captain looked back. She had remained there watching him.

At the bugle's order, the troopers standing beside their horses swung briskly into the saddle. The lieutenant said to the first sergeant:

"Williams, did they ever meet before?"

"Hanged if I know!"

"Well, say—"

The captain saw a curtain move at one of the windows. He cantered from his position at the head of the column and steered his horse between two flower beds.

"Well, good-bye!"

The squadron trampled slowly past.

"Good-bye!"

They shook hands.

He evidently had something enormously important to say to her, but it seems that he could not manage it. He struggled heroically. The bay charger, with his great mystically solemn eyes, looked around the corner of his shoulder at the girl.

The captain studied a pine tree. The girl inspected the grass beneath the window. The captain said hoarsely, "I don't suppose—I don't suppose—I'll ever see you again!"

She looked at him affrightedly and shrank back from the window. He seemed to have woefully expected a reception of this kind for his question. He gave her instantly a glance of appeal.

She said: "Why, no, I don't suppose we will."

"Never?"

"Why, no, 'tain't possible. You—you are a—Yankee!"

"Oh, I know it, but—" Eventually he continued, "Well, some day, you know, when there's no more fighting, we might—" He observed that she had again withdrawn suddenly into the shadow, so he said, "Well, good-bye!"

When he held her fingers she bowed her head, and he saw a pink blush steal over the curves of her cheek and neck.

"Am I never going to see you again?"

She made no reply.

"Never?" he repeated.

After a long time, he bent over to hear a faint reply: "Sometimes—when there are no troops in the neighborhood—grandpa don't mind if I—walk over as far as that old oak tree yonder—in the afternoons."

It appeared that the captain's grip was very strong, for she uttered an exclamation and looked at her fingers as if she expected to find them mere fragments. He rode away.

The bay horse leaped a flower bed. They were almost to the drive when the girl uttered a panic-stricken cry.

The captain wheeled his horse violently and upon this return journey went straight through a flower bed.

The girl had clasped her hands. She beseeched him wildly with her eyes. "Oh, please, don't believe it! I never walk to the old oak tree. Indeed, I don't! I never—never—never walk there."

The bridle drooped on the bay charger's neck. The captain's figure seemed limp. With an expression of profound dejection and gloom he stared off at where the leaden sky met the dark green line of the woods. The long-impending rain began to fall with a mournful patter, drop and drop. There was a silence.

At last a low voice said, "Well—I might—sometimes I might—perhaps—but only once in a great while—I might walk to the old tree—in the afternoons."

Stephen Crane

from *The Little Regiment, and Other Stories of the American Civil War* (1896)

AN EPISODE OF WAR

The lieutenant's rubber blanket lay on the ground, and upon it he had poured the company's supply of coffee. Corporals and other representatives of the grimy and hot-throated men who lined the breast-work had come for each squad's portion.

The lieutenant was frowning and serious at this task of division. His lips pursed as he drew with his sword various crevices in the heap until brown squares of coffee, astoundingly equal in size, appeared on the blanket. He was on the verge of a great triumph in mathematics and the corporals were thronging forward, each to reap a little square, when suddenly the lieutenant cried out and looked quickly at a man near him as if he suspected it was a case of personal assault. The others cried out also when they saw blood upon the lieutenant's sleeve.

He had winced like a man stung, swayed dangerously, and then straightened. The sound of his hoarse breathing was plainly audible. He looked sadly, mystically, over the breast-work at the green face of a wood where now were many little puffs of white smoke. During this moment, the men about him gazed statue-like and silent, astonished and awed by this catastrophe which had happened when catastrophes were not expected—when they had leisure to observe it.

As the lieutenant stared at the wood, they too swung their heads so that for another moment all hands, still silent, contemplated the distant forest as if their minds were fixed upon the mystery of a bullet's journey.

The officer had, of course, been compelled to take his sword at once into his left hand. He did not hold it by the hilt. He gripped it at the middle of the blade, awkwardly. Turning his eyes from the hostile wood, he looked at the sword as he held it there, and seemed puzzled as to what to do with it, where to put it. In short this weapon had of a sudden become a strange thing to him. He looked at it in a kind of stupefaction, as if he had been miraculously endowed with a trident, a sceptre, or a spade.

Finally, he tried to sheath it. To sheath a sword held by the left hand, at the middle of the blade, in a scabbard hung at the left hip, is a feat worthy of a sawdust ring. This wounded officer engaged in a desperate struggle with the sword and the wobbling scabbard, and during the time of it, he breathed like a wrestler.

But at this instant the men, the spectators, awoke from their stone-like poses and crowded forward sympathetically. The orderly-sergeant took the sword and tenderly placed it in the scabbard. At the time, he leaned nervously backward, and did not allow even his finger to brush the body of the lieutenant. A wound gives strange dignity to him who bears it. Well men shy from this new and terrible majesty. It is as if the wounded man's hand is upon the curtain which hangs before the revelations of all existence—the meaning of ants, potentates, wars, cities, sunshine, snow, a feather dropped from a bird's wing; and the power of it sheds radiance upon a bloody form, and makes the other men understand sometimes that they are little. His comrades look at him with large eyes thoughtfully. Moreover, they fear vaguely that the weight of a finger upon him might send him headlong, precipitate the tragedy, hurl him at once into the dim, grey unknown. And so the orderly-sergeant, while sheathing the sword, leaned nervously backward.

There were others who proffered assistance. One timidly presented his shoulder and asked the lieutenant if he cared to lean upon it, but the latter waved them away mournfully. He wore the look of one who knows he is the victim of a terrible disease and understands his helplessness. He again stared over the breast-work at the forest, and then turning went slowly rearward. He held his right wrist tenderly in his left hand, as if the wounded arm was made of very brittle glass.

And the men in silence stared at the wood, then at the departing lieutenant; then at the wood, then at the lieutenant.

As the wounded officer passed from the line of battle, he was enabled to see many things which as a participant in the fight were unknown to him. He saw a general on a black horse gazing over the lines of blue infantry at the green woods which veiled his problems. An aide galloped furiously, dragged his horse suddenly to a halt, saluted, and presented a paper. It was, for a wonder, precisely like a historical painting.

To the rear of the general and his staff, a group, composed of a bugler, two or three orderlies, and the bearer of the corps standard, all upon maniacal horses, were working like slaves to hold their ground, preserve their respectful interval, while the shells bloomed in the air about them, and caused their chargers to make furious quivering leaps.

A battery, a tumultuous and shining mass, was swirling toward the right. The wild thud of hoofs, the cries of the riders shouting blame and praise, menace and encouragement, and, last, the roar of the wheels, the slant of the glistening guns, brought the lieutenant to an intent pause. The battery swept in curves that stirred the heart; it made halts as dramatic as the crash of a wave on the rocks, and when it fled onward, this aggregation of wheels, levers, motors, had a beautiful unity, as if it were a missile. The sound of it was a war-chorus that reached into the depths of man's emotion.

The lieutenant, still holding his arm as if it were of glass, stood watching this battery until all detail of it was lost, save the figures of the riders, which rose and fell and waved lashes over the black mass.

Later, he turned his eyes toward the battle, where the shooting sometimes crackled like bush-fires, sometimes sputtered with exasperating irregularity, and sometimes reverberated like the thunder. He saw the smoke rolling upward and saw crowds of men who ran and cheered, or stood and blazed away at the inscrutable distance.

He came upon some stragglers and they told him how to find the field hospital. They described its exact location. In fact, these men, no longer having part in the battle, knew more of it than others. They told the performance of every corps, every division, the opinion of every general. The lieutenant, carrying his wounded arm rearward, looked upon them with wonder.

At the roadside a brigade was making coffee and buzzing with talk like a girls' boarding-school. Several officers came out to him and inquired concerning things of which he knew nothing. One, seeing his arm, began to scold. "Why, man, that's no way to do. You want to fix that thing." He appropriated the lieutenant and the lieutenant's wound. He cut the sleeve and laid bare the arm, every nerve of which softly fluttered under his touch. He bound his handkerchief over the wound, scolding away in the meantime. His tone allowed one to think that he was in the habit of being wounded every day. The lieutenant hung his head, feeling, in this presence, that he did not know how to be correctly wounded.

The low white tents of the hospital were grouped around an old schoolhouse. There was here a singular commotion. In the foreground two ambulances interlocked wheels in the deep mud. The drivers were tossing the blame of it back and forth, gesticulating and berating, while from the ambulances, both crammed with wounded, there came an occasional groan. An interminable crowd of bandaged men were coming and going. Great numbers sat under the trees nursing heads or arms or legs. There was a dispute of some kind raging on the steps of the school-house. Sitting with his back against a tree a man with a face as grey as a new army blanket was serenely smoking a corn-cob pipe. The lieutenant wished to rush forward and inform him that he was dying.

A busy surgeon was passing near the lieutenant. "Good-morning," he said, with a friendly smile. Then he caught sight of the lieutenant's arm, and his face at once changed. "Well, let's have a look at it." He seemed possessed suddenly of a great contempt for the lieutenant. This wound evidently placed the latter on a very low social plane. The doctor cried out impatiently: "What mutton-head had tied it up that way anyhow." The lieutenant answered: "Oh, a man."

When the wound was disclosed the doctor fingered it disdainfully. "Humph," he said. "You come along with me and I'll 'tend to you." His voice contained the same scorn as if he were saying: "You will have to go to jail."

The lieutenant had been very meek, but now his face flushed, and he looked into the doctor's eyes. "I guess I won't have it amputated," he said.

"Nonsense, man! Nonsense! Nonsense!" cried the doctor. "Come along, now. I won't amputate it. Come along. Don't be a baby."

"Let go of me," said the lieutenant, holding back wrathfully. His glance fixed upon the door of the old schoolhouse, as sinister to him as the portals of death.

And this is the story of how the lieutenant lost his arm. When he reached home, his sisters, his mother, his wife, sobbed for a long time at the sight of the flat sleeve. "Oh, well," he said, standing shamefaced amid these tears, "I don't suppose it matters so much as all that."

Stephen Crane

from *The Little Regiment, and Other Stories of the American Civil War* (1896)

A MYSTERY OF HEROISM

The dark uniforms of the men were so coated with dust from the incessant wrestling of the two armies that the regiment almost seemed a part of the clay bank which shielded them from the shells. On the top of the hill a battery was arguing in tremendous roars with some other guns and to the eye of the infantry, the artillerymen, the guns, the caissons, the horses, were distinctly outlined upon the blue sky. When a piece was fired, a red streak as round as a log flashed low in the heavens, like a monstrous bolt of lightning. The men of the battery wore white duck trousers, which somehow emphasized their legs; and when they ran and crowded in little groups at the bidding of the shouting officers, it was more impressive than usual to the infantry.

Fred Collins, of A Company, was saying: "Thunder! I wisht I had a drink. Ain't there any water round here?" Then somebody yelled, "There goes th' bugler!"

As the eyes of half of the regiment swept in one machinelike movement there was an instant's picture of a horse in a great convulsive leap of a death wound and a rider leaning back with a crooked arm and spread fingers before his face. On the ground was the crimson terror of an exploding shell, with fibres of flame that seemed like lances. A glittering bugle swung clear of the rider's back as fell headlong the horse and the man. In the air was an odour as from a conflagration.

Sometimes they of the infantry looked down at a fair little meadow which spread at their feet. Its long, green grass was rippling gently in a breeze. Beyond it was the gray form of a house half torn to pieces by shells and by the busy axes of soldiers who had pursued firewood. The line of an old fence was now dimly marked by long weeds and by an occasional post. A shell had blown the well-house to fragments. Little lines of grey smoke ribboning upward from some embers indicated the place where had stood the barn.

From beyond a curtain of green woods there came the sound of some stupendous scuffle, as if two animals of the size of islands were fighting. At a distance there were occasional appearances of swift-moving men, horses, batteries, flags, and, with the crashing of infantry volleys were heard, often, wild and frenzied cheers. In the midst of it all, Smith and Ferguson, two privates of A Company, were engaged in a heated discussion, which involved the greatest questions of the national existence.

The battery on the hill presently engaged in a frightful duel. The white legs of the gunners scampered this way and that way and the officers redoubled their shouts. The guns, with their demeanors of stolidity and courage, were typical of something infinitely self-possessed in this clamour of death that swirled around the hill.

One of a "swing" team was suddenly smitten quivering to the ground, and his maddened brethren dragged his torn body in their struggle to escape from this turmoil and danger. A young soldier astride one of the leaders swore and fumed in his saddle, and furiously jerked at the bridle. An officer screamed out an order so violently that his voice broke and ended the sentence in a falsetto shriek.

The leading company of the infantry regiment was somewhat exposed, and the colonel ordered it moved more fully under the shelter of the hill. There was the clank of steel against steel.

A lieutenant of the battery rode down and passed them, holding his right arm carefully in his left hand. And it was as if this arm was not at all a part of him, but belonged to another man. His sober and reflective charger went slowly. The officer's face was grimy and perspiring, and his uniform was tousled as if he had been in direct grapple with an enemy. He smiled grimly when the men stared at him. He turned his horse toward the meadow.

Collins, of A Company, said: "I wisht I had a drink. I bet there's water in that there ol' well yonder!"

"Yes; but how you goin' to git it?"

For the little meadow which intervened was now suffering a terrible onslaught of shells. Its green and beautiful calm had vanished utterly. Brown earth was being flung in monstrous handfuls. And there was a massacre of the young blades of grass. They were being torn, burned, obliterated. Some curious fortune of the battle had made this gentle little meadow the object of the red hate of the shells, and each one as it exploded seemed like an imprecation in the face of a maiden.

The wounded officer who was riding across this expanse said to himself, "Why, they couldn't shoot any harder if the whole army was massed here!"

A shell struck the grey ruins of the house and as, after the roar, the shattered wall fell in fragments, there was a noise which resembled the flapping of shutters during a wild gale of winter. Indeed, the infantry paused in the shelter of the bank, appeared as men standing upon a shore contemplating a madness of the sea. The angel of calamity had under its glance the battery upon the hill. Fewer white-legged men laboured about the guns. A shell had smitten one of the pieces and after the flare, the smoke, the dust, the wrath of this blow was gone, it was possible to see white legs stretched horizontally upon the ground. And at that interval to the rear, where it is the business of battery horses to stand with their noses to the fight awaiting the command to drag their guns out of the destruction or into it or wheresoever these incomprehensible humans demanded with whip and spur—in this line of passive and dumb spectators, whose fluttering hearts yet would not let them forget the iron laws of man's control of them—in this rank of brute-soldiers there had been relentless and hideous carnage. From the ruck of bleeding and prostrate horses, the men of the infantry could see one animal raising its stricken body with its forelegs, and turning its nose with mystic and profound eloquence toward the sky.

Some comrades joked Collins about his thirst. "Well, if yeh want a drink so bad, why don't yeh go git it!"

"Well, I will in a minnet, if yeh don't shut up!"

A lieutenant of artillery floundered his horse straight down the hill with as great concern as if it were level ground. As he galloped past the colonel of the infantry, he threw up his hand in swift salute. "We've got to get out of that," he roared angrily. He was a black-bearded officer, and his eyes, which resembled beads, sparkled like those of an insane man. His jumping horse sped along the column of infantry.

The fat major, standing carelessly with his sword held horizontally behind him and with his legs far apart, looked after the receding horseman and laughed. "He wants to get back with orders pretty quick, or there'll be no batt'ry left," he observed.

The wise young captain of the second company hazarded to the lieutenant colonel that the enemy's infantry would probably soon attack the hill, and the lieutenant colonel snubbed him.

A private in one of the rear companies looked out over the meadow and then turned to a companion and said, "Look there, Jim!" It was the wounded officer from the battery, who some time before had started to ride across the meadow, supporting his right arm carefully with his left hand. This man had encountered a shell apparently at a time when no one perceived him, and he could now be seen lying face downward with a stirruped foot stretched across the body of his dead horse. A leg of the charger extended slantingly upward precisely as stiff as a stake. Around this motionless pair the shells still howled.

There was a quarrel in A Company. Collins was shaking his fist in the faces of some laughing comrades. "Dern yeh! I ain't afraid t' go. If yeh say much, I will go!"

"Of course, yeh will! You'll run through that there medder, won't yeh?"

Collins said, in a terrible voice: "You see, now!" At this ominous threat his comrades broke into renewed jeers.

Collins gave them a dark scowl and went to find his captain. The latter was conversing with the colonel of the regiment.

"Captain," said Collins, saluting and standing at attention—in those days all trousers bagged at the knees—"captain, I want t' git permission to go git some water from that there well over yonder!"

The colonel and the captain swung about simultaneously and stared across the meadow. The captain laughed. "You must be pretty thirsty, Collins?"

"Yes, sir, I am."

"Well—ah," said the captain. After a moment he asked: "Can't you wait?"

"No, sir."

The colonel was watching Collins's face. "Look here, my lad," he said, in a pious sort of a voice—"look here, my lad"—Collins was not a lad—"don't you think that's taking pretty big risks for a little drink of water?"

"I dunno," said Collins, uncomfortably. Some of the resentment toward his companions, which perhaps had forced him into this affair, was beginning to fade. "I dunno wether 'tis."

The colonel and the captain contemplated him for a time.

"Well," said the captain finally.

"Well," said the colonel, "if you want to go, why go."

Collins saluted. "Much obliged t' yeh."

As he moved away the colonel called after him. "Take some of the other boys' canteens with you an' hurry back now."

"Yes, sir, I will."

The colonel and the captain looked at each other then, for it had suddenly occurred that they could not for the life of them tell whether Collins wanted to go or whether he did not.

They turned to regard Collins, and as they perceived him surrounded by gesticulating comrades, the colonel said: "Well, by thunder! I guess he's going."

Collins appeared as a man dreaming. In the midst of the questions, the advice, the warnings, all the excited talk of his company mates, he maintained a curious silence.

They were very busy in preparing him for his ordeal. When they inspected him carefully it was somewhat like the examination that grooms give a horse before a race; and they were amazed, staggered by the whole affair. Their astonishment found vent in strange repetitions.

"Are yeh sure a-goin'?" they demanded again and again.

"Certainly I am," cried Collins, at last furiously.

He strode sullenly away from them. He was swinging five or six canteens by their cords. It seemed that his cap would not remain firmly on his head, and often he reached and pulled it down over his brow.

There was a general movement in the compact column. The long animal-like thing moved slightly. Its four hundred eyes were turned upon the figure of Collins.

"Well, sir, if that ain't th' derndest thing! I never thought Fred Collins had the blood in him for that kind of business."

"What's he goin' to do, anyhow?"

"He's goin' to that well there after water."

"We ain't dyin' of thirst, are we? That's foolishness."

"Well, somebody put him up to it, an' he's doin' it."

"Say, he must be a desperate cuss."

When Collins faced the meadow and walked away from the regiment, he was vaguely conscious that a chasm, the deep valley of all prides, was suddenly between him and his comrades. It was provisional, but the provision was that he return as a victor. He had blindly been led by quaint emotions, and laid himself under an obligation to walk squarely up to the face of death.

But he was not sure that he wished to make a retraction, even if he could do so without shame. As a matter of truth, he was sure of very little. He was mainly surprised.

It seemed to him supernaturally strange that he had allowed his mind to manœuver his body into such a situation. He understood that it might be called dramatically great.

However, he had no full appreciation of anything excepting that he was actually conscious of being dazed. He could feel his dulled mind groping after the form and color of this incident. He wondered why he did not feel some keen agony of fear cutting his sense like a knife. He wondered at this, because human expression had said loudly for centuries that men should feel afraid of certain things, and that all men who did not feel this fear were phenomena—heroes.

He was, then, a hero. He suffered that disappointment which we would all have if we discovered that we were ourselves capable of those deeds which we most admire in history and legend. This, then, was a hero. After all, heroes were not much.

No, it could not be true. He was not a hero. Heroes had no shames in their lives, and, as for him, he remembered borrowing fifteen dollars from a friend and promising to pay it back the next day, and then avoiding that friend for ten months. When at home his mother had aroused him for the early labor of his life on the farm, it had often been his fashion to be irritable, childish, diabolical; and his mother had died since he had come to the war.

He saw that, in this matter of the well, the canteens, the shells, he was an intruder in the land of fine deeds.

He was now about thirty paces from his comrades. The regiment had just turned its many faces toward him.

From the forest of terrific noises there suddenly emerged a little uneven line of men. They fired fiercely and rapidly at distant foliage on which appeared little puffs of white smoke. The spatter of skirmish firing was added to the thunder of the guns on the hill. The little line of men ran forward. A colour sergeant fell flat with his flag as if he had slipped on ice. There was hoarse cheering from this distant field.

Collins suddenly felt that two demon fingers were pressed into his ears. He could see nothing but flying arrows, flaming red. He lurched from the shock of this explosion, but he made a mad rush for the house, which he viewed as a man submerged to the neck in a boiling surf might view the shore. In the air, little pieces of shell howled and the earth-quake explosions drove him insane with the menace of their roar. As he ran the canteens knocked together with a rhythmical tinkling.

As he neared the house, each detail of the scene became vivid to him. He was aware of some bricks of the vanished chimney lying on the sod. There was a door which hung by one hinge.

Rifle bullets called forth by the insistent skirmishers came from the far-off bank of foliage. They mingled with the shells and the pieces of shells until the air was torn in all directions by hootings, yells, howls. The sky was full of fiends who directed all their wild rage at his head.

When he came to the well, he flung himself face downward and peered into its dark-ness. There were furtive silver glintings some feet from the surface. He grabbed one of the canteens and, unfastening its cap, swung it down by the cord. The water flowed slowly in with an indolent gurgle.

And now as he lay with his face turned away he was suddenly smitten with the terror. It came upon his heart like the grasp of claws. All the power faded from his muscles. For an instant he was no more than a dead man.

The canteen filled with a maddening slowness, in the manner of all bottles. Presently he recovered his strength and addressed a screaming oath to it. He leaned over until it seemed as if he intended to try to push water into it with his hands. His eyes as he gazed down into the well shone like two pieces of metal and in their expression was a great appeal and a great curse. The stupid water derided him.

There was the blaring thunder of a shell. Crimson light shone through the swift-boiling smoke and made a pink reflection on part of the wall of the well. Collins jerked out his arm and canteen with the same motion that a man would use in withdrawing his head from a furnace.

He scrambled erect and glared and hesitated. On the ground near him lay the old well bucket, with a length of rusty chain. He lowered it swiftly into the well. The bucket struck the water and then, turning lazily over, sank. When, with hand reaching tremblingly over hand, he hauled it out, it knocked often against the walls of the well and spilled some of its contents.

In running with a filled bucket, a man can adopt but one kind of gait. So through this terrible field over which screamed practical angels of death Collins ran in the manner of a farmer chased out of a dairy by a bull.

His face went staring white with anticipation—anticipation of a blow that would whirl him around and down. He would fall as he had seen other men fall, the life knocked out of them so suddenly that their knees were no more quick to touch the ground than their heads. He saw the long blue line of the regiment, but his comrades were standing looking at him from the edge of an impossible star. He was aware of some deep wheel ruts and hoof prints in the sod beneath his feet.

The artillery officer who had fallen in this meadow had been making groans in the teeth of the tempest of sound. These futile cries, wrenched from him by his agony, were heard only by shells, bullets. When wild-eyed Collins came running, this officer raised himself. His face contorted and blanched from pain, he was about to utter some great beseeching cry. But suddenly his face straightened and he called: "Say, young man, give me a drink of water, will you?"

Collins had no room amid his emotions for surprise. He was mad from the threats of destruction.

"I can't," he screamed, and in this reply was a full description of his quaking apprehension. His cap was gone and his hair was riotous. His clothes made it appear that he had been dragged over the ground by the heels. He ran on.

The officer's head sank down and one elbow crooked. His foot in its brass-bound stirrup still stretched over the body of his horse and the other leg was under the steed.

But Collins turned. He came dashing back. His face had now turned gray and in his eyes was all terror. "Here it is! here it is!"

The officer was as a man gone in drink. His arm bent like a twig. His head drooped as if his neck was of willow. He was sinking to the ground, to lie face downward.

Collins grabbed him by the shoulder. "Here it is. Here's your drink. Turn over. Turn over, man, for God's sake!"

With Collins hauling at his shoulder, the officer twisted his body and fell with his face turned toward that region where lived the unspeakable noises of the swirling missiles. There was the faintest shadow of a smile on his lips as he looked at Collins. He gave a sigh, a little primitive breath like that from a child.

Collins tried to hold the bucket steadily, but his shaking hands caused the water to splash all over the face of the dying man. Then he jerked it away and ran on.

The regiment gave him a welcoming roar. The grimed faces were wrinkled in laughter.

His captain waved the bucket away. "Give it to the men!"

The two genial, skylarking young lieutenants were the first to gain possession of it. They played over it in their fashion.

When one tried to drink the other teasingly knocked his elbow. "Don't, Billie! You'll make me spill it," said the one. The other laughed.

Suddenly there was an oath, the thud of wood on the ground, and a swift murmur of astonishment from the ranks. The two lieutenants glared at each other. The bucket lay on the ground empty.

Ulysses S. Grant

from *Personal Memoirs of U. S. Grant* (1885-86)

CHAPTER 67: NEGOTIATIONS AT APPOMATTOX –

INTERVIEW WITH LEE AT MCLEAN'S HOUSE – THE TERMS OF SURRENDER –

LEE'S SURRENDER – INTERVIEW WITH LEE AFTER THE SURRENDER

On the 8th I had followed the Army of the Potomac in rear of Lee. I was suffering very severely with a sick headache, and stopped at a farmhouse on the road some distance in rear of the main body of the army. I spent the night in bathing my feet in hot water and mustard, and putting mustard plasters on my wrists and the back part of my neck, hoping to be cured by morning. During the night I received Lee's answer to my letter of the 8th, inviting and interview between the lines on the following morning. But it was for a different purpose from that of surrendering his army, and I answered him as follows:

> Headquarters Armies of the U.S.,
> April 9, 1865.

> General R. E. Lee,
> Commanding C. S. A.

> Your note of yesterday is received. As I have no authority to treat on the subject of peace, the meeting proposed for ten A.M. to-day could lead to no good. I will state, however, General, that I am equally anxious for peace with yourself, and the whole North entertains the same feeling. The terms upon which peace can be had are well understood. By the South laying down their arms they will hasten that most desirable event, save thousands of human lives, and hundreds of millions of property not yet destroyed. Sincerely hoping that all our difficulties may be settled without the loss of another life, I subscribe myself, etc.,

> U. S. Grant,
> Lieutenant-General.

I proceeded at an early hour in the morning, still suffering with the headache, to get to the head of the column. I was not more than two or three miles from Appomattox Court House at the time, but to go direct I would have to pass through Lee's army, or a portion of it. I had therefore to move south in order to get upon a road coming up from another direction.

When the white flag was put out by Lee, as already described, I was in this way moving towards Appomattox Court House, and consequently could not be communicated with immediately, and be informed of what Lee had done. Lee, therefore, sent a flag to the rear to advise Meade and one to the front to Sheridan, saying that he had sent a message to me for the purpose of having a meeting to consult about the surrender of his army, and asked for a suspension of hostilities until I could be communicated with. As they had heard nothing of this until the fighting had got to be severe and all going against Lee, both of these commanders hesitated very considerably about suspending hostilities at all. They were afraid it was not in good faith, and we had the Army of Northern Virginia where it could not escape except by some deception. They, however, finally consented to a suspension of hostilities for two hours to give an opportunity of communicating with me in that time, if possible. It was found that, from the route I had taken, they would probably not be able to communicate with me and get an answer back within the time fixed unless the messenger should pass through the rebel lines.

Lee, therefore, sent an escort with the officer bearing this message through his lines to me.

April 9, 1865.

General: — I received your note of this morning on the picket-line whither I had come to meet you and ascertain definitely what terms were embraced in your proposal of yesterday with reference to the surrender of this army. I now request an interview in accordance with the offer contained in your letter of yesterday for that purpose.

R. E. Lee, General.

Lieutenant-General U. S. Grant,
Commanding U. S. Armies

When the officer reached me I was still suffering with the sick headache; but the instant I saw the contents of the note I was cured. I wrote the following note in reply and hastened on:

April 9, 1865.

General R. E. Lee,
Commanding C. S. Armies.

Your note of this date is but this moment (11.50 A.M.) received, in consequence of my having passed from the Richmond and Lynchburg road to the Farmville and Lynchburg road. I am at this writing about four miles west of Walker's Church and will push forward to the front for the purpose of meeting you. Notice sent to me on this road where you wish the interview to take place will meet me.

U. S. Grant,
Lieutenant-General.

I was conducted at once to where Sheridan was located with his troops drawn up in line of battle facing the Confederate army near by. They were very much excited, and expressed their view that this was all a ruse employed to enable the Confederates to get away. They said they believed that Johnston was marching up from North Carolina now, and Lee was moving to join him; and they would whip the rebels where they now were in five minutes if I would only let them go in. But I had not doubt about the good faith of Lee, and pretty soon was conducted to where he was. I found him at the house of a Mr. McLean, at Appomattox Court House, with Colonel Marshall,[37] one of his staff officers, awaiting my arrival. The head of his column was occupying a hill, on a portion of which was an apple orchard, beyond a little valley which separated it from that on the crest of which Sheridan's forces were drawn up in line of battle to the south.

Before stating what took place between General Lee and myself, I will give all there is of the story of the famous apple tree.

Wars produce many stories of fiction, some of which are told until they are believed to be true. The war of the rebellion was no exception to this rule, and the story of the apple tree is one of those fictions based on a slight foundation of fact. As I have said, there was an apple orchard on the side of the hill occupied by the Confederate forces. Running diagonally up the hill was a wagon road, which, at one point, ran very near one of the trees, so that the wheels of vehicles had, on that side, cut off the roots of this tree, leaving a little embankment. General Babcock,[38] of my staff, reported to me that when he first met General Lee he was sitting upon this embankment with his feet in the road below and his back resting against the tree. The story had no other foundation than that. Like many other stories, it would be very good if it was only true.

I had known General Lee in the old army, and had served with him in the Mexican War; but did not suppose, owing to the difference in our age and rank, that he would remember me; while I would more naturally remember him distinctly, because he was the chief of staff of General Scott in the Mexican War.

When I had left camp that morning I had not expected so soon the result that was then taking place, and consequently was in rough garb. I was without a sword, as I usually was when on horseback on the field, and wore a soldier's blouse for a coat, with the shoulder straps of my rank to indicate to the army who I was. When I went into the house I found General Lee. We greeted each other, and after shaking hands took our seats. I had my staff with me, a good portion of whom were in the room during the whole of the interview.

What General Lee's feelings were I do not know. As he was a man of much dignity, with an impassible [sic] face, it was impossible to say whether he felt inwardly glad that the end had finally come, or felt sad over the result, and was too manly to show it. Whatever his feelings, they were entirely concealed from my observation; but my own feelings, which had been quite jubilant on the receipt of his letter, were sad and depressed. I felt like anything rather than rejoicing at the downfall of a foe who had fought so long and valiantly, and had suffered so much for a cause, though that cause was, I believe, one of the worst for which a people ever fought, and one for which there was the least excuse. I do not question, however, the sincerity of the great mass of those who were opposed to us.

General Lee was dressed in a full uniform which was entirely new, and was wearing a sword of considerable value, very likely the sword which had been presented by the State of Virginia; at all events, it was an entirely different sword from the one that would ordinarily be worn in the field. In my rough traveling suit, the uniform of a private with the straps of a lieutenant-general, I must have contrasted very strangely with a man so handsomely dressed, six feet high and of faultless form. But this was not a matter that I thought of until afterwards.

We soon fell into a conversation about old army times. He remarked that he remembered me very well in the old army; and I told him that as a matter of course I remembered him perfectly, but from the difference in our rank and years (there being about sixteen years' difference in our ages), I had thought it very likely that I had not attracted his attention sufficiently to be remembered by him after such a long interval. Our conversation grew so pleasant that I almost forgot the object of our meeting. After the conversation had run on in this style for some time, General Lee called my attention to the object of our meeting, and said that he had asked for this interview for the purpose of getting from me the terms I proposed to give his army. I said that I meant merely that his army should lay down their arms, not to take them up again during the continuance of the war unless duly and properly exchanged. He said that he had so understood my letter.

Then we gradually fell off again into conversation about matters foreign to the subject which had brought us together. This continued for some little time, when General Lee again interrupted the course of the conversation by suggesting that the terms I proposed to give his army ought to be written out. I called to General Parker, secretary on my staff, for writing materials, and commenced writing out the following terms:

Appomattox C. H., Va.,
Ap[ri]l 9th, 1865.

Gen. R. E. Lee,
Comd'g C. S. A.

Gen: In accordance with the substance of my letter to you of the 8th inst., I propose to receive the surrender of the Army of N. Va. on the following terms, to wit: Rolls of all the officers and men to be made in duplicate. One copy to be given to an officer designated by me, the other to be retained by such officer or officers as you may designate. The officers to give their individual paroles not to take up arms against the Government of the United States until properly exchanged, and each company or regimental commander sign a like parole for the men of their commands. The arms, artillery and public property to be parked and stacked, and turned over to the officer appointed by me to receive them. This will not embrace the side-arms of the officers, nor their private horses or baggage. This done, each officer and man will be allowed to return to their homes, not to be disturbed by United States authority so long as they observe their paroles and the laws in force where they may reside.

Very respectfully,
U. S. Grant,
Lt. Gen.

When I put my pen to the paper I did not know the first word that I should make use of in writing the terms. I only knew what was in my mind, and I wished to express it clearly, so that there could be no mistaking it. As I wrote on, the thought occurred to me that the officers had their own private horses and effects, which were important to them, but of no value to us; also that it would be an unnecessary humiliation to call upon them to deliver their side arms.

No conversation, not one word, passed between General Lee and myself, either about private property, side arms, or kindred subjects. He appeared to have no objections to the terms first proposed; or if he had a point to make against them he wished to wait until they were in writing to make it. When he read over that part of the terms about side arms, horses and private property of the officers, he remarked, with some feeling, I thought, that this would have a happy effect upon his army.

Then, after a little further conversation, General Lee remarked to me again that their army was organized a little differently from the army of the United States (still maintaining by implication that we were two countries); that in their army the cavalrymen and artillerists owned their own horses; and he asked if he was to understand that the men who so owned their horses were to be permitted to retain them. I told him that as the terms were written they would not; that only the officers were permitted to take their private property. He then, after reading over the terms a second time, remarked that that was clear.

I then said to him that I thought this would be about the last battle of the war—I sincerely hoped so; and I said further I took it that most of the men in the ranks were small farmers. The whole country had been so raided by the two armies that it was doubtful whether they would be able to put in a crop to carry themselves and their families through the next winter without the aid of the horses they were then riding. The United States did not want them and I would, therefore, instruct the officers I left behind to receive the paroles of his troops to let every man of the Confederate army who claimed to own a horse or mule take the animal to his home. Lee remarked again that this would have a happy effect.

He then sat down and wrote out the following letter:

Headquarters Army of Northern Virginia,
April 9, 1865.

General: — I received your letter of this date containing the terms of the surrender of the Army of Northern Virginia as proposed by you. As they are substantially the same as those expressed in your letter of the 8th inst., they are accepted. I will proceed to designate the proper officers to carry the stipulations into effect.

R. E. Lee, General.

Lieut.-General U. S. Grant

While duplicates of the two letters were being made, the Union generals present were severally presented to General Lee.

The much talked of surrendering of Lee's sword and my handing it back, this and much more that has been said about it is the purest romance. The word sword or side arms was not mentioned by either of us until I wrote it in the terms. There was no premeditation, and it did not occur to me until the moment I wrote it down. If I had happened to omit it, and General Lee had called my attention to it, I should have put it in the terms precisely as I acceded to the provision about the soldiers retaining their horses.

General Lee, after all was completed and before taking his leave, remarked that his army was in a very bad condition for want of food, and that they were without forage; that his men had been living for some days on parched corn exclusively, and that he would have to ask me for rations and forage. I told him "certainly," and asked for how many men he wanted rations. His answer was "about twenty-five thousand": and I authorized him to send his own commissary and quartermaster to Appomattox Station, two or three miles away, where he could have, out of the trains we had stopped, all the provisions wanted. As for forage, we had ourselves depended almost entirely upon the country for that.

Generals Gibbon, Griffin and Merritt[39] were designated by me to carry into effect the paroling of Lee's troops before they should start for their homes—General Lee leaving Generals Longstreet, Gordon and Pendleton[40] for them to confer with in order to facilitate this work. Lee and I then separated as cordially as we had met, he returning to his own lines, and all went into bivouac for the night at Appomattox.

Soon after Lee's departure I telegraphed to Washington as follows:

> Headquarters Appomattox C. H., Va.,
> April 9th, 1865, 4.30 P.M.
>
> Hon. E. M. Stanton, Secretary of War,
>   Washington.
>
> General Lee surrendered the Army of Northern Virginia this afternoon on terms proposed by myself. The accompanying additional correspondence will show the conditions fully.
>
> U. S. Grant,
> Lieut.-General.

When news of the surrender first reached our lines our men commenced firing a salute of a hundred guns in honor of the victory. I at once sent word, however, to have it stopped. The Confederates were now our prisoners, and we did not want to exult over their downfall.

I determined to return to Washington at once, with a view to putting a stop to the purchase of supplies, and what I now deemed other useless outlay of money. Before leaving, however, I thought I would like to see General Lee again; so next morning I rode out beyond our lines towards his headquarters, preceded by a bugler and a staff officer carrying a white flag.

Lee soon mounted his horse, seeing who it was, and met me. We had there between the lines, sitting on horseback, a very pleasant conversation of over half an hour, in the course of which Lee said to me that the South was a big country and that we might have to march over it three or four times before the war entirely ended, but that we would now be able to do it as they could no longer resist us. He expressed it as his earnest hope, however, that we would not be called upon to cause more loss and sacrifice of life; but he could not foretell the result. I then suggested to General Lee that there was not a man in the Confederacy whose influence with the soldiery and the whole people was as great as his, and that if he would now advise the surrender of all the armies I had no doubt his advice would be followed with alacrity. But Lee said, that he could not do that without consulting the President[41] first. I knew there was no use to urge him to do anything against his ideas of what was right.

I was accompanied by my staff and other officers, some of whom seemed to have a great desire to go inside the Confederate lines. They finally asked permission of Lee to do so for the purpose of seeing some of their old army friends, and the permission was granted. They went over, had a very pleasant time with their old friends, and brought some of them back with them when they returned.

When Lee and I separated he went back to his lines and I returned to the house of Mr. McLean. Here the officers of both armies cam in great numbers, and seemed to enjoy the meeting as much as though they had been friends separated for a long time while fighting battles under the same flag. For the time being it looked very much as if all thought of the war had escaped their minds. After an hour pleasantly passed in this way I set out on horseback, accompanied by my staff and a small escort, for Burkesville Junction, up to which point the railroad had by this time been repaired.

William T. Sherman

from *Memoirs of General William T. Sherman* (1875)

CHAPTER 24: CONCLUSION – MILITARY LESSONS OF THE WAR

Having thus recorded a summary of events, mostly under my own personal supervision, during the years from 1846 to 1865, it seems proper that I should add an opinion of some of the useful military lessons to be derived therefrom.

That civil war, by reason of the existence of slavery, was apprehended by most of the leading statesmen of the half-century preceding its outbreak, is a matter of notoriety. General Scott told me on my arrival at New York, as early as 1850, that the country was on the eve of civil war; and the Southern politicians openly asserted that it was their purpose to accept as a *casus belli* the election of General Fremont in 1856; but, fortunately or unfortunately, he was beaten by Mr. Buchanan, which simply postponed its occurrence for four years. Mr. Seward had also publicly declared that no government could possibly exist half slave and half free; yet the Government made no military preparation, and the Northern people generally paid no attention, took no warning of its coming, and would not realize its existence till Fort Sumter was fired on by batteries of artillery, handled by declared enemies, from the surrounding islands and from the city of Charleston.

General Bragg, who certainly was a man of intelligence, and who, in early life, ridiculed a thousand times, in my hearing, the threats of the people of South Carolina to secede from the Federal Union, said to me in New Orleans, in February, 1861, that he was convinced that the feeling between the slave and free States had become so embittered that it was better to part in peace; better to part anyhow; and, as a separation was inevitable, that the South should begin at once, because the possibility of a successful effort was yearly lessened by the rapid and increasing inequality between the two sections, from the fact that all the European immigrants were coming to the Northern States and Territories, and none to the Southern.

The slave population in 1860 was near four millions, and the money value thereof not far from twenty-five hundred million dollars. Now, ignoring the moral side of the question, a cause that endangered so vast a moneyed interest was an adequate cause of anxiety and preparation, and the Northern leaders surely ought to have foreseen the danger and prepared for it. After the election of Mr. Lincoln in 1860, there was no concealment of the declaration and preparation for war in the South. In Louisiana, as I have related, men were openly enlisted, officers were appointed, and war was actually begun, in January, 1861. The forts at the mouth of the Mississippi were seized, and occupied by garrisons that hauled down the United States flag and hoisted that of the State. The United States Arsenal at Baton Rouge was captured by New Orleans militia, its garrison ignominiously sent off, and the contents of the arsenal distributed. These were as much acts of war as was the subsequent firing on Fort Sumter, yet no public notice was taken thereof; and when, months afterward, I came North, I found not one single sign of preparation. It was for this reason, somewhat, that the people of the South became convinced that those of the North were pusillanimous and cowardly, and the Southern leaders were thereby enabled to commit their people to the war, nominally in defense of their slave property. Up to the hour of the firing on Fort Sumter, in April, 1861, it does seem to me that our public men, our politicians, were blamable for not sounding the note of alarm.

Then, when war was actually begun, it was by a call for seventy-five thousand "ninety-day" men, I suppose to fulfill Mr. Seward's prophecy that the war would last but ninety days.

The earlier steps by our political Government were extremely wavering and weak, for which an excuse can be found in the fact that many of the Southern representatives remained in Congress, sharing in the public councils, and influencing legislation. But as soon as Mr. Lincoln was installed, there was no longer any reason why Congress and the cabinet should have hesitated. They should have measured the cause, provided the means, and left the Executive to apply the remedy.

At the time of Mr. Lincoln's inauguration, viz., March 4, 1861, the Regular Army, by law, consisted of two regiments of dragoons, two regiments of cavalry, one regiment of mounted rifles, four regiments of artillery, and ten regiments of infantry, admitting of an aggregate strength of thirteen thousand and twenty-four officers and men. On the subsequent 4th of May the President, by his own orders (afterward sanctioned by Congress), added a regiment of cavalry, a regiment of artillery, and eight regiments of infantry, which, with the former army, admitted of a strength of thirty-nine thousand nine hundred and seventy-three; but at no time during the war did the Regular Army attain a strength of twenty-five thousand men.

To the new regiments of infantry was given an organization differing from any that had heretofore prevailed in this country—of three battalions of eight companies each; but at no time did more than one of these regiments attain its full standard; nor in the vast army of volunteers that was raised during the war were any of the regiments of infantry formed on the three-battalion system, but these were universally single battalions of ten companies; so that, on the reorganization of the Regular Army at the close of the war, Congress adopted the form of twelve companies for the regiments of cavalry and artillery, and that of ten companies for the infantry, which is the present standard.

Inasmuch as the Regular Army will naturally form the standard of organization for any increase or for new regiments of volunteers, it becomes important to study this subject in the light of past experience, and to select that form which is best for peace as well as war.

A cavalry regiment is now composed of twelve companies, usually divided into six squadrons, of two companies each, or better subdivided into three battalions of four companies each. This is an excellent form, easily admitting of subdivision as well as union into larger masses.

A single battalion of four companies, with a field-officer, will compose a good body for a garrison, for a separate expedition, or for a detachment; and, in war, three regiments would compose a good brigade, three brigades a division, and three divisions a strong cavalry corps, such as was formed and fought by Generals Sheridan and Wilson[42] during the war.

In the artillery arm, the officers differ widely in their opinion of the true organization. A single company forms a battery, and habitually each battery acts separately, though sometimes several are united or "massed;" but these always act in concert with cavalry or infantry.

Nevertheless, the regimental organization for artillery has always been maintained in this country for classification and promotion. Twelve companies compose a regiment, and, though probably no colonel ever commanded his full regiment in the form of twelve batteries, yet in peace they occupy our heavy sea-coast forts or act as infantry; then the regimental organization is both necessary and convenient.

But the infantry composes the great mass of all armies, and the true form of the regiment or unit has been the subject of infinite discussion; and, as I have stated, during the civil war the regiment was a single battalion of ten companies. In olden times the regiment was composed of eight battalion companies and two flank companies. The first and tenth companies were armed with rifles, and were styled and used as "skirmishers;" but during the war they were never used exclusively for that special purpose, and in fact no distinction existed between them and the other eight companies.

The ten-company organization is awkward in practice, and I am satisfied that the infantry regiment should have the same identical organization as exists for the cavalry and artillery, viz., twelve companies, so as to be susceptible of division into three battalions of four companies each.

These companies should habitually be about one hundred men strong, giving twelve hundred to a regiment, which in practice would settle down to about one thousand men.

Three such regiments would compose a brigade, three brigades a division, and three divisions a corps. Then, by allowing to an infantry corps a brigade of cavalry and six batteries of field-artillery, we would have an efficient *corps d'armée* of thirty thousand men, whose organization would be simple and most efficient, and whose strength should never be allowed to fall below twenty-five thousand men.

The corps is the true unit for grand campaigns and battle, should have a full and perfect staff, and every thing requisite for separate action, ready at all times to be detached and sent off for any nature of service. The general in command should have the rank of lieutenant-general, and should be, by experience and education, equal to any thing in war. Habitually with us he was a major-general, specially selected and assigned to the command by an order of the President, constituting, in fact, a separate grade.

The division is the unit of administration, and is the legitimate command of a major-general.

The brigade is the next subdivision, and is commanded by a brigadier-general.

The regiment is the family. The colonel, as the father, should have a personal acquaintance with every officer and man, and should instill a feeling of pride and affection for himself, so that his officers and men would naturally look to him for personal advice and instruction. In war the regiment should never be subdivided, but should always be maintained entire. In peace this is impossible.

The company is the true unit of discipline, and the captain is the company. A good captain makes a good company, and he should have the power to reward as well as punish. The fact that soldiers would naturally like to have a good fellow for their captain is the best reason why he should be appointed by the colonel, or by some superior authority, instead of being elected by the men.[43]

In the United States the people are the "sovereign," all power originally proceeds from them, and therefore the election of officers by the men is the common rule. This is wrong, because an army is not a popular organization, but an animated machine, an instrument in the hands of the Executive for enforcing the law, and maintaining the honor and dignity of the nation; and the President, as the constitutional commander-in-chief of the army and navy, should exercise the power of appointment (subject to the confirmation of the Senate) of the officers of "volunteers," as well as of "regulars."

No army can be efficient unless it be a unit for action; and the power must come from above, not from below: the President usually delegates his power to the commander-in-chief, and he to the next, and so on down to the lowest actual commander of troops, however small the detachment. No matter how troops come together, when once united, the highest officer in rank is held responsible, and should be consequently armed with the fullest power of the Executive, subject only to law and existing orders. The more simple the principle, the greater the likelihood of determined action; and the less a commanding officer is circumscribed by bounds or by precedent, the greater is the probability that he will make the best use of his command and achieve the best results.

The Regular Army and the Military Academy at West Point have in the past provided, and doubtless will in the future provide an ample supply of good officers for future wars; but, should their numbers be insufficient, we can always safely rely on the great number of young men of education and force of character throughout the country, to supplement them. At the close of our civil war, lasting four years, some of our best corps and division generals, as well as staff-officers, were from civil life; but I cannot recall any of the most successful who did not express a regret that he had not received in early life instruction in the elementary principles of the art of war, instead of being forced to acquire this knowledge in the dangerous and expensive school of actual war.

But the real difficulty was, and will be again, to obtain an adequate number of good soldiers. We tried almost every system known to modern nations, all with more or less success—voluntary enlistments, the draft, and bought substitutes[44]—and I think that all officers of experience will confirm my assertion that the men who voluntarily enlisted at the outbreak of the war were the best, better than the conscript, and far better than the bought substitute. When a regiment is once organized in a State, and mustered into the service of the United States, the officers and men become subject to the same laws of discipline and government as the regular troops. They are in no sense "militia," but compose a part of the Army of the United States, only retain their State title for convenience, and yet may be principally recruited from the neighborhood of their original organization. Once organized, the regiment should be kept full by recruits, and when it becomes difficult to obtain more recruits the pay should be raised by Congress, instead of tempting new men by exaggerated bounties. I believe it would have been more economical to have raised the pay of the soldier to thirty or even fifty dollars a month than to have held out the promise of three hundred and even six hundred dollars in the form of bounty. Toward the close of the war, I have often heard the soldiers complain that the "stay-at-home" men got better pay, bounties, and food, than they who were exposed to all the dangers and vicissitudes of the battles and marches at the front. The feeling of the soldier should be that, in every event, the sympathy and preference of his government is for him who fights, rather than for him who is on provost or guard duty to the rear, and, like most men, he measures this by the amount of pay. Of course, the soldier must be trained to obedience, and should be "content with his wages;" but whoever has commanded an army in the field knows the difference between a willing, contented mass of men, and one that feels a cause of grievance. There is a soul to an army as well as to the individual man, and no general can accomplish the full work of his army unless he commands the soul of his men, as well as their bodies and legs.

The greatest mistake made in our civil war was in the mode of recruitment and promotion. When a regiment became reduced by the necessary wear and tear of service, instead of being filled up at the bottom, and the vacancies among the officers filled from the best non-commissioned officers and men, the habit was to raise new regiments, with new colonels, captains, and men, leaving the old and experienced battalions to dwindle away into mere skeleton organizations. I believe with the volunteers this matter was left to the States exclusively, and I remember that Wisconsin kept her regiments filled with recruits, whereas other States generally filled their quotas by new regiments, and the result was that we estimated a Wisconsin regiment equal to an ordinary brigade. I believe that five hundred new men added to an old and experienced regiment were more valuable than a thousand men in the form of a new regiment, for the former by association with good, experienced captains, lieutenants, and non-commissioned officers, soon became veterans, whereas the latter were generally unavailable for a year. The German method of recruitment is simply perfect, and there is no good reason why we should not follow it substantially.

On a road, marching by the flank, it would be considered "good order" to have five thousand men to a mile, so that a full corps of thirty thousand men would extend six miles, but with the average trains and batteries of artillery the probabilities are that it would draw out to ten miles. On a long and regular march the divisions and brigades should alternate in the lead, the leading division should be on the road by the earliest dawn, and march at the rate of about two miles, or, at most, two and a half miles an hour, so as to reach camp by noon. Even then the rear divisions and trains will hardly reach camp much before night. Theoretically, a marching column should preserve such order that by simply halting and facing to the right or left, it would be in line of battle; but this is rarely the case, and generally deployments are made "forward," by conducting each brigade by the flank obliquely to the right or left to its approximate position in line of battle, and there deployed. In such a line of battle, a brigade of three thousand infantry would occupy a mile of "front;" but for a strong line of battle five thousand men with two batteries should be allowed to each mile, or a division would habitually constitute a double line with skirmishers and a reserve on a mile of "front."

The "feeding" of an army is a matter of the most vital importance, and demands the earliest attention of the general entrusted with a campaign. To be strong, healthy, and capable of the largest measure of physical effort, the soldier needs about three pounds gross of food per day, and the horse or mule about twenty pounds. When a general first estimates the quantity of food and forage needed for an army of fifty or one hundred thousand men, he is apt to be dismayed, and here a good staff is indispensable, though the general cannot throw off on them the responsibility. He must give the subject his personal attention, for the army reposes in him alone, and should never doubt the fact that their existence overrides in importance all other considerations. Once satisfied of this, and that all has been done that can be, the soldiers are always willing to bear the largest measure of privation. Probably no army ever had a more varied experience in this regard than the one I commanded in 1864–'65.

Our base of supply was at Nashville, supplied by railways and the Cumberland River, thence by rail to Chattanooga, a "secondary base," and thence forward a single-track railroad. The stores came forward daily, but I endeavored to have on hand a full supply for twenty days in advance. These stores were habitually in the wagon-trains, distributed to corps, divisions, and regiments, in charge of experienced quartermasters and commissaries, and became subject to the orders of the generals commanding these bodies. They were generally issued on provision returns, but these had to be closely scrutinized, for too often the colonels would make requisitions for provisions for more men than they reported for battle. Of course, there are always a good many non-combatants with an army, but, after careful study, I limited their amount to twenty-five per cent of the "effective strength," and that was found to be liberal. An ordinary army-wagon drawn by six mules may be counted on to carry three thousand pounds net, equal to the food of a full regiment for one day, but, by driving along beef-cattle, a commissary may safely count the contents of one wagon as sufficient for two days' food for a regiment of a thousand men; and as a corps should have food on hand for twenty days ready for detachment, it should have three hundred such wagons, as a provision-train; and for forage, ammunition, clothing, and other necessary stores, it was found necessary to have three hundred more wagons, or six hundred wagons in all, for a *corps d'armée.*

These should be absolutely under the immediate control of the corps commander, who will, however, find it economical to distribute them in due proportion to his divisions, brigades, and even regiments. Each regiment ought usually to have at least one wagon for convenience to distribute stores, and each company two pack-mules, so that the regiment may always be certain of a meal on reaching camp without waiting for the larger trains.

On long marches the artillery and wagon-trains should always have the right of way, and the troops should improvise roads to one side, unless forced to use a bridge in common, and all trains should have escorts to protect them, and to assist them in bad places. To this end there is nothing like actual experience, only, unless the officers in command give the subject their personal attention, they will find their wagon-trains loaded down with tents, personal baggage, and even the arms and knapsacks of the escort. Each soldier should, if not actually "sick or wounded," carry his musket and equipments [sic] containing from forty to sixty rounds of ammunition, his shelter-tent, a blanket or overcoat, and an extra pair of pants, socks, and drawers, in the form of a scarf, worn from the left shoulder to the right side in lieu of knapsack, and in his haversack he should carry some bread, cooked meat, salt, and coffee. I do not believe a soldier should be loaded down too much, but, including his clothing, arms, and equipment, he can carry about fifty pounds without impairing his health or activity. A simple calculation will show that by such a distribution a corps will thus carry the equivalent of five hundred wagon-loads—an immense relief to the trains.

Where an army is near one of our many large navigable rivers, or has the safe use of a railway, it can usually be supplied with the full army ration, which is by far the best furnished to any army in America or Europe; but when it is compelled to operate away from such a base, and is dependent on its own train of wagons, the commanding officer must exercise a wise discretion in the selection of his stores. In my opinion there is no better food for man than beef-cattle driven on the hoof, issued liberally, with salt, bacon, and bread. Coffee has also become almost indispensable, though many substitutes were found for it, such as Indian-corn, roasted, ground, and boiled as coffee; the sweet-potato, and the seed of the okra-plant prepared in the same way. All these were used by the people of the South, who for years could procure no coffee, but I noticed that the women always begged of us some *real* coffee, which seems to satisfy a natural yearning or craving more powerful than can be accounted for on the theory of habit. Therefore I would always advise that the coffee and sugar ration be carried along, even at the expense of bread, for which there are many substitutes. Of these, Indian-corn is the best and most abundant. Parched in a frying-pan, it is excellent food, or if ground, or pounded and boiled with meat of any sort, it makes a most nutritious meal. The potato, both Irish and sweet, forms an excellent substitute for bread, and at Savannah we found the rice also suitable, both for men and animals. For the former it should be cleaned of its husk in a hominy block, easily prepared out of a log, and sifted with a coarse corn bag; but for horses it should be fed in the straw. During the Atlanta campaign we were supplied by our regular commissaries with all sorts of patent compounds, such as desiccated vegetables, and concentrated milk, meat-biscuit, and sausages, but somehow the men preferred the simpler and more familiar forms of food, and usually styled these "desecrated vegetables and consecrated milk." We were also supplied liberally with lime-juice, sauerkraut, and pickles, as an antidote to scurvy, and I now recall the extreme anxiety of my medical director, Dr. Kittoe,[45] about the scurvy, which he reported at one time as spreading and imperiling the army. This occurred at a crisis about Kenesaw, [sic] when the railroad was taxed to its utmost capacity to provide the necessary ammunition, food, and forage, and could not possibly bring us an adequate supply of potatoes and cabbage, the usual antiscorbutics, when providentially the black-berries ripened and proved an admirable antidote, and I have known the skirmish-line, without orders, to fight a respectable battle for the possession of some old fields that were full of blackberries. Soon, thereafter, the green corn or roasting-ear came into season, and I heard no more of the scurvy. Our country abounds with plants which can be utilized for a prevention to the scurvy; besides the above are the persimmon, the sassafras root and bud, the wild-mustard, the "agave," turnip-tops, the dandelion cooked as greens, and a decoction of the ordinary pine-leaf.

For the more delicate and costly articles of food for the sick we relied mostly on the agents of the Sanitary Commission. I do not wish to doubt the value of these organizations, which gained so much applause during our civil war, for no one can question the motives of these charitable and generous people; but to be honest I must record an opinion that the Sanitary Commission should limit its operations to the hospitals at the rear, and should never appear at the front. They were generally local in feeling, aimed to furnish their personal friends and neighbors with a better class of food than the Government supplied, and the consequence was, that one regiment of a brigade would receive potatoes and fruit which would be denied another regiment close by. Jealousy would be the inevitable result, and in an army all parts should be equal; there should be no "partiality, favor, or affection."[46] The Government should supply all essential wants, and in the hospitals to the rear will be found abundant opportunities for the exercise of all possible charity and generosity. During the war I several times gained the ill-will of the agents of the Sanitary Commission because I forbade their coming to the front unless they would consent to distribute their stores equally among all, regardless of the parties who had contributed them.

The sick, wounded, and dead of an army are the subjects of the greatest possible anxiety, and add an immense amount of labor to the well men. Each regiment in an active campaign should have a surgeon and two assistants always close at hand, and each brigade and division should have an experienced surgeon as a medical director. The great majority of wounds and of sickness should be treated by the regimental surgeon, on the ground, under the eye of the colonel. As few should be sent to the brigade or division hospital as possible, for the men always receive better care with their own regiment than with strangers, and as a rule the cure is more certain; but when men receive disabling wounds, or have sickness likely to become permanent, the sooner they go far to the rear the better for all. The tent or the shelter of a tree is a better hospital than a house, whose walls absorb fetid and poisonous emanations, and then give them back to the atmosphere. To men accustomed to the open air, who live on the plainest food, wounds seem to give less pain, and are attended with less danger to life than to ordinary soldiers in barracks.

Wounds which, in 1861, would have sent a man to the hospital for months, in 1865 were regarded as mere scratches, rather the subject of a joke than of sorrow. To new soldiers the sight of blood and death always has a sickening effect, but soon men become accustomed to it, and I have heard them exclaim on seeing a dead comrade borne to the rear, "Well, Bill has turned up *his* toes to the daisies." Of course, during a skirmish or battle, armed men should *never* leave their ranks to attend a dead or wounded comrade—this should be seen to in advance by the colonel, who should designate his musicians or company cooks as hospital attendants, with a white rag on their arm to indicate their office. A wounded man should go himself (if able) to the surgeon near at hand, or, if he need help, he should receive it from one of the attendants and not a comrade. It is wonderful how soon the men accustom themselves to these simple rules. In great battles these matters call for a more enlarged attention, and then it becomes the duty of the division general to see that proper stretchers and field-hospitals are ready for the wounded, and trenches are dug for the dead. There should be no real neglect of the dead, because it has a bad effect on the living; for each soldier values himself and comrade as highly as though he were living in a good house at home.

The regimental chaplain, if any, usually attends the burials from the hospital, should make notes and communicate details to the captain of the company, and to the family at home. Of course it is usually impossible to mark the grave with names, dates, etc., and consequently the names of the "unknown" in our national cemeteries equal about one-half of all the dead.

Very few of the battles in which I have participated were fought as described in European text-books, viz., in great masses, in perfect order, manœuvring by corps, divisions, and brigades. We were generally in a wooded country, and, though our lines were deployed according to tactics, the men generally fought in strong skirmish-lines, taking advantage of the shape of ground, and of every cover. We were generally the assailants, and in wooded and broken countries the "defensive" had a positive advantage over us, for they were always ready, had cover, and always knew the ground to their immediate front; whereas we, their assailants, had to grope our way over unknown ground, and generally found a cleared field or prepared entanglements that held us for a time under a close and withering fire. Rarely did the opposing lines in compact order come into actual contact, but when, as at Peach-Tree Creek and Atlanta,[47] the lines did become commingled, the men fought individually in every possible style, more frequently with the musket clubbed than with the bayonet, and in some instances the men clinched like wrestlers, and went to the ground together. Europeans frequently criticised our war, because we did not always take full advantage of a victory; the true reason was, that habitually the woods served as a screen, and we often did not realize the fact that our enemy had retreated till he was already miles away and was again intrenched, having left a mere skirmish-line to cover the movement, in turn to fall back to the new position.

Our war was fought with the muzzle-loading rifle. Toward the close I had one brigade (Walcutt's[48]) armed with breech-loading "Spencer's;" the cavalry generally had breach-loading [sic] carbines, "Spencer's" and "Sharp's," both of which were good arms.

The only change that breech-loading arms will probably make in the art and practice of war will be to increase the amount of ammunition to be expended, and necessarily to be carried along; to still further "thin out" the lines of attack, and to reduce battles to short, quick, decisive conflicts. It does not in the least affect the grand strategy, or the necessity for perfect organization, drill, and discipline. The companies and battalions will be more dispersed, and the men will be less under the immediate eye of their officers, and therefore a higher order of intelligence and courage on the part of the individual soldier will be an element of strength.

When a regiment is deployed as skirmishers, and crosses an open field or woods, under heavy fire, if each man runs forward from tree to tree, or stump to stump, and yet preserves a good general alignment, it gives great confidence to the men themselves, for they always keep their eyes well to the right and left, and watch their comrades; but when some few hold back, stick too close or too long to a comfortable log, it often stops the line and defeats the whole object. Therefore, the more we improve the fire-arm the more will be the necessity for good organization, good discipline and intelligence on the part of the individual soldier and officer. There is, of course, such a thing as individual courage, which has a value in war, but familiarity with danger, experience in war and its common attendants, and personal habit, are equally valuable traits, and these are the qualities with which we usually have to deal in war. All men naturally shrink from pain and danger, and only incur their risk from some higher motive, or from habit; so that I would define true courage to be a perfect sensibility of the measure of danger, and a mental willingness to incur it, rather than that insensibility to danger of which I have heard far more than I have seen. The most courageous men are generally unconscious of possessing the quality; therefore, when one professes it too openly, by words or bearing, there is reason to mistrust it. I would further illustrate my meaning by describing a man of true courage to be one who possesses all his faculties and senses perfectly when serious danger is actually present.

Modern wars have not materially changed the relative values or proportions of the several arms of service: infantry, artillery, cavalry, and engineers. If any thing, the infantry has been increased in value. The danger of cavalry attempting to charge infantry armed with breech-loading rifles was fully illustrated at Sedan, and with us very frequently. So improbable has such a thing become that we have omitted the infantry-square from our recent tactics. Still, cavalry against cavalry, and as auxiliary to infantry, will always be valuable, while all great wars will, as heretofore, depend chiefly on the infantry. Artillery is more valuable with new and inexperienced troops than with veterans. In the early stages of the war the field-guns often bore the proportion of six to a thousand men; but toward the close of the war one gun, or at most two, to a thousand men, was deemed enough. Sieges, such as characterized the wars of the last century, are too slow for this period of the world, and the Prussians recently almost ignored them altogether, penetrated France between the forts, and left a superior force "in observation," to watch the garrison and accept its surrender when the greater events of the war ahead made further resistance useless;[49] but earth-forts, and especially field-works, will hereafter play an important part in wars, because they enable a minor force to hold a superior one in check for a *time,* and time is a most valuable element in all wars. It was one of Prof. Mahan's[50] maxims that the spade was as useful in war as the musket, and to this I will add the axe. The habit of entrenching certainly does have the effect of making new troops timid. When a line of battle is once covered by a good parapet, made by the engineers or by the labor of the men themselves, it does require an effort to make them leave it in the face of danger; but when the enemy is entrenched, it becomes absolutely necessary to permit each brigade and division of the troops immediately opposed to throw up a corresponding trench for their own protection in case of a sudden sally. We invariably did this in all our recent campaigns, and it had no ill effect, though sometimes our troops were a little too slow in leaving their well-covered lines to assail the enemy in position or on retreat. Even our skirmishers were in the habit of rolling logs together, or of making a lunette of rails, with dirt in front, to cover their bodies; and, though it revealed their position, I cannot say that it worked a bad effect; so that, as a rule, it may safely be left to the men themselves. On the "defensive," there is no doubt of the propriety of fortifying; but in the assailing army the general must watch closely to see that his men do not neglect an opportunity to drop his precautionary defenses, and act promptly on the "offensive" at every chance.

I have many a time crept forward to the skirmish-line to avail myself of the cover of the pickets' "little fort," to observe more closely some expected result; and always talked familiarly with the men, and was astonished to see how well they comprehended the general object, and how accurately they were informed of the state of facts existing miles away from their particular corps. Soldiers are very quick to catch the general drift and purpose of a campaign, and are always sensible when they are well commanded or well cared for. Once impressed with this fact, and that they are making progress, they bear cheerfully any amount of labor and privation.

In camp, and especially in the presence of an active enemy, it is much easier to maintain discipline than in barracks in time of peace. Crime and breaches of discipline are much less frequent, and the necessity for courts-martial far less. The captain can usually inflict all the punishment necessary, and the colonel *should* always. The field-officers' court is the best form for war, viz., one of the field-officers—the lieutenant-colonel or major—can examine the case and report his verdict, and the colonel should execute it. Of course, there are statutory offenses which demand a general court-martial, and these must be ordered by the division or corps commander; but the presence of one of our regular civilian judge-advocates in an army in the field would be a first-class nuisance, for technical courts always work mischief. Too many courts-martial in any command are evidence of poor discipline and inefficient officers.

For the rapid transmission of orders in an army covering a large space of ground, the magnetic telegraph is by far the best, though habitually the paper and pencil, with good mounted orderlies, answer every purpose. I have little faith in the signal-service by flags and torches, though we always used them; because, almost invariably when they were most needed, the view was cut off by intervening trees, or by mists and fogs. There was one notable instance in my experience, when the signal-flags carried a message of vital importance over the heads of Hood's army, which had interposed between me and Allatoona, and had broken the telegraph-wires—as recorded in Chapter XIX;[51] but the value of the magnetic telegraph in war cannot be exaggerated, as was illustrated by the perfect concert of action between the armies in Virginia and Georgia during 1864. Hardly a day intervened when General Grant did not know the exact state of facts with me, more than fifteen hundred miles away as the wires ran. So on the field a thin insulated wire may be run on improvised stakes or from tree to tree for six or more miles in a couple of hours, and I have seen operators so skillful, that by cutting the wire they would receive a message with their tongues from a distant station. As a matter of course, the ordinary commercial wires along the railways form the usual telegraph-lines for an array, and these are easily repaired and extended as the army advances, but each army and wing should have a small party of skilled men to put up the field-wire, and take it down when done. This is far better than the signal-flags and torches. Our commercial telegraph-lines will always supply for war enough skillful operators.

The value of railways is also fully recognized in war quite as much as, if not more so than, in peace. The Atlanta campaign would simply have been impossible without the use of the railroads from Louisville to Nashville—one hundred and eighty-five miles—from Nashville to Chattanooga—one hundred and fiftyone miles—and from Chattanooga to Atlanta—one hundred and thirty-seven miles. Every mile of this "single track" was so delicate, that one man could in a minute have broken or moved a rail, but our trains usually carried along the tools and means to repair such a break. We had, however, to maintain strong guards and garrisons at each important bridge or trestle—the destruction of which would have necessitated time for rebuilding. For the protection of a bridge, one or two log block-houses, two stories high, with a piece of ordnance and a small infantry guard, usually sufficed. The block-house had a small parapet and ditch about it, and the roof was made shot-proof by earth piled on. These points could usually be reached only by a dash of the enemy's cavalry, and many of these block-houses successfully resisted serious attacks by both cavalry and artillery. The only block-house that was actually captured on the main was the one described near Allatoona.

Our trains from Nashville forward were operated under military rules, and ran about ten miles an hour in gangs of four trains of ten cars each. Four such groups of trains daily made one hundred and sixty cars, of ten tons each, carrying sixteen hundred tons, which exceeded the absolute necessity of the army, and allowed for the accidents that were common and inevitable. But, as I have recorded, that single stem of railroad, four hundred and seventy-three miles long, supplied an army of one hundred thousand men and thirty-five thousand animals for the period of one hundred and ninety-six days, viz., from May 1 to November 12, 1864. To have delivered regularly that amount of food and forage by ordinary wagons would have required thirty-six thousand eight hundred wagons of six mules each, allowing each wagon to have hauled two tons twenty miles each day, a simple impossibility in roads such as then existed in that region of country. Therefore, I reiterate that the Atlanta campaign was an impossibility without these railroads; and only then, because we had the men and means to maintain and defend them, in addition to what were necessary to overcome the enemy. Habitually, a passenger-car will carry fifty men with their necessary baggage. Box-cars, and even platform-cars, answer the purpose well enough, but they should always have rough board-seats. For sick and wounded men, box-cars filled with straw or bushes were usually employed. Personally, I saw but little of the practical working of the railroads, for I only turned back once as far as Resaca; but I had daily reports from the engineer in charge, and officers who came from the rear often explained to me the whole thing, with a description of the wrecked trains all the way from Nashville to Atlanta. I am convinced that the risk to life to the engineers and men on that railroad fully equaled that on the skirmish-line, called for as high an order of courage, and fully equaled it in importance. Still, I doubt if there be any necessity in time of peace to organize a corps specially to work the military railroads in time of war, because in peace these same men gain all the necessary experience, possess all the daring and courage of soldiers, and only need the occasional protection and assistance of the necessary train-guard, which may be composed of the furloughed men coming and going, or of details made from the local garrisons to the rear.

For the transfer of large armies by rail, from one theatre of action to another by the rear—the cases of the transfer of the Eleventh and Twelfth Corps—General Hooker, twenty-three thousand men—from the East to Chattanooga, eleven hundred and ninety-two miles in seven days, in the fall of 1863; and that of the Army of the Ohio—General Schofield,[52] fifteen thousand men—from the valley of the Tennessee to Washington, fourteen hundred miles in eleven days, *en route* to North Carolina in January, 1865, are the best examples of which I have any knowledge, and reference to these is made in the report of the Secretary of War, Mr. Stanton, dated November 22, 1865.

Engineer troops attached to an army are habitually employed in supervising the construction of forts or field works of a nature more permanent than the lines used by the troops in motion, and in repairing roads and making bridges. I had several regiments of this kind that were most useful, but as a rule we used the infantry, or employed parties of freedmen, who worked on the trenches at night while the soldiers slept, and these in turn rested by day. Habitually the repair of the railroad and its bridges was committed to hired laborers, like the English navvies, [sic] under the supervision of Colonel W. W. Wright,[53] a railroad-engineer, who was in the military service at the time, and his successful labors were frequently referred to in the official reports of the campaign.

For the passage of rivers, each army corps had a pontoon-train with a detachment of engineers, and, on reaching a river, the leading infantry division was charged with the labor of putting it down. Generally the single pontoon-train could provide for nine hundred feet of bridge, which sufficed; but when the rivers were very wide two such trains would be brought together, or the single train was supplemented by a trestle-bridge, or bridges made on crib-work, out of timber found near the place. The pontoons in general use were skeleton frames, made with a hinge, so as to fold back and constitute a wagon-body. In this same wagon were carried the cotton canvas cover, the anchor and chains, and a due proportion of the balks, chesses, and lashings.[54] All the troops became very familiar with their mechanism and use, and we were rarely delayed by reason of a river, however broad. I saw, recently, in Aldershot, England, a very complete pontoon-train; the boats were sheathed with wood and felt, made very light; but I think these were more liable to chafing and damage in rough handling than were our less expensive and rougher boats. On the whole, I would prefer the skeleton frame and canvas cover to any style of pontoon that I have ever seen.

In relation to guards, pickets, and vedettes, I doubt if any discoveries or improvements were made during our war, or in any of the modern wars in Europe. These precautions vary with the nature of the country and the situation of each army. When advancing or retreating in line of battle, the usual skirmish-line constitutes the picket-line, and may have "reserves," but usually the main line of battle constitutes the reserve; and in this connection I will state that the recent innovation introduced into the new infantry tactics by General Upton[55] is admirable, for by it each regiment, brigade, and division deployed, sends forward as "skirmishers" the one man of each set of fours, to cover its own front, and these can be recalled or reënforced at pleasure by the bugle-signal.

For flank-guards and rear-guards, one or more companies should be detached under their own officers, instead of making up the guard by detailing men from the several companies.

For regimental or camp guards, the details should be made according to existing army regulations; and all the guards should be posted early in the evening, so as to afford each sentinel or vedette a chance to study his ground before it becomes too dark.

In like manner as to the staff. The more intimately it comes into contact with the troops, the more useful and valuable it becomes. The almost entire separation of the staff from the line, as now practised by us, and hitherto by the French, has proved mischievous, and the great retinues of staff-officers with which some of our earlier generals began the war were simply ridiculous. I don't believe in a chief of staff at all, and any general commanding an army, corps, or division, that has a staff-officer who professes to know more than his chief, is to be pitied. Each regiment should have a competent adjutant, quartermaster, and commissary, with two or three medical officers. Each brigade commander should have the same staff, with the addition of a couple of young aides-de-camp, habitually selected from the subalterns of the brigade, who should be good riders, and intelligent enough to give and explain the orders of their general.

The same staff will answer for a division. The general in command of a separate army, and of a *corps d'armée,* should have the same professional assistance, with two or more good engineers, and his adjutant-general should exercise all the functions usually ascribed to a chief of staff, viz., he should possess the ability to comprehend the scope of operations, and to make verbally and in writing all the orders and details necessary to carry into effect the views of his general, as well as to keep the returns and records of events for the information of the next higher authority, and for history. A bulky staff implies a division of responsibility, slowness of action, and indecision, whereas a small staff implies activity and concentration of purpose. The smallness of General Grant's staff throughout the civil war forms the best model for future imitation. So of tents, officers' furniture, etc., etc. In real war these should all be discarded, and an army is efficient for action and motion exactly in the inverse ratio of its *impedimenta.* Tents should be omitted altogether, save one to a regiment for an office, and a few for the division hospital. Officers should be content with a tent fly, improvising poles and shelter out of bushes. The *tente d'abri,* or shelter-tent, carried by the soldier himself, is all-sufficient. Officers should never seek for houses, but share the condition of their men.

A recent message (July 18, 1874) made to the French Assembly by Marshal MacMahon, President of the French Republic, submits a *projet de loi,* with a report prepared by a board of French generals on "army administration," which is full of information, and is as applicable to us as to the French.[56] I quote from its very beginning: "The misfortunes of the campaign of 1870 have demonstrated the inferiority of our system.... Two separate organizations existed with parallel functions—the 'general' more occupied in giving direction to his troops than in providing for their material wants, which he regarded as the special province of the staff, and the 'intendant' (staff) often working at random, taking on his shoulders a crushing burden of functions and duties, exhausting himself with useless efforts, and aiming to accomplish an insufficient service, to the disappointment of everybody. This separation of the administration and command, this coexistence of two wills, each independent of the other, which paralyzed both and annulled the dualism," was condemned. It was decided by the board that this error should be "proscribed" in the new military system. The report then goes on at great length discussing the provisions of the "new law," which is described to be a radical change from the old one on the same subject. While conceding to the Minister of War in Paris the general control and supervision of the entire military establishment primarily, especially of the annual estimates or budget, and the great depots of supply, it distributes to the commanders of the *corps d'armée* in time of peace, and to all army commanders generally in time of war, the absolute command of the money, provisions, and stores, with the necessary staff-officers to receive, issue, and account for them. I quote further: "The object of this law is to confer on the commander of troops whatever liberty of action the case demands. He has the power even to go beyond the regulations, in circumstances of urgency and pressing necessity. The extraordinary measures he may take on these occasions may require their execution without delay. The staff-officer has but one duty before obeying, and that is to submit his observations to the general, and to ask his orders in writing. With this formality his responsibility ceases, and the responsibility for the extraordinary act falls solely on the general who gives the order. The officers and agents charged with supplies are placed under the orders of the general in command of the troops, that is, they are obliged both in war and peace to obey, with the single qualification above named, of first making their observations and securing the written order of the general."

With us, to-day, the law and regulations are that, no matter what may be the emergency, the commanding general in Texas, New Mexico, and the remote frontiers, cannot draw from the arsenals a pistol-cartridge, or any sort of ordnance-stores, without first procuring an order of the Secretary of War in Washington. The commanding general—though intrusted with the lives of his soldiers and with the safety of a frontier in a condition of chronic war—cannot touch or be trusted with ordnance-stores or property, and that is declared to be the law! Every officer of the old army remembers how, in 1861, we were hampered with the old blue army-regulations,[57] which tied our hands, and that to do any thing positive and necessary we had to tear it all to pieces—cut the red-tape, as it was called—a dangerous thing for an army to do, for it was calculated to bring the law and authority into contempt; but war was upon us, and overwhelming necessity overrides all law.

This French report is well worth the study of our army-officers, of all grades and classes, and I will only refer again, casually, to another part, wherein it discusses the subject of military correspondence: whether the staff-officer should correspond directly with his chief in Paris, submitting to his general copies, or whether he should be required to carry on his correspondence through his general, so that the latter could promptly forward the communication, indorsed with his own remarks and opinions. The latter is declared by the board to be the only safe rule, because "the general should never be ignorant of any thing that is transpiring that concerns his command."

In this country, as in France, Congress controls the great questions of war and peace, makes all laws for the creation and government of armies, and votes the necessary supplies, leaving to the President to execute and apply these laws, especially the harder task of limiting the expenditure of public money to the amount of the annual appropriations. The executive power is further subdivided into the seven great departments, and to the Secretary of War is confided the general care of the military establishment, and his powers are further subdivided into ten distinct and separate bureaus.

The chiefs of these bureaus are under the immediate orders of the Secretary of War, who, through them, in fact commands the army from "his office," but cannot do so "in the field"—an absurdity in military if not civil law.

The subordinates of these staff-corps and departments are selected and chosen from the army itself, or fresh from West Point, and too commonly construe themselves into the *élite*, as made of better clay than the common soldier. Thus they separate themselves more and more from their comrades of the line, and in process of time realize the condition of that old officer of artillery who thought the army would be a delightful place for a gentleman if it were not for the d——d soldier; or, better still, the conclusion of the young lord in "Henry IV.," who told Harry Percy (Hotspur) that "but for these vile guns he would himself have been a soldier."[58] This is all wrong; utterly at variance with our democratic form of government and of universal experience; and now that the French, from whom we had copied the system, have utterly "proscribed" it, I hope that our Congress will follow suit. I admit, in its fullest force, the strength of the maxim that the civil law should be superior to the military in time of peace; that the army should be at all times subject to the direct control of Congress; and I assert that, from the formation of our Government to the present day, the Regular Army has set the highest example of obedience to law and authority; but, for the very reason that our army is comparatively so very small, I hold that it should be the best possible, organized and governed on true military principles, and that in time of peace we should preserve the "habits and usages of war," so that, when war does come, we may not again be compelled to suffer the disgrace, confusion, and disorder of 1861.

The commanding officers of divisions, departments, and posts, should have the amplest powers, not only to command their troops, but all the stores designed for their use, and the officers of the staff necessary to administer them, within the area of their command; and then with fairness they could be held to the most perfect responsibility. The President and Secretary of War can command the army quite as well through these generals as through the subordinate staff-officers. Of course, the Secretary would, as now, distribute the funds according to the appropriation bills, and reserve to himself the absolute control and supervision of the larger arsenals and depots of supply. The error lies in the law, or in the judicial interpretation thereof, and no code of army regulations can be made that meets the case, until Congress, like the French *Corps Législatif*, utterly annihilates and "proscribes" the old law and the system which has grown up under it.

It is related of Napoleon that his last words were, "Tête-d'armée!" Doubtless, as the shadow of death obscured his memory, the last thought that remained for speech was of some event when he was directing an important "head of column." I believe that every general who has handled armies in battle must recall from his own experience the intensity of thought on some similar occasion, when by a single command he had given the finishing stroke to some complicated action; but to me recurs another thought that is worthy of record, and may encourage others who are to follow us in our profession. I never saw the rear of an army engaged in battle but I feared that some calamity had happened at the front—the apparent confusion, broken wagons, crippled horses, men lying about dead and maimed, parties hastening to and fro in seeming disorder, and a general apprehension of something dreadful about to ensue; all these signs, however, lessened as I neared the front, and there the contrast was complete—perfect order, men and horses full of confidence, and it was not unusual for general hilarity, laughing, and cheering. Although cannon might be firing, the musketry clattering, and the enemy's shot hitting close, there reigned a general feeling of strength and security that bore a marked contrast to the bloody signs that had drifted rapidly to the rear; therefore, for comfort and safety, I surely would rather be at the front than the rear line of battle. So also on the march, the head of a column moves on steadily, while the rear is alternately halting and then rushing forward to close up the gap; and all sorts of rumors, especially the worst, float back to the rear. Old troops invariably deem it a special privilege to be in the front—to be at the "head of column"—because experience has taught them that it is the easiest and most comfortable place, and danger only adds zest and stimulus to this fact.

The hardest task in war is to lie in support of some position or battery, under fire without the privilege of returning it; or to guard some train left in the rear, within hearing but out of danger; or to provide for the wounded and dead of some corps which is too busy ahead to care for its own.

To be at the head of a strong column of troops, in the execution of some task that requires brain, is the highest pleasure of war—a grim one and terrible, but which leaves on the mind and memory the strongest mark; to detect the weak point of an enemy's line; to break through with vehemence and thus lead to victory; or to discover some key-point and hold it with tenacity; or to do some other distinct act which is afterward recognized as the real cause of success. These all become matters that are never forgotten. Other great difficulties, experienced by every general, are to measure truly the thousand-and-one reports that come to him in the midst of conflict; to preserve a clear and well-defined purpose at every instant of time, and to cause all efforts to converge to that end.

To do these things he must know perfectly the strength and quality of each part of his own army, as well as that of his opponent, and must be where he can personally see and observe with his own eyes, and judge with his own mind. No man can properly command an army from the rear, he must be "at its front;" and when a detachment is made, the commander thereof should be informed of the object to be accomplished, and left as free as possible to execute it in his own way; and when an army is divided up into several parts, the superior should always attend that one which he regards as most important. Some men think that modern armies may be so regulated that a general can sit in an office and play on his several columns as on the keys of a piano; this is a fearful mistake. The directing mind must be at the very head of the army—must be seen there, and the effect of his mind and personal energy must be felt by every officer and man present with it, to secure the best results. Every attempt to make war easy and safe will result in humiliation and disaster.

Lastly, mail facilities should be kept up with an army if possible, that officers and men may receive and send letters to their friends, this maintaining the home influence of infinite assistance to discipline. Newspaper correspondents with an army, as a rule, are mischievous. They are the world's gossips, pick up and retail the camp scandal, and gradually drift to the headquarters of some general, who finds it easier to make reputation at home than with his own corps or division. They are also tempted to prophesy events and state facts which, to an enemy, reveal a purpose in time to guard against it. Moreover, they are always bound to see facts colored by the partisan or political character of their own patrons, and thus bring army officers into the political controversies of the day, which are always mischievous and wrong. Yet, so greedy are the people at large for war news, that it is doubtful whether any army commander can exclude all reporters, without bringing down on himself a clamor that may imperil his own safety. Time and moderation must bring a just solution to this modern difficulty.

THE TEXTS

Herman Melville, selections from *Battle-Pieces and Aspects of the War*. Source: *The Works of Herman Melville*. Vol. 16 (London: Constable and Company Ltd., 1924). Originally published in *Battle-Pieces and Aspects of the War* (New York: Harper & Bros., 1866).

George Moses Horton, selections from *Naked Genius*. Source: *Naked Genius: By George Moses Horton, The Colored Bard of North Carolina* (Raleigh, N.C.: Wm. B. Smith & Co., Southern Field and Fireside Book Publishing House, 1865).

Sarah Morgan Piatt, "Hearing the Battle." Source: *Palace-Burner: The Selected Poetry of Sarah Piatt*, ed. Paula Bernat Bennett (Urbana: University of Illinois Press, 2001). Originally published in John James Piatt and Sarah M. B. Piatt, *The Nests at Washington, and Other Poems* (New York: W. Low; London: S. Low, Son & Co., 1864).

Henry Wadsworth Longfellow, "The Cumberland" and "Killed at the Ford." Source: *The Complete Poetical Works of Longfellow* (Cambridge, Mass.: Riverside Press, 1922). Originally published, respectively, in *The Atlantic Monthly*, vol. 10, no. 62 (December 1862) and *The Atlantic Monthly*, vol. 17, no. 102 (April 1866).

Lucy Larcom, "The Sinking of the Merrimack." Source: *The Poetical Works of Lucy Larcom. Household Edition. With Illustrations* (Boston and New York: Houghton, Mifflin and Company, 1890).

Walt Whitman, selections from *Specimen Days*. Source: *Specimen Days and Collect* (Philadelphia: D. McKay, 1882–83).

Walt Whitman, selections from *Drum-Taps*. Source: *Walt Whitman's Drum-Taps* (New York, s.n., 1865). In *Leaves of Grass*, Whitman retitled "The Dresser" "The Wound-Dresser" and made two significant revisions to the poem. The first was to add, as lines 4–6, the following: "(Arous'd and angry, I'd thought to beat the alarum, and urge relentless war, / But soon my fingers fail'd me, my face droop'd and I resign'd myself, / To sit by the wounded and soothe them, or silently watch the dead;)". The second was to delete the phrase "In nature's reverie sad" from the start of line 20 (before "With hinged knees").

S. Weir Mitchell, "The Case of George Dedlow." Source: *The Autobiography of a Quack and Other Stories*. Author's Definitive Edition (New York: The Century Co., 1905). Originally published in *The Atlantic Monthly*, vol. 18, no. 105 (July 1866). Mitchell included the following "Introduction" in his 1905 collection:

"The first two tales in this little volume ['The Autobiography of a Quack' and 'The Case of George Dedlow'] appeared originally in the 'Atlantic Monthly' as anonymous contributions. I owe to the present owners of that journal pemission to use them. 'The Autobiography of a Quack' has been recast with large additions.

"'The Case of George Dedlow' was not written with any intention that it should appear in print. I lent the manuscript to the Rev. Dr. Furness and forgot it. This gentleman sent it to the Rev. Edward Everett Hale.[59] He, presuming, I fancy, that every one desired to appear in the 'Atlantic,' offered it to that journal. To my surprise, soon afterwards I received a proof and a check. The story was inserted as a leading article without my name. It was at once accepted by many as the description of a real case. Money was collected in several places to assist the unfortunate man, and benevolent persons went to see the 'Stump Hospital,' in Philadelphia, to see the sufferer and to offer him aid. The spiritual incident at the end of the story was received with joy by the spiritualists as a valuable proof off the truth of their beliefs."

Helen Hunt Jackson, "Songs of Battle." Source: *Poems by Helen Jackson* (Boston: Little, Brown and Company, 1902). Originally published in *The Century*, vol. 31, no. 1 (Nov. 1885), with the footnote: "Suggested by La Farge's 'Battle' window for Memorial Hall, Cambridge, Mass." Included in *Sonnets and Lyrics, By Helen Jackson* (Boston: Roberts Brothers, 1886).

Abraham Lincoln, Address at the Dedication of the Gettysburg National Cemetery. Source: *Complete Works of Abraham Lincoln, Comprising his Speeches, Letters, State Papers, and Miscellaneous Writings*, ed. John G. Nicolay and John Hay. Vol. 2 (New York: The Century Company, 1920).

Louisa May Alcott, *Hospital Sketches*, Chapter 3 ("A Day"). Source: *Hospital Sketches* (Boston: James Redpath, 1863).

Emily Dickinson, poems #138, #465, #468, #545, #616, #629, #871, #704. Source: *The Poems of Emily Dickinson*, ed. R. W. Franklin (Cambridge: The Belknap Press of Harvard University Press, 1999).

Ambrose Bierce, "On a Mountain." Source: *The Collected Works of Ambrose Bierce*. Vol. 1 ("Bits of Autobiography") (New York: Neale Publishing Co., 1909).

Ambrose Bierce, "A Horseman in the Sky," "A Son of the Gods," and "One of the Missing." Source: *The Collected Works of Ambrose Bierce*, Vol. 2 ("In the Midst of Life") (New York: Neale Publishing Co., 1909). Originally published in *Tales of Soldiers and Civilians* (San Francisco: E.L.G. Steele, 1891; New York: Lovell, Coryell, 1891; New York: United States Book Co., 1891).

Ambrose Bierce, "A Tough Tussle." Source: *Collected Works of Ambrose Bierce*. Vol. 3 ("Can Such Things Be?") (New York: Neale Publishing Co., 1910). *Can Such Things Be?* was originally published in New York by The Cassell Pub. Co. in 1893.

Stephen Crane, "A Gray Sleeve." Source: *The Little Regiment, and Other Episodes of the American Civil War* (New York: D. Appleton and Company, 1896). Originally syndicated in October 1895 in several different newspapers. Other editions of the story change "gray" to "grey."

Stephen Crane, "A Mystery of Heroism." Source: *The Little Regiment, and Other Episodes of the American Civil War* (New York: D. Appleton and Company, 1896). Originally syndicated in August 1895 in several different newspapers.

Stephen Crane, "An Episode of War." Source: *The Work of Stephen Crane.* Vol. 9 ("Wounds in the Rain, and Other Impressions of War"), ed. Wilson Follett (New York: Alfred A. Knopf, 1925). Originally published in the British magazine *The Gentlewoman* (Dec. 1899), pp. 24–25. Probably sold to the *Youth's Companion* as "The Loss of an Arm" in late 1896, but never published there. See Fredson Bowers, textual introduction to *The Works of Stephen Crane.* Vol. 6 ("Tales of War") (Charlottesville: University of Virginia Press, 1970), pp. lxxx–lxxxii.

Ulysses S. Grant, from *Personal Memoirs.* Source: *Personal Memoirs of U. S. Grant.* Vol. 2. (New York: Charles L. Webster & Co., 1886).

William T. Sherman, from *Memoirs.* Source: *Memoirs of Gen. W. T. Sherman, Written By Himself.* Vol. 2. 4th ed. (New York: Charles L. Webster & Co., 1892).

NOTES

1. The Swamp Angel was an 8-inch, 200-pound rifled cannon, or Parrott gun, used during the Union bombardment of Charleston in August 1863. Several of its rounds were filled with "Greek fire," a combination of flammable substances. The heavier Parrott guns occasionally cracked or burst during firing – as did the Swamp Angel on August 23, after two days of use.

2. The battle of Belmont actually took place on November 7, 1861.

3. Union Gen. John Sedgwick (1813–1864), fondly nicknamed "Uncle John" by his men, killed at Spotsylvania.

4. Union Gen. Hiram Gregory Berry (1824–1863), fatally shot during a counter-charge at Chancellorsville.

5. John Singleton Mosby (1833–1916), Confederate cavalry leader. After resigning from service under Jeb Stuart, Mosby formed and led a semi-autonomous cavalry group, "Mosby's Rangers," that gained fame leading raids against Union troops and capturing federal resources. Upperville, in northern Virginia, was the scene of a minor battle on June 21, 1863.

6. William S. Prentiss was evidently a private in the Confederate 2nd Maryland Infantry, although *The Medical and Surgical History of the Civil War* (Wilmington, NC: Broadfoot, 1991–92; orig. Washington: Government Printing Office, 1870–1888) identifies him as Union (Index Vol. 1, p. 176). The *Medical and Surgical History* also gives his age as 26, lists his admittance date as April 2, 1865, and records June 23, 1865, as the date of his death (Vol. 11, p. 239).

7. Whitman appears to have gotten the rank wrong. Clifton K. Prentiss joined the Sixth Maryland Infantry as a Captain and mustered out as a Major.

8. The 79th Indiana was organized in late summer, 1862, and served in both the Army of the Ohio and the Army of the Cumberland.

9. "Regiment lost during service 3 Officers and 50 Enlisted men killed and mortally wounded and 2 Officers and 147 Enlisted men by disease. Total 202" (Frederick H. Dyer, *A Compendium of the War of the Rebellion* [New York: Thomas Yoseloff, 1959; orig. 1908], Vol. 3, p. 1147).

10. The system of such prisoner exchanges broke down in the summer of 1863 over the South's refusal to treat captured black soldiers as prisoners of war on an equal basis with whites.

11. The 79th Indiana contributed to the battle of Chickamauga by capturing, with heavy losses, a Confederate artillery battery.

12. Glenna R. Schroeder-Lein writes that Dr. David Wendel Yandell, medical director to Gen. Albert Sidney Johnston, "set up thirteen hospitals in Nashville during the fall of 1861," which ultimately "had beds for about 13,000" (*Confederate Hospitals on the Move: Samuel H. Stout and the Army of Tennessee.* Columbia: University of South Carolina Press [1994], pp. 45–46). The Confederates began vacating Nasville in February 1862.

13. Presumably Benjamin F. Palmer, who developed a prosthetic leg of relatively high mobility which was honored at the World's Fair in London in 1851.

14. Also known as Turner's Lane Hospital, this clinical research facility in north Philadelphia closed in fall 1864 (Ira M. Rutkow, *Bleeding Blue and Gray: Civil War Surgery and the Evolution of American Medicine* [New York: Random House, 2005], pp. 252–54).

15. "The absent ones are always wrong."

16. U.S. Surgeon General William Hammond established the Army Medical Museum in 1862 in order to collect specimens from wounded soldiers for research purposes; it also archived photographs and case histories. The AMM is now the National Museum of Health and Medicine of the Armed Forces Institute of Pathology.

17. Shakespeare, *Richard III*, Act V, scene iii, lines xxx: "Conscience avaunt, Richard's himself again." (Bessie Z. Jones, editor of the 1960 edition by the Belknap Press of Harvard University Press).

18. Sairey Gamp is the drunken nurse and midwife from Charles Dickens's *Martin Chuzzlewit* (1844).

19. "By force and arms" (Cicero, "Pro Caecina").

20. Alfred Lord Tennyson's "The Charge of the Light Brigade," written in 1854 and published in 1855 in *Maud, and Other Poems*, memorialized a heroically disastrous attack by a British cavalry unit in the Battle of Balaclava in the Crimean War (1854–56). The original stanza Alcott parodies reads: "Cannon to right of them, / Cannon to left of them, / Cannon behind them / Volley'd and thunder'd; / Storm'd at with shot and shell, / While horse and hero fell, / They that had fought so well / Came thro' the jaws of Death, / Back from the mouth of Hell, / All that was left of them, / Left of six hundred." Florence Nightingale, an inspiration and legend among American Civil War nurses, served in the Crimea.

21. I.e., an extravagant tale of adventure, from Baron Munchausen.

22. "Biddy" was a common nickname for Irish servant girls.

23. Slightly misquoted from William Thackeray's *Vanity Fair* (1847), vol. 1, ch. 24. The young ensign's letters, Thackeray writes, were "full of love and heartiness, and pluck and bad spelling. Ah! there were many anxious hearts beating through England at that time; and mothers' prayers and tears flowing in many homesteads."

24. In western Virginia, where the Union army in 1861 was engaged in driving out the Confederates.

25. See Alfred Lord Tennyson's "The Lotos-Eaters": "In the afternoon they came unto a land / In which it seemed always afternoon."

26. From Edgar Allan Poe's "Ulalume" (1847). In this poem, the speaker and "Psyche, my Soul" roam through the "ghoul-haunted woodland of Weir" and find a "legended tomb" where the speaker had earlier buried his "lost Ulalume."

27. On April 15, 1861, before it became obvious that the war would last much longer than three months, Lincoln issued a call for 75,000 Northern militiamen who would each serve for ninety days.

28. A minor engagement at Philippi, Virginia, on 3 June 1861, this was actually the first *land* battle of the war, and although trivial in military terms, it helped prepare for the political separation of West Virginia from Virginia. Previous engagements included the firing on Fort Sumter and minor naval skirmishes at Sewell's Point and Aquia Creek, Virginia.

29. The battle of Carrick's Ford, in Virginia, on 13 July 1861, following the Confederate retreat from Laurel Hill, was a minor tactical Union victory but contributed to the expulsion of Southern troops from the western part of the state.

30. Thomas Campbell's "The Pleasures of Hope" (1799) opens: "At summer eve, when Heaven's ethereal bow / Spans with bright arch the glittering hills below, / Why to yon mountain turns the musing eye, / Whose sun-bright summit mingles with the sky? / Why do those clifts of shadowy tint appear / More sweet than all the landscape smiling near? 'T is distance lends enchantment to the view, / And robes the mountain in its azure hue. / Thus, with delight, we linger to survey / The promised joys of life's unmeasured way;"

31. The western part of the state began the process of separation in the summer of 1861, and formally entered the Union as a new state on 20 June 1863.

32. From Milton's description of Satan's spear in Book I of *Paradise Lost*.

33. I.e., the standing U.S. Army, in contradistinction to State volunteer units.

34. Robert Kelley Weeks (1840–1876).

35. Perhaps Gen. James B. McPherson (1828–1864), who participated in the battle of Kennesaw Mountain and was known for his caution.

36. These were a series of battles in the successful Union campaign, under George McClellan, in the summer and early fall of 1861, to drive Confederate forces out of western Virginia.

37. Lt. Col. adjutant Charles Marshall, Lee's aide-de-camp, who arranged for the meeting between Grant and Lee to take place in the house of Wilmer McLean, a resident of Appomattox Court House.

38. Orville Elias Babcock (1835–1884), an aide-de-camp who delivered Grant's surrender offer to Lee. Babcock was brevetted brigadier general at war's end. He later became embroiled in the financial scandals in the Grant administration.

39. Gen. John Gibbon (1827–1896); Gen. Charles Griffin (1825–1867); Gen. Wesley Merritt (1837–1910).

40. Gen. James Longstreet (1821–1904); Gen. John Brown Gordon (1832–1904); Gen. William Nelson Pendleton (1809–1883).

41. I.e., Jefferson Davis.

42. James Harrison Wilson (1837–1925) served successfully under Grant in the West and then commanded cavalry under Sherman. In the spring of 1865, Wilson's three-division cavalry corps undertook a successful campaign from Tennessee, through Georgia, and into Alabama, routing Nathan Bedford Forrest's cavalry and capturing both Selma and Montgomery.

43. The practice of having enlisted men elect officers was common in both North and South during the early phase of the war. Although this democratic approach could heighten unit cohesion, it soon became clear that many elected officers were poorly qualified, and both militaries began phasing out the practice by 1862, an important step toward full professionalization of the army.

44. The Confederate Congress enacted a draft law in the spring of 1862, the U.S. Congress in the spring of 1863. Both conscription acts allowed for men whose names were called to hire substitutes to fight in their place, a form of exemption that seemed to allow the wealthy to avoid service. Facing public opposition to the practice, the South repealed substitution in December 1863, the North in July 1864.

45. Dr. Edward Dominicus Kittoe (1814–1887), of Galena, Illinois, held a series of appointments during the war, eventually rising to chief medical inspector for the Army of the Cumberland and then the Army of the Tennessee.

46. This phrase, governing the prosecution of courts-martial, dates to the Articles of War drafted in the 1776 journals of the Continental Congress, and became standard language in American military regulations.

47. The battle at Peachtree Creek (July 20, 1864) was a last-ditch attempt by the Confederates, under Gen. John Bell Hood, to protect Atlanta from advancing federal armies under Gens. Sherman, George Thomas, and John Schofield. The fighting, in heavily wooded terrain, was fierce but confused, and resulted in heavy Southern losses. On July 22, from just outside Atlanta, Hood attacked again, but to little effect.

48. Brig. General Charles C. Walcutt (1838–1898), commander of the 2nd Brigade, 1st Division, XV Corps, Army of the Tennessee.

49. In the Franco-Prussian War (1870–71), German forces captured Napoleon III and 100,000 men at the battle of Sedan in September 1870, forced the surrender of the garrison of Marshal Bazaine in October, and laid siege to Paris, which capitulated in January 1871.

50. Dennis Hart Mahan (1802–1871), Professor of Tactics and Engineering at the United States Military Academy.

51. In chapter 19 ("The Capture of Atlanta"), Sherman discusses Confederate Gen. John Hood's unsuccessful attempts to resist the Union occupation of Atlanta, including the destruction of railroads and disruption of communication lines.

52. John McAllister Schofield (1831–1906), after assisting Sherman in the Tennessee-Georgia campaign, especially with a major victory at the battle of Franklin, travelled to Wilmington in January 1865 to take command of the Department of North Carolina.

53. William Wierman Wright (1824–1882), a specialist in railroad construction and repair, assisted Sherman as head of the U.S. Military Railroad Construction Corps during Sherman's 1865 operations.

54. Balks and chesses were the timbers and planks used in a pontoon bridge.

55. Emory Upton (1839–1881), former Union brigadier general, instructor at West Point, and author of *A New System of Infantry Tactics, Double and Single Rank, Adapted to American Topography and Improved Fire-arms* (1866).

56. The monarchist and field marshal Marie Edmé Patrice de MacMahon (1808–1893) became President of the Third Republic in 1873, two years after France's ruinous defeat in the Franco-Prussian war.

57. The United States Army Regulations of 1861 (revised in 1863) comprised 52 articles governing the details of military life and the conduct of both officers and enlisted men.

58. Shakespeare, *The First Part of King Henry the Fourth*, Act I, scene iii, lines 63–64.

59. William Henry Furness (1802–1896) was a liberal Unitarian minister whose theological work *Remarks on the Four Gospels* (1836) was an important early text in the emergence of Transcendentalism. In 1866, Furness was pastor of the First Unitarian Church in Philadelphia. Edward Everett Hale (1822–1909), another liberal Unitarian clergyman, was also a journalist, editor, and author of fiction and non-fiction.

III

AFRICAN
AMERICAN
EXPERIENCE

Company E, 4th U.S. Colored Infantry, Ft. Lincoln, defenses of Washington.

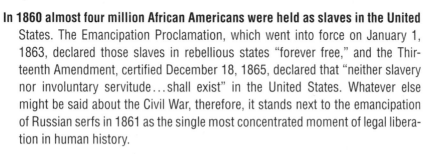

3

INTRODUCTION

In 1860 almost four million African Americans were held as slaves in the United States. The Emancipation Proclamation, which went into force on January 1, 1863, declared those slaves in rebellious states "forever free," and the Thirteenth Amendment, certified December 18, 1865, declared that "neither slavery nor involuntary servitude…shall exist" in the United States. Whatever else might be said about the Civil War, therefore, it stands next to the emancipation of Russian serfs in 1861 as the single most concentrated moment of legal liberation in human history.

Genuine freedom was another matter, of course. The inability of post-war Reconstruction to secure African American civil rights, indeed survival, in more than a theoretical sense meant that the long, hard struggle for practical liberty and equal citizenship had only just begun. It is also important to remember that the Civil War was not originally, and arguably not ever primarily, a war of liberation; that racism was common among Union soldiers, many of whom bristled at the notion that they risked their lives for "niggers"; and that officially sanctioned unequal treatment of black soldiers persisted in the federal military. American emancipation is thus a story of great hope and great accomplishment clouded by disappointment, violence, and hatred.

As the war took hold in the South, siphoning off adult males and disrupting civil order and the plantation system, slaves began to escape in greater numbers, and the Union soon discovered that it had a problem on its hands: what to do with those who ended up in federally held territory. The solution that emerged—one which African American leaders had been calling for all along—was to employ escaped slaves and freedmen in the war effort. The pivotal year was 1862, which saw an early attempt by Gen. David Hunter to organize a black regiment; Gen. Benjamin Butler's designation of ex-slaves as "contrabands of war"; and the preliminary emancipation proclamation of Sept. 22, which Lincoln justified as "a fit and necessary war measure." The Congressional militia act of July 1862 authorized the enlistment of black soldiers, and in August, the first official black regiment, the First South Carolina Volunteers, was formed. Although resistance accompanied all of these developments, the moral and military arguments in favor of raising African American troops proved irresistible, and in May 1863, the War Department established a Bureau of Colored Troops. Recruitment accelerated, and by the end of the war, almost 180,000 African Americans had served as enlisted men, and about 100 as officers.

Their service was not easy. Black soldiers faced an array of difficulties: lower pay than their white counterparts ($10.00 per month instead of $13.00); inferior supplies and medical care; much higher rates of fatal disease and combat casualties; harassment by white soldiers; and reprisals at the hands of Confederate captors. Even so, African American troops—along with many blacks serving in unofficial capacities such as reconnaissance and construction—made significant contributions to the Union war effort, particularly along the coastal regions of the Confederacy, and their performance cured many Northerners of their skepticism about the value of black citizenship.

African American troops saw significant action during the siege of Port Hudson, Louisiana, during the late spring and summer of 1863. The 1st Louisiana Native Guards (later the First Corps de Afrique and then the 73rd United States Colored Troops) and the 3rd Louisiana Native Guards sustained heavy casualties here but proved their combat mettle.

It was in the Sea Islands area of South Carolina, however, that black regiments would gain their fame. The Union bases at Port Royal and Beaufort—central to the overall strategy of taking advantage of Northern naval superiority, blockading the South, and moving against Charleston—were in an area inhabited by large communities of former slaves. In the so-called Port Royal Experiment, the U.S. military, with the help of Northern abolitionists, began organizing African American units and deploying them in raids along the coast and upriver. In November, 1862, Rufus Saxton, brigadier general in the Department of the South, asked Thomas Wentworth Higginson to take command of the recently formed 1st South Carolina Volunteers at Beaufort River. The regiment participated in various military expeditions and in the temporary occupation of Jacksonville, Florida, but its main significance consisted in the unprecedented cross-cultural contact between Northern whites and Southern blacks living together and fighting, literally, for the same goal. This remarkable collaboration is recorded in post-war memoirs both by Higginson and by Susie King Taylor, a former slave who volunteered as a general aide for the 1st South Carolina.

In the summer of 1863, in the wake of a failed assault on Charleston, Gen. Quincy Gillmore replaced Gen. David Hunter as commander of the Department of the South and prepared for further operations against the iconic Confederate city, which was under the command of Gen. P. G. T. Beauregard. After taking Morris Island, near the Charleston Harbor, Gillmore then moved against the Confederate battery at Fort Wagner. On July 18, 1863, a major charge on the fort, led by the 54th Massachusetts Infantry, a black regiment under the command of Col. Robert Gould Shaw, was a disaster in military terms, but burned the image of African American heroism into the Northern imagination. Although Fort

Wagner and Fort Sumter capitulated in the autumn, Charleston would hold out against Union pressure until February 1865, when the fall of Columbia to William T. Sherman's marauding army put the writing on the wall. Throughout this period, the interaction of whites and blacks was one of the war's vital but largely unremarked themes.

In March 1865, anticipating the need for major post-war assistance for Southern blacks, the United States created the Bureau of Refugees, Freedmen, and Abandoned Lands, under the command of Maj. Gen. Oliver Otis Howard. The exceedingly difficult work of the Freedmen's Bureau, and its mixed record in providing education, legal advice, property assistance, and material goods, are fully explained by W. E. B. Du Bois in *The Souls of Black Folk*. Suffice it here to say that, etiolated by insufficient funding, tepid executive support, and fierce Southern resistance, the Bureau had run its course by 1872—leaving Southern blacks effectively alone for the hard and bloody climb to follow. Many simply moved North, where the economic opportunities were greater and the racism less violent. Others, for a variety of reasons, stayed in the South and made a go of it, in spite of their second-class citizenship and physical and economic vulnerability. A few chose to write.

Representing the Civil War and its aftermath posed a challenge for any American writer, but more so for African American authors, whose efforts to record their experience faithfully ran into social and institutional resistance on all sides. Foremost among these was the widespread national desire for reconciliation, for *moving beyond* the conflict, and the concomitant desire of American publishers to print literature that declined to dwell on problems of race. Maintaining a focus on the racial dimensions of the war, and on the post-war struggles of African Americans, thus required of black writers careful strategies of representational parry-and-thrust; of subtle acquiescence to some, but not all, of the publishing industry's expectations; of rendering individual experience so as to affirm, or to seem to affirm, the national story.

Such experience, in the war and after, was incredibly varied, and the phrase "African American experience" means no more than to suggest a few tiles of the larger mosaic. Part of that collective experience, for better and worse, had to do with the representation of blacks by whites—since representation always plays a role in real-world social relations—and this section therefore includes several texts by non-African American writers. Taken together, the following selections should convey something of the sweeping range of feeling, action, and attitude with which black Americans responded to the Civil War, and to the complex fugue of possibility and peril that it inaugurated.

SUGGESTED READING

Blight, David W. *Frederick Douglass' Civil War: Keeping Faith in Jubilee*. Baton Rouge: Louisiana State University Press, 1989.

Cornish, Dudley T. *The Sable Arm: Negro Troops in the Union Army, 1861–1865*. New York: Norton, 1966.

Durden, Robert F. *The Gray and the Black: The Confederate Debate on Emancipation*. Baton Rouge: Louisiana State University Press, 1972, 2000.

Franklin, John Hope. *The Emancipation Proclamation*. New York: Anchor, 1965.

Glatthaar, Joseph T. *Forged in Battle: The Civil War Alliance of Black Soldiers and White Officers*. New York: Free Press; London: Collier Macmillan, 1990.

McPherson, James. *The Negro's Civil War: How American Blacks Felt and Acted During the War for the Union*. 1965. New York: Ballantine Books, 1991.

Rose, Willie Lee. *Rehearsal for Reconstruction: The Port Royal Experiment*. Indianapolis: Bobbs-Merrill, 1964.

Shaffer, Donald R. *After the Glory: The Struggles of Black Civil War Veterans*. Lawrence: University of Kansas Press, 2004.

Trudeau, Noah Andre. *Like Men of War: Black Troops in the Civil War, 1862-1865*. Boston: Little, Brown and Company, 1998.

Urwin, Gregory J. W., ed. *Black Flag Over Dixie: Racial Atrocities and Reprisals in the Civil War*. Carbondale: Southern Illinois University Press, 2004.

Westwood, Howard C. *Black Troops, White Commanders, and Freedmen During the Civil War*. Carbondale: Southern Illinois University Press, 1992.

Wise, Stephen R. *Gate of Hell: Campaign for Charleston Harbor, 1863*. Columbia: University of South Carolina Press, 1994.

George Moses Horton

from *Naked Genius* (1865)

THE SLAVE

What right divine has mortal man received,
    To domineer with uncontroll'd command?
What philosophic wight has thus believed
    That Heaven entailed on him the weaker band?

If Africa was fraught with weaker light,
    Whilst to the tribes of Europe more was given,
Does this impart to them a lawful right
    To counterfeit the golden rule of Heaven?

Did sovereign justice give to robbery birth,
    And bid the fools to theft their rights betray,
To spread the seeds of slavery o'er the earth,
    That you should hold them as your lawful prey?

Why did the Almighty God the land divide,
    And bid each nation to maintain her own,
Rolling between the deep, the wind and tide,
    With all their rage to make his order known?

The sad phylactory bound on rebel Cain,
    For killing Abel is in blood reveal'd,
For which the soldier falls among the slain,
    A victim on the sanguinary field.

Thus, in the cause of vile and sordid gain;
    To gratify their lust is all the plea;
Like Cain you've your consanguine brother slain,
    And robbed him of his birthright—Liberty.

Why do ye not the Ishmealites [sic] enslave,
    Or artful red man in his rude attire,
As well as with the Black man, split the wave,
    And to his progeny with rage aspire.

Because the brood-sow's left side pigs were black,
    Whose sable tincture was by nature struck,
Are you by justice bound to pull them back
    And leave the sandy colored pigs to suck?

Or can you deem that God does not intend
    His kingdom through creation to display,
The sacred right of nature to defend,
    And show to mortals who shall bear the sway?

Then suffer Heaven to vindicate the cause;
    The wrong abolish and the right restore;
To make a sacrifice of cruel laws,
    And slavish murmurs will be heard no more.

Susie King Taylor

Reminiscences of My Life in Camp

TO COLONEL T. W. HIGGINSON THESE PAGES ARE GRATEFULLY DEDICATED[1]

Preface

I have been asked many times by my friends, and also by members of the Grand Army of the Republic and Women's Relief Corps,[2] to write a book of my army life, during the war of 1861–65, with the regiment of the 1st South Carolina Colored Troops, later called 33d United States Colored Infantry.

At first I did not think I would, but as the years rolled on and my friends were still urging me to start with it, I wrote to Colonel C. T. Trowbridge[3] (who had command of this regiment), asking his opinion and advice on the matter. His answer to me was, "Go ahead! write it; that is just what I should do, were I in your place, and I will give you all the assistance you may need, whenever you require it." This inspired me very much.

In 1900 I received a letter from a gentleman, sent from the Executive Mansion at St. Paul, Minn., saying Colonel Trowbridge had told him I was about to write a book, and when it was published he wanted one of the first copies. This, coming from a total stranger, gave me more confidence, so I now present these reminiscences to you, hoping they may prove of some interest, and show how much service and good we can do to each other, and what sacrifices we can make for our liberty and rights, and that there were "loyal women," as well as men, in those days, who did not fear shell or shot, who cared for the sick and dying; women who camped and fared as the boys did, and who are still caring for the comrades in their declining years.

So, with the hope that the following pages will accomplish some good and instruction for its readers, I shall proceed with my narrative.

Susie King Taylor

Boston, 1902.

Introduction

Actual military life is rarely described by a woman, and this is especially true of a woman whose place was in the ranks, as the wife of a soldier and herself a regimental laundress. No such description has ever been given, I am sure, by one thus connected with a colored regiment; so that the nearly 200,000 black soldiers (178,975) of our Civil War have never before been delineated from the woman's point of view. All this gives peculiar interest to this little volume, relating wholly to the career of the very earliest of these regiments,—the one described by myself, from a wholly different point of view, in my volume "Army Life in a Black Regiment," long since translated into French by the Comtesse de Gasparin under the title "Vie Militaire dans un Regiment Noir."[4]

The writer of the present book was very exceptional among the colored laundresses, in that she could read and write and had taught children to do the same; and her whole life and career were most estimable, both during the war and in the later period during which she has lived in Boston and has made many friends. I may add that I did not see the book until the sheets were in print, and have left it wholly untouched, except as to a few errors in proper names. I commend the narrative to those who love the plain record of simple lives, led in stormy periods.

> Thomas Wentworth Higginson,
> *Former Colonel 1st S. C. Volunteers*
> (*afterwards 33d U. S. Colored Infantry*).

Cambridge, Mass.,
November 3, 1902.

Letter from Col. C. T. Trowbridge

St. Paul, Minn., April 7, 1902.

Mrs. Susan King Taylor:

Dear Madam,—The manuscript of the story of your army life reached me to-day. I have read it with much care and interest, and I most willingly and cordially indorse it as a truthful account of your unselfish devotion and service through more than three long years of war in which the 33d Regiment bore a conspicuous part in the great conflict for human liberty and the restoration of the Union. I most sincerely regret that through a technicality you are debarred from having your name placed on the roll of pensioners, as an Army Nurse; for among all the number of heroic women whom the government is now rewarding, I know of no one more deserving than yourself.

Yours in F. C.&L.,

> C. T. Trowbridge,
> Late Lt.-Col. 33d U. S. C. T.

· *Reminiscences*

I

A Brief Sketch of My Ancestors

My great-great-grandmother was 120 years old when she died. She had seven children, and five of her boys were in the Revolutionary War. She was from Virginia, and was half Indian. She was so old she had to be held in the sun to help restore or prolong her vitality.

My great-grandmother, one of her daughters, named Susanna, was married to Peter Simons, and was one hundred years old when she died, from a stroke of paralysis in Savannah. She was the mother of twenty-four children, twenty-three being girls. She was one of the noted midwives of her day. In 1820 my grandmother was born, and named after her grandmother, Dolly, and in 1833 she married Fortune Lambert Reed. Two children blessed their union, James and Hagar Ann. James died at the age of twelve years.

My mother was born in 1834. She married Raymond Baker in 1847. Nine children were born to them, three dying in infancy. I was the first born. I was born on the Grest Farm (which was on an island known as Isle of Wight), Liberty County, about thirty-five miles from Savannah, Ga., on August 6, 1848, my mother being waitress for the Grest family. I have often been told by mother of the care Mrs. Grest took of me. She was very fond of me, and I remember when my brother and I were small children, and Mr. Grest would go away on business, Mrs. Grest would place us at the foot of her bed to sleep and keep her company. Sometimes he would return home earlier than he had expected to; then she would put us on the floor.

When I was about seven years old, Mr. Grest allowed my grandmother to take my brother and me to live with her in Savannah. There were no railroad connections in those days between this place and Savannah; all travel was by stagecoaches. I remember, as if it were yesterday, the coach which ran in from Savannah, with its driver, whose beard nearly reached his knees. His name was Shakespeare, and often I would go to the stable where he kept his horses, on Barnard Street in front of the old Arsenal, just to look at his wonderful beard.

My grandmother went every three months to see my mother. She would hire a wagon to carry bacon, tobacco, flour, molasses, and sugar. These she would trade with people in the neighboring places, for eggs, chickens, or cash, if they had it. These, in turn, she carried back to the city market, where she had a customer who sold them for her. The profit from these, together with laundry work and care of some bachelors' rooms, made a good living for her.

The hardest blow to her was the failure of the Freedmen's Savings Bank in Savannah, for in that bank she had placed her savings, about three thousand dollars, the result of her hard labor and self-denial before the war, and which, by dint of shrewdness and care, she kept together all through the war. She felt it more keenly, coming as it did in her old age, when her life was too far spent to begin anew; but she took a practical view of the matter, for she said, "I will leave it all in God's hand. If the Yankees did take all our money, they freed my race; God will take care of us."

In 1888 she wrote me here (Boston), asking me to visit her, as she was getting very feeble and wanted to see me once before she passed away. I made up my mind to leave at once, but about the time I planned to go, in March, a fearful blizzard swept our country, and travel was at a standstill for nearly two weeks; but March 15 I left on the first through steamer from New York, en route for the South, where I again saw my grandmother, and we felt thankful that we were spared to meet each other once more. This was the last time I saw her, for in May, 1889, she died.

II

My Childhood

I was born under the slave law in Georgia, in 1848, and was brought up by my grandmother in Savannah. There were three of us with her, my younger sister and brother. My brother and I being the two eldest, we were sent to a friend of my grandmother, Mrs. Woodhouse, a widow, to learn to read and write. She was a free woman and lived on Bay Lane, between Habersham and Price streets, about half a mile from my house. We went every day about nine o'clock, with our books wrapped in paper to prevent the police or white persons from seeing them. We went in, one at a time, through the gate, into the yard to the L kitchen, which was the schoolroom. She had twenty-five or thirty children whom she taught, assisted by her daughter, Mary Jane. The neighbors would see us going in sometimes, but they supposed we were there learning trades, as it was the custom to give children a trade of some kind. After school we left the same way we entered, one by one, when we would go to a square, about a block from the school, and wait for each other. We would gather laurel leaves and pop them on our hands, on our way home. I remained at her school for two years or more, when I was sent to a Mrs. Mary Beasley, where I continued until May, 1860, when she told my grandmother she had taught me all she knew, and grandmother had better get some one else who could teach me more, so I stopped my studies for a while.

I had a white playmate about this time, named Katie O'Connor, who lived on the next corner of the street from my house, and who attended a convent. One day she told me, if I would promise not to tell her father, she would give me some lessons. On my promise not to do so, and getting her mother's consent, she gave me lessons about four months, every evening. At the end of this time she was put into the convent permanently, and I have never seen her since.

A month after this, James Blouis, our landlord's son, was attending the High School, and was very fond of grandmother, so she asked him to give me a few lessons, which he did until the middle of 1861, when the Savannah Volunteer Guards, to which he and his brother belonged, were ordered to the front under General Barton.[5] In the first battle of Manassas, his brother Eugene was killed, and James deserted over to the Union side, and at the close of the war went to Washington, D. C., where he has since resided.

I often wrote passes for my grandmother, for all colored persons, free or slaves, were compelled to have a pass; free colored people having a guardian in place of a master. These passes were good until 10 or 10.30 P. M. for one night or every night for one month. The pass read as follows:—

SAVANNAH, GA., March 1st, 1860.

Pass the bearer—from 9 to 10.30. P. M.

Valentine Grest

Every person had to have this pass, for at nine o'clock each night a bell was rung, and any colored persons found on the street after this hour were arrested by the watchman, and put in the guard-house until next morning, when their owners would pay their fines and release them. I knew a number of persons who went out at any time at night and were never arrested, as the watchman knew them so well he never stopped them, and seldom asked to see their passes, only stopping them long enough, sometimes, to say "Howdy," and then telling them to go along.

About this time I had been reading so much about the "Yankees" I was very anxious to see them. The whites would tell their colored people not to go to the Yankees, for they would harness them to carts and make them pull the carts around, in place of horses. I asked grandmother, one day, if this was true. She replied, "Certainly not!" that the white people did not want slaves to go over to the Yankees, and told them these things to frighten them. "Don't you see those signs pasted about the streets? one reading, 'I am a rattlesnake; if you touch me I will strike!' Another reads, 'I am a wild-cat! Beware,' etc. These are warnings to the North; so don't mind what the white people say." I wanted to see these wonderful "Yankees" so much, as I heard my parents say the Yankee was going to set all the slaves free. Oh, how those people prayed for freedom! I remember, one night, my grandmother went out into the suburbs of the city to a church meeting, and they were fervently singing this old hymn,—

"Yes, we all shall be free,
Yes, we all shall be free,
Yes, we all shall be free,
When the Lord shall appear,"

—when the police came in and arrested all who were there, saying they were planning freedom, and sang "the Lord," in place of "Yankee," to blind any one who might be listening. Grandmother never forgot that night, although she did not stay in the guard-house, as she sent to her guardian, who came at once for her; but this was the last meeting she ever attended out of the city proper.

On April 1, 1862, about the time the Union soldiers were firing on Fort Pulaski, I was sent out into the country to my mother. I remember what a roar and din the guns made. They jarred the earth for miles. The fort was at last taken by them. Two days after the taking of Fort Pulaski, my uncle took his family of seven and myself to St. Catherine Island. We landed under the protection of the Union fleet, and remained there two weeks, when about thirty of us were taken aboard the gunboat P—, to be transferred to St. Simon's Island; and at last, to my unbounded joy, I saw the "Yankee."

After we were all settled aboard and started on our journey, Captain Whitmore, commanding the boat, asked me where I was from. I told him Savannah, Ga. He asked if I could read; I said, "Yes!" "Can you write?" he next asked. "Yes, I can do that also," I replied, and as if he had some doubts of my answers he handed me a book and a pencil and told me to write my name and where I was from. I did this; when he wanted to know if I could sew. On hearing I could, he asked me to hem some napkins for him. He was surprised at my accomplishments (for they were such in those days), for he said he did not know there were any negroes in the South able to read or write. He said, "You seem to be so different from the other colored people who came from the same place you did." "No!" I replied, "the only difference is, they were reared in the country and I in the city, as was a man from Darien, Ga., named Edward King." That seemed to satisfy him, and we had no further conversation that day on the subject.

In the afternoon the captain spied a boat in the distance, and as it drew nearer he noticed it had a white flag hoisted, but before it had reached the Putumoka he ordered all passengers between decks, so we could not be seen, for he thought they might be spies. The boat finally drew alongside of our boat, and had Mr. Edward Donegall on board, who wanted his two servants, Nick and Judith. He wanted these, as they were his own children. Our captain told him he knew nothing of them, which was true, for at the time they were on St. Simon's, and not, as their father supposed, on our boat. After the boat left, we were allowed to come up on deck again.

III

On St. Simon's Island

1862

Next morning we arrived at St. Simon's, and the captain told Commodore Goldsborough[6] about this affair, and his reply was, "Captain Whitmore, you should not have allowed them to return; you should have kept them." After I had been on St. Simon's about three days, Commodore Goldsborough heard of me, and came to Gaston Bluff to see me. I found him very cordial. He said Captain Whitmore had spoken to him of me, and that he was pleased to hear of my being so capable, etc., and wished me to take charge of a school for the children on the island. I told him I would gladly do so, if I could have some books. He said I should have them, and in a week or two I received two large boxes of books and testaments from the North. I had about forty children to teach, beside a number of adults who came to me nights, all of them so eager to learn to read, to read above anything else. Chaplain French,[7] of Boston, would come to the school, sometimes, and lecture to the pupils on Boston and the North.

About the first of June we were told that there was going to be a settlement of the war. Those who were on the Union side would remain free, and those in bondage were to work three days for their masters and three for themselves. It was a gloomy time for us all, and we were to be sent to Liberia.[8] Chaplain French asked me would I rather go back to Savannah or go to Liberia. I told him the latter place by all means. We did not know when this would be, but we were prepared in case this settlement should be reached. However, the Confederates would not agree to the arrangement, or else it was one of the many rumors flying about at the time, as we heard nothing further of the matter. There were a number of settlements on this island of St. Simon's, just like little villages, and we would go from one to the other on business, to call, or only for a walk.

One Sunday, two men, Adam Miller and Daniel Spaulding, were chased by some rebels as they were coming from Hope Place (which was between the Beach and Gaston Bluff), but the latter were unable to catch them. When they reached the Beach and told this, all the men on the place, about ninety, armed themselves, and next day (Monday), with Charles O'Neal as their leader, skirmished the island for the "rebs." In a short while they discovered them in the woods, hidden behind a large log, among the thick underbrush. Charles O'Neal was the first to see them, and he was killed; also John Brown, and their bodies were never found. Charles O'Neal was an uncle of Edward King, who later was my husband and a sergeant in Co. E., U. S. I. Another man was shot, but not found for three days. On Tuesday, the second day, Captain Trowbridge and some soldiers landed, and assisted the skirmishers. Word having been sent by the mail-boat Uncas to Hilton Head, later in the day Commodore Goldsborough, who was in command of the naval station, landed about three hundred marines, and joined the others to oust the rebels. On Wednesday, John Baker, the man shot on Monday, was found in a terrible condition by Henry Batchlott, who carried him to the Beach, where he was attended by the surgeon. He told us how, after being shot, he lay quiet for a day. On the second day he managed to reach some wild grapes growing near him. These he ate, to satisfy his hunger and intense thirst, then he crawled slowly, every movement causing agony, until he got to the side of the road. He lived only three months after they found him.

On the second day of the skirmish the troops captured a boat which they knew the Confederates had used to land in, and having this in their possession, the "rebs" could not return; so pickets were stationed all around the island. There was an old man, Henry Capers, who had been left on one of the places by his old master, Mr. Hazzard, as he was too old to carry away. These rebels went to his house in the night, and he hid them up in the loft. On Tuesday all hands went to this man's house with a determination to burn it down, but Henry Batchlott pleaded with the men to spare it. The rebels were in hiding, still, waiting a chance to get off the island. They searched his house, but neglected to go up into the loft, and in so doing missed the rebels concealed there. Late in the night Henry Capers gave them his boat to escape in, and they got off all right. This old man was allowed by the men in charge of the island to cut grass for his horse, and to have a boat to carry this grass to his home, and so they were not detected, our men thinking it was Capers using the boat. After Commodore Goldsborough left the island, Commodore Judon sent the old man over to the mainland and would not allow him to remain on the island.

There were about six hundred men, women, and children on St. Simon's, the women and children being in the majority, and we were afraid to go very far from our own quarters in the daytime, and at night even to go out of the house for a long time, although the men were on the watch all the time; for there were not any soldiers on the island, only the marines who were on the gunboats along the coast. The rebels, knowing this, could steal by them under cover of the night, and getting on the island would capture any persons venturing out alone and carry them to the mainland. Several of the men disappeared, and as they were never heard from we came to the conclusion they had been carried off in this way.

The latter part of August, 1862, Captain C. T. Trowbridge, with his brother John and Lieutenant Walker,[9] came to St. Simon's Island from Hilton Head, by order of General Hunter, to get all the men possible to finish filling his regiment which he had organized in March, 1862. He had heard of the skirmish on this island, and was very much pleased at the bravery shown by these men. He found me at Gaston Bluff teaching my little school, and was much interested in it. When I knew him better I found him to be a thorough gentleman and a staunch friend to my race.

Captain Trowbridge remained with us until October, when the order was received to evacuate, and so we boarded the Ben-De-Ford, a transport, for Beaufort, S. C. When we arrived in Beaufort, Captain Trowbridge and the men he had enlisted went to camp at Old Fort, which they named "Camp Saxton." I was enrolled as laundress.

The first suits worn by the boys were red coats and pants, which they disliked very much, for, they said, "The rebels see us, miles away."

The first colored troops did not receive any pay for eighteen months, and the men had to depend wholly on what they received from the commissary, established by General Saxton. A great many of these men had large families, and as they had no money to give them, their wives were obliged to support themselves and children by washing for the officers of the gunboats and the soldiers, and making cakes and pies which they sold to the boys in camp. Finally, in 1863, the government decided to give them half pay, but the men would not accept this. They wanted "full pay" or nothing. They preferred rather to give their services to the state, which they did until 1864, when the government granted them full pay, with all the back pay due.

I remember hearing Captain Heasley telling his company, one day, "Boys, stand up for your full pay! I am with you, and so are all the officers." This captain was from Pennsylvania, and was a very good man; all the men liked him. N. G. Parker, our first lieutenant, was from Massachusetts. H. A. Beach was from New York. He was very delicate, and had to resign in 1864 on account of ill health.[10]

I had a number of relatives in this regiment,—several uncles, some cousins, and a husband in Company E, and a number of cousins in other companies. Major Strong, of this regiment, started home on a furlough, but the vessel he was aboard was lost, and he never reached his home. He was one of the best officers we had. After his death, Captain C. T. Trowbridge was promoted major, August, 1863, and filled Major Strong's place until December, 1864, when he was promoted lieutenant-colonel, which he remained until he was mustered out, February 6, 1866.

In February, 1863, several cases of varioloid [small-pox] broke out among the boys, which caused some anxiety in camp. Edward Davis, of Company E (the company I was with), had it very badly. He was put into a tent apart from the rest of the men, and only the doctor and camp steward, James Cummings, were allowed to see or attend him; but I went to see this man every day and nursed him. The last thing at night, I always went in to see that he was comfortable, but in spite of the good care and attention he received, he succumbed to the disease.

I was not in the least afraid of the small-pox. I had been vaccinated, and I drank sassafras tea constantly, which kept my blood purged and prevented me from contracting this dread scourge, and no one need fear getting it if they will only keep their blood in good condition with this sassafras tea, and take it before going where the patient is.

IV

Camp Saxton—Proclamation and Barbecue

1863

On the first of January, 1863, we held services for the purpose of listening to the reading of President Lincoln's proclamation by Dr. W. H. Brisbane,[11] and the presentation of two beautiful stands of colors, one from a lady in Connecticut, and the other from Rev. Mr. Cheever.[12] The presentation speech was made by Chaplain French. It was a glorious day for us all, and we enjoyed every minute of it, and as a fitting close and the crowning event of this occasion we had a grand barbecue. A number of oxen were roasted whole, and we had a fine feast. Although not served as tastily or correctly as it would have been at home, yet it was enjoyed with keen appetites and relish. The soldiers had a good time. They sang or shouted "Hurrah!" all through the camp, and seemed overflowing with fun and frolic until taps were sounded, when many, no doubt, dreamt of this memorable day.

I had rather an amusing experience; that is, it seems amusing now, as I look back, but at the time it occurred it was a most serious one to me. When our regiment left Beaufort for Seabrooke, I left some of my things with a neighbor who lived outside of the camp. After I had been at Seabrooke about a week, I decided to return to Camp Saxton and get them. So one morning, with Mary Shaw, a friend who was in the company at that time, I started off. There was no way for us to get to Beaufort other than to walk, except we rode on the commissary wagon. This we did, and reached Beaufort about one o'clock. We then had more than two miles to walk before reaching our old camp, and expected to be able to accomplish this and return in time to meet the wagon again by three o'clock that afternoon, and so be taken back. We failed to do this, however, for when we got to Beaufort the wagon was gone. We did not know what to do. I did not wish to remain overnight, neither did my friend, although we might easily have stayed, as both had relatives in the town.

It was in the springtime, and the days were long, and as the sun looked so bright, we concluded to walk back, thinking we should reach camp before dark. So off we started on our ten-mile tramp. We had not gone many miles, however, before we were all tired out and began to regret our undertaking. The sun was getting low, and we grew more frightened, fearful of meeting some animal or of treading on a snake on our way. We did not meet a person, and we were frightened almost to death. Our feet were so sore we could hardly walk. Finally we took off our shoes and tried walking in our stocking feet, but this made them worse. We had gone about six miles when night overtook us. There we were, nothing around us but dense woods, and as there was no house or any place to stop at, there was nothing for us to do but continue on. We were afraid to speak to each other.

Meantime at the camp, seeing no signs of us by dusk, they concluded we had decided to remain over until next day, and so had no idea of our plight. Imagine their surprise when we reached camp about eleven P. M. The guard challenged us, "Who comes there?" My answer was, "A friend without a countersign." He approached and saw who it was, reported, and we were admitted into the lines. They had the joke on us that night, and for a long time after would tease us; and sometimes some of the men who were on guard that night would call us deserters. They used to laugh at us, but we joined with them too, especially when we would tell them our experience on our way to camp. I did not undertake that trip again, as there was no way of getting in or out except one took the provision wagon, and there was not much dependence to be put in that returning to camp. Perhaps the driver would say one hour and he might be there earlier or later. Of course it was not his fault, as it depended when the order was filled at the Commissary Department; therefore I did not go any more until the regiment was ordered to our new camp, which was named after our hero, Colonel Shaw, who at that time was at Beaufort with his regiment, the 54th Massachusetts.[13]

I taught a great many of the comrades in Company E to read and write, when they were off duty. Nearly all were anxious to learn. My husband taught some also when it was convenient for him. I was very happy to know my efforts were successful in camp, and also felt grateful for the appreciation of my services. I gave my services willingly for four years and three months without receiving a dollar. I was glad, however, to be allowed to go with the regiment, to care for the sick and afflicted comrades.

V

Military Expeditions, and Life in Camp

In the latter part of 1862 the regiment made an expedition into Darien, Georgia, and up the Ridge, and on January 23, 1863, another up St. Mary's River, capturing a number of stores for the government; then on to Fernandina, Florida. They were gone ten or twelve days, at the end of which time they returned to camp.

March 10, 1863, we were ordered to Jacksonville, Florida. Leaving Camp Saxton between four and five o'clock, we arrived at Jacksonville about eight o'clock next morning, accompanied by three or four gunboats. When the rebels saw these boats, they ran out of the city, leaving the women behind, and we found out afterwards that they thought we had a much larger fleet than we really had. Our regiment was kept out of sight until we made fast at the wharf where it landed, and while the gunboats were shelling up the river and as far inland as possible, the regiment landed and marched up the street, where they spied the rebels who had fled from the city. They were hiding behind a house about a mile or so away, their faces blackened to disguise themselves as negroes, and our boys, as they advanced toward them, halted a second, saying, "They are black men! Let them come to us, or we will make them know who we are." With this, the firing was opened and several of our men were wounded and killed. The rebels had a number wounded and killed. It was through this way the discovery was made that they were white men. Our men drove them some distance in retreat and then threw out their pickets.

While the fighting was on, a friend, Lizzie Lancaster, and I stopped at several of the rebel homes, and after talking with some of the women and children we asked them if they had any food. They claimed to have only some hard-tack, and evidently did not care to give us anything to eat, but this was not surprising. They were bitterly against our people and had no mercy or sympathy for us.

The second day, our boys were reinforced by a regiment of white soldiers, a Maine regiment, and by cavalry, and had quite a fight. On the third day, Edward Herron, who was a fine gunner on the steamer John Adams, came on shore, bringing a small cannon, which the men pulled along for more than five miles. This cannon was the only piece for shelling. On coming upon the enemy, all secured their places, and they had a lively fight, which lasted several hours, and our boys were nearly captured by the Confederates; but the Union boys carried out all their plans that day, and succeeded in driving the enemy back. After this skirmish, every afternoon between four and five o'clock the Confederate General Finegan[14] would send a flag of truce to Colonel Higginson, warning him to send all women and children out of the city, and threatening to bombard it if this was not done. Our colonel allowed all to go who wished, at first, but as General Finegan grew more hostile and kept sending these communications for nearly a week, Colonel Higginson thought it not best or necessary to send any more out of the city, and so informed General Finegan. This angered the general, for that night the rebels shelled directly toward Colonel Higginson's headquarters. The shelling was so heavy that the colonel told my captain to have me taken up into the town to a hotel, which was used as a hospital. As my quarters were just in the rear of the colonel's, he was compelled to leave his also before the night was over. I expected every moment to be killed by a shell, but on arriving at the hospital I knew I was safe, for the shells could not reach us there. It was plainly to be seen now, the ruse of the flag of truce coming so often to us. The bearer was evidently a spy getting the location of the headquarters, etc., for the shells were sent too accurately to be at random.

Next morning Colonel Higginson took the cavalry and a regiment on another tramp after the rebels. They were gone several days and had the hardest fight they had had, for they wanted to go as far as a station which was some distance from the city. The gunboats were of little assistance to them, yet notwithstanding this drawback our boys returned with only a few killed and wounded, and after this we were not troubled with General Finegan.

We remained here a few weeks longer, when, about April first, the regiment was ordered back to Camp Saxton, where it stayed a week, when the order came to go to Port

Royal Ferry on picket duty. It was a gay day for the boys. By seven o'clock all tents were down, and each company, with a commissary wagon, marched up the shell road, which is a beautiful avenue ten or twelve miles out of Beaufort. We arrived at Seabrooke at about four o'clock, where our tents were pitched and the men put on duty. We were here a few weeks, when Company E was ordered to Barnwell plantation[15] for picket duty.

Some mornings I would go along the picket line, and I could see the rebels on the opposite side of the river. Sometimes as they were changing pickets they would call over to our men and ask for something to eat, or for tobacco, and our men would tell them to come over. Sometimes one or two would desert to us, saying, they "had no negroes to fight for." Others would shoot across at our picket, but as the river was so wide there was never any damage done, and the Confederates never attempted to shell us while we were there.

I learned to handle a musket very well while in the regiment, and could shoot straight and often hit the target. I assisted in cleaning the guns and used to fire them off, to see if the cartridges were dry, before cleaning and reloading, each day. I thought this great fun. I was also able to take a gun all apart, and put it together again.

Between Barnwell and the mainland was Hall Island. I went over there several times with Sergeant King and other comrades. One night there was a stir in camp when it was found that the rebels were trying to cross, and next morning Lieutenant Parker told me he thought they were on Hall Island; so after that I did not go over again.

While planning for the expedition up the Edisto River, Colonel Higginson was a whole night in the water, trying to locate the rebels and where their picket lines were situated. About July the boys went up the Edisto to destroy a bridge on the Charleston and Savannah road. This expedition was twenty or more miles into the mainland. Colonel Higginson was wounded in this fight and the regiment nearly captured. The steamboat John Adams always assisted us, carrying soldiers, provisions, etc. She carried several guns and a good gunner, Edward Herron. Henry Batchlott, a relative of mine, was a steward on this boat. There were two smaller boats, Governor Milton and the Enoch Dean, in the fleet, as these could go up the river better than the larger ones could. I often went aboard the John Adams. It went with us into Jacksonville, to Cole and Folly Island, and Gunner Herron was always ready to send a shell at the enemy.

One night, Companies K and E, on their way to Pocotaligo to destroy a battery that was situated down the river, captured several prisoners. The rebels nearly captured Sergeant King, who, as he sprang and caught a "reb," fell over an embankment. In falling he did not release his hold on his prisoner. Although his hip was severely injured, he held fast until some of his comrades came to his aid and pulled them up. These expeditions were very dangerous. Sometimes the men had to go five or ten miles during the night over on the rebel side and capture or destroy whatever they could find.

While at Camp Shaw, there was a deserter who came into Beaufort. He was allowed his freedom about the city and was not molested. He remained about the place a little while and returned to the rebels again. On his return to Beaufort a second time, he was held as a spy, tried, and sentenced to death, for he was a traitor. The day he was shot, he was placed on a hearse with his coffin inside, a guard was placed either side of the hearse, and he was driven through the town. All the soldiers and people in town were out, as this was to be a warning to the soldiers. Our regiment was in line on dress parade. They drove with him to the rear of our camp, where he was shot. I shall never forget this scene.

While at Camp Shaw, Chaplain Fowler, Robert Defoe, and several of our boys were captured while tapping some telegraph wires. Robert Defoe was confined in the jail at Walterborough, S. C., for about twenty months. When Sherman's army reached Pocotaligo he made his escape and joined his company (Company G). He had not been paid, as he had refused the reduced pay offered by the government. Before we got to camp, where the pay-rolls could be made out, he sickened and died of small-pox, and was buried at Savannah, never having been paid one cent for nearly three years of service. He left no heirs and his account was never settled.

In winter, when it was very cold, I would take a mess-pan, put a little earth in the bottom, and go to the cook-shed and fill it nearly full of coals, carry it back to my tent and put another pan over it; so when the provost guard went through camp after taps, they would not see the light, as it was against the rules to have a light after taps. In this way I was heated and kept very warm.

A mess-pan is made of sheet iron, something like our roasting pans, only they are nearly as large round as a peck measure, but not so deep. We had fresh beef once in awhile, and we would have soup, and the vegetables they put in this soup were dried and pressed. They looked like hops. Salt beef was our stand-by. Sometimes the men would have what we called slap-jacks. This was flour, made into bread and spread thin on the bottom of the mess-pan to cook. Each man had one of them, with a pint of tea, for his supper, or a pint of tea and five or six hard-tack. I often got my own meals, and would fix some dishes for the non-commissioned officers also.

Mrs. Chamberlain, our quartermaster's wife, was with us here. She was a beautiful woman; I can see her pleasant face before me now, as she, with Captain Trowbridge, would sit and converse with me in my tent two or three hours at a time. She was also with me on Cole Island, and I think we were the only women with the regiment while there. I remember well how, when she first came into camp, Captain Trowbridge brought her to my tent and introduced her to me. I found her then, as she remained ever after, a lovely person, and I always admired her cordial and friendly ways.

Our boys would say to me sometimes "Mrs. King, why is it you are so kind to us? you treat us just as you do the boys in your own company." I replied, "Well, you know, all the boys in other companies are the same to me as those in my Company E; you are all doing the same duty, and I will do just the same for you." "Yes," they would say, "we know that, because you were the first woman we saw when we came into camp, and you took an interest in us boys ever since we have been here, and we are very grateful for all you do for us."

When at Camp Shaw, I visited the hospital in Beaufort, where I met Clara Barton.[16] There were a number of sick and wounded soldiers there, and I went often to see the comrades. Miss Barton was always very cordial toward me, and I honored her for her devotion and care of those men.

There was a man, John Johnson, who with his family was taken by our regiment at Edisto. This man afterwards worked in the hospital and was well known to Miss Barton. I have been told since that when she went South, in 1883, she tried to look this man up, but learned he was dead. His son is living in Edisto, Rev. J. J. Johnson, and is the president of an industrial school on that island and a very intelligent man. He was a small child when his father and family were captured by our regiment at Edisto.

VI

On Morris and Other Islands

Fort Wagner being only a mile from our camp, I went there two or three times a week, and would go up on the ramparts to watch the gunners send their shells into Charleston (which they did every fifteen minutes), and had a full view of the city from that point. Outside of the fort were many skulls lying about; I have often moved them one side [sic] out of the path. The comrades and I would have quite a debate as to which side the men fought on. Some thought they were the skulls of our boys; others thought they were the enemy's; but as there was no definite way to know, it was never decided which could lay claim to them. They were a gruesome sight, those fleshless heads and grinning jaws, but by this time I had become accustomed to worse things and did not feel as I might have earlier in my camp life.

It seems strange how our aversion to seeing suffering is overcome in war,—how we are able to see the most sickening sights, such as men with their limbs blown off and mangled by the deadly shells, without a shudder; and instead of turning away, how we hurry to assist in alleviating their pain, bind up their wounds, and press the cool water to their parched lips, with feelings only of sympathy and pity.

About the first of June, 1864, the regiment was ordered to Folly Island, staying there until the latter part of the month, when it was ordered to Morris Island.[17] We landed on Morris Island between June and July, 1864. This island was a narrow strip of sandy soil, nothing growing on it but a few bushes and shrubs. The camp was one mile from the boat landing, called Pawnell Landing, and the landing one mile from Fort Wagner.

Colonel Higginson had left us in May of this year, on account of wounds received at Edisto. All the men were sorry to lose him. They did not want him to go, they loved him so. He was kind and devoted to his men, thoughtful for their comfort, and we missed his genial presence from the camp.

The regiment under Colonel Trowbridge did garrison duty, but they had troublesome times from Fort Gregg, on James Island,[18] for the rebels would throw a shell over on our island every now and then. Finally orders were received for the boys to prepare to take Fort Gregg, each man to take 150 rounds of cartridges, canteens of water, hard-tack, and salt beef. This order was sent three days prior to starting, to allow them to be in readiness. I helped as many as I could to pack haversacks and cartridge boxes.

The fourth day, about five o'clock in the afternoon, the call was sounded, and I heard the first sergeant say, "Fall in, boys, fall in," and they were not long obeying the command. Each company marched out of its street, in front of their colonel's headquarters, where they rested for half an hour, as it was not dark enough, and they did not want the enemy to have a chance to spy their movements. At the end of this time the line was formed with the 103d New York (white) in the rear, and off they started, eager to get to work. It was quite dark by the time they reached Pawnell Landing. I have never forgotten the good-bys of that day, as they left camp. Colonel Trowbridge said to me as he left, "Good-by, Mrs. King, take care of yourself if you don't see us again." I went with them as far as the landing, and watched them until they got out of sight, and then I returned to the camp. There was no one at camp but those left on picket and a few disabled soldiers, and one woman, a friend of mine, Mary Shaw, and it was lonesome and sad, now that the boys were gone, some never to return.

Mary Shaw shared my tent that night, and we went to bed, but not to sleep, for the fleas nearly ate us alive. We caught a few, but it did seem, now that the men were gone, that every flea in camp had located my tent, and caused us to vacate. Sleep being out of the question, we sat up the remainder of the night.

About four o'clock, July 2, the charge was made. The firing could be plainly heard in camp. I hastened down to the landing and remained there until eight o'clock that morning. When the wounded arrived, or rather began to arrive, the first one brought in was Samuel Anderson of our company. He was badly wounded. Then others of our boys, some with their legs off, arm gone, foot off, and wounds of all kinds imaginable. They had to wade through creeks and marshes, as they were discovered by the enemy and shelled very badly. A number of the men were lost, some got fastened in the mud and had to cut off the legs of their pants, to free themselves. The 103d New York suffered the most, as their men were very badly wounded.

My work now began. I gave my assistance to try to alleviate their sufferings. I asked the doctor at the hospital what I could get for them to eat. They wanted soup, but that I could not get; but I had a few cans of condensed milk and some turtle eggs, so I thought I would try to make some custard. I had doubts as to my success, for cooking with turtle eggs was something new to me, but the adage has it, "Nothing ventured, nothing done," so I made a venture and the result was a very delicious custard. This I carried to the men, who enjoyed it very much. My services were given at all times for the comfort of these men. I was on hand to assist whenever needed. I was enrolled as company laundress, but I did very little of it, because I was always busy doing other things through camp, and was employed all the time doing something for the officers and comrades.

After this fight, the regiment did not return to the camp for one month. They were ordered to Cole Island in September, where they remained until October. About November 1, 1864, six companies were detailed to go to Gregg Landing, Port Royal Ferry, and the rebels in some way found out some of our forces had been removed and gave our boys in camp a hard time of it, for several nights. In fact, one night it was thought the boys would have to retreat. The colonel told me to go down to the landing, and if they were obliged to retreat, I could go aboard one of our gunboats. One of the gunboats got in the rear, and began to shell General Beauregard's force, which helped our boys retain their possession.

About November 15, I received a letter from Sergeant King, saying the boys were still lying three miles from Gregg Landing and had not had a fight yet; that the rebels were waiting on them and they on the rebels, and each were holding their own; also that General Sherman had taken Fort McAllister, eight miles from Savannah.[19] After receiving this letter I wanted to get to Beaufort, so I could be near to them and so be able to get news from my husband. November 23 I got a pass for Beaufort. I arrived at Hilton Head about three o'clock next day, but there had been a battle, and a steamer arrived with a number of wounded men; so I could not get a transfer to Beaufort. The doctor wished me to remain over until Monday. I did not want to stay. I was anxious to get off, as I knew no one at Hilton Head.

I must mention a pet pig we had on Cole Island. Colonel Trowbridge brought into camp, one day, a poor, thin little pig, which a German soldier brought back with him on his return from a furlough. His regiment, the 74th Pennsylvania, was just embarking for the North, where it was ordered to join the 10th corps, and he could not take the pig back with him, so he gave it to our colonel. That pig grew to be the pet of the camp, and was the special care of the drummer boys, who taught him many tricks; and so well did they train him that every day at practice and dress parade, his pigship would march out with them, keeping perfect time with their music. The drummers would often disturb the devotions by riding this pig into the midst of evening praise meeting, and many were the complaints made to the colonel, but he was always very lenient towards the boys, for he knew they only did this for mischief. I shall never forget the fun we had in camp with "Piggie."

VII

Cast Away

There was a yacht that carried passengers from Hilton Head to Beaufort. There were also five small boats which carried people over. The only people here, beside the soldiers, were Mrs. Lizzie Brown, who came over on a permit to see her husband, who was at this place, and was very ill (he died while she was there), Corporal Walker's wife, with her two years old child, and Mrs. Seabrooke. As soon as we could get the yacht, these persons I have mentioned, together with a comrade just discharged, an officer's boy, and myself, took passage on it for Beaufort. It was nearly dark before we had gone any distance, and about eight o'clock we were cast away and were only saved through the mercy of God. I remember going down twice. As I rose the second time, I caught hold of the sail and managed to hold fast. Mrs. Walker held on to her child with one hand, while with the other she managed to hold fast to some part of the boat, and we drifted and shouted as loud as we could, trying to attract the attention of some of the government boats which were going up and down the river. But it was in vain, we could not make ourselves heard, and just when we gave up all hope, and in the last moment (as we thought) gave one more despairing cry, we were heard at Ladies' Island. Two boats were put off and a search was made, to locate our distressed boat. They found us at last, nearly dead from exposure. In fact, the poor little baby was dead, although her mother still held her by her clothing, with her teeth. The soldier was drowned, having been caught under the sail and pinned down. The rest of us were saved. I had to be carried bodily, as I was thoroughly exhausted. We were given the best attention that we could get at this place where we were picked up. The men who saved us were surprised when they found me among the passengers, as one of them, William Geary, of Darien, Georgia, was a friend of my husband. His mother lived about two miles from where we were picked up, and she told me she had heard cries for a long time that night, and was very uneasy about it. Finally, she said to her son, "I think some poor souls are cast away." "I don't think so, mother," he replied; "I saw some people going down the river to-day. You know this is Christmas, and they are having a good time." But she still persisted that these were cries of distress, and not of joy, and begged him to go out and see. So to satisfy her, he went outside and listened, and then he heard them also, and hastened to get the boats off to find us. We were capsized about 8.15 P. M. and it was near midnight when they found us. Next day, they kept a sharp lookout on the beach for anything that might be washed in from the yacht, and got a trunk and several other things. Had the tide been going out, we should have been carried to sea and lost.

I was very ill and under the doctor's care for some time, in Beaufort. The doctor said I ought to have been rolled, as I had swallowed so much water. In January, 1865, I went back to Cole Island, where I could be attended by my doctor, Dr. Miner, who did all in his power to alleviate my suffering, for I was swollen very much. This he reduced and I recovered, but had a severe cough for a long time afterward.

VIII

A Flag of Truce

In October, 1864, six companies of the regiment were ordered to Gregg Landing, S. C. Captain L. W. Metcalf, of Co. G, was appointed on General Saxton's staff as provost captain, Lieutenant James B. West acting as assistant general. As in some way our mail had been sent over to the Confederate side and their mail to us, Captain Metcalf and Lieutenant West were detailed to exchange these letters under a flag of truce. So, with an escort of six men of the companies at Port Royal Ferry, the flag was unfurled and the message shouted across the river to the Confederates. Captain Metcalf asked them to come over to our side under the protection of our flag of truce. This the Confederates refused to do, having for their excuse that their boat was too far up the river and so they had no way to cross the river to us. They asked Metcalf to cross to them. He at once ordered his men to "stack arms," the Confederates following suit, and his boys in blue rowed him over, and he delivered the message, after having introduced himself to the rebel officers. One of these officers was Major Jones, of Alabama, the other Lieutenant Scott, of South Carolina. Major Jones was very cordial to our captain, but Lieutenant Scott would not extend his hand, and stood aside, in sullen silence, looking as if he would like to take revenge then and there. Major Jones said to Captain Metcalf, "We have no one to fight for. Should I meet you again, I shall not forget we have met before." With this he extended his hand to Metcalf and bade him good-by, but Lieutenant Scott stood by and looked as cross as he possibly could. The letters were exchanged, but it seemed a mystery just how those letters got missent to the opposite sides. Captain Metcalf said he did not feel a mite comfortable while he was on the Confederate soil; as for his men, you can imagine their thoughts. I asked them how they felt on the other side, and they said, "We would have felt much better if we had had our guns with us." It was a little risky, for sometimes the flag of truce is not regarded, but even among the enemy there are some good and loyal persons.

Captain Metcalf is still living in Medford. He is 71 years old, and just as loyal to the old flag and the G. A. R. as he was from 1861 to 1866, when he was mustered out. He was a brave captain, a good officer, and was honored and beloved by all in the regiment.

IX

Capture of Charleston

On February 28, 1865, the remainder of the regiment were ordered to Charleston, as there were signs of the rebels evacuating that city.[20] Leaving Cole Island, we arrived in Charleston between nine and ten o'clock in the morning, and found the "rebs" had set fire to the city and fled, leaving women and children behind to suffer and perish in the flames. The fire had been burning fiercely for a day and night. When we landed, under a flag of truce, our regiment went to work assisting the citizens in subduing the flames. It was a terrible scene. For three or four days the men fought the fire, saving the property and effects of the people, yet these white men and women could not tolerate our black Union soldiers, for many of them had formerly been their slaves; and although these brave men risked life and limb to assist them in their distress, men and even women would sneer and molest them whenever they met them.

I had quarters assigned me at a residence on South Battery Street, one of the most aristocratic parts of the city, where I assisted in caring for the sick and injured comrades. After getting the fire under control, the regiment marched out to the race track, where they camped until March 12, when we were ordered to Savannah, Ga. We arrived there on the 13th, about eight o'clock in the evening, and marched out to Fairlong, near the A.&G. R. R., where we remained about ten days, when we were ordered to Augusta, Ga., where Captain Alexander Heasley, of Co. E, was shot and killed by a Confederate. After his death Lieutenant Parker was made captain of the company, and was with us until the regiment was mustered out. He often told me about Massachusetts, but I had no thought at that time that I should ever see that State, and stand in the "Cradle of Liberty."

The regiment remained in Augusta for thirty days, when it was ordered to Hamburg, S. C., and then on to Charleston. It was while on their march through the country, to the latter city, that they came in contact with the bushwhackers (as the rebels were called), who hid in the bushes and would shoot the Union boys every chance they got. Other times they would conceal themselves in the cars used to transfer our soldiers, and when our boys, worn out and tired, would fall asleep, these men would come out from their hiding places and cut their throats. Several of our men were killed in this way, but it could not be found out who was committing these murders until one night one of the rebels was caught in the act, trying to cut the throat of a sleeping soldier. He was put under guard, court-martialed, and shot at Wall Hollow.

First Lieutenant Jerome T. Furman and a number of soldiers were killed by these South Carolina bushwhackers at Wall Hollow. After this man was shot, however, the regiment marched through unmolested to Charleston.

X

Mustered Out

The regiment, under Colonel Trowbridge, reached Charleston in November, 1865, and camped on the race track until January, when they returned to Morris Island, and on February 9, 1866, the following "General Orders " were received and the regiment mustered out.

They were delighted to go home, but oh! how they hated to part from their commanding chief, Colonel C. T. Trowbridge. He was the very first officer to take charge of black soldiers. We thought there was no one like him, for he was a "man" among his soldiers. All in the regiment knew him personally, and many were the jokes he used to tell them. I shall never forget his friendship and kindness toward me, from the first time I met him to the end of the war. There was never any one from the North who came into our camp but he would bring them to see me.

While on a visit South in 1888, I met a comrade of the regiment, who often said to me, "You up North, Mrs. King, do you ever see Colonel Trowbridge? How I should like to see him! I don't see why he does not come South sometime. Why, I would take a day off and look up all the 'boys' I could find, if I knew he was coming." I knew this man meant what he said, for the men of the regiment knew Colonel Trowbridge first of all the other officers. He was with them on St. Simon and at Camp Saxton. I remember when the company was being formed, we wished Captain C. T. was our captain, because most of the men in Co. E were the men he brought with him from St. Simon, and they were attached to him. He was always jolly and pleasing with all. I remember, when going into Savannah in 1865, he said that he had been there before the war, and told me many things I did not know about the river. Although this was my home, I had never been on it before. No officer in the army was more beloved than our late lieutenant-colonel, C. T. Trowbridge.

[Copy of General Orders.]
"GENERAL ORDERS.

"HEADQUARTERS 33D U. S. C. T.,
"LATE 1ST SO. CAROLINA VOLUNTEERS,
"MORRIS ISLAND, S. C., Feb. 9, 1866.

"*General Order,*
"*No.* 1.

"Comrades: The hour is at hand when we must separate forever, and nothing can take from us the pride we feel, when we look upon the history of the 'First South Carolina Volunteers,' the first black regiment that ever bore arms in defense of freedom on the continent of America.

"On the 9th day of May, 1862, at which time there were nearly four millions of your race in bondage, sanctioned by the laws of the land and protected by our flag,—on that day, in the face of the floods of prejudice that well-nigh deluged every avenue to manhood and true liberty, you came forth to do battle for your country and kindred.

"For long and weary months, without pay or even the privilege of being recognized as soldiers, you labored on, only to be disbanded and sent to your homes without even a hope of reward, and when our country, necessitated by the deadly struggle with armed traitors, finally granted you the opportunity again to come forth in defense of the nation's life, the alacrity with which you responded to the call gave abundant evidence of your readiness to strike a manly blow for the liberty of your race. And from that little band of hopeful, trusting, and brave men who gathered at Camp Saxton, on Port Royal Island, in the fall of '62, amidst the terrible prejudices that surrounded us, has grown an army of a hundred and forty thousand black soldiers, whose valor and heroism has won for your race a name which will live as long as the undying pages of history shall endure; and by whose efforts, united with those of the white man, armed rebellion has been conquered, the millions of bondsmen have been emancipated, and the fundamental law of the land has been so altered as to remove forever the possibility of human slavery being established within the borders of redeemed America. The flag of our fathers, restored to its rightful significance, now floats over every foot of our territory, from Maine to California, and beholds only free men! The prejudices which formerly existed against you are well-nigh rooted out.

"Soldiers, you have done your duty and acquitted yourselves like men who, actuated by such ennobling motives, could not fail; and as the result of your fidelity and obedience you have won your freedom, and oh, how great the reward! It seems fitting to me that the last hours of our existence as a regiment should be passed amidst the unmarked graves of your comrades, at Fort Wagner. Near you rest the bones of Colonel Shaw, buried by an enemy's hand in the same grave with his black soldiers who fell at his side; where in the future your children's children will come on pilgrimages to do homage to the ashes of those who fell in this glorious struggle.

"The flag which was presented to us by the Rev. George B. Cheever and his congregation, of New York city, on the 1st of January, 1863,—the day when Lincoln's immortal proclamation of freedom was given to the world,—and which you have borne so nobly through the war, is now to be rolled up forever and deposited in our nation's capital. And while there it shall rest, with the battles in which you have participated inscribed upon its folds, it will be a source of pride to us all to remember that it has never been disgraced by a cowardly faltering in the hour of danger, or polluted by a traitor's touch.

"Now that you are to lay aside your arms, I adjure you, by the associations and history of the past, and the love you bear for your liberties, to harbor no feelings of hatred toward your former masters, but to seek in the paths of honesty, virtue, sobriety, and industry, and by a willing obedience to the laws of the land, to grow up to the full stature of American citizens. The church, the school-house, and the right forever to be free are now secured to you, and every prospect before you is full of hope and encouragement. The nation guarantees to you full protection and justice, and will require from you in return that respect for the laws and orderly deportment which will prove to every one your right to all the privileges of freemen. To the officers of the regiment I would say, your toils are ended, your mission is fulfilled, and we separate forever. The fidelity, patience, and patriotism with which you have discharged your duties to your men and to your country entitle you to a far higher tribute than any words of thankfulness which I can give you from the bottom of my heart. You will find your reward in the proud conviction that the cause for which you have battled so nobly has been crowned with abundant success.

"Officers and soldiers of the 33d U. S. Colored Troops, once the First So. Carolina Volunteers, I bid you all farewell!

"By order of

"Lt. Colonel C. T. Trowbridge,
"*Commanding regiment.*

"E. W. Hyde,
"1st Lieut. 33d U. S. C. T. and acting adjutant."

I have one of the original copies of these orders still in my possession.

My dear friends! do we understand the meaning of war? Do we know or think of that war of '61? No, we do not, only those brave soldiers, and those who had occasion to be in it, can realize what it was. I can and shall never forget that terrible war until my eyes close in death. The scenes are just as fresh in my mind to-day as in '61. I see now each scene,—the roll-call, the drum tap, "lights out," the call at night when there was danger from the enemy, the double force of pickets, the cold and rain. How anxious I would be, not knowing what would happen before morning! Many times I would dress, not sure but all would be captured. Other times I would stand at my tent door and try to see what was going on, because night was the time the rebels would try to get into our lines and capture some of the boys. It was mostly at night that our men went out for their scouts, and often had a hand to hand fight with the rebels, and although our men came out sometimes with a few killed or wounded, none of them ever were captured.

We do not, as the black race, properly appreciate the old veterans, white or black, as we ought to. I know what they went through, especially those black men, for the Confederates had no mercy on them; neither did they show any toward the white Union soldiers. I have seen the terrors of that war. I was the wife of one of those men who did not get a penny for eighteen months for their services, only their rations and clothing.

I cannot praise General David Hunter too highly, for he was the first man to arm the black man, in the beginning of 1862. He had a hard struggle to hold all the southern division, with so few men, so he applied to Congress; but the answer to him was, "Do not bother us," which was very discouraging. As the general needed more men to protect the islands and do garrison duty, he organized two companies.

I look around now and see the comforts that our younger generation enjoy, and think of the blood that was shed to make these comforts possible for them, and see how little some of them appreciate the old soldiers. My heart burns within me, at this want of appreciation. There are only a few of them left now, so let us all, as the ranks close, take a deeper interest in them. Let the younger generation take an interest also, and remember that it was through the efforts of these veterans that they and we older ones enjoy our liberty to-day.

XI

After the War

In 1866, the steamers which ran from Savannah to Darien would not take colored people unless they stayed in a certain part of the boat, away from the white people; so some of the colored citizens and ex-soldiers decided to form a syndicate and buy a steamer of their own. They finally bought a large one of a New York company. It arrived in fine shape, apparently, and made its first trip to Darien. The next trip was to Beaufort. I went on this trip, as the pilot, James Cook, was a friend of my family, and I thought I would enjoy the trip; and I did, getting back in safety. The next trip was to go to Florida, but it never reached there, for on the way down the boat ran upon St. John bar and went entirely to pieces. They found out afterwards that they had been swindled, as the boat was a condemned one, and the company took advantage of them; and as they carried no insurance on the boat they lost all the money they had invested in it. The best people of the city expressed great sympathy for them in their loss, as it promised to prove a great investment at first.

At the close of the war, my husband and I returned to Savannah, a number of the comrades returning at the same time. A new life was before us now, all the old life left behind. After getting settled, I opened a school at my home on South Broad Street, now called Oglethorpe Avenue, as there was not any public school for negro children. I had twenty children at my school, and received one dollar a month for each pupil, I also had a few older ones who came at night. There were several other private schools besides mine. Mrs. Lucinda Jackson had one on the same street I lived on.

I taught almost a year, when the Beach Institute opened, which took a number of my scholars, as this was a free school.[21] On September 16, 1866, my husband, Sergeant King, died, leaving me soon to welcome a little stranger alone. He was a boss carpenter, but being just mustered out of the army, and the prejudice against his race being still too strong to insure him much work at his trade, he took contracts for unloading vessels, and hired a number of men to assist him. He was much respected by the citizens, and was a general favorite with his associates.

In December, 1866, I was obliged to give up teaching, but in April, 1867, I opened a school in Liberty County, Georgia, and taught there one year; but country life did not agree with me, so I returned to the city, and Mrs. Susie Carrier took charge of my school.

On my return to Savannah, I found that the free school had taken all my former pupils, so I opened a night school, where I taught a number of adults. This, together with other things I could get to do and the assistance of my brother-in-law, supported me. I taught this school until the fall of 1868, when a free night school opened at the Beach Institute, and again my scholars left me to attend this free school. So I had to close my school. I put my baby with my mother and entered in the employ of a family, where I lived quite a while, but had to leave, as the work was too hard.

In 1872 I put in a claim for my husband's bounty and received one hundred dollars, some of which I put in the Freedmen's Savings Bank. In the fall of 1872 I went to work for a very wealthy lady, Mrs. Charles Green, as laundress. In the spring of 1873, Mr. and Mrs. Green came North to Rye Beach for the summer, and as their cook did not care to go so far from home, I went with them in her place. While there, I won a prize for excellent cooking at a fair which the ladies who were summering there had held to raise funds to build an Episcopal Church, and Mrs. Green was one of the energetic workers to make this fair a success; and it was a success in every respect and a tidy sum was netted.

I returned South with Mrs. Green, and soon after, she went to Europe. I returned to Boston again in 1874, through the kindness of Mrs. Barnard, a daughter of ex-Mayor Otis of Boston. She was accompanied by her husband, Mr. James Barnard (who was an agent for the line of steamers), her six children, the nurse, and myself. We left Savannah on the steamship Seminole, under Captain Matthews, and when we had passed Hatteras some distance, she broke her shaft. The captain had the sails hoisted and we drifted along, there being a stiff breeze, which was greatly in our favor. Captain Matthews said the nearest point he could make was Cape Henry Light. About noon, Mr. Barnard spied the light and told the captain if he would give him a boat and some of the crew, he would row to the light for help. This was done, the boat was manned and they put off. They made the light, then they made for Norfolk, which was eight miles from the light, and did not reach the city until eight o'clock that night.

Next morning he returned with a tug, to tow us into Norfolk for repairs; but the tug was too small to move the steamer, so it went back for more help, but before it returned, a Norfolk steamer, on its way to Boston, stopped to see what was the matter with our steamer. Our trouble was explained to them, and almost all the passengers were transferred to this steamer. Mr. Barnard remained on the steamer, and Mrs. Barnard deciding to remain with him, I went aboard this other steamer with the rest of the passengers. We left them at anchor, waiting for the tugs to return.

This accident brought back very vividly the time previous to this, when I was in that other wreck in 1864, and I wondered if they would reach port safe, for it is a terrible thing to be cast away; but on arriving in Boston, about two days later, I was delighted to hear of the arrival of their steamer at T Wharf, with all on board safe.

Soon after I got to Boston, I entered the service of Mr. Thomas Smith's family, on Walnut Avenue, Boston Highlands, where I remained until the death of Mrs. Smith. I next lived with Mrs. Gorham Gray, Beacon Street, where I remained until I was married, in 1879, to Russell L. Taylor.

In 1880 I had another experience in steamer accidents. Mr. Taylor and I started for New York on the steamer Stonington. We were in bed when, sometime in the night, the Narragansett collided with our boat. I was awakened by the crash. I was in the ladies' cabin. There were about thirty-five or forty others in the cabin. I sprang out of my berth, dressed as quickly as I could, and tried to reach the deck, but we found the cabin door locked, and two men stood outside and would not let us out. About twenty minutes after, they opened the doors and we went up on deck, and a terrible scene was before us. The Narragansett was on fire, in a bright blaze; the water was lighted as far as one could see, the passengers shrieking, groaning, running about, leaping into the water, panic-stricken. A steamer came to our assistance; they put the life-rafts off and saved a great many from the burning steamer, and picked a number up from the water. A colored man saved his wife and child by giving each a chair and having them jump overboard. These chairs kept them afloat until they were taken aboard by the life-raft. The steamer was burned to the water's edge. The passengers on board our steamer were transferred to another one and got to New York at 9.30 the next morning. A number of lives were lost in this accident, and the bow of the Stonington was badly damaged. I was thankful for my escape, for I had been in two similar experiences and got off safely, and I have come to the conclusion I shall never have a watery grave.

XII

The Women's Relief Corps

All this time my interest in the boys in blue had not abated. I was still loyal and true, whether they were black or white. My hands have never left undone anything they could do towards their aid and comfort in the twilight of their lives. In 1886 I helped to organize Corps 67, Women's Relief Corps, auxiliary to the G. A. R., and it is a very flourishing corps to-day. I have been Guard, Secretary, Treasurer for three years, and in 1893 I was made President of this corps, Mrs. Emily Clark being Department President this year. In 1896, in response to an order sent out by the Department W. R. C. to take a census to secure a complete roster of the Union Veterans of the War of the Rebellion now residing in Massachusetts, I was allotted the West End district, which (with the assistance of Mrs. Lizzie L. Johnson, a member of Corps 67, and widow of a soldier of the 54th Mass. Volunteers) I canvassed with splendid success, and found a great many comrades who were not attached to any post in the city or State.

In 1898 the Department of Mass. W. R. C. gave a grand fair at Music Hall. I made a large quilt of red, white, and blue ribbon that made quite a sensation. The quilt was voted for and was awarded to the Department President, Mrs. E. L. W. Waterman, of Boston.

XIII

Thoughts on Present Conditions

Living here in Boston where the black man is given equal justice, I must say a word on the general treatment of my race, both in the North and South, in this twentieth century. I wonder if our white fellow men realize the true sense or meaning of brotherhood? For two hundred years we had toiled for them; the war of 1861 came and was ended, and we thought our race was forever freed from bondage, and that the two races could live in unity with each other, but when we read almost every day of what is being done to my race by some whites in the South, I sometimes ask, "Was the war in vain? Has it brought freedom, in the full sense of the word, or has it not made our condition more hopeless?"

In this "land of the free" we are burned, tortured, and denied a fair trial, murdered for any imaginary wrong conceived in the brain of the negro-hating white man. There is no redress for us from a government which promised to protect all under its flag. It seems a mystery to me. They say, "One flag, one nation, one country indivisible." Is this true? Can we say this truthfully, when one race is allowed to burn, hang, and inflict the most horrible torture weekly, monthly, on another? No, we cannot sing "My country, 'tis of thee, Sweet land of Liberty"![22] It is hollow mockery. The Southland laws are all on the side of the white, and they do just as they like to the negro, whether in the right or not.

I do not uphold my race when they do wrong. They ought to be punished, but the innocent are made to suffer as well as the guilty, and I hope the time will hasten when it will be stopped forever. Let us remember God says, "He that sheds blood, his blood shall be required again."[23] I may not live to see it, but the time is approaching when the South will again have cause to repent for the blood it has shed of innocent black men, for their blood cries out for vengeance. For the South still cherishes a hatred toward the blacks, although there are some true Southern gentlemen left who abhor the stigma brought upon them, and feel it very keenly, and I hope the day is not far distant when the two races will reside in peace in the Southland, and we will sing with sincere and truthful hearts, "My country, 't is of thee, Sweet land of Liberty, of thee I sing."

I have been in many States and cities, and in each I have looked for liberty and justice, equal for the black as for the white; but it was not until I was within the borders of New England, and reached old Massachusetts, that I found it. Here is found liberty in the full sense of the word, liberty for the stranger within her gates, irrespective of race or creed, liberty and justice for all.

We have before us still another problem to solve. With the close of the Spanish war, and on the entrance of the Americans into Cuba, the same conditions confront us as the war of 1861 left. The Cubans are free, but it is a limited freedom, for prejudice, deep-rooted, has been brought to them and a separation made between the white and black Cubans, a thing that had never existed between them before; but to-day there is the same intense hatred toward the negro in Cuba that there is in some parts of this country.

I helped to furnish and pack boxes to be sent to the soldiers and hospitals during the first part of the Spanish war; there were black soldiers there too. At the battle of San Juan Hill, they were in the front, just as brave, loyal, and true as those other black men who fought for freedom and the right; and yet their bravery and faithfulness were reluctantly acknowledged, and praise grudgingly given.[24] All we ask for is "equal justice," the same that is accorded to all other races who come to this country, of their free will (not forced to, as we were), and are allowed to enjoy every privilege, unrestricted, while we are denied what is rightfully our own in a country which the labor of our forefathers helped to make what it is.

One thing I have noticed among my people in the South: they have accumulated a large amount of real estate, far surpassing the colored owners in the North, who seem to let their opportunity slip by them. Nearly all of Brownsville (a suburb of Savannah) is owned by colored people, and so it is in a great many other places throughout the State, and all that is needed is the protection of the law as citizens.

In 1867, soon after the death of my father, who had served on a gunboat during the war, my mother opened a grocery store, where she kept general merchandise always on hand. These she traded for cash or would exchange for crops of cotton, corn, or rice, which she would ship once a month, to F. Lloyd & Co., or Johnson & Jackson, in Savannah. These were colored merchants, doing business on Bay Street in that city. Mother bought her first property, which contained ten acres. She next purchased fifty acres of land. Then she had a chance to get a place with seven hundred acres of land, and she bought this.

In 1870, Colonel Hamilton and Major Devendorft, of Oswego, N. Y., came to the town and bought up a tract of land at a place called Doctortown, and started a mill. Mrs. Devendorft heard of my mother and went to see her, and persuaded her to come to live with her, assuring her she would be as one of the family. Mother went with her, but after a few months she went to Doctortown, where she has been since, and now owns the largest settlement there. All trains going to Florida pass her place, just across the Altamaha River. She is well known by both white and black; the people are fond of her, and will not allow any one to harm her.

Mr. Devendorft sold out his place in 1880 and went back to New York, where later he died.

I read an article, which said the ex-Confederate Daughters had sent a petition to the managers of the local theatres in Tennessee to prohibit the performance of "Uncle Tom's Cabin," claiming it was exaggerated (that is, the treatment of the slaves), and would have a very bad effect on the children who might see the drama.[25] I paused and thought back a few years of the heart-rending scenes I have witnessed; I have seen many times, when I was a mere girl, thirty or forty men, handcuffed, and as many women and children, come every first Tuesday of each month from Mr. Wiley's trade office to the auction blocks, one of them being situated on Drayton Street and Court Lane, the other on Bryant Street, near the Pulaski House. The route was down our principal street, Bull Street, to the courthouse, which was only a block from where I resided.

All people in those days got all their water from the city pumps, which stood about a block apart throughout the city. The one we used to get water from was opposite the courthouse, on Bull Street. I remember, as if it were yesterday, seeing droves of negroes going to be sold, and I often went to look at them, and I could hear the auctioneer very plainly from my house, auctioning these poor people off.

Do these Confederate Daughters ever send petitions to prohibit the atrocious lynchings and wholesale murdering and torture of the negro? Do you ever hear of them fearing this would have a bad effect on the children? Which of these two, the drama or the present state of affairs, makes a degrading impression upon the minds of our young generation? In my opinion it is not "Uncle Tom's Cabin," but it should be the one that has caused the world to cry "Shame!" It does not seem as if our land is yet civilized. It is like times long past, when rulers and high officers had to flee for their lives, and the negro has been dealt with in the same way since the war by those he lived with and toiled for two hundred years or more. I do not condemn all the Caucasian race because the negro is badly treated by a few of the race. No! for had it not been for the true whites, assisted by God and the prayers of our forefathers, I should not be here to-day.

There are still good friends to the negro. Why, there are still thousands that have not bowed to Baal. So it is with us. Man thinks two hundred years is a long time, and it is, too; but it is only as a week to God, and in his own time—I know I shall not live to see the day, but it will come—the South will be like the North, and when it comes it will be prized higher than we prize the North to-day. God is just; when he created man he made him in his image, and never intended one should misuse the other. All men are born free and equal in his sight.

I am pleased to know at this writing that the officers and comrades of my regiment stand ready to render me assistance whenever required. It seems like "bread cast upon the water,"[26] and it has returned after many days, when it is most needed. I have received letters from some of the comrades, since we parted in 1866, with expressions of gratitude and thanks to me for teaching them their first letters. One of them, Peter Waggall, is a minister in Jacksonville, Fla. Another is in the government service at Washington, D. C. Others are in Darien and Savannah, Ga., and all are doing well.

There are many people who do not know what some of the colored women did during the war. There were hundreds of them who assisted the Union soldiers by hiding them and helping them to escape. Many were punished for taking food to the prison stockades for the prisoners. When I went into Savannah, in 1865, I was told of one of these stockades which was in the suburbs of the city,[27] and they said it was an awful place. The Union soldiers were in it, worse than pigs, without any shelter from sun or storm, and the colored women would take food there at night and pass it to them, through the holes in the fence. The soldiers were starving, and these women did all they could towards relieving those men, although they knew the penalty, should they be caught giving them aid. Others assisted in various ways the Union army. These things should be kept in history before the people. There has never been a greater war in the United States than the one of 1861, where so many lives were lost,—not men alone but noble women as well.

Let us not forget that terrible war, or our brave soldiers who were thrown into Andersonville and Libby prisons,[28] the awful agony they went through, and the most brutal treatment they received in those loathsome dens, the worst ever given human beings; and if the white soldiers were subjected to such treatment, what must have been the horrors inflicted on the negro soldiers in their prison pens? Can we forget those cruelties? No, though we try to forgive and say, "No North, no South," and hope to see it in reality before the last comrade passes away.

XIV

A Visit to Louisiana

The inevitable always happens. On February 3, 1898, I was called to Shreveport, La., to the bedside of my son, who was very ill. He was traveling with Nickens and Company, with "The Lion's Bride," when he fell ill, and had been ill two weeks when they sent to me. I tried to have him brought home to Boston, but they could not send him, as he was not able to sit and ride this long distance; so on the sixth of February I left Boston to go to him. I reached Cincinnati on the eighth, where I took the train for the south. I asked a white man standing near (before I got my train) what car I should take. "Take that one," he said, pointing to one. "But that is a smoking car!" "Well," he replied, "that is the car for colored people." I went to this car, and on entering it all my courage failed me. I have ridden in many coaches, but I was never in such as these. I wanted to return home again, but when I thought of my sick boy I said, "Well, others ride in these cars and I must do likewise," and tried to be resigned, for I wanted to reach my boy, as I did not know whether I should find him alive. I arrived in Chattanooga at eight o'clock in the evening, where the porter took my baggage to the train which was to leave for Marion, Miss. Soon after I was seated, just before the train pulled out, two tall men with slouch hats on walked through the car, and on through the train. Finally they came back to our car and stopping at my seat said, "Where are those men who were with you?" I did not know to whom they were speaking, as there was another woman in the car, so I made no reply. Again they asked me, standing directly in front of my seat, "Where are those men who came in with you?" "Are you speaking to me?" I said. "Yes!" they said. "I have not seen any men," I replied. They looked at me a moment, and one of them asked where I was from. I told him Boston; he hesitated a minute and walked out of our car to the other car.

When the conductor came around I told him what these men had said, and asked him if they allowed persons to enter the car and insult passengers. He only smiled. Later, when the porter came in, I mentioned it to him. He said, "Lady, I see you do not belong here; where are you from?" I told him. He said, "I have often heard of Massachusetts. I want to see that place." "Yes!" I said, "you can ride there on the cars, and no person would be allowed to speak to you as those men did to me." He explained that those men were constables, who were in search of a man who had eloped with another man's wife. "That is the way they do here. Each morning you can hear of some negro being lynched;" and on seeing my surprise, he said, "Oh, that is nothing; it is done all the time. We have no rights here. I have been on this road for fifteen years and have seen some terrible things." He wanted to know what I was doing down there, and I told him it was only the illness of my son that brought me there.

I was a little surprised at the way the poor whites were made to ride on this road. They put them all together by themselves in a car, between the colored people's coach and the first-class coach, and it looked like the "laborers' car" used in Boston to carry the different day laborers to and from their work.

I got to Marion, Miss., at two o'clock in the morning, arrived at Vicksburg at noon, and at Shreveport about eight o'clock in the evening, and found my son just recovering from a severe hemorrhage. He was very anxious to come home, and I tried to secure a berth for him on a sleeper, but they would not sell me one, and he was not strong enough to travel otherwise. If I could only have gotten him to Cincinnati, I might have brought him home, but as I could not I was forced to let him remain where he was. It seemed very hard, when his father fought to protect the Union and our flag, and yet his boy was denied, under this same flag, a berth to carry him home to die, because he was a negro.

Shreveport is a little town, made up largely of Jews and Germans and a few Southerners, the negroes being in the majority. Its sidewalks are sand except on the main street. Almost all the stores are kept either by the Jews or Germans. They know a stranger in a minute, as the town is small and the citizens know each other; if not personally, their faces are familiar.

I went into a jewelry store one day to have a crystal put in my watch, and the attendant remarked, "You are a stranger." I asked him how he knew that. He said he had watched me for a week or so. I told him yes, I was a stranger and from Boston. "Oh! I have heard of

Boston," he said. "You will not find this place like it is there. How do you like this town?" "Not very well," I replied.

I found that the people who had lived in Massachusetts and were settled in Shreveport were very cordial to me and glad to see me. There was a man murdered in cold blood for nothing. He was a colored man and a "porter" in a store in this town. A clerk had left his umbrella at home. It had begun to rain when he started for home, and on looking for the umbrella he could not, of course, find it. He asked the porter if he had seen it. He said no, he had not. "You answer very saucy," said the clerk, and drawing his revolver, he shot the colored man dead. He was taken up the street to an office where he was placed under one thousand dollars bond for his appearance and released, and that was the end of the case. I was surprised at this, but I was told by several white and colored persons that this was a common occurrence, and the persons were never punished if they were white, but no mercy was shown to negroes.

I met several comrades, white and colored, there, and noticed that the colored comrades did not wear their buttons. I asked one of them why this was, and was told, should they wear it, they could not get work. Still some would wear their buttons in spite of the feeling against it. I met a newsman from New York on the train. He was a veteran, and said that Sherman ought to come back and go into that part of the country.

Shreveport is a horrid place when it rains. The earth is red and sticks to your shoes, and it is impossible to keep rubbers on, for the mud pulls them off. Going across the Mississippi River, I was amazed to see how the houses were built, so close to the shore, or else on low land; and when the river rises, it flows into these houses and must make it very disagreeable and unhealthy for the inmates.

After the death of my son, while on my way back to Boston, I came to Clarksdale, one of the stations on the road from Vicksburg. In this town a Mr. Hancock, of New York, had a large cotton plantation, and the Chinese intermarry with the blacks.

At Clarksdale, I saw a man hanged. It was a terrible sight, and I felt alarmed for my own safety down there. When I reached Memphis I found conditions of travel much better. The people were mostly Western and Northern here; the cars were nice, but separate for colored persons until we reached the Ohio River, when the door was opened and the porter passed through, saying, "The Ohio River! change to the other car." I thought, "What does he mean? We have been riding all this distance in separate cars, and now we are all to sit together." It certainly seemed a peculiar arrangement. Why not let the negroes, if their appearance and respectability warrant it, be allowed to ride as they do in the North, East, or West?

There are others beside the blacks, in the South and North, that should be put in separate cars while traveling, just as they put my race. Many black people in the South do not wish to be thrown into a car because all are colored, as there are many of their race very objectionable to them, being of an entirely different class; but they have to adapt themselves to the circumstances and ride with them, because they are all negroes. There is no such division with the whites. Except in one place I saw, the workingman and the millionaire ride in the same coaches together. Why not allow the respectable, law-abiding classes of the blacks the same privilege? We hope for better conditions in the future, and feel sure they will come in time, surely if slowly.

While in Shreveport, I visited ex-Senator Harper's house. He is a colored man and owns a large business block, besides a fine residence on Cado Street and several good building lots. Another family, the Pages, living on the same street, were quite wealthy, and a large number of colored families owned their homes, and were industrious, refined people; and if they were only allowed justice, the South would be the only place for our people to live.

We are similar to the children of Israel, who, after many weary years in bondage, were led into that land of promise, there to thrive and be forever free from persecution; and I don't despair, for the Book which is our guide through life declares, "Ethiopia shall stretch forth her hand."

What a wonderful revolution! In 1861 the Southern papers were full of advertisements for "slaves," but now, despite all the hindrances and "race problems," my people are striving to attain the full standard of all other races born free in the sight of God, and in a number of instances have succeeded. Justice we ask,—to be citizens of these United States, where so many of our people have shed their blood with their white comrades, that the stars and stripes should never be polluted.

Thomas Wentworth Higginson

from *Army Life in a Black Regiment* (1869)

CAMP DIARY

November 27, 1862.

Thanksgiving-Day; it is the first moment I have had for writing during these three days, which have installed me into a new mode of life so thoroughly that they seem three years. Scarcely pausing in New York or in Beaufort, there seems to have been for me but one step from the camp of a Massachusetts regiment to this, and that step over leagues of waves.[29]

It is a holiday wherever General Saxton's proclamation[30] reaches. The chilly sunshine and the pale blue river seems like New England, but those alone. The air is full of noisy drumming, and of gunshots; for the prize-shooting is our great celebration of the day, and the drumming is chronic. My young barbarians are all at play. I look out from the broken windows of this forlorn plantation-house, through avenues of great live-oaks, with their hard, shining leaves, and their branches hung with a universal drapery of soft, long moss, like fringe-trees struck with grayness. Below, the sandy soil, scantly covered with coarse grass, bristles with sharp palmettoes and aloes; all the vegetation is stiff, shining, semi-tropical, with nothing soft or delicate in its texture. Numerous plantation-buildings totter around, all slovenly and unattractive, while the interspaces are filled with all manner of wreck and refuse, pigs, fowls, dogs, and omnipresent Ethiopian[31] infancy. All this is the universal Southern panorama; but five minutes' walk beyond the hovels and the live-oaks will bring one to something so un-Southern that the whole Southern coast at this moment trembles at the suggestion of such a thing,—the camp of a regiment of freed slaves.

One adapts one's self so readily to new surroundings that already the full zest of the novelty seems passing away from my perceptions, and I write these lines in an eager effort to retain all I can. Already I am growing used to the experience, at first so novel, of living among five hundred men, and scarce a white face to be seen,—of seeing them go through all their daily processes, eating, frolicking, talking, just as if they were white. Each day at dress-parade I stand with the customary folding of the arms before a regimental line of countenances so black that I can hardly tell whether the men stand steadily or not; black is every hand which moves in ready cadence as I vociferate, "Battalion! Shoulder arms!" nor is it till the line of white officers moves forward, as parade is dismissed, that I am reminded that my own face is not the color of coal.

The first few days on duty with a new regiment must be devoted almost wholly to tightening reins; in this process one deals chiefly with the officers, and I have as yet had but little personal intercourse with the men. They concern me chiefly in bulk, as so many consumers of rations, wearers of uniforms, bearers of muskets. But as the machine comes into shape, I am beginning to decipher the individual parts. At first, of course, they all looked just alike; the variety comes afterwards, and they are just as distinguishable, the officers say, as so many whites. Most of them are wholly raw, but there are many who have already been for months in camp in the abortive "Hunter Regiment," yet in that loose kind of way which, like average militia training, is a doubtful advantage. I notice that some companies, too, look darker than others, though all are purer African than I expected. This is said to be partly a geographical difference between the South Carolina and Florida men. When the Rebels evacuated this region they probably took with them the house-servants, including most of the mixed blood, so that the residuum seems very black. But the men brought from Fernandina[32] the other day average lighter in complexion, and look more intelligent, and they certainly take wonderfully to the drill.

It needs but a few days to show the absurdity of distrusting the military availability of these people. They have quite as much average comprehension as whites of the need of the thing, as much courage (I doubt not), as much previous knowledge of the gun, and, above all, a readiness of ear and of imitation, which, for purposes of drill, counterbalances any defect of mental training. To learn the drill, one does not want a set of college professors; one wants a squad of eager, active, pliant school-boys; and the more childlike these pupils are the better. There is no trouble about the drill; they will surpass whites in that. As to camp-life, they have little to sacrifice; they are better fed, housed, and clothed than ever in their lives before, and they appear to have few inconvenient vices. They are simple, docile, and affectionate almost to the point of absurdity. The same men who stood fire in open field with perfect coolness, on the late expedition, have come to me blubbering in the most irresistibly ludicrous manner on being transferred from one company in the regiment to another.

In noticing the squad-drills I perceive that the men learn less laboriously than whites that "double, double, toil and trouble," which is the elementary vexation of the drill-master,—that they more rarely mistake their left for their right,—and are more grave and sedate while under instruction. The extremes of jollity and sobriety, being greater with them, are less liable to be intermingled; these companies can be driven with a looser rein than my former one, for they restrain themselves; but the moment they are dismissed from drill every tongue is relaxed and every ivory tooth visible. This morning I wandered about where the different companies were target-shooting, and their glee was contagious. Such exulting shouts of "Ki! ole man," when some steady old turkey-shooter brought his gun down for an instant's aim, and then unerringly hit the mark; and then, when some unwary youth fired his piece into the ground at half-cock such guffawing and delight, such rolling over and over on the grass, such dances of ecstasy, as made the "Ethiopian minstrelsy"[33] of the stage appear a feeble imitation.

Evening.—Better still was a scene on which I stumbled to-night. Strolling in the cool moonlight, I was attracted by a brilliant light beneath the trees, and cautiously approached it. A circle of thirty or forty soldiers sat around a roaring fire, while one old uncle, Cato by name, was narrating an interminable tale, to the insatiable delight of his audience. I came up into the dusky background, perceived only by a few, and he still continued. It was a narrative, dramatized to the last degree, of his adventures in escaping from his master to the Union vessels; and even I, who have heard the stories of Harriet Tubman, and such wonderful slave-comedians, never witnessed such a piece of acting. When I came upon the scene he had just come unexpectedly upon a plantation-house, and, putting a bold face upon it, had walked up to the door.

"Den I go up to de white man, berry humble, and say, would he please gib ole man a mouthful for eat?

"He say he must hab de valeration ob half a dollar.

"Den I look berry sorry, and turn for go away.

"Den he say I might gib him dat hatchet I had.

"Den I say" (this in a tragic vein) "dat I must hab dat hatchet for defend myself *from de dogs!*"

(Immense applause, and one appreciating auditor says, chuckling, "Dat was your *arms*, ole man," which brings down the house again.)

"Den he say de Yankee pickets was near by, and I must be very keerful.

"Den I say, `Good Lord, Mas'r, am dey?'"

Words cannot express the complete dissimulation with which these accents of terror were uttered,—this being precisely the piece of information he wished to obtain.

Then he narrated his devices to get into the house at night and obtain some food,— how a dog flew at him, how the whole household, black and white, rose in pursuit,—how he scrambled under a hedge and over a high fence, etc.,—all in a style of which Gough[34] alone among orators can give the faintest impression, so thoroughly dramatized was every syllable.

Then he described his reaching the river-side at last, and trying to decide whether certain vessels held friends or foes.

"Den I see guns on board, and sure sartin he Union boat, and I pop my head up. Den I been-a-tink (think) Seceshkey [sic] hab guns too, and my head go down again. Den I hide in de bush till morning. Den I open my bundle, and take ole white shirt and tie him on ole pole and wave him, and ebry time de wind blow, I been-a-tremble, and drap down in de bushes,"—because, being between two fires, he doubted whether friend or foe would see his signal first. And so on, with a succession of tricks beyond Molière, of acts of caution, foresight, patient cunning, which were listened to with infinite gusto and perfect comprehension by every listener.

And all this to a bivouac of negro soldiers, with the brilliant fire lighting up their red trousers and gleaming from their shining black faces,—eyes and teeth all white with tumultuous glee. Overhead, the mighty limbs of a great live-oak, with the weird moss swaying in the smoke, and the high moon gleaming faintly through.

Yet to-morrow strangers will remark on the hopeless, impenetrable stupidity in the daylight faces of many of these very men, the solid mask under which Nature has concealed all this wealth of mother-wit. This very comedian is one to whom one might point, as he hoed lazily in a cotton-field, as a being the light of whose brain had utterly gone out; and this scene seems like coming by night upon some conclave of black beetles, and finding them engaged, with green-room and foot-lights, in enacting "Poor Pillicoddy."[35] This is their university; every young Sambo before me, as he turned over the sweet potatoes and peanuts which were roasting in the ashes, listened with reverence to the wiles of the ancient Ulysses, and meditated the same. It is Nature's compensation; oppression simply crushes the upper faculties of the head, and crowds every-thing into the perceptive organs. Cato, thou reasonest well! When I get into any serious scrape, in an enemy's country, may I be lucky enough to have you at my elbow, to pull me out of it!

The men seem to have enjoyed the novel event of Thanksgiving-Day; they have had company and regimental prize-shootings, a minimum of speeches and a maximum of dinner. Bill of fare: two beef-cattle and a thousand oranges. The oranges cost a cent apiece, and the cattle were Secesh, bestowed by General Saxby, as they all call him.

December 1, 1862.

How absurd is the impression bequeathed by Slavery in regard to these Southern blacks, that they are sluggish and inefficient in labor! Last night, after a hard day's work (our guns and the remainder of our tents being just issued), an order came from Beaufort that we should be ready in the evening to unload a steamboat's cargo of boards, being some of those captured by them a few weeks since, and now assigned for their use. I wondered if the men would grumble at the night-work; but the steamboat arrived by seven, and it was bright moonlight when they went at it. Never have I beheld such a jolly scene of labor. Tugging these wet and heavy boards over a bridge of boats ashore, then across the slimy beach at low tide, then up a steep bank, and all in one great uproar of merriment for two hours. Running most of the time, chattering all the time, snatching the boards from each other's backs as if they were some coveted treasure, getting up eager rivalries between different companies, pouring great choruses of ridicule on the heads of all shirkers, they made the whole scene so enlivening that I gladly stayed out in the moonlight for the whole time to watch it. And all this without any urging or any promised reward, but simply as the most natural way of doing the thing. The steamboat captain declared that they unloaded the ten thousand feet of boards quicker than any white gang could have done it; and they felt it so little, that, when, later in the night, I reproached one whom I found sitting by a campfire, cooking a surreptitious opossum, telling him that he ought to be asleep after such a job of work, he answered, with the broadest grin,—

"O no, Cunnel, da's no work at all, Cunnel; dat only jess enough *for stretch we*."

December 2, 1862.

I believe I have not yet enumerated the probable drawbacks to the success of this regiment, if any. We are exposed to no direct annoyance from the white regiments, being out of their way; and we have as yet no discomforts or privations which we do not share with them. I do not as yet see the slightest obstacle, in the nature of the blacks, to making them good soldiers, but rather the contrary. They take readily to drill, and do not object to discipline; they are not especially dull or inattentive; they seem fully to understand the importance of the contest, and of their share in it. They show no jealousy or suspicion towards their officers.

They do show these feelings, however, towards the Government itself; and no one can wonder. Here lies the drawback to rapid recruiting. Were this a wholly new regiment, it would have been full to overflowing, I am satisfied, ere now. The trouble is in the legacy of bitter distrust bequeathed by the abortive regiment of General Hunter,—into which they were driven like cattle, kept for several months in camp, and then turned off without a shilling, by order of the War Department. The formation of that regiment was, on the whole, a great injury to this one; and the men who came from it, though the best soldiers we have in other respects, are the least sanguine and cheerful; while those who now refuse to enlist have a great influence in deterring others. Our soldiers are constantly twitted by their families and friends with their prospect of risking their lives in the service, and being paid nothing; and it is in vain that we read them the instructions of the Secretary of War to General Saxton, promising them the full pay of soldiers. They only half believe it.*

Another drawback is that some of the white soldiers delight in frightening the women on the plantations with doleful tales of plans for putting us in the front rank in all battles, and such silly talk,—the object being perhaps, to prevent our being employed on active service at all. All these considerations they feel precisely as white men would,—no less, no more; and it is the comparative freedom from such unfavorable influences which makes the Florida men seem more bold and manly, as they undoubtedly do. To-day General Saxton has returned from Fernandina with seventy-six recruits, and the eagerness of the captains to secure them was a sight to see. Yet they cannot deny that some of the very best men in the regiment are South Carolinians.

December 3, 1862.—7 P.M.

What a life is this I lead! It is a dark, mild, drizzling evening, and as the foggy air breeds sand-flies, so it calls out melodies and strange antics from this mysterious race of grown-up children with whom my lot is cast. All over the camp the lights glimmer in the tents, and as I sit at my desk in the open doorway, there come mingled sounds of stir and glee. Boys laugh and shout,—a feeble flute stirs somewhere in some tent, not an officer's,—a drum throbs far away in another,—wild kildeer-plover flit and wail above us, like the haunting souls of dead slave-masters,—and from a neighboring cook-fire comes the monotonous sound of that strange festival, half pow-wow, half prayer-meeting, which they know only as a "shout." These fires are usually enclosed in a little booth, made neatly of palm-leaves and covered in at top, a regular native African hut, in short, such as is pictured in books, and such as I once got up from dried palm-leaves for a fair at home. This hut is now crammed with men, singing at the top of their voices, in one of their quaint, monotonous, endless, negro-Methodist chants, with obscure syllables recurring constantly, and slight variations interwoven, all accompanied with a regular drumming of the feet and clapping of the hands, like castanets. Then the excitement spreads: inside and outside the enclosure men begin to quiver and dance, others join, a circle forms, winding monotonously round some one in the centre; some "heel and toe" tumultuously, others merely tremble and stagger on, others stoop and rise, others whirl, others caper sideways, all keep steadily circling like dervishes; spectators applaud special strokes of skill; my approach only enlivens the scene; the circle enlarges, louder grows the singing, rousing shouts of encouragement come in, half bacchanalian, half devout, "Wake 'em, brudder!" "Stan' up to 'em, brudder!"—and still the ceaseless drumming and clapping, in perfect cadence, goes steadily on. Suddenly there comes a sort of *snap*, and the spell breaks, amid general sighing and laughter. And this not rarely and occasionally, but night after night, while in other parts of the camp the soberest prayers and exhortations are proceeding sedately.

A simple and lovable people, whose graces seem to come by nature, and whose vices by training. Some of the best superintendents confirm the first tales of innocence, and Dr.

---

* With what utter humiliation were we, their officers, obliged to confess to them, eighteen months afterwards, that it was their distrust which was wise, and our faith in the pledges of the United States Government which was foolishness!

Zachos[36] told me last night that on his plantation, a sequestered one, "they had absolutely no vices." Nor have these men of mine yet shown any worth mentioning; since I took command I have heard of no man intoxicated, and there has been but one small quarrel. I suppose that scarcely a white regiment in the army shows so little swearing. Take the "Progressive Friends"[37] and put them in red trousers, and I verily believe they would fill a guard-house sooner than these men. If camp regulations are violated, it seems to be usually through heedlessness. They love passionately three things besides their spiritual incantations; namely, sugar, home, and tobacco. This last affection brings tears to their eyes, almost, when they speak of their urgent need of pay; they speak of their last-remembered quid as if it were some deceased relative, too early lost, and to be mourned forever. As for sugar, no white man can drink coffee after they have sweetened it to their liking.

I see that the pride which military life creates may cause the plantation trickeries to diminish. For instance, these men make the most admirable sentinels. It is far harder to pass the camp lines at night than in the camp from which I came; and I have seen none of that disposition to connive at the offences of members of one's own company which is so troublesome among white soldiers. Nor are they lazy, either about work or drill; in all respects they seem better material for soldiers than I had dared to hope.

There is one company in particular, all Florida men, which I certainly think the finest-looking company I ever saw, white or black; they range admirably in size, have remarkable erectness and ease of carriage, and really march splendidly. Not a visitor but notices them; yet they have been under drill only a fortnight, and a part only two days. They have all been slaves, and very few are even mulattoes.

December 4, 1862.

"Dwelling in tents, with Abraham, Isaac, and Jacob."[38] This condition is certainly mine,— and with a multitude of patriarchs beside, not to mention Cæsar and Pompey, Hercules and Bacchus.

A moving life, tented at night, this experience has been mine in civil society, if society be civil before the luxurious forest fires of Maine and the Adirondack, or upon the lonely prairies of Kansas. But a stationary tent life, deliberately going to housekeeping under canvas, I have never had before, though in our barrack life at "Camp Wool"[39] I often wished for it.

The accommodations here are about as liberal as my quarters there, two wall-tents being placed end to end, for office and bedroom, and separated at will by a "fly" of canvas. There is a good board floor and mop-board, effectually excluding dampness and draughts, and everything but sand, which on windy days penetrates everywhere. The office furniture consists of a good desk or secretary, a very clumsy and disastrous settee, and a remarkable chair. The desk is a bequest of the slaveholders, and the settee of the slaves, being ecclesiastical in its origin, and appertaining to the little old church or "praise-house," now used for commissary purposes. The chair is a composite structure: I found a cane seat on a dust-heap, which a black sergeant combined with two legs from a broken bedstead and two more from an oak-bough. I sit on it with a pride of conscious invention, mitigated by profound insecurity. Bedroom furniture, a couch made of gun-boxes covered with condemned blankets, another settee, two pails, a tin cup, tin basin (we prize any tin or wooden ware as savages prize iron), and a valise, regulation size. Seriously considered, nothing more appears needful, unless ambition might crave another chair for company, and, perhaps, something for a wash-stand higher than a settee.

To-day it rains hard, and the wind quivers through the closed canvas, and makes one feel at sea. All the talk of the camp outside is fused into a cheerful and indistinguishable murmur, pierced through at every moment by the wail of the hovering plover. Sometimes a face, black or white, peers through the entrance with some message. Since the light readily penetrates, though the rain cannot, the tent conveys a feeling of charmed security, as if an invisible boundary checked the pattering drops and held the moaning wind. The front tent I share, as yet, with my adjutant; in the inner apartment I reign supreme, bounded in a nutshell, with no bad dreams.

In all pleasant weather the outer "fly" is open, and men pass and repass, a chattering throng. I think of Emerson's Saadi,[40] "As thou sittest at thy door, on the desert's yellow floor,"—for these bare sand-plains, gray above, are always yellow when upturned, and there seems a tinge of Orientalism in all our life.

Thrice a day we go to the plantation-houses for our meals, camp-arrangements being yet very imperfect. The officers board in different messes, the adjutant and I still clinging to the household of William Washington,—William the quiet and the courteous, the pattern of house-servants, William the noiseless, the observing, the discriminating, who knows everything that can be got, and how to cook it. William and his tidy, lady-like little spouse Hetty—a pair of wedded lovers, if ever I saw one—set our table in their one room, halfway between an unglazed window and a large wood-fire, such as is often welcome. Thanks to the adjutant, we are provided with the social magnificence of napkins; while (lest pride take too high a flight) our table-cloth consists of two "New York Tribunes" and a "Leslie's Pictorial."[41] Every steamer brings us a clean table-cloth. Here are we forever supplied with pork and oysters and sweet potatoes and rice and hominy and corn-bread and milk; also mysterious griddle-cakes of corn and pumpkin; also preserves made of pumpkin-chips, and other fanciful productions of Ethiop art. Mr. E.[42] promised the plantation-superintendents who should come down here "all the luxuries of home," and we certainly have much apparent, if little real variety. Once William produced with some palpitation something fricasseed, which he boldly termed chicken; it was very small, and seemed in some undeveloped condition of ante-natal toughness. After the meal he frankly avowed it for a squirrel.

December 5, 1862.

Give these people their tongues, their feet, and their leisure, and they are happy. At every twilight the air is full of singing, talking, and clapping of hands in unison. One of their favorite songs is full of plaintive cadences; it is not, I think, a Methodist tune, and I wonder where they obtained a chant of such beauty.

"I can't stay behind, my Lord, I can't stay behind!
O, my father is gone, my father is gone,
My father is gone into heaven, my Lord!
   I can't stay behind!
Dere's room enough, room enough,
Room enough in de heaven for de sojer:
Can't stay behind!"[43]

It always excites them to have us looking on, yet they sing these songs at all times and seasons. I have heard this very song dimly droning on near midnight, and, tracing it into the recesses of a cook-house, have found an old fellow coiled away among the pots and provisions, chanting away with his "Can't stay behind, sinner," till I made him leave his song behind.

This evening, after working themselves up to the highest pitch, a party suddenly rushed off, got a barrel, and mounted some man upon it, who said, "Gib anoder song, boys, and I'se gib you a speech." After some hesitation and sundry shouts of "Rise de sing, somebody," and "Stan' up for Jesus, brudder," irreverently put in by the juveniles, they got upon the John Brown song,[44] always a favorite, adding a jubilant verse which I had never before heard,—"We'll beat Beauregard on de clare battlefield." Then came the promised speech, and then no less than seven other speeches by as many men, on a variety of barrels, each orator being affectionately tugged to the pedestal and set on end by his special constituency. Every speech was good, without exception; with the queerest oddities of phrase and pronunciation, there was an invariable enthusiasm, a pungency of statement, and an understanding of the points at issue, which made them all rather thrilling. Those long-winded slaves in "Among the Pines"[45] seemed rather fictitious and literary in comparison. The most eloquent, perhaps, was Corporal Price Lambkin, just arrived from Fernandina, who evidently had a previous reputation among them. His historical references were very interesting. He reminded them that he had predicted this war ever since Fremont's time, to which some of the crowd assented; he gave a very intelligent account of that Presidential campaign, and then described most impressively the secret anxiety of the slaves in Florida to know all about President Lincoln's election, and told how they all refused to work on the fourth of March, expecting their freedom to date from that day. He finally brought out one of the few really impressive appeals for the American flag that I have ever heard. "Our mas'rs dey hab lib under de flag, dey got dere wealth under it, and ebryting beautiful for dere chilen. Under it dey hab grind us up, and put us in dere pocket for money. But de fus' minute dey tink dat ole flag mean freedom for we colored people, dey pull it right down, and run up de rag ob dere own." (Immense applause). "But we'll neber desert de ole flag, boys, neber; we hab lib under it for *eighteen hundred sixty-two years*, and we'll die for it now." With which overpowering discharge of chronology-at-long-range, this most effective of stump-speeches closed. I see already with relief that there will be small demand in this regiment for harangues from the officers; give the men an empty barrel for a stump, and they will do their own exhortation.

December 11, 1862.

Haroun Alraschid,[46] wandering in disguise through his imperial streets, scarcely happened upon a greater variety of groups than I, in my evening strolls among our own camp-fires.

Beside some of these fires the men are cleaning their guns or rehearsing their drill,—beside others, smoking in silence their very scanty supply of the beloved tobacco,—beside others, telling stories and shouting with laughter over the broadest mimicry, in which they excel, and in which the officers come in for a full share. The everlasting "shout" is always within hearing, with its mixture of piety and polka, and its castanet-like clapping of the hands. Then there are quieter prayer-meetings, with pious invocations and slow psalms, "deaconed out" from memory by the leader, two lines at a time, in a sort of wailing chant. Elsewhere, there are *conversazioni* around fires, with a woman for queen of the circle,—her Nubian face, gay headdress, gilt necklace, and white teeth, all resplendent in the glowing light. Sometimes the woman is spelling slow monosyllables out of a primer, a feat which always commands all ears,—they rightly recognizing a mighty spell, equal to the overthrowing of monarchs, in the magic assonance of *cat, hat, pat, bat,* and the rest of it. Elsewhere, it is some solitary old cook, some aged Uncle Tiff, with enormous spectacles, who is perusing a hymn-book by the light of a pine splinter, in his deserted cooking booth of palmetto leaves. By another fire there is an actual dance, red-legged soldiers doing right-and-left, and "now-lead-de-lady-ober," to the music of a violin which is rather artistically played, and which may have guided the steps, in other days, of Barnwells and Hugers.[47] And yonder is a stump-orator perched on his barrel, pouring out his exhortations to fidelity in war and in religion. To-night for the first time I have heard a harangue in a different strain, quite saucy, sceptical, and defiant, appealing to them in a sort of French materialistic style, and claiming some personal experience of warfare. "You don't know notin' about it, boys. You tink you's brave enough; how you tink, if you stan' clar in de open field,—here you, and dar de Secesh? You's got to hab de right ting inside o' you. You must hab it 'served (preserved) in you, like dese yer sour plums dey 'serve in de barr'l; you's got to harden it down inside o' you, or it's notin." Then he hit hard at the religionists: "When a man's got de sperit ob de Lord in him, it weakens him all out, can't hoe de corn." He had a great deal of broad sense in his speech; but presently some others began praying vociferously close by, as if to drown this free-thinker, when at last he exclaimed, "I mean to fight de war through, an' die a good sojer wid de last kick,—dat's *my* prayer!" and suddenly jumped off the barrel. I was quite interested at discovering this reverse side of the temperament, the devotional side preponderates so enormously, and the greatest scamps kneel and groan in their prayer-meetings with such entire zest. It shows that there is some individuality developed among them, and that they will not become too exclusively pietistic.

Their love of the spelling-book is perfectly inexhaustible,—they stumbling on by themselves, or the blind leading the blind, with the same pathetic patience which they carry into everything. The chaplain is getting up a schoolhouse, where he will soon teach them as regularly as he can. But the alphabet must always be a very incidental business in a camp.

January 1, 1863 (evening).[48]

A happy New Year to civilized people,—mere white folks. Our festival has come and gone, with perfect success, and our good General has been altogether satisfied. Last night the great fires were kept smouldering in the pit, and the beeves were cooked more or less, chiefly more,—during which time they had to be carefully watched, and the great spits turned by main force. Happy were the merry fellows who were permitted to sit up all night, and watch the glimmering flames that threw a thousand fantastic shadows among the great gnarled oaks. And such a chattering as I was sure to hear whenever I awoke that night!

My first greeting to-day was from one of the most stylish sergeants, who approached me with the following little speech, evidently the result of some elaboration:

"I tink myself happy, dis New Year's Day, for salute my own Cunnel. Dis day las' year I was servant to a Cunnel ob Secesh; but now I hab de privilege for salute my own Cunnel."

That officer, with the utmost sincerity, reciprocated the sentiment.

About ten o'clock the people began to collect by land, and also by water,—in steamers sent by General Saxton for the purpose; and from that time all the avenues of approach were thronged. The multitude were chiefly colored women, with gay handkerchiefs on their heads, and a sprinkling of men, with that peculiarly respectable look which these people always have on Sundays and holidays. There were many white visitors also,—ladies on horseback and in carriages, superintendents and teachers, officers, and cavalry-men. Our companies were marched to the neighborhood of the platform, and allowed to sit or stand, as at the Sunday services; the platform was occupied by ladies and dignitaries, and by the band of the Eighth Maine, which kindly volunteered for the occasion; the colored people filled up all the vacant openings in the beautiful grove around, and there was a cordon of mounted visitors beyond. Above, the great live-oak branches and their trailing moss; beyond the people, a glimpse of the blue river.

The services began at half past eleven o'clock, with prayer by our chaplain, Mr. Fowler,[49] who is always, on such occasions, simple, reverential, and impressive. Then the President's Proclamation was read by Dr. W. H. Brisbane,[50] a thing infinitely appropriate, a South Carolinian addressing South Carolinians; for he was reared among these very islands, and here long since emancipated his own slaves. Then the colors were presented to us by the Rev. Mr. French,[51] a chaplain who brought them from the donors in New York. All this was according to the programme. Then followed an incident so simple, so touching, so utterly unexpected and startling, that I can scarcely believe it on recalling, though it gave the keynote to the whole day. The very moment the speaker had ceased, and just as I took and waved the flag, which now for the first time meant anything to these poor people, there suddenly arose, close beside the platform, a strong male voice (but rather cracked and elderly), into which two women's voices instantly blended, singing, as if by an impulse that could no more be repressed than the morning note of the song-sparrow.

"My Country, 'tis of thee,
Sweet land of liberty,
Of thee I sing!"[52]

People looked at each other, and then at us on the platform, to see whence came this interruption, not set down in the bills. Firmly and irrepressibly the quavering voices sang on, verse after verse; others of the colored people joined in; some whites on the platform began, but I motioned them to silence. I never saw anything so electric; it made all other words cheap; it seemed the choked voice of a race at last unloosed. Nothing could be more wonderfully unconscious; art could not have dreamed of a tribute to the day of jubilee that should be so affecting; history will not believe it; and when I came to speak of it, after it was ended, tears were everywhere. If you could have heard how quaint and innocent it was! Old Tiff and his children might have sung it; and close before me was a little slave-boy, almost white, who seemed to belong to the party, and even he must join in. Just think of it!—the first day they had ever had a country, the first flag they had ever seen which promised anything to their people, and here, while mere spectators stood in silence, waiting for my stupid words, these simple souls burst out in their lay, as if they were by their own hearths at home! When they stopped, there was nothing to do for it but to speak, and I went on; but the life of the whole day was in those unknown people's song.

Receiving the flags, I gave them into the hands of two fine-looking men, jet black, as color-guard, and they also spoke, and very effectively,—Sergeant Prince Rivers and Corporal Robert Sutton.[53] The regiment sang "Marching Along," and then General Saxton spoke, in his own simple, manly way, and Mrs. Francis D. Gage[54] spoke very sensibly to the women, and Judge Stickney, from Florida, added something; then some gentleman sang an ode, and the regiment the John Brown song, and then they went to their beef and molasses. Everything was very orderly, and they seemed to have a very gay time. Most of the visitors had far to go, and so dispersed before dress-parade, though the band stayed to enliven it. In the evening we had letters from home, and General Saxton had a reception at his house, from which I excused myself; and so ended one of the most enthusiastic and happy gatherings I ever knew. The day was perfect, and there was nothing but success.

I forgot to say, that, in the midst of the services, it was announced that General Fremont was appointed Commander-in-Chief,—an announcement which was received with immense cheering, as would have been almost anything else, I verily believe, at that moment of high tide. It was shouted across by the pickets above,—a way in which we often receive news, but not always trustworthy.

January 12.

Many things glide by without time to narrate them. On Saturday we had a mail with the President's Second Message of Emancipation, and the next day it was read to the men. The words themselves did not stir them very much, because they have been often told that they were free, especially on New Year's Day, and, being unversed in politics, they do not understand, as well as we do, the importance of each additional guaranty. But the chaplain spoke to them afterwards very effectively, as usual; and then I proposed to them to hold up their hands and pledge themselves to be faithful to those still in bondage. They entered heartily into this, and the scene was quite impressive, beneath the great oak-branches. I heard afterwards that only one man refused to raise his hand, saying bluntly that his wife was out of slavery with him, and he did not care to fight. The other soldiers of his company were very indignant, and shoved him about among them while marching back to their quarters, calling him "Coward." I was glad of their exhibition of feeling, though it is very possible that the one who had thus the moral courage to stand alone among his comrades might be more reliable, on a pinch, than some who yielded a more ready assent. But the whole response, on their part, was very hearty, and will be a good thing to which to hold them hereafter, at any time of discouragement or demoralization,—which was my chief reason for proposing it. With their simple natures it is a great thing to tie them to some definite committal; they never forget a marked occurrence, and never seem disposed to evade a pledge.

It is this capacity of honor and fidelity which gives me such entire faith in them as soldiers. Without it all their religious demonstration would be mere sentimentality. For instance, every one who visits the camp is struck with their bearing as sentinels. They exhibit, in this capacity, not an upstart conceit, but a steady, conscientious devotion to duty. They would stop their idolized General Saxton, if he attempted to cross their beat contrary to orders: I have seen them. No feeble or incompetent race could do this. The officers tell many amusing instances of this fidelity, but I think mine the best.

It was very dark the other night,—an unusual thing here,—and the rain fell in torrents; so I put on my India-rubber suit, and went the rounds of the sentinels, incognito, to test them. I can only say that I shall never try such an experiment again and have cautioned my officers against it. 'Tis a wonder I escaped with life and limb,—such a charging of bayonets and clicking of gun-locks. Sometimes I tempted them by refusing to give any countersign, but offering them a piece of tobacco, which they could not accept without allowing me nearer than the prescribed bayonet's distance. Tobacco is more than gold to them, and it was touching to watch the struggle in their minds; but they always did their duty at last, and I never could persuade them. One man, as if wishing to crush all his inward vacillation at one fell stroke, told me stoutly that he never used tobacco, though I found next day that he loved it as much as any one of them. It seemed wrong thus to tamper with their fidelity; yet it was a vital matter to me to know how far it could be trusted, out of my sight. It was so intensely dark that not more than one or two knew me, even after I had talked with the very next sentinel, especially as they had never seen me in India-rubber clothing, and I can always disguise my voice. It was easy to distinguish those who did make the discovery; they were always conscious and simpering when their turn came; while the others were stout and irreverent till I revealed myself, and then rather cowed and anxious, fearing to have offended.

It rained harder and harder, and when I had nearly made the rounds I had had enough of it, and, simply giving the countersign to the challenging sentinel, undertook to pass within the lines.

"Halt!" exclaimed this dusky man and brother, bringing down his bayonet, "de countersign not correck."

Now the magic word, in this case, was "Vicksburg," in honor of a rumored victory. But as I knew that these hard names became quite transformed upon their lips, "Carthage" being familiarized into Cartridge, and "Concord" into Corncob, how could I possibly tell what shade of pronunciation my friend might prefer for this particular proper name?

"Vicksburg," I repeated, blandly, but authoritatively, endeavoring, as zealously as one of Christy's Minstrels,[55] to assimilate my speech to any supposed predilection of the Ethiop vocal organs.

"Halt dar! Countersign not correck," was the only answer.

The bayonet still maintained a position which, in a military point of view, was impressive.

I tried persuasion, orthography, threats, tobacco, all in vain. I could not pass in. Of course my pride was up; for was I to defer to an untutored African on a point of pronunciation? Classic shades of Harvard, forbid! Affecting scornful indifference, I tried to edge away, proposing to myself to enter the camp at some other point, where my elocution would be better appreciated. Not a step could I stir.

"Halt!" shouted my gentleman again, still holding me at his bayonet's point, and I wincing and halting.

I explained to him the extreme absurdity of this proceeding, called his attention to the state of the weather, which, indeed, spoke for itself so loudly that we could hardly hear each other speak, and requested permission to withdraw. The bayonet, with mute eloquence, refused the application.

There flashed into my mind, with more enjoyment in the retrospect than I had experienced at the time, an adventure on a lecturing tour in other years, when I had spent an hour in trying to scramble into a country tavern, after bed-time, on the coldest night of winter. On that occasion I ultimately found myself stuck midway in the window, with my head in a temperature of 80°, and my heels in a temperature of -10°, with a heavy windowsash pinioning the small of my back. However, I had got safe out of that dilemma, and it was time to put an end to this one.

"Call the corporal of the guard," said I at last, with dignity, unwilling to make a night of it or to yield my incognito.

"Corporal ob de guard!" he shouted, lustily,—"Post Number Two!" while I could hear another sentinel chuckling with laughter. This last was a special guard, placed over a tent, with a prisoner in charge. Presently he broke silence.

"Who am dat?" he asked, in a stage whisper. "Am he a buckra (white man)?"

"Dunno whether he been a buckra or not," responded, doggedly, my Cerberus in uniform; "but I's bound to keep him here till de corporal ob de guard come."

Yet, when that dignitary arrived, and I revealed myself, poor Number Two appeared utterly transfixed with terror, and seemed to look for nothing less than immediate execution. Of course I praised his fidelity, and the next day complimented him before the guard, and mentioned him to his captain; and the whole affair was very good for them all. Hereafter, if Satan himself should approach them in darkness and storm, they will take him for "de Cunnel," and treat him with special severity.

January 13.

In many ways the childish nature of this people shows itself. I have just had to make a change of officers in a company which has constantly complained, and with good reason, of neglect and improper treatment. Two excellent officers have been assigned to them; and yet they sent a deputation to me in the evening, in a state of utter wretchedness. "We's bery grieved dis evening, Cunnel; 'pears like we couldn't bear it, to lose de Cap'n and de Lieutenant, all two togeder." Argument was useless; and I could only fall back on the general theory, that I knew what was best for them, which had much more effect; and I also could cite the instance of another company, which had been much improved by a new captain, as they readily admitted. So with the promise that the new officers should not be "savage to we," which was the one thing they deprecated, I assuaged their woes. Twenty-four hours have passed, and I hear them singing most merrily all down that company street.

I often notice how their griefs may be dispelled, like those of children, merely by permission to utter them: if they can tell their sorrows, they go away happy, even without asking to have anything done about them. I observe also a peculiar dislike of all *intermediate* control: they always wish to pass by the company officer, and deal with me personally for everything. General Saxton notices the same thing with the people on the plantations as regards himself. I suppose this proceeds partly from the old habit of appealing to the master against the overseer. Kind words would cost the master nothing, and he could easily put off any non-fulfilment upon the overseer. Moreover, the negroes have acquired such constitutional distrust of white people, that it is perhaps as much as they can do to trust more than one person at a time. Meanwhile this constant personal intercourse is out of the question in a well-ordered regiment; and the remedy for it is to introduce by degrees more and more of system, so that their immediate officers will become all-sufficient for the daily routine.

It is perfectly true (as I find everybody takes for granted) that the first essential for an officer of colored troops is to gain their confidence. But it is equally true, though many persons do not appreciate it, that the admirable methods and proprieties of the regular army are equally available for all troops, and that the sublimest philanthropist, if he does not appreciate this, is unfit to command them.

Another childlike attribute in these men, which is less agreeable, is a sort of blunt insensibility to giving physical pain. If they are cruel to animals, for instance, it always reminds me of children pulling off flies' legs, in a sort of pitiless, untaught, experimental way. Yet I should not fear any wanton outrage from them. After all their wrongs, they are not really revengeful; and I would far rather enter a captured city with them than with white troops, for they would be more subordinate. But for mere physical suffering they would have no fine sympathies. The cruel things they have seen and undergone have helped to blunt them; and if I ordered them to put to death a dozen prisoners, I think they would do it without remonstrance.

Yet their religious spirit grows more beautiful to me in living longer with them; it is certainly far more so than at first, when it seemed rather a matter of phrase and habit. It influences them both on the negative and the positive side. That is, it cultivates the feminine virtues first,—makes them patient, meek, resigned. This is very evident in the hospital; there is nothing of the restless, defiant habit of white invalids. Perhaps, if they had more of this, they would resist disease better. Imbued from childhood with the habit of submission, drinking in through every pore that other-world trust which is the one spirit of their songs, they can endure everything. This I expected; but I am relieved to find that their religion strengthens them on the positive side also, gives zeal, energy, daring. They could easily be made fanatics, if I chose; but I do not choose. Their whole mood is essentially Mohammedan, perhaps, in its strength and its weakness; and I feel the same degree of sympathy that I should if I had a Turkish command,—that is, a sort of sympathetic admiration, not tending towards agreement, but towards cooperation. Their philosophizing is often the highest form of mysticism; and our dear surgeon declares that they are all natural transcendentalists. The white camps seem rough and secular, after this; and I hear our men talk about "a religious army," "a Gospel army," in their prayer-meetings. They are certainly evangelizing the chaplain, who was rather a heretic at the beginning; at least, this is his own admission. We have recruits on their way from St. Augustine, where the negroes are chiefly Roman Catholics; and it will be interesting to see how their type of character combines with that elder creed.

It is time for rest; and I have just looked out into the night, where the eternal stars shut down, in concave protection, over the yet glimmering camp, and Orion hangs above my tent-door, giving to me the sense of strength and assurance which these simple children obtain from their Moses and the Prophets. Yet external Nature does its share in their training; witness that most poetic of all their songs, which always reminds me of the "Lyke-Wake Dirge" in the "Scottish Border Minstrelsy,"[56]—

> "I know moon-rise, I know star-rise;
>   Lay dis body down.
> I walk in de moonlight, I walk in de starlight,
>   To lay dis body down.
> I'll walk in de graveyard, I'll walk through de graveyard,
>   To lay dis body down.

I'll lie in de grave and stretch out my arms;
*   Lay dis body down.*
I go to de Judgment in de evening ob de day
*   When I lay dis body down;*
And my soul and your soul will meet in de day
*   When I lay dis body down."*

January 14.

In speaking of the military qualities of the blacks, I should add, that the only point where I am disappointed is one I have never seen raised by the most incredulous newspaper critics,—namely, their physical condition. To be sure they often look magnificently to my gymnasium-trained eye; and I always like to observe them when bathing,—such splendid muscular development, set off by that smooth coating of adipose tissue which makes them, like the South-Sea Islanders appear even more muscular than they are. Their skins are also of finer grain than those of whites, the surgeons say, and certainly are smoother and far more free from hair. But their weakness is pulmonary; pneumonia and pleurisy are their besetting ailments; they are easily made ill, and easily cured, if promptly treated: childish organizations again.[57] Guard-duty injures them more than whites, apparently; and double-quick movements, in choking dust, set them coughing badly. But then it is to be remembered that this is their sickly season, from January to March, and that their healthy season will come in summer, when the whites break down. Still my conviction of the physical superiority of more highly civilized races is strengthened on the whole, not weakened, by observing them. As to availability for military drill and duty in other respects, the only question I ever hear debated among the officers is, whether they are equal or superior to whites. I have never heard it suggested that they were inferior, although I expected frequently to hear such complaints from hasty or unsuccessful officers.

Of one thing I am sure, that their best qualities will be wasted by merely keeping them for garrison duty. They seem peculiarly fitted for offensive operations, and especially for partisan warfare; they have so much dash and such abundant resources, combined with such an Indian-like knowledge of the country and its ways. These traits have been often illustrated in expeditions sent after deserters. For instance, I despatched one of my best lieutenants and my best sergeant with a squad of men to search a certain plantation, where there were two separate negro villages. They went by night, and the force was divided. The lieutenant took one set of huts, the sergeant the other. Before the lieutenant had reached his first house, every man in the village was in the woods, innocent and guilty alike. But the sergeant's mode of operation was thus described by a corporal from a white regiment who happened to be in one of the negro houses. He said that not a sound was heard until suddenly a red leg appeared in the open doorway, and a voice outside said, "Rally." Going to the door, he observed a similar pair of red legs before every hut, and not a person was allowed to go out, until the quarters had been thoroughly searched, and the three deserters found. This was managed by Sergeant Prince Rivers, our color-sergeant, who is provost-sergeant also, and has entire charge of the prisoners and of the daily policing of the camp. He is a man of distinguished appearance, and in old times was the crack coachman of Beaufort, in which capacity he once drove Beauregard from this plantation to Charleston, I believe. They tell me that he was once allowed to present a petition to the Governor of South Carolina in behalf of slaves, for the redress of certain grievances; and that a placard, offering two thousand dollars for his recapture, is still to be seen by the wayside between here and Charleston. He was a sergeant in the old "Hunter Regiment," and was taken by General Hunter to New York last spring, where the *chevrons* on his arm brought a mob upon him in Broadway, whom he kept off till the police interfered. There is not a white officer in this regiment who has more administrative ability, or more absolute authority over the men; they do not love him, but his mere presence has controlling power over them. He writes well enough to prepare for me a daily report of his duties in the camp; if his education reached a higher point, I see no reason why he should not command the Army of the Potomac. He is jet-black, or rather, I should say, *wine-black*; his complexion, like that of others of my darkest men, having a sort of rich, clear depth, without a trace of sootiness, and to my eye very handsome. His features are tolerably regular, and full of command, and his figure superior to that of any of our white officers,—being six feet high, perfectly proportioned, and of apparently inexhaustible strength and activity. His gait is like a panther's; I never saw such a tread. No anti-slavery novel has described a man of such marked ability. He makes Toussaint[58] perfectly intelligible; and if there should ever be a black monarchy in South Carolina, he will be its king.

Rebecca Harding Davis

JOHN LAMAR
(1862)

The guard-house was, in fact, nothing but a shed in the middle of a stubble-field. It had been built for a cider-press last summer; but since Captain Dorr had gone into the army, his regiment had camped over half his plantation, and the shed was boarded up, with heavy wickets at either end, to hold whatever prisoners might fall into their hands from Floyd's forces. It was a strong point for the Federal troops, his farm,—a sort of wedge in the Rebel Cheat counties[59] of Western Virginia. Only one prisoner was in the guard-house now. The sentry, a raw boat-hand from Illinois, gaped incessantly at him through the bars, not sure if the "Secesh" were limbed and headed like other men; but the November fog was so thick that he could discern nothing but a short, squat man, in brown clothes and white hat, heavily striding to and fro. A negro was crouching outside, his knees cuddled in his arms to keep warm: a field-hand, you could be sure from the face, a grisly patch of flabby black, with a dull eluding word of something, you could not tell what, in the points of eyes,—treachery or gloom. The prisoner stopped, cursing him about something: the only answer was a lazy rub of the heels.

"Got any 'baccy, Mars' John?" he whined, in the middle of the hottest oath.

The man stopped abruptly, turning his pockets inside out.

"That's all, Ben," he said, kindly enough. "Now begone, you black devil!"

"Dem's um, Mars'! Goin' 'mediate,"—catching the tobacco, and lolling down full length as his master turned off again.

Dave Hall, the sentry, stared reflectively, and sat down.

"Ben? Who air you next?"—nursing his musket across his knees, baby-fashion.

Ben measured him with one eye, polished the quid in his greasy hand, and looked at it.

"Pris'ner o' war," he mumbled, finally,—contemptuously; for Dave's trousers were in rags like his own, and his chilblained toes stuck through the shoe-tops. Cheap white trash, clearly.

"Yer master's some at swearin'. Heow many, neow, hes he like you, down to Georgy?"

The boatman's bony face was gathering a woful pity. He had enlisted to free the Uncle Toms, and carry God's vengeance to the Legrees. Here they were, a pair of them.[60]

Ben squinted another critical survey of the "miss'able Linkinite."

"How many wells hev *yer* poisoned since yer set out?" he muttered.

The sentry stopped.

"How many 'longin' to de Lamars? 'Bout as many as der's dam' Yankees in Richmond 'baccy-houses!"

Something in Dave's shrewd, whitish eye warned him off.

"Ki yi! yer white nigger, yer!" he chuckled, shuffling down the stubble.

Dave clicked his musket,—then, choking down an oath into a grim Methodist psalm, resumed his walk, looking askance at the coarse-moulded face of that prisoner peering through the bars, and the diamond studs in his shirt,—bought with human blood, doubtless. The man was the black curse of slavery itself in the flesh, in his thought some-how, and he hated him accordingly. Our men of the Northwest have enough brawny Covenanter muscle in their religion to make them good haters for opinion's sake.[61]

Lamar, the prisoner, watched him with a lazy drollery in his sluggish black eyes. It died out into sternness, as he looked beyond the sentry. He had seen this Cheat country before; this very plantation was his grandfather's a year ago, when he had come up from Georgia here, and loitered out the summer months with his Virginia cousins, hunting. That was a pleasant summer! Something in the remembrance of it flashed into his eyes, dewy, genial; the man's leather-covered face reddened like a child's. Only a year ago,—and now—The plantation was Charley Dorr's now, who had married Ruth. This very shed he and Dorr had planned last spring, and now Charley held him a prisoner in it. The very thought of Charley Dorr warmed his heart. Why, he could thank God there were such men. True grit, every inch of his little body! There, last summer, how he had avoided Ruth until the day when he (Lamar) was going away!—then he told him he meant to try and win her. "She cared most for you always," Lamar had said, bitterly; "why have you waited so long?" "You loved her first, John, you know." That was like a man! He remembered that even that day, when his pain was breathless and sharp, the words made him know that Dorr was fit to be her husband.

Dorr was his friend. The word meant much to John Lamar. He thought less meanly of himself when he remembered it. Charley's prisoner! An odd chance! Better that than to have met in battle. He thrust hack the thought, the sweat oozing out on his face,—something within him muttering, "For Liberty! I would have killed him, so help me God!"

He had brought despatches to General Lee, that he might see Charley, and the old place, and—Ruth again; there was a gnawing hunger in his heart to see them. Fool! what was he to them? The man's face grew slowly pale, as that of a savage or an animal does, when the wound is deep and inward.

The November day was dead, sunless: since morning the sky had had only enough life in it to sweat out a few muddy drops, that froze as they fell: the cold numbed his mouth as he breathed it. This stubbly slope was where he and his grandfather had headed the deer: it was covered with hundreds of dirty, yellow tents now. Around there were hills like uncouth monsters, swathed in ice, holding up the soggy sky; shivering pine-forests; un-meaning, dreary flats; and the Cheat, coiled about the frozen sinews of the hills, limp and cold, like a cord tying a dead man's jaws. Whatever outlook of joy or worship this region had borne on its face in time gone, it turned to him to-day nothing but stagnation, a great death. He wondered idly, looking at it, (for the old Huguenot brain of the man was full of morbid fancies,) if it were winter alone that had deadened color and pulse out of these full-blooded hills, or if they could know the colder horror crossing their threshold, and forgot to praise God as it came.

Over that farthest ridge the house had stood. The guard (he had been taken by a band of Snake-hunters, back in the hills) had brought him past it. It was a heap of charred rafters. "Burned in the night," they said, "when the old Colonel was alone." They were very willing to show him this, as it was done by his own party, the Secession "Bush-whackers"; took him to the wood-pile to show him where his grandfather had been murdered, (there was a red mark,) and buried, his old hands above the ground. "Colonel said 't was a job fur us to pay up; so we went to the village an' hed a scrimmage,"—pointing to gaps in the hedges where the dead Bush-whackers yet lay unburied. He looked at them, and at the besotted faces about him, coolly. Snake-hunters and Bush-whackers, he knew, both armies used in Virginia as tools for rapine and murder: the sooner the Devil called home his own, the better. And yet, it was not God's fault, surely, that there were such tools in the North, any more than that in the South Ben was—Ben. Something was rotten in freer States than Denmark, he thought.

One of the men went into the hedge, and brought out a child's golden ringlet as a trophy. Lamar glanced in, and saw the small face in its woollen hood, dimpled yet, though dead for days. He remembered it. Jessy Birt, the ferryman's little girl. She used to come up to the house every day for milk. He wondered for which flag *she* died. Ruth was teaching her to write. *Ruth*! Some old pain hurt him just then, nearer than even the blood of the old man or the girl crying to God from the ground. The sergeant mistook the look. "They'll be buried," he said, gruffly. "Ye brought it on yerselves." And so led him to the Federal camp.

The afternoon grew colder, as he stood looking out of the guard-house. Snow began to whiten through the gray. He thrust out his arm through the wicket, his face kindling with childish pleasure, as he looked closer at the fairy stars and crowns on his shaggy sleeve. If Floy were here! She never had seen snow. When the flakes had melted off, he took a case out of his pocket to look at Floy. His sister,—a little girl who had no mother, nor father, nor lover, but Lamar. The man among his brother officers in Richmond was coarse, arrogant, of dogged courage, keen palate at the table, as keen eye on the turf. Sickly little Floy, down at home, knew the way to something below all this: just as they of the Rommany blood see below the muddy boulders of the streets the enchanted land of Boabdil bare beneath. Lamar polished the ivory painting with his breath, remembering that he had drunk nothing for days. A child's face, of about twelve, delicate,—a breath of fever or cold would shatter such weak beauty; big, dark eyes, (her mother was pure Castilian,) out of which her little life looked irresolute into the world, uncertain what to do there. The painter, with an unapt fancy, had clustered about the Southern face the Southern emblem, buds of the magnolia, unstained, as yet, as pearl. It angered Lamar, remembering how the creamy whiteness of the full-blown flower exhaled passion of which the crimsonest rose knew nothing,—a content, ecstasy, in animal life. Would Floy—Well, God help them both! they needed help. Three hundred souls was a heavy weight for those thin little hands to hold sway over,—to lead to hell or heaven. Up North they could have worked for her, and gained only her money. So Lamar reasoned, like a Georgian: scribbling a letter to "My Baby" on the wrapper of a newspaper,—drawing the shapes of the snow-flakes,—telling her he had reached their grandfather's plantation, but "have not seen our Cousin Ruth yet, of whom you may remember I have told you, Floy. When you grow up, I should like you to be just such a woman; so remember, my darling, if I"—He scratched the last words out: why should he hint to her that he could die? Holding his life loose in his hand, though, had brought things closer to him lately,—God and death, this war, the meaning of it all. But he would keep his brawny body between these terrible realities and Floy, yet awhile. "I want you," he wrote, "to leave the plantation, and go with your old maumer to the village. It will be safer there." He was sure the letter would reach her. He had a plan to escape to-night, and he could put it into a post inside the lines. Ben was to get a small hand-saw that would open the wicket; the guards were not hard to elude. Glancing up, he saw the negro stretched by a camp-fire, listening to the gaunt boatman, who was off duty. Preaching Abolitionism, doubtless: he could hear Ben's derisive shouts of laughter. "And so, good bye, Baby Florence!" he scrawled. "I wish I could send you some of this snow, to show you what the floor of heaven is like."

While the snow fell faster without, he stopped writing, and began idly drawing a map of Georgia on the tan-bark with a stick. Here the Federal troops could effect a landing: he knew the defences at that point. If they did? He thought of these Snake-hunters[62] who had found in the war a peculiar road for themselves downward with no gallows to stumble over, fancied he saw them skulking through the fields at Cedar Creek, closing around the house, and behind them a mass of black faces and bloody bayonets. Floy alone, and he here,—like a rat in a trap! "God keep my little girl!" he wrote, unsteadily. "God bless you, Floy!" He gasped for breath, as if he had been writing with his heart's blood. Folding up the paper, he hid it inside his shirt and began his dogged walk, calculating the chances of escape. Once out of this shed, he could baffle a blood-hound, he knew the hills so well.

His head bent down, he did not see a man who stood looking at him over the wicket. Captain Dorr. A puny little man, with thin yellow hair, and womanish face: but not the less the hero of his men,—they having found out, somehow, that muscle was not the solidest thing to travel on in war-times. Our regiments of "roughs" were not altogether crowned with laurel at Manassas! So the men built more on the old Greatheart soul in the man's blue eyes: one of those souls born and bred pure, sent to teach, that can find breath only in the free North. His hearty "Hillo!" startled Lamar.

"How are you, old fellow?" he said, unlocking the gate and coming in.

Lamar threw off his wretched thoughts, glad to do it. What need to borrow trouble? He liked a laugh,—had a lazy, jolly humor of his own. Dorr had finished drill, and come up, as he did every day, to freshen himself with an hour's talk to this warm, blundering fellow. In this dismal war-work, (though his whole soul was in that, too,) it was like putting your hands to a big blaze. Dorr had no near relations; Lamar—they had played marbles together—stood to him where a younger brother might have stood. Yet, as they talked, he could not help his keen eye seeing him just as he was.

Poor John! he thought: the same uncouth-looking effort of humanity that he had been at Yale. No wonder the Northern boys jeered him, with his sloth-ways, his mouthed English, torpid eyes, and brain shut up in that worst of mud-moulds,—belief in caste. Even now, going up and down the tan-bark, his step was dead, sodden, like that of a man in whose life God had not yet wakened the full live soul. It was wakening, though, Dorr thought. Some pain or passion was bringing the man in him out of the flesh, vigilant, alert, aspirant. A different man from Dorr.

In fact, Lamar was just beginning to think for himself and of course his thoughts were defiant, intolerant. He did not comprehend how his companion could give his heresies such quiet welcome, and pronounce sentence of death on them so coolly. Because Dorr had gone farther up the mountain, had he the right to make him follow in the same steps? The right,—that was it. By brute force, too? Human freedom, eh? Consequently, their talks were stormy enough. To-day, however, they were on trivial matters.

"I've brought the General's order for your release at last, John. It confines you to this district, however."

Lamar shook his head.

"No parole for me! My stake outside is too heavy for me to remain a prisoner on anything but compulsion. I mean to escape, if I can. Floy has nobody but me, you know, Charley."

There was a moment's silence.

"I wish," said Dorr, half to himself, "the child was with her cousin Ruth. If she could make her a woman like herself!"

"You are kind," Lamar forced out, thinking of what might have been a year ago.

Dorr had forgotten. He had just kissed little Ruth at the door-step, coming away: thinking, as he walked up to camp, how her clear thought, narrow as it was, was making his own higher, more just; wondering if the tears on her face last night, when she got up from her knees after prayer, might not help as much in the great cause of truth as the life he was ready to give. He was so used to his little wife now, that he could look to no hour of his past life, nor of the future coming ages of event and work, where she was not present,—very flesh of his flesh, heart of his heart. A gulf lay between them and the rest of the world. It was hardly probable he could see her as a woman towards whom another man looked across the gulf, dumb, hopeless, defrauded of his right.

"She sent you some flowers, by the way, John,—the last in the yard,—and bade me be sure and bring you down with me. Your own colors, you see?—to put you in mind of home,"—pointing to the crimson asters flaked with snow.

The man smiled faintly: the smell of the flowers choked him: he laid them aside. God knows he was trying to wring out this bitter old thought: he could not look in Dorr's frank eyes while it was there. He must escape to-night: he never would come near them again, in this world, or beyond death,—never! He thought of that like a man going to drag through eternity with half his soul gone. Very well: there was man enough left in him to work honestly and bravely, and to thank God for that good pure love he yet had. He turned to Dorr with a flushed face, and began talking of Floy in hearty earnest,—glancing at Ben coming up the hill, thinking that escape depended on him.

"I ordered your man up," said Captain Dorr. "Some canting Abolitionist had him open-mouthed down there."

The negro came in, and stood in the corner, listening while they talked. A gigantic fellow, with a gladiator's muscles. Stronger than that Yankee captain, he thought,—than either of them: better breathed,—drawing the air into his brawny chest. "A man and a brother."[63] Did the fool think he didn't know that before? He had a contempt for Dave and his like. Lamar would have told you Dave's words were true, but despised the man as a crude, unlicked bigot. Ben did the same, with no words for the idea. The negro instinct in him recognized gentle blood by any of its signs,—the transparent animal life, the reticent eye, the mastered voice: he had better men than Lamar at home to learn it from. It is a trait of serfdom, the keen eye to measure the inherent rights of a man to be master. A negro or a Catholic Irishman does not need "Sartor Resartus"[64] to help him to see through any clothes. Ben leaned, half-asleep, against the wall, some old thoughts creeping out of their hiding-places through the torpor, like rats to the sunshine: the boatman's slang had been hot and true enough to rouse them in his brain.

"So, Ben," said his master, as he passed once, "your friend has been persuading you to exchange the cotton-fields at Cedar Creek for New-York alleys, eh?"

"Ki!" laughed Ben, "white darkey. Mind ole dad, Mars' John, as took off in der swamp? Um asked dat Linkinite ef him saw dad up Norf. Guess him's free now. Ki! ole dad!"

"The swamp was the place for him," said Lamar. "I remember."

"Dunno," said the negro, surlily: "him's dad, af'er all: tink him's free now,"—and mumbled down into a monotonous drone about

"Oh yo, bredern, is yer gwine ober Jordern?"

Half-asleep, they thought,—but with dull questionings at work in his brain, some queer notions about freedom, of that unknown North, mostly mixed with his remembrance of his father, a vicious old negro, that in Pennsylvania would have worked out his salvation in the under cell of the penitentiary, but in Georgia, whipped into heroism, had betaken himself into the swamp, and never returned. Tradition among the Lamar slaves said he had got off to Ohio, of which they had as clear an idea as most of us have of heaven. At any rate, old Kite became a mystery, to be mentioned with awe at fish-bakes and barbecues. He was this uncouth wretch's father,—do you understand? The flabby-faced boy, flogged in the cotton-field for whining after his dad, or hiding away part of his fitch and molasses for months in hopes the old man would come back, was rather a comical object, you would have thought. Very different his, from the feeling with which you left your mother's grave,—though as yet we have not invented names for the emotions of those people. We'll grant that it hurt Ben a little, however. Even the young polypus, when it is torn from the old one, bleeds a drop or two, they say. As he grew up, the great North glimmered through his thought, a sort of big field,—a paradise of no work, no flogging, and white bread every day, where the old man sat and ate his fill.

The second point in Ben's history was that he fell in love. Just as you did,—with the difference, of course: though the hot sun, or the perpetual foot upon his breast, does not make our black Prometheus less fierce in his agony of hope or jealousy than you, I am afraid. It was Nan, a pale mulatto house-servant, that the field-hand took into his dull, lonesome heart to make life of with true-love defiance of caste. I think Nan liked him very truly. She was lame and sickly, and if Ben was black and a picker, and stayed in the quarters, he was strong, like a master to her in some ways: the only thing she could call hers in the world was the love the clumsy boy gave her. White women feel in that way sometimes, and it makes them very tender to men not their equals. However, old Mrs. Lamar, before she died, gave her house-servants their free papers, and Nan was among them. So she set off, with all the finery little Floy could give her: went up into that great, dim North. She never came again.

The North swallowed up all Ben knew or felt outside of his hot, hated work, his dread of a lashing on Saturday night. All the pleasure left him was 'possum and hominy for Sunday's dinner. It did not content him. The spasmodic religion of the field-negro does not teach endurance. So it came, that the slow tide of discontent ebbing in everybody's heart towards some unreached sea set in his ignorant brooding towards that vague country which the only two who cared for him had found. If he forgot it through the dogged, sultry days, he remembered it when the overseer scourged the dull tiger-look into his eyes, or when, husking corn with the others at night, the smothered negro-soul, into which their masters dared not look, broke out in their wild, melancholy songs. Aimless, unappealing, yet no prayer goes up to God more keen in its pathos. You find, perhaps, in Beethoven's seventh symphony the secrets of your heart made manifest, and suddenly think of a Somewhere to come, where your hope waits for you with late fulfilment. Do not laugh at Ben, then, if he dully told in his song the story of all he had lost, or gave to his heaven a local habitation and a name.

From the place where he stood now, as his master and Dorr walked up and down, he could see the purplish haze beyond which the sentry had told him lay the North. The

North! Just beyond the ridge. There was a pain in his head, looking at it; his nerves grew cold and rigid, as yours do when something wrings your heart sharply: for there are nerves in these black carcasses, thicker, more quickly stung to madness than yours. Yet if any savage longing, smouldering for years, was heating to madness now in his brain, there was no sign of it in his face. Vapid, with sordid content, the huge jaws munching tobacco slowly, only now and then the beady eye shot a sharp glance after Dorr. The sentry had told him the Northern army had come to set the slaves free; he watched the Federal officer keenly.

"What ails you, Ben?" said his master. "Thinking over your friend's sermon?"

Ben's stolid laugh was ready.

"Done forgot dat, Mars'. Would n't go, nohow. Since Mars' sold dat cussed Joe, gorry good times 't home. Dam' Abolitioner say we ums all goin' Norf,"—with a stealthy glance at Dorr.

"That's more than your philanthropy bargains for, Charley," laughed Lamar.

The men stopped; the negro skulked nearer, his whole senses sharpened into hearing. Dorr's clear face was clouded.

"This slave question must be kept out of the war. It puts a false face on it."

"I thought one face was what it needed," said Lamar. "You have too many slogans. Strong government, tariff, Sumter, a bit of bunting, eleven dollars a month. It ought to be a vital truth that would give soul and *vim* to a body with the differing members of your army. You, with your ideal theory, and Billy Wilson with his 'Blood and Baltimore!' Try human freedom. That's high and sharp and broad."

Ben drew a step closer.

"You are shrewd, Lamar. I am to go below all constitutions or expediency or existing rights, and tell Ben here that he is free? When once the Government accepts that doctrine, you, as a Rebel, must be let alone."

The slave was hid back in the shade.

"Dorr," said Lamar, "you know I'm a groping, ignorant fellow, but it seems to me that prating of constitutions and existing rights is surface talk; there is a broad common-sense underneath, by whose laws the world is governed, which your statesmen don't touch often. You in the North, in your dream of what shall be, shut your eyes to what is. You want a republic where every man's voice shall be heard in the council, and the majority shall rule. Granting that the free population are educated to a fitness for this,—(God forbid I should grant it with the Snake-hunters before my eyes !)—look here!"

He turned round, and drew the slave out into the light: he crouched down, gaping vacantly at them.

"There is Ben. What, in God's name, will you do with him? Keep him a slave, and chatter about self-government? Pah! The country is paying in blood for the lie, to-day. Educate him for freedom, by putting a musket in his hands? We have this mass of heathendom drifted on our shores by your will as well as mine. Try to bring them to a level with the whites by a wrench, and you'll waken out of your dream to a sharp reality. Your Northern philosophy ought to be old enough to teach you that spasms in the body-politic shake off no atom of disease,—that reform, to be enduring, must be patient, gradual, inflexible as the Great Reformer. 'The mills of God,' the old proverb says, 'grind surely.' But, Dorr, they grind exceeding slow!"

Dorr watched Lamar with an amused smile. It pleased him to see his brain waking up, eager, vehement. As for Ben, crouching there, if they talked of him like a clod, heedless that his face deepened in stupor, that his eyes had caught a strange, gloomy treachery,—we all do the same, you know.

"What is your remedy, Lamar? You have no belief in the right of Secession, I know," said Dorr.

"It's a bad instrument for a good end. Let the white Georgian come out of his sloth, and the black will rise with him. Jefferson Davis may not intend it, but God does. When we have our Lowell,[65] our New York, when we are a self-sustaining people instead of lazy land-princes, Ben here will have climbed the second of the great steps of Humanity. Do you laugh at us?" said Lamar, with a quiet self-reliance. "Charley, it needs only work and ambition to cut the brute away from my face, and it will leave traits very like your own. Ben's father was a Guinea fetich-worshipper; when we stand where New England does, Ben's son will be ready for his freedom."

"And while you theorize," laughed Dorr, "I hold you a prisoner, John, and Ben knows it is his right to be free. He will not wait for the grinding of the mill, I fancy."

Lamar did not smile. It was womanish in the man, when the life of great nations hung in doubt before them, to go back so constantly to little Floy sitting in the lap of her old black maumer. But he did it,—with the quick thought that to-night he must escape, that death lay in delay.

While Dorr talked, Lamar glanced significantly at Ben. The negro was not slow to understand,—with a broad grin, touching his pocket, from which projected the dull end of a hand-saw. I wonder what sudden pain made the negro rise just then, and come close to his master, touching him with a strange affection and remorse in his tired face, as though he had done him some deadly wrong.

"What is it, old fellow?" said Lamar, in his boyish way. "Homesick, eh? There's a little girl in Georgia that will be glad to see you and your master, and take precious good care of us when she gets us safe again. That's true, Ben!" laying his hand kindly on the man's shoulder, while his eyes went wandering off to the hills lying South.

"'Yes, Mars," said Ben, in a low voice, suddenly bringing a blacking-brush, and beginning to polish his master's shoes,—thinking, while he did it, of how often Mars' John had interfered with the over-seers to save him from a flogging,—(Lamar, in his lazy way, was kind to his slaves,)—thinking of little Mist' Floy with an odd tenderness and awe, as a gorilla might of a white dove: trying to think thus,—the simple, kindly nature of the negro struggling madly with something beneath, new and horrible. He understood enough of the talk of the white men to know that there was no help for him,—none. Always a slave. Neither you nor I can know what those words meant to him. The pale purple mist where the North lay was never to be passed. His dull eyes turned to it constantly,—with a strange look, such as the lost women might have turned to the door, when Jesus shut it: they forever outside. There was a way to help himself? The stubby black fingers holding the brush grew cold and clammy,—noting withal, the poor wretch in his slavish way, that his master's clothes were finer than the Northern captain's, his hands whiter, and proud that it was so,—holding Lamar's foot daintily, trying to see himself in the shoe, smoothing down the trousers with a boorish, affectionate touch,—with the same fierce whisper in his ear, Would the shoes ever be cleaned again? would the foot move to-morrow?

It grew late. Lamar's supper was brought up from Captain Dorr's, and placed on the bench. He poured out a goblet of water.

"Come, Charley, let's drink. To Liberty! It is a war-cry for Satan or Michael."

They drank, laughing, while Ben stood watching. Dorr turned to go, but Lamar called him back,—stood resting his hand on his shoulder: he never thought to see him again, you know.

"Look at Ruth, yonder," said Dorr, his face lighting. "She is coming to meet us. She thought you would be with me."

Lamar looked gravely down at the low field-house and the figure at the gate. He thought he could see the small face and earnest eyes, though it was far off and night was closing.

"She is waiting for you, Charley. Go down. Good night, old chum!"

If it cost any effort to say it, Dorr saw nothing of it.

"Good night, Lamar! I'll see you in the morning."

He lingered. His old comrade looked strangely alone and desolate.

"John!"

"What is it, Dorr?"

"If I could tell the Colonel you would take the oath? For Floy's sake."

The man's rough face reddened.

"You should know me better. Good bye."

"Well, well, you are mad. Have you no message for Ruth?"

There was a moment's silence.

"Tell her I say, God bless her!"

Dorr stopped and looked keenly in his face,—then, coming back, shook hands again, in a different way from before, speaking in a lower voice,—

"God help us all, John! Good night!"—and went slowly down the hill.

It was nearly night, and bitter cold. Lamar stood where the snow drifted in on him, looking out through the horizonless gray.

"Come out o' dem cold, Mars' John," whined Ben, pulling at his coat.

As the night gathered, the negro was haunted with a terrified wish to be kind to his master. Something told him that the time was short. Here and there through the far night some tent-fire glowed in a cone of ruddy haze, through which the thick-falling snow shivered like flakes of light. Lamar watched only the square block of shadow where Dorr's house stood. The door opened at last, and a broad, cheerful gleam shot out red darts across the white waste without; then he saw two figures go in together. They paused a moment; he put his head against the bars, straining his eyes, and saw that the woman turned, shading her eyes with her hand, and looked up to the side of the mountain where the guard-house lay,—with a kindly look, perhaps, for the prisoner out in the cold. A kind look: that was all. The door shut on them. Forever: so, good night, Ruth!

He stood there for an hour or two, leaning his head against the muddy planks, smoking. Perhaps, in his coarse fashion, he took the trouble of his manhood back to the same God he used to pray to long ago. When he turned at last, and spoke, it was with a quiet, strong voice, like one who would fight through life in a manly way. There was a grating sound at the back of the shed: it was Ben, sawing through the wicket, the guard having lounged off to supper. Lamar watched him, noticing that the negro was unusually silent. The plank splintered, and hung loose.

"Done gone, Mars' John, now,"—leaving it, and beginning to replenish the fire.

"That's right, Ben. We'll start in the morning. That sentry at two o'clock sleeps regularly."

Ben chuckled, heaping up the sticks.

"Go on down to the camp, as usual. At two, Ben, remember! We will be free to-night, old boy!"

The black face looked up from the clogging smoke with a curious stare.

"Ki! we'll be free to-night, Mars'!"—gulping his breath.

Soon after, the sentry unlocked the gate, and he shambled off out into the night. Lamar, left alone, went closer to the fire, and worked busily at some papers he drew from his pocket: maps and schedules. He intended to write until two o'clock; but the blaze dying down, he wrapped his blanket about him, and lay down on the heaped straw, going on sleepily, in his brain, with his calculations.

The negro, in the shadow of the shed, watched him. A vague fear beset him,—of the vast, white cold,—the glowering mountains,—of himself; he clung to the familiar face, like a man drifting out into an unknown sea, clutching some relic of the shore. When Lamar fell asleep, he wandered uncertainly towards the tents. The world had grown new, strange; was he Ben, picking cotton in the swamp-edge?—plunging his fingers with a shudder in the icy drifts. Down in the glowing torpor of the Santilla flats, where the Lamar plantations lay, Ben had slept off as maddening hunger for life and freedom as this of to-day; but here, with the winter air stinging every nerve to life, with the perpetual mystery of the mountains terrifying his bestial nature down, the strength of the man stood up: groping, blind, malignant, it may be; but whose fault was that? He was half-frozen: the physical pain sharpened the keen doubt conquering his thought. He sat down in the crusted snow, looking vacantly about him, a man, at last,—but wakening, like a new-born soul, into a world of unutterable solitude. Wakened dully, slowly; sitting there far into the night, pondering stupidly on his old life; crushing down and out the old parasite affection for his master, the old fears, the old weight threatening to press out his thin life; the muddy blood heating, firing with the same heroic dream that bade Tell and Garibaldi[66] lift up their hands to God, and cry aloud that they were men and free: the same,—God-given, burning in the imbruted veins of a Guinea slave. To what end? May God be merciful to America while she answers the question! He sat, rubbing his cracked, bleeding feet, glancing stealthily at the southern hills. Beyond them lay all that was past; in an hour he would follow Lamar back to—what? He lifted his hands up to the sky, in his silly way sobbing hot tears. "Gor-a'mighty, Mars' Lord, I'se tired," was all the prayer he made. The pale purple mist was gone from the North; the ridge behind which love, freedom waited, struck black across the sky, a wall of iron. He looked at it drearily. Utterly alone: he had always been alone. He got up at last, with a sigh.

"It 's a big world,"—with a bitter chuckle,—"but der's no room in it fur poor Ben."

He dragged himself through the snow to a light in a tent where a voice in a wild drone, like that he had heard at negro camp-meetings, attracted him. He did not go in: stood at the tent-door, listening. Two or three of the guard [sic] stood around, leaning on their muskets; in the vivid fire-light rose the gaunt figure of the Illinois boatman, swaying to and fro as he preached. For the men were honest, God-fearing souls, members of the same church, and Dave, in all integrity of purpose, read aloud to them,—the cry of Jeremiah against the foul splendors of the doomed city,[67]—waving, as he spoke, his bony arm to the

South. The shrill voice was that of a man wrestling with his Maker. The negro's fired brain caught the terrible meaning of the words,—found speech in it: the wide, dark night, the solemn silence of the men, were only fitting audience.

The man caught sight of the slave, and, laying down his book, began one of those strange exhortations in the manner of his sect. Slow at first, full of unutterable pity. There was room for pity. Pointing to the human brute crouching there, made once in the image of God,—the saddest wreck on his green foot-stool: to the great stealthy body, the revengeful jaws, the foreboding eyes. Soul, brains,—a man, wifeless, homeless, nationless, hawked, flung from trader to trader for a handful of dirty shinplasters. "Lord God of hosts," cried the man, lifting up his trembling hands, "lay not this sin to our charge!" There was a scar on Ben's back where the lash had buried itself: it stung now in the cold. He pulled his clothes tighter, that they should not see it; the scar and the words burned into his heart: the childish nature of the man was gone; the vague darkness in it took a shape and name. The boatman had been praying for him; the low words seemed to shake the night:—

"Hear the prayer of Thy servant, and his supplications! Is not this what Thou hast chosen: to loose the bands, to undo the heavy burdens, and let the oppressed go free? O Lord, hear! O Lord, hearken and do! Defer not for Thine own sake, O my God!"

"What shall I do?" said the slave, standing up.

The boatman paced slowly to and fro, his voice chording in its dull monotone with the smothered savage muttering in the negro's brain.

"The day of the Lord cometh; it is nigh at hand. Who can abide it? What saith the prophet Jeremiah? 'Take up a burden against the South. Cry aloud, spare not. Woe unto Babylon, for the day of her vengeance is come, the day of her visitation! Call together the archers against Babylon; camp against it round about; let none thereof escape. Recompense her: as she hath done unto my people, be it done unto her. A sword is upon Babylon: it shall break in pieces the shepherd and his flock, the man and the woman, the young man and the maid. I will render unto her the evil she hath done in my sight, saith the Lord.'"

It was the voice of God: the scar burned fiercer; the slave came forward boldly,—

"Mars'er, what shall I do?"

"Give the poor devil a musket," said one of the men. "Let him come with us, and strike a blow for freedom."

He took a knife from his belt, and threw it to him, then sauntered off to his tent.

"A blow for freedom?" mumbled Ben, taking it up.

"Let us sing to the praise of God," said the boatman, "the sixty-eighth psalm," lining it out while they sang,—the scattered men joining, partly to keep themselves awake. In old times David's harp charmed away the demon from a human heart. It roused one now, never to be laid again. A dull, droning chant, telling how the God of Vengeance rode upon the wind, swift to loose the fetters of the chained, to make desert the rebellious land; with a chorus, or refrain, in which Ben's wild, melancholy cry sounded like the wail of an avenging spirit:—

> *"That in the blood of enemies*
> *Thy foot imbrued may he:*
> *And of thy dogs dipped in the same*
> *The tongues thou mayest see."*

The meaning of that was plain; he sang it lower and more steadily each time, his body swaying in cadence, the glitter in his eye more steely.

Lamar, asleep in his prison, was wakened by the far-off plaintive song: he roused himself, leaning on one elbow, listening with a half-smile. It was Naomi they sang, he thought,—an old-fashioned Methodist air that Floy had caught from the negroes, and used to sing to him sometimes. Every night, down at home, she would come to his parlor-door to say good-night: he thought he could see the little figure now in its white night-gown, and hear the bare feet pattering on the matting. When he was alone, she would come in, and sit on his lap awhile, and kneel down before she went away, her head on his knee, to say her prayers, as she called it. Only God knew how many times he had remained alone after hearing those prayers, saved from nights of drunken debauch. He thought he felt Floy's pure little hand on his forehead now, as if she were saying her usual "Good night, Bud." He lay down to sleep again, with a genial smile on his face, listening to the hymn.

"It's the same God," he said,—"Floy's and theirs."

Outside, as he slept, a dark figure watched him. The song of the men ceased. Midnight, white and silent, covered the earth. He could hear only the slow breathing of the sleeper. Ben's black face grew ashy pale, but he did not tremble, as he crept, cat-like, up to the wicket, his blubber lips apart, the white teeth clenched.

"It's for Freedom, Mars' Lord!" he gasped, looking up to the sky, as if he expected an answer. "Gor-a'mighty, it's for Freedom!" And went in.

A belated bird swooped through the cold moonlight into the valley, and vanished in the far mountain-cliffs with a low, fearing cry, as though it had passed through Hades.

They had broken down the wicket: he saw them lay the heavy body on the lumber outside, the black figures hurrying over the snow. He laughed low, savagely, watching them. Free now! The best of them despised him; the years past of cruelty and oppression turned back, fused in a slow, deadly current of revenge and hate, against the race that had trodden him down. He felt the iron muscles of his fingers, looked close at the glittering knife he held, chuckling at the strange smell it bore. Would the Illinois boatman blame him, if it maddened him? And if Ben took the fancy to put it to his throat, what right has he to complain? Has not he also been a dweller in Babylon? He hesitated a moment in the cleft of the hill, choosing his way, exultantly. He did not watch the North now; the quiet old dream of content was gone; his thick blood throbbed and surged with passions of which you and I know nothing: he had a lost life to avenge. His native air, torrid, heavy with latent impurity, drew him back: a fitter breath than this cold snow for the animal in his body, the demon in his soul, to triumph and wallow in. He panted, thinking of the saffron hues of the Santilla flats, of the white, stately dwellings, the men that went in and out from them, quiet, dominant,—feeling the edge of his knife. It was his turn to be master now! He ploughed his way doggedly through the snow,—panting, as he went,—a hotter glow in his gloomy eyes. It was his turn for pleasure now: he would have his fill! Their wine and their gardens and—He did not need to choose a wife from his own color now. He stopped, thinking of little Floy, with her curls and great listening eyes, watching at the door for her brother. He had watched her climb up into his arms and kiss his cheek. She never would do that again! He laughed aloud, shrilly. By God! she should keep the kiss for other lips! Why should he not say it?

Up on the hill the night-air throbbed colder and holier. The guards stood about in the snow, silent, troubled. This was not like a death in battle: it put them in mind of home, somehow. All that the dying man said was, "Water," now and then. He had been sleeping, when struck, and never had thoroughly wakened from his dream. Captain Poole, of the Snake-hunters, had wrapped him in his own blanket, finding nothing more could be done. He went off to have the Colonel summoned now, muttering that it was "a damned shame." They put snow to Lamar's lips constantly, being hot and parched; a woman, Dorr's wife, was crouching on the ground beside him, chafing his hands, keeping down her sobs for fear they would disturb him. He opened his eyes at last, and knew Dorr, who held his head.

"Unfasten my coat, Charley. What makes it so close here?"

Dorr could not speak.

"Shall I lift you up, Captain Lamar?" asked Dave Hall, who stood leaning on his rifle.

He spoke in a subdued tone, Babylon being far off for the moment. Lamar dozed again before he could answer.

"Don't try to move him,—it is too late," said Dorr, sharply.

The moonlight steeped mountain and sky in a fresh whiteness. Lamar's face, paling every moment, hardening, looked in it like some solemn work of an untaught sculptor. There was a breathless silence. Ruth, kneeling beside him, felt his hand grow slowly colder than the snow. He moaned, his voice going fast,—

"At two, Ben, old fellow! We'll be free to-night!"

Dave, stooping to wrap the blanket, felt his hand wet: he wiped it with a shudder.

"As he hath done unto My people, be it done unto him!" he muttered, but the words did not comfort him.

Lamar moved, half-smiling.

"That's right, Floy. What is it she says? 'Now I lay me down'—I forget. Good night. Kiss me, Floy."

He waited,—looked up uneasily. Dorr looked at his wife: she stooped, and kissed his lips. Charley smoothed back the hair from the damp face with as tender a touch as a woman's. Was he dead? The white moonlight was not more still than the calm face.

Suddenly the night-air was shattered by a wild, revengeful laugh from the hill. The departing soul rushed back, at the sound, to life, full consciousness. Lamar started from their hold,—sat up.

"It was Ben," he said, slowly.

In that dying flash of comprehension, it may be, the wrongs of the white man and the black stood clearer to his eyes than ours: the two lives trampled down. The stern face of the boatman bent over him: he was trying to stanch the flowing blood. Lamar looked at him: Hall saw no bitterness in the look,—a quiet, sad question rather, before which his soul lay bare. He felt the cold hand touch his shoulder, saw the pale lips move.

"Was this well done?" they said.

Before Lamar's eyes the rounded arch of gray receded, faded into dark; the negro's fierce laugh filled his ear: some woful thought at the sound wrung his soul, as it halted at the gate. It caught at the simple faith his mother taught him.

"Yea," he said aloud, "though I walk through the valley of the shadow of death, I will fear no evil: for Thou art with me."

Dorr gently drew down the uplifted hand. He was dead.

"It was a manly soul," said the Northern captain, his voice choking, as he straightened the limp hair.

"He trusted in God? A strange delusion!" muttered the boatman.

Yet he did not like that they should leave him alone with Lamar, as they did, going down for help. He paced to and fro, his rifle on his shoulder, arming his heart with strength to accomplish the vengeance of the Lord against Babylon. Yet he could not forget the murdered man sitting there in the calm moonlight, the dead face turned towards the North,—the dead face, whereon little Floy's tears should never fall. The grave, unmoving eyes seemed to the boatman to turn to him with the same awful question. "Was this well done?" they said. He thought in eternity they would rise before him, sad, unanswered. The earth, he fancied, lay whiter, colder,—the heaven farther off; the war, which had become a daily business, stood suddenly before him in all its terrible meaning. God, he thought, had met in judgment with His people. Yet he uttered no cry of vengeance against the doomed city. With the dead face before him, he bent his eyes to the ground, humble, uncertain,— speaking out of the ignorance of his own weak, human soul.

"The day of the Lord is nigh," he said; "it is at hand; and who can abide it?"

Abraham Lincoln

FINAL EMANCIPATION PROCLAMATION
January 1, 1863

By the President of the United States of America:

A Proclamation

Whereas, on the twenty-second day of September, in the year of our Lord one thousand eight hundred and sixty-two, a proclamation was issued by the President of the United States, containing, among other things, the following, to wit:

"That on the first day of January, in the year of our Lord one thousand eight hundred and sixty-three, all persons held as slaves within any State, or designated part of a State, the people whereof shall then be in rebellion against the United States, shall be then, thenceforward, and forever free; and the Executive Government of the United States, including the military and naval authority thereof, will recognize and maintain the freedom of such persons, and will do no act or acts to repress such persons, or any of them, in any efforts they may make for their actual freedom.

"That the Executive will, on the first day of January aforesaid, by proclamation, designate the States and parts of States, if any, in which the people thereof, respectively, shall then be in rebellion against the United States; and the fact that any State, or the people thereof, shall on that day be in good faith represented in the Congress of the United States by members chosen thereto at elections wherein a majority of the qualified voters of such State shall have participated, shall in the absence of strong countervailing testimony be deemed conclusive evidence that such State and the people thereof are not then in rebellion against the United States."

Now, therefore, I, Abraham Lincoln, President of the United States, by virtue of the power in me vested as commander-in-chief of the army and navy of the United States, in time of actual armed rebellion against authority and government of the United States, and as a fit and necessary war measure for suppressing said rebellion, do, on this first day of January, in the year of our Lord one thousand eight hundred and sixty-three, and in accordance with my purpose so to do, publicly proclaimed for the full period of 100 days, from the day first above mentioned, order and designate as the States and parts of States wherein the people thereof, respectively, are this day in rebellion against the United States, the following, to wit:

Arkansas, Texas, Louisiana, (except the Parishes of St. Bernard; Plaquemines, Jefferson, St. Johns, St. Charles, St. James, Ascension, Assumption, Terre Bonne, Lafourche, St. Mary, St. Martin, and Orleans, including the city of New Orleans), Mississippi, Alabama, Florida, Georgia, South Carolina, North Carolina, and Virginia (except the forty-eight counties designated as West Virginia, and also the counties of Berkley, Accomac, Northampton, Elizabeth City, York, Princess Ann, and Norfolk, including the cities of Norfolk and Portsmouth), and which excepted parts are for the present left precisely as if this proclamation were not issued.

And by virtue of the power and for the purpose aforesaid, I do order and declare that all persons held as slaves within said designated States and parts of States are, and henceforward shall be, free; and that the Executive Government of the United States, including the military and naval authorities thereof, will recognize and maintain the freedom of said persons.

And I hereby enjoin upon the people so declared to be free to abstain from all violence, unless in necessary self-defense; and I recommend to them that, in all cases when allowed, they labor faithfully for reasonable wages.

And I further declare and make known that such persons of suitable condition will be received into the armed service of the United States to garrison forts, positions, stations, and other places, and to man vessels of all sorts in said service.

And upon this act, sincerely believed to be an act of justice, warranted by the Constitution upon military necessity, I invoke the considerate judgment of mankind and the gracious favor of Almighty God.

In witness whereof, I have hereunto set my hand, and caused the seal of the United States to be affixed.

Done at the city of Washington, this first day of January, in the year of our Lord one thousand eight hundred and sixty-three, and of the independence of the United States of America the eighty-seventh.

ABRAHAM LINCOLN

By the President: WILLIAM H. SEWARD, Secretary of State.

Ralph Waldo Emerson

The Emancipation Proclamation

AN ADDRESS DELIVERED IN BOSTON IN SEPTEMBER 1862

In so many arid forms which states encrust themselves with, once in a century, if so often, a poetic act and record occur. These are the jets of thought into affairs, when, roused by danger or inspired by genius, the political leaders of the day break the else insurmountable routine of class and local legislation, and take a step forward in the direction of catholic and universal interests. Every step in the history of political liberty is a sally of the human mind into the untried Future, and has the interest of genius, and is fruitful in heroic anecdotes. Liberty is a slow fruit. It comes, like religion, for short periods, and in rare conditions, as if awaiting a culture of the race which shall make it organic and permanent. Such moments of expansion in modern history were the Confession of Augsburg,[68] the plantation of America, the English Commonwealth of 1648, the Declaration of American Independence in 1776, the British emancipation of slaves in the West Indies, the passage of the Reform Bill, the repeal of the Corn-Laws, the Magnetic Ocean Telegraph, though yet imperfect, the passage of the Homestead Bill in the last Congress,[69] and now, eminently, President Lincoln's Proclamation on the twenty-second of September. These are acts of great scope, working on a long future and on permanent interests, and honoring alike those who initiate and those who receive them. These measures provoke no noisy joy, but are received into a sympathy so deep as to apprise us that mankind are greater and better than we know. At such times it appears as if a new public were created to greet the new event. It is as when an orator, having ended the compliments and pleasantries with which he conciliated attention, and having run over the superficial fitness and commodities of the measure he urges, suddenly, lending himself to some happy inspiration, announces with vibrating voice the grand human principles involved;—the bravos and wits who greeted him loudly thus far are surprised and overawed; a new audience is found in the heart of the assembly,—an audience hitherto passive and unconcerned, now at last so searched and kindled that they come forward, every one a representative of mankind, standing for all nationalities.

The extreme moderation with which the President advanced to his design,—his long-avowed expectant policy, as if he chose to be strictly the executive of the best public sentiment of the country, waiting only till it should be unmistakably pronounced,—so fair a mind that none ever listened so patiently to such extreme varieties of opinion,—so reticent that his decision has taken all parties by surprise, whilst yet it is just the sequel of his prior acts,—the firm tone in which he announces it, without inflation or surplusage,—all these have bespoken such favor to the act that, great as the popularity of the President has been, we are beginning to think that we have underestimated the capacity and virtue which the Divine Providence has made an instrument of benefit so vast. He has been permitted to do more for America than any other American man. He is well entitled to the most indulgent construction. Forget all that we thought shortcomings, every mistake, every delay. In the extreme embarrassments of his part, call these endurance, wisdom, magnanimity; illuminated, as they now are, by this dazzling success.

When we consider the immense opposition that has been neutralized or converted by the progress of the war (for it is not long since the President anticipated the resignation of a large number of officers in the army, and the secession of three states,[70] on the promulgation of this policy),—when we see how the great stake which foreign nations hold in our affairs has recently brought every European power as a client into this court, and it became every day more apparent what gigantic and what remote interests were to be affected by the decision of the President,—one can hardly say the deliberation was too long. Against all timorous counsels he had the courage to seize the moment; and such was his position, and such the felicity attending the action, that he has replaced government in the good graces of mankind. "Better is virtue in the sovereign than plenty in the season," say the Chinese. 'Tis wonderful what power is, and how ill it is used, and how its ill use makes life mean, and the sunshine dark. Life in America had lost much of its attraction in the later years. The virtues of a good magistrate undo a world of mischief, and, because Nature works with rectitude, seem vastly more potent than the acts of bad governors, which are ever tempered by the good nature in the people, and the incessant resistance which fraud and violence encounter. The acts of good governors work a geometrical ratio, as one midsummer day seems to repair the damage of a year of war.

A day which most of us dared not hope to see, an event worth the dreadful war, worth its costs and uncertainties, seems now to be close before us. October, November, December will have passed over beating hearts and plotting brains: then the hour will strike, and all men of African descent who have faculty enough to find their way to our lines are assured of the protection of American law.

It is by no means necessary that this measure should be suddenly marked by any signal results on the negroes or on the rebel masters. The force of the act is that it commits the country to this justice,—that it compels the innumerable officers, civil, military, naval, of the Republic to range themselves on the line of this equity. It draws the fashion to this side. It is not a measure that admits of being taken back. Done, it cannot be undone by a new administration. For slavery overpowers the disgust of the moral sentiment only through immemorial usage. It cannot be introduced as an improvement of the nineteenth century. This act makes that the lives of our heroes have not been sacrificed in vain. It makes a victory of our defeats. Our hurts are healed; the health of the nation is repaired. With a victory like this, we can stand many disasters. It does not promise the redemption of the black race; that lies not with us: but it relieves it of our opposition. The President by this act has paroled all the slaves in America; they will no more fight against us: and it relieves our race once for all of its crime and false position. The first condition of success is secured in putting ourselves right. We have recovered ourselves from our false position, and planted ourselves on a law of Nature:—

> "If that fail,
> The pillared firmament is rottenness,
> And earth's base built on stubble."[71]

The government has assured itself of the best constituency in the world: every spark of intellect, every virtuous feeling, every religious heart, every man of honor, every poet, every philosopher, the generosity of the cities, the health of the country, the strong arms of the mechanic, the endurance of farmers, the passionate conscience of women, the sympathy of distant nations,—all rally to its support.

Of course, we are assuming the firmness of the policy thus declared. It must not be a paper proclamation. We confide that Mr. Lincoln is in earnest, and as he has been slow in making up his mind, has resisted the importunacy of parties and of events to the latest moment, he will be as absolute in his adhesion. Not only will he repeat and follow up his stroke, but the nation will add its irresistible strength. If the ruler has duties, so has the citizen. In times like these, when the nation is imperilled, what man can, without shame, receive good news from day to day without giving good news of himself? What right has any one to read in the journals tidings of victories, if he has not bought them by his own valor, treasure, personal sacrifice, or by service as good in his own department? With this blot removed from our national honor, this heavy load lifted off the national heart, we shall not fear henceforward to show our faces among mankind. We shall cease to be hypocrites and pretenders, but what we have styled our free institutions will be such.

In the light of this event the public distress begins to be removed. What if the brokers' quotations show our stocks discredited, and the gold dollar costs one hundred and twenty-seven cents? These tables are fallacious. Every acre in the free states gained substantial value on the twenty-second of September. The cause of disunion and war has been reached and begun to be removed. Every man's house-lot and garden are relieved of the malaria which the purest winds and strongest sunshine could not penetrate and purge. The territory of the Union shines to-day with a lustre which every European emigrant can discern from far; a sign of inmost security and permanence. Is it feared that taxes will check immigration? That depends on what the taxes are spent for. If they go to fill up this yawning Dismal Swamp, which engulfed armies and populations, and created plague, and neutralized hitherto all the vast capabilities of this continent,—then this taxation, which makes the land wholesome and habitable, and will draw all men unto it, is the best investment in which property-holder ever lodged his earnings.

Whilst we have pointed out the opportuneness of the Proclamation, it remains to be said that the President had no choice. He might look wistfully for what variety of courses lay open to him; every line but one was closed up with fire. This one, too, bristled with danger, but through it was the sole safety. The measure he has adopted was imperative. It is wonderful to see the unseasonable senility of what is called the Peace Party, through all its masks, blinding their eyes to the main feature of the war, namely, its inevitableness. The war existed long before the cannonade of Sumter, and could not be postponed. It might have begun otherwise or elsewhere, but war was in the minds and bones of the combatants, it was written on the iron leaf, and you might as easily dodge gravitation. If we had consented to a peaceable secession of the rebels, the divided sentiment of the border states made peaceable secession impossible, the insatiable temper of the South made it impossible, and the slaves on the border, wherever the border might be, were an incessant fuel to rekindle the fire. Give the Confederacy New Orleans, Charleston, and Richmond, and they would have demanded St. Louis and Baltimore. Give them these, and they would have insisted on Washington. Give them Washington, and they would have assumed the army and navy, and, through these, Philadelphia, New York, and Boston. It looks as if the battle-field would have been at least as large in that event as it is now. The war was formidable, but could not be avoided. The war was and is an immense mischief, but brought with it the immense benefit of drawing a line and rallying the free states to fix it impassably,—preventing the whole force of Southern connection and influence throughout the North from distracting every city with endless confusion, detaching that force and reducing it to handfuls, and, in the progress of hostilities, disinfecting us of our habitual proclivity, through the affection of trade and the traditions of the Democratic party, to follow Southern leading.

These necessities which have dictated the conduct of the federal government are overlooked especially by our foreign critics. The popular statement of the opponents of the war abroad is the impossibility of our success. "If you could add," say they, "to your strength the whole army of England, of France and of Austria, you could not coerce eight millions of people to come under this government against their will." This is an odd thing for an Englishman, a Frenchman or an Austrian to say, who remembers Europe of the last seventy years,—the condition of Italy, until 1859,—of Poland, since 1793,—of France, of French Algiers,—of British Ireland, and British India.[72] But granting the truth, rightly read, of the historical aphorism, that "the people always conquer," it is to be noted that, in the Southern States, the tenure of land and the local laws, with slavery, give the social system not a democratic but an aristocratic complexion; and those states have shown every year a more hostile and aggressive temper, until the instinct of self-preservation forced us into the war. And the aim of the war on our part is indicated by the aim of the President's Proclamation, namely, to break up the false combination of Southern society, to destroy the piratic feature in it which makes it our enemy only as it is the enemy of the human race, and so allow its reconstruction on a just and healthful basis. Then new affinities will act, the old repulsion will cease, and, the cause of war being removed, Nature and trade may be trusted to establish a lasting peace.

We think we cannot overstate the wisdom and benefit of this act of the government. The malignant cry of the Secession press within the free states,[73] and the recent action of the Confederate Congress, are decisive as to its efficiency and correctness of aim. Not less so is the silent joy which has greeted it in all generous hearts, and the new hope it has breathed into the world. It was well to delay the steamers at the wharves until this edict could be put on board. It will be an insurance to the ship as it goes plunging through the sea with glad tidings to all people. Happy are the young, who find the pestilence cleansed out of the earth, leaving open to them an honest career. Happy the old, who see Nature purified before they depart. Do not let the dying die: hold them back to this world, until you have charged their ear and heart with this message to other spiritual societies, announcing the melioration of our planet:

> "Incertainties now crown themselves assured,
> And Peace proclaims olives of endless age."[74]

Meantime that ill-fated, much-injured race which the Proclamation respects will lose somewhat of the dejection sculptured for ages in their bronzed countenance, uttered in the wailing of their plaintive music,—a race naturally benevolent, docile, industrious, and whose very miseries sprang from their great talent for usefulness, which, in a more moral age, will not only defend their independence, but will give them a rank among nations.

Ralph Waldo Emerson

BOSTON HYMN (1863)

The word of the Lord by night
To the watching Pilgrims came,
As they sat by the sea-side,
And filled their hearts with flame.

God said,—I am tired of kings,
I suffer them no more;
Up to my ear the morning brings
The outrage of the poor.

Think ye I made this ball
A field of havoc and war,
Where tyrants great and tyrants small
Might harry the weak and poor?

My angel,—his name is Freedom,
Choose him to be your king;
He shall cut pathways east and west,
And fend you with his wing.

Lo! I uncover the land
Which I hid of old time in the West,
As the sculptor uncovers his statue,
When he has wrought his best.

I show Columbia, of the rocks
Which dip their foot in the seas
And soar to the air-borne flocks
Of clouds, and the boreal fleece.

I will divide my goods,
Call in the wretch and slave:
None shall rule but the humble,
And none but Toil shall have.

I will have never a noble,
No lineage counted great:
Fishers and choppers and ploughmen
Shall constitute a State.

Go, cut down trees in the forest,
And trim the straightest boughs;
Cut down trees in the forest,
And build me a wooden house.

Call the people together,
The young men and the sires,
The digger in the harvest-field,
Hireling, and him that hires.

And here in a pine state-house
They shall choose men to rule
In every needful faculty,
In church, and state, and school.

Lo, now! if these poor men
Can govern the land and sea,
And make just laws below the sun,
As planets faithful be.

And ye shall succor men;
'T is nobleness to serve;
Help them who cannot help again;
Beware from right to swerve.

I break your bonds and masterships,
And I unchain the slave:
Free be his heart and hand henceforth,
As wind and wandering wave.

I cause from every creature
His proper good to flow:
So much as he is and doeth,
So much he shall bestow.

But, laying his hands on another
To coin his labor and sweat,
He goes in pawn to his victim
For eternal years in debt.

Pay ransom to the owner,
And fill the bag to the brim.
Who is the owner? The slave is owner,
And ever was. Pay him.

O North! give him beauty for rags,
And honor, O South! for his shame;
Nevada! coin thy golden crags
With Freedom's image and name.

Up! and the dusky race
That sat in darkness long,—
Be swift their feet as antelopes,
And as behemoth strong.

Come, East, and West, and North,
By races, as snow-flakes,
And carry my purpose forth,
Which neither halts nor shakes.

My will fulfilled shall be,
For, in daylight or in dark,
My thunderbolt has eyes to see
His way home to the mark.

Ralph Waldo Emerson

VOLUNTARIES (1863)

I.

Low and mournful be the strain,
Haughty thought be far from me;
Tones of penitence and pain,
Moanings of the Tropic sea;
Low and tender in the cell
Where a captive sits in chains,
Crooning ditties treasured well
From his Afric's torrid plains.
Sole estate his sire bequeathed—
Hapless sire to hapless son—
Was the wailing song he breathed,
And his chain when life was done.

What his fault, or what his crime?
Or what ill planet crossed his prime?
Heart too soft and will too weak
To front the fate that crouches near,—
Dove beneath the vulture's beak;—
Will song dissuade the thirsty spear?
Dragged from his mother's arms and breast,
Displaced, disfurnished here,
His wistful toil to do his best
Chilled by a ribald jeer.
Great men in the Senate sate,
Sage and hero, side by side,
Building for their sons the State,
Which they shall rule with pride.
They forbore to break the chain
Which bound the dusky tribe,
Checked by the owners' fierce disdain,
Lured by "Union" as the bribe.
Destiny sat by, and said,
"Pang for pang your seed shall pay,
Hide in false peace your coward head,
I bring round the harvest-day."

II.

Freedom all winged expands,
Nor perches in a narrow place,
Her broad van seeks unplanted lands,

She loves a poor and virtuous race.
Clinging to the colder zone
Whose dark sky sheds the snow-flake down,
The snow-flake is her banner's star,
Her stripes the boreal streamers are.
Long she loved the Northman well;
Now the iron age is done,
She will not refuse to dwell
With the offspring of the Sun.
Foundling of the desert far,
Where palms plume and siroccos blaze,
He roves unhurt the burning ways
In climates of the summer star.
He has avenues to God
Hid from men of northern brain,
Far beholding, without cloud,
What these with slowest steps attain.
If once the generous chief arrive
To lead him willing to be led,
For freedom he will strike and strive,
And drain his heart till he be dead.

III.

In an age of fops and toys,
Wanting wisdom, void of right,
Who shall nerve heroic boys
To hazard all in Freedom's fight,—
Break sharply off their jolly games,
Forsake their comrades gay,
And quit proud homes and youthful dames,
For famine, toil, and fray?
Yet on the nimble air benign
Speed nimbler messages,
That waft the breath of grace divine
To hearts in sloth and ease.
So nigh is grandeur to our dust,
So near is God to man,
When Duty whispers low, *Thou must,*
The youth replies, *I can.*

IV.

Oh, well for the fortunate soul
Which Music's wings infold,
Stealing away the memory
Of sorrows new and old!

Frederick Douglass

The Mission of the War

DELIVERED IN CONCERT HALL: PHILADELPHIA 1863

Ladies and Gentlemen:

By the mission of the war, I mean nothing occult, nothing difficult to understand; but simply the accomplishment of those great changes in the condition of the American people, which are demanded by the situation of the country, and involved in the nature of the war, and which, if the war is conducted in accordance with sound principles, it is naturally and logically fitted to accomplish.

Speaking in the name of Providence, some men tell us that slavery is already dead; that the first gun fired at Sumter, put an end to slavery. This may be so, but I do not share the confidence with which it is asserted. In a grand crisis like this, I prefer to look facts squarely in the face, and accept their verdict.

I shall do this whether it shall bless or blast me. I look for no miracle to abolish slavery. The war looms before me simply as a grand National opportunity, which may be improved to National salvation, or neglected to National destruction.

I hope much from the skill and bravery of our armies, but vain is the might of armies, if they fail to profit by experience, and refuse to listen to the suggestions of wisdom and justice. The hopeful fact of the hour is, that we are now in a salutary school, the school of affliction. If sharp and signal and wide-sweeping and overwhelming retribution, long delayed and long protracted, can teach a great nation respect for the cruelly despised and neglected claims of justice, surely we shall be taught now and for all time to come. But if on the other hand, this school of affliction, this potent teacher, whose lessons are written in characters of blood, and thundered in our ears from the blazing cannon's mouth, shall fail, we shall go down, as we deserve to go down, a warning to all other nations which shall come after us.

It is less pleasant to contemplate the present hour as one of danger, than to contemplate it as one of security and safety, but it may be wiser to consider the danger and warn men against it.

The acorn involves the oak, but the commonest accident may destroy its potential character, and defeat its natural destiny. One wave brings a treasure from the briny deep, but another often sweeps it back to its primal depths. The saying that revolutions never go backward must be taken with limitations.

The revolution of 1848 was one of the grandest that ever dazzled a gazing world. It sent Louis Philippe into exile; upset the French throne; inaugurated a glorious republic; and shook every throne in Europe,—but was followed by reaction. Looking on from a distance, the friends of democratic Liberty saw in the convulsion, the death of king craft in Europe. Great was their disappointment. Almost in the twinkling of an eye the latent forces of despotism rallied. The Republic disappeared. Her noblest defenders were sent into exile, and the hopes of Constitutional liberty were blasted in the very moment of their bloom! Politics and perfidy proved, in that contest, too strong for the principles of justice and liberty.

I wish I could say that no such liabilities darken the horizon around us. But this example is too recent and the case too plain for such a conclusion. The same elements are involved here as there, and although the portents indicate that we shall flourish, it is too much to assume that we are out of danger. The price of liberty is eternal vigilence.

Our destiny is not taken out of our own hands, and it will not do to shuffle off our responsibilities upon the shoulders of Providence. We are now wading deep into the third year of conflict with a fierce and sanguinary rebellion: one which one of our most sagacious political prophets[75] assured us at its beginning, would end in less than ninety days. We are struggling with a rebellion which, in its worst features, stands alone among rebellions; which in its solitary and ghastly horror is without parallel in the history of any nation, ancient or modern; a rebellion inspired by no love of liberty and no hatred of oppression, and therefore indefensible upon any moral or social grounds; a rebellion which openly and shamelessly sets at defiance the worlds [sic] judgment of right and wrongs, appeals from light to darkness, from intelligence to ignorance, from the ever increasing prospects and blessings of a high civilization to the cold and withering blast of a naked barbarism; a rebellion which draws all its assistance and power from a system of bondage, too inhuman, too monstrous, and too indecent to be described, and of which sensitive and just minds can only think with horror; a rebellion which, even at this unfinished stage, counts its slain, not by thousands nor by tens of thousands, but by hundreds of thousands; a rebellion which, in the destruction of human life and property, rivals the earth-quake, the whirlwind, and the pestilence that walketh in darkness; a rebellion which, in two short years, has planted the bitterest agony at a million hearth-stones, thronged our streets with weeds of mourning, filled our land with mere stumps of men, ridged our soil with two hundred thousand rudely formed graves, and mantled it all over as with the shadow of death; a rebellion which has arrested the wheels of industry, checked the peaceful commerce of the world, and piled up a frightful debt, heavier than a mountain of gold, to weigh down the necks of our children's children; a rebellion which has blasted the hopes of European democracy, given joy to tyrants, brought ruin at home, and contempt abroad: which has cooled our friends, heated our enemies, and endangered the very existence of this great Nation!

Now for what is all this desolation, ruin, shame, and sorrow?

Here is the answer: It has been given a hundred times, and it has never been denied, by the only men who could have denied it, were it deniable. Less than half a million of Southern slaveholders, holding in bondage four millions of slaves, finding themselves outvoted in the effort to get possession of the United States Government, have now resorted to the sword. They have undertaken for the preservation of slavery, to accomplish by bullets what they failed to do by ballots.

It should be remarked here, that this rebellion was not originally intended to be a war for secession, but a war for subversion; a war to supplant a Republican Government by a slaveholding Oligarchy. Its aim was not Richmond but Washington,—not the South merely, but the whole United States.

Whence came the guilty ambition equal to this atrocious crime? From SLAVERY! SLAVERY, that robs the slave of his manhood, and the master of his just consideration for the rights and happiness of his fellow-men; which pays for labor by covering the laborer's back with bloody stripes, has prepared the guilty slave-holder for all the infernal concomitants of this terrible war. But for this curse of curses, the internal peace of this great country had flowed on for the next half century as it flowed on through the last half century. From no source less foul and wicked than slavery, could such a rebellion come. No argument is needed at this point. The country knows the story by heart.

I am one of those who think that this rebellion, inaugurated and carried on for a cause so unspeakably guilty, is quite enough for the whole lifetime of any Nation, even though that lifetime cover the space of a thousand years. We cannot want a repetition of it. Looking at the matter from no higher ground than patriotism, and setting aside the high conditions of justice and liberty, the American people,—let the war cost little or much; let its duration be short or long,—should resolve as one man, that this rebellion shall be the last slave-holding rebellion that shall ever curse the shores of America. The work now begun should suffer no pause till it is done, NOW AND FOREVER.

I know that many are appalled and disappointed by the apparently interminable character of this war. I am neither appalled nor disappointed by this feature of the contest. Without pretending to any higher wisdom than other men, I knew well enough, and often said it, that if once the north and the south confronted each other on the battle field, the contest would be fierce, long and bloody; and the longer the better, if it must be so, in order to put an end to the hell black cause out of which the rebellion has risen.

Say not that I am indifferent to the horrors of war. In common with the American people generally, I feel this prolongation of the war to be a heavy calamity, private as well as public. There are vacant places at my hearthstone, which I shall rejoice to see filled again by the boys who once occupied them, but which must remain sadly vacant while war shall last; and, possibly, forever; for my sons enlisted for the entire war![76] But even from the length of this war, we, who mourn over it, may draw some consolation, when we reflect on the vastness and grandeur of its mission.

The world has witnessed many struggles, and history records and perpetuates their memory, but never was one nobler and grander than that which the loyal people of this country are now maintaining against the slaveholders rebellion. In the long chain of human events; in the allotments and destinies of nations, we seem to have been especially chosen to strike this last blow to releive [sic] the world of slavery. We stand in our place today and wage war, not merely for our selves, but for the whole world; not for this generation, but for unborn generations, and for all time. We are writing the statutes of eternal justice and liberty, in the blood of tyrants, as a warning to all future cruel ambition. Ours is a high mission. Let us not mourn over it, but rather rejoice that we have in any measure been able to answer the high demands of this mighty crisis.

It is true that the war seems long. But this very slow progress is essential to its effectiveness. As in tardy convalescence of some patients, the fault is less due to the treatment than to the nature of the disease. We were in a very low condition before the remedy could be applied. We had been dragged nearly to death by pro-slavery compromises. A radical change was needed in the morals and manners of the people. Nothing is better calculated to make this change than the slow and steady progress of the war. I know that this idea is not consoling to the peace Democracy.[77] I was not sent, and have not come, to console that branch of the political church. To them, this grand moral revolution in the mind and heart of the nation, is the most distressing attribute of the war. In view of it they howl like certain characters of whom we read who thought themselves tormented before their time. In utter helplessness, they charge that this war is no longer waged on Constitutional principles. They charge that it was not intended to establish the Union as it was!

They charge that this is a war for the subjugation of the south, a war for the overthrow of Southern Institutions: in a word, an abolition war.

For one, I am not careful to deny this charge; but it is instructive to observe how it is brought, and how it is not. Both warn us of danger. Why is the war fiercely denounced as an abolition war? I answer, because the nation has long and bitterly hated abolition, and the enemies of the war confidently rely upon this hatred, to serve the ends of treason. Why do the loyal people deny the charge? I answer because they know that abolition, though now a vast power, is still odious. But the charge and the denial tell how the people despise the only measure that can save the country.

An abolition war! Well, let us thank the Democracy for teaching us this word. The charge, in a comprehensive sense, is true, and it is not a pity that it is true, but it would be a vast pity if it were not true. Would that it were more true than it is.

When our Government and people shall bravely avow this to be an abolition war, then the country will be safe; then our work will be fairly mapped out; then the uplifted arm of the nation will swing unfettered, and the spirit, pride and power of the rebellion will be broken.

Had slavery been broken down in the border states at the very beginning of this war, as it ought to have been, there would now be no rebellion in the southern states. Instead of having to watch Kentucky and Maryland, our armies would have marched in

overpowering numbers upon the rebels, and overwhelmed them. I now hold that a sacred regard for truth, as well as a sound policy, makes it our duty to own and avow before heaven and Earth, that this war is, and of right ought to be, an abolition war. This is its central principle and comprehensive character, and includes everything else which this struggle involves.

It is a war for the Union, a war for the Constitution, and a war for Republican Institutions, I admit; but it is logically such a war, only in the sense that the greater includes the lesser. Slavery has proved itself the strong element of our national life. In every rebel state it has proved itself stronger than the Union, the Constitution, and Republican Institutions. This strong element must be bound and cast out of our national life before union, the Constitution, and Republican Institutions can become possible. An abolition war therefore includes union, Constitution, and Republican Institutions and all else that goes to make up the greatness and glory of our common country.

The position of the Democratic party in relation to the war ought to surprise no one. It is consistent with the history of the party for thirty years past. Slavery, and only slavery, has been its recognized master during all that time. It early won for itself the title of being the natural ally of the South, and of slavery. It has always been for peace or against peace, for war or against war, precisely as dictated by slavery.

Ask why it was for the Florida war, and its answer is "Slavery;" ask why it was for the Mexican war, and it answers "Slavery;" ask why it was for the annexation of Texas, and it answers "Slavery;" ask why it was opposed to the habeas corpus when a negro was the applicant, and it answers "Slavery;" Ask why it is now in favor of the habeas corpus when traitors and repels are the applicants for its benefit, and it answers "Slavery!"

Ask why it was for mobbing down freedom of speech a few years ago, when that freedom was claimed by abolitionists and "Slavery!" is the answer. Ask why it now furiously asserts freedom of speech when sympathizers with traitors claim that freedom, and again "Slavery!" is the answer. Ask why it denied the right of a state to protect itself and its citizens from possible abuses of the fugitive slave bill, and you have the same old answer. Ask why it now asserts the sovereignty of the states separately, as against the states united, and again "Slavery!" is the answer. Ask why it was opposed to giving persons claimed as fugitive slaves a jury trial before returning them to slavery? Ask why it is now in favor of giving jury trial to traitors before sending them to the forts for safe keeping? Ask why it was for war with England at the beginning of our civil war? Ask why it has attempted to hinder and embarrass the loyal Government at every step of its progress, and you have but one answer, and that answer is again and again, "Slavery!"

The fact is that the party in question, I say nothing of individual men who were once members of it, has had but one vital and animating principle for thirty years, and that has been the same old horrible and hell black principle of negro slavery.

It has now assumed a saintly character, and desires to recieve [sic] the benediction due to peacemakers. It would stop bloodshed at the South, by inaugurating a bloody revolution at the North. The livery of peace is a beautiful livery, but, in this case, it is a stolen livery, and stolen to serve the ends of treason and slavery.

These new apostles of peace call themselves peace Democrats, and boast that they belong to the only party which can restore the country to peace. I neither dispute their title, nor the pretention founded upon it. All that can be said of the peace making ability of this class of men, is, that it consists in known treachery to the loyal government. That upon which they are most proud is their most killing condemnation, with all soundly loyal men. They have but to cross the rebel lines to he hailed by the rebels as fellow countrymen, clansmen, kinsmen, and brothers beloved in a common conspiracy.

But, fellow citizens, I have far less solicitude about the position and influence of this party, than I have about that of the great loyal party of the country. We have much less to fear from the bold and shameless wickedness of the Democratic party, than from the timid and short sighted policy of the great loyal party.

I know we have recently gained a great political victory,[78] but it remains to be seen whether we shall wisely avail ourselves of its manifest advantages. There is danger that, like some of our generals in the field, who, after soundly whipping the foe, generously allow him to retreat, reorganize, and entrench himself in a new and stronger position where it will require more power and skill to dislodge him than was required to vanquish him in the first instance, we, although the game is now in our own hands, shall be [likewise led to give it over to the enemy?]

I hold, that, while the Democratic party has an existence as an organization, we are in danger of a slaveholding peace and, therefore, a rebel victory and a rebel rule. There is but one way to destroy this danger and avert this calamity, and that is, to destroy slavery and enfranchise the black man. While there is a vistage [sic] of slavery remaining, it will command the political support of the whole South and of the Democratic party of the North. The South united, and the North divided, we shall be hereafter, as heretofore, under the heels of the South.

Now how shall we meet this danger? How shall we avert this calamity? I answer, Let these be our principles, and let our practice conform to them.

First:—

That this war which we are compelled to wage against slaveholding rebels and traitors, shall be, and of right ought to be, an abolition war.

Second:—

That the loyal people of the North and of the whole country, shall offer no peace, and accept no peace, which shall not be to all intents and purposes, an abolition peace.

Third:—

That the colored people of the whole country, in the loyal as well as in the disloyal states, shall be at once declared, unconditionally, and forever, free.

Fourth:—

That the emancipated slaves of the south shall enjoy the most perfect civil and political equality, including the right of voting and being voted for, in common with all other citizens.

Fifth:—

That this Government shall oppose all schemes for colonizing colored Americans or any part of them, in Africa or elsewhere: that, in peace, the black man is needed as a laborer: that, in war he is needed as a warrior, and that it is the duty of the Government and people to render him valuable in both relations, by paying him equal wages and giving him an equal chance to rise.

Sixth:—

That the freedom and elevation of white men are neither subserved nor shall be purchased by the degradation of black men, but the contrary.

There was a time when I hoped that events, unaided by discussion, would couple the rebellion and slavery in a common grave. But the facts of the present do not come up to our hopes. The question, What shall be done with slavery?, and, especially, What shall be done with the negro?, is an open one.

It is true that we have the proclamation of Jan. 1863. It was a vast and glorious step. But, unhappily, excellent as that paper is, it settles nothing permanently. It is still open to decision by court, by Congress, and by cannon. I applauded it and do now applaud it; but I detest the principle upon which it proceeds, namely: that *only* loyal men shall enjoy the luxury of holding and flogging negroes.[79]

Our danger lies in the absence of all moral feeling in the utterances of our rulers. In his letter to Mr. Greely, [sic] the President has told the country that, if he could save the Union with slavery he would do that; if he could save it without the abolition of slavery, he would do that. In his last message he shows the same indifference as to slavery, by saying that he hoped that the rebellion could be put down without the abolition of slavery. When the late Stephen A. Douglass [sic] uttered the sentiment that he did not care whether slavery were voted up or voted down in the territories, we thought him lost to all genuine feeling on the subject of slavery, and no man more than Mr. Lincoln denounced that sentiment. But to day, after nearly three years of slaveholding rebellion, we find Mr. Lincoln uttering something like the same sentiment. Douglas wanted his popular sovereignty, and cared nothing for the fortunes of the slave. Mr. Lincoln wanted the Union, and would accept that, with or without slavery. Had a warm heart and high moral feeling controlled his utterance, he would have welcomed with joy unspeakable and full of glory, the opportunity afforded by the rebellion to free his country from the matchless crime and infamy of slavery. But policy, policy, everlasting policy has robbed our statesmanship of broad soul moving utterance.

The great misfortune is, and has been, through all the progress of this grand struggle, that the government and the loyal people of the country have not fully understood and accepted the true mission of the war. Hence we have been floundering in the depths of dead issues endeavoring to impose old and worn out conditions upon new relations; putting new wine into old bottles and new cloth into old garments and thus making the rent worse than before.

We have failed to recognize the war as at once the signal and the necessity for a new order of social and political relations.

Hence, we have been talking of carrying on the war within the limits of a Constitution, already broken down by the very people in whose behalf the Constitution is pleaded. Hence, we have, from the first, been deluding ourselves with the miserable dream that the old Union can be revived in the States where it has been abolished.

Now we of the North have seen many strange things and may see more; but that *old* Union whose cannonized [sic] bones we saw hearsed in death and inurned under the walls of Sumter, we shall never see again while the world stands. The issue before us is a living issue. We are not fighting for the dead past, but for the living present and the glorious future. We are not fighting for the old Union as it was, but for something ten thousand times more important, and that thing, crisply rendered, is *National Unity*. Both sections have tried union and it has failed. The lesson for the statesmen at, this hour is, to find out and apply some principle which shall produce unity of sentiment, unity of idea, unity of purpose, and unity of object. Such unity alone can give and support national unity. Union without unity, is body without soul; marriage without love, a barrel without hoops, and will fall at the first touch.

The statesmen of the South understood this matter better and earlier than did the statesmen of the North. The dissolution of the Union on the old basis of compromise, was plainly seen thirty years ago. Mr. Calhoun, and not Mr. Seward, was the author of the irrepressible conflict. The South is logical and consistent. Under the teachings of their great leader, they admit into their form of Government, no disturbing force. They have based their confederacy squarely upon slavery as their corner stone. Their two great and all commanding ideas are, that slavery is right, and that slave holders are superior to all other classes of men. Around these, their religion, their morals, their manners, and their politics, revolve. Slavery being right, every thing inconsistent with it is wrong, and ought to be put down. I say they are strictly logical in their theory and definite in their ideas of fundamental principles. They first endeavored to have the Federal Government stand on their accursed corner stone, and we barely escaped the calamity. Fugitive slave laws, slavery extension laws, and Dred Scott decisions [sic] were but vain endeavors to get the nation squarely upon the corner stone now chosen by the Confederate States.

The loyal North is less logical, less consistent, and less definite, in regard to the necessity of fundamental principles of National unity; yet, unconsciously to ourselves and against our own protestations, we are in reality, like the south, fighting for National unity; a unity of which the great principles of liberty and equality, and not slavery and class superiority, are the corner stone.

Long before this rude and terrible war came to tell us of a broken Constitution and a dead Union, the better portion of the loyal people had outlived and outgrown what they had been taught to believe were the requirements of the old Union. We had come to detest the principle by which slavery had a strong representation in Congress. We had come to abhor the idea of being called upon to suppress slave insurrections. We had come to be ashamed of slave hunting and of being the watch dogs of the slave holders who were too proud to scent out and hunt down their slaves for themselves. We had, four years ago, so far outlived the old Union that we thought the little finger of the hero of Harper's Ferry of more value to the world struggling for liberty, than all the first families of old Va. put together.[80]

What business have we to be pouring out our treasure and shedding our blood like water for that old worn out dead and buried Union, which had already become a calamity and a curse. The fact is, we are not fighting for any such thing, and we ought to come out under our own true colors and let the South and the whole world know that we do not want, and will not have, the old Union, nor anything analogous to the old Union.

What we now want is a country, a free country: a country nowhere saddened and defaced by the footprints of a single slave, and nowhere cursed by the presence of a slaveholder.

We want a country, and we are fighting for a country, which shall not brand the Declaration of Independence as a lie. We want a country whose fundamental institutions we can proudly defend before the highest intelligence and civilization of the age. Hitherto we have opposed European scorn of our slavery, with the blush of shame as our best defence. We now want a country in which the obligation of patriotism shall not conflict with fidelity to justice and liberty.

We want a country and are fighting for a country which shall be free from sectional political parties; free from sectional religious denominations; free from sectional religious associations; free from every kind and description of combination of a sectional character.

We want a country where men may assemble from any part of it, and in any part of it, without prejudice to their interests or peril to their persons.

We are, in fact and from absolute necessity, transplanting the whole south with the higher civilization of the North. The New England school house is to take the place of the Southern whipping post; not because we love the negro, but because we love the nation; not because we prefer to do it, but because we must do it, or give up the contest and the country.

We want a country, and are fighting for a country, where social intercourse and commercial relations shall neither be embarrassed nor imbittered by the imperious exactions of an insolent slaveholding oligarchy, requiring Northern merchants to sell their souls as a condition of selling their goods.

We want a country, and are fighting for a country, through the length and breadth of which, the literature of any section of it may float to its extremities unimpaired, and thus become the common property of all the people; a country in which no man shall be fined for reading a book, or imprisoned for selling a book; a country where no man can he imprisoned, or flogged, or sold, for learning to read, or for teaching a fellow mortal to read! We want a country, and are fighting for a country, in any part of which, to be called an American citizen, shall mean as much, as it meant to be called a Roman citizen, in the palmest days of the Roman Empire.

We have in other days heard much of manifest destiny—I do not go all the length to which such theories are pressed, but I do believe, that it is the manifest destiny of this war, to unify and reorganize the morals, manners, and institutions of this country; and that herein is the secret of the strength, the patient fortitude, the persistent energy, and the sacred significance of this contest of [xxx]. Strike out the high ends and aims thus indicated, and the war would appear, to the impartial eye of an onlooking world, little better than a gigantic enterprise for shedding human blood.

A most interesting and gratifying confirmation of this theory of the mission of the war, is furnished in the history of the great struggle itself. In just proportion of progress made in taking upon itself the character I have ascribed to it, just in that proportion has our cause prospered, and that of the rebels, correspondingly lost ground. Justice and liberty, though often overpowered and crushed, are of themselves mighty forces; and the cause supported by them, must triumph at last. A war waged merely for power, as our seemed at first to be, repels sympathy and invites abhorrence, although backed by legitimacy. If Ireland should strike for Independence to-morrow, the sympathy of the world would go with her, and I doubt if American statesmen would be quite as discreet in the expressions of their opinions concerning the merits of such a contest, as English statesmen have been in respect of our war, in its early days.

But now the world begins to see, in the cause of the North, something more than legitimacy. It sees something more than National pride. It sees National wisdom, aiming at National unity, and National justice breaking the chains of bondmen and giving liberty to millions.

This new complexion of affairs, warms our hearts and strengthens our hands at home, while it equally disarms opposition, and increases our friends and supporters abroad. It is this which, more than all else, has carried alarm and consternation into every blood-stained hall of the South, and, like a strong angel, has gone through the world on the wings of the lighting, paralizing [sic] rebel press and tongues, sealing the fiery lips of the Robucks and Lindsays in England, and causing the eloquent Mr. Gladstone to restrain the expression of his admiration for Jefferson Davis and the Southern Confederacy![81] It has placed the sharp eye of British suspicion upon the prow of the Rebel rams in the Mersey and performed a like service for those in France! It has given a new meaning to British neutrality, and driven Mr. Mason,[82] the shameless negro hunter, from London, where he should never have been tolerated for an hour, except, as blood-hounds are tolerated in Regent Park, for exhibition. Depend upon it my friends, the more completely we fill out this high mission of the war, the more certain will be our success in waging it, and the more wide spread and glorious will be the results of our triumph at last. It is the fact that this war is a war for humanity, a war for a united Union based upon liberty, which has brought to our cause the powerful aid of John Bright, Richard Cobden, Wm. Edward Forster and other liberal British Statesmen. They outran us in comprehending this fact.

I know we are not to be praised for this changed character of the war. It came not of our choice nor of our seeking, but rather against both. The truth is the American people and Government did at the beginning, design that this war should have but one object, and that object should be simply the restoration of the old Union; and for a time the war was kept to that object, strictly, and you know full well, with what results. I do not stop here to cast blame. Many of the blunders and disasters of the past might have been avoided, had our armies and generals not repelled the only people in the rebel states likely to he friendly to the loyal cause.

But let that pass. Few men, however great their wisdom, are permitted to see the end from the beginning. The history of this war teaches that events are mightier than men, and that these Divine forces have, with over powering logic, fixed upon this war the comprehensive character I have ascribed to it. Even Mr. Lincoln can no longer, as at first, regard the war as a war for the repossession of a few forts and arsenals which the rebels had captured in their flight out of the Union.

This has, in every sense of the term, been a growing war. It began weak and has risen strong. It began low and has risen high and broad. It began with few, and now behold our country filled with armed men, ready to carry out, with courage and fortitude, the all controlling idea of their country men.

Let, then, the war proceed in its high, broad and strong course, till the rebellion is put down and our country is saved, and saved beyond the necessity of being saved again.

I have already hinted of our danger. Let me be a little more direct and pronounced.

The Democratic party at the North, though defeated in the election of last, fall, is still a power not to be despised. It is the still the ready, organized, and living nucleus of a powerful proslavery and pro-rebel reaction. Though it has lost its numbers, it retains all the elements of its characteristic mischief and malevolence. A slight change in the balance of power, and it can turn the guns now levelled at traitors and rebels, at the breasts of the loyal enemies of slavery, where they would rather aim them.

That party has five strong points in its favor, and its public men, headed by Horatio Seymour,[83] know well enough how to take advantage of them.

First: there is, on the part of the great mass of loyal people, an absence of any deep moral feeling against slavery itself. They hate it, not because it is a crime against human nature, but because it has made war upon the Government and broken up the Union.

Second: the vast expense of the war and the heavy taxes in money and men required for its prosecution. We know that loyalty has a strong back, but it is a back often broken by heavy taxation, and the hardships of prolonged warfare.

Third: the earnest desire for the return of peace which is shared by all classes, except Government contractors who are making fortunes out of the misfortunes of their country. This feeling, which is silent in victory, becomes vehement and powerful in reverses to our arms.

Fourth: the fact that an abolitionist is an object of popular dislike. The Democratic party knows that a man in earnest against slavery is more hated by the rabble who control the elections in large cities, than is the guilty slave-holder who, with broad blade and bloody hands, is seeking to destroy the life of the Republic.

Fifth: The Democratic party has on its side the National prejudice, (shared alike by union men and disunion men) against the colored people of the country; a prejudice which has done more to encourage the hopes of the rebels than all other powers at the North combined. It was this feeling which enabled the rebels to convert New York into a hell and its lower orders into fiends, last summer, while Lee was overrunning Pennsylvania and threatening Philadelphia.[84]

By skillful management of the conditions indicated in these five points, the Democratic party has strong hopes of placing itself into power, and, I may say, not without reason.

We have the game in our hands, but we are playing badly; playing against ourselves.

While our Government has the unspeakable meanness and injustice to call upon the colored men of the North, to leave their homes, their families and good wages, to share with their white fellow citizens the perils and hardships of war, it takes pains to insult and degrade them in the presence of their fellow soldiers, by offering them only half the pay received by white soldiers. The pro-slavery Democracy may well enough play upon the string of popular prejudice. While the Government at Washington refuses to reward the valour of its brave black soldiers with the hope of promotion, the Democratic party may well enough presume upon the strength of popular prejudice against the negro, and scent victory in the distance.

Since the war department at Washington degraded colored officers at New Orleans, simply because Yankee officers would not salute them, according to their rank, the Democratic party may well enough hope to bring about an anti-abolition peace. I warn the Union party now, as at the beginning of this war, that, if they are to win, they are to do so with the aid of their black cards. The nearer we approach the standard of justice in our treatment of the black man, the more certain we are of putting down the rebellion, retaining the reins of power and saving the country.

Our Republican friends tell us that the days of compromise with slavery are past. I wish I could feel sure of that.

The Northern people have always been remarkably confident of the strength and constancy of their virtue, just before they gave away to some tempting iniquity.

Twenty years ago we hoped that Texas could not be annexed; but it was annexed. We then hoped that, though annexed, it would be made a free state; but it was not made a free state. Thirteen years ago we were quite sure that no such abomination as the fugitive slave bill could get itself on our National Statute book; but it did get itself on our National statute book. We then hoped it could never be enforced; but it was enforced, and with all the sanctities of Law and Religion. Four years ago we were sure that the slave States would not rebel; but they did rebel. Then we were very sure it would be a very short rebellion; nevertheless, we are nearing the edge of the fourth year of the war.

I know that times have changed very rapidly, and that we have changed with them; yet I know also, that we are the same old American people, and that what we have once done we may possibly do again. The leaven of compromise is among us. It has become almost second nature with us.

I repeat that, while we have a Democratic party at the North trimming its sails to catch the Southern breeze in the next presidential election, we are in danger of compromise.

Tell me not of amnesties, of Oaths of Allegiance. Tell me not of the loyal people of the South. They are valueless and powerless in the presence of twenty hundred millions invested in human flesh.

Let but the little finger of slavery get hack into this Union, and, in one year, you shall see its whole body upon our backs.

While a respectable colored man or woman can be kicked out of the commonest street car in New York, while any white ruffian may ride unquestioned, we are in danger of a compromise with slavery. While the North is full of such papers as the New York World, Express and Herald,[85] firing the Nation's heart with hatred toward negroes and abolitionists, we are in danger of a slave holding peace. While the major part of all anti-slavery profession is based upon devotion to the Union rather than opposition to slavery, the country is in danger of a slave holding peace.

My friends, until we shall see the election of November next, and know that it has resulted in the election of a sound antislaveryman [sic] as President, we shall be in danger of a slave-holding peace. Indeed, so long as slavery has any life in it, any where in the country, we are in danger of such a peace. Then, look again at the danger arising from the impatience of the people, on account of the prolongation of the war. I know the American People.

They are an impatient people; impatient of delay; clamorous for change, and often look for results out of all proportion to the means employed in attaining them.

You and I know that the mission of this war is National regeneration. We know and consider that a nation is not born in a day. We know that, large bodies move slowly, and often seem to move thus, when, could we perceive their actual velocity, we should be astonished at its greatness. A great battle lost or won is easily described, understood and appreciated, but the moral growth of a great nation, requires reflection as well as observation. There are vast numbers of voters who make no account of the moral growth of the Nation, and care nothing for the interests of humanity, or of civilization; who look at the war only as a calamity to be endured so long as they have no power to arrest it, and no longer.

Now this is just the sort of people whose votes may turn the scale against us in the last event. Thoughts of this kind tell me that there was never a time, when anti-slavery work was more needed than now. The day that shall see the rebels at our feet, their weapons flung away, will be the day of trial. We have need to prepare for that trial. We have long been saved a pro-slavery peace, by the stubborn, unbending persistence of the rebels; but let them bend as they will bend, then will come the test of our sternest virtues.

I have now given, very briefly and imperfectly, some of the sources of danger.

A word now as to the ground of hope, The best that can be offered is, that we have made some progress; vast and striking progress within the last two years.

President Lincoln introduced his Administration to the country, as one which would faithfully catch, hold, and return runaway slaves to their masters. He avowed his determination to protect and defend the slave holders right to plunder the black laborer of his hard earnings. Europe was early assured by Mr. Seward that no slave should gain his freedom by this war. Both the President and the Secretary of State have made some progress since then.

Our Generals at the beginning of the war were horribly pro-slavery. They took to slave catching and slave killing, as a duck takes to water. They are now very generally and very earnestly in favor of putting an end to slavery; some of them, like Hunter and Butler, because they hate slavery on its own account; and others, because slavery is in arms against the Government. The rebellion has been a rapid educator. Congress was the first to respond to the instructive judgment of the people and to fix the broad brand of its reprobation upon slave hunting in shoulder straps. Then came very temperate talk about confiscation, which soon came to be pretty radical talk. Then came a proposition for border state gradual, [sic] compensated, and colonized emancipation. Then came the shadow of a proclamation in the shape of a threat, and then came the proclamation itself.

Meanwhile the negro had passed silently along from a loyal spade, pickaxe, and pike, to a Springfield rifle; the greatest sign of progress seen yet.[86]

Hayti and Liberia are recognized. Slavery is humbled in Maryland; threatened in Tennessee; stunned nearly to death in Western Virginia; doomed by the noble Germans in Missouri;[87] trembling in Kentucky; and is gradually melting away before our guns in the rebellious States.

The hour is one of hope, as well as of danger. We should take counsel of both.

But whatever may come to pass, one thing is clear; the principle involved in this contest; the necessities of both sections of the country; the obvious requirements of the age, and every suggestion of enlightened policy, demand the utter extirpation of slavery from every foot of American soil, and the complete enfranchisement of the entire colored population of the country.

Finis.

Louisa May Alcott

from *Hospital Sketches; and Camp and Fireside Stories* (1869)

MY CONTRABAND

Doctor Franck came in as I sat sewing up the rents in an old shirt, that Tom might go tidily to his grave. New shirts were needed for the living, and there was no wife or mother to "dress him handsome when he went to meet the Lord," as one woman said, describing the fine funeral she had pinched herself to give her son.

"Miss Dane, I'm in a quandary," began the Doctor, with that expression of countenance which says as plainly as words, "I want to ask a favor, but I wish you'd save me the trouble."

"Can I help you out of it?"

"Faith! I don't like to propose it, but you certainly can, if you please."

"Then name it, I beg."

"You see a Reb has just been brought in crazy with typhoid;[88] a bad case every way; a drunken, rascally little captain somebody took the trouble to capture, but whom nobody wants to take the trouble to cure. The wards are full, the ladies worked to death, and willing to be for our own boys, but rather slow to risk their lives for a Reb. Now, you've had the fever, you like queer patients, your mate will see to your ward for a while, and I will find you a good attendant. The fellow won't last long, I fancy; but he can't die without some sort of care, you know. I've put him in the fourth story of the west wing, away from the rest. It is airy, quiet, and comfortable there. I'm on that ward, and will do my best for you in every way. Now, then, will you go?"

"Of course I will, out of perversity, if not common charity; for some of these people think that because I'm an abolitionist I am also a heathen, and I should rather like to show them that, though I cannot quite love my enemies, I am willing to take care of them."

"Very good; I thought you'd go; and speaking of abolition reminds me that you can have a contraband for servant, if you like. It is that fine mulatto fellow who was found burying his rebel master after the fight, and, being badly cut over the head, our boys brought him along. Will you have him?"

"By all means,—for I'll stand to my guns on that point, as on the other; these black boys are far more faithful and handy than some of the white scamps given me to serve, instead of being served by. But is this man well enough?"

"Yes, for that sort of work, and I think you'll like him. He must have been a handsome fellow before he got his face slashed; not much darker than myself; his master's son, I dare say, and the white blood makes him rather high and haughty about some things. He was in a bad way when he came in, but vowed he'd die in the street rather than turn in with the black fellows below; so I put him up in the west wing, to be out of the way, and he's seen to the captain all the morning. When can you go up?"

"As soon as Tom is laid out, Skinner moved, Haywood washed, Marble dressed, Charley rubbed, Downs taken up, Upham laid down, and the whole forty fed."

We both laughed, though the Doctor was on his way to the dead-house and I held a shroud on my lap. But in a hospital one learns that cheerfulness is one's salvation; for, in an atmosphere of suffering and death, heaviness of heart would soon paralyze usefulness of hand, if the blessed gift of smiles had been denied us.

In an hour I took possession of my new charge, finding a dissipated-looking boy of nineteen or twenty raving in the solitary little room, with no one near him but the contraband in the room adjoining. Feeling decidedly more interest in the black man than in the white, yet remembering the Doctor's hint of his being "high and haughty," I glanced furtively at him as I scattered chloride of lime about the room to purify the air, and settled matters to suit myself. I had seen many contrabands, but never one so attractive as this. All colored men are called "boys," even if their heads are white; this boy was five-and-twenty at least, strong-limbed and manly, and had the look of one who never had been cowed by abuse or worn with oppressive labor. He sat on his bed doing nothing; no book, no pipe, no pen or paper anywhere appeared, yet anything less indolent or listless than his attitude and expression I never saw. Erect he sat, with a hand on either knee, and eyes fixed on the bare wall opposite, so rapt in some absorbing thought as to be unconscious of my presence, though the door stood wide open and my movements were by no means noiseless. His face was half averted, but I instantly approved the Doctor's taste, for the profile which I saw possessed all the attributes of comeliness belonging to his mixed race. He was more quadroon than mulatto, with Saxon features, Spanish complexion darkened by exposure, color in lips and cheek, waving hair, and an eye full of the passionate melancholy which in such men always seems to utter a mute protest against the broken law that doomed them at their birth. What could he be thinking of? The sick boy cursed and raved, I rustled to and fro, steps passed the door, bells rang, and the steady rumble of army-wagons came up from the street, still he never stirred. I had seen colored people in what they call "the black sulks," when, for days, they neither smiled nor spoke, and scarcely ate. But this was something more than that; for the man was not dully brooding over some small grievance; he seemed to see an all-absorbing fact or fancy recorded on the wall, which was a blank to me. I wondered if it were some deep wrong or sorrow, kept alive by memory and impotent regret; if he mourned for the dead master to whom he had been faithful to the end; or if the liberty now his were robbed of half its sweetness by the knowledge that some one near and dear to him still languished in the hell from which he had escaped. My heart quite warmed to him at that idea; I wanted to know and comfort him; and, following the impulse of the moment, I went in and touched him on the shoulder.

In an instant the man vanished and the slave appeared. Freedom was too new a boon to have wrought its blessed changes yet; and as he started up, with his hand at his temple, and an obsequious "Yes, Missis," any romance that had gathered round him fled away, leaving the saddest of all sad facts in living guise before me. Not only did the manhood seem to die out of him, but the comeliness that first attracted me; for, as he turned, I saw the ghastly wound that had laid open cheek and forehead. Being partly healed, it was no longer bandaged, but held together with strips of that transparent plaster which I never see without a shiver, and swift recollections of the scenes with which it is associated in my mind. Part of his black hair had been shorn away, and one eye was nearly closed; pain so distorted, and the cruel sabre-cut so marred that portion of his face, that, when I saw it, I felt as if a fine medal had been suddenly reversed, showing me a far more striking type of human suffering and wrong than Michael Angelo's bronze prisoner.[89] By one of those inexplicable processes that often teach us how little we understand ourselves, my purpose was suddenly changed; and, though I went in to offer comfort as a friend, I merely gave an order as a mistress.

"Will you open these windows? this man needs more air."

He obeyed at once, and, as he slowly urged up the unruly sash, the handsome profile was again turned toward me, and again I was possessed by my first impression so strongly that I involuntarily said,—

"Thank you."

Perhaps it was fancy, but I thought that in the look of mingled surprise and something like reproach which he gave me, there was also a trace of grateful pleasure. But he said, in that tone of spiritless humility these poor souls learn so soon,—

"I isn't a white man, Missis, I'se a contraband."

"Yes, I know it; but a contraband is a free man, and I heartily congratulate you."

He liked that; his face shone, he squared his shoulders, lifted his head, and looked me full in the eye with a brisk,—

"Thank ye, Missis; anything more to do fer yer?"

"Doctor Franck thought you would help me with this man, as there are many patients and few nurses or attendants. Have you had the fever?"

"No, Missis."

"They should have thought of that when they put him here; wounds and fevers should not be together. I'll try to get you moved."

He laughed a sudden laugh: if he had been a white man, I should have called it scornful; as he was a few shades darker than myself, I suppose it must be considered an insolent, or at least an unmannerly one.

"It don't matter, Missis. I'd rather be up here with the fever than down with those niggers; and there isn't no other place fer me."

Poor fellow! that was true. No ward in all the hospital would take him in to lie side by side with the most miserable white wreck there. Like the bat in Æsop's fable,[90] he belonged to neither race; and the pride of one and the helplessness of the other, kept him hovering alone in the twilight a great sin has brought to overshadow the whole land.

"You shall stay, then; for I would far rather have you than my lazy Jack. But are you well and strong enough?"

"I guess I'll do, Missis."

He spoke with a passive sort of acquiescence,—as if it did not much matter if he were not able, and no one would particularly rejoice if he were.

"Yes, I think you will. By what name shall I call you?"

"Bob, Missis."

Every woman has her pet whim; one of mine was to teach the men self-respect by treating them respectfully. Tom, Dick, and Harry would pass, when lads rejoiced in those familiar abbreviations; but to address men often old enough to be my father in that style did not suit my old-fashioned ideas of propriety. This "Bob" would never do; I should have found it as easy to call the chaplain "Gus" as my tragical-looking contraband by a title so strongly associated with the tail of a kite.

"What is your other name?" I asked. "I like to call my attendants by their last names rather than by their first."

"I'se got no other, Missis; we has our masters' names, or do without. Mine's dead, and I won't have anything of his 'bout me."

"Well, I'll call you Robert, then, and you may fill this pitcher for me, if you will be so kind."

He went; but, through all the tame obedience years of servitude had taught him, I could see that the proud spirit his father gave him was not yet subdued, for the look and gesture with which he repudiated his master's name were a more effective declaration of independence than any Fourth-of-July orator could have prepared.

We spent a curious week together. Robert seldom left his room, except upon my errands; and I was a prisoner all day, often all night, by the bedside of the rebel. The fever burned itself rapidly away, for there seemed little vitality to feed it in the feeble frame of this old young man, whose life had been none of the most righteous, judging from the revelations made by his unconscious lips; since more than once Robert authoritatively silenced him, when my gentler hushings were of no avail, and blasphemous wanderings or ribald camp-songs made my cheeks burn and Robert's face assume an aspect of disgust. The captain was a gentleman in the world's eye, but the contraband was the gentleman in mine;—I was a fanatic, and that accounts for such depravity of taste, I hope. I never asked Robert of himself, feeling that somewhere there was a spot still too sore to bear the lightest touch; but, from his language, manner, and intelligence, I inferred that his color had procured for him the few advantages within the reach of a quick-witted, kindly-treated slave. Silent, grave, and thoughtful, but most serviceable, was my contraband; glad of the books I brought him, faithful in the performance of the duties I assigned to him, grateful for the friendliness I could not but feel and show toward him. Often I longed to ask what purpose was so visibly altering his aspect with such daily deepening gloom. But I never dared, and no one else had either time or desire to pry into the past of this specimen of one branch of the chivalrous "F.F.Vs."[91]

On the seventh night, Dr. Franck suggested that it would be well for some one, besides the general watchman of the ward, to be with the captain, as it might be his last. Although the greater part of the two preceding nights had been spent there, of course I offered to remain,—for there is a strange fascination in these scenes, which renders one careless of fatigue and unconscious of fear until the crisis is past.

"Give him water as long as he can drink, and if he drops into a natural sleep, it may save him. I'll look in at midnight, when some change will probably take place. Nothing but sleep or a miracle will keep him now. Good-night."

Away went the Doctor; and, devouring a whole mouthful of grapes, I lowered the lamp, wet the captain's head, and sat down on a hard stool to begin my watch. The captain lay with his hot, haggard face turned toward me, filling the air with his poisonous breath, and feebly muttering, with lips and tongue so parched that the sanest speech would have been difficult to understand. Robert was stretched on his bed in the inner room, the door of which stood ajar, that a fresh draught from his open window might carry the fever-fumes away through mine. I could just see a long, dark figure, with the lighter outline of a face, and, having little else to do just then, I fell to thinking of this curious contraband, who evidently prized his freedom highly, yet seemed in no haste to enjoy it. Dr. Franck had offered to send him on to safer quarters, but he had said, "No, thank yer, sir, not yet," and then had gone away to fall into one of those black moods of his, which began to disturb me, because I had no power to lighten them. As I sat listening to the clocks from the steeples all about us, I amused myself with planning Robert's future, as I often did my own, and had dealt out to him a generous hand of trumps wherewith to play this game of life which hitherto had gone so cruelly against him, when a harsh choked voice called,—

"Lucy!"

It was the captain, and some new terror seemed to have gifted him with momentary strength.

"Yes, here's Lucy," I answered, hoping that by following the fancy I might quiet him,— for his face was damp with the clammy moisture, and his frame shaken with the nervous tremor that so often precedes death. His dull eye fixed upon me, dilating with a bewildered look of incredulity and wrath, till he broke out fiercely,—

"That's a lie! she's dead,—and so's Bob, damn him!"

Finding speech a failure, I began to sing the quiet tune that had often soothed delirium like this; but hardly had the line,—

"*See gentle patience smile on pain,*"

passed my lips, when he clutched me by the wrist, whispering like one in mortal fear,—

"Hush! she used to sing that way to Bob, but she never would to me. I swore I'd whip the devil out of her, and I did; but you know before she cut her throat she said she'd haunt me, and there she is!"

He pointed behind me with an aspect of such pale dismay, that I involuntarily glanced over my shoulder and started as if I had seen a veritable ghost; for, peering from the gloom of that inner room, I saw a shadowy face, with dark hair all about it, and a glimpse of scarlet at the throat. An instant showed me that it was only Robert leaning from his bed's foot, wrapped in a gray army-blanket, with his red shirt just visible above it, and his long hair disordered by sleep. But what a strange expression was on his face! The unmarred side was toward me, fixed and motionless as when I first observed it,—less absorbed now, but more intent. His eye glittered, his lips were apart like one who listened with every sense, and his whole aspect reminded me of a hound to which some wind had brought the scent of unsuspected prey.

"Do you know him, Robert? Does he mean you?"

"Laws, no, Missis; they all own half-a-dozen Bobs: but hearin' my name woke me; that's all."

He spoke quite naturally, and lay down again, while I returned to my charge, thinking that this paroxysm was probably his last. But by another hour I perceived a hopeful change; for the tremor had subsided, the cold dew was gone, his breathing was more regular, and Sleep, the healer, had descended to save or take him gently away. Doctor Franck looked in at midnight, bade me keep all cool and quiet, and not fail to administer a certain draught as soon as the captain woke. Very much relieved, I laid my head on my arms, uncomfortably folded on the little table, and fancied I was about to perform one of the feats which practice renders possible,—"sleeping with one eye open," as we say: a half-and-half doze, for all senses sleep but that of hearing; the faintest murmur, sigh, or motion will break it, and give one back one's wits much brightened by the brief permission to "stand at ease." On this night the experiment was a failure, for previous vigils, confinement, and much care had rendered naps a dangerous indulgence. Having roused half-a-dozen times in an hour to find all quiet, I dropped my heavy head on my arms, and, drowsily resolving to look up again in fifteen minutes, fell fast asleep.

The striking of a deep-voiced clock awoke me with a start. "That is one," thought I; but, to my dismay, two more strokes followed, and in remorseful haste I sprang up to see what harm my long oblivion had done. A strong hand put me back into my seat, and held me there. It was Robert. The instant my eye met his my heart began to beat, and all along my nerves tingled that electric flash which foretells a danger that we cannot see. He was very pale, his mouth grim, and both eyes full of sombre fire; for even the wounded one was open now, all the more sinister for the deep scar above and below. But his touch was steady, his voice quiet, as he said,—

"Sit still, Missis; I won't hurt yer, nor scare yer, ef I can help it, but yer waked too soon."

"Let me go, Robert,—the captain is stirring,—I must give him something."

"No, Missis, yer can't stir an inch. Look here!"

Holding me with one hand, with the other he took up the glass in which I had left the draught, and showed me it was empty.

"Has he taken it?" I asked, more and more bewildered.

"I flung it out o' winder, Missis; he'll have to do without."

"But why, Robert? why did you do it?"

"'Kase I hate him!"

Impossible to doubt the truth of that; his whole face showed it, as he spoke through his set teeth, and launched a fiery glance at the unconscious captain. I could only hold my breath and stare blankly at him, wondering what mad act was coming next. I suppose I shook and turned white, as women have a foolish habit of doing when sudden danger daunts them; for Robert released my arm, sat down upon the bedside just in front of me, and said, with the ominous quietude that made me cold to see and hear,—

"Don't yer be frightened, Missis; don't try to run away, fer the door's locked and the key in my pocket; don't yer cry out, fer yer'd have to scream a long while, with my hand on yer mouth, 'efore yer was heard. Be still, an' I'll tell yer what I'm gwine to do."

"Lord help us! he has taken the fever in some sudden, violent way, and is out of his head. I must humor him till some one comes"; in pursuance of which swift determination, I tried to say, quite composedly,—

"I will be still and hear you; but open the window. Why did you shut it?"

"I'm sorry I can't do it, Missis; but yer'd jump out, or call, if I did, an' I'm not ready yet. I shut it to make yer sleep, an' heat would do it quicker'n anything else I could do."

The captain moved, and feebly muttered "Water!" Instinctively I rose to give it to him, but the heavy hand came down upon my shoulder, and in the same decided tone Robert said,—

"The water went with the physic; let him call."

"Do let me go to him! he'll die without care!"

"I mean he shall;—don't yer meddle, if yer please, Missis."

In spite of his quiet tone and respectful manner, I saw murder in his eyes, and turned faint with fear; yet the fear excited me, and, hardly knowing what I did, I seized the hands that had seized me, crying,—

"No, no; you shall not kill him! It is base to hurt a helpless man. Why do you hate him? He is not your master."

"He's my brother."

I felt that answer from head to foot, and seemed to fathom what was coming, with a prescience vague, but unmistakable. One appeal was left to me, and I made it.

"Robert, tell me what it means? Do not commit a crime and make me accessory to it. There is a better way of righting wrong than by violence;—let me help you find it."

My voice trembled as I spoke, and I heard the frightened flutter of my heart; so did he, and if any little act of mine had ever won affection or respect from him, the memory of it served me then. He looked down, and seemed to put some question to himself; whatever it was, the answer was in my favor, for when his eyes rose, again, they were gloomy, but not desperate.

"I *will* tell yer, Missis; but mind, this makes no difference; the boy is mine. I'll give the Lord a chance to take him fust: if He don't, I shall."

"Oh, no! remember he is your brother."

An unwise speech; I felt it as it passed my lips, for a black frown gathered on Robert's face, and his strong hands closed with an ugly sort of grip. But he did not touch the poor soul gasping there behind him, and seemed content to let the slow suffocation of that stifling room end his frail life.

"I'm not like to forget dat, Missis, when I've been thinkin' of it all this week. I knew him when they fetched him in, an' would 'a' done it long 'fore this, but I wanted to ask where Lucy was; he knows,—he told to-night,—an' now he's done for."

"Who is Lucy?" I asked hurriedly, intent on keeping his mind busy with any thought but murder.

With one of the swift transitions of a mixed temperament like this, at my question Robert's deep eyes filled, the clenched hands were spread before his face, and all I heard were the broken words,—

"My wife,—he took her—"

In that instant every thought of fear was swallowed up in burning indignation for the wrong, and a perfect passion of pity for the desperate man so tempted to avenge an injury for which there seemed no redress but this. He was no longer slave or contraband, no drop of black blood marred him in my sight, but an infinite compassion yearned to save, to help, to comfort him. Words seemed so powerless I offered none, only put my hand on his poor head, wounded, homeless, bowed down with grief for which I had no cure, and softly smoothed the long, neglected hair, pitifully wondering the while where was the wife who must have loved this tender-hearted man so well.

The captain moaned again, and faintly whispered, "Air!" but I never stirred. God forgive me! just then I hated him as only a woman thinking of a sister woman's wrong could hate. Robert looked up; his eyes were dry again, his mouth grim. I saw that, said, "Tell me more," and he did; for sympathy is a gift the poorest may give, the proudest stoop to receive.

"Yer see, Missis, his father,—I might say ours, ef I warn't ashamed of both of 'em,—his father died two years ago, an' left us all to Marster Ned,—that's him here, eighteen then. He always hated me, I looked so like old Marster: he don't,—only the light skin an' hair. Old Marster was kind to all of us, me 'specially, an' bought Lucy off the next plantation down there in South Car'lina, when he found I liked her. I married her, all I could; it warn't much, but we was true to one another till Marster Ned come home a year after an' made hell fer both of us. He sent my old mother to be used up in his rice-swamp in Georgy; he found me with my pretty Lucy, an' though young Miss cried, an' I prayed to him on my knees, an' Lucy run away, he wouldn't have no mercy; he brought her back, an'—took her."

"Oh, what did you do?" I cried, hot with helpless pain and passion.

How the man's outraged heart sent the blood flaming up into his face and deepened the tones of his impetuous voice, as he stretched his arm across the bed, saying, with a terribly expressive gesture,—

"I half murdered him, an' to-night I'll finish."

"Yes, yes,—but go on now; what came next?"

He gave me a look that showed no white man could have felt a deeper degradation in remembering and confessing these last acts of brotherly oppression.

"They whipped me till I couldn't stand, an' then they sold me further South. Yer thought I was a white man once,—look here!"

With a sudden wrench he tore the shirt from neck to waist, and on his strong, brown shoulders showed me furrows deeply ploughed, wounds which, though healed, were ghastlier to me than any in that house. I could not speak to him, and, with the pathetic dignity a great grief lends the humblest sufferer, he ended his brief tragedy by simply saying,—

"That's all, Missis. I'se never seen her since, an' now I never shall in this world,—maybe not in t'other."

"But, Robert, why think her dead? The captain was wandering when he said those sad things; perhaps he will retract them when he is sane. Don't despair; don't give up yet."

"No, Missis, I 'spect he's right; she was too proud to bear that long. It's like her to kill herself. I told her to, if there was no other way; an' she always minded me, Lucy did. My poor girl! Oh, it warn't right! No, by God, it warn't!"

As the memory of this bitter wrong, this double bereavement, burned in his sore heart, the devil that lurks in every strong man's blood leaped up; he put his hand upon his brother's throat, and, watching the white face before him, muttered low between his teeth,—

"I'm lettin' him go too easy; there's no pain in this; we a'n't even yet. I wish he knew me. Marster Ned! it's Bob; where's Lucy?"

From the captain's lips there came a long faint sigh, and nothing but a flutter of the eyelids showed that he still lived. A strange stillness filled the room as the elder brother held the younger's life suspended in his hand, while wavering between a dim hope and a deadly hate. In the whirl of thoughts that went on in my brain, only one was clear enough to act upon. I must prevent murder, if I could,—but how? What could I do up there alone, locked in with a dying man and a lunatic?—for any mind yielded utterly to any unrighteous impulse is mad while the impulse rules it. Strength I had not, nor much courage, neither time nor wit for stratagem, and chance only could bring me help before it was too late. But one weapon I possessed,—a tongue,—often a woman's best defence; and sympathy, stronger than fear, gave me power to use it. What I said Heaven only knows, but surely Heaven helped me; words burned on my lips, tears streamed from my eyes, and some good angel prompted me to use the one name that had power to arrest my hearer's hand and touch his heart. For at that moment I heartily believed that Lucy lived, and this earnest faith roused in him a like belief.

He listened with the lowering look of one in whom brute instinct was sovereign for the time,—a look that makes the noblest countenance base. He was but a man,—a poor, untaught, outcast, outraged man. Life had few joys for him; the world offered him no honors, no success, no home, no love. What future would this crime mar? and why should he deny himself that sweet, yet bitter morsel called revenge? How many white men, with all New England's freedom, culture, Christianity, would not have felt as he felt then? Should I have reproached him for a human anguish, a human longing for redress, all now left him from the ruin of his few poor hopes? Who had taught him that self-control, self-sacrifice, are attributes that make men masters of the earth, and lift them nearer heaven? Should I have urged the beauty of forgiveness, the duty of devout submission? He had no religion, for he was no saintly "Uncle Tom,"[92] and Slavery's black shadow seemed to darken all the world to him, and shut out God. Should I have warned him of penalties, of judgments, and the potency of law? What did he know of justice, or the mercy that should temper that stern virtue, when every law, human and divine, had been broken on his hearthstone? Should I have tried to touch him by appeals to filial duty, to brotherly love? How had his appeals been answered? What memories had father and brother stored up in his heart to plead for either now? No,—all these influences, these associations, would have proved worse than useless, had I been calm enough to try them. I was not; but instinct, subtler than reason, showed me the one safe clue by which to lead this troubled soul from the labyrinth in which it groped and nearly fell. When I paused, breathless, Robert turned to me, asking, as if human assurances could strengthen his faith in Divine Omnipotence,—"Do you believe, if I let Marster Ned live, the Lord will give me back my Lucy?"

"As surely as there is a Lord, you will find her here or in the beautiful hereafter, where there is no black or white, no master and no slave."

He took his hand from his brother's throat, lifted his eyes from my face to the wintry sky beyond, as if searching for that blessed country, happier even than the happy North. Alas, it was the darkest hour before the dawn!—there was no star above, no light below but the pale glimmer of the lamp that showed the brother who had made him desolate. Like a blind man who believes there is a sun, yet cannot see it, he shook his head, let his arms drop nervelessly upon his knees, and sat there dumbly asking that question which many a soul whose faith is firmer fixed than his has asked in hours less dark than this,—"Where is God?" I saw the tide had turned, and strenuously tried to keep this rudderless life-boat from slipping back into the whirlpool wherein it had been so nearly lost.

"I have listened to you, Robert; now hear me, and heed what I say, because my heart is full of pity for you, full of hope for your future, and a desire to help you now. I want you to go away from here, from the temptation of this place, and the sad thoughts that haunt it. You have conquered yourself once, and I honor you for it, because, the harder the battle, the more glorious the victory; but it is safer to put a greater distance between you and this man. I will write you letters, give you money, and send you to good old Massachusetts to begin your new life a freeman,—yes, and a happy man; for when the captain is himself again, I will learn where Lucy is, and move heaven and earth to find and give her back to you. Will you do this, Robert?"

Slowly, very slowly, the answer came; for the purpose of a week, perhaps a year, was hard to relinquish in an hour.

"Yes, Missis, I will."

"Good! Now you are the man I thought you, and I'll work for you with all my heart. You need sleep, my poor fellow; go, and try to forget. The captain is alive, and as yet you are spared that sin. No, don't look there; I'll care for him. Come, Robert, for Lucy's sake."

Thank Heaven for the immortality of love! for when all other means of salvation failed, a spark of this vital fire softened the man's iron will, until a woman's hand could bend it. He let me take from him the key, let me draw him gently away, and lead him to the solitude which now was the most healing balm I could bestow. Once in his little room, he fell down on his bed and lay there, as if spent with the sharpest conflict of his life. I slipped the bolt across his door, and unlocked my own, flung up the window, steadied myself with a breath of air, then rushed to Doctor Franck. He came; and till dawn we worked together, saving one brother's life, and taking earnest thought how best to secure the other's liberty. When the sun came up as blithely as if it shone only upon happy homes, the Doctor went to Robert. For an hour I heard the murmur of their voices; once I caught the sound of heavy sobs, and for a time a reverent hush, as if in the silence that good man were ministering to soul as well as body. When he departed he took Robert with him, pausing to tell me he should get him off as soon as possible, but not before we met again.

Nothing more was seen of them all day; another surgeon came to see the captain, and another attendant came to fill the empty place. I tried to rest, but could not, with the thought of poor Lucy tugging at my heart, and was soon back at my post again, anxiously hoping that my contraband had not been too hastily spirited away. Just as night fell there came a tap, and, opening, I saw Robert literally "clothed, and in his right mind."[93] The Doctor had replaced the ragged suit with tidy garments, and no trace of that tempestuous night remained but deeper lines upon the forehead, and the docile look of a repentant child. He did not cross the threshold, did not offer me his hand,—only took off his cap, saying, with a traitorous falter in his voice,—

"God bless yer, Missis! I'm gwine."

I put out both my hands, and held his fast.

"Good-by, Robert! Keep up good heart, and when I come home to Massachusetts we'll meet in a happier place than this. Are you quite ready, quite comfortable for your journey?"

"Yes, Missis, yes; the Doctor's fixed everything; I'se gwine with a friend of his; my papers are all right, an' I'm as happy as I can be till I find"—

He stopped there; then went on, with a glance into the room,—

"I'm glad I didn't do it, an' I thank yer, Missis, fer hinderin' me,—thank yer hearty; but I'm afraid I hate him jest the same."

Of course he did; and so did I; for these faulty hearts of ours cannot turn perfect in a night, but need frost and fire, wind and rain, to ripen and make them ready for the great harvest-home. Wishing to divert his mind, I put my poor mite into his hand, and, remembering the magic of a certain little book, I gave him mine, on whose dark cover whitely shone the Virgin Mother and the Child, the grand history of whose life the book contained. The money went into Robert's pocket with a grateful murmur, the book into his bosom, with a long look and a tremulous—

"I never saw my baby, Missis."

I broke down then; and though my eyes were too dim to see, I felt the touch of lips upon my hands, heard the sound of departing feet, and knew my contraband was gone.

When one feels an intense dislike, the less one says about the subject of it the better; therefore I shall merely record that the captain lived,—in time was exchanged; and that, whoever the other party was, I am convinced the Government got the best of the bargain. But long before this occurred, I had fulfilled my promise to Robert; for as soon as my patient recovered strength of memory enough to make his answer trustworthy, I asked, without any circumlocution,—

"Captain Fairfax, where is Lucy?"

And too feeble to be angry, surprised, or insincere, he straightway answered,—

"Dead, Miss Dane."

"And she killed herself when you sold Bob?"

"How the devil did you know that?" he muttered, with an expression half-remorseful, half-amazed; but I was satisfied, and said no more.

Of course this went to Robert, waiting far away there, in a lonely home,—waiting, working, hoping for his Lucy. It almost broke my heart to do it; but delay was weak, deceit was wicked; so I sent the heavy tidings, and very soon the answer came,—only three lines; but I felt that the sustaining power of the man's life was gone.

"I tort I'd never see her any more; I'm glad to know she's out of trouble. I thank yer, Missis; an' if they let us, I'll fight fer yer till I'm killed, which I hope will be 'fore long."

Six months later he had his wish, and kept his word.

Every one knows the story of the attack on Fort Wagner; but we should not tire yet of recalling how our Fifty-Fourth, spent with three sleepless nights, a day's fast, and a march under the July sun, stormed the fort as night fell, facing death in many shapes, following their brave leaders through a fiery rain of shot and shell, fighting valiantly for "God and Governor Andrew,"[94]—how the regiment that went into action seven hundred strong, came out having had nearly half its number captured, killed, or wounded, leaving their young commander to be buried, like a chief of earlier times, with his body-guard around him, faithful to the death. Surely, the insult turns to honor, and the wide grave needs no monument but the heroism that consecrates it in our sight; surely, the hearts that held him nearest, see through their tears a noble victory in the seeming sad defeat; and surely, God's benediction was bestowed, when this loyal soul answered, as Death called the roll, "Lord, here am I, with the brothers Thou hast given me!"

The future must show how well that fight was fought; for though Fort Wagner once defied us, public prejudice is down; and through the cannon-smoke of that black night, the manhood of the colored race shines before many eyes that would not see, rings in many ears that would not hear, wins many hearts that would not hitherto believe.

When the news came that we were needed, there was none so glad as I to leave teaching contrabands, the new work I had taken up, and go to nurse "our boys," as my dusky flock so proudly called the wounded of the Fifty-Fourth. Feeling more satisfaction, as I assumed my big apron and turned up my cuffs, than if dressing for the President's levee, I fell to work in Hospital No. 10 at Beaufort. The scene was most familiar, and yet strange; for only dark faces looked up at me from the pallets so thickly laid along the floor, and I missed the sharp accent of my Yankee boys in the slower, softer voices calling cheerily to one another, or answering my questions with a stout, "'We'll never give it up, Missis, till the last Reb's dead,'" or, "If our people's free, we can afford to die."

Passing from bed to bed, intent on making one pair of hands do the work of three, at least, I gradually washed, fed, and bandaged my way down the long line of sable heroes, and coming to the very last, found that he was my contraband. So old, so worn, so deathly weak and wan, I never should have known him but for the deep scar on his cheek. That side lay uppermost, and caught my eye at once; but even then I doubted, such an awful change had come upon him, when, turning to the ticket just above his head, I saw the name, "Robert Dane." That both assured and touched me, for, remembering that he had no name, I knew that he had taken mine. I longed for him to speak to me, to tell how he had fared since I lost sight of him, and let me perform some little service for him in return for many he had done for me; but he seemed asleep; and as I stood re-living that strange night again, a bright lad, who lay next him softly waving an old fan across both beds, looked up and said,—

"I guess you know him, Missis?"

"You are right. Do you?"

"As much as any one was able to, Missis."

"Why do you say 'was,' as if the man were dead and gone?"

"I s'pose because I know he'll have to go. He's got a bad jab in the breast, an' is bleedin' inside, the Doctor says. He don't suffer any, only gets weaker 'n' weaker every minute. I've been fannin' him this long while, an' he's talked a little; but he don't know me now, so he's most gone, I guess."

There was so much sorrow and affection in the boy's face, that I remembered something, and asked, with redoubled interest—

"Are you the one that brought him off? I was told about a boy who nearly lost his life in saving that of his mate."

I dare say the young fellow blushed, as any modest lad might have done; I could not see it, but I heard the chuckle of satisfaction that escaped him, as he glanced from his shattered arm and bandaged side to the pale figure opposite.

"Lord, Missis, that's nothin'; we boys always stan' by one another, an' I warn't goin' to leave him to be tormented any more by them cussed Rebs. He's been a slave once, though he don't look half so much like it as me, an' I was born in Boston."

He did not; for the speaker was as black as the ace of spades,—being a sturdy specimen, the knave of clubs would perhaps be a fitter representative,—but the dark freeman looked at the white slave with the pitiful, yet puzzled expression I have so often seen on the faces of our wisest men, when this tangled question of Slavery presented itself, asking to be cut or patiently undone.

"Tell me what you know of this man; for, even if he were awake, he is too weak to talk."

"I never saw him till I joined the regiment, an' no one 'peared to have got much out of him. He was a shut-up sort of feller, an' didn't seem to care for anything but gettin' at the Rebs. Some say he was the fust man of us that enlisted; I know he fretted till we were off, an' when we pitched into old Wagner, he fought like the devil."

"Were you with him when he was wounded? How was it?"

"Yes, Missis. There was somethin' queer about it; for he 'peared to know the chap that killed him, an' the chap knew him. I don't dare to ask, but I rather guess one owned the other some time; for, when they clinched, the chap sung out, 'Bob!' an' Dane, 'Marster Ned!'—then they went at it."

I sat down suddenly, for the old anger and compassion struggled in my heart, and I both longed and feared to hear what was to follow.

"You see, when the Colonel,—Lord keep an' send him back to us!—it a'n't certain yet, you know, Missis, though it's two days ago we lost him,—well, when the Colonel shouted, 'Rush on, boys, rush on!' Dane tore away as if he was goin' to take the fort alone; I was next him, an' kept close as we went through the ditch an' up the wall. Hi! warn't that a rusher!"

and the boy flung up his well arm with a whoop, as if the mere memory of that stirring moment came over him in a gust of irrepressible excitement.

"Were you afraid?" I said, asking the question women often put, and receiving the answer they seldom fail to get.

"No, Missis!"—emphasis on the "Missis"—"I never thought of anything but the damn' Rebs, that scalp, slash, an' cut our ears off, when they git us. I was bound to let daylight into one of 'em at least, an' I did. Hope he liked it!"

"It is evident that you did. Now go on about Robert, for I should be at work."

"He was one of the fust up; I was just behind, an' though the whole thing happened in a minute, I remember how it was, for all I was yellin' an' knockin' round like mad. Just where we were, some sort of an officer was wavin' his sword an' cheerin' on his men; Dane saw him by a big flash that come by; he flung away his gun, give a leap, an' went at that feller as if he was Jeff, Beauregard, an' Lee, all in one. I scrabbled after as quick as I could, but was only up in time to see him git the sword straight through him an' drop into the ditch. You needn't ask what I did next, Missis, for I don't quite know myself; all I'm clear about is, that I managed somehow to pitch that Reb into the fort as dead as Moses, git hold of Dane, an' bring him off. Poor old feller! we said we went in to live or die; he said he went in to die, an' he's done it."

I had been intently watching the excited speaker; but as he regretfully added those last words I turned again, and Robert's eyes met mine,—those melancholy eyes, so full of an intelligence that proved he had heard, remembered, and reflected with that preternatural power which often outlives all other faculties. He knew me, yet gave no greeting; was glad to see a woman's face, yet had no smile wherewith to welcome it; felt that he was dying, yet uttered no farewell. He was too far across the river to return or linger now; departing thought, strength, breath, were spent in one grateful look, one murmur of submission to the last pang he could ever feel. His lips moved, and, bending to them, a whisper chilled my cheek, as it shaped the broken words,—

"I'd 'a' done it,—but it's better so,—I'm satisfied."

Ah! well he might be,—for, as he turned his face from the shadow of the life that was, the sunshine of the life to be touched it with a beautiful content, and in the drawing of a breath my contraband found wife and home, eternal liberty and God.

Charles Chesnutt

from *The Wife of His Youth, and Other Stories of the Color Line* (1899)

CICELY'S DREAM

I

The old woman stood at the back door of the cabin, shading her eyes with her hand, and looking across the vegetable garden that ran up to the very door. Beyond the garden she saw, bathed in the sunlight, a field of corn, just in the ear, stretching for half a mile, its yellow, pollen-laden tassels over-topping the dark green mass of broad glistening blades; and in the distance, through the faint morning haze of evaporating dew, the line of the woods, of a still darker green, meeting the clear blue of the summer sky. Old Dinah saw, going down the path, a tall, brown girl, in a homespun frock, swinging a slat-bonnet in one hand and a splint basket in the other.

"Oh, Cicely!" she called.

The girl turned and answered in a resonant voice, vibrating with youth and life,—

"Yes, granny!"

"Be sho' and pick a good mess er peas, chile, fer yo' gran'daddy's gwine ter be home ter dinner ter-day."

The old woman stood a moment longer and then turned to go into the house. What she had not seen was that the girl was not only young, but lithe and shapely as a sculptor's model; that her bare feet seemed to spurn the earth as they struck it; that though brown, she was not so brown but that her cheek was darkly red with the blood of another race than that which gave her her name and station in life; and the old woman did not see that Cicely's face was as comely as her figure was superb, and that her eyes were dreamy with vague yearnings.

Cicely climbed the low fence between the garden and the cornfield, and started down one of the long rows leading directly away from the house. Old Needham was a good ploughman, and straight as an arrow ran the furrow between the rows of corn, until it vanished in the distant perspective. The peas were planted beside alternate hills of corn, the corn-stalks serving as supports for the climbing pea-vines. The vines nearest the house had been picked more or less clear of the long green pods, and Cicely walked down the row for a quarter of a mile, to where the peas were more plentiful. And as she walked she thought of her dream of the night before.

She had dreamed a beautiful dream. The fact that it was a beautiful dream, a delightful dream, her memory retained very vividly. She was troubled because she could not remember just what her dream had been about. Of one other fact she was certain, that in her dream she had found something, and that her happiness had been bound up with the thing she had found. As she walked down the corn-row she ran over in her mind the various things with which she had always associated happiness. Had she found a gold ring? No, it was not a gold ring—of that she felt sure. Was it a soft, curly plume for her hat? She had seen town people with them, and had indulged in day-dreams on the subject; but it was not a feather. Was it a bright-colored silk dress? No; as much as she had always wanted one, it was not a silk dress. For an instant, in a dream, she had tasted some great and novel happiness, and when she awoke it was dashed from her lips, and she could not even enjoy the memory of it, except in a vague, indefinite, and tantalizing way.

Cicely was troubled, too, because dreams were serious things. Dreams had certain meanings, most of them, and some dreams went by contraries. If her dream had been a prophecy of some good thing, she had by forgetting it lost the pleasure of anticipation. If her dream had been one of those that go by contraries, the warning would be in vain, because she would not know against what evil to provide. So, with a sigh, Cicely said to herself that it was a troubled world, more or less; and having come to a promising point, began to pick the tenderest pea-pods and throw them into her basket.

By the time she had reached the end of the line the basket was nearly full. Glancing toward the pine woods beyond the rail fence, she saw a brier bush loaded with large, luscious blackberries. Cicely was fond of blackberries, so she set her basket down, climbed the fence, and was soon busily engaged in gathering the fruit, delicious even in its wild state.

She had soon eaten all she cared for. But the berries were still numerous, and it occurred to her that her granddaddy would like a blackberry pudding for dinner. Catching up her apron, and using it as a receptacle for the berries, she had gathered scarcely more than a handful when she heard a groan.

Cicely was not timid, and her curiosity being aroused by the sound, she stood erect, and remained in a listening attitude. In a moment the sound was repeated, and, gauging the point from which it came, she plunged resolutely into the thick underbrush of the forest. She had gone but a few yards when she stopped short with an exclamation of surprise and concern.

Upon the ground, under the shadow of the towering pines, a man lay at full length,—a young man, several years under thirty, apparently, so far as his age could be guessed from a face that wore a short soft beard, and was so begrimed with dust and incrusted with blood that little could be seen of the underlying integument. What was visible showed a skin browned by nature or by exposure. His hands were of even a darker brown, almost as dark as Cicely's own. A tangled mass of very curly black hair, matted with burs, dank with dew, and clotted with blood, fell partly over his forehead, on the edge of which, extending back into the hair, an ugly scalp wound was gaping, and, though apparently not just inflicted, was still bleeding slowly, as though reluctant to stop, in spite of the coagulation that had almost closed it.

Cicely with a glance took in all this and more. But, first of all, she saw the man was wounded and bleeding, and the nurse latent in all womankind awoke in her to the requirements of the situation. She knew there was a spring a few rods away, and ran swiftly to it. There was usually a gourd at the spring, but now it was gone. Pouring out the blackberries in a little heap where they could be found again, she took off her apron, dipped one end of it into the spring, and ran back to the wounded man. The apron was clean, and she squeezed a little stream of water from it into the man's mouth. He swallowed it with avidity. Cicely then knelt by his side, and with the wet end of her apron washed the blood from the wound lightly, and the dust from the man's face. Then she looked at her apron a moment, debating whether she should tear it or not.

"I'm feared granny'll be mad," she said to herself. "I reckon I'll jes' use de whole apron."

So she bound the apron around his head as well as she could, and then sat down a moment on a fallen tree trunk, to think what she should do next. The man already seemed more comfortable; he had ceased moaning, and lay quiet, though breathing heavily.

"What shall I do with that man?" she reflected. "I don' know whether he's a w'ite man or a black man. Ef he's a w'ite man, I oughter go an' tell de w'ite folks up at de big house, an' dey'd take keer of 'im. If he 's a black man, I oughter go tell granny. He don' look lack a black man somehow er nuther, an' yet he don' look lack a w'ite man; he's too dahk, an' his hair's too curly. But I mus' do somethin' wid 'im. He can't be lef' here ter die in de woods all by hisse'f. Reckon I'll go an' tell granny."

She scaled the fence, caught up the basket of peas from where she had left it, and ran, lightly and swiftly as a deer, toward the house. Her short skirt did not impede her progress, and in a few minutes she had covered the half mile and was at the cabin door, a slight heaving of her full and yet youthful breast being the only sign of any unusual exertion.

Her story was told in a moment. The old woman took down a black bottle from a high shelf, and set out with Cicely across the cornfield, toward the wounded man.

As they went through the corn Cicely recalled part of her dream. She had dreamed that under some strange circumstances—what they had been was still obscure—she had met a young man—a young man whiter than she and yet not all white—and that he had loved her and courted her and married her. Her dream had been all the sweeter because in it she had first tasted the sweetness of love, and she had not recalled it before because only in her dream had she known or thought of love as something supremely desirable.

With the memory of her dream, however, her fears revived. Dreams were solemn things. To Cicely the fabric of a vision was by no means baseless. Her trouble arose from her not being able to recall, though she was well versed in dream-lore, just what event was foreshadowed by a dream of finding a wounded man. If the wounded man were of her own race, her dream would thus far have been realized, and having met the young man, the other joys might be expected to follow. If he should turn out to be a white man, then her dream was clearly one of the kind that go by contraries, and she could expect only sorrow and trouble and pain as the proper sequences of this fateful discovery.

II

The two women reached the fence that separated the cornfield from the pine woods.

"How is I gwine ter git ovuh dat fence, chile?" asked the old woman.

"Wait a minute, granny," said Cicely; "I'll take it down."

It was only an eight-rail fence, and it was a matter of but a few minutes for the girl to lift down and lay to either side the ends of the rails that formed one of the angles. This done, the old woman easily stepped across the remaining two or three rails. It was only a moment before they stood by the wounded man. He was lying still, breathing regularly, and seemingly asleep.

"What is he, granny," asked the girl anxiously, "a w'ite man, or not?"

Old Dinah pushed back the matted hair from the wounded man's brow, and looked at the skin beneath. It was fairer there, but yet of a decided brown. She raised his hand, pushed back the tattered sleeve from his wrist, and then she laid his hand down gently.

"Mos' lackly he 's a mulatter man f'om up de country somewhar. He don' look lack dese yer niggers roun' yere, ner yet lack a w'ite man. But de po' boy 's in a bad fix, w'ateber he is, an' I 'spec's we bettah do w'at we kin fer 'im, an' w'en he comes to he'll tell us w'at he is—er w'at he calls hisse'f. Hol' 'is head up, chile, an' I 'll po' a drop er dis yer liquor down his th'oat; dat 'll bring 'im to quicker 'n anything e'se I knows."

Cicely lifted the sick man's head, and Dinah poured a few drops of the whiskey between his teeth. He swallowed it readily enough. In a few minutes he opened his eyes and stared blankly at the two women. Cicely saw that his eyes were large and black, and glistening with fever.

"How you feelin', suh?" asked the old woman.

There was no answer.

"Is you feelin' bettah now?"

The wounded man kept on staring blankly. Suddenly he essayed to put his hand to his head, gave a deep groan, and fell back again unconscious.

"He 's gone ag'in," said Dinah. "I reckon we'll hafter tote 'im up ter de house and take keer er 'im dere. W'ite folks would n't want ter fool wid a nigger man, an' we doan know who his folks is. He 's outer his head an' will be fer some time yet, an' we can't tell nuthin' 'bout 'im tel he comes ter his senses."

Cicely lifted the wounded man by the arms and shoulders. She was strong, with the strength of youth and a sturdy race. The man was pitifully emaciated; how much, the two women had not suspected until they raised him. They had no difficulty whatever, except for the awkwardness of such a burden, in lifting him over the fence and carrying him through the cornfield to the cabin.

They laid him on Cicely's bed in the little lean-to shed that formed a room separate from the main apartment of the cabin. The old woman sent Cicely to cook the dinner, while she gave her own attention exclusively to the still unconscious man. She brought water and washed him as though he were a child.

"Po' boy," she said, "he doan feel lack he's be'n eatin' nuff to feed a sparrer. He 'pears ter be mos' starved ter def."

She washed his wound more carefully, made some lint,—the art was well known in the sixties,—and dressed his wound with a fair degree of skill.

"Somebody must 'a' be'n tryin' ter put yo' light out, chile," she muttered to herself as she adjusted the bandage around his head. "A little higher er a little lower, an' you would n' 'a' be'n yere ter tell de tale. Dem clo's," she argued, lifting the tattered garments she had removed from her patient, "don' b'long 'roun' yere. Dat kinder weavin' come f'om down to'ds Souf Ca'lina. I wish Needham 'u'd come erlong. He kin tell who dis man is, an' all erbout 'im."

She made a bowl of gruel, and fed it, drop by drop, to the sick man. This roused him somewhat from his stupor, but when Dinah thought he had enough of the gruel, and stopped feeding him, he closed his eyes again and relapsed into a heavy sleep that was so closely akin to unconsciousness as to be scarcely distinguishable from it.

When old Needham came home at noon, his wife, who had been anxiously awaiting his return, told him in a few words the story of Cicely's discovery and of the subsequent events.

Needham inspected the stranger with a professional eye. He had been something of a plantation doctor in his day, and was known far and wide for his knowledge of simple remedies. The negroes all around, as well as many of the poorer white people, came to him for the treatment of common ailments.

"He's got a fevuh," he said, after feeling the patient's pulse and laying his hand on his brow, "an' we'll hafter gib 'im some yarb tea an' nuss 'im tel de fevuh w'ars off. I 'spec'," he added, "dat I knows whar dis boy come f'om. He's mos' lackly one er dem bright mulatters, f 'om Robeson County—some of 'em call deyse'ves Croatan Injins—w'at's been conscripted an' sent ter wu'k on de fo'tifications down at Wimbleton er some'er's er nuther, an' done 'scaped, and got mos' killed gittin' erway, an' wuz n' none too well fed befo', an' nigh 'bout starved ter def sence. We'll hafter hide dis man, er e'se we is lackly ter git inter trouble ou'se'ves by harb'rin' 'im. Ef dey ketch 'im yere, dey's liable ter take 'im out an' shoot 'im—an' des ez lackly us too."

Cicely was listening with bated breath.

"Oh, gran'daddy," she cried with trembling voice, "don' let 'em ketch 'im! Hide 'im somewhar."

"I reckon we'll leave 'im yere fer a day er so. Ef he had come f'om roun' yere I'd be skeered ter keep 'im, fer de w'ite folks 'u'd prob'ly be lookin' fer 'im. But I knows ev'ybody w'at's be'n conscripted fer ten miles 'roun', an' dis yere boy don' b'long in dis neighborhood. W'en 'e gits so 'e kin he'p 'isse'f we'll put 'im up in de lof' an' hide 'im till de Yankees come. Fer dey're comin' sho'. I dremp' las' night dey wuz close ter han', and I hears de w'ite folks talkin' ter deyse'ves 'bout it. An' de time is comin' w'en de good Lawd gwine ter set His people free, an' it ain' gwine ter be long, nuther."

Needham's prophecy proved true. In less than a week the Confederate garrison evacuated the arsenal in the neighboring town of Patesville,[95] blew up the buildings, destroyed the ordnance and stores, and retreated across the Cape Fear River, burning the river bridge behind them,—two acts of war afterwards unjustly attributed to General Sherman's army, which followed close upon the heels of the retreating Confederates.

When there was no longer any fear for the stranger's safety, no more pains were taken to conceal him. His wound had healed rapidly, and in a week he had been able with some help to climb up the ladder into the loft. In all this time, however, though apparently conscious, he had said no word to any one, nor had he seemed to comprehend a word that was spoken to him.

Cicely had been his constant attendant. After the first day, during which her granny had nursed him, she had sat by his bedside, had fanned his fevered brow, had held food and water and medicine to his lips. When it was safe for him to come down from the loft and sit in a chair under a spreading oak, Cicely supported him until he was strong enough to walk about the yard. When his strength had increased sufficiently to permit of greater exertion, she accompanied him on long rambles in the fields and woods.

In spite of his gain in physical strength, the newcomer changed very little in other respects. For a long time he neither spoke nor smiled. To questions put to him he simply gave no reply, but looked at his questioner with the blank unconsciousness of an infant. By and by he began to recognize Cicely, and to smile at her approach. The next step in returning consciousness was but another manifestation of the same sentiment. When Cicely would leave him he would look his regret, and be restless and uneasy until she returned.

The family were at a loss what to call him. To any inquiry as to his name he answered no more than to other questions.

"He come jes' befo' Sherman," said Needham, after a few weeks, "lack John de Baptis' befo' de Lawd. I reckon we bettah call 'im John."

So they called him John. He soon learned the name. As time went on Cicely found that he was quick at learning things. She taught him to speak her own negro English, which he pronounced with absolute fidelity to her intonations; so that barring the quality of his voice, his speech was an echo of Cicely's own.

The summer wore away and the autumn came. John and Cicely wandered in the woods together and gathered walnuts, and chinquapins and wild grapes. When harvest time came, they worked in the fields side by side,—plucked the corn, pulled the fodder, and gathered the dried peas from the yellow pea-vines. Cicely was a phenomenal cotton-picker, and John accompanied her to the fields and stayed by her hours at a time, though occasionally he would complain of his head, and sit under a tree and rest part of the day while Cicely worked, the two keeping one another always in sight.

They did not have a great deal of intercourse with other people. Young men came to the cabin sometimes to see Cicely, but when they found her entirely absorbed in the stranger they ceased their visits. For a time Cicely kept him away, as much as possible, from others, because she did not wish them to see that there was anything wrong about him. This was her motive at first, but after a while she kept him to herself simply because she was happier so. He was hers—hers alone. She had found him, as Pharaoh's daughter had found Moses in the bulrushes; she had taught him to speak, to think, to love. She had not taught him to remember; she would not have wished him to; she would have been jealous of any past to which he might have proved bound by other ties. Her dream so far had come true. She had found him; he loved her. The rest of it would as surely follow, and that before long. For dreams were serious things, and time had proved hers to have been not a presage of misfortune, but one of the beneficent visions that are sent, that we may enjoy by anticipation the good things that are in store for us.

III

But a short interval of time elapsed after the passage of the warlike host that swept through North Carolina, until there appeared upon the scene the vanguard of a second army, which came to bring light and the fruits of liberty to a land which slavery and the havoc of war had brought to ruin. It is fashionable to assume that those who undertook the political rehabilitation of the Southern States merely rounded out the ruin that the war had wrought—merely ploughed up the desolate land and sowed it with salt. Perhaps the gentler judgments of the future may recognize that their task was a difficult one, and that wiser and honester men might have failed as egregiously. It may even, in time, be conceded that some good came out of the carpet-bag governments, as, for instance, the establishment of a system of popular education in the former slave States. Where it had been a crime to teach people to read or write, a schoolhouse dotted every hillside, and the State provided education for rich and poor, for white and black alike. Let us lay at least this token upon the grave of the carpet-baggers. The evil they did lives after them, and the statute of limitations does not seem to run against it. It is but just that we should not forget the good.

Long, however, before the work of political reconstruction had begun, a brigade of Yankee schoolmasters and schoolma'ams had invaded Dixie, and one of the latter had opened a Freedman's Bureau School in the town of Patesville, about four miles from Needham Green's cabin on the neighboring sandhills.

It had been quite a surprise to Miss Chandler's Boston friends when she had announced her intention of going South to teach the freedmen. Rich, accomplished, beautiful, and a social favorite, she was giving up the comforts and luxuries of Northern life to go among hostile strangers, where her associates would be mostly ignorant negroes. Perhaps she might meet occasionally an officer of some Federal garrison, or a traveler from the North; but to all intents and purposes her friends considered her as going into voluntary exile. But heroism was not rare in those days, and Martha Chandler was only one of the great multitude whose hearts went out toward an oppressed race, and who freely poured out their talents, their money, their lives,—whatever God had given them,—in the sublime and not unfruitful effort to transform three millions of slaves into intelligent freemen. Miss Chandler's friends knew, too, that she had met a great sorrow, and more than suspected that out of it had grown her determination to go South.

When Cicely Green heard that a school for colored people had been opened at Patesville she combed her hair, put on her Sunday frock and such bits of finery as she possessed, and set out for town early the next Monday morning.

There were many who came to learn the new gospel of education, which was to be the cure for all the freedmen's ills. The old and gray-haired, the full-grown man and woman, the toddling infant,—they came to acquire the new and wonderful learning that was to make them the equals of the white people. It was the teacher's task, by no means an easy one, to select from this incongruous mass the most promising material, and to distribute among them the second-hand books and clothing that were sent, largely by her Boston friends, to aid her in her work; to find out what they knew, to classify them by their intelligence rather than by their knowledge, for they were all lamentably ignorant. Some among them were the children of parents who had been free before the war, and of these some few could read and one or two could write. One paragon, who could repeat the multiplication table, was immediately promoted to the position of pupil teacher.

Miss Chandler took a liking to the tall girl who had come so far to sit under her instruction. There was a fine, free air in her bearing, a lightness in her step, a sparkle in her eye, that spoke of good blood,—whether fused by nature in its own alembic, out of material despised and spurned of men, or whether some obscure ancestral strain, the teacher could not tell. The girl proved intelligent and learned rapidly, indeed seemed almost feverishly anxious to learn. She was quiet, and was, though utterly untrained, instinctively polite, and profited from the first day by the example of her teacher's quiet elegance. The teacher dressed in simple black. When Cicely came back to school the second day, she had left off her glass beads and her red ribbon, and had arranged her hair as nearly like the teacher's as her skill and its quality would permit.

The teacher was touched by these efforts at imitation, and by the intense devotion Cicely soon manifested toward her. It was not a sycophantic, troublesome devotion, that made itself a burden to its object. It found expression in little things done rather than in any words the girl said. To the degree that the attraction was mutual, Martha recognized in it a sort of freemasonry of temperament that drew them together in spite of the differences between them. Martha felt sometimes, in the vague way that one speculates about the impossible, that if she were brown, and had been brought up in North Carolina, she would be like Cicely; and that if Cicely's ancestors had come over in the *Mayflower*, and Cicely had been reared on Beacon Street, in the shadow of the State House dome, Cicely would have been very much like herself.

Miss Chandler was lonely sometimes. Her duties kept her occupied all day. On Sundays she taught a Bible class in the school-room. Correspondence with bureau officials and friends at home furnished her with additional occupation. At times, nevertheless, she felt a longing for the company of women of her own race; but the white ladies of the town did not call, even in the most formal way, upon the Yankee school-teacher. Miss Chandler was therefore fain to do the best she could with such companionship as was available.

She took Cicely to her home occasionally, and asked her once to stay all night. Thinking, however, that she detected a reluctance on the girl's part to remain away from home, she did not repeat her invitation.

Cicely, indeed, was filling a double rôle. The learning acquired from Miss Chandler she imparted to John at home. Every evening, by the light of the pine-knots blazing on Needham's ample hearth, she taught John to read the simple words she had learned during the day. Why she did not take him to school she had never asked herself; there were several other pupils as old as he seemed to be. Perhaps she still thought it necessary to protect him from curious remark. He worked with Needham by day, and she could see him at night, and all of Saturdays and Sundays. Perhaps it was the jealous selfishness of love. She had found him; he was hers. In the spring, when school was over, her granny had said that she might marry him. Till then her dream would not yet have come true, and she must keep him to herself. And yet she did not wish him to lose this golden key to the avenues of opportunity. She would not take him to school, but she would teach him each day all that she herself had learned. He was not difficult to teach, but learned, indeed, with what seemed to Cicely marvelous ease,—always, however, by her lead, and never of his own initiative. For while he could do a man's work, he was in most things but a child, without a child's curiosity. His love for Cicely appeared the only thing for which he needed no suggestion; and even that possessed an element of childish dependence that would have seemed, to minds trained to thoughtful observation, infinitely pathetic.

The spring came and cotton-planting time. The children began to drop out of Miss Chandler's school one by one, as their services were required at home. Cicely was among those who intended to remain in school until the term closed with the "exhibition," in which she was assigned a leading part. She had selected her recitation, or "speech," from among half a dozen poems that her teacher had suggested, and to memorizing it she devoted considerable time and study. The exhibition, as the first of its kind, was sure to be a notable event. The parents and friends of the children were invited to attend, and a colored church, recently erected,—the largest available building,—was secured as the place where the exercises should take place.

On the morning of the eventful day, uncle Needham, assisted by John, harnessed the mule to the two-wheeled cart, on which a couple of splint-bottomed chairs were fastened to accommodate Dinah and Cicely. John put on his best clothes,—an ill-fitting suit of blue jeans,—a round wool hat, a pair of coarse brogans, a homespun shirt, and a bright blue necktie. Cicely wore her best frock, a red ribbon at her throat, another in her hair, and carried a bunch of flowers in her hand. Uncle Needham and aunt Dinah were also in holiday array. Needham and John took their seats on opposite sides of the cart-frame, with their feet dangling down, and thus the equipage set out leisurely for the town.

Cicely had long looked forward impatiently to this day. She was going to marry John the next week, and then her dream would have come entirely true. But even this anticipated happiness did not overshadow the importance of the present occasion, which would be an epoch in her life, a day of joy and triumph. She knew her speech perfectly, and timidity was not one of her weaknesses. She knew that the red ribbons set off her dark beauty effectively, and that her dress fitted neatly the curves of her shapely figure. She confidently expected to win the first prize, a large morocco-covered Bible, offered by Miss Chandler for the best exercise.

Cicely and her companions soon arrived at Patesville. Their entrance into the church made quite a sensation, for Cicely was not only an acknowledged belle, but a general favorite, and to John there attached a tinge of mystery which inspired a respect not bestowed upon those who had grown up in the neighborhood. Cicely secured a seat in the front part of the church, next to the aisle, in the place reserved for the pupils. As the house was already partly filled by townspeople when the party from the country arrived, Needham and his wife and John were forced to content themselves with places somewhat in the rear of the room, from which they could see and hear what took place on the platform, but where they were not at all conspicuously visible to those at the front of the church.

The schoolmistress had not yet arrived, and order was preserved in the audience by two of the elder pupils, adorned with large rosettes of red, white, and blue, who ushered the most important visitors to the seats reserved for them. A national flag was gracefully draped over the platform, and under it hung a lithograph of the Great Emancipator, for it was thus these people thought of him. He had saved the Union, but the Union had never meant anything good to them. He had proclaimed liberty to the captive, which meant all to them; and to them he was and would ever be the Great Emancipator.

The schoolmistress came in at a rear door and took her seat upon the platform. Martha was dressed in white; for once she had laid aside the sombre garb in which alone she had been seen since her arrival at Patesville. She wore a yellow rose at her throat, a bunch of jasmine in her belt. A sense of responsibility for the success of the exhibition had deepened the habitual seriousness of her face, yet she greeted the audience with a smile.

"Don' Miss Chan'ler look sweet," whispered the little girls to one another, devouring her beauty with sparkling eyes, their lips parted over a wealth of ivory.

"De Lawd will bress dat chile," said one old woman, in soliloquy. "I t'ank de good Marster I's libbed ter see dis day."

Even envy could not hide its noisome head: a pretty quadroon whispered to her neighbor:—

"I don't b'liebe she's natch'ly ez white ez dat. I 'spec' she's be'n powd'rin'! An' I know all dat hair can't be her'n; she's got on a switch, sho's you bawn."

"You knows dat ain' so, Ma'y 'Liza Smif," rejoined the other, with a look of stern disapproval; "you *knows* dat ain' so. You'd gib yo' everlastin' soul 'f you wuz ez white ez Miss Chan'ler, en yo' ha'r wuz ez long ez her'n."

"By Jove, Maxwell!" exclaimed a young officer, who belonged to the Federal garrison stationed in the town, "but that girl is a beauty." The speaker and a companion were in fatigue uniform, and had merely dropped in for an hour between garrison duty. The ushers had wished to give them seats on the platform, but they had declined, thinking that perhaps their presence there might embarrass the teacher. They sought rather to avoid observation by sitting behind a pillar in the rear of the room, around which they could see without attracting undue attention.

"To think," the lieutenant went on, "of that Junonian figure, those lustrous orbs, that golden coronal, that flower of Northern civilization, being wasted on these barbarians!" The speaker uttered an exaggerated but suppressed groan.

His companion, a young man of clean-shaven face and serious aspect, nodded assent, but whispered reprovingly,—

"'Sh! some one will hear you. The exercises are going to begin."

When Miss Chandler stepped forward to announce the hymn to be sung by the school as the first exercise, every eye in the room was fixed upon her, except John's, which saw only Cicely. When the teacher had uttered a few words, he looked up to her, and from that moment did not take his eyes off Martha's face.

After the singing, a little girl, dressed in white, crossed by ribbons of red and blue, recited with much spirit a patriotic poem.

When Martha announced the third exercise, John's face took on a more than usually animated expression, and there was a perceptible deepening of the troubled look in his eyes, never entirely absent since Cicely had found him in the woods.

A little yellow boy, with long curls, and a frightened air, next ascended the platform.

"Now, Jimmie, be a man, and speak right out," whispered his teacher, tapping his arm reassuringly with her fan as he passed her.

Jimmie essayed to recite the lines so familiar to a past generation of schoolchildren:—

"I knew a widow very poor,
Who four small children had;
The eldest was but six years old,
A gentle, modest lad."

He ducked his head hurriedly in a futile attempt at a bow; then, following instructions previously given him, fixed his eyes upon a large cardboard motto hanging on the rear wall of the room, which admonished him in bright red letters to

"ALWAYS SPEAK THE TRUTH,"

and started off with assumed confidence—

"I knew a widow very poor,
Who"—

At this point, drawn by an irresistible impulse, his eyes sought the level of the audience. Ah, fatal blunder! He stammered, but with an effort raised his eyes and began again:

"I knew a widow very poor,
Who four"—
Again his treacherous eyes fell, and his little remaining self-possession utterly forsook him. He made one more despairing effort:—

"I knew a widow very poor,
Who four small"—

and then, bursting into tears, turned and fled amid a murmur of sympathy.

Jimmie's inglorious retreat was covered by the singing in chorus of "The Star-spangled Banner," after which Cicely Green came forward to recite her poem.

"By Jove, Maxwell!" whispered the young officer, who was evidently a connoisseur of female beauty, "that is n't bad for a bronze Venus. I'll tell you"—

"'Sh!" said the other. "Keep still."

When Cicely finished her recitation, the young officers began to applaud, but stopped suddenly in some confusion as they realized that they were the only ones in the audience so engaged. The colored people had either not learned how to express their approval in orthodox fashion, or else their respect for the sacred character of the edifice forbade any such demonstration. Their enthusiasm found vent, however, in a subdued murmur, emphasized by numerous nods and winks and suppressed exclamations. During the singing that followed Cicely's recitation the two officers quietly withdrew, their duties calling them away at this hour.

At the close of the exercises, a committee on prizes met in the vestibule, and unanimously decided that Cicely Green was entitled to the first prize. Proudly erect, with sparkling eyes and cheeks flushed with victory, Cicely advanced to the platform to receive the coveted reward. As she turned away, her eyes, shining with gratified vanity, sought those of her lover.

John sat bent slightly forward in an attitude of strained attention; and Cicely's triumph lost half its value when she saw that it was not at her, but at Miss Chandler, that his look was directed. Though she watched him thenceforward, not one glance did he vouchsafe to his jealous sweetheart, and never for an instant withdrew his eyes from Martha, or relaxed the unnatural intentness of his gaze. The imprisoned mind, stirred to unwonted effort, was struggling for liberty; and from Martha had come the first ray of outer light that had penetrated its dungeon.

Before the audience was dismissed, the teacher rose to bid her school farewell. Her intention was to take a vacation of three months; but what might happen in that time she did not know, and there were duties at home of such apparent urgency as to render her return to North Carolina at least doubtful; so that in her own heart her *au revoir* sounded very much like a farewell.

She spoke to them of the hopeful progress they had made, and praised them for their eager desire to learn. She told them of the serious duties of life, and of the use they should make of their acquirements. With prophetic finger she pointed them to the upward way which they must climb with patient feet to raise themselves out of the depths.

Then, an unusual thing with her, she spoke of herself. Her heart was full; it was with difficulty that she maintained her composure; for the faces that confronted her were kindly faces, and not critical, and some of them she had learned to love right well.

"I am going away from you, my children," she said; "but before I go I want to tell you how I came to be in North Carolina; so that if I have been able to do anything here among you for which you might feel inclined, in your good nature, to thank me, you may thank not me alone, but another who came before me, and whose work I have but taken up where *he* laid it down. I had a friend,—a dear friend,—why should I be ashamed to say it?—a lover, to whom I was to be married,—as I hope all you girls may some day be happily married. His country needed him, and I gave him up. He came to fight for the Union and for Freedom, for he believed that all men are brothers. He did not come back again—he gave up his life for you. Could I do less than he? I came to the land that he sanctified by his death, and I have tried in my weak way to tend the plant he watered with his blood, and which, in the fullness of time, will blossom forth into the perfect flower of liberty."

She could say no more, and as the whole audience thrilled in sympathy with her emotion, there was a hoarse cry from the men's side of the room, and John forced his way to the aisle and rushed forward to the platform.

"Martha! Martha!"

"Arthur! O Arthur!"

Pent-up love burst the flood-gates of despair and oblivion, and caught these two young hearts in its torrent. Captain Arthur Carey, of the 1st Massachusetts,[96] long since reported missing, and mourned as dead, was restored to reason and to his world.

It seemed to him but yesterday that he had escaped from the Confederate prison at Salisbury;[97] that in an encounter with a guard he had received a wound in the head; that he had wandered on in the woods, keeping himself alive by means of wild berries, with now and then a piece of bread or a potato from a friendly negro. It seemed but the night before that he had laid himself down, tortured with fever, weak from loss of blood, and with no hope that he would ever rise again. From that moment his memory of the past was a blank until he recognized Martha on the platform and took up again the thread of his former existence where it had been broken off.

And Cicely? Well, there is often another woman, and Cicely, all unwittingly to Carey or to Martha, had been the other woman. For, after all, her beautiful dream had been one of the kind that go by contraries.

Paul Laurence Dunbar

from *Lyrics of Lowly Life* (1895)

THE DESERTED PLANTATION

Oh, de grubbin'-hoe 's a-rustin' in de co'nah,
    An' de plow 's a-tumblin' down in de fiel',
While de whippo'will 's a-wailin' lak a mou'nah
    When his stubbo'n hea't is tryin' ha'd to yiel'.

In de furrers whah de co'n was allus wavin',
    Now de weeds is grown' green an' rank an' tall;
An' de swallers roun' de whole place is a-bravin'
    Lak dey thought deir folks had allus owned it all.

An' de big house stan's all quiet lak an' solemn,
    Not a blessed soul in pa'lor, po'ch, er lawn;
Not a guest, ner not a ca'iage lef' to haul 'em,
    Fu' de ones dat tu'ned de latch-string out air gone.

An' de banjo's voice is silent in de qua'ters,
    D' ain't a hymn ner co'n-song ringin' in de air;
But de murmur of a branch's passin' waters
    Is de only soun' dat breks de stillness dere.

Whah 's de da'kies, dem dat used to be a-dancin'
    Evry night befo' de ole cabin do'?
Whah 's de chillun, dem dat used to be a-prancin'
    Er a-rollin' in de san' er on de flo'?

Whah 's ole Uncle Mordecai an' Uncle Aaron?
    Whah 's Aunt Doshy, Sam, an' Kit, an' all de res'?
Whah 's ole Tom de da'ky fiddlah, how 's he farin'?
    Whah 's de gals dat used to sing an' dance de bes'?

Gone! not one o' dem is lef' to tell de story;
    Dey have lef' de deah ole place to fall away.
Could n't one o' dem dat seed it in its glory
    Stay to watch it in de hour of decay?

Dey have lef' de ole plantation to de swallers,
    But it ho's in me a lover till de las';
Fu' I fin' hyeah in de memory dat follers
    All dat loved me an' dat I loved in de pas'.

So I 'll stay an' watch de deah ole place an' tend it
    Ez I used to in de happy days gone by.
'Twell de othah Mastah thinks it 's time to end it,
    An' calls me to my qua'ters in de sky.

Paul Laurence Dunbar

WHEN DEY 'LISTED COLORED SOLDIERS (August 1899)

Dey was talkin' in de cabin, dey was talkin' in de hall;
But I listened kin' o' keerless, not a-t'inkin' 'bout it all;
An' on Sunday, too, I noticed, dey was whisp'rin' mighty much,
Stan'in' all erroun' de roadside w'en dey let us out o' chu'ch.
But I didn't t'ink erbout it 'twell de middle of de week,
An' my 'Lias come to see me, an' somehow he couldn't speak.
Den I seed all in a minute whut he'd come to see me for; —
Dey had 'listed colo'ed sojers an' my 'Lias gwine to wah.

Oh, I hugged him, an' I kissed him, an' I baiged him not to go;
But he tol' me dat his conscience, hit was callin' to him so,
An' he could n't baih to lingah w'en he had a chanst to fight
For de freedom dey had gin him an' de glory of de right.
So he kissed me, an' he lef' me, w'en I'd p'omised to be true;
An' dey put a knapsack on him, an' a coat all colo'ed blue.
So I gin him pap's ol' Bible f'om de bottom of de draw', —
W'en dey 'listed colo'ed sojers an' my 'Lias went to wah.

But I t'ought of all de weary miles dat he would have to tramp,
An' I could n't be contented w'en dey tuk him to de camp.
W'y my hea't nigh broke wid grievin' 'twell I seed him on de street;
Den I felt lak I could go an' th'ow my body at his feet.
For his buttons was a-shinin', an' his face was shinin', too,
An' he looked so strong an' mighty in his coat o' sojer blue,
Dat I hollahed, "Step up, manny," dough my th'oat was so' an' raw, —
W'en dey 'listed colo'ed sojers an' my 'Lias went to wah.

Ol' Mis' cried w'en mastah lef' huh, young Miss mou'ned huh brothah Ned,
An' I did n't know dey feelin's is de ve'y wo'ds dey said
W'en I tol' 'em I was so'y. Dey had done gin up dey all;
But dey only seemed mo' proudah dat dey men had hyeahed de call.
Bofe my mastahs went in gray suits, an' I loved de Yankee blue,
But I t'ought dat I could sorrer for de losin' of 'em too;
But I could n't, for I did n't know de ha'f o' whut I saw,
'Twell dey 'listed colo'ed sojers an' my 'Lias went to wah.

Mastah Jack come home all sickly; he was broke for life, dey said;
An' dey lef' my po' young mastah some'r's on de roadside,—dead.
W'en de women cried an' mou'ned 'em, I could feel it thoo an' thoo,
For I had a loved un fightin' in de way o' dangah, too.
Den dey tol' me dey had laid him some'r's way down souf to res',
Wid de flag dat he had fit for shinin' daih acrost his breas'.
Well, I cried, but den I reckon dat 's whut Gawd had called him for,
W'en dey 'listed colo'ed sojers an' my 'Lias went to wah.

Paul Laurence Dunbar

ROBERT GOULD SHAW (October 1900)

Why was it that the thunder voice of Fate
    Should call thee, studious, from the classic groves,
    Where calm-eyed Pallas with still footstep roves,
And charge thee seek the turmoil of the state?
What bade thee hear the voice and rise elate,
    Leave home and kindred and thy spicy loaves,
    To lead th' unlettered and despised droves
To manhood's home and thunder at the gate?

Far better the slow blaze of Learning's light,
    The cool and quiet of her dearer fane,
Than this hot terror of a hopeless fight,
    This cold endurance of the final pain,—
Since thou and those who with thee died for right
    Have died, the Present teaches, but in vain!

W. E. B. Du Bois

from *The Souls of Black Folk* (1903)

CHAPTER 1: OF OUR SPIRITUAL STRIVINGS

O water, voice of my heart, crying in the sand,
　　All night long crying with a mournful cry,
As I lie and listen, and cannot understand
　　　　The voice of my heart in my side or the voice of the sea,
　　O water, crying for rest, is it I, is it I?
　　　　All night long the water is crying to me.

Unresting water, there shall never be rest
　　Till the last moon droop and the last tide fail,
And the fire of the end begin to burn in the west;
　　　　And the heart shall be weary and wonder and cry like the sea,
　　All life long crying without avail,
　　　　As the water all night long is crying to me.

　　　　　　　　　　　　　　　　　Arthur Symons[98]

Between me and the other world there is ever an unasked question: unasked by some through feelings of delicacy; by others through the difficulty of rightly framing it. All, nevertheless, flutter round it. They approach me in a half-hesitant sort of way, eye me curiously or compassionately, and then, instead of saying directly, How does it feel to be a problem? they say, I know an excellent colored man in my town; or, I fought at Mechan-icsville;[99] or, Do not these Southern outrages make your blood boil? At these I smile, or am interested, or reduce the boiling to a simmer, as the occasion may require. To the real question, How does it feel to be a problem? I answer seldom a word.

And yet, being a problem is a strange experience,—peculiar even for one who has never been anything else, save perhaps in babyhood and in Europe. It is in the early days of rollicking boyhood that the revelation first bursts upon one, all in a day, as it were. I remember well when the shadow swept across me. I was a little thing, away up in the hills of New England, where the dark Housatonic winds between Hoosac and Taghkanic to the sea. In a wee wooden schoolhouse, something put it into the boys' and girls' heads to buy gorgeous visiting-cards—ten cents a package—and exchange. The exchange was merry, till one girl, a tall newcomer, refused my card—refused it peremptorily, with a glance. Then it dawned upon me with a certain suddenness that I was different from the others; or like, mayhap, in heart and life and longing, but shut out from their world by a vast veil. I had thereafter no desire to tear down that veil, to creep through; I held all beyond it in com-mon contempt, and lived above it in a region of blue sky and great wandering shadows. That sky was bluest when I could beat my mates at examination-time, or beat them at a foot-race, or even beat their stringy heads. Alas, with the years all this fine contempt began to fade; for the worlds I longed for, and all their dazzling opportunities, were theirs, not mine. But they should not keep these prizes, I said; some, all, I would wrest from them.

Just how I would do it I could never decide: by reading law, by healing the sick, by telling the wonderful tales that swam in my head,—some way. With other black boys the strife was not so fiercely sunny: their youth shrunk into tasteless sycophancy, or into silent hatred of the pale world about them and mocking distrust of everything white; or wasted itself in a bitter cry, Why did God make me an outcast and a stranger in mine own house? The shades of the prison-house closed round about us all: walls strait and stubborn to the whitest, but relentlessly narrow, tall, and unscalable to sons of night who must plod darkly on in resignation, or beat unavailing palms against the stone, or steadily, half hopelessly, watch the streak of blue above.

After the Egyptian and Indian, the Greek and Roman, the Teuton and Mongolian, the Negro is a sort of seventh son, born with a veil, and gifted with second-sight in this American world,—a world which yields him no true self-consciousness, but only lets him see himself through the revelation of the other world. It is a peculiar sensation, this double-consciousness, this sense of always looking at one's self through the eyes of others, of measuring one's soul by the tape of a world that looks on in amused contempt and pity. One ever feels his two-ness,—an American, a Negro; two souls, two thoughts, two unreconciled strivings; two warring ideals in one dark body, whose dogged strength alone keeps it from being torn asunder.

The history of the American Negro is the history of this strife,—this longing to attain self-conscious manhood, to merge his double self into a better and truer self. In this merging he wishes neither of the older selves to be lost. He would not Africanize America, for America has too much to teach the world and Africa. He would not bleach his Negro soul in a flood of white Americanism, for he knows that Negro blood has a message for the world. He simply wishes to make it possible for a man to be both a Negro and an American, without being cursed and spit upon by his fellows, without having the doors of Opportunity closed roughly in his face.

This, then, is the end of his striving: to be a co-worker in the kingdom of culture, to escape both death and isolation, to husband and use his best powers and his latent genius. These powers of body and mind have in the past been strangely wasted, dispersed, or forgotten. The shadow of a mighty Negro past flits through the tale of Ethiopia the Shadowy and of Egypt the Sphinx. Throughout history, the powers of single black men flash here and there like falling stars, and die sometimes before the world has rightly gauged their brightness. Here in America, in the few days since Emancipation, the black man's turning hither and thither in hesitant and doubtful striving has often made his very strength to lose effectiveness, to seem like absence of power, like weakness. And yet it is not weakness,—it is the contradiction of double aims. The double-aimed struggle of the black artisan—on the one hand to escape white contempt for a nation of mere hewers of wood and drawers of water, and on the other hand to plough and nail and dig for a poverty-stricken horde—could only result in making him a poor craftsman, for he had but half a heart in either cause. By the poverty and ignorance of his people, the Negro minister or doctor was tempted toward quackery and demagogy; and by the criticism of the other world, toward ideals that made him ashamed of his lowly tasks. The would-be black *savant* was confronted by the paradox that the knowledge his people needed was a twice-told tale to his white neighbors, while the knowledge which would teach the white world was Greek to his own flesh and blood. The innate love of harmony and beauty that set the ruder sols of his people a-dancing and a-singing raised but confusion and doubt in the soul of the black artist; for the beauty revealed to him was the soul-beauty of a race which his larger audience despised, and he could not articulate the message of another people. This waste of double aims, this seeking to satisfy two unreconciled ideals, has wrought sad havoc with the courage and faith and deeds of ten thousand thousand people,—has sent them often wooing false gods and invoking false means of salvation, and at times has even seemed about to make them ashamed of themselves.

Away back in the days of bondage, they thought to see in one divine event the end of all doubt and disappointment; few men ever worshipped Freedom with half such unquestioning faith as did the American Negro for two centuries. To him, so far as he thought and dreamed, slavery was indeed the sum of all villainies, the cause of all sorrow, the root of all prejudice; Emancipation was the key to a promised land of sweeter beauty than ever stretched before the eyes of wearied Israelites. In song and exhortation swelled one refrain —Liberty; in his tears and curses the God he implored had Freedom in his right hand. At last it came,—suddenly, fearfully, like a dream. With one wild carnival of blood and passion came the message in his own plaintive cadences:—

"Shout, O Children!
Shout, you're free!
For God has bought your liberty!"[100]

Years have passed away since then,—ten, twenty, forty; forty years of national life, forty years of renewal and development, and yet the swarthy spectre sits in its accustomed seat at the Nation's feast. In vain do we cry to this our vastest social problem:—

"Take any shape but that, and my firm nerves
Shall never tremble!"[101]

The Nation has not yet found peace from its sins; the freedman has not yet found in freedom his promised land. Whatever of good may have come in these years of change, the shadow of a deep disappointment rests upon the Negro people,—a disappointment all the more bitter because the unattained ideal was unbounded save by the simple ignorance of a lowly people.

The first decade was merely a prolongation of the vain search for freedom, the boon that seemed ever barely to elude their grasp,—like a tantalizing will-o'-the-wisp, maddening and misleading the headless host. The holocaust of war, the terrors of the Ku-Klux Klan, the lies of carpet-baggers, the disorganization of industry, and the contradictory advice of friends and foes, left the bewildered serf with no new watchword beyond the old cry for freedom. As the time flew, however, he began to grasp a new idea. The ideal of liberty demanded for its attainment powerful means, and these the Fifteenth Amendment gave him.[102] The ballot, which before he had looked upon as a visible sign of freedom, he now regarded as the chief means of gaining and perfecting the liberty with which war had partially endowed him. And why not? Had not votes made war and emancipated millions? Had not votes enfranchised the freedmen? Was anything impossible to a power that had done all this? A million black men started with renewed zeal to vote themselves into the kingdom. So the decade flew away, the revolution of 1876 came, and left the half-free serf weary, wondering, but still inspired.[103] Slowly but steadily, in the following years, a new vision began gradually to replace the dream of political power,—a powerful movement, the rise of another ideal to guide the unguided, another pillar of fire by night after a clouded day. It was the ideal of "book-learning"; the curiosity, born of compulsory ignorance, to know and test the power of the cabalistic letters of the white man, the longing to know. Here at last seemed to have been discovered the mountain path to Canaan; longer than the highway of Emancipation and law, steep and rugged, but straight, leading to heights high enough to overlook life.

Up the new path the advance guard toiled, slowly, heavily, doggedly; only those who have watched and guided the faltering feet, the misty minds, the dull understandings, of the dark pupils of these schools know how faithfully, how piteously, this people strove to learn. It was weary work. The cold statistician wrote down the inches of progress here and there, noted also where here and there a foot had slipped or some one had fallen. To the tired climbers, the horizon was ever dark, the mists were often cold, the Canaan was always dim and far away. If, however, the vistas disclosed as yet no goal, no resting-place, little but flattery and criticism, the journey at least gave leisure for reflection and self-examination; it changed the child of Emancipation to the youth with dawning self-consciousness, self-realization, self-respect. In those sombre forests of his striving his own soul rose before him, and he saw himself,—darkly as through a veil; and yet he saw in himself some faint revelation of his power, of his mission. He began to have a dim feeling that, to attain his place in the world, he must be himself, and not another. For the first time he sought to analyze the burden he bore upon his back, that dead-weight of social degradation partially masked behind a half-named Negro problem. He felt his poverty; without a cent, without a home, without land, tools, or savings, he had entered into competition with rich, landed, skilled neighbors. To be a poor man is hard, but to be a poor race in a land of dollars is the very bottom of hardships. He felt the weight of his ignorance,—not simply of letters, but of life, of business, of the humanities; the accumulated sloth and shirking and awkwardness of decades and centuries shackled his hands and feet. Nor was his burden all poverty and ignorance. The red stain of bastardy, which two centuries of systematic legal defilement of Negro women had stamped upon his race, meant not only the loss of ancient African chastity, but also the hereditary weight of a mass of corruption from white adulterers, threatening almost the obliteration of the Negro home.

A people thus handicapped ought not to be asked to race with the world, but rather allowed to give all its time and thought to its own social problems. But alas! while sociologists gleefully count his bastards and his prostitutes, the very soul of the toiling, sweating black man is darkened by the shadow of a vast despair. Men call the shadow prejudice, and learnedly explain it as the natural defence of culture against barbarism, learning against ignorance, purity against crime, the "higher" against the "lower" races. To which the Negro cries Amen! and swears that to so much of this strange prejudice as is founded on just homage to civilization, culture, righteousness, and progress, he humbly bows and meekly does obeisance. But before that nameless prejudice that leaps beyond all this he stands helpless, dismayed, and well-nigh speechless; before that personal disrespect and mockery, the ridicule and systematic humiliation, the distortion of fact and wanton license of fancy, the cynical ignoring of the better and the boisterous welcoming of the worse, the all-pervading desire to inculcate disdain for everything black, from Toussaint[104] to the devil,—before this there rises a sickening despair that would disarm and discourage any nation save that black host to whom "discouragement" is an unwritten word.

But the facing of so vast a prejudice could not but bring the inevitable self-questioning, self-disparagement, and lowering of ideals which ever accompany repression and breed in an atmosphere of contempt and hate. Whisperings and portents came borne upon the four winds: Lo! we are diseased and dying, cried the dark hosts; we cannot write, our voting is vain; what need of education, since we must always cook and serve? And the Nation echoed and enforced this self-criticism, saying: Be content to be servants, and nothing more; what need of higher culture for half-men? Away with the black man's ballot, by force or fraud,—and behold the suicide of a race! Nevertheless, out of the evil came something of good,—the more careful adjustment of education to real life, the clearer perception of the Negroes' social responsibilities, and the sobering realization of the meaning of progress.

So dawned the time of *Sturm und Drang*: storm and stress to-day rocks our little boat on the mad waters of the world-sea; there is within and without the sound of conflict, the burning of body and rending of soul; inspiration strives with doubt, and faith with vain questionings. The bright ideals of the past,—physical freedom, political power, the training of brains and the training of hands,—all these in turn have waxed and waned, until even the last grows dim and overcast. Are they all wrong,—all false? No, not that, but each alone was over-simple and incomplete,—the dreams of a credulous race-childhood, or the fond imaginings of the other world which does not know and does not want to know our power. To be really true, all these ideals must be melted and welded into one. The training of the schools we need to-day more than ever,—the training of deft hands, quick eyes and ears, and above all the broader, deeper, higher culture of gifted minds and pure hearts. The power of the ballot we need in sheer self-defence,—else what shall save us from a second slavery? Freedom, too, the long-sought, we still seek,—the freedom of life and limb, the freedom to work and think, the freedom to love and aspire. Work, culture, liberty,—all these we need, not singly but together, not successively but together, each growing and aiding each, and all striving toward that vaster ideal that swims before the Negro people, the ideal of human brotherhood, gained through the unifying ideal of Race; the ideal of fostering and developing the traits and talents of the Negro, not in opposition to or contempt for other races, but rather in large conformity to the greater ideals of the American Republic, in order that some day on American soil two world-races may give each to each those characteristics both so sadly lack. We the darker ones come even now not altogether empty-handed: there are to-day no truer exponents of the pure human spirit of the Declaration of Independence than the American Negroes; there is no true American music but the wild sweet melodies of the Negro slave; the American fairy tales and folk-lore are Indian and African; and, all in all, we black men seem the sole oasis of simple faith and reverence in a dusty desert of dollars and smartness. Will America be poorer if she replace her brutal dyspeptic blundering with light-hearted but determined Negro humility? or her coarse and cruel wit with loving jovial good-humor? or her vulgar music with the soul of the Sorrow Songs?

Merely a concrete test of the underlying principles of the great republic is the Negro Problem, and the spiritual striving of the freedmen's sons is the travail of souls whose burden is almost beyond the measure of their strength, but who bear it in the name of an historic race, in the name of this the land of their fathers' fathers, and in the name of human opportunity.

And now what I have briefly sketched in large outline let me on coming pages tell again in many ways, with loving emphasis and deeper detail, that men may listen to the striving in the souls of black folk.

W. E. B. Du Bois

from *The Souls of Black Folk* (1903)

CHAPTER 2: OF THE DAWN OF FREEDOM

Careless seems the great Avenger;
　　History's lessons but record
One death-grapple in the darkness
　　'Twixt old systems and the Word;
Truth forever on the scaffold,
　　Wrong forever on the throne;
Yet that scaffold sways the future,
　　And behind the dim unknown
Standeth God within the shadow
　　Keeping watch above His own.

Lowell.[105]

The problem of the twentieth century is the problem of the color-line,—the relation of the darker to the lighter races of men in Asia and Africa, in America and the islands of the sea. It was a phase of this problem that caused the Civil War; and however much they who marched South and North in 1861 may have fixed on the technical points of union and local autonomy as a shibboleth, all nevertheless knew, as we know, that the question of Negro slavery was the real cause of the conflict. Curious it was, too, how this deeper question ever forced itself to the surface despite effort and disclaimer. No sooner had Northern armies touched Southern soil than this old question, newly guised, sprang from the earth,—What shall be done with Negroes? Peremptory military commands, this way and that, could not answer the query; the Emancipation Proclamation seemed but to broaden and intensify the difficulties; and the War Amendments made the Negro problems of to-day.

It is the aim of this essay to study the period of history from 1861 to 1872 so far as it relates to the American Negro. In effect, this tale of the dawn of Freedom is an account of that government of men called the Freedmen's Bureau,—one of the most singular and interesting of the attempts made by a great nation to grapple with vast problems of race and social condition.

The war has naught to do with slaves, cried Congress, the President, and the Nation; and yet no sooner had the armies, East and West, penetrated Virginia and Tennessee than fugitive slaves appeared within their lines. They came at night, when the flickering camp-fires shone like vast unsteady stars along the black horizon: old men and thin, with gray and tufted hair; women, with frightened eyes, dragging whimpering hungry children; men and girls, stalwart and gaunt,—a horde of starving vagabonds, homeless, helpless, and pitiable, in their dark distress. Two methods of treating these newcomers seemed equally logical to opposite sorts of minds. Ben Butler, in Virginia, quickly declared slave property contraband of war, and put the fugitives to work; while Fremont, in Missouri, declared the slaves free under martial law. Butler's action was approved, but Fremont's was hastily countermanded, and his successor, Halleck, saw things differently. "Hereafter," he commanded, "no slaves should be allowed to come into your lines at all; if any come without your knowledge, when owners call for them deliver them." Such a policy was difficult to enforce; some of the black refugees declared themselves freemen, others showed that their masters had deserted them, and still others were captured with forts and plantations. Evidently, too, slaves were a source of strength to the Confederacy, and were being used as laborers and producers. "They constitute a military resource," wrote Secretary Cameron, late in 1861; "and being such, that they should not be turned over to the enemy is too plain to discuss." So gradually the tone of the army chiefs changed; Congress forbade the rendition of fugitives, and Butler's "contrabands" were welcomed as military laborers. This complicated rather than solved the problem, for now the scattering fugitives became a steady stream, which flowed faster as the armies marched.

Then the long-headed man with care-chiselled face who sat in the White House saw the inevitable, and emancipated the slaves of rebels on New Year's, 1863. A month later Congress called earnestly for the Negro soldiers whom the act of July, 1862, had half grudgingly allowed to enlist. Thus the barriers were levelled and the deed was done. The stream of fugitives swelled to a flood, and anxious army officers kept inquiring: "What must be done with slaves, arriving almost daily? Are we to find food and shelter for women and children?"

It was a Pierce of Boston who pointed out the way, and thus became in a sense the founder of the Freedmen's Bureau. He was a firm friend of Secretary Chase; and when, in 1861, the care of slaves and abandoned lands devolved upon the Treasury officials, Pierce was specially detailed from the ranks to study the conditions. First, he cared for the refugees at Fortress Monroe; and then, after Sherman had captured Hilton Head, Pierce was sent there to found his Port Royal experiment of making free workingmen out of slaves. Before his experiment was barely started, however, the problem of the fugitives had assumed such proportions that it was taken from the hands of the over-burdened Treasury Department and given to the army officials. Already centres of massed freedmen were forming at Fortress Monroe, Washington, New Orleans, Vicksburg and Corinth, Columbus, Ky., and Cairo, Ill., as well as at Port Royal. Army chaplains found here new and fruitful fields; "superintendents of contrabands" multiplied, and some attempt at systematic work was made by enlisting the able-bodied men and giving work to the others.

Then came the Freedmen's Aid societies, born of the touching appeals from Pierce and from these other centres of distress. There was the American Missionary Association, sprung from the Amistad,[106] and now full-grown for work; the various church organizations, the National Freedmen's Relief Association, the American Freedmen's Union, the Western Freedmen's Aid Commission,—in all fifty or more active organizations, which sent clothes, money, school-books, and teachers southward. All they did was needed, for the destitution of the freedmen was often reported as "too appalling for belief," and the situation was daily growing worse rather than better.

And daily, too, it seemed more plain that this was no ordinary matter of temporary relief, but a national crisis; for here loomed a labor problem of vast dimensions. Masses of Negroes stood idle, or, if they worked spasmodically, were never sure of pay; and if perchance they received pay, squandered the new thing thoughtlessly. In these and other ways were camp-life and the new liberty demoralizing the freedmen. The broader economic organization thus clearly demanded sprang up here and there as accident and local conditions determined. Here it was that Pierce's Port Royal plan of leased plantations and guided workmen pointed out the rough way. In Washington the military governor, at the urgent appeal of the superintendent, opened confiscated estates to the cultivation of the fugitives, and there in the shadow of the dome gathered black farm villages. General Dix[107] gave over estates to the freedmen of Fortress Monroe, and so on, South and West. The government and benevolent societies furnished the means of cultivation, and the Negro turned again slowly to work. The systems of control, thus started, rapidly grew, here and there, into strange little governments, like that of General Banks in Louisiana, with its ninety thousand black subjects, its fifty thousand guided laborers, and its annual budget of one hundred thousand dollars and more. It made out four thousand pay-rolls a year, registered all freedmen, inquired into grievances and redressed them, laid and collected taxes, and established a system of public schools. So, too, Colonel Eaton,[108] the superintendent of Tennessee and Arkansas, ruled over one hundred thousand freedmen, leased and cultivated seven thousand acres of cotton land, and fed ten thousand paupers a year. In South Carolina was General Saxton, with his deep interest in black folk. He succeeded Pierce and the Treasury officials, and sold forfeited estates, leased abandoned plantations, encouraged schools, and received from Sherman, after that terribly picturesque march to the sea, thousands of the wretched camp followers.

Three characteristic things one might have seen in Sherman's raid through Georgia, which threw the new situation in shadowy relief: the Conqueror, the Conquered, and the Negro. Some see all significance in the grim front of the destroyer, and some in the bitter sufferers of the Lost Cause. But to me neither soldier nor fugitive speaks with so deep a meaning as that dark human cloud that clung like remorse on the rear of those swift columns, swelling at times to half their size, almost engulfing and choking them. In vain were they ordered back, in vain were bridges hewn from beneath their feet; on they trudged and writhed and surged, until they rolled into Savannah, a starved and naked horde of tens of thousands. There too came the characteristic military remedy: "The islands from Charleston south, the abandoned rice-fields along the rivers for thirty miles back from the sea, and the country bordering the St. John's River, Florida, are reserved and set apart for the settlement of Negroes now made free by act of war." So read the celebrated "Field-order Number Fifteen."[109]

All these experiments, orders, and systems were bound to attract and perplex the government and the nation. Directly after the Emancipation Proclamation, Representative Eliot had introduced a bill creating a Bureau of Emancipation; but it was never reported. The following June a committee of inquiry, appointed by the Secretary of War [Edwin Stanton], reported in favor of a temporary bureau for the "improvement, protection, and employment of refugee freedmen," on much the same lines as were afterwards followed. Petitions came in to President Lincoln from distinguished citizens and organizations, strongly urging a comprehensive and unified plan of dealing with the freedmen, under a bureau which should be "charged with the study of plans and execution of measures for easily guiding, and in every way judiciously and humanely aiding, the passage of our emancipated and yet to be emancipated blacks from the old condition of forced labor to their new state of voluntary industry."

Some half-hearted steps were taken to accomplish this, in part, by putting the whole matter again in charge of the special Treasury agents. Laws of 1863 and 1864 directed them to take charge of and lease abandoned lands for periods not exceeding twelve months, and to "provide in such leases, or otherwise, for the employment and general welfare" of the freedmen. Most of the army officers greeted this as a welcome relief from perplexing "Negro affairs," and Secretary Fessenden, July 29, 1864, issued an excellent system of regulations, which were afterward closely followed by General Howard.[110] Under Treasury agents, large quantities of land were leased in the Mississippi Valley, and many Negroes were employed; but in August, 1864, the new regulations were suspended for reasons of "public policy," and the army was again in control.

Meanwhile Congress had turned its attention to the subject; and in March the House passed a bill by a majority of two establishing a Bureau for Freedmen in the War Department. Charles Sumner, who had charge of the bill in the Senate, argued that freedmen and abandoned lands ought to be under the same department, and reported a substitute for the House bill attaching the Bureau to the Treasury Department. This bill passed, but too late for action by the House. The debates wandered over the whole policy of the administration and the general question of slavery, without touching very closely the specific merits of the measure in hand. Then the national election took place; and the administration, with a vote of renewed confidence from the country, addressed itself to the matter more seriously. A conference between the two branches of Congress agreed upon a carefully drawn measure which contained the chief provisions of Sumner's bill, but made the proposed organization a department independent of both the War and the Treasury officials. The bill was conservative, giving the new department "general superintendence of all freedmen." Its purpose was to "establish regulations" for them, protect them, lease them lands, adjust their wages, and appear in civil and military courts as their "next friend." There were many limitations attached to the powers thus granted, and the organization was made permanent. Nevertheless, the Senate defeated the bill, and a new conference committee was appointed. This committee reported a new bill, February 28, which was whirled through just as the session closed, and became the act of 1865 establishing in the War Department a "Bureau of Refugees, Freedmen, and Abandoned Lands."

This last compromise was a hasty bit of legislation, vague and uncertain in outline. A Bureau was created, "to continue during the present War of Rebellion, and for one year thereafter," to which was given "the supervision and management of all abandoned lands and the control of all subjects relating to refugees and freedmen," under "such rules and regulations as may be presented by the head of the Bureau and approved by the President." A Commissioner, appointed by the President and Senate, was to control the Bureau, with an office force not exceeding ten clerks. The President might also appoint assistant commissioners in the seceded States, and to all these offices military officials might be detailed at regular pay. The Secretary of War could issue rations, clothing, and fuel to the destitute, and all abandoned property was placed in the hands of the Bureau for eventual lease and sale to ex-slaves in forty-acre parcels.

Thus did the United States government definitely assume charge of the emancipated Negro as the ward of the nation. It was a tremendous undertaking. Here at a stroke of the pen was erected a government of millions of men,—and not ordinary men either, but black men emasculated by a peculiarly complete system of slavery, centuries old; and now, suddenly, violently, they come into a new birthright, at a time of war and passion, in the midst of the stricken and embittered population of their former masters. Any man might well have hesitated to assume charge of such a work, with vast responsibilities, indefinite powers, and limited resources. Probably no one but a soldier would have answered such a call promptly; and, indeed, no one but a soldier could be called, for Congress had appropriated no money for salaries and expenses.

Less than a month after the weary Emancipator passed to his rest, his successor assigned Major-Gen. Oliver O. Howard to duty as Commissioner of the new Bureau. He was a Maine man, then only thirty-five years of age. He had marched with Sherman to the sea, had fought well at Gettysburg, and but the year before had been assigned to the command of the Department of Tennessee. An honest man, with too much faith in human nature, little aptitude for business and intricate detail, he had had large opportunity of becoming acquainted at first hand with much of the work before him. And of that work it has been truly said that "no approximately correct history of civilization can ever be written which does not throw out in bold relief, as one of the great landmarks of political and social progress, the organization and administration of the Freedmen's Bureau."

On May 12, 1865, Howard was appointed; and he assumed the duties of his office promptly on the 15th, and began examining the field of work. A curious mess he looked upon: little despotisms, communistic experiments, slavery, peonage, business speculations, organized charity, unorganized almsgiving,—all reeling on under the guise of helping the freedmen, and all enshrined in the smoke and blood of war and the cursing and silence of angry men. On May 19 the new government—for a government it really was—issued its constitution; commissioners were to be appointed in each of the seceded States, who were to take charge of "all subjects relating to refugees and freedmen," and all relief and rations were to be given by their consent alone. The Bureau invited continued cooperation with benevolent societies, and declared: "It will be the object of all commissioners to introduce practicable systems of compensated labor," and to establish schools. Forthwith nine assistant commissioners were appointed. They were to hasten to their fields of work; seek gradually to close relief establishments, and make the destitute self-supporting; act as courts of law where there were no courts, or where Negroes were not recognized in them as free; establish the institution of marriage among ex-slaves, and keep records; see that freedmen were free to choose their employers, and help in making fair contracts for them; and finally, the circular said: "Simple good faith, for which we hope on all hands for those concerned in the passing away of slavery, will especially relieve the assistant commissioners in the discharge of their duties toward the freedmen, as well as promote the general welfare."

No sooner was the work thus started, and the general system and local organization in some measure begun, than two grave difficulties appeared which changed largely the theory and outcome of Bureau work. First, there were the abandoned lands of the South. It had long been the more or less definitely expressed theory of the North that all the chief problems of Emancipation might be settled by establishing the slaves on the forfeited lands of their masters,—a sort of poetic justice, said some. But this poetry done into solemn prose meant either wholesale confiscation of private property in the South, or vast appropriations. Now Congress had not appropriated a cent, and no sooner did the proclamations of general amnesty appear than the eight hundred thousand acres of abandoned lands in the hands of the Freedmen's Bureau melted quickly away. The second difficulty lay in perfecting the local organization of the Bureau throughout the wide field of work. Making a new machine and sending out officials of duly ascertained fitness for a great work of social reform is no child's task; but this task was even harder, for a new central organization had to be fitted on a heterogeneous and confused but already existing system of relief and control of ex-slaves; and the agents available for this work must be sought for in an army still busy with war operations,—men in the very nature of the case ill fitted for delicate social work,—or among the questionable camp followers of an invading host. Thus, after a year's work, vigorously as it was pushed, the problem looked even more difficult to grasp and solve than at the beginning. Nevertheless, three things that year's work did, well worth the doing: it relieved a vast amount of physical suffering; it transported seven thousand fugitives from congested centres back to the farm; and, best of all, it inaugurated the crusade of the New England schoolma'am.

The annals of this Ninth Crusade are yet to be written,—the tale of a mission that seemed to our age far more quixotic than the quest of St. Louis seemed to his. Behind the mists of ruin and rapine waved the calico dresses of women who dared, and after the hoarse mouthings of the field guns rang the rhythm of the alphabet. Rich and poor they were, serious and curious. Bereaved now of a father, now of a brother, now of more than these, they came seeking a life work in planting New England schoolhouses among the white and black of the South. They, did their work well. In that first year they taught one hundred thousand souls, and more.

Evidently, Congress must soon legislate again on the hastily organized Bureau, which had so quickly grown into wide significance and vast possibilities. An institution such as that was well-nigh as difficult to end as to begin. Early in 1866 Congress took up the matter, when Senator Trumbull, of Illinois, introduced a bill to extend the Bureau and enlarge its powers. This measure received, at the hands of Congress, far more thorough discussion and attention than its predecessor. The war cloud had thinned enough to allow a clearer conception of the work of Emancipation. The champions of the bill argued that the strengthening of the Freedmen's Bureau was still a military necessity; that it was needed for the proper carrying out of the Thirteenth Amendment, and was a work of sheer justice to the ex-slave, at a trifling cost to the government. The opponents of the measure declared that the war was over, and the necessity for war measures past; that the Bureau, by reason of its extraordinary powers, was clearly unconstitutional in time of peace, and was destined to irritate the South and pauperize the freedmen, at a final cost of possibly hundreds of millions. These two arguments were unanswered, and indeed unanswerable: the one that the extraordinary powers of the Bureau threatened the civil rights of all citizens; and the other that the government must have power to do what manifestly must be done, and that present abandonment of the freedmen meant their practical reenslavement. The bill which finally passed enlarged and made permanent the Freedmen's Bureau. It was promptly vetoed by President Johnson as "unconstitutional," "unnecessary," and "extrajudicial," and failed of passage over the veto. Meantime, however, the breach between Congress and the President began to broaden, and a modified form of the lost bill was finally passed over the President's second veto, July 16.

The act of 1866 gave the Freedmen's Bureau its final form,—the form by which it will be known to posterity and judged of men. It extended the existence of the Bureau to July, 1868; it authorized additional assistant commissioners, the retention of army officers mustered out of regular service, the sale of certain forfeited lands to freedmen on nominal terms, the sale of Confederate public property for Negro schools, and a wider field of judicial interpretation and cognizance. The government of the unreconstructed South was thus put very largely in the hands of the Freedmen's Bureau, especially as in many cases the departmental military commander was now made also assistant commissioner. It was thus that the Freedmen's Bureau became a full-fledged government of men. It made laws, executed them and interpreted them; it laid and collected taxes, defined and, punished crime, maintained and used military force, and dictated such measures as it thought necessary and proper for the accomplishment of its varied ends. Naturally, all these powers were not exercised continuously nor to their fullest extent; and yet, as General Howard has said, "scarcely any subject that has to be legislated upon in civil society failed, at one time or another, to demand the action of this singular Bureau."

To understand and criticise intelligently so vast a work, one must not forget an instant the drift of things in the later sixties. Lee had surrendered, Lincoln was dead; and Johnson and Congress were at loggerheads; the Thirteenth Amendment was adopted, the Fourteenth pending, and the Fifteenth declared in force in 1870. Guerrilla raiding, the ever-present flickering after-flame of war, was spending its force against the Negroes, and all the Southern land was awakening as from some wild dream to poverty and social revolution. In a time of perfect calm, amid willing neighbors and streaming wealth, the social uplifting of four million slaves to an assured and self-sustaining place in the body politic and economic would have been a herculean task; but when to the inherent difficulties of so delicate and nice a social operation were added the spite and hate of conflict, the hell of war; when suspicion and cruelty were rife, and gaunt Hunger wept beside Bereavement,—in such a case, the work of any instrument of social regeneration was in large part foredoomed to failure. The very name of the Bureau stood for a thing in the South which for two centuries and better men had refused even to argue,—that life amid free Negroes was simply unthinkable, the maddest of experiments.

The agents that the Bureau could command varied all the way from unselfish philanthropists to narrow-minded busybodies and thieves; and even though it be true that the average was far better than the worst, it was the occasional fly that helped spoil the ointment.

Then amid all crouched the freed slave, bewildered between friend and foe. He had emerged from slavery,—not the worst slavery in the world, not a slavery that made all life unbearable, rather a slavery that had here and there something of kindliness, fidelity, and happiness,—but withal slavery, which, so far as human aspiration and desert were concerned, classed the black man and the ox together. And the Negro knew full well that, whatever their deeper convictions may have been, Southern men had fought with desperate energy to perpetuate this slavery under which the black masses, with half-articulate thought, had writhed and shivered. They welcomed freedom with a cry. They shrank from the master who still strove for their chains; they fled to the friends that had freed them, even though those friends stood ready to use them as a club for driving the recalcitrant South back into loyalty. So the cleft between the white and black South grew. Idle to say it never should have been; it was as inevitable as its results were pitiable. Curiously incongruous elements were left arrayed against each other,—the North, the government, the carpet-bagger, and the slave, here; and there, all the South that was white, whether gentleman or vagabond, honest man or rascal, lawless murderer or martyr to duty.

Thus it is doubly difficult to write of this period calmly, so intense was the feeling, so mighty the human passions that swayed and blinded men. Amid it all, two figures ever stand to typify that day to coming ages,—the one, a gray-haired gentleman, whose fathers had quit themselves like men, whose sons lay in nameless graves; who bowed to the evil of slavery because its abolition threatened untold ill to all; who stood at last, in the evening of life, a blighted, ruined form, with hate in his eyes;—and the other, a form hovering dark and mother-like, her awful face black with the mists of centuries, had aforetime quailed at that white master's command, had bent in love over the cradles of his sons and daughters, and closed in death the sunken eyes of his wife,—aye, too, at his behest had laid herself low to his lust, and borne a tawny man-child to the world, only to see her dark boy's limbs scattered to the winds by midnight marauders riding after "damned Niggers." These were the saddest sights of that woful day; and no man clasped the hands of these two passing figures of the present-past; but, hating, they went to their long home, and, hating, their children's children live to-day.

Here, then, was the field of work for the Freedmen's Bureau; and since, with some hesitation, it was continued by the act of 1868 until 1869, let us look upon four years of its work as a whole. There were, in 1868, nine hundred Bureau officials scattered from Washington to Texas, ruling, directly and indirectly, many millions of men. The deeds of these rulers fall mainly under seven heads: the relief of physical suffering, the overseeing of the beginnings of free labor, the buying and selling of land, the establishment of schools, the paying of bounties, the administration of justice, and the financiering of all these activities.

Up to June, 1869, over half a million patients had been treated by Bureau physicians and surgeons, and sixty hospitals and asylums had been in operation. In fifty months twenty-one million free rations were distributed at a cost of over four million dollars. Next came the difficult question of labor. First, thirty thousand black men were transported from the refuges and relief stations back to the farms, back to the critical trial of a new way of working. Plain instructions went out from Washington: the laborers must be free to choose their employers, no fixed rate of wages was prescribed, and there was to be no peonage or forced labor. So far, so good; but where local agents differed *toto cœlo* in capacity and character, where the *personnel* was continually changing, the outcome was necessarily varied. The largest element of success lay in the fact that the majority of the freedmen were willing, even eager, to work. So labor contracts were written,—fifty thousand in a single State,—laborers advised, wages guaranteed, and employers supplied. In truth, the organization became a vast labor bureau,—not perfect, indeed, notably defective here and there, but on the whole successful beyond the dreams of thoughtful men. The two great obstacles which confronted the officials were the tyrant and the idler,—the slaveholder who was determined to perpetuate slavery under another name; and the freedman who regarded freedom as perpetual rest,—the Devil and the Deep Sea.

In the work of establishing the Negroes as peasant proprietors, the Bureau was from the first handicapped and at last absolutely checked. Something was done, and larger things were planned; abandoned lands were leased so long as they remained in the hands of the Bureau, and a total revenue of nearly half a million dollars derived from black tenants. Some other lands to which the nation had gained title were sold on easy terms, and public lands were opened for settlement to the very few freedmen who had tools and capital. But the vision of "forty acres and a mule"—the righteous and reasonable ambition to become a landholder, which the nation had all but categorically promised the freedmen—was destined in most cases to bitter disappointment. And those men of marvellous hindsight who are today seeking to preach the Negro back to the present peonage of the soil know well, or ought to know, that the opportunity of binding the Negro peasant willingly to the soil was lost on that day when the Commissioner of the Freedmen's Bureau had to go to South

Carolina and tell the weeping freedmen, after their years of toil, that their land was not theirs, that there was a mistake—somewhere. If by 1874 the Georgia Negro alone owned three hundred and fifty thousand acres of land, it was by grace of his thrift rather than by bounty of the government.

The greatest success of the Freedmen's Bureau lay in the planting of the free school among Negroes, and the idea of free elementary education among all classes in the South. It not only called the school-mistresses through the benevolent agencies and built them schoolhouses, but it helped discover and support such apostles of human culture as Edmund Ware, Samuel Armstrong, and Erastus Cravath. The opposition to Negro education in the South was at first bitter, and showed itself in ashes, insult, and blood; for the South believed an educated Negro to be a dangerous Negro. And the South was not wholly wrong; for education among all kinds of men always has had, and always will have, an element of danger and revolution, of dissatisfaction and discontent. Nevertheless, men strive to know. Perhaps some inkling of this paradox, even in the unquiet days of the Bureau, helped the bayonets allay an opposition to human training which still to-day lies smouldering in the South, but not flaming. Fisk, Atlanta, Howard, and Hampton were founded in these days, and six million dollars were expended for educational work, seven hundred and fifty thousand dollars of which the freedmen themselves gave of their poverty.

Such contributions, together with the buying of land and various other enterprises, showed that the ex-slave was handling some free capital already. The chief initial source of this was labor in the army, and his pay and bounty as a soldier. Payments to Negro soldiers were at first complicated by the ignorance of the recipients, and the fact that the quotas of colored regiments from Northern States were largely filled by recruits from the South, unknown to their fellow soldiers. Consequently, payments were accompanied by such frauds that Congress, by joint resolution in 1867, put the whole matter in the hands of the Freedmen's Bureau. In two years six million dollars was thus distributed to five thousand claimants, and in the end the sum exceeded eight million dollars. Even in this system fraud was frequent; but still the work put needed capital in the hands of practical paupers, and some, at least, was well spent.

The most perplexing and least successful part of the Bureau's work lay in the exercise of its judicial functions. The regular Bureau court consisted of one representative of the employer, one of the Negro, and one of the Bureau. If the Bureau could have maintained a perfectly judicial attitude, this arrangement would have been ideal, and must in time have gained confidence; but the nature of its other activities and the character of its *personnel* prejudiced the Bureau in favor of the black litigants, and led without doubt to much injustice and annoyance. On the other hand, to leave the Negro in the hands of Southern courts was impossible. In a distracted land where slavery had hardly fallen, to keep the strong from wanton abuse of the weak, and the weak from gloating insolently over the half-shorn strength of the strong, was a thankless, hopeless task. The former masters of the land were peremptorily ordered about, seized, and imprisoned, and punished over and again, with scant courtesy from army officers. The former slaves were intimidated, beaten, raped, and butchered by angry and revengeful men. Bureau courts tended to become centres simply for punishing whites, while the regular civil courts tended to become solely institutions for perpetuating the slavery of blacks. Almost every law and method ingenuity could devise was employed by the legislatures to reduce the Negroes to serfdom,—to make them the slaves of the State, if not of individual owners; while the Bureau officials too often were found striving to put the "bottom rail on top," and give the freedmen a power and independence which they could not yet use. It is all well enough for us of another generation to wax wise with advice to those who bore the burden in the heat of the day. It is full easy now to see that the man who lost home, fortune, and family at a stroke, and saw his land ruled by "mules and niggers," was really benefited by the passing of slavery. It is not difficult now to say to the young freedman, cheated and cuffed about, who has seen his father's head beaten to a jelly and his own mother namelessly assaulted, that the meek shall inherit the earth. Above all, nothing is more convenient than to heap on the Freedmen's Bureau all the evils of that evil day, and damn it utterly for every mistake and blunder that was made.

All this is easy, but it is neither sensible nor just. Some one had blundered, but that was long before Oliver Howard was born; there was criminal aggression and heedless neglect, but without some system of control there would have been far more than there was. Had that control been from within, the Negro would have been re-enslaved, to all intents and purposes. Coming as the control did from without, perfect men and methods would have bettered all things; and even with imperfect agents and questionable methods, the work accomplished was not undeserving of commendation.

Such was the dawn of Freedom; such was the work of the Freedmen's Bureau, which, summed up in brief, may be epitomized thus: For some fifteen million dollars, beside the sums spent before 1865, and the dole of benevolent societies, this Bureau set going a system of free labor, established a beginning of peasant proprietorship, secured the recognition of black freedmen before courts of law, and founded the free common school in the South. On the other hand, it failed to begin the establishment of good-will between ex-masters and freedmen, to guard its work wholly from paternalistic methods which discouraged self-reliance, and to carry out to any considerable extent its implied promises to furnish the freedmen with land. Its successes were the result of hard work, supplemented by the aid of philanthropists and the eager striving of black men. Its failures were the result of bad local agents, the inherent difficulties of the work, and national neglect.

Such an institution, from its wide powers, great responsibilities, large control of moneys, and generally conspicuous position, was naturally open to repeated and bitter attack. It sustained a searching Congressional investigation at the instance of Fernando Wood in 1870.[111] Its archives and few remaining functions were with blunt discourtesy transferred from Howard's control, in his absence, to the supervision of Secretary of War [William] Belknap in 1872, on the Secretary's recommendation. Finally, in consequence of grave intimations of wrong-doing made by the Secretary and his subordinates, General Howard was court-martialed in 1874. In both of these trials the Commissioner of the Freedmen's Bureau was officially exonerated from any wilful misdoing, and his work commended. Nevertheless, many unpleasant things were brought to light,—the methods of transacting the business of the Bureau were faulty; several cases of defalcation were proved, and other frauds strongly suspected; there were some business transactions which savored of dangerous speculation, if not dishonesty; and around it all lay the smirch of the Freedmen's Bank.

Morally and practically, the Freedmen's Bank was part of the Freedmen's Bureau, although it had no legal connection with it. With the prestige of the government back of it, and a directing board of unusual respectability and national reputation, this banking institution had made a remarkable start in the development of that thrift among black folk which slavery had kept them from knowing. Then in one sad day came the crash,[112]—all the hard-earned dollars of the freedmen disappeared; but that was the least of the loss,—all the faith in saving went too, and much of the faith in men; and that was a loss that a Nation which to-day sneers at Negro shiftlessness has never yet made good. Not even ten additional years of slavery could have done so much to throttle the thrift of the freedmen as the mismanagement and bankruptcy of the series of savings banks chartered by the Nation for their especial aid. Where all the blame should rest, it is hard to say; whether the Bureau and the Bank died chiefly by reason of the blows of its selfish friends or the dark machinations of its foes, perhaps even time will never reveal, for here lies unwritten history.

Of the foes without the Bureau, the bitterest were those who attacked not so much its conduct or policy under the law as the necessity for any such institution at all. Such attacks came primarily from the Border States and the South; and they were summed up by Senator [Garrett] Davis, of Kentucky, when he moved to entitle the act of 1866 a bill "to promote strife and conflict between the white and black races…by a grant of unconstitutional power." The argument gathered tremendous strength South and North; but its very strength was its weakness. For, argued the plain common-sense of the nation, if it is unconstitutional, unpractical, and futile for the nation to stand guardian over its helpless wards, then there is left but one alternative,—to make those wards their own guardians by arming them with the ballot. Moreover, the path of the practical politician pointed the same way; for, argued this opportunist, if we cannot peacefully reconstruct the South with white votes, we certainly can with black votes. So justice and force joined hands.

The alternative thus offered the nation was not between full and restricted Negro suffrage; else every sensible man, black and white, would easily have chosen the latter. It was rather a choice between suffrage and slavery, after endless blood and gold had flowed to sweep human bondage away. Not a single Southern legislature stood ready to admit a Negro, under any conditions, to the polls; not a single Southern legislature believed free Negro labor was possible without a system of restrictions that took all its freedom away; there was scarcely a white man in the South who did not honestly regard Emancipation as a crime, and its practical nullification as a duty. In such a situation, the granting of the ballot to the black man was a necessity, the very least a guilty nation could grant a wronged race, and the only method of compelling the South to accept the results of the war. Thus Negro suffrage ended a civil war by beginning a race feud. And some felt gratitude toward the race thus sacrificed in its swaddling clothes on the altar of national integrity; and some felt and feel only indifference and contempt.

Had political exigencies been less pressing, the opposition to government guardianship of Negroes less bitter, and the attachment to the slave system less strong, the social seer can well imagine a far better policy,—a permanent Freedmen's Bureau, with a national system of Negro schools; a carefully supervised employment and labor office; a system of impartial protection before the regular courts; and such institutions for social betterment as savings-banks, land and building associations, and social settlements. All this vast expenditure of money and brains might have formed a great school of prospective citizenship, and solved in a way we have not yet solved the most perplexing and persistent of the Negro problems.

That such an institution was unthinkable in 1870 was due in part to certain acts of the Freedmen's Bureau itself. It came to regard its work as merely temporary, and Negro suffrage as a final answer to all present perplexities. The political ambition of many of its agents and *protégés* led it far afield into questionable activities, until the South, nursing its own deep prejudices, came easily to ignore all the good deeds of the Bureau and hate its very name with perfect hatred. So the Freedmen's Bureau died, and its child was the Fifteenth Amendment.

The passing of a great human institution before its work is done, like the untimely passing of a single soul, but leaves a legacy of striving for other men. The legacy of the Freedmen's Bureau is the heavy heritage of this generation. To-day, when new and vaster problems are destined to strain every fibre of the national mind and soul, would it not be well to count this legacy honestly and carefully? For this much all men know: despite compromise, war, and struggle, the Negro is not free. In the backwoods of the Gulf States, for miles and miles, he may not leave the plantation of his birth; in well-nigh the whole rural South the black farmers are peons, bound by law and custom to an economic slavery, from which the only escape is death or the penitentiary. In the most cultured sections and cities of the South the Negroes are a segregated servile caste, with restricted rights and privileges. Before the courts, both in law and custom, they stand on a different and peculiar basis. Taxation without representation is the rule of their political life. And the result of all this is, and in nature must have been, lawlessness and crime. That is the large legacy of the Freedmen's Bureau, the work it did not do because it could not.

I have seen a land right merry with the sun, where children sing, and rolling hills lie like passioned women wanton with harvest. And there in the King's Highway sat and sits a figure veiled and bowed, by which the traveller's footsteps hasten as they go. On the tainted air broods fear. Three centuries' thought has been the raising and unveiling of that bowed human heart, and now behold a century new for the duty and the deed. The problem of the Twentieth Century is the problem of the color-line.

THE TEXTS

George Moses Horton, "The Slave." Source: *Naked Genius: By George Moses Horton, The Colored Bard of North Carolina* (Raleigh, N.C.: Wm. B. Smith & Co., Southern Field and Fireside Book Publishing House, 1865).

Susie King Taylor, from *Reminiscences of My Life in Camp*. Source: *Reminiscences of My Life in Camp with the 33d United States Colored Troops Late 1st S. C. Volunteers* (Boston: The author, 1902).

Thomas Wentworth Higginson, "Camp Diary." Source: *The Magnificent Activist: The Writings of Thomas Wentworth Higginson (1823–1911)*, ed. Howard N. Meyer (New York: Da Capo Press, 2000). Originally published as "Leaves from an Officer's Journal" in *The Atlantic Monthly*, Nov/Dec 1864 and Jan. 1865, and subsequently incorporated into *Army Life in a Black Regiment* (Boston: Lee and Shepard; New York: C. T. Dillingham, 1869; Boston: Fields, Osgood, 1870), based on the journal Higginson kept while commanding the 1st South Carolina.

Abraham Lincoln, Final Emancipation Proclamation. Source: *Complete Works of Abraham Lincoln, Comprising his Speeches, Letters, State Papers, and Miscellaneous Writings*, ed. John G. Nicolay and John Hay. Vol. 2 (New York: The Century Company, 1920).

Ralph Waldo Emerson, "Emancipation Proclamation." Source: *The Complete Works of Ralph Waldo Emerson*, Vol. 11 (*Miscellanies*), ed. Edward Emerson (Boston and New York: Houghton, Mifflin and Co., 1911). Originally published in *The Atlantic Monthly*, vol. 10, no. 61 (Nov. 1862), pp. 638–642, without the poetry epigraph, as "The President's Proclamation."

Ralph Waldo Emerson, "Boston Hymn." Source: *The Atlantic Monthly* vol. 11, no. 64 (Feb. 1863), pp. 227-228.

Ralph Waldo Emerson, "Voluntaries." Source: *The Atlantic Monthly*, vol. 12, no. 71 (Sept. 1863), pp. 504–506.

Rebecca Harding Davis, "John Lamar." Source: *The Atlantic Monthly*, vol. 9 no. 54 (April 1862), pp. 411–423.

Frederick Douglass, "The Mission of the War." Source: The Frederick Douglass Papers at the Library of Congress. Delivered repeatedly as a lecture during the winter of 1863–64.

Louisa May Alcott, "My Contraband." Source: *Hospital Sketches; and Camp and Fireside Stories* (Boston: Roberts Bros., 1869).

Charles Chesnutt, "Cicely's Dream." Source: *The Wife of His Youth, and Other Stories of the Color Line* (Boston and New York: Houghton, Mifflin and Co., 1899).

Paul Laurence Dunbar, poems. Source: *The Complete Poems of Paul Laurence Dunbar*, ed. William Dean Howells (New York: Dodd, Mead & Co., 1922). "The Deserted Plantation" was originally published in *Lyrics of Lowly Life* (New York: Young People's Missionary Movement of the United States and Canada, 1895; New York: Dodd, Mead, and Co., 1896). "When Dey 'Listed Colored Soldiers" was originally published in the *New England Magazine*, Aug. 1899; "Robert Gould Shaw" was originally published in *The Atlantic Monthly*, Oct. 1900; both were included in *Lyrics of Love and Laughter* (New York: Dodd, Mead, and Co., 1903).

W. E. B. Du Bois, from *The Souls of Black Folk*. Source: *The Souls of Black Folk: Essays and Sketches by W. E. Burghardt Du Bois*. 3rd ed. (Chicago: A. C. McClurg & Co., 1903).

NOTES

1. Higginson took command of the 1st South Carolina Volunteer Infantry on November 10, 1862, when it was reorganized under Gen. Rufus Saxton. The regiment was renamed the 33rd United States Colored Troops in February 1864. Higginson led the regiment until May 1864, after being wounded during an expedition up the Edisto River.

2. The Grand Army of the Republic, or G.A.R., was an organization of Union veterans founded in 1866 that, at its peak, claimed more than 400,000 members. The Women's Relief Corps began in 1883 as an auxiliary to the G.A.R. through which women could provide services to veterans and veterans' families.

3. Charles Tyler Trowbridge commanded Company A after the 1st South Carolina Volunteers were reorganized under Higginson in November 1862. Promoted from Captain to Major in 1863, Trowbridge took functional command of the 33rd U.S. Colored Infantry (Col. William Bennett was official commander) after Higginson was wounded at Edisto. He mustered out in 1865 at the rank of Lt. Colonel.

4. Catherine Valérie Boissier Gasparin, comtesse de, *Vie militaire dans un régiment noir; aventures et pages intimes…* Paris: Fishbacher, 1884.

5. The Savannah Volunteer Guards, originally organized in 1802, saw service in the War of 1812, and went through a variety of organizational and name changes before and during the Civil War.

6. Louis Malesherbes Goldsborough (1805-1877) commanded the North Atlantic Blockading Squadron. In 1862, his fleet participated in Ambrose Burnside's capture of Roanoke Island and the successful Union campaign against the North Carolina coast.

7. Rev. Mansfield French (1810-1876) was a preacher, antislavery activist, educator, and editor. In 1862–63 he participated in the training of freedmen at Port Royal.

8. Liberia was a settlement of American freedmen on the west coast of Africa, founded by the American Colonization Society in 1822 for motives both humanitarian (African American uplift) and self-serving (removing from the United States a potential source of "trouble"). The colony grew steadily, and was formally recognized by the U.S. as the Republic of Liberia in 1862.

9. Lt. John Augustine Trowbridge; Lt. George D. Walker.

10. Capt. Alexander Heasley (killed at August, Georgia, Sept. 6, 1865); Lt. Niles G. Parker (promoted to Captain February 1865); Lt. Henry A. Beach.

11. William Henry Brisbane (1803? –1878) was a Baptist pastor and former planter from Beaufort County, South Carolina, who renounced slavery in the 1830s and moved to Wisconsin in 1853. During the war, Brisbane served as chaplain in the 2nd Wisconsin Cavalry and as a tax commissioner in South Carolina.

12. George Barrell Cheever (1807–1890) was the author of a number of books denouncing slavery, of which *God Against Slavery* (1857) is the best known.

13. Robert Gould Shaw (1837–1863), scion of Boston's elite, abolitionist, and skilled soldier, organized and commanded the 54th Massachusetts Infantry, the North's legendary African American regiment. He died on 18 July 1863 while leading the unsuccessful attack on Fort Wager, South Carolina.

14. Joseph Finegan (1810? –1885) started the Civil War as captain of the Fernandina Volunteers of Florida and rose to brigadier general commanding the District of East Florida in November 1862. During 1863–64, his troops fought repeated engagements in northern Florida.

15. William Barnwell was a wealthy planter in Beaufort county. (See Higginson's mention on p. 231)

16. The diminutive Clara Barton (1821–1912) earned a towering reputation during the war through her essentially freelance relief efforts on behalf of Union soldiers.

17. Folly Island and Morris Island lie along the South Carolina coast, just south of Charleston Harbor.

18. James Island lies inland from Morris Island, just south of Charleston.

19. After his "march to the sea," Union forces under Sherman attacked and captured Fort McAllister on December 13, 1864, preparing for the occupation of Savannah later that month.

20. Taylor might mean February 18. After Sherman's northward-bound army swept into Columbia, South Carolina, on 17 February 1865, the fate of Charleston was sealed, and that evening Confederate Gen. William Hardee ordered the evacuation of the city that had withstood an 18-month siege.

21. The Beach Institute in Savannah was founded in 1867 by the American Missionary Association and the Freedmen's Bureau to promote African American education. It was named for Alfred Beach, the editor of *Scientific American* who provided funds for the purchase of the school site.

22. See page 325, note 52.

23. See Gen. 9:6 and Leviticus 24:17.

24. Taylor refers to the so-called "Buffalo Soldiers" (the 9th and 10th Cavalry, and the 24th and 25th Infantry) who fought with Theodore Roosevelt's "Rough Riders" in the American campaign in Cuba during the Spanish-American war, including the famous charge up San Juan Hill on July 1, 1898. Their contributions were applauded in a number of contemporary books and magazine articles. See Edward Van Zile Scott, *The Unwept: Black American Soldiers and the Spanish-American War* (Montogmery, Ala.: Black Belt Press, 1996); and Frank Schubert, *Black Valor: Buffalo Soldiers and the Medal of Honor, 1870--1898* (Wilmington, Del.: Scholarly Resources, 1997).

25. Harriet Beecher Stowe's best-selling, landmark antislavery novel of 1852 received frequent theatrical stagings even after the Civil War. The Southern criticism that it "exaggerated" the plight of slaves dated to its publication. The "ex-Confederate Daughters" may be the Memorial Association organized by Confederate women in Nashville in 1870. The Tennessee-based Ladies Auxiliary of the Confederate Soldiers' Home was not founded until 1890, and changed its name to "Daughters of the Confederacy" in 1892. The National Association of the Daughters of the Confederacy was established in 1894. See Karen L. Cox, *Dixie's Daughters: The United Daughters of the Confederacy and the Preservation of Confederate Culture* (Gainesville: University Press of Florida, 2003).

26. Ecclesiastes 11:1.

27. Camp Davidson, built in July 1864 to transfer prisoners away from Andersonville.

28. Libby Prison, in Richmond, was converted for military use from a tobacco factory in 1861 and by 1863 was overcrowded with captured Union soldiers. Conditions were not as bad as at Andersonville, but prisoners still faced severe shortages of food, water, and clothing.

29. Higginson received a commission to raise the 51st Massachusetts Volunteers in September 1862, but resigned his captainship to lead the First South Carolina Volunteers, the Union Army's first African American regiment.

30. "Saxton issued a Thanksgiving Proclamation declaring November 27, 1862, to be a general holiday in celebration of military victories and the freedom of slaves in the Port Royal region" (Christopher Looby, *The Complete*

Civil War Journal and Selected Letters of Thomas Wentworth Higginson [Chicago: University of Chicago Press, 1999], p. 46, n. 33).

31. I.e., of African descent.

32. "On their periodic raids along the coast, one of the objectives of the 1st South Carolina was to recruit soldiers from among the slaves and refugees they encountered" (Looby, p. 47, n. 35).

33. I.e., blackface minstrelsy.

34. John Bartholomew Gough (1817–1886) was a famous British-born temperance orator.

35. A long-running nineteenth-century theatrical farce.

36. John Celivergos Zachos (1820–1898), assistant surgeon in the Union army.

37. The Progressive Friends were a radical abolitionist Quaker group founded in 1853 in Pennsylvania.

38. See Genesis 4:20, 9:27, 25:27.

39. Camp Wool was the base of Higginson's former regiment, the 51st Massachusetts.

40. Emerson's poem "Saadi" (1847) represents the thirteenth-century Persian poet as oracular and remote, yet compassionate.

41. First launched in 1855, *Frank Leslie's Illustrated Newspaper* quickly became a highly popular, general interest periodical. During the Civil War, *Leslie's* increasingly emphasized visual journalism, employing a team of artists to dramatically illustrate the personalities, scenes, and events of the conflict. In 1861 and 1862, Leslie published four "pictorial" compilations of the newspaper's war coverage to date.

42. "George B. Emerson, longtime member of the General Committee of the Educational Commission, sponsors of the Port Royal Experiment" (Looby, p. 61, n. 67).

43. Given the title "Room in There" by Higginson (see ch. 4, p. 356), and the title "I Can't Stay Behind" by William Francis Allen, Charles Pickard Ware, and Lucy McKim Garrison in *Slave Songs of the United States* (New York, 1867).

44. "John Brown's Body" (see p. 336).

45. James R. Gilmore's abolitionist *Among the Pines: or, South in Secession Time* (New York, 1862) is a fictionalized account of a tour through the South and includes graphic descriptions of slave life. Gilmore's African American characters speak in heavy dialect.

46. Harun Al-Rashid (763-809), the fifth Abassid caliph, oversaw the golden age of Baghdad, inspiring a number of the stories in *The Thousand and One Nights*. Higginson has apparently taken the spelling from Alfred Lord Tennyson's "Recollections of the Arabian Nights" (1830).

47. The Barnwells and Hugers were wealthy planter families in South Carolina.

48. The day the Emancipation Proclamation went into force.

49. Rev. James H. Fowler was also a volunteer nurse at Judiciary Square Hospital in Washington, D.C.

50. "Dr. William Henry Brisbane, a native Sea Island planter and convert to abolitionism, he abandoned South Carolina in the 1830s, but returned later after his political awakening to buy back his slaves and convey them to freedom in the North; in 1862 he was appointed as federal tax commissioner in Beaufort, supervising the sale of confiscated Confederate plantations" (Looby, p. 76, n. 96).

51. See page 323, note 7.

52. These lyrics were written by Boston native Samuel F. Smith in 1832; the melody, by Siegfried Mahlmann, dates from approximately 1740.

53. "Corporal, later Sergeant, Prince Rivers, later a member of the South Carolina Constitutional Convention, and a member of the state legislature; Corporal, later Sergeant, Robert Sutton, later court-martialed for an alleged act of mutiny (which, however, TWH and his officers disbelieved), then pardoned and restored to his place in the regiment" (Looby, p. 77, n. 99)

54. Frances Dana Gage (1808-1884) was a prominent antislavery and women's rights activist. She is best known for her written recollections of Sojourner Truth's address at the 1851 woman's rights convention in Akron, Ohio.

55. A highly successful, influential blackface minstrelsy troupe from Buffalo, founded by Edwin Pearce Christy in 1843. The group's heyday ran from 1846 to 1854, during its tenure at Mechanics Hall in New York.

56. Higginson is referring to *Minstrelsy of the Scottish Border* (1802-03) by the Scottish novelist Sir Walter Scott (1771–1832).

57. Black troops actually suffered a much higher rate of disease than the Union army as a whole, primarily because they disproportionately served in unhealthy climates and received poor medical care.

58. Toussaint L'Ouverture was a prominent leader of the successful slave revolt on the French island colony of Saint-Domingue in 1791, which set in motion the events leading to Haitian independence in 1804.

59. See Ambrose Bierce's "On a Mountain," page 117.

60. Simon Legree is the degenerate, cruel, slave-owning villain of Harriet Beecher Stowe's *Uncle Tom's Cabin* (1852). Uncle Tom, his Christ-like victim, embodies the virtues (vices?) of pacifist resignation and faith in the hereafter.

61. From a sixteenth- and seventeenth-century Scottish Presbyterian resistance movement known for its zeal.

62. The "Snake-hunters" were federal anti-guerrilla squads from western Virginia and Missouri.

63. The motto of the eighteenth-century British anti-slave-trade movement, subsequently adopted by American abolitionists, was "Am I Not a Man and a Brother?"

64. Thomas Carlyle's *Sartor Resartus* (1833–34) developed, in incredibly baroque fashion, its author's ideas of continual philososphical and social renewal, imaged by the ongoing retailoring of outworn clothes ("the tailor retailored").

65. Lowell, Massachusetts, a center of Northern industry.

66. On Tell, see page 590, note 6. Giuseppe Garibaldi (1807–1882) led the movement for Italian unification.

67. In Jeremiah 29:1-32, in his letter to the captive Judeans in Babylon, the prophet Jeremiah instructs them as to how to live, and warns of the destruction of Babylon.

68. The Confession of Augsburg, the principal statement of the Luthern faith, was presented to the Holy Roman Emperor at the Diet of Augsburg in 1530.

69. Among other Republican Congressional reforms, the Homestead Act of 1862, which emerged after years of free-soil politics, was meant to encourage Western settlement and free labor by providing for the distribution of 160 acres of public land to any individual who would inhabit and use the land. The act was meant to promote the settlement of Western territories by non-slaveholders. Despite a variety of obstacles, the homesteading program by 1890 had given about 270 million acres to about 1.6 million homesteaders.

70. I.e., Maryland, Kentucky, and Missouri, border states with slaves and much secesisonist sentiment, but which had remained in the union.

71. From Milton's *Comus* (1637), lines 597–599. The Elder Brother is referring to the triumph of good over evil, which "on itself shall back recoil, / And mix no more with goodness."

72. Emersons' examples are of military subjugation. Italy's victory over Austria in 1859 culminated its second war for independence and paved the way for Italian unification during the 1860s. In 1793, in its second partition, Poland was divided between Austria, Prussia, and Russia; a national uprising in 1794 was inspiring but unsuccessful. The French occupied Algiers in 1830. Ireland, long under the heel of the British, officially became part of the United Kingdom in 1801. Britain had ruled colonial territories in India since the 18th century, and was expanding that rule in the nineteenth.

73. Pro-Southern and/or Democratic newspapers in the North declaimed ferociously against the Emancipation Proclamation. For instance, the proclamation prompted Samuel Medary, the editor of *The Crisis* (Columbus, Ohio), to call Lincoln a "half-witted usurper" (quoted in David Sachsman et al., eds., *The Civil War and the Press*, 297).

74. Shakespeare, sonnet 107

75. I.e., Secretary of State William Seward.

76. Sgt. Major Lewis H. Douglass and Pvt. Charles R. Douglass served in the 54th Massachusetts Infantry.

77. I.e., Northern Peace Democrats.

78. I.e., the Emancipation Proclamation.

79. Since Lincoln justified emancipation on the basis of military necessity rather than constitutional authority, it applied to "States and parts of States" which "are this day in rebellion against the United States," while exempting Tennessee and areas of both Virginia and Louisiana deemed loyal or non-resisting.

80. The "First Families of Virginia," or F.F.V.s, in a strict sense comprised the clans that originally settled the Virginia colony; in the nineteenth century, it took on a looser meaning, signalling the quasi-aristocratic lineage of well-established Virginia families. This latter meaning, however, elided the social heterogeneity of the F.F.V.s. As George Willison observes: "Among those who founded the first families of Virginia were men from many lands – *vignerons* from France, glassmakers from Italy, woodworkers from Poland, carpenters from Germany, Negroes from the West Indies and the Gold Coast. But most were English and, with few exceptions, very poor" (*Behold Virginia: The Fifth Crown*. New York: Harcourt, Brace and Company, 1951).

81. William Gladstone (1809–1898), British Parliamentarian and Chancellor of the Exchequer, who wanted to maintain the flow of Southern cotton to England advocated recognizing the Confederacy. He made the case in an October 1862 speech "Jefferson Davis and other leaders of the South have made an army; they are making it appears, a navy; and they have made what is more than either; they have made a nation" (quoted in James McPherson, *Battle Cry of Freedom*, p. 552).

82. Former Democratic Senator James M. Mason was a Confederate minister sent to London in 1861 to try to secure diplomatic recognition.

83. Horatio Seymour (1810–1886), who served as governor of New York from (1853–1868?), was a moderate Democrat whose political ideas emphasized both unionism and federal restraint; he opposed emancipation and conscription.

84.   Douglass is referring to the New York draft riots of 1863, triggered by the federal Enrollment Act, and encouraged by anti-administration Democrats. While rioting against the draft took place in many towns and cities, the violence in New York claimed more than 1,000 lives.

85.   The New York *World*, the New York *Express*, and the New York *Herald* all leaned sharply southward and Democratic in their editorial sympathies, and could be blatantly racist. In one 1862 report, for example, the *Herald* wrote that the education of blacks on the South Carolina coast would "create Negro insurrection, and result in the indiscriminate slaughter of the white race, of every age and sex, in every section of the South" (quoted in Brayton Harris, *Blue and Gray in Black and White* [Washington: Brassey's, 1999], p. 194).

86.   The reliable, rifled Springfield musket, manufactured at the Springfield Armory in Massachusetts, was the most common firearm used in the Civil War.

87.   Of the approximately 1.3 million German Americans living in the U.S. in 1860, the vast majority lived in non-seceding states, and about 15 percent fought in the war, many of them veterans of the European revolutions of 1848–49. Missouri, with a large German population in St. Louis, sent six all-German regiments into combat, the most prominent of which were the 3rd Infantry, under Franz Sigel, and the 12th Infantry, under Peter J. Osterhaus. See Bruce Levine, *The Spirit of 1848: German Immigrants, Labor Conflict, and the Coming of the Civil War* (Urbana: University of Illinois Press, 1992).

88.   Confederate soldiers in South Carolina contracted typhoid fever less frequently than did Union troops, for whom the disease was "a major military liability" (Paul E. Steiner, *Disease in the Civil War: Natural Biological Warfare in 1861–1865* [Springfield, Ill.: C.C. Thomas, 1968], p. 78), but it was nonetheless common, and often fatal.

89.   Alcott may be referring to Michelangelo's unfinished *Awakening Prisoner* (marble, c. 1525).

90.   In "The Bat, the Birds, and the Beasts," the bat fails to choose sides in the conflict between the birds and the beasts, and ends up spurned and friendless.

91.   The First Families of Virginia. See page 326, note 80.

92.   See page 324, note 25, and page 325, note 60.

93.   Mark 5:15.

94.   John Albion Andrew (1818–1867), the popular governor of Massachusetts, was an early and vocal advocate of African American military service, and made a pivotal decision in choosing Robert Gould Shaw to lead the 54th Massachusetts Infantry.

95.   "Patesville" is Chesnutt's fictionalized version of Fayetteville, NC, which also appears in other of his works, including "The Goophered Grapevine" and *The House Behind the Cedars*. The massive federal arsenal at Fayetteville, seized by North Carolina troops in April 1861, became one of the Confederacy's military gems, specializing in the manufacture of rifles. Chesnutt's history is not quite accurate, however: Confederate troops did remove stores and destroy some equipment as Sherman advanced on Fayetteville, but it remains true that the Union general ordered its completed destruction in March, 1865.

96.   The First Massachusetts Volunteer Cavalry. Its sharpest combat experience came at the battle of Aldie, Virginia, on 17 June 1863, where it suffered 66 casualties, including a Lt. Hugh Carey, and lost 88 prisoners.

97.   Located in the small town of Salisbury, North Carolina, this prison camp, like its larger, more infamous counterpart at Andersonville, became a graveyard for thousands of Union troops. After the breakdown of prisoner exchanges in 1864, Salisbury was quickly overrun by inmates, many of whom escaped by tunneling out, but many more of whom succumbed to disease and malnourishment.

98.   From "The Crying of Water" (1900) by the Welsh symbolist Arthur Symons (1865–1945).

99.   The battle of Mechanicsville, Virginia (26 June 1862), was a Confederate defeat that inaugurated the Seven Days' battles.

100.   From the spiritual "Shout, O Children!"

101.   *Macbeth*, Act 3, scene 4, lines 103–104. Macbeth is speaking to the ghost of the murdered Banquo, which he has seen at the royal banquet.

102.   "Section 1. The right of citizens of the United States to vote shall not be denied or abridged by the United States or by any State on account of race, color, or previous condition of servitude. Section 2. The Congress shall have power to enforce this article by appropriate legislation."

103.   Du Bois is referring to the disputed Presidential election of 1876, which pitted Democrat Samuel J. Tilden against Republican Rutherford B. Hayes. Although early signs pointed to a Tilden victory, Hayes was declared the winner after returns in South Carolina, Florida, and Louisiana gave him a one-vote electoral college majority. A political crisis ensued when Southern Democrats sought to invalidate the results, the so-called "revolution" of 1876. Following the baroque compromise fashioned by Congress that winter, Hayes became President but the Republican commitment to Reconstruction was curtailed to the vanishing point, and Southern "home rule" became the order of the day. In Eric Foner's words, the first year of Hayes's Presidency "marked a decisive

retreat from the idea, born during the Civil War, of a powerful national state protecting the fundamental rights of American citizens" (*Reconstruction*, p. 582).

104. See page 325, note 58.

105. From James Russell Lowell's "The Present Crisis" (1844), from which the NAACP later took the name for its periodical newspaper, *The Crisis*.

106. The American Missionary Association was a religious antislavery organization founded in 1846; a number of its leaders had participated in the legal defense of the Africans who had rebelled aboard the slave ship *Amistad* in 1839.

107. Maj. Gen. John Adams Dix (1798–1879) commanded the Department of Eastern Virginia, headquartered at Fortress Monroe, from May 1862 to July 1863.

108. Col. John Eaton served as superintendent of contrabands in the Missisippi Valley.

109. Sherman issued this order on January 16, 1865. Like the Emancipation Proclamation, it was justified on the basis of military necessity.

110. Gen. Oliver Otis Howard (1830–1909) was appointed commissioner of the Freedmen's Bureau in May 1865 and served there until it closed in 1872.

111. Fernando Wood (1812–1881), the former mayor of New York, was a Democratic Congressman and Southern sympathizer who in 1870 called for an investigation of Oliver Howard's transferral of $600,000 from the Freedman's Bureau to the Department of Education. Howard was exonerated by Congress in 1871.

112. The Panic of 1873 devastated the American financial system and led to the most severe economic depression before the 1930s. Particularly hard hit was the agricultural sector and its most vulnerable workers, black farmers and sharecroppers.

Portrait of a musician, 2d Regulars, U.S. Cavalry. Reprinted with permission of Marius Péladeau.

4

INTRODUCTION

Only Vietnam had a greater impact on American music than did the Civil War.
Hundreds of songs came out of the 1860s: marching songs, camp songs, patriotic songs, parade songs, sentimental ballads, spirituals. Many of these musical
pieces have faded from the national memory, but together they would permanently reshape the American musical tradition.

Two related factors underlay the flourishing of Civil War music. First, in keeping with American publishing generally, the sheet music industry had come of
age in the 1830s and 1840s. The cities of Boston, New York, and Philadelphia
dominated the scene, but other cities in the Midwest and South, including New
Orleans, Chicago, and Baltimore, also supported music publishers. By the early
1850s, according to Richard Crawford, American sheet music firms were printing on the order of 5,000 pieces a year, or about three times more than they
had a decade earlier.[1] Second, what helped drive that rate of publishing was the
increasing demand for music on the part of the American middle class. In the
antebellum years, rising standards of living gave more Americans greater access to musical instruments, particularly the piano, which became a fixture in
many parlors and a focal point of communal entertainment. In a way that is less
familiar to us today, social singing was a central form of cultural experience in
nineteenth-century America, and publishers rushed to provide the sheet music
that made it possible.

During the Civil War itself, music did much to shape perceptions of the conflict,
to sustain soldiers in the fighting of it, and to help Americans cope with its horrific toll. For both soldiers and civilians, music provided a measure of social
cohesion and emotional comfort in the midst of chaos. For soldiers, singing was
a way of wiling away the time, boosting morale, relieving the grind of marching
or the monotony of camp, feeling reconnected to home and, to some extent,
resisting the ideological pressure under which they were expected to fight for a
cause. For civilians, music could salve the pain of separation, anxiety, and loss,
and it could define the war in terms that made sense to those far removed from
the front lines and from the centers of power. For military authorities, we might
note, music occasionally represented subversion, and at least two composers—
William Hays Shakespeare and Septimus Winner—were arrested because of
their "seditious" songs.

The lyrics of Civil War songs tended to focus on a few recurrent themes: the cause that people fought for, the realities of military life and death, the feelings of those left at home, the meaning of emancipation. Like much popular literature of the day, these songs were meant to be accessible to a broad public, and the lyrics tend to reflect the digestible poetics that the nineteenth century preferred. In musical terms, most of the songs are fairly simple, with formulaic structures, regular eight-bar phrases, predictable refrains and rhythms, unchallenging melodies and harmonies.

Many Civil War songs have a murky textual and musical history. A number of these songs emerged from folk tradition, with unclear origins. Often a song would generate lyrical variants, involving contributions by different people, and often the music would go through a series of changes. In these cases, the process of publication involved setting down one version of the lyrics and one version of the music, in effect authorizing that rendition, and then printing it on broadsheets for distribution to local booksellers.

The relation between folk tradition and published music becomes particularly complicated when we consider the spirituals and slave songs of the era. African Americans, particularly in the South, had already developed a rich musical tradition by the nineteenth century, one which drew on both European and African influences. Yet antebellum blacks had little or no access to the tools of literacy, let alone the publishing industry, and African American music thus existed almost entirely beyond the awareness of white America. This would change during the Civil War.

On the Union-occupied Sea Islands of South Carolina, federal troops and white Northern activists were exposed, in a sustained fashion, to the singing of freedmen and runaway slaves. Some of these Northerners, notably Thomas Wentworth Higginson and Lucy McKim, recognized the musical value in what they heard, and began writing it down. Higginson's resulting essay, "Negro Spirituals," is included here. In 1867, Lucy McKim Garrison (now married) joined William Francis Allen and Charles Pickard Ware in publishing *Slave Songs of the United States*, a seminal work in what we would today call ethnomusicology (and one which incorporated Higginson's material). Both texts raise difficult questions regarding the problem of white interference in or appropriation of African American cultural expression. But they nonetheless gave white America its first serious introduction to the music performed by black America.

Out of the trials of civil war, then, two major musical legacies emerged. First, the war bequeathed to American music dozens of songs that, beyond simply commemorating the conflict, have transcended their historical origins to become touchstones of a shared cultural identity. In that sense, the Civil War accelerated the development of a truly indigenous musical tradition, helping to liberate American music from its European past, especially when it came to lyrics. Yet the rhythmic, melodic, and tonal norms of European music still held sway.

So the Civil War's second, less remarked, legacy for American music may be the more significant. The intercultural contact the war occasioned, however limited, began a gradual process of listening and exchanging that would have profound implications for the later evolution of American music. The spirituals and slave songs told a tale of woe and triumph that touched a deep cultural nerve, and they did so through music that, drawing on African as well as European musical practices, contributed several vital musical elements to the American palette: syncopation, the shout, the blue note. It would take decades of experimentation and resistance, a perpetual dance of give and take, of musical homogenization and dissent, but the signs were there. Although Dena Epstein has observed that the country "did not seem to be ready for the music of the slaves, unrefined by genteel adaptors," at least one contemporary reviewer of *Slave Songs of the United States* recognized that "whatever of nationality there is in the music of America she owes to her dusky children."[2] This truth would need much repeating, but already the note had sounded.

NOTES

1.   Richard Crawford, *America's Musical Life* (New York: Norton, 2001) p. 32.
2.   Dena J. Epstein, *Sinful Tunes and Spirituals: Black Folk Music to the Civil War*, p. 40. "Slave Songs of the United States," [unsigned review] *The Nation* 5 (Nov. 21, 1867): 411, quoted in Epstein, p. 337.

SUGGESTED READING

Cornelius, Steven H. *Music of the Civil War Era*. Westport, CT: Greenwood Press, 2004.

Crawford, Richard. *America's Musical Life*. New York: W.W. Norton, 2001.

Currie, Stephen. *Music in the Civil War*. Cincinnati, OH: Betterway Books, 1992.

Eaklor, Vicki. *American Antislavery Songs: A Collection and Analysis*. Westport, CT: Greenwood Press, 1988.

Epstein, Dena J. *Sinful Tunes and Spirituals: Black Folk Music to the Civil War*. Urbana: University of Illinois Press, 1977.

Glass, Paul and Louis C. Singer. *Singing Soldiers: A History of the Civil War in Song*. New York: Da Capo Press, 1975.

Harwell, Richard. *Confederate Music*. Chapel Hill: University of North Carolina Press, 1950.

Heaps, Willard A. and Porter W. Heaps. *The Singing Sixties: The Spirit of Civil War Days Drawn from the Music of the Times*. Norman: University of Oklahoma Press, 1960.

Loesser, Arthur. *Men, Women and Pianos: A Social History*. New York: Simon & Schuster, 1954.

Olson, Kenneth E. *Music and Musket: Bands and Bandsmen of the American Civil War*. Westport, CT: Greenwood Press, 1981.

Sanjek, Russell. *American Popular Music and Its Business: The First Four Hundred Years, Vol. II: From 1790 to 1909*. New York: Oxford University Press, 1988.

Southern, Eileen. *The Music of Black Americans: A History*. 3rd ed. New York: W.W. Norton, 1997.

Daniel Emmett

DIXIE'S LAND (1859, 1860)

I wish I was in de land ob cotton,
Old times dar am not forgotten,
    Look away! Look away! Look away!
In Dixie Land where I was born in
Early on one frosty mornin'
    Look away! Look away! Look away!

[Chorus:]
Den I wish I was in Dixie,
Hooray! Hooray!
In Dixie Land, I'll take my stand,
To lib and die in Dixie,
Away! Away!
Away down south in Dixie.

Old Missus marry "Will-de-weaber,"
Willium was a gay deceaber;
    Look away! Look away! Look away!
But when he put his arms around 'er
He smiled as fierce as a forty-pounder,
    Look away! Look away! Look away!

[Chorus]

His face was sharp as a butcher's cleaber,
But dat did not seem to greab 'er;
    Look away! Look away! Look away!
Old Missus acted de foolish part,
And died for a man dat broke her heart,
    Look away! Look away! Look away!

[Chorus]

Now here's a health to de next old Missus,
And all de gals dat want to kiss us;
    Look away! Look away! Look away!
But if you want to drive 'way sorrow,
Come and hear dis song tomorrow,
    Look away! Look away! Look away!

[Chorus]

Dar's buckwheat cakes an' Injen batter,
Makes you fat or a little fatter;
    Look away! Look away! Look away!
Den hoe it down and scratch your grabble,
To Dixie's Land I'm bound to trabble,
    Look away! Look away! Look away!

[Chorus]

Anonymous

JOHN BROWN'S BODY (1859?)

John Brown's body lies a-mould'ring in the grave,
John Brown's body lies a-mould'ring in the grave,
John Brown's body lies a-mould'ring in the grave,
    His soul is marching on!

[Chorus:]
Glory! glory hallelujah!
Glory! glory hallelujah!
Glory! glory hallelujah!
    His soul is marching on.

He's gone to be a soldier in the army of the Lord!
He's gone to be a soldier in the army of the Lord!
He's gone to be a soldier in the army of the Lord!
    His soul is marching on.

John Brown's knapsack is strapped upon his back,
John Brown's knapsack is strapped upon his back,
John Brown's knapsack is strapped upon his back,
    His soul is marching on.

His pet lambs will meet him on the way,
His pet lambs will meet him on the way,
His pet lambs will meet him on the way,
    And they'll go marching on.

They'll hang Jeff Davis on a sour apple tree,
They'll hang Jeff Davis on a sour apple tree,
They'll hang Jeff Davis on a sour apple tree,
    As they go marching on.

Now for the Union let's give three rousing cheers,
Now for the Union let's give three rousing cheers,
Now for the Union let's give three rousing cheers,
    As we go marching on.
        Hip, hip, hip, hip, Hurrah!

Septimus Winner

ABRAHAM'S DAUGHTER (RAW RECRUITS) (1861)

Oh! kind folks listen to my song, it is no idle story,
It's all about a volunteer who's goin' to fight for glory;
Now don't you think that I am right, for I am nothin' shorter,
And I belong to the Fire Zou-Zous,[1] and don't you think I oughter,
We're goin' down to Washington to fight for Abraham's daughter.

Oh! should you ask me who she am, Columbia is her name, sir,
She is the child of Abraham, or Uncle Sam, the same, sir,
Now if I fight, why aint I right, and don't you think I oughter;
The volunteers are a pouring in from every loyal quarter,
And I'm goin' long to Washington, to fight for Abraham's daughter.

They say we have no officers, but ah! they are mistaken;
And soon you'll see the Rebels run, with all the fuss they're makin';
For there is one who just spring up, he'll show the foe no quarter.
(McClellan is the man I mean,) you know he hadn't oughter,
For he's gone down to Washington, to fight for Abraham's daughter.

We'll have a spree with Johnny Bull, perhaps, some day or other,
And won't he have his fingers full, if not a deal of bother;
For Yankee boys are just the lads upon the land and water,
And won't we have a "bully" fight, and don't you think we oughter,
If he is caught at any time insulting Abraham's daughter.

But let us lay all jokes aside, it is a sorry question;
The man who would these States divide, should hang for his suggestion.
Our Country and one Flag, I say, whoe'er the war may slaughter,
So I'm going as a Fire Zou-a, and don't you think I oughter;
I'm going down to Washington, to fight for Abraham's daughter.

A. E. Blackmar

ALLONS ENFANS (THE SOUTHERN MARSEILLAISE) (1861)

Sons of the South awake to glory,
    A thousand voices bid you rise,
Your children, wives and grandsires hoary,
    Gaze on you now with trusting eyes,
    Gaze on you now with trusting eyes;
Your country ev'ry strong arm calling,
    To meet the hireling Northern band
    That comes to desolate the land
With fire and blood and scenes appalling,
    To arms, to arms, ye brave;
    Th' avenging sword unsheath!

March on! March on! All hearts resolved on victory or death.
March on! March on! All hearts resolved on victory or death.

Now, now, the dang'rous storm is rolling,
    Which treacherous brothers madly raise,
The dogs of war let loose, are howling
    And soon our peaceful towns may blaze,
    And soon our peaceful towns may blaze.
Shall fiends who basely plot our ruin,
    Unchecked, advance with guilty stride
    To spread destruction far and wide,
With Southrons' blood their hands embruing?
    To arms, to arms, ye brave!
    Th' avenging sword unsheath!

March on! March on! All hearts resolved on victory or death.
March on! March on! All hearts resolved on victory or death.

With needy, starving mobs surrounded,
    The jealous, blind fanatics dare
To offer, in their zeal unbounded,
    Our happy slaves their tender care,
    Our happy slaves their tender care.
The South, though deepest wrongs bewailing,
    Long yielded all to Union name;
    But Independence now we claim,
And all their threats are unavailing.
    To arms, to arms, ye brave!
    Th' avenging sword unsheath!

March on! March on! All hearts resolved on victory or death.
March on! March on! All hearts resolved on victory or death.

William B. Bradbury

MARCHING ALONG (1861)

The army is gath'ring from near and from far;
The trumpet is sounding the call for the war;
McClellan's our leader, he's gallant and strong;
We'll gird on our armor and be marching along.

[Chorus:]
Marching along, we are marching along,
Gird on the armor and be marching along
McClellan's our leader, he's gallant and strong;
For God and our country we're marching along.

[Chorus]

The foe is before us in battle array,
But let us not waver, nor turn from the way;
The Lord is our strength and the Union's our song;
With courage and faith we are marching along.

[Chorus]

We sigh for our country, we mourn for our dead,
For them now our last trop [sic] of blood will be shed;
Our cause is the right one—our foe's in the wrong;
Then gladly we'll sing as we're marching along.

[Chorus]

Our wives and our children we leave in your care,
We know you will help them their sorrows to bear;
'Tis hard thus to part, but we hope 'twon't be long,
We'll keep up our heart as we're marching along.

[Chorus]

The flag of our country is floating on high,
We'll stand by that flag till we conquer or die;
McClellan's our leader, he's gallant and strong,
We'll gird on our armor and be marching along.

[Chorus]

Ethel Lynn Beers

ALL QUIET ALONG THE POTOMAC (1861)

"All quiet along the Potomac," they say,
    "Except here and there a stray picket
Is shot, as he walks on his beat, to and fro,
    By a rifleman hid in the thicket.

'Tis nothing—a private or two now and then
    Will not count in the news of the battle;
Not an officer lost, only one of the men
    Moaning out all alone the death rattle."

All quiet along the Potomac to-night,
    Where the soldiers lie peacefully dreaming,
Their tents in the rays of the clear autumn moon,
    And the light of their watch-fires are gleaming.

A tremulous sigh, as the gentle night wind
    Through the forest leaves softly is creeping,
While the stars up above, with their glittery eyes,
    Keep guard, for the army is sleeping.

There's only the sound of the lone sentry's tread,
    As he tramps from the rock to the fountain,
And thinks of the two on the low trundle bed,
    Far away in the cot on the mountain.

His musket falls slack—his face, dark and grim,
    Grows gentle with memories tender,
As he mutters a prayer for the children asleep,
    And their mother—"may Heaven defend her."

Then drawing his sleeve roughly over his eyes,
    He dashes off tears that are welling;
And gathers his gun closer up to his breast,
    As if to keep down the heart's swelling.

He passes the fountain, the blasted pine tree,
    And his footstep is lagging and weary:
Yet onward he goes, through the broad belt of light,
    Toward the shades of the forest so dreary.

Hark! was it the night wind that rustles the leaves?
    Was it the moonlight so wondrously flashing?
It looked like a rifle! "Ha! Mary, good-bye!"
    And his lifeblood is ebbing and splashing.

"All quiet along the Potomac to-night,"
    No sound save the rush of the river;
While soft falls the dew on the face of the dead,
    The picket's off duty forever.

Harry McCarthy

THE BONNIE BLUE FLAG (1861)

We are a band of brothers, and native to the soil,
Fighting for our liberty, with treasure, blood and toil;
And when our rights were threatened, the cry rose near and far,
Hurrah for the Bonnie Blue Flag that bears a Single Star!

[Chorus:]
Hurrah! Hurrah! For Southern Rights, Hurrah!
Hurrah! for the Bonnie Blue Flag that bears a Single Star!

As long as the Union was faithful to her trust,
Like friends and brethren kind were we and just;
But now, when Northern treachery attempts our rights to mar,
We hoist on high the Bonnie Blue Flag that bears a Single Star.

[Chorus]

First, gallant South Carolina nobly made the stand;
Then came Alabama and took her by the hand;
Next, quickly, Mississippi, Georgia, and Florida,
All raised on high the Bonnie Blue Flag that bears a Single Star.

[Chorus]

Ye men of valor, gather round the banner of the right,
Texas and fair Louisiana join us in the fight;
Davis, our loved President, and Stephens statesmen rare,
Now rally round the Bonnie Blue Flag that bears a Single Star.

[Chorus]

And here's to brave Virginia! the Old Dominion State,
With the young Confederacy at length has link'd her fate;
Impelled by her example, now other States prepare,
To hoist on high the Bonnie Blue Flag that bears a Single Star.

[Chorus]

Then cheer, boys, cheer, raise the joyous shout,
For Arkansas and North Carolina now have both gone out;
And let another rousing cheer for Tennessee be given,
The Single Star of the Bonnie Blue Flag has grown to be Eleven.

[Chorus]

Then here's to our Confederacy, strong we are and brave,
Like patriots of old, we'll fight, our heritage to save;
And rather than submit to shame, to die we would prefer,
So cheer for the Bonnie Blue Flag that bears a Single Star.

Julia Ward Howe

THE BATTLE HYMN OF THE REPUBLIC (1862)

Mine eyes have seen the glory of the coming of the Lord:
He is trampling out the vintage where the grapes of wrath are stored;
He hath loosed the fateful lightning of his terrible swift sword:
    His truth is marching on.

I have seen him in the watchfires of a hundred circling camps;
They have builded him an altar in the evening dews and damps;
I can read his righteous sentence by the dim and flaring lamps;
    His day is marching on.

I have read a fiery gospel writ in burnished rows of steel;
"As ye deal with my contemners, so with you my grace shall deal;
Let the Hero, born of woman, crush the serpent with his heel,
    Since God is marching on."

He has sounded from the trumpet that shall never call retreat;
He is sifting out the hearts of men before his judgment-seat:
Oh, be swift, my soul, to answer him! be jubilant, my feet!
    Our God is marching on.

In the beauty of the lilies Christ was born across the sea,
With a glory in his bosom that transfigures you and me;
As he died to make men holy, let us die to make men free,
    While God is marching on.

Walter Kittredge

TENTING ON THE OLD CAMPGROUND (1862)

We're tenting to-night on the old camp ground;
Give us a song to cheer
Our weary hearts, a song of home,
And friend we love so dear.

[Chorus:]
Many are the hearts that are weary to-night,
Wishing for the war to cease,
Many are the hearts, looking for the right,
To see the dawn of peace.
Tenting to-night, tenting to-night,
Tenting on the old camp ground.

We've been tenting to-night on the old camp ground,
Thinking of days gone by,
Of the loved ones at home, that gave us the hand,
And the tear that said "Good-bye!"

[Chorus]

We are tired of war on the old camp ground,
Many are dead and gone,
Of the brave and true who've left their homes,
Others been wounded long.

[Chorus]

We've been fighting to-day on the old camp ground,
Many are lying near;
Some are dead, and some are dying,
Many are in tears.

Charles Carroll Sawyer and Henry Tucker

WEEPING, SAD AND LONELY; OR,
WHEN THIS CRUEL WAR IS OVER (1862)

Dearest love, do you remember,
When we last did meet,
How you told me that you lov'd me,
Kneeling at my feet?
Oh! how proud you stood before me,
In your suit of blue,
When you vow'd to me and country
Ever to be true.

[Chorus:]
Weeping, sad and lonely,
Hopes and fears how vain!
When this cruel war is over,
Praying that we meet again!

When the summer breeze is sighing,
Mournfully along;
Or when autumn leaves are falling,
Sadly breathes the song.
Oft in dreams I see thee lying
On the battle plain,
Lonely, wounded, even dying,
Calling, but in vain.

[Chorus]

If amid the din of battle
Nobly you should fall,
Far away from those who love you,
None to hear you call—
Who would whisper words of comfort
Who would soothe your pain?
Ah! the many cruel fancies,
Ever in my brain.

But our country call'd you, darling,
Angels cheer your way;
While our nation's sons are fighting,
We can only pray.
Nobly strike for God and liberty,
Let all nations see
How we love the starry banner,
Emblem of the free.

Anonymous

PARODY ON WHEN THIS CRUEL WAR IS OVER

Och, Biddy dear, do you remember
    Whin we last did meet?
'Twas at Paddy Murphy's party,
    Down in Baxter street;
And there all the boys did envy me,
    And the girls envy'd you—
Whin they saw my great big bounty
    In Green-Backs, all new.

[Chorus:]

Och, weepin', Biddy darlin',
For the Pay-Master's tin;
Whin this cruel war is over,
Praying...for a good horn of gin.

Next day, I shoulder'd my ould musket,
    Braver thin Ould Mars;
And, with spirits light and airy.
    Marched off to the wars;
But now me drame of glory's over,
    I'm home sick, I fear;
I'd give this world for a substitute,
    To take my place here.

[Chorus]

Och, Biddy darlin', things are changing,
    Since I left New-York;
There, I got good beef steak plenty—
    Now I get salt pork;
And the crackers, Biddy jewel,
    For to tell the truth,
They are harder than a brick-bat,
    And wud break yer tooth.

[Chorus]

Whin the cabbages are blooming,
    Beautiful and strong:
Or whin whisky-punch is brewin'—
    Mournful is my song;
In me drames, I often see ye walking
    With that black-guard Tim;
Oh! if I could only get a furlough,
    Wouldn't I slather him?

[Chorus]

A. E. Blackmar

GOOBER PEAS (1866)

Sitting by the roadside on a summer day,
Chatting with my mess-mates, passing time away,
Lying in the shadows, underneath the trees,
Goodness, how delicious, eating goober peas!

[Chorus:]
Peas! Peas! Peas! Peas! eating goober peas!
Goodness, how delicious, eating goober peas!

When a horseman passes the soldiers have a rule
To cry out at their loudest "Mister, here's your mule,"
But another pleasure enchantinger than these,
Is wearing out your grinders, eating goober peas!

[Chorus]

Just before the battle, the General hears a row;
He says, "The Yanks are coming, I hear their rifles now"
He turns around in wonder, and what do you think he sees?
The Georgia Militia, eating goober peas!

[Chorus]

I think my song had lasted almost long enough,
The subject's interesting, but rhymes are mighty rough,
I wish this war was over, when free from rags and fleas,
We'd kiss our wives and sweethearts and gobble goober peas!

M. B. Smith

THE BATTLE OF SHILOH HILL (1863)

Come, all ye valiant soldiers, and a story I will tell,
It is of a noted battle you all remember well;
It was an awful strife, and will cause your blood to chill,
It was the famous battle that was fought on Shiloh Hill!

It was the sixth of April, just at the break of day,
The drums and fifes were playing for us to march away;
The feeling of that hour I do remember still,
For the wounded and the dying that lay on Shiloh Hill.

About the hour of sunrise the battle it began,
And before the day had vanished we fought them hand to hand;
The horrors of the field did my heart with anguish fill,
For the wounded and the dying that lay on Shiloh Hill.

There were men of every nation laid on those rocky plains,
Fathers, sons and brothers were numbered with the slain,
That has caused so many homes with deep mourning to be filled,
All from the bloody battle that was fought on Shiloh Hill.

The wounded men were crying for help from everywhere,
While others, who were dying, were offering God their prayer:
"Protect my wife and children, if it is Thy holy will!"
Such were the prayers I heard that night on Shiloh Hill.

And early the next morning, we were called to arms again,
Unmindful of the wounded and unmindful of the slain,
The struggle was renewed, and ten thousand men were killed;
This was the second conflict of the famous Shiloh Hill.

The battle it raged on, though dead and dying men,
Lay thick all o'er the ground, on the hill and in the glen,
And from their deadly wounds their blood ran like a rill;
Such were the mournful sights that I saw on Shiloh Hill.

Before the day was ended the battle ceased to roar,
And thousands of brave soldiers had fall'n to rise no more;
They left their vacant ranks for some other ones to fill,
And how their mouldering bodies all lie on Shiloh Hill.

And now my song is ended about these bloody plains,
I hope the sight by mortal man may ne'er be seen again;
But I pray to God, the Saviour, "if consistent with Thy will,"
To save the souls of all who fell on bloody Shiloh Hill.

Patrick S. Gilmore

WHEN JOHNNY COMES MARCHING HOME (1863)

When Johnny comes marching home again,
    Hurrah! hurrah!
We'll give him a hearty welcome then,
    Hurrah! hurrah!
The men will cheer, the boys will shout,
The ladies, they will all turn out,
And we'll all feel gay,
When Johnny comes marching home.

The old church bell will peal with joy,
    Hurrah! hurrah!
To welcome home our darling boy,
    Hurrah! hurrah!
The village lads and lassies say,
With roses they will strew the way;
And we'll all feel gay,
When Johnny comes marching home.

Get ready for the Jubilee,
    Hurrah! hurrah!
We'll give the hero three times three,
    Hurrah! hurrah!
The laurel-wreath is ready now,
To place upon his loyal brow,
And we'll all feel gay,
When Johnny comes marching home.

Let love and friendship on that day,
    Hurrah! hurrah!
Their choicest treasures then display,
    Hurrah! hurrah!
And let each one perform some part,
To fill with joy the warrior's heart;
And we'll all feel gay,
When Johnny comes marching home.

George F. Root

TRAMP! TRAMP! TRAMP!
(THE PRISONER'S HOPE) (1863)

In the prison cell I sit,
Thinking, Mother dear, of you,
And our bright and happy home so far away,
And the tears they fill my eyes
Spite of all that I can do,
Tho' I try to cheer my comrades and be gay.

[Chorus:]
Tramp, tramp, tramp, the boys are marching,
Cheer up comrades, they will come,
And beneath the starry flag,
We shall breathe the air again,
Of the free-land in our own beloved home.

In the battle front we stood
When their fiercest charge they made,
And they swept us off a hundred men or more,
But before we reached their lines,
They were beaten back dismayed,
And we heard the cry of vict'ry o'er and o'er.

[Chorus]

So within the prison cell,
We are waiting for the day
That shall come to open wide the iron door,
And the hollow eye grows bright,
And the poor heart almost gay,
As we think of seeing home and friends once more.

[Chorus]

George F. Root

JUST BEFORE THE BATTLE, MOTHER

Just before the battle, mother,
    I am thinking most of you,
While upon the field we're watching,
    With the enemy in view—
Comrades brave are round me lying,
    Fill'd with tho't of home and God;
For well they know that on the morrow,
    Some will sleep beneath the sod.
       Farewell, mother, you may never
       Press me to your heart again;
       But oh, you'll not forget me, m other,
       If I'm number'd with the slain.

Oh I long to see you, mother,
    And the loving ones at home,
But I'll never leave our banner
    Till in honor I can come.
Tell the traitors all around you,
    That their cruel words, we know,
In ev'ry battle kill our soldiers
    By the help they give the foe.

Hark! I hear the bugles sounding,
    'Tis the signal for the fight,
Now may God protect us, mother,
    As he ever does the right.
Hear the "Battle Cry of Freedom,"
    How it swells upon the air,
Oh, yes, we'll rally round the standard,
    Or we'll perish nobly there.

Henry Clay Work

MARCHING THROUGH GEORGIA (1865)

Bring the good ol' bugle, boys, we'll sing another song,
Sing it with a spirit that will start the world along,
Sing it like we used to sing it fifty thousand strong,
While we were marching through Georgia.

[Chorus:]
Hurrah! hurrah! We bring the jubilee!
Hurrah! hurrah! The flag that makes you free!
So we sang the chorus from Atlanta to the sea
While we were marching through Georgia.

How the darkies shouted when they heard the joyful sound!
How the turkeys gobbled which our commissary found!
How the sweet potatoes even started from the ground,
While we were marching through Georgia.

[Chorus]

Yes, and there were Union men who wept with joyful tears,
When they saw the honored flag they had not seen for years.
Hardly could they be restrained from breaking forth in cheers,
While we were marching through Georgia.

[Chorus]

 "Sherman's dashing Yankee boys will never reach the coast!"
So the saucy rebels said, and 'twas a handsome boast,
Had they not forgot, alas, to reckon with the host,
While we were marching through Georgia.

[Chorus]

So we made a thoroughfare for Freedom and her train,
Sixty miles in latitude, three hundred to the main;
Treason fled before us, for resistance was in vain,
While we were marching through Georgia.

Thomas Wentworth Higginson

NEGRO SPIRITUALS
(1867)

The war brought to some of us, besides its direct experiences, many a strange fulfilment of dreams of other days. For instance, the present writer has been a faithful student of the Scottish ballads, and had always envied Sir Walter the delight of tracing them out amid their own heather, and of writing them down piecemeal from the lips of aged crones. It was a strange enjoyment, therefore, to be suddenly brought into the midst of a kindred world of unwritten songs, as simple and indigenous as the Border Minstrelsy,[2] more uniformly plaintive, almost always more quaint, and often as essentially poetic.

This interest was rather increased by the fact that I had for many years heard of this class of songs under the name of "Negro Spirituals," and had even heard some of them sung by friends from South Carolina. I could now gather on their own soil these strange plants, which I had before seen as in museums alone. True, the individual songs rarely coincided; there was a line here, a chorus there,—just enough to fix the class, but this was unmistakable. It was not strange that they differed, for the range seemed almost endless, and South Carolina, Georgia, and Florida seemed to have nothing but the generic character in common, until all were mingled in the united stock of camp-melodies.

Often in the starlit evening I have returned from some lonely ride by the swift river, or on the plover-haunted barrens, and, entering the camp, have silently approached some glimmering fire, round which the dusky figures moved in the rhythmical barbaric dance the negroes call a "shout," chanting, often harshly, but always in the most perfect time, some monotonous refrain. Writing down in the darkness, as I best could—perhaps with my hand in the safe covert of my pocket,—the words of the song, I have afterwards carried it to my tent, like some captured bird or insect, and then, after examination, put it by. Or, summoning one of the men at some period of leisure,—Corporal Robert Sutton,[3] for instance, whose iron memory held all the details of a song as if it were a ford or a forest,—I have completed the new specimen by supplying the absent parts. The music I could only retain by ear, and though the more common strains were repeated often enough to fix their impression, there were others that occurred only once or twice.

The words will be here given, as nearly as possible, in the original dialect; and if the spelling seems sometimes inconsistent, or the misspelling insufficient, it is because I could get no nearer. I wished to avoid what seems to me the only error of Lowell's "Biglow Papers"[4] in respect to dialect,—the occasional use of an extreme misspelling, which merely confuses the eye, without taking us any closer to the peculiarity of sound.

The favorite song in camp was the following,—sung with no accompaniment but the measured clapping of hands and the clatter of many feet. It was sung perhaps twice as often as any other. This was partly due to the fact that it properly consisted of a chorus alone, with which the verses of other songs might be combined at random.

I. Hold Your Light.

"Hold your light, Brudder Robert,—
    Hold your light,
Hold your light on Canaan's shore.

"What make ole Satan for follow me so?
Satan ain't got notin' for do wid me.
    Hold your light,
    Hold your light,
Hold your light on Canaan's shore."

This would be sung for half an hour at a time, perhaps, each person present being named in turn. It seemed the simplest primitive type of "spiritual." The next in popularity was almost as elementary, and, like this, named successively each one of the circle. It was, however, much more resounding and convivial in its music.

II. Bound To Go.

"Jordan River, I 'm bound to go,
    Bound to go, bound to go,—
Jordan River, I 'm bound to go,
    And bid 'em fare ye well.

"My Brudder Robert, I 'm bound to go,
    Bound to go, &c.

"My Sister Lucy, I 'm bound to go,
    Bound to go," &c.

Sometimes it was "tink 'em " (think them) "fare ye well." The *ye* was so detached, that I thought at first it was "very" or "vary well."

Another picturesque song, which seemed immensely popular, was at first very bewildering to me. I could not make out the first words of the chorus, and called it the "Romandàr," being reminded of some Romaic song which I had formerly heard. That association quite fell in with the Orientalism of the new tent-life.

III. Room in There.

"O, my mudder is gone! my mudder is gone!
My mudder is gone into heaven, my Lord!
    I can't stay behind!
Dere's room in dar, room in dar,
Room in dar, in de heaven, my Lord!
    I can't stay behind,
Can't stay behind, my dear,
    I can't stay behind!

"O, my fader is gone!" &c.

"O, de angels are gone!" &c.

"O, I 'se been on de road! I 'se been on de road!
I 'se been on de road into heaven, my Lord!
    I can't stay behind!
O, room in dar, room in dar,
Room in dar, in de heaven, my Lord!
    I can't stay behind!"

By this time every man within hearing, from oldest to youngest, would be wriggling and shuffling, as if through some magic piper's bewitchment; for even those who at first affected contemptuous indifference would be drawn into the vortex erelong.

Next to these in popularity ranked a class of songs belonging emphatically to the Church Militant, and available for camp purposes with very little strain upon their symbolism. This, for instance, had a true companion-in-arms heartiness about it, not impaired by the feminine invocation at the end.

IV. Hail Mary.

"One more valiant soldier here,
    One more valiant soldier here,
One more valiant soldier here,
    To help me bear de cross.
O hail, Mary, hail!
    Hail!, Mary, hail!
Hail!, Mary, hail!
    To help me bear de cross."

I fancied that the original reading might have been "soul," instead of "soldier,"—with some other syllable inserted, to fill out the metre,—and that the "Hail, Mary," might denote a Roman Catholic origin, as I had several men from St. Augustine who held in a dim way to that faith. It was a very ringing song, though not so grandly jubilant as the next, which was really impressive as the singers pealed it out, when marching or rowing or embarking.

V. My Army Cross Over.

"My army cross over,
My army cross over.
O, Pharaoh's army drownded!
My army cross over.

"We 'll cross de mighty river,
    My army cross over;
We 'll cross de river Jordan,
    My army cross over;
We 'll cross de danger water,
    My army cross over;

We 'll cross de mighty Myo,
>   My army cross over. (*Thrice.*)
>   O, Pharaoh's army drownded!
>   My army cross over."

I could get no explanation of the "mighty Myo," except that one of the old men thought it meant the river of death. Perhaps it is an African word. In the Cameroon dialect, "Mawa" signifies "to die."[5]

The next also has a military ring about it, and the first line is well matched by the music. The rest is conglomerate, and one or two lines show a more Northern origin. "Done" is a Virginia shibboleth, quite distinct from the "been" which replaces it in South Carolina. Yet one of their best choruses, without any fixed words, was, "De bell done ringing," for which, in proper South Carolina dialect, would have been substituted, "De bell been a-ring." This refrain may have gone South with our army.

VI. *Ride In, Kind Savior.*

"Ride in, kind Saviour!
>   No man can hinder me.
O, Jesus is a mighty man!
>   No man, &c.
We 're marching through Virginny fields.
>   No man, &c.
O, Satan is a busy man,
>   No Man, &c.
And he has his sword and shield,
>   No man, &c.
O, old Secesh done come and gone!
>   No man can hinder me."

Sometimes they substituted "hinder *we*," which was more spicy to the ear, and more in keeping with the usual head-over-heels arrangement of their pronouns.

Almost all their songs were thoroughly religious in their tone, however quaint their expression, and were in a minor key, both as to words and music. The attitude is always the same, and, as a commentary on the life of the race, is infinitely pathetic. Nothing but patience for this life,—nothing but triumph in the next. Sometimes the present predominates, sometimes the future; but the combination is always implied. In the following, for instance, we hear simply the patience.

VII. *This World Almost Done.*

"Brudder, keep your lamp trimmin' and a-burnin',
Keep your lamp trimmin' and a-burnin',
Keep your lamp trimmin' and a-burnin',
>   For dis world most done.
So keep your lamp, &c.
>   Dis world most done."

But in the next, the final reward of patience is proclaimed as plaintively.

VIII. I Want to Go Home.

"Dere's no rain to wet you,
        O, yes, I want to go home.
Dere's no sun to burn you,
        O, yes, I want to go home;
O, push along, believers,
        O, yes, &c.
Dere's no hard trials,
        O, yes, &c.
Dere's no whips a-crackin',
        O, yes, &c.
My brudder on de wayside,
        O, yes, &c.
O, push along, my brudder,
        O, yes, &c.
Where dere's no stormy weather,
        O, yes, &c.
Dere's no tribulation,
        O, yes, &c."

This next was a boat-song, and timed well with the tug of the oar.

IX. The Coming Day.

"I want to go to Canaan,
I want to go to Canaan,
I want to go to Canaan,
        To meet 'em at de comin' day.
O, remember, let me go to Canaan, (*Thrice.*)
        To meet 'em, &c.
O brudder, let me go to Canaan, (*Thrice.*)
        To meet 'em, &c.
My brudder, you—oh!—remember (*Thrice.*)
        To meet 'em at de comin' day."

The following begins with a startling affirmation, yet the last line quite outdoes the first. This, too, was a capital boat-song.

X. One More River.

"O, Jordan bank was a great old bank!
        Dere ain't but one more river to cross.
We have some valiant soldier here,
        Dere ain't, &c.

O, Jordan stream will never run dry,
    Dere ain't, &c.
Dere's a hill on my leff, and he catch on my right,
    Dere ain't but one more river to cross."

I could get no explanation of this last riddle, except, "Dat mean, if you go on de leff, go to 'struction, and if you go on de right, go to God, for sure."

In others, more of spiritual conflict is implied, as in this next.

XI. O The Dying Lamb!

"I wants to go where Moses trod,
    O de dying Lamb!
For Moses gone to de promised land,
    O de dying Lamb!
To drink from springs dat never run dry,
    O, &c.
Cry O my Lord!
    O, &c.
Before I 'll stay in hell one day,
    O, &c.
I 'm in hopes to pray my sins away,
    O, &c.
Cry O my Lord!
    O, &c.
Brudder Moses promised for be dar too,
    O &c.
To drink from streams dat never run dry,
    O de dying Lamb!"

In the next, the conflict is at its height, and the lurid imagery of the Apocalypse is brought to bear. This book, with the books of Moses, constituted their Bible; all that lay between, even the narratives of the life of Jesus, they hardly cared to read or to hear.

XII. Down in the Valley.

"We 'll run and never tire,
We 'll run and never tire,
We 'll run and never tire,
    Jesus set poor sinners free.
Way down in de valley,
    Who will rise and go with me?
You 've heern talk of Jesus,
    Who set poor sinners free.

"De lightnin' and de flashin',
De lightnin' and de flashin'

De lightnin' and de flashin'
    Jesus set poor sinners free.
I can't stand de fire. (*Thrice.*)
    Jesus set poor sinners free,
De green trees a-flamin'. (*Thrice.*)
    Jesus set poor sinners free,
        Way down in de valley,
            Who will rise and go with me?
        You 've heern talk of Jesus
            Who set poor sinners free."

"De valley" and "de lonesome valley" were familiar words in their religious experience. To descend into that region implied the same process with the "anxious-seat" of the camp-meeting. When a young girl was supposed to enter it, she bound a handkerchief by a peculiar knot over her head, and made it a point of honor not to change a single garment till the day of her baptism, so that she was sure of being in physical readiness for the cleansing rite, whatever her spiritual mood might be. More than once, in noticing a damsel thus mystically kerchiefed, I have asked some dusky attendant its meaning, and have received the unfailing answer,—framed with their usual indifference to the genders of pronouns,—"He in de lonesome valley, sa."

The next gives the same dramatic conflict, while its detached and impersonal refrain gives it strikingly the character of the Scotch and Scandinavian ballads.

XIII. Cry Holy.

"Cry holy, holy!
    Look at de people dat is born of God.
And I run down de valley, and I run down to pray,
    Says, look at de people dat is born of God.
When I get dar, Cappen Satan was dar,
    Says, look at, &c.
Says, young man, young man, dere 's no use for pray,
    Says, look at, &c.
For Jesus is dead, and God gone away,
    Says, look at, &c.
And I made him out a liar and I went my way,
    Says, look at, &c.
        Sing holy, holy!

"O, Mary was a woman, and he had a one Son,
    Says, look at, &c.
And de Jews and de Romans had him hung,
    Says, look at, &c.
        Cry holy, holy!

"And I tell you, sinner, you had better had pray,
    Says look at, &c.

For hell is a dark and dismal place,
    Says, look at, &c.
And I tell you, sinner, and I would n't go dar!
    Says, look at, &c.
      Cry holy, holy!"

Here is an infinitely quaint description of the length of the heavenly road:—

XIV. O'er the Crossing.

"Yonder 's my old mudder,
    Been a-waggin' at de hill so long.
It 's about time she 'll cross over;
    Get home bimeby.
Keep prayin', I do believe
    We 're a long time waggin' o'er de crossin'.
Keep prayin' I do believe
    We 'll get home to heaven bimeby.

"Hear dat mournful thunder
    Roll front door to door,
Calling home God's children;
    Get home bimeby.
Little chil'en, I do believe
    We 're a long time, &c.
Little chil'en, I do believe
    We 'll get home, &c.

"See dat forked lightning
    Flash from tree to tree,
Callin' home God's chil'en;
    Get home bimeby.
True believer, I do believe
    We 're a long time, &c.
O brudders, I do believe,
    We 'll get home to heaven bimeby."

One of the most singular pictures of future joys, and with a fine flavor of hospitality about it, was this:—

XV. Walk 'em Easy.

"O, walk 'em easy round de heaven,
Walk 'em easy round de heaven,
Walk 'em easy round de heaven,
    Dat all de people may join de band.

Walk 'em easy round de heaven. (*Thrice.*)
    O, shout glory till 'em join dat band!"

The chorus was usually the greater part of the song, and often came in paradoxically, thus:—

XVI. O Yes, Lord.

"O, must I be like de foolish mans?
    O yes, Lord!
Will build de house on de sandy hill.
    O yes, Lord!
I 'll build my house on Zion hill,
    O yes, Lord!
No wind nor rain can blow me down
    O yes, Lord!"

The next is very graceful and lyrical, and with more variety of rhythm than usual:—

XVII. Bow Low, Mary.

"Bow low, Mary, bow low, Martha,
    For Jesus come and lock de door,
    And carry de keys away.
Sail, sail, over yonder,
And view de promised land.
    For Jesus come, &c.
Weep, O Mary, bow low, Martha,
    For Jesus come, &c.
Sail, sail, my true believer;
Sail, sail over yonder;
Mary bow low, Martha, bow low,
    For Jesus come and lock de door
    And carry de keys away."

But of all the "spirituals" that which surprised me the most, I think—perhaps because it was that in which external nature furnished the images most directly,—was this. With all my experience of their ideal ways of speech, I was startled when first I came on such a flower of poetry in that dark soil.

XVIII. I Know Moon-Rise.

"I know moon-rise, I know star-rise,
    Lay dis body down.
I walk in de moonlight, I walk in de starlight,
    To lay dis body down.

> I 'll walk in de graveyard, I 'll walk through de graveyard,
>   To lay dis body down.
> I 'll lie in de grave and stretch out my arms;
>   Lay dis body down.
> I go to de judgment in de evenin' of de day,
>   When I lay dis body down;
> And my soul and your soul will meet in de day
>   When I lay dis body down."

"I 'll lie in de grave and stretch out my arms." Never, it seems to me, since man first lived and suffered, was his infinite longing for peace uttered more plaintively than in that line.

The next is one of the wildest and most striking of the whole series: there is a mystical effect and a passionate striving throughout the whole. The Scriptural struggle between Jacob and the angel, which is only dimly expressed in the words, seems all uttered in the music. I think it impressed my imagination more powerfully than any other of these songs.

XIX. *Wrestling Jacob.*

> "O wrestlin' Jacob, Jacob, day 's a-breakin';
>   I will not let thee go!
> O wrestlin' Jacob, Jacob, day 's a-breakin';
>   He will not let me go!
> O, I hold my brudder wid a tremblin' hand;
>   I would not let him go!
> I hold my sister wid a tremblin' hand;
>   I would not let her go!
>
> "O, Jacob do hang from a tremblin' limb,
>   He would not let him go!
> O, Jacob do hang from a tremblin' limb;
>   De Lord will bless my soul.
> O wrestlin' Jacob, Jacob," &c.

Of "occasional hymns," properly so called, I noticed but one, a funeral hymn for an infant, which is sung plaintively over and over, without variety of words.

XX. *The Baby Gone Home.*

> "De little baby gone home,
> De little baby gone home,
> De little baby gone along,
>   For to climb up Jacob's ladder.
> And I wish I 'd been dar,
> I wish I 'd been dar,
> I wish I 'd been dar, my Lord,
>   For to climb up Jacob's ladder "

Still simpler is this, which is yet quite sweet and touching.

XXI. *Jesus With Us.*

"He have been wid us, Jesus,
    He still wid us, Jesus,
He will be wid us, Jesus,
    Be wid us to the end."

The next seemed to be a favorite about Christmas time, when meditations on "de rollin' year" were frequent among them.

XXII. *Lord, Remember Me!*

"O do Lord, remember me!
    O do, Lord, remember me!
O, do remember me, until de year roll round!
    Do, Lord, remember me!

"If you want to die like Jesus died,
    Lay in de grave,
You would fold your arms and close your eyes
    And die wid a free good will.

"For Death is a simple ting,
    And he go from door to door
And he knock down some, and he cripple up some,
    And he leave some here to pray.

"O do, Lord, remember me!
    O do, Lord, remember me!
My old fader 's gone till de year roll round;
    Do, Lord, remember me!"

The next was sung in such an operatic and rollicking way that it was quite hard to fancy it a religious performance, which, however, it was. I heard it but once.

XXIII. *Early in the Morning.*

"I meet little Rosa early in de mornin',
    O Jerusalem! early in de mornin';
And I ax her, How you do, my darter?
    O Jerusalem! early in de mornin'.

"I meet my mudder early in de mornin',
    O Jerusalem! &c.
And I ax her, How you do, my mudder?
    O Jerusalem! &c.

"I meet Budder Robert early in de mornin'
    O Jerusalem! &c.
And I ax him, How you do, my sonny?
    O Jerusalem! &c.

"I meet Tittawisa early in de mornin',
    O Jerusalem! &c.
And I ax her, how you do, my darter?
    O Jerusalem!" &c.

"Tittawisa" means "Sister Louisa." In songs of this class the name of every person present successively appears.

Their best marching song, and one which was invaluable to lift their feet along, as they expressed it, was the following. There was a kind of spring and *lilt* to it, quite indescribable by words.

XXIV. *Go in the Wilderness.*

"Jesus call you. Go in de wilderness,
    Go in de wilderness, go in de wilderness,
Jesus call you. Go in de wilderness
    To wait upon de Lord.
Go wait upon do Lord,
Go wait upon de Lord,
Go wait upon de Lord, my God,
    He take away de sins of de world.

"Jesus a-waitin'. Go in de wilderness,
    Go, &c.
All dem chil'en go in de wilderness
    To wait upon de Lord."

The next was one of those which I had heard in boyish days, brought North from Charleston. But the chorus alone was identical; the words were mainly different, and those here given are quaint enough.

XXV. *Blow Your Trumpet, Gabriel.*

"O, blow your trumpet, Gabriel,
    Blow your trumpet louder;
And I want dat trumpet to blow me home
    To my new Jerusalem.

"De prettiest ting dat ever I done
Was to serve de Lord when I was young.
    So blow your trumpet, Gabriel, &c.

"O, Satan is a liar, and he conjure too,
And if you don't mind, he 'll conjure you.
    So blow your trumpet, Gabriel, &c.

"O, I was lost in de wilderness,
King Jesus hand me de candle down.
    So blow your trumpet, Gabriel," &c.

The following contains one of those odd transformations of proper names with which their Scriptural citations were often enriched. It rivals their text, "Paul may plant, and may polish wid water," which I have elsewhere quoted,[6] and in which the sainted Apollos [sic] would hardly have recognized himself.

XXVI. *In the Morning.*

"In de mornin',
In de mornin',
Chil'en? Yes, my Lord!
    Don't you hear de trumpet sound?
If I had a-died when I was young,
I never would had de race for run.
    Don't you hear de trumpet sound?

"O Sam and Peter was fishin' in de sea,
And dey drop de net and follow my Lord.
    Don't you hear de trumpet sound?

"Dere 's a silver spade for to dig my grave
And a golden chain for to let me down.
    Don't you hear de trumpet sound?
In de mornin',
In de mornin',
Chil'en? Yes, my Lord!
    Don't you hear de trumpet sound?"

These golden and silver fancies remind one of the King of Spain's daughter in "Mother Goose," and the golden apple, and the silver pear, which are doubtless themselves but the vestiges of some simple early composition like this. The next has a humbler and more domestic style of fancy.

XXVII. *Fare Ye Well.*

"My true believers, fare ye well,
Fare ye well, fare ye well,
Fare ye well, by de grace of God,
    For I 'm going home.

"Massa Jesus give me a little broom
For to sweep my heart clean,
And I will try, by de grace of God,
      To win my way home."

Among the songs not available for marching, but requiring the concentrated enthusiasm of the camp, was "The Ship of Zion," of which they had three wholly distinct versions, all quite exuberant and tumultuous.

XXVIII. *The Ship of Zion.*

"Come along, come along,
And let us go home,
O, glory, hallelujah!
Dis de ole ship o' Zion,
      Halleloo! Halleloo!
Dis de ole ship o' Zion,
      Hallelujah!

"She has landed many a tousand,
She can land as many more.
      O, glory, hallelujah! &c.

"Do you tink she will be able
For to take us all home?
      O, glory, hallelujah! &c.

"You can tell 'em I 'm a coming,
      Halleloo! Halleloo!
You can tell 'em I 'm a coming
      Hallelujah!
Come along, come along," & c.

XXIX. *The Ship of Zion.* (*Second version.*)

"Dis de good ole ship o' Zion,
Dis de good ole ship o' Zion,
Dis de good ole ship o' Zion,
      And she 's makin' for de Promise Land.
She hab angels for de sailors, (*Thrice.*)
      And she 's, &c.
And how you know dey 's angels? (*Thrice.*)
      And she 's, &c.
Good lord, shall I be de one? (*Thrice.*)
      And she 's, &c.

"Dat ship is out a-sailin', sailin', sailin',
    And she 's, &c.
She 's a-sailin' mighty steady, steady, steady,
    And she 's, &c.
She 'll neither reel nor totter, totter, totter,
    And she 's, &c.
She 's a-sailin' away cold Jordan, Jordan, Jordan,
    And she 's, &c.
King Jesus is de captain, captain, captain,
    And she 's making for de Promise Land."

XXX. The Ship of Zion. (Third Version.)

"De Gospel ship is sailin',
    Hosann—sann.
O, Jesus is de captain,
    Hosann—sann.
De angels are de sailors,
    Hosann—sann.
O, is your bundle ready?
    Hosann—sann.
O, have you got your ticket?
    Hosann—sann."

This abbreviated chorus is given with unspeakable unction.

The three just given are modifications of an old camp-meeting melody; and the same may be true of the three following, although I cannot find them in the Methodist hymn-books. Each, however, has its characteristic modifications, which make it well worth giving. In the second verse of this next, for instance, "Saviour" evidently has become "soldier."

XXXI. Sweet Music.

"Sweet music in heaven,
    Just beginning for to roll.
Don't you love God?
    Glory, hallelujah!

"Yes, late I heard my soldier say,
Come, heavy soul, I am de way.
    Don't you love God?
    Glory, hallelujah!

"I 'll go and tell to sinners round
What a kind Saviour I have found.
    Don't you love God?
    Glory, hallelujah!

"My grief my burden long has been,
Because I was not cease from sin.
　　Don't you love God?
　　Glory, hallelujah!"

XXXII. *Good News.*

"O, good news! O, good news!
　　De angels brought de tidings down,
　　Just comin' from de trone.

"As grief from out my soul shall fly,
　　Just comin' from de trone;
I 'll shout salvation when I die,
　　Good news, O, good news!
　　Just comin' from de trone.

"Lord, I want to go to heaven when I die,
Good news, O, good news! &c.

"De white folks call us a noisy crew,
　　Good news, O, good news!
But dis I know, we are happy too,
　　Just comin' from de trone."

XXXIII. *The Heavenly Road.*

"You may talk of my name as much as you please,
　　And carry my name abroad,
But I really do believe I 'm a child of God
　　As I walk in de heavenly road.
O, won't you go wid me? (*Thrice.*)
　　For to keep our garments clean.

"O, Satan is a mighty busy ole man,
　　And roll rocks in my way;
But Jesus is my bosom friend,
　　And roll 'em out of de way.
O, won't you go wid me? (*Thrice.*)
　　For to keep our garments clean.

"Come, my brudder, if you never did pray,
　　I hope you may pray to-night;
For I really believe I 'm a child of God
　　As I walk in de heavenly road.
O, won't you," &c.

Some of the songs had played an historic part during the war. For singing the next, for instance, the negroes had been put in jail in Georgetown, S. C., at the outbreak of the Rebellion. "We 'll soon be free," was too dangerous an assertion; and though the chant was an old one, it was no doubt sung with redoubled emphasis during the new events. "De Lord will call us home," was evidently thought to be a symbolical verse; for, as a little drummer-boy explained to me, showing all his white teeth as he sat in the moonlight by the door of my tent, "Dey tink *de Lord* mean for say *de Yankees*."

XXXIV. *We 'll Soon Be Free.*

"We 'll soon be free,
We 'll soon be free,
We 'll soon be free,
    When de Lord will call us home.
My brudder, how long,
My brudder, how long,
My brudder, how long,
    'Fore we done sufferin' here?
It won't be long (*Thrice.*)
    'Fore de Lord will call us home.
We 'll walk de miry road (*Thrice.*)
    Where pleasure never dies.
We 'll walk de golden street (*Thrice.*)
    Where pleasure never dies.
My brudder, how long (*Thrice.*)
    'Fore we done sufferin' here?
We 'll soon be free (*Thrice.*)
    When Jesus sets me free.
We 'll fight for liberty (*Thrice.*)
    When de Lord will call us home."

The suspicion in this case was unfounded, but they had another song to which the Rebellion had actually given rise. This was composed by nobody knew whom,—though it was the most recent, doubtless, of all these "spirituals,"—and had been sung in secret to avoid detection. It is certainly plaintive enough. The peck of corn and pint of salt were slavery's rations.

XXXV. *Many Thousand Go.*

"No more peck o' corn for me,
    No more, no more,—
No more peck o' corn for me,
    Many tousand go.

"No more driver's lash for me, (*Twice.*)
    No more, &c.

"No more pint o' salt for me, (*Twice.*)
    No more, &c.

"No more hundred lash for me, (*Twice.*)
    No more, &c.

"No more mistress' call for me,
    No more, No more,—
No more mistress' call for me,
    Many tousand go."

Even of this last composition, however, we have only the approximate date, and know nothing of the mode of composition. Allan Ramsay says of the Scotch songs, that, no matter who made them, they were soon attributed to the minister of the parish whence they sprang.[7] And I always wondered, about these, whether they had always a conscious and definite origin in some leading mind, or whether they grew by gradual accretion in an almost unconscious way. On this point I could get no information, though I asked many questions, until at last, one day when I was being rowed across from Beaufort to Ladies' Island, I found myself, with delight, on the actual trail of a song. One of the oarsmen, a brisk young fellow, not a soldier, on being asked for his theory of the matter, dropped out a coy confession. "Some good sperituals," he said, "are start jess out o' curiosity. I been a-raise a sing, [sic] myself, once."

My dream was fulfilled, and I had traced out, not the poem alone, but the poet. I implored him to proceed.

"Once we boys." he said, "went for tote some rice, and de nigger-driver, he keep a-callin' on us; and I say, 'O, de ole nigger-driver!' Den anudder said, 'Fust ting my mammy tole me was, notin' so bad as nigger-driver.' Den I made a sing, just puttin' a word, and den anudder word."

Then he began singing and the men, after listening a moment, joined in at the chorus as if it were an old acquaintance, though they evidently had never heard it before. I saw how easily a new "sing" took root among them.

XXXVI. *The Driver.*

"O, de ole nigger-driver!
    O, gwine away!
Fust ting my mammy tell me,
    O, gwine away!
Tell me 'bout de nigger-driver,
    O, gwine away!
Nigger-driver second devil,
    O, gwine away!
Best ting for do he driver,
    O, gwine away!
Knock he down and spoil he labor,
    O, gwine away! "

It will be observed that, although this song is quite secular in its character, its author yet called it a "spiritual." I heard but two songs among them, at any time, to which they would not, perhaps, have given this generic name. One of these consisted simply in the endless repetition—after the manner of certain college songs—of the mysterious line,

"Rain fall and wet Becky Martin."

But who Becky Martin was, and why she should or should not be wet, and whether the dryness was a reward or a penalty, none could say. I got the impression that, in either case, the event was posthumous and that there was some tradition of grass not growing over the grave of a sinner; but even this was vague, and all else vaguer.

The other song I heard but once, on a morning when a squad of men came in from picket duty, and chanted it in the most rousing way. It had been a stormy and comfortless night, and the picket station was very exposed. It still rained in the morning when I strolled to the edge of the camp, looking out for the men, and wondering how they had stood it. Presently they came striding along the road, at a great pace, with their shining rubber blankets worn as cloaks around them, the rain streaming from these and from their equally shining faces, which were almost all upon the broad grin, as they pealed out this remarkable ditty:—

Hangman Johnny.

"O, dey call me Hangman Johnny!
    O, ho! O, ho!
But I never hang nobody,
    O, hang, boys, hang!

"O, dey call me Hangman Johnny!
    O, ho! O, ho!
But we 'll all hang togedder,
    O, hang, boys, hang!"

My presence apparently checked the performance of another verse, beginning, "De buckra 'list for money," apparently in reference to the controversy about the pay-question, then just beginning, and to the more mercenary aims they attributed to the white soldiers. But "Hangman Johnny" remained always a myth as inscrutable as "Becky Martin."

As they learned all their songs by ear, they often strayed into wholly new versions, which sometimes became popular, and entirely banished the others. This was amusingly the case, for instance, with one phrase in the popular camp-song of "Marching Along," which was entirely new to them until our quartermaster taught it to them, at my request. The words, "Gird on the armor," were to them a stumbling-block, and no wonder, until some ingenious ear substituted, "Guide on de army," which was at once accepted, and became universal.

"We 'll guide on de army, and be marching along,"

is now the established version on the Sea Islands.

These quaint religious songs were to the men more than a source of relaxation; they were a stimulus to courage and a tie to heaven. I never overheard in camp a profane or vulgar song. With the trifling exceptions given, all had a religious motive, while the most secular melody could not have been more exciting. A few youths from Savannah, who were comparatively men of the world, had learned some of the "Ethiopian Minstrel" ditties, imported from the North. These took no hold upon the mass; and, on the other hand, they sang reluctantly, even on Sunday, the long and short metres of the hymn-books, always gladly yielding to the more potent excitement of their own "spirituals." By these they could sing themselves, as had their fathers before them, out of the contemplation of their own low estate, into the sublime scenery of the Apocalypse. I remember that this minor-keyed pathos used to seem to me almost too sad to dwell upon, while slavery seemed destined to last for generations; but now that their patience has had its perfect work, history cannot afford to lose this portion of its record. There is no parallel instance of an oppressed race thus sustained by the religious sentiment alone. These songs are but the vocal expression of the simplicity of their faith and the sublimity of their long resignation.

THE TEXTS

Daniel Emmett, "Dixie's Land." Source: *Immortal Songs of Camp and Field*, ed. Rev. Louis Albert Banks (Cleveland: The Burrows Brothers Co., 1899). Words and music by Emmett in 1859, while working with the Dan Bryant Minstrel Company in New York. Sheet music verison published by Firth, Pond & Co., New York, 1860. Steven Cornelius, in *Music of the Civil War Era*, identifies the following as the original opening verse, deleted before the song's first performance, in New York: "Dis worl' was made is jiss six days, / An' finished up in various ways, / Look away! Look away! Look away! Dixie land. / Dey den made Dixie trim and nice, / But Adam called it 'paradise,' / Look away! Look away! Look away! Dixie land."

Anonymous, "John Brown's Body." Source: *American War Ballads and Lyrics*, ed. George Cary Eggleston (New York: G. P. Putnam's Sons, 1889). The exact origins of the song are murky and several variants exist. The "original" written lyrics were composed by Edna Dean Proctor, with four principal lines: "John Brown's body lies mouldering in the grave! / The stars of heaven are looking kindly down! / He's gone to be a soldier in the army of the Lord! / John Brown's knapsack is strapped upon his back!" The popular Northern version here dates from 1861, when a Massachusetts regiment adapted the original lyrics; the final written form is attributed to Charles Sprague Hall.

Septimus Winner, "Abraham's Daughter." Source: "Abraham's Daughter" song sheet (Philadelphia: J. H. Johnson, 1861). Library of Congress Rare Book and Special Collections Division. Words and music by Winner, although a Tony Emmett is listed on song leaflets. Occasionally parenthetically subtitled "Raw Recruits."

A. E. Blackmar, "Allons Enfans (The Southern Marseillaise)." Source: *Southern War Songs: Camp-Fire, Patriotic, and Sentimental*, ed. W. L. Fagan (New York: M. T. Richardson & Co., 1890).

William B. Bradbury, "Marching Along." Source: "Marching along No. 1" song sheet (New York: Charles Magnus, 1861). Library of Congress Rare Book and Special Collections Division. Words and music by Bradbury, although several other variants exist.

Ethel Lynn Beers, "All Quiet Along the Potomac." Source: *Famous Songs and Those Who Made Them*, ed. Helen K. Johnson and Frederic Dean (New York: Bryan, Taylor & Co., 1895). Words by Beers to music by John Hill Hewitt. Originally published in *Harper's Weekly*, Nov. 30, 1861, as "The Picket Guard." Sheet music edition published by Miller & Beacham, Baltimore, 1863.

Harry Macarthy, "The Bonnie Blue Flag." Source: *Southern War Songs: Camp-Fire, Patriotic, and Sentimental*, ed. W. L. Fagan (New York: M. T. Richardson & Co., 1890). Words by Macarthy to the tune of "The Irish Jaunting Car." Sheet music edition published by A. E. Blackmar & Bro., New Orleans, 1861. Irwin Silber, in *Songs of the Civil War*, gives the second line as: "Fighting for the property we have gained by honest toil;"

Julia Ward Howe, "Battle Hymn of the Republic." Source: *Immortal Songs of Camp and Field*, ed. Rev. Louis Albert Banks (Cleveland: The Burrows Brothers Co., 1899). Words by Howe to the music of "John Brown's Body." Originally published in *The Atlantic Monthly*, vol. 9, no. 52 (February 1862), p. 10. Sheet music edition published by Oliver Ditson & Co. Boston, 1862. Howe reportedly wrote the lyrics after visiting Washington D.C. in Nov. 1861 and hearing Union soldiers singing "John Brown's Body."

Walter Kittredge, "Tenting on the Old Camp Ground." Source: *Immortal Songs of Camp and Field*, ed. Rev. Louis Albert Banks (Cleveland: The Burrows Brothers Co., 1899). Words and music by Kittredge. Sheet music edition published by Oliver Ditson & Co., Boston, 1864. Steven Cornelius, in *Music of the Civil War Era*, gives the last refrain as: "Many are the hearts that are weary to-night, / Wishing for the war to cease, / Many are the hearts looking for the right, / To see the dawn of peace. / Dying to-night, dying to-night, / Dying on the old camp ground."

Charles Carroll Sawyer, "Weeping, Sad and Lonely; or, When This Cruel War Is Over." Source: *Immortal Songs of Camp and Field*, ed. Rev. Louis Albert Banks (Cleveland: The Burrows Brothers Co., 1899). Words by Sawyer; music by Henry Tucker. Sheet music edition published by Sawyer & Thompson, Brooklyn, 1862.

Anonymous, "Parody on When this Cruel War is Over." Source: "Parody on When this Cruel War is Over" song sheet (Philadelphia: J. H. Johnson, n.d.). Library of Congress Rare Book and Special Collections Division.

A. E. Blackmar, "Goober Peas." Source: *Songs of the Confederacy*, ed. Richard Barksdale Harwell (New York: Broadcast Music, Inc., 1951). Camp song evidently transcribed by Blackmar. Sheet music edition published by A. E. Blackmar & Bro., New Orleans, 1866, with the music attributed to "P. Nutt, Esq." and the words to "A. Pindar, Esq." "Gouba" and "pinda" are Gullah words for peanut.

M. B. Smith, "The Battle of Shiloh Hill." Source: Source: *Southern War Songs: Camp-Fire, Patriotic, and Sentimental*, ed. W. L. Fagan (New York: M. T. Richardson & Co., 1890). Ed. note: "By M. B. Smith, of Co. C., Second Regiment Texas Volunteers."

Patrick S. Gilmore, "When Johnny Comes Marching Home." Source: *American War Songs* (Philadelphia: National Society of the Colonial Dames of America, 1925). Words and music by Gilmore, possibly as an adaptation of an old Irish folk song. Sheet music edition published by Henry Tolman & Co., Boston, 1863, under the pseudonym "Louis Lambert." Lambert (1835–1910) was actually a Roman Catholic priest in Illinois, chaplain of 18th Illinois Infantry, and a lyricist in his own right.

George F. Root, "Tramp! Tramp! Tramp! (The Prisoner's Hope)." Source: *American War Songs* (Philadelphia: National Society of the Colonial Dames of America, 1925). Words and music by Root. Sheet music edition published by Root & Cady, Chicago, 1864.

George F. Root, "Just Before the Battle, Mother." Source: *Immortal Songs of Camp and Field*, ed. Rev. Louis Albert Banks (Cleveland: The Burrows Brothers Co., 1899). Words and music by Root.

Henry Clay Work, "Marching Through Georgia" (1865). Source: *Immortal Songs of Camp and Field*, ed. Rev. Louis Albert Banks (Cleveland: The Burrows Brothers Co., 1899). Words and music by Work. Sheet music edition published by Root & Cady, Chicago, 1865.

Thomas Wentworth Higginson, "Negro Spirituals." Source: *The Atlantic Monthly*, vol. 19, no. 116 (June 1867), pp. 685-694. Republished as Chapter 9 of *Army Life in a Black Regiment* (Boston: Lee and Shepard; New York: C. T. Dillingham, 1869). Incorporated into *Slave Songs of the United States*, ed. William Francis Allen, Charles Pickard Ware, and Lucy McKim Garrison (New York: A. Simpson, 1867). In a June 11, 1867, letter to Wendell Garrison, James H. Wilson wrote: "It seems to me that Mr. Higginson has 'finished' out a good many of these he has published in the Atlantic, with a good deal more of elaboration than the negroes sang them—but…in their general characteristics he has given them admirably" (quoted in Epstein, *Sinful Tunes and Spirituals*, pp. 329).

NOTES

1. The 114th Pennsylvania Volunteers, who resembled Zouaves.
2. See page 325, note 56.
3. See page 325, note 53.
4. In *The Biglow Papers* (serialized in the *Boston Courier* 1846-48; published as a book in 1848), James Russell Lowell (1819-1891) fashioned a heavy Yankee dialect in which his rustic narrator, Hosea Biglow, criticized the Mexican American war in such lines as: "Thet air flag's a leetle rotten, / Hope it aint your Sunday's best;— / Fact! it takes a sight o' cotton / To stuff out a soger's chest." Lowell published a second series of the "Biglow Papers" in *The Atlantic* during the Civil War.
5. In *Slave Songs of the United States* (New York, 1867), edited by William Francis Allen, Charles Pickard Ware, and Lucy McKim Garrison, we are told that "Lt. Col. Trowbridge feels very confident that ['mawa'] is merely a corruption of 'bayou.'"
6. In his December 14, 1862, "Camp Diary" entry.
7. Allan Ramsay Sr. (1686–1758) published three volumes of Scottish ballads collectively called the *Tea-Table Miscellany* (1724–27).

"Home again." Lithograph by Endicott & Co., 1866.

5

INTRODUCTION

Because it was fought entirely on American soil, and because it absorbed the full energies of both North and South, the Civil War affected civilian life in far-reaching ways. Every state had an economic and political stake in the conflict; every state sent soldiers into the fray; and millions of families found their lives directly affected by events both near and far. In contrast to America's foreign wars, civilians participated and suffered in the Civil War in ways that few could have anticipated. The civilian experience in the Civil War entailed an array of changes—some minor and some major, some short-lived and some long-lasting—in both daily life and the broader framework of cultural attitudes that Americans had traditionally brought to their work, their homes, and their social relations.

Most directly, the war effort affected civilians by turning some of them into combatants—not always with their consent. As it became clear that the initial call-up of voluntary enlistments in 1861 would not suffice, both militaries turned to other means of recruitment, the most prominent being conscription (or the threat of conscription) and bounties (i.e., direct payments to new enlistees). By the end of the war, more than 3 million Americans, or about 10 percent of the total population, had fought. These soldiers represented a broad swath of the American public. The vast majority were native-born white men in their twenties and thirties, although immigrants made up about a quarter of the Union army and about 10 percent of the Confederate army. About half of the North's soldiers were farmers or farm laborers, compared to about two-thirds of Southern soldiers, while the rest hailed from a variety of social backgrounds, including a good number of skilled laborers and professionals.

What this meant was that very few families or towns could avoid the loss of sons, husbands, fathers, and productive workers. Maris Vinovski has estimated that about 6 percent of Northern white males aged 13 to 43 in 1860 died in the Civil War, compared to about 18 percent of their Southern counterparts.[1] (Since the North had a much larger total population, it suffered a lower proportional rate of casualties). Moreover, since many units were raised from the same geographic area, some communities could be particularly hard hit if a local regiment suffered high losses in combat.

Although the Civil War evolved into a "total war" in the sense that entire societies, not just military forces, contended for victory, a relatively small number of civilians were actually killed during the conflict. Rather, they found their daily lives affected in other ways. Inflation, stagnant wages, the disruption of commerce, and the destruction or diversion of necessary goods, took an economic toll on many families. Particularly vulnerable were civilians in the Southern border states, where much of the fighting took place, and in Georgia and South Carolina, where late in the war Gen. William T. Sherman waged a campaign against the Southern economic and military infrastructure. Meanwhile, both sides—the North more aggressively—instituted restrictions on free speech and political dissent, suspending the writ of habeas corpus and making arrests for activities deemed seditious or treasonous. And the war, in profound ways, affected children; James Marten writes that it "burdened them with greater responsibilities, opened them to greater autonomy and freedom, and politicized them."[2]

In the midst of these difficulties, ordinary Americans worked to support the front-line militaries, raising money to purchase supplies, sending goods to soldiers in camp, and volunteering at hospitals and in benevolent organizations such as the United States Sanitary Commission. It is possible that this intensified public activity translated into various forms of post-war political activism, particularly on the part of women. Civilians also sustained a vital correspondence with soldiers at the front, and at times traveled to hospitals to find wounded family members or to encampments to get first-hand knowledge. Recounting their experiences, write Paul Cimbala and Randall Miller, enabled both civilians and soldiers to preserve intact a sense of community: "Keeping diaries, letters, and memoirs, and telling and re-telling the stories of the men and women who joined in the great cause sealed the union of home front and soldier after the war."[3]

Civilians also benefited from a roisterous press, getting news about the war from a rich variety of newspapers, magazines, and illustrated weeklies. This proved significant. The Civil War was, in a fundamental sense, an information war. Not only did photography and the publishing industry make the realities of war available for public consumption, but the information people took in affected public opinion, and public opinion in turn had a bearing on the military and political decisions that war leaders made. Behind many of these decisions—from Lincoln's timing of the Emancipation Proclamation to Robert E. Lee's decision to invade Pennsylvania—the pressure of the public mood could be felt, and that mood depended largely on what people read in the periodicals.

Tangible changes in daily life inevitably created intangible changes in cultural attitudes, but these are much more difficult to measure. Did shared military service, for instance, help to reduce class and ethnic tensions among soldiers from different backgrounds? Or might it have reinforced antagonism and prejudice? What about shared sacrifice by civilians? How did the war change public perceptions of political leaders? At a more personal level, how did the war affect Americans' thinking about mortality, and about the fragility of the human body?

These are issues that cultural historians have only begun to address, but they promise to be a fruitful vein of study.

Much more work has looked at the Civil War's impact on gender roles and the family, and while a consensus has formed that the war challenged the traditional models, the extent to which it did so remains an open question. Since many women during the war had to move outside of their customary economic and social responsibilities, working on farms and in factories and hospitals, some scholars have suggested that the war brought about a "crisis in gender" and a "crisis of domesticity."[4] Joan E. Cashin, for instance, maintains that the war "unsettled, undermined, and sometimes destroyed traditional gender roles, in all regions, forcing people to reconsider their assumptions about appropriate behavior for men and women of both races."[5] But revolutions produce counter-revolutions, and—in the South particularly—the desire for pre-war stability may have led people to cling to familiar traditions in the face of upheaval. As George Rable observes, "the struggle for survival . . . provided the social context for both women and men to redefine—or, more accurately, re-establish—'proper' female roles."[6] What is certain is that, across the country, it would take decades before women began joining the labor force in large numbers, and decades before they began voting.

As in any war, finally, veterans returned home to find a world changed, and they faced the challenge of reintegrating into civilian life. For many Southern veterans there was little left—except, perhaps, the sense of having fought honorably. Some veterans returned as heroes and some returned as deserters. All veterans found their relation to their communities and families changed, in subtle ways and dramatic ways. They were civilians again, and yet no longer civilians.

NOTES

1. Maris A. Vinovskis, "Have Social Historians Lost the Civil War? Some Preliminary Demographic Specula-tions," in Vinovskis, ed., *Toward a Social History of the American Civil War*, pp. 1–30.
2. James Marten, *The Children's Civil War* (Chapel Hill: University of North Carolina Press, 1998), p. 2.
3. Paul A. Cimbala and Randall M. Miller, eds. *Union Soldiers and the Northern Home Front: Wartime Experi-ences, Postwar Adjustments* (New York: Fordham University Press, 2002), p. xii.
4. LeeAnn Whites, "The Civil War as a Crisis in Gender" and Jeanie Attie, "Warwork and the Crisis of Domestic-ity in the North," in Catherine Clinton and Nina Silber, eds., *Divided Houses: Gender and the Civil War* (Oxford University Press, 1992).
5. Joan E. Cashin, ed., *The War Was You and Me: Civilians in the American Civil War* (Princeton, NJ: Princeton University Press, 2002), p. 3.
6. George C. Rable, *Civil Wars: Women and the Crisis of Southern Nationalism* (Urbana: University of Illinois Pres, 1989), p. 241.

SUGGESTED READING

Cashin, Joan E., ed. *The War Was You and Me: Civilians in the American Civil War*. Princeton, NJ: Princeton University Press, 2002.

Cimbala, Paul A., and Randall M. Miller, eds. *Union Soldiers and the Northern Home Front: Wartime Experiences, Postwar Adjustments*. New York: Fordham University Press, 2002.

Clinton, Catherine, and Nina Silber, eds. *Divided Houses: Gender and the Civil War*. New York: Oxford University Press, 1992.

Faust, Drew Gilpin. *Mothers of Invention: Women of the Slaveholding South in the American Civil War*. Chapel Hill: University of North Carolina Press, 1996.

Leonard, Elizabeth D. *Yankee Women: Gender Battles in the Civil War*. New York: W.W. Norton, 1994.

Marten, James. *The Children's Civil War*. Chapel Hill: University of North Carolina Press, 1998.

Rable, George C. *Civil Wars: Women and the Crisis of Southern Nationalism*. Urbana: University of Illinois Press, 1989.

Vinovskis, Maris, ed. *Toward a Social History of the American Civil War: Exploratory Essays*. Cambridge: Cambridge University Press, 1990.

Volo, Dorothy Denneen, and James M. Volo. *Daily Life in Civil War America*. Westport, Conn.: Greenwood Press, 1998.

Harriet Beecher Stowe

THE CHIMNEY-CORNER
(January 1865)

Here comes the First of January, Eighteen Hundred and Sixty-Five, and we are all settled comfortably into our winter places, with our winter surroundings and belongings; all cracks and openings are calked and listed, the double windows are in, the furnace dragon in the cellar is ruddy and in good liking, sending up his warming respirations through every pipe and register in the house; and yet, though an artificial summer reigns everywhere, like bees, we have our swarming-place,—in my library. There is my chimney-corner, and my table permanently established on one side of the hearth; and each of the female genus has, so to speak, pitched her own winter-tent within sight of the blaze of my camp-fire. I discerned to-day that Jennie had surreptitiously appropriated one of the drawers of my study-table to knitting-needles and worsted; and wicker work-baskets and stands of various heights and sizes seem to be planted here and there for permanence among the bookcases. The canary-bird has a sunny window, and the plants spread out their leaves and unfold their blossoms as if there were no ice and snow in the street, and Rover makes a hearth-rug of himself in winking satisfaction in front of my fire, except when Jennie is taken with a fit of discipline, when he beats a retreat, and secretes [sic] himself under my table.

Peaceable, ah, how peaceable, home and quiet and warmth in winter! And how, when we hear the wind whistle, we think of you, O our brave brothers, our saviours and defenders, who for our sake have no home but the muddy camp, the hard pillow of the barrack, the weary march, the uncertain fare,—you, the rank and file, the thousand unnoticed ones, who have left warm fires, dear wives, loving little children, without even the hope of glory or fame,—without even the hope of doing anything remarkable or perceptible for the cause you love,—resigned only to fill the ditch or bridge the chasm over which your country shall walk to peace and joy! Good men and true, brave unknown hearts, we salute you, and feel that we, in our soft peace and security, are not worthy of you! When we think of you, our simple comforts seem luxuries all too good for us, who give so little when you give all!

But there are others to whom from our bright homes, our cheerful firesides, we would fain say a word, if we dared.

Think of a mother receiving a letter with such a passage as this in it! It is extracted from one we have just seen, written by a private in the army of Sheridan, describing the death of a private. "He fell instantly, gave a peculiar smile and look, and then closed his eyes. We laid him down gently at the foot of a large tree. I crossed his hands over his breast, closed his eyelids down, but the smile was still on his face. I wrapped him in his tent, spread my pocket-handkerchief over his face, wrote his name on a piece of paper, and pinned it on his breast, and there we left him: we could not find pick or shovel to dig a grave." There it is!—a history that is multiplying itself by hundreds daily, the substance of what has come to so many homes, and must come to so many more before the great price of our ransom is paid!

What can we say to you, in those many, many homes where the light has gone out forever?—you, O fathers, mothers, wives, sisters, haunted by a name that has ceased to be spoken on earth,—you, for whom there is no more news from the camp, no more reading of lists, no more tracing of maps, no more letters, but only a blank, dead silence! The battle-cry goes on, but for you it is passed by! The victory comes, but, oh, never more to bring him back to you! your offering to this great cause has been made, and been taken; you have thrown into it *all* your living, even all that you had, and from henceforth your house is left unto you desolate! O ye watchers of the cross, ye waiters by the sepulchre, what can be said to you? We could almost extinguish our own home-fires, that seem too bright when we think of your darkness; the laugh dies on our lip, the lamp burns dim through our tears, and we seem scarcely worthy to speak words of comfort, lest we seem as those who mock a grief they cannot know.

But is there no consolation? Is it nothing to have had such a treasure to give, and to have given it freely for the noblest cause for which ever battle was set,—for the salvation of your country, for the freedom of all mankind? Had he died a fruitless death, in the track of common life, blasted by fever, smitten or rent by crushing accident, then might his most precious life seem to be as water spilled upon the ground; but now it has been given for a cause and a purpose worthy even the anguish of your loss and sacrifice. He has been counted worthy to be numbered with those who stood with precious incense between the living and the dead, that the plague which was consuming us might be stayed. The blood of these young martyrs shall be the seed of the future church of liberty, and from every drop shall spring up flowers of healing. O widow! O mother! Blessed among bereaved women! There remains to you a treasure that belongs not to those who have lost in any other wise,—the power to say, "He died for his country." In all the good that comes of this anguish you shall have a right and share by virtue of this sacrifice. The joy of freedmen bursting from chains, the glory of a nation new-born, the assurance of a triumphant future for your country and the world,—all these become yours by the purchase-money of that precious blood.

Besides this, there are other treasures that come through sorrow, and sorrow alone. There are celestial plants of root so long and so deep that the land must be torn and furrowed, ploughed up from the very foundation, before they can strike and flourish; and when we see how God's plough is driving backward and forward and across this nation, rending, tearing up tender shoots, and burying soft wild-flowers, we ask ourselves, What is He going to plant?

Not the first year, nor the second, after the ground has been broken up, does the purpose of the husbandman appear. At first we see only what is uprooted and ploughed in,—the daisy drabbled, and the violet crushed,—and the first trees planted amid the unsightly furrows stand dumb and disconsolate, irresolute in leaf, and without flower or fruit. Their work is under the ground. In darkness and silence they are putting forth long fibers, searching hither and thither under the black soil for the strength that years hence shall burst into bloom and bearing.

What is true of nations is true of individuals. It may seem now winter and desolation with you. Your hearts have been ploughed and harrowed and are now frozen up. There is not a flower left, not a blade of grass, not a bird to sing,—and it is hard to believe that any brighter flowers, any greener herbage, shall spring up, than those which have been torn away: and yet there will. Nature herself teaches you today. Out-doors nothing but bare branches and shrouding snow; and yet you know that there is not a tree that is not patiently holding out at the end of its boughs next year's buds, frozen indeed, but unkilled. The rhododendron and the lilac have their blossoms all ready, wrapped in cere-cloth, waiting in patient faith. Under the frozen ground the crocus and the hyacinth and the tulip hide in their hearts the perfect forms of future flowers. And it is even so with you: your leaf-buds of the future are frozen, but not killed; the soil of your heart has many flowers under it cold and still now, but they will yet come up and bloom.

The dear old book of comfort tells of no present healing for sorrow. No chastening for the present seemeth joyous, but grievous, but *afterwards* it yieldeth peaceable fruits of righteousness. We, as individuals, as a nation, need to have faith in that AFTERWARDS. It is sure to come,—sure as spring and summer to follow winter.

There is a certain amount of suffering which must follow the rending of the great chords of life, suffering which is natural and inevitable; it cannot be argued down; it cannot be stilled; it can no more be soothed by any effort of faith and reason than the pain of a fractured limb, or the agony of fire on the living flesh. All that we can do is to brace ourselves to bear it, calling on God, as the martyrs did in the fire, and resigning ourselves to let it burn on. We must be willing to suffer, since God so wills. There are just so many waves to go over us, just so many arrows of stinging thought to be shot into our soul, just so many faintings and sinkings and revivings only to suffer again, belonging to and inherent in our portion of sorrow; and there is a work of healing that God has placed in the bands of Time alone.

Time heals all things at last; yet it depends much on us in our suffering, whether time shall send us forth healed, indeed, but maimed and crippled and callous, or whether, looking to the great Physician of sorrows, and coworking with him, we come forth stronger and fairer even for our wounds.

We call ourselves a Christian people, and the peculiarity of Christianity is that it is a worship and doctrine of sorrow. The five wounds of Jesus, the instruments of the passion, the cross, the sepulchre,—these are its emblems and watchwords. In thousands of churches, amid gold and gems and altars fragrant with perfume, are seen the crown of thorns, the nails, the spear, the cup of vinegar mingled with gall, the sponge that could not slake that burning death-thirst; and in a voice choked with anguish the Church in many lands and divers tongues prays from age to age,—"By thine agony and bloody sweat, by thy cross and passion, by thy precious death and burial!"—mighty words of comfort, whose meaning reveals itself only to souls fainting in the cold death-sweat of mortal anguish! They tell all Christians that by uttermost distress alone was the Captain of their salvation made perfect as a Saviour.

Sorrow brings us into the true unity of the Church,—that unity which underlies all external creeds, and unites all hearts that have suffered deeply enough to know that when sorrow is at its utmost there is but one kind of sorrow, and but one remedy. What matter, *in extremis*, whether we be called Romanist, or Protestant, or Greek, or Calvinist?

We suffer, and Christ suffered; we die, and Christ died; he conquered suffering and death, he rose and lives and reigns,—and we shall conquer, rise, live, and reign; the hours on the cross were long, the thirst was bitter, the darkness and horror real,—*but they ended.* After the wail, "My God, why hast thou forsaken me?" came the calm, "It is finished"; pledge to us all that our "It is finished" shall come also.

Christ arose, fresh, joyous, no more to die; and it is written, that, when the disciples were gathered together in fear and sorrow, he stood in the midst of them, and showed unto them his hands and his side; and then were they glad. Already had the healed wounds of Jesus become pledges of consolation to innumerable thousands; and those who, like Christ, have suffered the weary struggles, the dim horrors of the cross,—who have lain, like him, cold and chilled in the hopeless sepulchre,—if his spirit wakes them to life, shall come forth with healing power for others who have suffered and are suffering.

Count the good and beautiful ministrations that have been wrought in this world of need and labor, and how many of them have been wrought by hands wounded and scarred, by hearts that had scarcely ceased to bleed!

How many priests of consolation is God now ordaining by the fiery imposition of sorrow! How many Sisters of the Bleeding Heart, Daughters of Mercy, Sisters of Charity, are receiving their first vocation in tears and blood!

The report of every battle strikes into some home; and heads fall low, and hearts are shattered, and only God sees the joy that is set before them, and that shall come out of their sorrow. He sees our morning at the same moment that He sees our night,—sees us comforted, healed, risen to a higher life, at the same moment that He sees us crushed and broken in the dust; and so, though tenderer than we, He bears our great sorrows for the joy that is set before us.

After the Napoleonic wars had desolated Europe, the country was, like all countries after war, full of shattered households, of widows and orphans and homeless wanderers. A nobleman of Silesia, the Baron von Kottwitz, who had lost his wife and all his family in the reverses and sorrows of the times, found himself alone in the world, which looked more dreary and miserable through the multiplying lenses of his own tears. But he was one of those whose heart had been quickened in its death anguish by the resurrection voice of Christ; and he came forth to life and comfort. He bravely resolved to do all that one man could to lessen the great sum of misery. He sold his estates in Silesia, bought in Berlin a large building that had been used as barracks for the soldiers, and, fitting it up in plain, commodious apartments, formed there a great family-establishment, into which he received the wrecks and fragments of families that had been broken up by the war,—orphan children, widowed and helpless women, decrepit old people, disabled soldiers. These he made his family, and constituted himself their father and chief. He abode with them, and cared for them as a parent. He had schools for the children; the more advanced he put to trades and employments; he set up a hospital for the sick; and for all he had the priestly ministrations of his own Christ-like heart. The celebrated Professor Tholuck,[1] one of the most learned men of modern Germany, was an early *protégé* of the old Baron's, who, discerning his talents, put him in the way of a liberal education. In his earlier years, like many others of the young who play with life, ignorant of its needs, Tholuck piqued himself on a lordly skepticism with regard to the commonly received Christianity, and even wrote an essay to prove the superiority of the Mohammedan to the Christian religion. In speaking of his conversion, he says,—"What moved me was no argument, nor any spoken reproof, but simply that divine image of the old Baron walking before my soul. That life was an argument always present to me, and which I never could answer; and so I became a Christian." In the life of this man we see the victory over sorrow. How many with means like his, when desolated by like bereavements, have lain coldly and idly gazing on the miseries of life, and weaving around themselves icy tissues of doubt and despair,—doubting the being of a God, doubting the reality of a Providence, doubting the divine love, embittered and rebellious against the power which they could not resist, yet to which they would not submit! In such a chill heart-freeze lies the danger of sorrow. And it is a mortal danger. It is a torpor that must be resisted, as the man in the whirling snows must bestir himself, or he will perish. The apathy of melancholy must be broken by an effort of religion and duty. The stagnant blood must be made to flow by active work, and the cold hand warmed by clasping the hands outstretched towards it in sympathy or supplication. One orphan child taken in, to be fed, clothed, and nurtured, may save a heart from freezing to death: and God knows this war is making but too many orphans!

It is easy to subscribe to an orphan asylum, and go on in one's despair and loneliness. Such ministries may do good to the children who are thereby saved from the street, but they impart little warmth and comfort to the giver. One destitute child housed, taught, cared for, and tended personally, will bring more solace to a suffering heart than a dozen maintained in an asylum. Not that the child will probably prove an angel, or even an uncommonly interesting mortal. It is a prosaic work, this bringing-up of children, and there can be little rosewater in it. The child may not appreciate what is done for him, may not be particularly grateful, may have disagreeable faults, and continue to have them after much pains on your part to eradicate them,—and yet it is a fact, that to redeem one human being from destitution and ruin, even in some homely every-day course of ministrations, is one of the best possible tonics and alteratives to a sick and wounded spirit.

But this is not the only avenue to beneficence which the war opens. We need but name the service of hospitals, the care and education of the freedmen,—for these are charities that have long been before the eyes of the community, and have employed thousands of busy hands: thousands of sick and dying beds to tend, a race to be educated, civilized, and Christianized, surely were work enough for one age; and yet this is not all. War shatters everything, and it is hard to say what in society will not need rebuilding and binding up and strengthening anew. Not the least of the evils of war are the vices which a great army engenders wherever it moves,—vices peculiar to military life, as others are peculiar to peace. The poor soldier perils for us not merely his body, but his soul. He leads a life of harassing and exhausting toil and privation, of violent strain on the nervous energies, alternating with sudden collapse, creating a craving for stimulants, and endangering the formation of fatal habits. What furies and harpies are those that follow the army, and that seek out the soldier in his tent, far from home, mother, wife, and sister, tired, disheartened, and tempt him to forget his troubles in a momentary exhilaration, that burns only to chill and to destroy! Evil angels are always active and indefatigable, and there must he good angels enlisted to face them; and here is employment for the slack hand of grief. Ah, we have known mothers bereft of sons in this war, who have seemed at once to open wide their hearts, and to become mothers to every brave soldier in the field. They have lived only to work,—and in place of one lost, their sons have been counted by thousands.

And not least of all the fields for exertion and Christian charity opened by this war is that presented by womanhood. The war is abstracting from the community its protecting and sheltering elements, and leaving the helpless and dependent in vast disproportion. For years to come, the average of lone women will be largely increased; and the demand, always great, for some means by which they may provide for themselves, in the rude jostle of the world, will become more urgent and imperative.

Will any one sit pining away in inert grief, when two streets off are the midnight dance-houses, where girls of twelve, thirteen, and fourteen are being lured into the way of swift destruction? How many of these are daughters of soldiers who have given their hearts' blood for us and our liberties!

Two noble women of the Society of Friends have lately been taking the gauge of suffering and misery in our land, visiting the hospitals at every accessible point, pausing in our great cities, and going in their purity to those midnight orgies where mere children are being trained for a life of vice and infamy. They have talked with these poor bewildered souls, entangled in toils as terrible and inexorable as those of the slave-market, and many of whom are frightened and distressed at the life they are beginning to lead, and earnestly looking for the means of escape. In the judgment of these holy women, at least one third of those with whom they have talked are children so recently entrapped, and so capable of reformation, that there would be the greatest hope in efforts for their salvation. While such things are to be done in our land, is there any reason why any one should die of grief? One soul redeemed will do more to lift the burden of sorrow than all the blandishments and diversions of art, all the alleviations of luxury, all the sympathy of friends.

In the Roman Catholic Church there is an order of women called the Sisters of the Good Shepherd, who have renounced the world to devote themselves, their talents and property, entirely to the work of seeking out and saving the fallen of their own sex; and the wonders worked by their self-denying love on the hearts and lives of even the most depraved are credible only to those who know that the Good Shepherd Himself ever lives and works with such spirits engaged in such a work. A similar order of women exists in New York, under the direction of the Episcopal Church, in connection with St. Luke's Hospital; and another in England, who tend the "House of Mercy" of Clewer.

Such benevolent associations offer objects of interest to that class which most needs something to fill the void made by bereavement. The wounds of grief are less apt to find a cure in that rank of life where the sufferer has wealth and leisure. The *poor* widow, whose husband was her all, *must* break the paralysis of grief. The hard necessities of life are her physicians; they send her out to unwelcome, yet friendly toil, which, hard as it seems, has yet its healing power. But the sufferer surrounded by the appliances of wealth and luxury may long indulge the baleful apathy, and remain in the damp shadows of the valley of death till strength and health are irrecoverably lost. How Christ-like is the thought of a woman, graceful, elegant, cultivated, refined, whose voice has been trained to melody, whose fingers can make sweet harmony with every touch, whose pencil and whose needle can awake the beautiful creations of art, devoting all these powers to the work of charming back to the sheepfold those wandering and bewildered lambs whom the Good Shepherd still calls his own! Jenny Lind, once, when she sang at a concert for destitute children, exclaimed in her enthusiasm, "Is it not beautiful that I can sing so?"[2] And so may not every woman feel, when her graces and accomplishments draw the wanderer, and charm away evil demons, and soothe the sore and sickened spirit, and make the Christian fold more attractive than the dizzy gardens of false pleasure?

In such associations, and others of kindred nature, how many of the stricken and bereaved women of our country might find at once a home and an object in life! Motherless hearts might be made glad in a better and higher motherhood; and the stock of earthly life that seemed cut off at the root, and dead past recovery, may be grafted upon with a shoot from the tree of life which is in the Paradise of God.

So the beginning of this eventful 1865, which finds us still treading the wine-press of our great conflict, should bring with it a serene and solemn hope, a joy such as those had with whom in the midst of the fiery furnace there walked one like unto the Son of God.

The great affliction that has come upon our country is so evidently the purifying chastening of a Father, rather than the avenging anger of a Destroyer, that all hearts may submit themselves in a solemn and holy calm still to bear the burning that shall make us clean from dross and bring us forth to a higher national life. Never, in the whole course of our history, have such teachings of the pure abstract Right been so commended and forced upon us by Providence. Never have public men been so constrained to humble themselves before God, and to acknowledge that there is a Judge that ruleth in the earth. Verily His inquisition for blood has been strict and awful; and for every stricken household of the poor and lowly, hundreds of households of the oppressor have been scattered. The land where the family of the slave was first annihilated, and the negro, with all the loves and hopes of a man, was proclaimed to be a beast to be bred and sold in market with the horse and the swine,—that land, with its fair name, Virginia, has been made a desolation so signal, so wonderful, that the blindest passer-by cannot but ask for what sin so awful a doom has been meted out. The prophetic visions of Nat Turner, who saw the leaves drop blood and the land darkened, have been fulfilled.[3] The work of justice which he predicted is being executed to the uttermost.

But when this strange work of judgment and justice is consummated, when our country, through a thousand battles and ten thousands of precious deaths, shall have come forth from this long agony, redeemed and regenerated, then God Himself shall return and dwell with us, and the Lord God shall wipe away all tears from all faces, and the rebuke of His people shall He utterly take away.

Nathaniel Hawthorne

CHIEFLY ABOUT WAR-MATTERS:
BY A PEACEABLE MAN
(July 1862)

This article appeared in the "Atlantic Monthly" for July 1862, and is now first reprinted among Hawthorne's collected writings. The editor of the magazine objected to sundry paragraphs in the manuscript, and these were cancelled with the consent of the author, who himself supplied all the foot-notes that accompanied the article when it was published. It has seemed best to retain them in the present reproduction. One of the suppressed passages, in which President Lincoln is described, has since been printed, and is therefore restored to its proper place in the following pages.—G. P. L.

There is no remoteness of life and thought, no hermetically sealed seclusion, except, possibly, that of the grave, into which the disturbing influences of this war do not penetrate. Of course, the general heart-quake of the country long ago knocked at my cottage-door, and compelled me, reluctantly, to suspend the contemplation of certain fantasies, to which, according to my harmless custom, I was endeavoring to give a sufficiently life-like aspect to admit of their figuring in a romance. As I make no pretensions to state-craft or soldier-ship, and could promote the common weal neither by valor nor counsel, it seemed, at first, a pity that I should be debarred from such unsubstantial business as I had contrived for myself, since nothing more genuine was to be substituted for it. But I magnanimously considered that there is a kind of treason in insulating one's self from the universal fear and sorrow, and thinking one's idle thoughts in the dread time of civil war; and could a man be so cold and hard-hearted he would better deserve to be sent to Fort Warren[4] than many who have found their way thither on the score of violent, but misdirected sympathies. I remembered the touching rebuke administered by King Charles to that rural squire the echo of whose hunting-horn came to the poor monarch's ear on the morning before a battle, where the sovereignty and constitution of England were to be set at a stake. So I gave myself up to reading newspapers and listening to the click of the telegraph, like other people; until, after a great many months of such pastime, it grew so abominably irksome that I determined to look a little more closely at matters with my own eyes.

Accordingly we set out—a friend and myself—towards Washington, while it was still the long, dreary January of our Northern year, though March in name; nor were we unwilling to clip a little margin off the five months' winter, during which there is nothing genial in New England save the fireside. It was a clear, frosty morning, when we started. The sun shone brightly on snow-covered hills in the neighborhood of Boston, and burnished the surface of frozen ponds; and the wintry weather kept along with us while we trundled through Worcester and Springfield, and all those old, familiar towns, and through the village-cities of Connecticut. In New York the streets were afloat with liquid mud and slosh.

Over New Jersey there was still a thin covering of snow, with the face of Nature visible through the rents in her white shroud, though with little or no symptom of reviving life. But when we reached Philadelphia, the air was mild and balmy; there was but a patch or two of dingy winter here and there, and the bare, brown fields about the city were ready to be green. We had met the Spring half-way, in her slow progress from the South; and if we kept onward at the same pace, and could get through the Rebel lines, we should soon come to fresh grass, fruit-blossoms, green peas, strawberries, and all such delights of early summer.

On our way, we heard many rumors of the war, but saw few signs of it. The people were staid and decorous, according to their ordinary fashion; and business seemed about as brisk as usual,—though, I suppose, it was considerably diverted from its customary channels into warlike ones. In the cities, especially in New York, there was a rather prominent display of military goods at the shop windows,—such as swords with gilded scabbards and trappings, epaulets, carbines, revolvers, and sometimes a great iron cannon at the edge of the pavement, as if Mars had dropped one of his pocket-pistols there, while hurrying to the field. As railway-companions, we had now and then a volunteer in his French-gray great-coat, returning from furlough, or a new-made officer traveling to join his regiment, in his new-made uniform, which was perhaps all of the military character that he had about him,—but proud of his eagle-buttons, and likely enough to do them honor before the gilt should be wholly dimmed. The country, in short, so far as bustle and movement went, was more quiet than in ordinary times, because so large a proportion of its restless elements had been drawn towards the seat of the conflict. But the air was full of a vague disturbance. To me, at least, it seemed so, emerging from such a solitude as has been hinted at, and the more impressible by rumors and indefinable presentiments, since I had not lived, like other men, in an atmosphere of continual talk about the war. A battle was momentarily expected on the Potomac; for, though our army was still on the hither side of the river, all of us were looking towards the mysterious and terrible Manassas, with the idea that somewhere in its neighborhood lay a ghastly battlefield, yet to be fought, but foredoomed of old to be bloodier than the one where we had reaped such shame. Of all haunted places, methinks such a destined field should be thickest thronged with ugly phantoms, ominous of mischief through ages beforehand.

Beyond Philadelphia there was a much greater abundance of military people. Between Baltimore and Washington a guard seemed to hold every station along the railroad; and frequently, on the hill-sides, we saw a collection of weather-beaten tents, the peaks of which, blackened with smoke, indicated that they had been made comfortable by stove-heat throughout the winter. At several commanding positions we saw fortifications, with the muzzles of cannon protruding from the ramparts, the slopes of which were made of the yellow earth of that region, and still unsodded; whereas, till these troublous times, there have been no forts but what were grass-grown with the lapse of at least a lifetime of peace. Our stopping-places were thronged with soldiers, some of whom came through the cars asking for newspapers that contained accounts of the battle between the Merrimack and Monitor, which had been fought the day before. A railway-train met us, conveying a regiment out of Washington to some unknown point; and reaching the capital, we filed out of the station between lines of soldiers, with shouldered muskets, putting us in mind of similar spectacles at the gates of European cities. It was not without sorrow that we saw the free circulation of the nation's life-blood (at the very heart, moreover) clogged with such strictures as these, which have caused chronic diseases in almost all countries save our own. Will the time ever come again, in America, when we may live half a score of years without once seeing the likeness of a soldier, except it be in the festal march of a company on its summer tour? Not in this generation, I fear, nor in the next, nor till the Millennium; and even that blessed epoch, as the prophecies seem to intimate, will advance to the sound of the trumpet.

One terrible idea occurs in reference to this matter. Even supposing the war should end to-morrow, and the army melt into the mass of the population within the year, what an incalculable preponderance will there be of military titles and pretensions for at least half a century to come! Every country-neighborhood will have its general or two, its three or four colonels, half a dozen majors, and captains without end,—besides non-commissioned officers and privates, more than the recruiting offices ever knew of,—all with their campaign-stories, which will become the staple of fireside-talk forevermore. Military merit, or rather, since that is not so readily estimated, military notoriety, will be the measure of all claims to civil distinction. One bullet-headed general will succeed another in the Presidential chair; and veterans will hold the offices at home and abroad, and sit in Congress and the state legislatures, and fill all the avenues of public life. And yet I do not speak of this deprecatingly, since, very likely, it may substitute something more real and genuine, instead of the many shams on which men have heretofore founded their claims to public regard; but it behooves civilians to consider their wretched prospects in the future, and assume the military button before it is too late.

We were not in time to see Washington as a camp. On the very day of our arrival sixty thousand men had crossed the Potomac on their march towards Manassas; and almost with their first step into the Virginia mud, the phantasmagory of a countless host and impregnable ramparts, before which they had so long remained quiescent, dissolved quite away. It was as if General McClellan had thrust his sword into a gigantic enemy, and, beholding him suddenly collapse, had discovered to himself and the world that he had merely punctured an enormously swollen bladder. There are instances of a similar character in old romances, where great armies are long kept at bay by the arts of necromancers, who build airy towers and battlements, and muster warriors of terrible aspect, and thus feign a defence of seeming impregnability, until some bolder champion of the besiegers dashes forward to try an encounter with the foremost foeman, and finds him melt away in the death-grapple. With such heroic adventures let the march upon Manassas be hereafter reckoned. The whole business, though connected with the destinies of a nation, takes inevitably a tinge of the ludicrous. The vast preparation of men and warlike material,—the majestic patience and docility with which the people waited through those weary and dreary months,—the martial skill, courage, and caution, with which our movement was ultimately made,—and, at last, the tremendous shock with which we were brought suddenly up against nothing at all! The Southerners show little sense of humor nowadays, but I think they must have meant provoke a laugh at our expense, when they planted those Quaker guns.[5] At all events, no other Rebel artillery has played upon us with such overwhelming effect.

The troops being gone, we had the better leisure and opportunity to look into other matters. It is natural enough to suppose that the centre and heart of Washington is the Capitol; and certainly, in its outward aspect, the world has not many statelier or more

beautiful edifices, nor any, I should suppose, more skilfully adapted to legislative purposes, and to all accompanying needs. But, etc., etc.*

* * * *

We found one man, however, at the Capitol, who was satisfactorily adequate to the
business which brought him thither. In quest of him, we went through halls, galleries, and
corridors, and ascended a noble staircase, balustraded with a dark and beautifully varie-
gated marble from Tennessee, the richness of which is quite a sufficient cause for objecting
to the secession of that State. At last we came to a barrier of pine boards, built right across
the stairs. Knocking at a rough, temporary door, we thrust a card beneath; and in a minute
or two it was opened by a person in his shirt-sleeves, a middle-aged figure, neither tall nor
short, of Teutonic build and aspect, with an ample beard of a ruddy tinge and chestnut
hair. He looked at us, in the first place, with keen and somewhat guarded eyes, as if it were
not his practice to vouchsafe any great warmth of greeting, except upon sure ground of
observation. Soon, however, his look grew kindly and genial (not that it had ever been in
the least degree repulsive, but only reserved), and Leutze[6] allowed us to gaze at the cartoon
of his great fresco, and talked about it unaffectedly, as only a man of true genius can speak
of his own works. Meanwhile the noble design spoke for itself upon the wall. A sketch in
color, which we saw afterwards, helped us to form some distant and flickering notion of
what the picture will be, a few months hence, when these bare outlines, already so rich in
thought and suggestiveness, shall glow with a fire of their own,—a fire which, I truly believe, will consume every other pictorial decoration of the Capitol, or, at least, will compel
us to banish those stiff and respectable productions to some less conspicuous gallery. The
work will be emphatically original and American, embracing characteristics that neither
art nor literature have yet dealt with, and producing new forms of artistic beauty from
the natural features of the Rocky-Mountain region, which Leutze seems to have studied
broadly and minutely. The garb of the hunters and wanderers of those deserts, too, under
his free and natural management is shown as the most picturesque of costumes. But it
would be doing this admirable painter no kind office to overlay his picture with any more
of my colorless and uncertain words; so I shall merely add that it looked full of energy,
hope, progress, irrepressible movement onward, all represented in a momentary pause of
triumph; and it was most cheering to feel its good augury at this dismal time, when our
country might seem to have arrived at such a deadly stand-still.

It was an absolute comfort, indeed, to find Leutze so quietly busy at this great national
work, which is destined to glow for centuries on the walls of the Capitol, if that edifice shall
stand, or must share its fate, if treason shall succeed in subverting it with the Union which
it represents. It was delightful to see him so calmly elaborating his design, while other men
doubted and feared, or hoped treacherously, and whispered to one another that the nation would exist only a little longer, or that, if a remnant still held together, its centre and
seat of government would be far northward and westward of Washington. But the artist
keeps right on, firm of heart and hand, drawing his outlines with an unwavering pencil,
beautifying and idealizing our rude, material life, and thus manifesting that we have an

---

* We omit several paragraphs here, in which the author speaks of some prominent Members of Congress with a
  freedom that seems to have been not unkindly meant, but might be liable to misconstruction. As he admits that he
  never listened to an important debate, we can hardly recognize his qualifications to estimate these gentlemen, in their
  legislative and oratorical capacities.

indefeasible claim to a more enduring national existence. In honest truth, what with the hope-inspiring influence of the design, and what with Leutze's undisturbed evolvement of it, I was exceedingly encouraged, and allowed these cheerful auguries to weigh against a sinister omen that was pointed out to me in another part of the Capitol. The freestone walls of the central edifice are pervaded with great cracks, and threaten to come thundering down, under the immense weight of the iron dome,—an appropriate catastrophe enough, if it should occur on the day when we drop the Southern stars out of our flag.

Everybody seems to be at Washington, and yet there is a singular dearth of imperatively noticeable people there. I question whether there are half a dozen individuals, in all kinds of eminence, at whom a stranger, wearied with the contact of a hundred moderate celebrities, would turn round to snatch a second glance. Secretary Seward, to be sure,—a pale, large-nosed, elderly man, of moderate stature, with a decided originality of gait and aspect, and a cigar in his mouth,—etc., etc.*

* * * *

Of course, there was one other personage, in the class of statesmen, whom I should have been truly mortified to leave Washington without seeing; since (temporarily, at least, and by force of circumstances) he was the man of men. But a private grief had built up a barrier about him, impeding the customary free intercourse of Americans with their chief magistrate; so that I might have come away without a glimpse of his very remarkable physiognomy, save for a semi-official opportunity of which I was glad to take advantage. The fact is, we were invited to annex ourselves, as supernumeraries, to a deputation that was about to wait upon the President, from a Massachusetts whip-factory, with a present of a splendid whip.

Our immediate party consisted only of four or five (including Major Ben Perley Poore,[7] with his notebook and pencil), but we were joined by several other persons, who seemed to have been lounging about the precincts of the White House, under the spacious porch, or within the hall, and who swarmed in with us to take the chances of a presentation. Nine o'clock had been appointed as the time for receiving the deputation, and we were punctual to the moment; but not so the President, who sent us word that he was eating his breakfast, and would come as soon as he could. His appetite, we were glad to think, must have been a pretty fair one; for we waited about half an hour in one of the antechamber, and then were ushered into a reception-room, in one corner of which sat the Secretaries of War and of the Treasury,[8] expecting, like ourselves, the termination of the Presidential breakfast. During this interval there were several new additions to our group, one or two of whom were in a working-garb, so that we formed a very miscellaneous collection of people, mostly unknown to each other, and without any common sponsor, but all with an equal right to look our head-servant in the face.

By and by there was a little stir on the staircase and in the passage-way, and in lounged a tall, loose-jointed figure, of an exaggerated Yankee port and demeanor, whom (as being about the homeliest man I ever saw, yet by no means repulsive or disagreeable) it was impossible not to recognize as Uncle Abe.

---

* We are again compelled to interfere with our friend's license of personal description and criticism. Even Cabinet Ministers (to whom the next few pages of the article wore devoted) had their private immunities, which ought to be conscientiously observed,—unless, indeed, the writer chanced to have some very piquant motives for violating them.

Unquestionably, Western man though he be, and Kentuckian by birth, President Lincoln is the essential representative of all Yankees, and the veritable specimen, physically, of what the world seems determined to regard as our characteristic qualities. It is the strangest and yet the fittest thing in the jumble of human vicissitudes, that he, out of so many millions, unlooked for, unselected by any intelligible process that could be based upon his genuine qualities, unknown to those who chose him, and unsuspected of what endowments may adapt him for his tremendous responsibility, should have found the way open for him to fling his lank personality into the chair of state,—where, I presume, it was his first impulse to throw his legs on the council-table, and tell the Cabinet Ministers a story. There is no describing his lengthy awkwardness, nor the uncouthness of his movement, and yet it seemed as if I had been in the habit of seeing him daily, and had shaken hands with him a thousand times inn some village street; so true was he to the aspect of the pattern American, though with a certain extravagance which, possibly, I exaggerated still further by the delighted eagerness with which I took it in. If put to guess his calling and livelihood, I should have taken him for a country schoolmaster as soon as anything else. He was dressed in a rusty black frock-coat and pantaloons, unbrushed, and worn so faithfully that the suit had adapted itself to the curves and angularities of his figure, and had grown to be an outer skin of the man. He had shabby slippers on his feet. His hair was black, still unmixed with gray, stiff, somewhat bushy, and had apparently been acquainted with neither brush nor comb that morning, after the disarrangement of the pillow; and as to a night-cap, Uncle Abe probably knows nothing of such effeminacies. His complexion is dark and sallow, betokening, I fear, an insalubrious atmosphere around the White House; he has thick black eyebrows and an impending brow; his nose is large, and the lines about his mouth are very strongly defined.

The whole physiognomy is as coarse a one as you would meet anywhere in the length and breadth of the States; but, withal, it is redeemed, illuminated, softened, and brightened by a kindly though serious look out of his eyes, and an expression of homely sagacity, that seems weighted with rich results of village experience. A great deal of native sense; no bookish cultivation, no refinement; honest at heart, and thoroughly so, and yet, in some sort, sly,—at least, endowed with a sort of tact and wisdom that are akin to craft, and would impel him, I think, to take an antagonist in flank rather than to make a bull-run at him right in front. But, on the whole, I like this sallow, queer, sagacious visage, with the homely human sympathies that warmed it; and, for my small share in the matter, would as lief have Uncle Abe for a ruler as any man whom it would have been practicable to put in his place.

Immediately on his entrance the President accosted our member of Congress, who had us in charge, and, with a comical twist of his face, made some jocular remark about the length of his breakfast. He then greeted us all round, not waiting for an introduction, but shaking and squeezing everybody's hand with the utmost cordiality, whether the individual's name was announced to him or not. His manner towards us was wholly without pretence, but yet had a kind of natural dignity, quite sufficient to keep the forwardest of us from clapping him on the shoulder and asking him for a story. A mutual acquaintance being established, our leader took the whip out of its case, and began to read the address of presentation. The whip was an exceedingly long one, its handle wrought in ivory (by some artist in the Massachusetts State Prison, I believe), and ornamented with a medallion of the President, and other equally beautiful devices; and along its whole length there was a succession of golden bands and ferrules. The address was shorter than the whip, but equally well made, consisting chiefly of an explanatory description of these artistic designs, and closing with a hint that the gift was a suggestive and emblematic one, and that the President would recognize the use to which such an instrument should be put.

This suggestion gave Uncle Abe rather a delicate task in his reply, because, slight as the matter seemed, it apparently called for some declaration, or intimation, or faint foreshadowing of policy in reference to the conduct of the war, and the final treatment of the Rebels. But the President's Yankee aptness and not-to-be-caughtness stood him in good stead, and he jerked or wiggled himself out of the dilemma with an uncouth dexterity that was entirely in character; although, without his gesticulation of eye and mouth,—and especially the flourish of the whip, with which he imagined himself touching up a pair of fat horses,—I doubt whether his words would be worth recording, even if I could remember them. The gist of the reply was, that he accepted the whip as an emblem of peace, not punishment; and, this great affair over, we retired out of the presence in high good-humor, only regretting that we could not have seen the President sit down and fold up his legs (which is said to be a most extraordinary spectacle), or have heard him tell one of those delectable stories for which he is so celebrated. A good many of them are afloat upon the common talk of Washington, and are certainly the aptest, pithiest, and funniest little things imaginable; though, to be sure, they smack of the frontier freedom, and would not always bear repetition in a drawing-room, or on the immaculate page of the Atlantic.*

Good Heavens! What liberties have I been taking with one of the potentates of the earth, and the man on whose conduct more important consequences depend than on that of any other historical personage of the century! But with whom is an American citizen entitled to take a liberty, if not with his own chief magistrate? However, lest the above allusions to President Lincoln's little peculiarities (already well known to the country and to the world) should be misinterpreted, I deem it proper to say a word or two in regard to him, of unfeigned respect and measurable confidence. He is evidently a man of keen faculties, and, what is still more to the purpose, of powerful character. As to his integrity, the people have that intuition of it which is never deceived. Before he actually entered upon his great office, and for a considerable time afterwards, there is no reason to suppose that he adequately estimated the gigantic task about to be imposed on him, or, at least, had any distinct idea how it was to be managed; and I presume there may have been more than one veteran politician who proposed to himself to take the power out of President Lincoln's hands into his own, leaving, our honest friend only the public responsibility for the good or ill success of the career. The extremely imperfect development of his statesmanly qualities, at that period, may have justified such designs. But the President is teachable by events, and has now spent a year in a very arduous course of education; he has a flexible mind, capable of much expansion, and convertible towards far loftier studies and activities than those of his early life; and if he came to Washington a back-woods humor-

---

* The above passage relating to President Lincoln was one of those omitted from the article as originally published, and the following note was appended to explain the omission, which had been indicated by a line of points—

We are compelled to omit two or three pages in which the author describes the interview and gives his idea of the personal appearance and deportment of the President. The sketch appears to have been written in a benign spirit and perhaps conveys a not inaccurate impression of its august subject; but it lacks reverence, and it pains us to see a gentleman of ripe age, and who has spent years under the corrective influence of foreign institutions, falling into the characteristic and most ominous fault of Young America.

ist, he has already transformed himself into as good a statesman (to speak moderately) as his prime-minister.

Among other excursions to camps and places of interest in the neighborhood of Washington, we went, one day, to Alexandria. It is a little port on the Potomac, with one or two shabby wharves and docks, resembling those of a fishing-village in New England, and the respectable old brick town rising gently behind. In peaceful times it no doubt bore an aspect of decorous quietude and dullness; but it was now thronged with the Northern soldiery, whose stir and bustle contrasted strikingly with the many closed warehouses, the absence of citizens from their customary haunts, and the lack of any symptom of healthy activity, while army-wagons trundled heavily over the pavements, and sentinels paced the sidewalks, and mounted dragoons dashed to and fro on military errands. I tried to imagine how very disagreeable the presence of a Southern army would be in a sober town of Massachusetts; and the thought considerably lessened my wonder at the cold and shy regards that are cast upon our troops, the gloom, the sullen demeanor, the declared or scarcely hidden sympathy with rebellion, which are so frequent here. It is a strange thing in human life, that the greatest errors both of men and women often spring from their sweetest and most generous qualities; and so, undoubtedly, thousands of warm-hearted, sympathetic, and impulsive persons have joined the Rebels, not from any real zeal for the cause, but because, between two conflicting loyalties, they chose that which necessarily lay nearest the heart. There never existed any other government against which treason was so easy, and could defend itself by such plausible arguments, as against that of the United States. The anomaly of two allegiances (of which that of the State comes nearest home to a man's feelings, and includes the altar and the hearth, while the General Government claims his devotion only to an airy mode of law, and has no symbol but a flag) is exceedingly mischievous in this point of view; for it has converted crowds of honest people into traitors, who seem to themselves not merely innocent, but patriotic, and who die for a bad cause with as quiet a conscience as if it were the best. In the vast extent of our country,—too vast by far to be taken into one small human heart,—we inevitably limit to our own State, or, at farthest, to our own section, that sentiment of physical love for the soil which renders an Englishman, for example, so intensely sensitive to the dignity and well-being of his little island, that one hostile foot, treading anywhere upon it, would make a bruise on each individual breast. If a man loves his own State, therefore, and is content to be ruined with her, let us shoot him, if we can, but allow him an honorable burial in the soil he fights for.*

In Alexandria, we visited the tavern in which Colonel Ellsworth was killed, and saw the spot where he fell, and the stairs below, whence Jackson fired the fatal shot, and where he himself was slain a moment afterwards; so that the assassin and his victim must have met on the threshold of the spirit-world, and perhaps came to a better understanding before they had taken many steps on the other side. Ellsworth was too generous to bear an immortal grudge for a deed like that, done in hot blood, and by no skulking enemy. The memorial-hunters have completely cut away the original wood-work around the spot, with their pocket-knives; and the staircase, balustrade, and floor, as well as the adjacent doors and door-frames, have recently been renewed; the walls, moreover, are covered with

---

* We do not thoroughly comprehend the author's drift in the foregoing paragraph, but are inclined to think its tone reprehensible, and its tendency impolitic in the present stage of our national difficulties.

new paper-hangings, the former having been torn off in tatters; and thus it becomes something like a metaphysical question whether the place of the murder actually exists.

Driving out of Alexandria, we stopped on the edge of the city to inspect an old slave-pen, which is one of the lions of the place, but a very poor one; and a little farther on, we came to a brick church where Washington used sometimes to attend service,—a pre-Revolutionary edifice, with ivy growing over its walls, though not very luxuriantly. Reaching the open country, we saw forts and camps on all sides; some of the tents being placed immediately on the ground, while others were raised over a basement of logs, laid lengthwise, like those of a log-hut, or driven vertically into the soil in a circle,—thus forming a solid wall, the chinks closed up with Virginia mud, and above it the pyramidal shelter of the tent. Here were in progress all the occupations, and all the idleness, of the soldier in the tented field; some were cooking the company-rations in pots hung over fires in the open air; some played at ball, or developed their muscular power by gymnastic exercise; some read newspapers; some smoked cigars or pipes; and many were cleaning their arms and accoutrements,—the more carefully, perhaps, because their division was to be reviewed by the Commander-in-Chief that afternoon; others sat on the ground, while their comrades cut their hair,—it being a soldierly fashion (and for excellent reasons) to crop it within an inch of the skull; others, finally, lay asleep in breast-high high tents, with their legs protruding into the open air.

We paid a visit to Fort Ellsworth,[9] and from its ramparts (which have been heaped up out of the muddy soil within the last few months, and will require still a year or two to make them verdant) we had a beautiful view of the Potomac, a truly majestic river, and the surrounding country. The fortifications, so numerous in all this region, and now so unsightly with their bare, precipitous sides, will remain as historic monuments, grass-grown and picturesque memorials of an epoch of terror and suffering: they will serve to make our country dearer and more interesting to us, and afford fit soil for poetry to root itself in: for this is a plant which thrives best in spots where blood has been spilt long ago, and grows in abundant clusters in old ditches, such as the moat around Fort Ellsworth will be a century hence. It may seem to be paying dear for what many will reckon but a worthless weed; but the more historical associations we can link with our localities, the richer will be the daily life that feeds upon the past, and the more valuable the things that have been long established: so that our children will be less prodigal than their fathers in sacrificing good institutions to passionate impulses and impracticable theories. This herb of grace, let us hope, may be found in the old footprints of the war.

Even in an aesthetic point of view, however, the war has done a great deal of enduring mischief, by causing the devastation of great tracts of woodland scenery, in which this part of Virginia would appear to have been very rich. Around all the encampments, and everywhere along the road, we saw the bare sites of what had evidently been tracts of hardwood forest, indicated by the unsightly stumps of well-grown trees, not smoothly felled by regular axe-men, but hacked, haggled, and unevenly amputated, as by a sword, or other miserable tool, in an unskilful hand. Fifty years will not repair this desolation! An army destroys everything before and around it, even to the very grass; for the sites of the encampments are converted into barren esplanades, like those of the squares in French cities, where not a blade of grass is allowed to grow. As to the other symptoms of devastation and obstruction, such as deserted houses, unfenced fields, and a general aspect of nakedness and ruin, I know not how much may be due to a normal lack of neatness in the rural life of

Virginia, which puts a squalid face even upon a prosperous state of things; but undoubtedly the war must have spoilt what was good, and made the bad a great deal worse. The carcasses of horses were scattered along the wayside.

One very pregnant token of a social system thoroughly disturbed was presented by a party of contrabands, escaping out of the mysterious depths of Secessia; and its strangeness consisted in the leisurely delay with which they trudged forward, as dreading no pursuer, and encountering nobody to turn them back. They were unlike the specimens of their race whom we are accustomed to see at the North, and, in my judgment, were far more agreeable. So rudely were they attired,—as if their garb had grown upon them spontaneously,—so picturesquely natural in manners, and wearing such a crust of primeval simplicity (which is quite polished away from the northern black man), that they seemed a kind of creature by themselves, not altogether human, but perhaps quite as good, and akin to the fauns and rustic deities of olden times. I wonder whether I shall excite anybody's wrath by saying this. It is no great matter. At all events, I felt most kindly towards these poor fugitives, but knew not precisely what to wish in their behalf, nor in the least how to help them. For the sake of the manhood which is latent in them, I would not have turned them back; but I should have felt almost as reluctant, on their own account, to hasten them forward to the stranger's land; and I think my prevalent idea was, that, whoever may be benefited by the results of this war, it will not be the present generation of negroes, the childhood of whose race is now gone forever, and who must henceforth fight a hard battle with the world, on very unequal terms. On behalf of my own race, I am glad and can only hope that an inscrutable Providence means good to both parties.

There is an historical circumstance, known to few, that connects the children of the Puritans with these Africans of Virginia in a very singular way. They are our brethren, as being lineal descendants from the Mayflower, the fated womb of which, in her first voyage, sent forth a brood of Pilgrims on Plymouth Rock, and, in a subsequent one, spawned slaves upon the Southern soil,—a monstrous birth, but with which we have an instinctive sense of kindred, and so are stirred by an irresistible impulse to attempt their rescue, even at the cost of blood and ruin. The character of our sacred ship, I fear, may suffer a little by this revelation; but we must let her white progeny offset her dark one,—and two such portents never sprang from an identical source before.[10]

While we drove onward, a young officer on horseback looked earnestly into the carriage, and recognized some faces that he had seen before; so he rode along by our side, and we pestered him with queries and observations, to which he responded more civilly than they deserved. He was on General McClellan's staff, and a gallant cavalier, high-booted, with a revolver in his belt, and mounted on a noble horse, which trotted hard and high without disturbing the rider in his accustomed seat. His face had a healthy hue of exposure and an expression of careless hardihood; and, as I looked at him, it seemed to me that the war had brought good fortune to the youth of this epoch, if to none beside; since they now make it their daily business to ride a horse and handle a sword, instead of lounging listlessly through the duties, occupations, pleasures—all tedious alike—to which the artificial state of society limits a peaceful generation. The atmosphere of the camp and the smoke of the battlefield are morally invigorating; the hardy virtues flourish in them, the nonsense dies like a wilted weed. The enervating effects of centuries of civilization vanish at once, and leave these young men to enjoy a life of hardship, and the exhilarating sense of danger,—to kill men blamelessly, or to be killed gloriously,—and to be happy in following out their native instincts of destruction, precisely in the spirit of Homer's heroes, only with some considerable change of mode. One touch of Nature makes not only the whole world, but all time, akin. Set men face to face, with weapons in their hands, and they are as ready to slaughter one another now, after playing at peace and good-will for so many years, as in the rudest ages, that never heard of peace-societies, and thought no wine so delicious as what they quaffed from an enemy's skull. Indeed, if the report of a Congressional committee may be trusted, that old-fashioned kind of goblet has again come into use, at the expense of our Northern head-pieces,—a costly drinking-cup to him that furnishes it! Heaven forgive me for seeming to jest upon such a subject!—only, it is so odd, when we measure our advances from barbarism, and find ourselves just here!*

We now approached General McClellan's headquarters, which, at that time, were established at Fairfield Seminary. The edifice was situated on a gentle elevation, amid very agreeable scenery, and, at a distance, looked like a gentleman's seat. Preparations were going forward for reviewing a division of ten or twelve thousand men, the various regiments composing which had begun to array themselves on an extensive plain, where, methought, there was a more convenient place for a battle than is usually found in this broken and difficult country. Two thousand cavalry made a portion of the troops to be reviewed. By and by we saw a pretty numerous troop of mounted officers, who were congregated on a distant part of the plain, and whom we finally ascertained to be the Commander-in-Chief's staff, with McClellan himself at their head. Our party managed to establish itself in a position conveniently close to the General, to whom, moreover, we had the honor of an introduction; and he bowed, on his horseback, with a good deal of dignity and martial courtesy, but no airs nor fuss nor pretension beyond what his character and rank inevitably gave him.

Now, at that juncture, and, in fact, up to the present moment, there was, and is, a most fierce and bitter outcry, and detraction loud and low, against General McClellan, accusing him of sloth, imbecility, cowardice, treasonable purposes, and, in short, utterly denying his ability as a soldier, and questioning his integrity as a man. Nor was this to be wondered at; for when before, in all history, do we find a general in command of half a million of men, and in presence of an enemy inferior in numbers and no better disciplined than his own troops, leaving it still debatable, after the better part of a year, whether he is a soldier or no? The question would seem to answer itself in the very asking. Nevertheless, being most profoundly ignorant of the art of war, like the majority of the General's critics, and, on the other hand, having some considerable impressibility by men's characters, I was glad of the opportunity to look him in the face, and to feel whatever influence might reach me from his sphere. So I stared at him, as the phrase goes, with all the eyes I had; and the reader shall have the benefit of what I saw,—to which he is the more welcome, because, in writing this article, I feel disposed to be singularly frank, and can scarcely restrain myself from telling truths the utterance of which I should get slender thanks for.

The General was dressed in a simple, dark-blue uniform, without epaulets, booted to the knee, and with a cloth cap upon his head; and, at first sight, you might have taken him for a corporal of dragoons, of particularly neat and soldier-like aspect, and in the prime of his age and strength. He is only of middling stature, but his build is very compact and

---

* We hardly expected this outbreak in favor of war from the Peaceable Man: but the justice of our cause makes us all soldiers at heart, however quiet in our outward life. We have heard of twenty Quakers in a single company of a Pennsylvania regiment.

sturdy, with broad shoulders and a look of great physical vigor, which, in fact, he is said to possess,—he and Beauregard having been rivals in that particular, and both distinguished above other men. His complexion is dark and sanguine, with dark hair. He has a strong, bold, soldierly face, full of decision; a Roman nose, by no means a thin prominence, but very thick and firm; and if he follows it (which I should think likely), it may be pretty confidently trusted to guide him aright. His profile would make a more effective likeness than the full face, which, however, is much better in the real man than in any photograph that I have seen. His forehead is not remarkably large, but comes forward at the eyebrows; it is not the brow nor countenance of a prominently intellectual man (not a natural student, I mean, or abstract thinker), but of one whose office it is to handle things practically and to bring about tangible results. His face looked capable of being very stern, but wore, in its repose, when I saw it, an aspect pleasant and dignified; it is not, in its character, an American face, nor an English one. The man on whom he fixes his eye is conscious of him. In his natural disposition, he seems calm and self-possessed, sustaining his great responsibilities cheerfully, without shrinking, or weariness, or spasmodic effort, or damage to his health, but all with quiet, deep-drawn breaths; just as his broad shoulders would bear up a heavy burden without aching beneath it.

After we had had sufficient time to peruse the man (so far as it could be done with one pair of very attentive eyes), the General rode off, followed by his cavalcade, and was lost to sight among the troops. They received him with loud shouts, by the eager uproar of which—now near, now in the centre, now on the outskirts of the division, and now sweeping back towards us in a great volume of sound—we could trace his progress through the ranks. If he is a coward, or a traitor, or a humbug, or anything less than a brave, true, and able man, that mass of intelligent soldiers, whose lives and honor he had in charge, were utterly deceived, and so was this present writer; for they believed in him, and so did I; and had I stood in the ranks, I should have shouted with the lustiest of them. Of course I may be mistaken; my opinion on such a point is worth nothing, although my impression may be worth a little more; neither do I consider the General's antecedents as bearing very decided testimony to his practical soldiership. A thorough knowledge of the science of war seems to be conceded to him; he is allowed to be a good military critic; but all this is possible without his possessing any positive qualities of a great general, just as a literary critic may show the profoundest acquaintance with the principles of epic poetry without being able to produce a single stanza of an epic poem. Nevertheless, I shall not give up my faith in General McClellan's soldiership until he is defeated, nor in his courage and integrity even then.

Another of our excursions was to Harper's Ferry,—the Directors of the Baltimore and Ohio Railroad having kindly invited us to accompany them on the first trip over the newly laid track, after its breaking up by the Rebels. It began to rain, in the early morning, pretty soon after we left Washington, and continued to pour a cataract throughout the day; so that the aspect of the country was dreary, where it would otherwise have been delightful, as we entered among the hill-scenery that is formed by the subsiding swells of the Alleghanies. The latter part of our journey lay along the shore of the Potomac, in its upper course, where the margin of that noble river is bordered by gray, overhanging crags, beneath which—and sometimes right through them—the railroad takes its way. In one place the Rebels had attempted to arrest a train by precipitating an immense mass of rock down upon the track, by the side of which it still lay, deeply imbedded in the ground, and looking as if it might have lain there since the Deluge. The scenery grew even more picturesque as we proceeded, the bluffs becoming very bold in their descent upon the river, which, at Harper's Ferry, presents as striking a vista among the hills as a painter could desire to see. But a beautiful landscape is a luxury, and luxuries are thrown away amid discomfort; and when we alighted into the tenacious mud and almost fathomless puddle, on the hither side of the Ferry (the ultimate point to which the cars proceeded, since the railroad bridge had been destroyed by the Rebels), I cannot remember that any very rapturous emotions were awakened by the scenery.

We paddled and floundered over the ruins of the track, and, scrambling down an embankment, crossed the Potomac by a pontoon-bridge, a thousand feet in length, over the narrow line of which—level with the river, and rising and subsiding with it—General Banks had recently led his whole army, with its ponderous artillery and heavily laden wagons. Yet our own tread made it vibrate. The broken bridge of the railroad was a little below us, and at the base of one of its massive piers, in the rocky bed of the river, lay a locomotive, which the Rebels had precipitated there.

As we passed over, we looked towards the Virginia shore, and beheld the little town of Harper's Ferry, gathered about the base of a round hill and climbing up its steep acclivity; so that it somewhat resembled the Etruscan cities which I have seen among the Apennines, rushing, as it were, down an apparently breakneck height. About midway of the ascent stood a shabby brick church, towards which a difficult path went scrambling up the precipice, indicating, one would say, a very fervent aspiration on the part of the worshippers, unless there was some easier mode of access in another direction. Immediately on the shore of the Potomac, and extending back towards the town, lay the dismal ruins of the United States arsenal and armory, consisting of piles of broken bricks and a waste of shapeless demolition, amid which we saw gun-barrels in heaps of hundreds together. They were the relics of the conflagration, bent with the heat of the fire and rusted with the wintry rain to which they had since been exposed. The brightest sunshine could not have made the scene cheerful, nor have taken away the gloom from the dilapidated town; for, besides the natural shabbiness, and decayed, unthrifty look of a Virginian village, it has an inexpressible forlornness resulting from the devastations of war and its occupation by both armies alternately. Yet there would be a less striking contrast between Southern and New-England villages, if the former were as much in the habit of using white paint as we are. It is prodigiously efficacious in putting a bright face upon a bad matter.

There was one small shop, which appeared to have nothing for sale. A single man and one or two boys were all the inhabitants in view, except the Yankee sentinels and soldiers, belonging to Massachusetts regiments, who were scattered about pretty numerously. A guard-house stood on the slope of the hill; and in the level street at its base were the offices of the Provost-Marshal and other military authorities, to whom we forthwith reported ourselves. The Provost-Marshal kindly sent a corporal to guide us to the little building which John Brown seized upon as his fortress, and which, after it was stormed by the United States marines, became his temporary prison. It is an old engine-house, rusty and shabby, like every other work of man's hands in this God-forsaken town, and stands fronting upon the river, only a short distance from the bank, nearly at the point where the pontoon-bridge touches the Virginia shore. In its front wall, on each side of the door, are two or three ragged loop-holes, which John Brown perforated for his defence, knocking out merely a brick or two, so as to give himself and his garrison a sight over their rifles.

Through these orifices the sturdy old man dealt a good deal of deadly mischief among his assailants, until they broke down the door by thrusting against it with a ladder, and tumbled headlong in upon him. I shall not pretend to be an admirer of old John Brown, any farther than sympathy with Whittier's excellent ballad about him may go;[11] nor did I expect ever to shrink so unutterably from any apophthegm [sic] of a sage, whose happy lips have uttered a hundred golden sentences, as from that saying (perhaps falsely attributed to so honored a source), that the death of this blood-stained fanatic has "made the Gallows as venerable as the Cross!" Nobody was ever more justly hanged. He won his martyrdom fairly, and took it firmly. He himself, I am persuaded (such was his natural integrity), would have acknowledged that Virginia had a right to take the life which he had staked and lost; although it would have been better for her, in the hour that is fast coming, if she could generously have forgotten the criminality of his attempt in its enormous folly. On the other hand, any common-sensible man, looking at the matter unsentimentally, must have felt a certain intellectual satisfaction in seeing him hanged, if it were only in requital of his preposterous miscalculation of possibilities.*

But, coolly as I seem to say these things, my Yankee heart stirred triumphantly when I saw the use to which John Brown's fortress and prison-house has now been put. What right have I to complain of any other man's foolish impulses, when I cannot possibly control my own? The engine-house is now a place of confinement for Rebel prisoners.

A Massachusetts soldier stood on guard, but readily permitted our whole party to enter. It was a wretched place. A room of perhaps twenty-five feet square occupied the whole interior of the building, having an iron stove in its centre, whence a rusty funnel ascended towards a hole in the roof, which served the purposes of ventilation, as well as for the exit of smoke. We found ourselves right in the midst of the Rebels, some of whom lay on heaps of straw, asleep, or, at all events, giving no sign of consciousness; others sat in the corners of the room, huddled close together, and staring with a lazy kind of interest at the visitors; two were astride of some planks, playing with the dirtiest pack of cards that I ever happened to see. There was only one figure in the least military among all these twenty prisoners of war,—a man with a dark, intelligent moustached face, wearing a shabby cotton uniform, which he had contrived to arrange with a degree of soldierly smartness, though it had evidently borne the brunt of a very filthy campaign. He stood erect, and talked freely with those who addressed him, telling them his place of residence, the number of his regiment, the circumstances of his capture, and such other particulars as their Northern inquisitiveness prompted them to ask. I liked the manliness of his deportment; he was neither ashamed, nor afraid, nor in the slightest degree sullen, peppery, or contumacious, but bore himself as if whatever animosity he had felt towards his enemies was left upon the battle-field, and would not be resumed till he had again a weapon in his hand.

Neither could I detect a trace of hostile feeling in the countenance, words, or manner of any prisoner there. Almost to a man, they were simple, bumpkin-like fellows, dressed in homespun clothes, with faces singularly vacant of meaning, but sufficiently good-humored a breed of men, in short, such as I did not suppose to exist in this country, although I have seen their like in some other parts of the world. They were peasants, and of a very low order: a class of people with whom our Northern rural population has not a single trait in common. They were exceedingly respectful,—more so than a rustic New-Englander ever

---

* Can it be a son of old Massachusetts who utters this abominable sentiment? For shame.

dreams of being towards anybody, except perhaps his minister; and had they worn any hats, they would probably have been self-constrained to take them off, under the unusual circumstance of being permitted to hold conversation with well-dressed persons. It is my belief that not a single bumpkin of them all (the moustached soldier always excepted) had the remotest comprehension of what they had been fighting for, or how they had deserved to be shut up in that dreary hole; nor, possibly, did they care to inquire into this latter mystery, but took it as a godsend to be suffered to lie here in a heap of unwashed human bodies, well warmed and well foddered to-day, and without the necessity of bothering themselves about the possible hunger and cold of to-morrow. Their dark prison-life may have seemed to them the sunshine of all their lifetime.

There was one poor wretch, a wild-beast of a man, at whom I gazed with greater interest than at his fellows; although I know not that each one of them, in their semi-barbarous moral state, might not have been capable of the same savage impulse that had made this particular individual a horror to all beholders. At the close of some battle or skirmish, a wounded Union soldier had crept on hands and knees to his feet, and besought his assistance,—not dreaming that any creature in human shape, in the Christian land where they had so recently been brethren, could refuse it. But this man (this fit fiend, if you prefer to call him so, though I would not advise it) flung a bitter curse at the poor Northerner, and absolutely trampled the soul out of his body, as he lay writhing beneath his feet. The fellow's face was horribly ugly; but I am not quite sure that I should have noticed it, if I had not known his story. He spoke not a word, and met nobody's eye, but kept staring upward into the smoky vacancy towards the ceiling, where, it might be, he beheld a continual portraiture of his victim's horror-stricken agonies. I rather fancy, however, that his moral sense was yet too torpid to trouble him with such remorseful visions, and that, for his own part, he might have had very agreeable reminiscences of the soldier's death, if other eyes had not been bent reproachfully upon him and warned him that something was amiss. It was this reproach in other men's eyes that made him look aside. He was a wild-beast, as I began with saying,—an unsophisticated wild-beast,—while the rest of us are partially tamed, though still the scent of blood excites some of the savage instincts of our nature. What this wretch needed, in order to make him capable of the degree of mercy and benevolence that exists in us, was simply such a measure of moral and intellectual development as we have received; and, in my mind, the present war is so well justified by no other consideration as by the probability that it will free this class of Southern whites from a thraldom in which they scarcely begin to be responsible beings. So far as the education of the heart is concerned, the negroes have apparently the advantage of them; and as to other schooling, it is practically unattainable by black or white.

Looking round at these poor prisoners, therefore, it struck me as an immense absurdity that they should fancy us their enemies; since, whether we intend it so or no, they have a far greater stake on our success than we can possibly have. For ourselves, the balance of advantages between defeat and triumph may admit of question. For them, all truly valuable things are dependent on our complete success; for thence would come the regeneration of a people,—the removal of a foul scurf that has overgrown their life, and keeps them in a state of disease and decrepitude, one of the chief symptoms of which is, that, the more they suffer and are debased, the more they imagine themselves strong and beautiful. No human effort, on a grand scale, has ever yet resulted according to the purpose of its projectors. The advantages are always incidental. Man's accidents are God's purposes. We miss the good we sought, and do the good we little cared for.*

Our Government evidently knows when and where to lay its finger upon its most available citizens; for, quite unexpectedly, we were joined with some other gentlemen, scarcely less competent than ourselves, in a commission to proceed to Fortress Monroe and examine into things in general. Of course, official propriety compels us to be extremely guarded in our description of the interesting objects which this expedition opened to our view. There can be no harm, however, in stating that we were received by the commander of the fortress[12] with a kind of acid good-nature, or mild cynicism, that indicated him to be a humorist, characterized by certain rather pungent peculiarities, yet of no unamiable cast. He is a small, thin old gentleman, set off by a large pair of brilliant epaulets,—the only pair, so far as my observation went, that adorn the shoulders of any officer in the Union army. Either for our inspection, or because the matter had already been arranged, he drew out a regiment of Zouaves that formed the principal part of his garrison, and appeared at their head, sitting on horseback with rigid perpendicularity, and affording us a vivid idea of the disciplinarian of Baron Steuben's school.[13]

There can be no question of the General's military qualities; he must have been especially useful in converting raw recruits into trained and efficient soldiers. But valor and martial skill are of so evanescent a character (hardly less fleeting than a woman's beauty), that Government has perhaps taken the safer course in assigning to this gallant officer, though distinguished in former wars, no more active duty than the guardianship of an apparently impregnable fortress. The ideas of military men solidify and fossilize so fast, while military science makes such rapid advances, that even here there might be a difficulty. An active, diversified, and therefore a youthful, ingenuity is required by the quick exigencies of this singular war. Fortress Monroe, for example, in spite of the massive solidity of its ramparts, its broad and deep moat, and all the contrivances of defence that were known at the not very remote epoch of its construction, is now pronounced absolutely incapable of resisting the novel modes of assault which may be brought to bear upon it. It can only be the flexible talent of a young man that will evolve a new efficiency out of its obsolete strength.

It is a pity that old men grow unfit for war, not only by their incapacity for new ideas, but by the peaceful and unadventurous tendencies that gradually possess themselves of the once turbulent disposition, which used to snuff the battle-smoke as its congenial atmosphere. It is a pity; because it would be such an economy of human existence, if time-stricken people (whose value I have the better right to estimate, as reckoning myself one of them) could snatch from their juniors the exclusive privilege of carrying on the war. In case of death upon the battle-field, how unequal would be the comparative sacrifice! On one part, a few unenjoyable years, the little remnant of a life grown torpid; on the many fervent summers of manhood in its spring and prime, with all that they include of possible benefit to mankind. Then, too, a bullet offers such a brief and easy way, such a pretty little orifice, through which the weary spirit might seize the opportunity to be exhaled! If I had the ordering of these matters, fifty should be the tenderest age at which a recruit might

---

* The author seems to imagine that he has compressed a great deal of meaning into these little, hard, dry pellets of aphoristic wisdom. We disagree with him. The counsels of wise and good men are often coincident with the purposes of Providence; and the present war promises to illustrate our remark.

be accepted for training; at fifty-five or sixty, I would consider him eligible for most kinds of military duty and exposure, excluding, that of a forlorn hope, which no soldier should be permitted to volunteer upon, short of the ripe age of seventy. As a general rule, these venerable combatants should have the preference for all dangerous and honorable service in the order of their seniority, with a distinction in favor of those whose infirmities might render their lives less worth the keeping. Methinks there would be no more Bull Runs; a warrior with gout in his toe, or rheumatism in his joints, or with one foot in the grave, would make a sorry fugitive!

On this admirable system, the productive part of the population would be undisturbed even by the bloodiest war; and, best of all, those thousands upon thousands of our Northern girls, whose proper mates will perish in camp-hospitals or on Southern battlefields, would avoid their doom of forlorn old-maidenhood. But, no doubt, the plan will he pooh-poohed down by the War Department; though it could scarcely be more disastrous than the one on which we began the war, when a young army was struck with paralysis through the age of its commander.

The waters around Fortress Monroe were thronged with a gallant array of ships of war and transports, wearing the Union flag,—"Old Glory," as I hear it called in these days.[14] A little withdrawn from our national fleet lay two French frigates, and, in another direction, an English sloop, under that banner which always makes itself visible, like a red portent in the air, wherever there is strife. In pursuance of our official duty (which had no ascertainable limits), we went on board the flag-ship, and were shown over every part of her, and down into her depths, inspecting her gallant crew, her powerful armament, her mighty engines, and her furnaces, where the fires are always kept burning, as well at midnight as at noon, so that it would require only five minutes to put the vessel under full steam. This vigilance has been felt necessary ever since the Merrimack made that terrible dash from Norfolk. Splendid as she is, however, and provided with all but the very latest improvements in naval armament, the Minnesota belongs to a class of vessels that will be built no more, nor ever fight another battle,—being as much a thing, of the past as any of the ships of Queen Elizabeth's time, which grappled with the galleons of the Spanish Armada.

On her quarter-deck, an elderly flag-officer was pacing to and fro, with a self-conscious dignity to which a touch of the gout or rheumatism perhaps contributed a little additional stiffness. He seemed to be a gallant gentleman, but of the old, slow, and pompous school of naval worthies, who have grown up amid rules, forms, and etiquette which were adopted full-blown from the British navy into ours, and are somewhat too cumbrous for the quick spirit of to-day. This order of nautical heroes will probably go down, along with the ships in which they fought valorously and strutted most intolerably. How can an admiral condescend to go to sea in an iron pot? What space and elbow-room can be found for quarter-deck dignity in the cramped lookout of the Monitor, or even in the twenty-feet diameter of her cheese-box? All the pomp and splendor of naval warfare are gone by. Henceforth there must come up a race of enginemen and smoke-blackened cannoneers, who will hammer away at their enemies under the direction of a single pair of eyes; and even heroism—so deadly a gripe is Science laying on our noble possibilities—will become a quality of very minor importance, when its possessor cannot break through the iron crust of his own armament and give the world a glimpse of it.

At no great distance from the Minnesota lay the strangest-looking craft I ever saw. It was a platform of iron, so nearly on a level with the water that the swash of the waves broke over it, under the impulse of a very moderate breeze; and on this platform was raised a circular structure, likewise of iron, and rather broad and capacious, but of no great height. It could not be called a vessel at all; it was a machine,—and I have seen one of somewhat similar appearance employed in cleaning out the docks, or, for lack of a better similitude, it looked like a gigantic rat-trap. It was ugly, questionable, suspicious, evidently mischievous,—nay, I will allow myself to call it devilish; for this was the new war-fiend, destined, along with others of the same breed, to annihilate whole navies and batter down old supremacies. The wooden walls of Old England cease to exist, and a whole history of naval renown reaches its period, now that the Monitor comes smoking into view; while the billows dash over what seems her deck, and storms bury even her turret in green water, as she burrows and snorts along, oftener under the surface than above. The singularity of the object has betrayed me into a more ambitious vein of description than I often indulge; and, after all, I might as well have contented myself with simply saying that she looked very queer.

Going on board, we were surprised at the extent and convenience of her interior accommodations. There is a spacious ward-room, nine or ten feet in height, besides a private cabin for the commander, and sleeping accommodations on an ample scale; the whole well lighted and ventilated, though beneath the surface of the water. Forward, or aft (for it is impossible to tell stem from stern), the crew are relatively quite as well provided for as the officers. It was like finding a palace, with all its conveniences, under the sea. The inaccessibility, the apparent impregnability, of this submerged iron fortress are most satisfactory; the officers and crew get down through a little hole in the deck, hermetically seal themselves, and go below; and until they see fit to reappear, there would seem to be no power given to man whereby they can be brought to light. A storm of cannon-shot damages them no more than a handful of dried peas. We saw the shot-marks made by the great artillery of the Merrimack on the outer casing of the iron tower; they were about the breadth and depth of shallow saucers, almost imperceptible dents, with no corresponding bulge on the interior surface. In fact, the thing looked altogether too safe; though it may not prove quite an agreeable predicament to be thus boxed up in impenetrable iron, with the possibility, one would imagine, of being sent to the bottom of the sea, and, even there, not drowned, but stifled. Nothing, however, can exceed the confidence of the officers in this new craft. It was pleasant to see their benign exultation in her powers of mischief, and the delight with which they exhibited the circumvolutory movement of the tower, the quick thrusting forth of the immense guns to deliver their ponderous missiles, and then the immediate recoil, and the security behind the closed port-holes. Yet even this will not long be the last and most terrible improvement in the science of war. Already we hear of vessels the armament of which is to act entirely beneath the surface of the water; so that, with no other external symptoms than a great bubbling and foaming, and gush of smoke, and belch of smothered thunder out of the yeasty waves, there shall be a deadly fight going on below,—and, by and by, a sucking whirlpool, as one of the ships goes down.

The Monitor was certainly an object of great interest; but on our way to Newport News, whither we next went, we saw a spectacle that affected us with far profounder emotion. It was the sight of the few sticks that are left of the frigate Congress, stranded near the shore,—and still more, the masts of the Cumberland rising midway out of the water, with a tattered rag of a pennant fluttering from one of them. The invisible hull of the latter ship seems to be careened over, so that the three masts stand slantwise; the rigging looks quite unimpaired, except that a few ropes dangle loosely from the yards. The flag (which never was struck, thanks Heaven!) is entirely hidden under the waters of the bay, but is still doubtless waving in its old place, although it floats to and fro with the swell and reflux of the tide, instead of rustling on the breeze. A remnant of the dead crew still man the sunken ship, and sometimes a drowned body floats up to the surface.

That was a noble fight. When was ever a better word spoken than that of Commodore Smith,[15] the father of the commander of the Congress, when he heard that his son's ship was surrendered? "Then Joe's dead!" said he; and so it proved. Nor can any warrior be more certain of enduring renown than the gallant Morris, who fought so well the final battle of the old system of naval warfare, and won glory for his country and himself out of inevitable disaster and defeat. That last gun from the Cumberland, when her deck was half submerged, sounded the requiem of many sinking ships. Then went down all the navies of Europe, and our own, Old Ironsides[16] and all, and Trafalgar and a thousand other fights became only a memory, never to be acted over again; and thus our brave countrymen come last in the long procession of heroic sailors that includes Blake and Nelson, and so many mariners of England, and other mariners as brave as they, whose renown is our native inheritance. There will be other battles, but no more such tests of seamanship and manhood as the battles of the past; and, moreover, the Millennium is certainly approaching, because human strife is to be transferred from the heart and personality of man into cunning contrivances of machinery, which by and by will fight out our wars with only the clank and smash of iron, strewing the field with broken engines, but damaging nobody's little finger except by accident. Such is obviously the tendency of modern improvement. But, in the meanwhile, so long as manhood retains any part of its pristine value, no country can afford to let gallantry like that of Morris and his crew, any more than that of the brave Worden, pass unhonored and unrewarded. If the Government do nothing, let the people take the matter into their own hands, and cities give him swords, gold boxes, festivals of triumph, and, if he needs it, heaps of gold. Let poets brood upon the theme, and make themselves sensible how much of the past and future is contained within its compass, till its spirit shall flash forth in the lightning of a song!

From these various excursions, and a good many others (including one to Manassas), we gained a pretty lively idea of what was going on; but, after all, if compelled to pass a rainy day in the hall and parlors of Willard's Hotel,[17] it proved about as profitably spent as if we had floundered miles of Virginia mud, in quest of interesting matter. This hotel, in fact, may be much more justly called the centre of Washington and the Union than either the Capitol, the White House, or the State Department. Everybody may be seen there. It is the meeting-place of the true representatives of the country,—not such as are chosen blindly and amiss by electors who take a folded ballot from the hand of a local politician, and thrust it into the ballot-box unread, but men who gravitate or are attracted hither by real business, or a native impulse to breathe the intensest atmosphere of the nation's life, or a genuine anxiety to see how this life-and-death struggle is going to deal with us. Nor these only, but all manner of loafers. Never, in any other spot, was there such a miscellany of people. You exchange nods with governors of sovereign States; you elbow illustrious men, and tread on the toes of generals; you hear statesmen and orators speaking in their familiar tones. You are mixed up with office-seekers, wire-pullers, inventors, artists, poets, prosers (including editors, army-correspondents, *attachés* of foreign journals, and long-winded talkers), clerks, diplomatists, mail-contractors, railway-directors, until your own identity is lost among them. Occasionally you talk with a man whom you have never before heard of, and are struck by the brightness of a thought, and fancy that there is more wisdom hidden among the obscure than is anywhere revealed among the famous. You adopt the universal habit of the place, and call for a mint julep, a whiskey-skin, a gin-cocktail, a brandy-smash, or a glass of pure Old Rye; for the conviviality of Washington sets in at an early hour, and, so far as I had an opportunity of observing, never terminates at any hour, and all these drinks are continually in request by almost all these people. A constant atmosphere of cigar-smoke, too, envelops the motley crowd, and forms a sympathetic medium, in which men meet more closely and talk more frankly than in any other kind of air. If legislators would smoke in session, they might speak truer words, and fewer of them, and bring about more valuable results.

It is curious to observe what antiquated figures and costumes sometimes make their appearance at Willard's. You meet elderly men with frilled shirt-fronts, for example, the fashion of which adornment passed away from among the people of this world half a century ago. It is as if one of Stuart's portraits were walking abroad.[18] I see no way of accounting for this, except that the trouble of the times, the impiety of traitors, and the peril of our sacred Union and Constitution have disturbed, in their honored graves, some of the venerable fathers of the country, and summoned them forth to protest against the meditated and half-accomplished sacrilege. If it be so, their wonted fires are not altogether extinguished in their ashes,—in their throats, I might rather say,—for I beheld one of these excellent old men quaffing such a horn of Bourbon whiskey as a toper the present century would be loath to venture upon. But, really, one would be glad to know where these strange figures come from. It shows, at any rate, how many remote, decaying villages and country-neighborhood of the North, and forest-nooks of the West, and old mansion-houses in cities, are shaken by the tremor of our native soil, so that men long hidden in retirement put on the garments of their youth and hurry out to inquire what is the matter. The old men whom we see here have generally more marked faces than the young ones, and naturally enough; since it must be an extraordinary vigor and renewability of life that can overcome the rusty sloth of age, and keep the senior flexible enough to take an interest in new things; whereas hundreds of commonplace young men come hither to stare with eyes of vacant wonder, and with vague hopes of finding out what they are fit for. And this war (we may say so much in its favor) has been the means of discovering that important secret to not a few.

We saw at Willard's many who had thus found out for themselves, that, when Nature gives a young man no other utilizable faculty, she must be understood as intending him for a soldier. The bulk of the army had moved out of Washington before we reached the city; yet it seemed to me that at least two thirds of the guests and idlers at the hotel wore one or another token of the military profession. Many of them, no doubt, were self-commissioned officers, and had put on the buttons and the shoulder-straps, and booted themselves to the knees, merely because captain, in these days, is so good a traveling-name. The majority, however, had been duly appointed by the President, but might be none the better warriors for that. It was pleasant, occasionally, to distinguish veteran among this crowd of carpet-knights,—the trained soldier of a lifetime, long ago from West Point, who had spent his prime upon the frontier, and very likely could show an Indian bullet-mark on his breast,—if such decorations, won in an obscure warfare, were worth the showing now.

The question often occurred to me,—and, to say the truth, it added an indefinable piquancy to the scene,—what proportion of all these people, whether soldiers or civilians, were true at heart to the Union, and what part were tainted, more or less, with treasonable sympathies and wishes, even if such had never blossomed into purpose. Traitors there were among them,—no doubt of that,—civil servants of the public. Very reputable persons, who yet deserved to dangle from a cord; or men who buttoned military coats over their breasts, hiding perilous secrets there, which might bring the gallant officer to stand pale-faced before a file of musketeers, with his open grave behind him. But, without insisting upon such picturesque criminality and punishment as this, an observer, who kept both his eyes and heart open, would find it by no means difficult to discern that many residents and visitors of Washington so far sided with the South as to desire nothing more nor better than to see everything reestablished a little worse than its former basis. If the cabinet of Richmond were transferred to the Federal city, and the North awfully snubbed, at least, and driven back within its old political limits, they would deem it a happy day. It is no wonder, and, if we look at the matter generously, no unpardonable crime. Very excellent people hereabouts remember the many dynasties in which the Southern character has been predominant, and contrast the genial courtesy, the warm and graceful freedom of that region, with what they call (though I utterly disagree with them) the frigidity of our Northern manners, and the Western plainness of the President. They have a conscientious, though mistaken belief, that the South was driven out of the Union by intolerable wrong on our part, and that we are responsible for having compelled true patriots to love only half their country instead of the whole, and brave soldiers to draw their swords against the Constitution which they would once have died for,—to draw them, too, with a bitterness of animosity which is the only symptom of brotherhood (since brothers hate each other best) that any longer exists. They whisper these things with tears in their eyes, and shake their heads, and stoop their poor old shoulders, at the tidings of another and another Northern victory, which, in their opinion, puts farther off the remote, the already impossible, chance of a reunion.

I am sorry for them, though it is by no means a sorrow without hope. Since the matter has gone so far, there seems to be no way but to go on winning victories, and establishing peace and a truer union in another generation, at the expense, probably, of greater trouble, in the present one, than any other people ever voluntarily suffered. We woo the South "as the Lion wooes his bride;" it is a rough courtship, but perhaps love and a quiet household may come of it at last. Or, if we stop short of that blessed consummation, heaven was heaven still, as Milton sings, after Lucifer and a third part of the angels had seceded from its golden palaces,—and perhaps all the more heavenly, because so many gloomy brows, and soured, vindictive hearts, had gone to plot ineffectual schemes of mischief elsewhere.*

---

* We regret the innuendo in the concluding sentence. The war can never be allowed to terminate, except in the complete triumph of Northern principles. We hold the event in our own hands, and may choose whether to terminate it by the methods already so successfully used, or by other means equally within our control, and calculated to be still more speedily efficacious. In truth, the work is already done.

We should be sorry to cast a doubt on the Peaceable Man's loyalty, but he will allow us to say that we consider him premature in his kindly feelings towards traitors and sympathizers with treason. As the author himself says of John Brown (and, so applied, we thought it an atrociously cold-blooded *dictum*), "any common-sensible man would feel an intellectual satisfaction in seeing them hanged, were it only for their preposterous miscalculation of possibilities." There are some degrees of absurdity that put Reason herself into a rage, and affect us like an intolerable crime,—which this Rebellion is, into the bargain.

Julia Ward Howe

OUR ORDERS (1865)

Weave no more silks, ye Lyons looms,[19]
 To deck our girls for gay delights!
The crimson flower of battle blooms,
 And solemn marches fill the nights.

Weave but the flag whose bars to-day
 Drooped heavy o'er our early dead,
And homely garments, coarse and gray,
 For orphans that must earn their bread!

Keep back your tunes, ye viols sweet,
 That poured delight from other lands!
Rouse there the dancer's restless feet:
 The trumpet leads our warrior bands.

And ye that wage the war of words
 With mystic fame and subtle power,
Go, chatter to the idle birds,
 Or teach the lesson of the hour!

Ye Sibyl Arts, in one stern knot
 Be all your offices combined!
Stand close, while Courage draws the lot,
 The destiny of human kind.

And if that destiny could fail,
 The sun should darken in the sky,
The eternal bloom of Nature pale,
 And God, and Truth, and Freedom die!

Lucy Larcom

WEAVING (1869)

All day she stands before her loom;
    The flying shuttles come and go:
By grassy fields, and trees in bloom,
    She sees the winding river flow:
And fancy's shuttle flieth wide,
And faster than the waters glide.

Is she entangled in her dreams,
    Like that fair weaver of Shalott,
Who left her mystic mirror's gleams,
    To gaze on Sir Lancelot?[20]
Her heart, a mirror sadly true,
Brings gloomier visions into view.

"I weave, and weave, the livelong day:
    The woof is strong, the warp is good:
I weave, to be my mother's stay;
    I weave, to win my daily food:
But ever as I weave," saith she,
"The world of women haunteth me.

"The river glides along, one thread
    In nature's mesh, so beautiful!
The stars are woven in; the red
    Of sunrise; and the rain-cloud dull.
Each seems a separate wonder wrought;
Each blends with some more wondrous thought.

"So, at the loom of life, we weave
    Our separate shreds, that varying fall,
Some stained, some fair; and passing, leave
    To God the gathering up of all,
In that full pattern, wherein man
Works blindly out the eternal plan.

"In his vast work, for good or ill,
    The undone and the done he blends:
With whatsoever woof we fill,
    To our weak hands His might He lends,
And gives the threads beneath His eye
The texture of eternity.

"Wind on, by willow and by pine,
     Thou blue, untroubled Merrimack!
Afar, by sunnier streams than thine,
     My sisters toil, with foreheads black;
And water with their blood this root,
Whereof we gather bounteous fruit.

"I think of women sad and poor;
     Women who walk in garments soiled:
Their shame, their sorrow, I endure;
     By their defect my hope is foiled:
The blot they bear is on my name;
Who sins, and I am not to blame?

"And how much of your wrong is mine,
     Dark women slaving at the South?
Of your stolen grapes I quaff the wine;
     The bread you starve for fills my mouth:
The beam unwinds, but every thread
With blood of strangled souls is red.

"If this be so, we win and wear
     A Nessus-robe of poisoned cloth;
Or weave them shrouds they may not wear,—
     Fathers and brothers falling both
On ghastly, death-sown fields, that lie
Beneath the tearless Southern sky.

"Alas! the weft has lost its white.
     It grows a hideous tapestry,
That pictures war's abhorrent sight:
     Unroll not, web of destiny!
Be the dark volume left unread,
The tale untold, the curse unsaid!"

So up and down before her loom
     She paces on, and to and fro,
Till sunset fills the dusty room,
     And makes the water redly glow,
As if the Merrimack's calm flood
Were changed into a stream of blood.

Too soon fulfilled, and all too true
     The words she murmured as she wrought:
But, weary weaver, not to you
     Alone was war's stern message brought:
"Woman!" it knelled from heart to heart,
"Thy sister's keeper know thou art!"

Lucy Larcom

A LOYAL WOMAN'S NO

No! is my answer from this cold, bleak ridge,
    Down to your valley: you may rest you there:
The gulf is wide, and none can build a bridge
    That your gross weight would safely hither bear.

Pity me, if you will. I look at you
    With something that is kinder far than scorn,
And think, "Ah, well! I might have grovelled, too;
    I might have walked there, fettered and forsworn."

I am of nature weak as others are;
    I might have chosen comfortable ways;
Once from these heights I shrank, beheld afar,
    In the soft lap of quiet, easy days.

I might,—I will not hide it,—once I might
    Have lost, in the warm whirlpools of your voice,
The sense of Evil, the stern cry of Right;
    But Truth has steered me free, and I rejoice.

Not with the triumph that looks back to jeer
    At the poor herd that call their misery bliss;
But as a mortal speaks when God is near,
    I drop you down my answer: it is this:

I am not yours, because you prize in me
    What is the lowest in my own esteem:
Only my flowery levels can you see,
    Nor of my heaven-smit summits do you dream.

I am not yours, because you love yourself:
    Your heart has scarcely room for me beside.
I will not be shut in with name and pelf;
    I spurn the shelter of your narrow pride!

Not yours,—because you are not man enough
    To grasp your country's measure of a man.
If such as you, when Freedom's ways are rough,
    Cannot walk in them, learn that women can!

Not yours,—because, in this the nation's need,
　　You stoop to bend her losses to your gain,
And do not feel the meanness of your deed:
　　I touch no palm defiled with such a stain!

Whether man's thought can find too lofty steeps
　　For woman's scaling, care not I to know;
But when he falters by her side, or creeps,
　　She must not clog her soul with him to go.

Who weds me, must at least with equal pace
　　Sometimes move with me at my being's height:
To follow him to his superior place,
　　His rare atmosphere, were keen delight.

You lure me to the valley: men should call
　　Up to the mountains, where the air is clear.
Win me and help me climbing, if at all!
　　Beyond these peaks great harmonies I hear:—

The morning chant of Liberty and Law!
　　The dawn pours in, to wash out Slavery's blot;
Fairer than aught the bright sun ever saw,
　　Rises a Nation without stain or spot!

The men and women mated for that time
　　Tread not the soothing mosses of the plain;
Their hands are joined in sacrifice sublime;
　　Their feet firm set in upward paths of pain.

Sleep your thick sleep, and go your drowsy way!
　　You cannot hear the voices in the air!
Ignoble souls will shrivel in that day;
　　The brightness of its coming can you bear?

For me, I do not walk these hills alone:
　　Heroes who poured their blood out for the truth,
Women whose hearts bled, martyrs all unknown,
　　Here catch the sunrise of an immortal youth

On their pale cheeks and consecrated brows:—
　　It charms me not, your call to rest below.
I press their hands, my lips pronounce their vows:
　　Take my life's silence for your answer: No!

Sarah Morgan Bryan Piatt

GIVING BACK THE FLOWER (1867)

So, because you chose to follow me into the subtle sadness of night,
    And to stand in the half-set moon with the weird fall-light on your
        glimmering hair,
Till your presence hid all of the earth and all of the sky from my sight,
    And to give me a little scarlet bud, that was dying of frost, to wear,

Say, must you taunt me forever, forever? You looked at my hand and you knew
    That I was the slave of the Ring, while you were as free as the wind is free.
When I saw your corpse in the coffin, I flung back your flower to you;
    It was all of yours that I ever had; you may keep it, and—keep from me.

Ah? so God is your witness. Has God, then, no world to look after but ours?
    May He not have been searching for that wild star, with the trailing plumage,
        that flew
Far over a part of our darkness while we were there by the freezing flowers,
    Or else brightening some planet's luminous rings, instead of thinking of you?

Or, if He was near us at all, do you think that He would sit listening there
    Because you sang "Hear me, Norma,"[21] to a woman in jewels and lace,
While, so close to us, down in another street, in the wet, unlighted air,
    There were children crying for bread and fire, and mothers who questioned
        His grace?

Or perhaps He had gone to the ghastly field where the fight had been that day,
    To number the bloody stabs that were there, to look at and judge the dead;
Or else to the place full of fever and moans where the wretched wounded lay;
    At least I do not believe that He cares to remember a word that you said.

So take back your flower, I tell you—of its sweetness I now have no need;
    Yes; take back your flower down into the stillness and mystery to keep;
When you wake I will take it, and God, then, perhaps will witness indeed,
    But go, now, and tell Death he must watch you, and not let you walk
        in your sleep.

Walt Whitman

from *Drum-Taps* (1865)

COME UP FROM THE FIELDS FATHER

Come up from the fields, father, here's a letter from our Pete;
And come to the front door, mother—here's a letter from thy dear son.

Lo, 'tis autumn;
Lo, where the trees, deeper green, yellower and redder,
Cool and sweeten Ohio's villages, with leaves fluttering in the moderate wind;
Where apples ripe in the orchards hang, and grapes on the trellis'd vines;
(Smell you the smell of the grapes on the vines?
Smell you the buckwheat, where the bees were lately buzzing?)

Above all, lo, the sky, so calm, so transparent after the rain, and with
    wondrous clouds;
Below, too, all calm, all vital and beautiful—and the farm prospers well.

Down in the fields all prospers well;
But now from the fields come, father—come at the daughter's call;
And come to the entry, mother—to the front door come, right away.

Fast as she can she hurries—something ominous—her steps trembling;
She does not tarry to smooth her white hair, nor adjust her cap.

Open the envelope quickly;
O this is not our son's writing, yet his name is sign'd;
O a strange hand writes for our dear son—O stricken mother's soul!
All swims before her eyes—flashes with black—she catches the main words only;
Sentences broken—*gun-shot wound in the breast, cavalry skirmish, taken to hospital,*
At present low, but will soon be better.

Ah, now the single figure to me,
Amid all teeming and wealthy Ohio, with all its cities and farms,
Sickly white in the face and dull in the head, very faint,
By the jamb of a door leans.

Grieve not so, dear mother, (the just-grown daughter speaks through her sobs;
The little sisters huddle around, speechless and dismay'd;)
See, dearest mother, the letter says Pete will soon be better.

Alas, poor boy, he will never be better, (nor may-be needs to be better, that brave
    and simple soul;)
While they stand at home at the door, he is dead already;
The only son is dead.

But the mother needs to be better;
She with thin form, presently drest in black;
By day her meals untouch'd—then at night fitfully sleeping, often waking,
In the midnight waking, weeping, longing with one deep longing,
O that she might withdraw unnoticed—silent from life, escape and withdraw,
To follow, to seek, to be with her dear dead son.

Kate Chopin

from *Bayou Folk* (1894)

A WIZARD FROM GETTYSBURG (1892)

It was one afternoon in April, not long ago, only the other day, and the shadows had already begun to lengthen.

Bertrand Delmandé, a fine, bright-looking boy of fourteen years,—fifteen, perhaps,—was mounted, and riding along a pleasant country road, upon a little Creole pony, such as boys in Louisiana usually ride when they have nothing better at hand. He had hunted, and carried his gun before him.

It is unpleasant to state that Bertrand was not so depressed as he should have been, in view of recent events that had come about. Within the past week he had been recalled from the college of Grand Coteau to his home, the Bon-Accueil plantation.

He had found his father and his grandmother depressed over money matters, awaiting certain legal developments that might result in his permanent withdrawal from school. That very day, directly after the early dinner, the two had driven to town, on this very business, to be absent till the late afternoon. Bertrand, then, had saddled Picayune and gone for a long jaunt, such as his heart delighted in.

He was returning now, and had approached the beginning of the great tangled Cherokee hedge that marked the boundary line of Bon-Accueil, and that twinkled with multiple white roses.

The pony started suddenly and violently at something there in the turn of the road, and just under the hedge. It looked like a bundle of rags at first. But it was a tramp, seated upon a broad, flat stone.

Bertrand had no maudlin consideration for tramps as a species; he had only that morning driven from the place one who was making himself unpleasant at the kitchen window.

But this tramp was old and feeble. His beard was long, and as white as new-ginned cotton, and when Bertrand saw him he was engaged in stanching a wound in his bare heel with a fistful of matted grass.

"What's wrong, old man?" asked the boy, kindly.

The tramp looked up at him with a bewildered glance, but did not answer.

"Well," thought Bertrand, "since it's decided that I 'm to be a physician some day, I can't begin to practice too early."

He dismounted, and examined the injured foot. It had an ugly gash. Bertrand acted mostly from impulse. Fortunately his impulses were not bad ones. So, nimbly, and as quickly as he could manage it, he had the old man astride Picayune, whilst he himself was leading the pony down the narrow lane.

The dark green hedge towered like a high and solid wall on one side. On the other was a broad, open field, where here and there appeared the flash and gleam of uplifted, polished hoes, that negroes were plying between the even rows of cotton and tender corn.

"This is the State of Louisiana," uttered the tramp, quaveringly.

"Yes, this is Louisiana," returned Bertrand cheerily.

"Yes, I know it is. I've been in all of them since Gettysburg. Sometimes it was too hot, and sometimes it was too cold; and with that bullet in my head—you don't remember? No, you don't remember Gettysburg."

"Well, no, not vividly," laughed Bertrand.

"Is it a hospital? It isn't a factory, is it?" the man questioned.

"Where we're going? Why, no, it's the Delmandé plantation—Bon-Accueil. Here we are. Wait, I'll open the gate."

This singular group entered the yard from the rear, and not far from the house. A big black woman, who sat just without a cabin door, picking a pile of rusty-looking moss, called out at sight of them:—

"W'at's dat you's bringin' in dis yard, boy? top dat hoss?"

She received no reply. Bertrand, indeed, took no notice of her inquiry.

"Fu' a boy w'at goes to school like you does—whar's yo' sense?" she went on, with a fine show of indignation; then, muttering to herself, "Ma'ame Bertrand an' Marse St. Ange ain't gwine stan' dat, I knows dey ain't. Dah! ef he ain't done sot 'im on de gall'ry, plumb down in his pa's rockin'-cheer!"

Which the boy had done; seated the tramp in a pleasant corner of the veranda, while he went in search of bandages for his wound.

The servants showed high disapproval, the housemaid following Bertrand into his grandmother's room, whither he had carried his investigations.

"W'at you tearin' yo' gra'ma's closit to pieces dat away, boy?" she complained in her high soprano.

"I 'm looking for bandages."

"Den w'y you don't ax fu' ban'ges, an' lef yo' gra'ma's closit 'lone? You want to listen to me; you gwine git shed o' dat tramp settin' dah naxt to de dinin'-room! W'en de silva be missin', 'tain' you w'at gwine git blame, it's me."

"The silver? Nonsense, 'Cindy; the man's wounded, and can't you see he's out of his head?"

"No mo' outen his head 'an I is. 'Tain' me w'at want to tres' [trust] 'im wid de sto'-room key, ef he is outen his head," she concluded with a disdainful shrug.

But Bertrand's protégé proved so unapproachable in his long-worn rags, that the boy concluded to leave him unmolested till his father's return, and then ask permission to turn the forlorn creature into the bath-house, and array him afterward in clean, fresh garments.

So there the old tramp sat in the veranda corner, stolidly content, when St. Ange Delmandé and his mother returned from town.

St. Ange was a dark, slender man of middle age, with a sensitive face, and a plentiful sprinkle of gray in his thick black hair; his mother, a portly woman, and an active one for her sixty-five years.

They were evidently in a despondent mood. Perhaps it was for the cheer of her sweet presence that they had brought with them from town a little girl, the child of Madame Delmandé's only daughter, who was married, and lived there.

Madame Delmandé and her son were astonished to find so uninviting an intruder in possession. But a few earnest words from Bertrand reassured them, and partly reconciled them to the man's presence; and it was with wholly indifferent though not unkindly glances that they passed him by when they entered. On any large plantation there are always nooks and corners where, for a night or more, even such a man as this tramp may be tolerated and given shelter.

When Bertrand went to bed that night, he lay long awake thinking of the man, and of what he had heard from his lips in the hushed starlight. The boy had heard of the awfulness of Gettysburg, till it was like something he could feel and quiver at.

On that field of battle this man had received a new and tragic birth. For all his existence that went before was a blank to him. There, in the black desolation of war, he was born again, without friends or kindred; without even a name he could know was his own. Then he had gone forth a wanderer; living more than half the time in hospitals; toiling when he could, starving when he had to.

Strangely enough, he had addressed Bertrand as "St. Ange," not once, but every time he had spoken to him. The boy wondered at this. Was it because he had heard Madame Delmandé address her son by that name, and fancied it?

So this nameless wanderer had drifted far down to the plantation of Bon-Accueil, and at last had found a human hand stretched out to him in kindness.

When the family assembled at breakfast on the following morning, the tramp was already settled in the chair, and in the corner which Bertrand's indulgence had made familiar to him.

If he had turned partly around, he would have faced the flower garden, with its graveled walks and trim parterres, where a tangle of color and perfume were holding high revelry this April morning; but he liked better to gaze into the back yard, where there was always movement: men and women coming and going, bearing implements of work; little negroes in scanty garments, darting here and there, and kicking up the dust in their exuberance.

Madame Delmandé could just catch a glimpse of him through the long window that opened to the floor, and near which he sat.

Mr. Delmandé had spoken to the man pleasantly; but he and his mother were wholly absorbed by their trouble, and talked constantly of that, while Bertrand went back and forth ministering to the old man's wants. The boy knew that the servants would have done the office with ill grace, and he chose to be cup-bearer himself to the unfortunate creature for whose presence he alone was responsible.

Once, when Bertrand went out to him with a second cup of coffee, steaming and fragrant, the old man whispered:—

"What are they saying in there?" pointing over his shoulder to the dining-room.

"Oh, money troubles that will force us to economize for a while," answered the boy. "What father and *mé-mère* feel worst about is that I shall have to leave college now."

"No, no! St. Ange must go to school. The war's over, the war's over! St. Ange and Florentine must go to school."

"But if there's no money," the boy insisted, smiling like one who humors the vagaries of a child.

"Money! money!" murmured the tramp. "The war's over—money! Money!"

His sleepy gaze had swept across the yard into the thick of the orchard beyond, and rested there.

Suddenly he pushed aside the light table that had been set before him, and rose, clutching Bertrand's arm.

"St. Ange, you must go to school!" he whispered. "The war's over," looking furtively around. "Come. Don't let them hear you. Don't let the negroes see us. Get a spade—the little spade that Buck Williams was digging his cistern with."

Still clutching the boy, he dragged him down the steps as he said this, and traversed the yard with long, limping strides, himself leading the way.

From under a shed where such things were to be found, Bertrand selected a spade, since the tramp's whim demanded that he should, and together they entered the orchard.

The grass was thick and tufted here, and wet with the morning dew. In long lines, forming pleasant avenues between, were peach-trees growing, and pear and apple and plum. Close against the fence was the pomegranate hedge, with its waxen blossoms, brick-red. Far down in the centre of the orchard stood a huge pecan-tree, twice the size of any other that was there, seeming to rule like an old-time king.

Here Bertrand and his guide stopped. The tramp had not once hesitated in his movements since grasping the arm of his young companion on the veranda. Now he went and leaned his back against the pecan-tree, where there was a deep knot, and looking steadily before him he took ten paces forward. Turning sharply to the right, he made five additional paces. Then pointing his finger downward, and looking at Bertrand, he commanded:—

"There, dig. I would do it myself, but for my wounded foot. For I 've turned many a spade of earth since Gettysburg. Dig, St. Ange, dig! The war's over; you must go to school."

Is there a boy of fifteen under the sun who would not have dug, even knowing he was following the insane dictates of a demented man? Bertrand entered with all the zest of his years and his spirit into the curious adventure; and he dug and dug, throwing great spade-fuls of the rich, fragrant earth from side to side.

The tramp, with body bent, and fingers like claws clasping his bony knees, stood watching with eager eyes, that never unfastened their steady gaze from the boy's rhythmic motions.

"That's it!" he muttered at intervals. "Dig, dig! The war's over. You must go to school, St. Ange."

Deep down in the earth, too deep for any ordinary turning of the soil with spade or plow to have reached it, was a box. It was of tin, apparently, something larger than a cigar box, and bound round and round with twine, rotted now and eaten away in places.

The tramp showed no surprise at seeing it there; he simply knelt upon the ground and lifted it from its long resting place.

Bertrand had let the spade fall from his hands, and was quivering with the awe of the thing he saw. Who could this wizard be that had come to him in the guise of a tramp, that walked in cabalistic paces upon his own father's ground, and pointed his finger like a divining-rod to the spot where boxes—may be treasures—lay? It was like a page from a wonder-book.

And walking behind this white-haired old man, who was again leading the way, something of childish superstition crept back into Bertrand's heart. It was the same feeling with which he had often sat, long ago, in the weird firelight of some negro's cabin, listening to tales of witches who came in the night to work uncanny spells at their will.

Madame Delmandé had never abandoned the custom of washing her own silver and dainty china. She sat, when the breakfast was over, with a pail of warm suds before her that 'Cindy had brought to her, with an abundance of soft linen cloths. Her little granddaughter stood beside her playing, as babies will, with the bright spoons and forks, and ranging them in rows on the polished mahogany. St. Ange was at the window making entries in a note-book, and frowning gloomily as he did so.

The group in the dining-room were so employed when the old tramp came staggering in, Bertrand close behind him.

He went and stood at the foot of the table, opposite to where Madame Delmandé sat, and let fall the box upon it.

The thing in falling shattered, and from its bursting sides gold came, clicking, spinning, gliding, some of it like oil; rolling along the table and off it to the floor, but heaped up, the bulk of it, before the tramp.

"Here's money!" he called out, plunging his old hand in the thick of it. "Who says St. Ange shall not go to school? The war's over—here's money! St. Ange, my boy," turning to Bertrand and speaking with quick authority, "Tell Buck Williams to hitch Black Bess to the buggy, and go bring Judge Parkerson here."

Judge Parkerson, indeed, who had been dead for twenty years and more!

"Tell him that—that"—and the hand that was not in the gold went up to the withered forehead, "that—Bertrand Delmandé needs him!"

Madame Delmandé, at sight of the man with his box and his gold, had given a sharp cry, such as might follow the plunge of a knife. She lay now in her son's arms, panting hoarsely.

"Your father, St. Ange,—come back from the dead—your father!"

"Be calm, mother!" the man implored. "You had such sure proof of his death in that terrible battle, this *may* not be he."

"I know him! I know your father, my son!" and disengaging herself from the arms that held her, she dragged herself as a wounded serpent might to where the old man stood.

His hand was still in the gold, and on his face was yet the flush which had come there when he shouted out the name Bertrand Delmandé.

"Husband," she gasped, "do you know me—your wife?"

The little girl was playing gleefully with the yellow coin.

Bertrand stood, pulseless almost, like a young Actæon cut in marble.

When the old man had looked long into the woman's imploring face, he made a courtly bow.

"Madame," he said, "an old soldier, wounded on the field of Gettysburg, craves for himself and his two little children your kind hospitality."

Henry James

THE STORY OF A YEAR
(March 1865)

I

My story begins as a great many stories have begun within the last three years, and indeed as a great many have ended; for, when the hero is despatched, does not the romance come to a stop?

In early May, two years ago, a young couple I wot of strolled homeward from an evening walk, a long ramble among the peaceful hills which inclosed their rustic home. Into these peaceful hills the young man had brought, not the rumor, (which was an old inhabitant,) but some of the reality of war,—a little whiff of gunpowder, the clanking of a sword; for, although Mr. John Ford had his campaign still before him, he wore a certain comely air of camp-life which stamped him a very Hector to the steady-going villagers, and a very pretty fellow to Miss Elizabeth Crowe, his companion in this sentimental stroll. And was he not attired in the great brightness of blue and gold which befits a freshly made lieutenant? This was a strange sight for these happy Northern glades; for, although the first Revolution had boomed awhile in their midst, the honest yeomen who defended them were clad in sober homespun, and it is well known that His Majesty's troops wore red.

These young people, I say, had been roaming. It was plain that they had wandered into spots where the brambles were thick and the dews heavy,—nay, into swamps and puddles where the April rains were still undried. Ford's boots and trousers had imbibed a deep foretaste of the Virginia mud; his companion's skirts were fearfully bedraggled. What great enthusiasm had made our friends so unmindful of their steps? What blinding ardor had kindled these strange phenomena: a young lieutenant scornful of his first uniform, a well-bred young lady reckless of her stockings?

Good reader, this narrative is averse to retrospect.

Elizabeth (as I shall not scruple to call her outright) was leaning upon her companion's arm, half moving in concert with him, and half allowing herself to be led, with that instinctive acknowledgment of dependence natural to a young girl who has just received the assurance of lifelong protection. Ford was lounging along with that calm, swinging stride which often bespeaks, when you can read it aright, the answering consciousness of a sudden rush of manhood. A spectator might have thought him at this moment profoundly conceited. The young girl's blue veil was dangling from his pocket; he had shouldered her sun-umbrella after the fashion of a musket on a march: he might carry these trifles. Was there not a vague longing expressed in the strong expansion of his stalwart shoulders, in the fond accommodation of his pace to hers,—her pace so submissive and slow, that, when he tried to match it, they almost came to a delightful standstill,—a silent desire for the whole fair burden?

They made their way up a long swelling mound, whose top commanded the sunset. The dim landscape which had been brightening all day to the green of spring was now darkening to the gray of evening. The lesser hills, the farms, the brooks, the fields, orchards, and woods, made a dusky gulf before the great splendor of the west. As Ford looked at the clouds, it seemed to him that their imagery was all of war, their great uneven masses were marshalled into the semblance of a battle. There were columns charging and columns flying and standards floating,—tatters of the reflected purple; and great captains on colossal horses, and a rolling canopy of cannon-smoke and fire and blood. The background of the clouds, indeed, was like a land on fire, or a battle-ground illumined by another sunset, a country of blackened villages and crimsoned pastures. The tumult of the clouds increased; it was hard to believe them inanimate. You might have fancied them an army of gigantic souls playing at football with the sun. They seemed to sway in confused splendor; the opposing squadrons bore each other down; and then suddenly they scattered, bowling with equal velocity towards north and south, and gradually fading into the pale evening sky. The purple pennons sailed away and sank out of sight, caught, doubtless, upon the brambles of the intervening plain. Day contracted itself into a fiery ball and vanished.

Ford and Elizabeth had quietly watched this great mystery of the heavens.

"That is an allegory," said the young man, as the sun went under, looking into his companion's face, where a pink flush seemed still to linger: "it means the end of the war. The forces on both sides are withdrawn. The blood that has been shed gathers itself into a vast globule and drops into the ocean."

"I'm afraid it means a shabby compromise," said Elizabeth. "Light disappears, too, and the land is in darkness."

"Only for a season," answered the other. "We mourn our dead. Then light comes again, stronger and brighter than ever. Perhaps you'll be crying for me, Lizzie, at that distant day."

"Oh, Jack, didn't you promise not to talk about that?" says Lizzie, threatening to anticipate the performance in question.

Jack took this rebuke in silence, gazing soberly at the empty sky. Soon the young girl's eyes stole up to his face. If he had been looking at anything in particular, I think she would have followed the direction of his glance; but as it seemed to be a very vacant one, she let her eyes rest.

"Jack," said she, after a pause, "I wonder how you'll look when you get back."

Ford's soberness gave way to a laugh.

"Uglier than ever. I shall be all incrusted with mud and gore. And then I shall be magnificently sun-burnt, and I shall have a beard."

"Oh, you dreadful!" and Lizzie gave a little shout. "Really, Jack, if you have a beard, you'll not look like a gentleman."

"Shall I look like a lady, pray?" says Jack.

"Are you serious?" asked Lizzie.

"To be sure. I mean to alter my face as you do your misfitting garments,—take in on one side and let out on the other. Isn't that the process? I shall crop my head and cultivate my chin."

"You've a very nice chin, my dear, and I think it's a shame to hide it."

"Yes, I know my chin's handsome; but wait till you see my beard."

"Oh, the vanity!" cried Lizzie, "the vanity of men in their faces! Talk of women!" and the silly creature looked up at her lover with most inconsistent satisfaction.

"Oh, the pride of women in their husbands!" said Jack, who of course knew what she was about.

"You're not my husband, Sir. There's many a slip"—But the young girl stopped short.

"'Twixt the cup and the lip," said Jack. "Go on. I can match your proverb with another. 'There's many a true word,' and so forth. No, my darling: I'm not your husband. Perhaps I never shall be. But if anything happens to me, you'll take comfort, won't you?"

"Never!" said Lizzie, tremulously.

"Oh, but you must; otherwise, Lizzie, I should think our engagement inexcusable. Stuff! who am I that you should cry for me?"

"You are the best and wisest of men. I don't care; you *are*."

"Thank you for your great love, my dear. That's a delightful illusion. But I hope Time will kill it, in his own good way, before it hurts any one. I know so many men who are worth infinitely more than I—men wise, generous, and brave—that I shall not feel as if I were leaving you in an empty world."

"Oh, my dear friend!" said Lizzie, after a pause, "I wish you could advise me all my life."

"Take care, take care," laughed Jack; "you don't know what you are bargaining for. But will you let me say a word now? If by chance I'm taken out of the world, I want you to beware of that tawdry sentiment which enjoins you to be 'constant to my memory.' My memory be hanged! Remember me at my best,—that is, fullest of the desire of humility. Don't inflict me on people. There are some widows and bereaved sweethearts who remind me of the peddler in that horrible murder-story, who carried a corpse in his pack. Really, it's their stock in trade. The only justification of a man's personality is his rights. What rights has a dead man?—Let's go down."

They turned southward and went jolting down the hill.

"Do you mind this talk, Lizzie?" asked Ford.

"No," said Lizzie, swallowing a sob, unnoticed by her companion in the sublime egotism of protection; "I like it."

"Very well," said the young man, "I want my memory to help you. When I am down in Virginia, I expect to get a vast deal of good from thinking of you,—to do my work better, and to keep straighter altogether. Like all lovers, I'm horribly selfish. I expect to see a vast deal of shabbiness and baseness and turmoil, and in the midst of it all I'm sure the inspiration of patriotism will sometimes fail. Then I'll think of you. I love you a thousand times better than my country, Liz.—Wicked? So much the worse. It's the truth. But if I find your memory makes a milksop of me, I shall thrust you out of the way, without ceremony,—I shall clap you into my box or between the leaves of my Bible, and only look at you on Sunday."

"I shall be very glad, Sir, if that makes you open your Bible frequently," says Elizabeth, rather demurely.

"I shall put one of your photographs against every page," cried Ford; "and then I think I shall not lack a text for my meditations. Don't you know how Catholics keep little pictures of their adored Lady in their prayer-books?"

"Yes, indeed," said Lizzie; "I should think it would be a very soul-stirring picture, when you are marching to the front, the night before a battle,—a poor, stupid girl, knitting stupid socks, in a stupid Yankee village."

Oh, the craft of artless tongues! Jack strode along in silence a few moments, splashing straight through a puddle; then, ere he was quite clear of it, he stretched out his arm and gave his companion a long embrace.

"And pray what am I to do," resumed Lizzie, wondering, rather proudly perhaps, at Jack's averted face, "While you are marching and countermarching in Virginia?"

"Your duty, of course," said Jack, in a steady voice, which belied a certain little conjecture of Lizzie's. "I think you will find the sun will rise in the east, my dear, just as it did before you were engaged."

"I'm sure I didn't suppose it wouldn't," says Lizzie.

"By duty I don't mean anything disagreeable, Liz," pursued the young man. "I hope you'll take your pleasure, too. I wish you might go to Boston, or even to Leatherborough, for a month or two."

"What for, pray?"

"What for? Why, for the fun of it: to 'go out,' as they say."

"Jack, do you think me capable of going to parties while you are in danger?"

"Why not? Why should I have all the fun?"

"Fun? I'm sure you're welcome to it all. As for me, I mean to make a new beginning."

"Of what?"

"Oh, of everything. In the first place, I shall begin to improve my mind. But don't you think it's horrid for women to be reasonable?"

"Hard, say you?"

"Horrid,—yes, and hard too. But I mean to become so. Oh, girls are such fools, Jack! I mean to learn to like boiled mutton and history and plain sewing, and all that. Yet, when a girl's engaged, she's not expected to do anything in particular."

Jack laughed, and said nothing; and Lizzie went on.

"I wonder what your mother will say to the news. I think I know."

"What?"

"She'll say you've been very unwise. No, she won't: she never speaks so to you. She'll say I've been very dishonest or indelicate, or something of that kind. No, she won't either: she does n't say such things, though I'm sure she thinks them. I don't know what she'll say."

"No, I think not, Lizzie, if you indulge in such conjectures. My mother never speaks without thinking. Let us hope that she may think favorably of our plan. Even if she does n't"—

Jack did not finish his sentence, nor did Lizzie urge him. She had a great respect for his hesitations. But in a moment he began again.

"I was going to say this, Lizzie: I think for the present our engagement had better be kept quiet."

Lizzie's heart sank with a sudden disappointment. Imagine the feelings of the damsel in the fairy-tale, whom the disguised enchantress had just empowered to utter diamonds and pearls, should the old beldame have straightway added that for the present mademoiselle had better hold her tongue. Yet the disappointment was brief. I think this enviable young lady would have tripped home talking very hard to herself, and have been not ill pleased to find her little mouth turning into a tightly clasped jewel-casket. Nay, would she not on this occasion have been thankful for a large mouth,—a mouth huge and unnatural,—stretching from ear to ear? Who wish to cast their pearls before swine? The young lady of the pearls was, after all, but a barnyard miss. Lizzie was too proud of Jack to be vain. It's well enough to wear our own hearts upon our sleeves; but for those of others, when intrusted to our keeping, I think we had better find a more secluded lodging.

"You see, I think secrecy would leave us much freer," said Jack,—"leave *you* much freer."

"Oh, Jack, how can you?" cried Lizzie. "Yes, of course; I shall be falling in love with some one else. Freer! Thank you, Sir!"

"Nay, Lizzie, what I'm saying is really kinder than it sounds. Perhaps you *will* thank me one of these days."

"Doubtless! I've already taken a great fancy to George Mackenzie."

"Will you let me enlarge on my suggestion?"

"Oh, certainly! You seem to have your mind quite made up."

"I confess I like to take account of possibilities. Don't you know mathematics are my hobby? Did you ever study algebra? I always have an eye on the unknown quantity."

"No, I never studied algebra. I agree with you, that we had better not speak of our engagement."

"That's right, my dear. You're always right. But mind, I don't want to bind you to secrecy. Hang it, do as you please! Do what comes easiest to you, and you'll do the best thing. What made me speak is my dread of the horrible publicity which clings to all this business. Nowadays, when a girl's engaged, it's no longer, 'Ask mamma,' simply; but, 'Ask Mrs. Brown, and Mrs. Jones, and my large circle of acquaintance,—Mrs. Grundy, in short.' I say nowadays, but I suppose it's always been so."

"Very well, we'll keep it all nice and quiet," said Lizzie, who would have been ready to celebrate her nuptials according to the rites of the Esquimaux, had Jack seen fit to suggest it.

"I know it doesn't look well for a lover to be so cautious," pursued Jack; "but you understand me, Lizzie, don't you?"

"I don't entirely understand you, but I quite trust you."

"God bless you! My prudence, you see, is my best strength. Now, if ever, I need my strength. When a man's a-wooing, Lizzie, he is all feeling, or he ought to be; when he's accepted, then he begins to think."

"And to repent, I suppose you mean."

"Nay, to devise means to keep his sweetheart from repenting. Let me be frank. Is it the greatest fools only that are the best lovers? There's no telling what may happen, Lizzie. I want you to marry me with your eyes open. I don't want you to feel tied down or taken in. You're very young, you know. You're responsible to yourself of a year hence. You're at an age when no girl can count safely from year's end to year's end."

"And you, Sir!" cries Lizzie; "one would think you were a grandfather."

"Well, I'm on the way to it. I'm a pretty old boy. I mean what I say. I may not be entirely frank, but I think I'm sincere. It seems to me as if I'd been fibbing all my life before I told you that your affection was necessary to my happiness. I mean it out and out. I never loved any one before, and I never will again. If you had refused me half an hour ago, I should have died a bachelor. I have no fear for myself. But I have for you. You said a few minutes ago that you wanted me to be your adviser. Now you know the function of an adviser is to perfect his victim in the art of walking with his eyes shut. I sha'n't be so cruel."

Lizzie saw fit to view these remarks in a humorous light. "How disinterested!" quoth she: "how very self-sacrificing! Bachelor indeed! For my part, I think I shall become a Mormon!"—I verily believe the poor misinformed creature fancied that in Utah it is the ladies who are guilty of polygamy.

Before many minutes they drew near home. There stood Mrs. Ford at the garden-gate, looking up and down the road, with a letter in her hand.

"Something for you, John," said his mother, as they approached. "It looks as if it came from camp.—Why, Elizabeth, look at your skirts!"

"I know it," says Lizzie, giving the articles in question a shake. "What is it, Jack?"

"Marching orders!" cried the young man. "The regiment leaves day after to-morrow. I must leave by the early train in the morning. Hurray!" And he diverted a sudden gleeful kiss into a filial salute.

They went in. The two women were silent, after the manner of women who suffer. But Jack did little else than laugh and talk and circumnavigate the parlor, sitting first here and then there,—close beside Lizzie and on the opposite side of the room. After a while Miss Crowe joined in his laughter, but I think her mirth might have been resolved into articulate heart-beats. After tea she went to bed, to give Jack opportunity for his last filial *épanchements*. How generous a man's intervention makes women! But Lizzie promised to see her lover off in the morning.

"Nonsense!" said Mrs. Ford. "You'll not be up. John will want to breakfast quietly."

"I shall see you off, Jack," repeated the young lady, from the threshold.

Elizabeth went up stairs buoyant with her young love. It had dawned upon her like a new life,—a life positively worth the living. Hereby she would subsist and cost nobody anything. In it she was boundlessly rich. She would make it the hidden spring of a hundred praiseworthy deeds. She would begin the career of duty: she would enjoy boundless equanimity: she would raise her whole being to the level of her sublime passion. She would practise charity, humility, piety,—in fine, all the virtues: together with certain *morceaux* of Beethoven and Chopin. She would walk the earth like one glorified. She would do homage to the best of men by inviolate secrecy. Here, by I know not what gentle transition, as she lay in the quiet darkness, Elizabeth covered her pillow with a flood of tears.

Meanwhile Ford, down-stairs, began in this fashion. He was lounging at his manly length on the sofa, in his slippers.

"May I light a pipe, mother?"

"Yes, my love. But please be careful of your ashes. There's a newspaper."

"Pipes don't make ashes.—Mother, what do you think?" he continued, between the puffs of his smoking; "I've got a piece of news."

"Ah?" said Mrs. Ford, fumbling for her scissors; "I hope it's good news."

"I hope you'll think it so. I've been engaging myself"—puff,—puff—"to Lizzie Crowe." A cloud of puffs between his mother's face and his own. When they cleared away, Jack felt his mother's eyes. Her work was in her lap. "To be married, you know," he added.

In Mrs. Ford's view, like the king in that of the British Constitution, her only son could do no wrong. Prejudice is a stout bulwark against surprise. Moreover, Mrs. Ford's motherly instinct had not been entirely at fault. Still, it had by no means kept pace with fact. She had been silent, partly from doubt, partly out of respect for her son. As long as John did not doubt of himself, he was right. Should he come to do so, she was sure he would speak. And now, when he told her the matter was settled, she persuaded herself that he was asking her advice.

"I've been expecting it," she said, at last.

"You have? Why didn't you speak?"

"Well, John, I can't say I've been hoping it."

"Why not?"

"I am not sure of Lizzie's heart," said Mrs. Ford, who, it may be well to add, was very sure of her own.

Jack began to laugh. "What's the matter with her heart?"

"I think Lizzie's shallow," said Mrs. Ford; and there was that in her tone which betokened some satisfaction with this adjective.

"Hang it! She is shallow," said Jack. "But when a thing's shallow, you can see to the bottom. Lizzie doesn't pretend to be deep. I want a wife, mother, that I can understand. That's the only wife I can love. Lizzie's the only girl I ever understood, and the first I ever loved. I love her very much,—more than I can explain to you."

"Yes, I confess it's inexplicable. It seems to me," she added, with a bad smile, "like infatuation."

Jack did not like the smile; he liked it even less than the remark. He smoked steadily for a few moments, and then he said,—

"Well, mother, love is notoriously obstinate, you know. We shall not be able to take the same view of this subject: suppose we drop it."

"Remember that this is your last evening at home, my son," said Mrs. Ford.

"I do remember. Therefore I wish to avoid disagreement."

There was a pause. The young man smoked, and his mother sewed, in silence.

"I think my position, as Lizzie's guardian," resumed Mrs. Ford, "entitles me to an interest in the matter."

"Certainly, I acknowledged your interest by telling you of our engagement."

Further pause.

"Will you allow me to say," said Mrs. Ford, after a while, "that I think this a little selfish?"

"Allow you? Certainly, if you particularly desire it. Though I confess it isn't very pleasant for a man to sit and hear his future wife pitched into,—by his own mother, too."

"John, I am surprised at your language."

"I beg your pardon," and John spoke more gently. "You must n't be surprised at anything from an accepted lover.—I'm sure you misconceive her. In fact, mother, I don't believe you know her."

Mrs. Ford nodded, with an infinite depth of meaning; and from the grimness with which she bit off the end of her thread it might have seemed that she fancied herself to be executing a human vengeance.

"Ah, I know her only too well!"

"And you don't like her?"

Mrs. Ford performed another decapitation of her thread.

"Well, I'm glad Lizzie has one friend in the world," said Jack.

"Her best friend," said Mrs. Ford, "is the one who flatters her least. I see it all, John. Her pretty face has done the business."

The young man flushed impatiently.

"Mother," said he, "you are very much mistaken. I'm not a boy nor a fool. You trust me in a great many things; why not trust me in this?"

"My dear son, you are throwing yourself away. You deserve for your companion in life a higher character than that girl."

I think Mrs. Ford, who had been an excellent mother, would have liked to give her son a wife fashioned on her own model.

"Oh, come, mother," said he, "that's twaddle. I should be thankful, if I were half as good as Lizzie."

"It's the truth, John, and your conduct—not only the step you've taken, but your talk about it—is a great disappointment to me. If I have cherished any wish of late, it is that my darling boy should get a wife worthy of him. The household governed by Elizabeth Crowe is not the home I should desire for any one I love."

"It's one to which you should always be welcome, Ma'am," said Jack.

"It's not a place I should feel at home in," replied his mother.

"I'm sorry," said Jack. And he got up and began to walk about the room. "Well, well, mother," he said at last, stopping in front of Mrs. Ford, "we don't understand each other. One of these days we shall. For the present let us have done with discussion. I'm half sorry I told you."

"I'm glad of such a proof of your confidence. But if you had n't, of course Elizabeth would have done so."

"No, Ma'am, I think not."

"Then she is even more reckless of her obligations than I thought her."

"I advised her to say nothing about it."

Mrs. Ford made no answer. She began slowly to fold up her work.

"I think we had better let the matter stand," continued her son. "I'm not afraid of time. But I wish to make a request of you: you won't mention this conversation to Lizzie, will you? Nor allow her to suppose that you know of our engagement? I have a particular reason."

Mrs. Ford went on smoothing out her work. Then she suddenly looked up.

"No, my dear, I'll keep your secret. Give me a kiss."

II

I have no intention of following Lieutenant Ford to the seat of war. The exploits of his campaign are recorded in the public journals of the day, where the curious may still peruse them. My own taste has always been for unwritten history, and my present business is with the reverse of the picture.

After Jack went off, the two ladies resumed their old homely life. But the homeliest life had now ceased to be repulsive to Elizabeth. Her common duties were no longer wearisome: for the first time, she experienced the delicious companionship of thought. Her chief task was still to sit by the window knitting soldiers' socks; but even Mrs. Ford could not help owning that she worked with a much greater diligence, yawned, rubbed her eyes, gazed up and down the road less, and indeed produced a much more comely article. Ah, me! if half the lovesome fancies that flitted through Lizzie's spirit in those busy hours could have found their way into the texture of the dingy yarn, as it was slowly wrought into shape, the eventual wearer of the socks would have been as light-footed as Mercury. I am afraid I should make the reader sneer, were I to rehearse some of this little fool's diversions. She passed several hours daily in Jack's old chamber: it was in this sanctuary, indeed, at the sunny south window, overlooking the long road, the wood-crowned heights, the gleaming river, that she worked with most pleasure and profit. Here she was removed from the untiring glance of the elder lady, from her jarring questions and commonplaces; here she was alone with her love,—that greatest commonplace in life. Lizzie felt in Jack's room a certain impress of his personality. The idle fancies of her mood were bodied forth in a dozen sacred relics. Some of these articles Elizabeth carefully cherished. It was rather late in the day for her to assert a literary taste,—her reading having begun and ended (naturally enough) with the ancient fiction of the "Scottish Chiefs."[22] So she could hardly help smiling, herself, sometimes, at her interest in Jack's old college tomes. She carried several of them to her own apartment, and placed them at the foot of her little bed, on a book-shelf adorned, besides, with a pot of spring violets, a portrait of General McClellan, and a likeness of Lieutenant Ford. She had a vague belief that a loving study of their well-thumbed verses would remedy, in some degree, her sad intellectual deficiencies. She was sorry she knew so little: as sorry, that is, as she might be, for we know that she was shallow. Jack's omniscience was one of his most awful attributes. And yet she comforted herself with the thought, that, as he had forgiven her ignorance, she herself might surely forget it. Happy Lizzie, I envy you this easy path to knowledge! The volume she most frequently consulted was an old German "Faust," over which she used to fumble with a battered lexicon. The secret of this preference was in certain marginal notes in pencil, signed "J." I hope they were really of Jack's making.

Lizzie was always a small walker. Until she knew Jack, this had been quite an unsuspected pleasure. She was afraid, too, of the cows, geese, and sheep,—all the agricultural *spectra* of the feminine imagination. But now her terrors were over. Might she not play the soldier, too, in her own humble way? Often with a beating heart, I fear, but still with resolute, elastic steps, she revisited Jack's old haunts; she tried to love Nature as he had seemed to love it; she gazed at his old sunsets; she fathomed his old pools with bright plummet glances, as if seeking some lingering trace of his features in their brown depths, stamped there as on a fond human heart; she sought out his dear name, scratched on the rocks and trees,—and when night came on, she studied, in her simple way, the great starlit canopy, under which, perhaps, her warrior lay sleeping; she wandered through the green glades, singing snatches of his old ballads in a clear voice, made tuneful with love,—and as she sang, there mingled with the everlasting murmur of the trees the faint sound of a muffled bass, borne upon the south wind like a distant drum-beat, responsive to a bugle. So she led for some months a very pleasant idyllic life, face to face with a strong, vivid memory, which gave everything and asked nothing. These were doubtless to be (and she half knew it) the happiest days of her life. Has life any bliss so great as this pensive ecstasy? To know that the golden sands are dropping one by one makes servitude freedom, and poverty riches.

In spite of a certain sense of loss, Lizzie passed a very blissful summer. She enjoyed the deep repose which, it is to be hoped, sanctifies all honest betrothals. Possible calamity weighed lightly upon her. We know that when the columns of battle-smoke leave the field, they journey through the heavy air to a thousand quiet homes, and play about the crackling blaze of as many firesides. But Lizzie's vision was never clouded. Mrs. Ford might gaze into the thickening summer dusk and wipe her spectacles; but her companion hummed her old ballad-ends with an unbroken voice. She no more ceased to smile under evil tidings than the brooklet ceases to ripple beneath the projected shadow of the roadside willow. The self-given promises of that tearful night of parting were forgotten. Vigilance had no place in Lizzie's scheme of heavenly idleness. The idea of moralizing in Elysium!

It must not be supposed that Mrs. Ford was indifferent to Lizzie's mood. She studied it watchfully, and kept note of all its variations. And among the things she learned was, that her companion knew of her scrutiny, and was, on the whole, indifferent to it. Of the full extent of Mrs. Ford's observation, however, I think Lizzie was hardly aware. She was like a reveller in a brilliantly lighted room, with a curtainless window, conscious, and yet heedless, of passers-by. And Mrs. Ford may not inaptly be compared to the chilly spectator on the dark side of the pane. Very few words passed on the topic of their common thoughts. From the first, as we have seen, Lizzie guessed at her guardian's probable view of her engagement: an abasement incurred by John. Lizzie lacked what is called a sense of duty; and, unlike the majority of such temperaments, which contrive to be buoyant on the glistening bubble of Dignity, she had likewise a modest estimate of her dues. Alack, my poor heroine had no pride! Mrs. Ford's silent censure awakened no resentment. It sounded in her ears like a dull, soporific hum. Lizzie was deeply enamored of what a French book terms her *aises intellectuelles*.[23] Her mental comfort lay in the ignoring of problems. She possessed a certain native insight which revealed many of the horrent [sic] inequalities of her pathway; but she found it so cruel and disenchanting a faculty, that blindness was infinitely preferable. She preferred repose to order, and mercy to justice. She was speculative, without being critical. She was continually wondering, but she never inquired. This world was the riddle; the next alone would be the answer.

So she never felt any desire to have an "understanding" with Mrs. Ford. Did the old lady misconceive her? It was her own business. Mrs. Ford apparently felt no desire to set herself right. You see, Lizzie was ignorant of her friend's promise. There were moments when Mrs. Ford's tongue itched to speak. There were others, it is true, when she dreaded any explanation which would compel her to forfeit her displeasure. Lizzie's happy self-sufficiency was most irritating. She grudged the young girl the dignity of her secret; her own actual knowledge of it rather increased her jealousy, by showing her the importance of the scheme from which she was excluded. Lizzie, being in perfect good-humor with the world and with herself, abated no jot of her personal deference to Mrs. Ford. Of Jack, as a good friend and her guardian's son, she spoke very freely. But Mrs. Ford was mistrustful of this semi-confidence. She would not, she often said to herself, be wheedled against her principles. Her principles! Oh for some shining blade of purpose to hew down such stubborn stakes! Lizzie had no thought of flattering her companion. She never deceived any one but herself. She could not bring herself to value Mrs. Ford's good-will. She knew that Jack often suffered from his mother's obstinacy. So her unbroken humility shielded no unavowed purpose. She was patient and kindly from nature, from habit. Yet I think, that, if Mrs. Ford could have measured her benignity, she would have preferred, on the whole, the most open defiance. "Of all things," she would sometimes mutter, "to be patronized by that little piece!" It was very disagreeable, for instance, to have to listen to *portions* of her own son's letters.

These letters came week by week, flying out of the South like white-winged carrier-doves. Many and many a time, for very pride, Lizzie would have liked a larger audience. Portions of them certainly deserved publicity. They were far too good for her. Were they not better than that stupid war-correspondence in the "Times," which she so often tried in vain to read? They contained long details of movements, plans of campaigns, military opinions and conjectures, expressed with the emphasis habitual to young sub-lieutenants. I doubt whether General Halleck's despatches laid down the law more absolutely than Lieutenant Ford's. Lizzie answered in her own fashion. It must be owned that hers was a dull pen. She told her dearest, dearest Jack how much she loved and honored him, and how much she missed him, and how delightful his last letter was, (with those beautifully drawn diagrams,) and the village gossip, and how stout and strong his mother continued to be,—and again, how she loved, etc., etc., and that she remained his loving L. Jack read these effusions as became one so beloved. I should not wonder if he thought them very brilliant.

The summer waned to its close, and through myriad silent stages began to darken into autumn. Who can tell the story of those red months? I have to chronicle another silent transition. But as I can find no words delicate and fine enough to describe the multifold changes of Nature, so, too, I must be content to give you the spiritual facts in gross.

John Ford became a veteran down by the Potomac. And, to tell the truth, Lizzie became a veteran at home. That is, her love and hope grew to be an old story. She gave way, as the strongest must, as the wisest will, to time. The passion which, in her simple, shallow way, she had confided to the woods and waters reflected their outward variations; she thought of her lover less, and with less positive pleasure. The golden sands had run out. Perfect rest was over. Mrs. Ford's tacit protest began to be annoying. In a rather resentful spirit, Lizzie forbore to read any more letters aloud. These were as regular as ever. One of them contained a rough camp-photograph of Jack's newly bearded visage. Lizzie declared it was "too ugly for anything," and thrust it out of sight. She found herself skipping his military dissertations, which were still as long and written in as handsome a hand as ever. The "too good," which used to be uttered rather proudly, was now rather a wearisome truth. When Lizzie in certain critical moods tried to qualify Jack's temperament, she said to herself that he was too literal. Once he gave her a little scolding for not writing oftener. "Jack can make no allowances," murmured Lizzie. "He can understand no feelings but his own. I remember he used to say that moods were diseases. His mind is too healthy for such things; his heart is too stout for ache or pain. The night before he went off he told me that Reason, as he calls it, was the rule of life. I suppose he thinks it the rule of love, too. But his heart is younger than mine,—younger and better. He has lived through awful scenes of danger and bloodshed and cruelty, yet his heart is purer." Lizzie had a horrible feeling of being *blasée* of this one affection. "Oh, God bless him!" she cried. She felt much better for the tears in which this soliloquy ended. I fear she had begun to doubt her ability to cry about Jack.

III

Christmas came. The Army of the Potomac had stacked its muskets and gone into winter-quarters. Miss Crowe received an invitation to pass the second fortnight in February at the great manufacturing town of Leatherborough. Leatherborough is on the railroad, two hours south of Glenham, at the mouth of the great river Tan, where this noble stream expands into its broadest smile, or gapes in too huge a fashion to be disguised by a bridge.

"Mrs. Littlefield kindly invites you for the last of the month," said Mrs. Ford, reading a letter behind the tea-urn.

It suited Mrs. Ford's purpose—a purpose which I have not space to elaborate—that her young charge should now go forth into society and pick up acquaintances.

Two sparks of pleasure gleamed in Elizabeth's eyes. But, as she had taught herself to do of late with her protectress, she mused before answering.

"It is my desire that you should go," said Mrs. Ford, taking silence for dissent.

The sparks went out.

"I intend to go," said Lizzie, rather grimly. "I am much obliged to Mrs. Littlefield."

Her companion looked up.

"I intend you shall. You will please to write this morning."

For the rest of the week the two stitched together over muslins and silks, and were very good friends. Lizzie could scarcely help wondering at Mrs. Ford's zeal on her behalf. Might she not have referred it to her guardian's principles? Her wardrobe, hitherto fashioned on the Glenham notion of elegance, was gradually raised to the Leatherborough standard of fitness. As she took up her bedroom candle the night before she left home, she said,—

"I thank you very much, Mrs. Ford, for having worked so hard for me,—for having taken so much interest in my outfit. If they ask me at Leatherborough who made my things, I shall certainly say it was you."

Mrs. Littlefield treated her young friend with great kindness. She was a good-natured, childless matron. She found Lizzie very ignorant and very pretty. She was glad to have so great a beauty and so many lions to show.

One evening Lizzie went to her room with one of the maids, carrying half a dozen candles between them. Heaven forbid that I should cross that virgin threshold—for the present! But we will wait. We will allow them two hours. At the end of that time, having gently knocked, we will enter the sanctuary. Glory of glories! The faithful attendant has done her work. Our lady is robed, crowned, ready for worshippers.

I trust I shall not be held to a minute description of our dear Lizzie's person and costume. Who is so great a recluse as never to have beheld young ladyhood in full dress? Many of us have sisters and daughters. Not a few of us, I hope, have female connections of another degree, yet no less dear. Others have looking-glasses. I give you my word for it that Elizabeth made as pretty a show as it is possible to see. She was of course well-dressed. Her skirt was of voluminous white, puffed and trimmed in wondrous sort. Her hair was profusely ornamented with curls and braids of its own rich substance. From her waist depended a ribbon, broad and blue. White with coral ornaments, as she wrote to Jack in the course of the week. Coral ornaments, forsooth! And pray, Miss, what of the other jewels with which your person was decorated,—the rubies, pearls, and sapphires? One by one Lizzie assumes her modest gimcracks: her bracelet, her gloves, her handkerchief, her fan, and then—her smile. Ah, that strange crowning smile!

An hour later, in Mrs. Littlefield['s] pretty drawing-room, amid music, lights, and talk, Miss Crowe was sweeping a grand curtsy before a tall, sallow man, whose name she caught from her hostess's redundant murmur as Bruce. Five minutes later, when the honest matron gave a glance at her newly started enterprise from the other side of the room, she said to herself that really, for a plain country-girl, Miss Crowe did this kind of thing very well. Her next glimpse of the couple showed them whirling round the room to the crashing thrum of the piano. At eleven o'clock she beheld them linked by their finger-tips in the dazzling mazes of the reel. At half-past eleven she discerned them charging shoulder to shoulder in the serried columns of the Lancers.[24] At midnight she tapped her young friend gently with her fan.

"Your sash is unpinned, my dear.—I think you have danced often enough with Mr. Bruce. If he asks you again, you had better refuse. It's not quite the thing.—Yes, my dear, I know.—Mr. Simpson, will you be so good as to take Miss Crowe down to supper?"

I'm afraid young Simpson had rather a snappish partner.

After the proper interval, Mr. Bruce called to pay his respects to Mrs. Littlefield. He found Miss Crowe also in the drawing-room. Lizzie and he met like old friends. Mrs. Littlefield was a willing listener; but it seemed to her that she had come in at the second act of the play. Bruce went off with Miss Crowe's promise to drive with him in the afternoon. In the afternoon he swept up to the door in a prancing, tinkling sleigh. After some minutes of hoarse jesting and silvery laughter in the keen wintry air, he swept away again with Lizzie curled up in the buffalo-robe beside him, like a kitten in a rug. It was dark when they returned. When Lizzie came in to the sitting-room fire, she was congratulated by her hostess upon having made a "conquest."

"I think he's a most gentlemanly man," says Lizzie.

"So he is, my dear," said Mrs. Littlefield; "Mr. Bruce is a perfect gentleman. He's one of the finest young men I know. He's not so young either. He's a little too yellow for my taste; but he's beautifully educated. I wish you could hear his French accent. He has been abroad I don't know how many years. The firm of Bruce and Robertson does an immense business."

"And I'm so glad," cries Lizzie, "he's coming to Glenham in March! He's going to take his sister to the water-cure."

"Really?—poor thing! She has very good manners."

"What do you think of his looks?" asked Lizzie, smoothing her feather.

"I was speaking of Jane Bruce. I think Mr. Bruce has fine eyes."

"I must say I like tall men," says Miss Crowe.

"Then Robert Bruce is your man," laughs Mr. Littlefield. "He's as tall as a bell-tower. And he's got a bell-clapper in his head, too."

"I believe I will go and take off my things," remarks Miss Crowe, flinging up her curls.

Of course it behooved Mr. Bruce to call the next day and see how Miss Crowe had stood her drive. He set a veto upon her intended departure, and presented an invitation from his sister for the following week. At Mrs. Littlefield's instance, Lizzie accepted the invitation, despatched a laconic note to Mrs. Ford, and stayed over for Miss Bruce's party. It was a grand affair. Miss Bruce was a very great lady: she treated Miss Crowe with every attention. Lizzie was thought by some persons to look prettier than ever. The vaporous gauze, the sunny hair, the coral, the sapphires, the smile, were displayed with renewed success. The master of the house was unable to dance; he was summoned to sterner duties. Nor could Miss Crowe be induced to perform, having hurt her foot on the ice. This was of course a disappointment; let us hope that her entertainers made it up to her.

On the second day after the party, Lizzie returned to Glenham. Good Mr. Littlefield took her to the station, stealing a moment from his precious business-hours.

"There are your checks," said he; "be sure you don't lose them. Put them in your glove."

Lizzie gave a little scream of merriment.

"Mr. Littlefield, how can you? I've a reticule, Sir. But I really don't want you to stay."

"Well, I confess," said her companion.—"Hullo! there's your Scottish chief! I'll get him to stay with you till the train leaves. He may be going. Bruce!"

"Oh, Mr. Littlefield, don't!" cries Lizzie. "Perhaps Mr. Bruce is engaged."

Bruce's tall figure came striding towards them. He was astounded to find that Miss Crowe was going by this train. Delightful! He had come to meet a friend who had not arrived.

"Littlefield," said he, "you can't be spared from your business. I will see Miss Crowe off."

When the elder gentleman had departed, Mr. Bruce conducted his companion into the car, and found her a comfortable seat, equidistant from the torrid stove and the frigid door. Then he stowed away her shawls, umbrella, and reticule. She would keep her muff? She did well. What a pretty fur!

"It's just like your collar," said Lizzie. "I wish I had a muff for my feet," she pursued, tapping on the floor.

"Why not use some of those shawls?" said Bruce; "let's see what we can make of them."

And he stooped down and arranged them as a rug, very neatly and kindly. And then he called himself a fool for not having used the next seat, which was empty; and the wrapping was done over again.

"I'm so afraid you'll be carried off!" said Lizzie. "What would you do?"

"I think I should make the best of it. And you?"

"I would tell you to sit down *there*"; and she indicated the seat facing her. He took it. "Now you'll be sure to," said Elizabeth.

"I'm afraid I shall, unless I put the newspaper between us." And he took it out of his pocket. "Have you seen the news?"

"No," says Lizzie, elongating her bonnet-ribbons. "What is it? Just look at that party."

"There's not much news. There's been a scrimmage on the Rappahannock. Two of our regiments engaged,—the Fifteenth and the Twenty-Eighth. Did n't you tell me you had a cousin or something in the Fifteenth?"

"Not a cousin, no relation, but an intimate friend,—my guardian's son. What does the paper say, please?" inquires Lizzie, very pale.

Bruce cast his eye over the report. "It does n't seem to have amounted to much; we drove back the enemy, and recrossed the river at our ease. Our loss only fifty. There are no names," he added, catching a glimpse of Lizzie's pallor,—"none in this paper at least."

In a few moments appeared a newsboy crying the New York journals.

"Do you think the New York papers would have any names?" asked Lizzie.

"We can try," said Bruce. And he bought a "Herald," and unfolded it. "Yes, there *is* a list," he continued, some time after he had opened out the sheet. "What's your friend's name?" he asked, from behind the paper.

"Ford,—John Ford, second lieutenant," said Lizzie.

There was a long pause.

At last Bruce lowered the sheet, and showed a face in which Lizzie's pallor seemed faintly reflected.

"There *is* such a name among the wounded," he said; and, folding the paper down, he held it out, and gently crossed to the seat beside her.

Lizzie took the paper, and held it close to her eyes. But Bruce could not help seeing that her temples had turned from white to crimson.

"Do you see it?" he asked; "I sincerely hope it's nothing very bad."

"*Severely*," whispered Lizzie.

"Yes, but that proves nothing. Those things are most unreliable. *Do* hope for the best."

Lizzie made no answer. Meanwhile passengers had been brushing in, and the car was full. The engine began to puff, and the conductor to shout. The train gave a jog.

"You'd better go, Sir, or you'll be carried off," said Lizzie, holding out her hand, with her face still hidden.

"May I go on to the next station with you?" said Bruce.

Lizzie gave him a rapid look, with a deepened flush. He had fancied that she was shedding tears. But those eyes were dry; they held fire rather than water.

"No, no, Sir; you must not. I insist. Good bye."

Bruce's offer had cost him a blush, too. He had been prepared to back it with the assurance that he had business ahead, and, indeed, to make a little business in order to satisfy his conscience. But Lizzie's answer was final.

"Very well," said he, "*good* bye. You have my real sympathy, Miss Crowe. Don't despair. We shall meet again."

The train rattled away. Lizzie caught a glimpse of a tall figure with lifted hat on the platform. But she sat motionless, with her head against the window-frame, her veil down, and her hands idle.

She had enough to do to think, or rather to feel. It is fortunate that the utmost shock of evil tidings often comes first. After that everything is for the better. Jack's name stood printed in that fatal column like a stern signal for despair. Lizzie felt conscious of a crisis which almost arrested her breath. Night had fallen at midday: what was the hour? A tragedy had stepped into her life: was she spectator or actor? She found herself face to face with death: was it not her own soul masquerading in a shroud? She sat in a half-stupor. She had been aroused from a dream into a waking nightmare. It was like hearing a murder-shriek while you turn the page of your novel. But I cannot describe these things. In time the crushing sense of calamity loosened its grasp. Feeling lashed her pinions. Thought struggled to rise. Passion was still, stunned, floored. She had recoiled like a receding wave for a stronger onset. A hundred ghastly fears and fancies strutted a moment, pecking at the young girl's naked heart, like sandpipers on the weltering beach. Then, as with a great murmurous rush, came the meaning of her grief. The flood-gates of emotion were opened.

At last passion exhausted itself, and Lizzie thought. Bruce's parting words rang in her ears. She did her best to hope. She reflected that wounds, even severe wounds, did not necessarily mean death. Death might easily be warded off. She would go to Jack; she would nurse him; she would watch by him; she would cure him. Even if Death had already beckoned, she would strike down his hand: if Life had already obeyed, she would issue the stronger mandate of Love. She would stanch his wounds; she would unseal his eyes with her kisses; she would call till he answered her.

Lizzie reached home and walked up the garden path. Mrs. Ford stood in the parlor as she entered, upright, pale, and rigid. Each read the other's countenance. Lizzie went towards her slowly and giddily. She must of course kiss her patroness. She took her listless hand and bent towards her stern lips. Habitually Mrs. Ford was the most undemonstrative of women. But as Lizzie looked closer into her face, she read the signs of a grief infinitely more potent than her own. The formal kiss gave way: the young girl leaned her head on the old woman's shoulder and burst into sobs. Mrs. Ford acknowledged those tears with a slow inclination of the head, full of a certain grim pathos: she put out her arms and pressed them closer to her heart.

At last Lizzie disengaged herself and sat down.

"I am going to him," said Mrs. Ford.

Lizzie's dizziness returned. Mrs. Ford was going,—and she, she?

"I am going to nurse him, and with God's help to save him."

"How did you hear?"

"I have a telegram from the surgeon of the regiment"; and Mrs. Ford held out a paper.

Lizzie took it and read: "Lieutenant Ford dangerously wounded in the action of yesterday. You had better come on."

"I should like to go myself," said Lizzie: "I think Jack would like to have me."

"Nonsense! A pretty place for a young girl! I am not going for sentiment; I am going for use."

Lizzie leaned her head back in her chair, and closed her eyes. From the moment they had fallen upon Mrs. Ford, she had felt a certain quiescence. And now it was a relief to have responsibility denied her. Like most weak persons, she was glad to step out of the current of life, now that it had begun to quicken into action. In emergencies, such persons are tacitly counted out; and they as tacitly consent to the arrangement. Even to the sensitive spirit there is a certain meditative rapture in standing on the quiet shore, (beside the ruminating cattle,) and watching the hurrying, eddying flood, which makes up for the loss of dignity. Lizzie's heart resumed its peaceful throbs. She sat, almost dreamily, with her eyes shut.

"I leave in an hour," said Mrs. Ford. "I am going to get ready.—Do you hear?"

The young girl's silence was a deeper consent than her companion supposed.

IV

It was a week before Lizzie heard from Mrs. Ford. The letter, when it came, was very brief. Jack still lived. The wounds were three in number, and very serious; he was unconscious; he had not recognized her; but still the chances either way were thought equal. They would be much greater for his recovery nearer home; but it was impossible to move him. "I write from the midst of horrible scenes," said the poor lady. Subjoined was a list of necessary medicines, comforts, and delicacies, to be boxed up and sent.

For a while Lizzie found occupation in writing a letter to Jack, to be read in his first lucid moment, as she told Mrs. Ford. This lady's man-of-business came up from the village to superintend the packing of the boxes. Her directions were strictly followed; and in no point were they found wanting. Mr. Mackenzie bespoke Lizzie's admiration for their friend's wonderful clearness of memory and judgment. "I wish we had that woman at the head of affairs," said he. "'Gad, I'd apply for a Brigadier-Generalship."—"I'd apply to be sent

South," thought Lizzie. When the boxes and letter were despatched, she sat down to await more news. Sat down, say I? Sat down, and rose, and wondered, and sat down again. These were lonely, weary days. Very different are the idleness of love and the idleness of grief. Very different is it to be alone with your hope and alone with your despair. Lizzie failed to rally her musings. I do not mean to say that her sorrow was very poignant, although she fancied it was. Habit was a great force in her simple nature; and her chief trouble now was that habit refused to work. Lizzie had to grapple with the stern tribulation of a decision to make, a problem to solve. She felt that there was some spiritual barrier between herself and repose. So she began in her usual fashion to build up a false repose on the hither side of belief. She might as well have tried to float on the Dead Sea. Peace eluding her, she tried to resign herself to tumult. She drank deep at the well of self-pity, but found its waters brackish. People are apt to think that they may temper the penalties of misconduct by self-commiseration, just as they season the long aftertaste of beneficence by a little spice of self-applause. But the Power of Good is a more grateful master than the Devil. What bliss to gaze into the smooth gurgling wake of a good deed, while the comely bark sails on with floating pennon! What horror to look into the muddy sediment which floats round the piratic keel! Go, sinner, and dissolve it with your tears! And you, scoffing friend, there is the way out! Or would you prefer the window? I'm an honest man forevermore.

One night Lizzie had a dream,—a rather disagreeable one,—which haunted her during many waking hours. It seemed to her that she was walking in a lonely place, with a tall, dark-eyed man who called her wife. Suddenly, in the shadow of a tree, they came upon an unburied corpse. Lizzie proposed to dig him a grave. They dug a great hole and took hold of the corpse to lift him in; when suddenly he opened his eyes. Then they saw that he was covered with wounds. He looked at them intently for some time, turning his eyes from one to the other. At last he solemnly said, "Amen!" and closed his eyes. Then she and her companion placed him in the grave, and shovelled the earth over him, and stamped it down with their feet.

He of the dark eyes and he of the wounds were the two constantly recurring figures of Lizzie's reveries. She could never think of John without thinking of the courteous Leatherborough gentleman, too. These were the *data* of her problem. These two figures stood like opposing knights, (the black and the white,) foremost on the great chess-board of fate. Lizzie was the wearied, puzzled player. She would idly finger the other pieces, and shift them carelessly hither and thither; but it was of no avail: the game lay between the two knights. She would shut her eyes and long for some kind hand to come and tamper with the board; she would open them and see the two knights standing immovable, face to face. It was nothing new. A fancy had come in and offered defiance to a fact; they must fight it out. Lizzie generously inclined to the fancy, the unknown champion, with a reputation to make. Call her *blasée*, if you like, this little girl, whose record told of a couple of dances and a single lover, heartless, old before her time. Perhaps she deserves your scorn. I confess she thought herself ill-used. By whom? By what? Wherein? These were questions Miss Crowe was not prepared to answer. Her intellect was unequal to the stern logic of human events. She expected two and two to make five: as why should they not for the nonce? She was like an actor who finds himself on the stage with a half-learned part and without sufficient wit to extemporize. Pray, where is the prompter? Alas, Elizabeth, that you had no mother! Young girls are prone to fancy that when once they have a lover, they have everything they need: a conclusion inconsistent with the belief entertained by many persons, that life begins with love. Lizzie's fortunes became old stories to her before she had half read them through. Jack's wounds and danger were an old story. Do not suppose that she had exhausted the lessons, the suggestions of these awful events, their inspirations, exhortations,—that she had wept as became the horror of the tragedy. No: the curtain had not yet fallen, yet our young lady had begun to yawn. To yawn? Ay, and to long for the afterpiece. Since the tragedy dragged, might she not divert herself with that well-bred man beside her?

Elizabeth was far from owning to herself that she had fallen away from her love. For my own part, I need no better proof of the fact than the dull persistency with which she denied it. What accusing voice broke out of the stillness? Jack's nobleness and magnanimity were the hourly theme of her clogged fancy. Again and again she declared to herself that she was unworthy of them, but that, if he would only recover and come home, she would be his eternal bond-slave. So she passed a very miserable month. Let us hope that her childish spirit was being tempered to some useful purpose. Let us hope so.

She roamed about the empty house with her footsteps tracked by an unlaid ghost. She cried aloud and said that she was very unhappy; she groaned and called herself wicked. Then, sometimes, appalled at her moral perplexities, she declared that she was neither wicked nor unhappy; she was contented, patient, and wise. Other girls had lost their lovers: it was the present way of life. Was she weaker than most women? Nay, but Jack was the best of men. If he would only come back directly, without delay, as he was, senseless, dying even, that she might look at him, touch him, speak to him! Then she would say that she could no longer answer for herself, and wonder (or pretend to wonder) whether she were not going mad. Suppose Mrs. Ford should come back and find her in an unswept room, pallid and insane? Or suppose she should die of her troubles? What if she should kill herself?—dismiss the servants, and close the house, and lock herself up with a knife? Then she would cut her arm to escape from dismay at what she had already done; and then her courage would ebb away with her blood, and, having so far pledged herself to despair, her life would ebb away with her courage; and then, alone, in darkness, with none to help her, she would vainly scream, and thrust the knife into her temple, and swoon to death. And Jack would come back, and burst into the house, and wander through the empty rooms, calling her name, and for all answer get a death-scent! These imaginings were the more creditable or discreditable to Lizzie, that she had never read "Romeo and Juliet." At any rate, they served to dissipate time,—heavy, weary time,—the more heavy and weary as it bore dark foreshadowings of some momentous event. If that event would only come, whatever it was, and sever this Gordian knot of doubt!

The days passed slowly: the leaden sands dropped one by one. The roads were too bad for walking; so Lizzie was obliged to confine her restlessness to the narrow bounds of the empty house, or to an occasional journey to the village, where people sickened her by their dull indifference to her spiritual agony. Still they could not fail to remark how poorly Miss Crowe was looking. This was true, and Lizzie knew it. I think she even took a certain comfort in her pallor and in her failing interest in her dress. There was some satisfaction in displaying her white roses amid the apple-cheeked prosperity of Main Street. At last Miss Cooper, the Doctor's sister, spoke to her:—

"How is it, Elizabeth, you look so pale, and thin, and worn out? What you been doing with yourself? Falling in love, eh? It is n't right to be so much alone. Come down and stay with us awhile,—till Mrs. Ford and John come back," added Miss Cooper, who wished to put a cheerful face on the matter.

For Miss Cooper, indeed, any other face would have been difficult. Lizzie agreed to come. Her hostess was a busy, unbeautiful old maid, sister and housekeeper of the village physician. Her occupation here below was to perform the forgotten tasks of her fellow-men,—to pick up their dropped stitches, as she herself declared. She was never idle, for her general cleverness was commensurate with mortal needs. Her own story was, that she kept moving, so that folks could n't see how ugly she was. And, in fact, her existence was manifest through her long train of good deeds,—just as the presence of a comet is shown by its tail. It was doubtless on the above principle that her visage was agitated by a perpetual laugh.

Meanwhile more news had been coming from Virginia. "What an absurdly long letter you sent John," wrote Mrs. Ford, in acknowledging the receipt of the boxes. "His first lucid moment would be very short, if he were to take upon himself to read your effusions. Pray keep your long stories till he gets well." For a fortnight the young soldier remained the same,—feverish, conscious only at intervals. Then came a change for the worse, which, for many weary days, however, resulted in nothing decisive. "If he could only be moved to Glenham, home, and old sights," said his mother, "I should have hope. But think of the journey!" By this time Lizzie had stayed out ten days of her visit.

One day Miss Cooper came in from a walk, radiant with tidings. Her face, as I have observed, wore a continual smile, being dimpled and punctured all over with merriment,—so that, when an unusual cheerfulness was super-diffused, it resembled a tempestuous little pool into which a great stone has been cast.

"Guess who's come," said she, going up to the piano, which Lizzie was carelessly fingering, and putting her hands on the young girl's shoulders. "Just guess!"

Lizzie looked up.

"Jack," she half gasped.

"Oh, dear, no, not that! How stupid of me! I mean Mr. Bruce, your Leatherborough admirer."

"Mr. Bruce! Mr. Bruce!" said Lizzie. "Really?"

"True as I live. He's come to bring his sister to the Water-Cure.[25] I met them at the post-office."

Lizzie felt a strange sensation of good news. Her finger-tips were on fire. She was deaf to her companion's rattling chronicle. She broke into the midst of it with a fragment of some triumphant, jubilant melody. The keys rang beneath her flashing hands. And then she suddenly stopped, and Miss Cooper, who was taking off her bonnet at the mirror, saw that her face was covered with a burning flush.

That evening, Mr. Bruce presented himself at Doctor Cooper's, with whom he had a slight acquaintance. To Lizzie he was infinitely courteous and tender. He assured her, in very pretty terms, of his profound sympathy with her in her cousin's danger,—her cousin he still called him,—and it seemed to Lizzie that until that moment no one had begun to be kind. And then he began to rebuke her, playfully and in excellent taste, for her pale cheeks.

"Is n't it dreadful?" said Miss Cooper. "She looks like a ghost. I guess she's in love."

"He must be a good-for-nothing lover to make his mistress look so sad. If I were you, I'd give him up, Miss Crowe."

"I did n't know I looked sad," said Lizzie.

"You don't now," said Miss Cooper. "You're smiling and blushing. A'n't she blushing, Mr. Bruce?"

"I think Miss Crowe has no more than her natural color," said Bruce, dropping his eye-glass. "What have you been doing all this while since we parted?"

"All this while? it's only six weeks. I don't know. Nothing. What have you?"

"I've been doing nothing, too. It's hard work."

"Have you been to any more parties?"

"Not one."

"Any more sleigh-rides?"

"Yes. I took one more dreary drive all alone,—over that same road, you know. And I stopped at the farm-house again, and saw the old woman we had the talk with. She remembered us, and asked me what had become of the young lady who was with me before. I told her you were gone home, but that I hoped soon to go and see you. So she sent you her love"—

"Oh, how nice!" exclaimed Lizzie.

"Was n't it? And then she made a certain little speech; I won't repeat it, or we shall have Miss Cooper talking about your blushes again."

"I know," cried the lady in question: "she said she was very"—

"Very what?" said Lizzie.

"Very h-a-n-d—what every one says."

"Very handy?" asked Lizzie. "I'm sure no one ever said that."

"Of course," said Bruce; "and I answered what every one answers."

"Have you seen Mrs. Littlefield lately?"

"Several times. I called on her the day before I left town, to see if she had any messages for you."

"Oh, thank you! I hope she's well."

"Oh, she's as jolly as ever. She sent you her love, and hoped you would come back to Leatherborough very soon again. I told her, that, however it might be with the first message, the second should be a joint one from both of us."

"You're very kind. I should like very much to go again.—Do you like Mrs. Littlefield?"

"Like her? Yes. Don't you? She's thought a very pleasing woman."

"Oh, she's very nice.—I don't think she has much conversation."

"Ah, I'm afraid you mean she does n't backbite. We've always found plenty to talk about."

"That's a very significant tone. What, for instance?"

"Well, we *have* talked about Miss Crowe."

"Oh, you have? Do you call that having plenty to talk about?"

"We *have* talked about Mr. Bruce,—have n't we, Elizabeth?" said Miss Cooper, who had her own notion of being agreeable.

It was not an altogether bad notion, perhaps; but Bruce found her interruptions rather annoying, and insensibly allowed them to shorten his visit. Yet, as it was, he sat till eleven o'clock,—a stay quite unprecedented at Glenham.

When he left the house, he went splashing down the road with a very elastic tread, springing over the starlit puddles, and trolling out some sentimental ditty. He reached the inn, and went up to his sister's sitting-room.

"Why, Robert, where have you been all this while?" said Miss Bruce.

"At Dr. Cooper's."

"Dr. Cooper's? I should think you had! Who's Dr. Cooper?"

"Where Miss Crowe's staying."

"Miss Crowe? Ah, Mrs. Littlefield's friend! Is she as pretty as ever?"

"Prettier,—prettier,—prettier. *Tara-ta! tara-ta!*"

"Oh, Robert, do stop that singing! You'll rouse the whole house."

V

Late one afternoon, at dusk, about three weeks after Mr. Bruce's arrival, Lizzie was sitting alone by the fire, in Miss Cooper's parlor, musing, as became the place and hour. The Doctor and his sister came in, dressed for a lecture.

"I'm sorry you won't go, my dear," said Miss Cooper. "It's a most interesting subject: 'A Year of the War.' All the battles and things described, you know."

"I'm tired of war," said Lizzie.

"Well, well, if you're tired of the war, we'll leave you in peace. Kiss me good-bye. What's the matter? You look sick. You are homesick, a'n't you?"

"No, no,—I'm very well."

"Would you like me to stay at home with you?"

"Oh, no! pray, don't!"

"Well, we'll tell you all about it. Will they have programmes, James? I'll bring her a programme.—But you really feel as if you were going to be ill. Feel of her skin, James."

"No, you need n't, Sir," said Lizzie. "How queer of you, Miss Cooper! I'm perfectly well."

And at last her friends departed. Before long the servant came with the lamp, ushering Mr. Mackenzie.

"Good evening, Miss," said he. "Bad news from Mrs. Ford."

"Bad news?"

"Yes, Miss. I've just got a letter stating that Mr. John is growing worse and worse, and that they look for his death from hour to hour.—It's very sad," he added, as Elizabeth was silent.

"Yes, it's very sad," said Lizzie.

"I thought you'd like to hear it."

"Thank you."

"He was a very noble young fellow," pursued Mr. Mackenzie.

Lizzie made no response.

"There's the letter," said. Mr. Mackenzie, handing it over to her.

Lizzie opened it.

"How long she is reading it!" thought her visitor. "You can't see so far from the light, can you, Miss?"

"Yes," said Lizzie.—"His poor mother! Poor woman!"

"Ay, indeed, Miss,—she's the one to be pitied."

"Yes, she's the one to be pitied," said Lizzie. "Well!" and she gave him back the letter.

"I thought you'd like to see it," said Mackenzie, drawing on his gloves; and then, after a pause,—"I'll call again, Miss, if I hear anything more. Good night!"

Lizzie got up and lowered the light, and then went back to her sofa by the fire.

Half an hour passed; it went slowly; but it passed. Still lying there in the dark room on the sofa, Lizzie heard a ring at the door-bell, a man's voice and a man's tread in the hall. She rose and went to the lamp. As she turned it up, the parlor-door opened. Bruce came in.

"I was sitting in the dark," said Lizzie; "but when I heard you coming, I raised the light."

"Are you afraid of me?" said Bruce.

"Oh, no! I'll put it down again. Sit down."

"I saw your friends going out," pursued Bruce; "so I knew I should find you alone.—What are you doing here in the dark?"

"I've just received very bad news from Mrs. Ford about her son. He's much worse, and will probably not live."

"Is it possible?"

"I was thinking about that."

"Dear me! Well that's a sad subject. I'm told he was a very fine young man."

"He was,—very," said Lizzie.

Bruce was silent awhile. He was a stranger to the young officer, and felt that he had nothing to offer beyond the commonplace expressions of sympathy and surprise. Nor had he exactly the measure of his companion's interest in him.

"If he dies," said Lizzie, "it will be under great injustice."

"Ah! what do you mean?"

"There was n't a braver man in the army."

"I suppose not."

"And, oh, Mr. Bruce," continued Lizzie, "he was so clever and good and generous! I wish you had known him."

"I wish I had. But what do you mean by injustice? Were these qualities denied him?"

"No indeed! Everyone that looked at him could see that he was perfect."

"Where's the injustice, then? It ought to be enough for him that you should think so highly of him."

"Oh, he knew that," said Lizzie.

Bruce was a little puzzled by his companion's manner. He watched her, as she sat with her cheek on her hand, looking at the fire. There was a long pause. Either they were too friendly or too thoughtful for the silence to be embarrassing. Bruce broke it at last.

"Miss Crowe," said he, "on a certain occasion, some time ago, when you first heard of Mr. Ford's wounds, I offered you my company, with the wish to console you as far as I might for what seemed a considerable shock. It was, perhaps, a bold offer for so new a friend; but, nevertheless, in it even then my heart spoke. You turned me off. Will you let me repeat it? Now, with a better right, will you let me speak out all my heart?"

Lizzie heard this speech, which was delivered in a slow and hesitating tone, without looking up or moving her head, except, perhaps, at the words "turned me off." After Bruce had ceased, she still kept her position.

"You'll not turn me off now?" added her companion.

She dropped her hand, raised her head, and looked at him a moment: he thought he saw the glow of tears in her eyes. Then she sank back upon the sofa with her face in the shadow of the mantel-piece.

"I don't understand you, Mr. Bruce," said she.

"Ah, Elizabeth! Am I such a poor speaker. How shall I make it plain? When I saw your friends leave home half an hour ago, and reflected that you would probably be alone, I determined to go right in and have a talk with you that I've long been wanting to have. But first I walked half a mile up the road, thinking hard,—thinking how I should say what I had to say. I made up my mind to nothing, but that somehow or other I should say it.

I would trust,—I *do* trust to your frankness, kindness, and sympathy, to a feeling corresponding to my own. Do you understand that feeling? Do you know that I love you? I do, I do, I do! You *must* know it. If you don't, I solemnly swear it. I solemnly ask you, Elizabeth, to take me for your husband."

While Bruce said these words, he rose, with their rising passion, and came and stood before Lizzie. Again she was motionless.

"Does it take you so long to think?" said he, trying to read her indistinct features; and he sat down on the sofa beside her and took her hand.

At last Lizzie spoke.

"Are you sure," said she, "that you love me?"

"As sure as that I breathe. Now, Elizabeth, make me as sure that I am loved in return."

"It seems very strange, Mr. Bruce," said Lizzie.

"What seems strange? Why should it? For a month I've been trying, in a hundred dumb ways, to make it plain; and now, when I swear it, it only seems strange!"

"What do you love me for?"

"For? For yourself, Elizabeth."

"Myself? I am nothing."

"I love you for what you are,—for your deep, kind heart,—for being so perfectly a woman."

Lizzie drew away her hand, and her lover rose and stood before her again. But now she looked up into his face, questioning when she should have answered, drinking strength from his entreaties for her replies. There he stood before her, in the glow of the firelight, in all his gentlemanhood, for her to accept or reject. She slowly rose and gave him the hand she had withdrawn.

"Mr. Bruce, I shall be very proud to love you," she said.

And then, as if this effort was beyond her strength, she half staggered back to the sofa again. And still holding her hand, he sat down beside her. And there they were still sitting when they heard the Doctor and his sister come in.

For three days Elizabeth saw nothing of Mr. Mackenzie. At last, on the fourth day, passing his office in the village, she went in and asked for him. He came out of his little back parlor with his mouth full and a beaming face.

"Good-day, Miss Crowe, and good news!"

"*Good* news?" cried Lizzie.

"Capital!" said he, looking hard at her, while he put on his spectacles. "She writes that Mr. John—won't you take a seat?—has taken a sudden and unexpected turn for the better. Now's the moment to save him; it's an equal risk. They were to start for the North the second day after date. The surgeon comes with them. So they'll be home—of course they'll travel slowly—in four or five days. Yes, Miss, it's a remarkable Providence. And that noble young man will be spared to the country, and to those who love him, as I do."

"I had better go back to the house and have it got ready," said Lizzie, for an answer.

"Yes, Miss, I think you had. In fact, Mrs. Ford made that request."

The request was obeyed. That same day Lizzie went home. For two days she found it her interest to overlook, assiduously, a general sweeping, scrubbing, and provisioning. She allowed herself no idle moment until bed-time. Then—But I would rather not be the chamberlain of her agony. It was the easier to work, as Mr. Bruce had gone to Leatherborough on business.

On the fourth evening, at twilight, John Ford was borne up to the door on his stretcher, with his mother stalking beside him in rigid grief, and kind, silent friends pressing about with helping hands.

> "Home they brought her warrior dead,
> She nor swooned nor uttered cry."[26]

It was, indeed, almost a question, whether Jack was not dead. Death is not thinner, paler, stiller. Lizzie moved about like one in a dream. Of course, when there are so many sympathetic friends, a man's family has nothing to do,—except exercise a little self-control. The women huddled Mrs. Ford to bed; rest was imperative; she was killing herself. And it was significant of her weakness that she did not resent this advice. In greeting her, Lizzie felt as if she were embracing the stone image on the top of a sepulchre. She, too, had her cares anticipated. Good Doctor Cooper and his sister stationed themselves at the young man's couch.

The Doctor prophesied wondrous things of the change of climate; he was certain of a recovery. Lizzie found herself very shortly dealt with as an obstacle to this consummation. Access to John was prohibited. "Perfect stillness, you know, my dear," whispered Miss Cooper, opening his chamber-door on a crack, in a pair of very creaking shoes. So for the first evening that her old friend was at home Lizzie caught but a glimpse of his pale, senseless face, as she hovered outside the long train of his attendants. If we may suppose any of these kind people to have had eyes for aught but the sufferer, we may be sure that they saw another visage equally sad and white. The sufferer? It was hardly Jack, after all.

When Lizzie was turned from Jack's door, she took a covering from a heap of draperies that had been hurriedly tossed down in the hall: it was an old army-blanket. She wrapped it round her, and went out on the verandah. It was nine o'clock; but the darkness was filled with light. A great wanton wind—the ghost of the raw blast which travels by day—had arisen, bearing long, soft gusts of inland spring. Scattered clouds were hurrying across the white sky. The bright moon, careering in their midst, seemed to have wandered forth in frantic quest of the hidden stars.

Lizzie nestled her head in the blanket, and sat down on the steps. A strange earthy smell lingered in that faded old rug, and with it a faint perfume of tobacco. Instantly the young girl's senses were transported as they had never been before to those far-off Southern battle-fields. She saw men lying in swamps, puffing their kindly pipes, drawing their blankets closer, canopied with the same luminous dusk that shone down upon her comfortable weakness. Her mind wandered amid these scenes till recalled to the present by the swinging of the garden-gate. She heard a firm, well-known tread crunching the gravel. Mr. Bruce came up the path. As he drew near the steps, Lizzie arose. The blanket fell back from her head, and Bruce started at recognizing her.

"Hullo! You, Elizabeth? What's the matter?"

Lizzie made no answer.

"Are you one of Mr. Ford's watchers?" he continued, coming up the steps; "how is he?"

Still she was silent. Bruce put out his hands to take hers, and bent forward as if to kiss her. She half shook him off, and retreated toward the door.

"Good heavens!" cried Bruce; "what's the matter? Are you moon-struck? Can't you speak?"

"No,—no,—not to-night," said Lizzie, in a choking voice. "Go away,—go away!"

She stood holding the door-handle, and motioning him off. He hesitated a moment, and then advanced. She opened the door rapidly, and went in. He heard her lock it. He stood looking at it stupidly for some time, and then slowly turned round and walked down the steps.

The next morning Lizzie arose with the early dawn, and came down stairs. She went into the room where Jack lay, and gently opened the door. Miss Cooper was dozing in her chair. Lizzie crossed the threshold, and stole up to the bed. Poor Ford lay peacefully sleeping. There was his old face, after all,—his strong, honest features refined, but not weakened, by pain. Lizzie softly drew up a low chair, and sat down beside him. She gazed into his face,—the dear and honored face into which she had so often gazed in health. It was strangely handsomer: body stood for less. It seemed to Lizzie, that, as the fabric of her lover's soul was more clearly revealed,—the veil of the temple rent wellnigh in twain,—she could read the justification of all her old worship. One of Jack's hands lay outside the sheets,—those strong, supple fingers, once so cunning in workmanship, so frank in friendship, now thinner and whiter than her own. After looking at it for some time, Lizzie gently grasped it. Jack slowly opened his eyes. Lizzie's heart began to throb; it was as if the stillness of the sanctuary had given a sign. At first there was no recognition in the young man's gaze. Then the dull pupils began visibly to brighten. There came to his lips the commencement of that strange moribund smile which seems so ineffably satirical of the things of this world. O imposing spectacle of death! O blessed soul, marked for promotion! What earthly favor is like thine? Lizzie sank down on her knees, and, still clasping John's hand, bent closer over him.

"Jack,—dear, dear Jack," she whispered, "do you know me?"

The smile grew more intense. The poor fellow drew out his other hand, and slowly, feebly placed it on Lizzie's head, stroking down her hair with his fingers.

"Yes, yes," she murmured; "you know me, don't you? I am Lizzie, Jack. Don't you remember Lizzie?"

Ford moved his lips inaudibly, and went on patting her head.

"This is home, you know," said Lizzie; "this is Glenham. You have n't forgotten Glenham? You are with your mother and me and your friends. Dear, darling Jack!"

Still he went on, stroking her head; and his feeble lips tried to emit some sound. Lizzie laid her head down on the pillow beside his own, and still his hand lingered caressingly on her hair.

"Yes, you know me," she pursued; "you are with your friends now forever,—with those who will love and take care of you, oh, forever!"

"I'm very badly wounded," murmured Jack, close to her ear.

"Yes, yes, my dear boy, but your wounds are healing. I will love you and nurse you forever."

"Yes, Lizzie, our old promise," said Jack: and his hand fell upon her neck, and with its feeble pressure he drew her closer, and she wet his face with her tears.

Then Miss Cooper, awakening, rose and drew Lizzie away.

"I am sure you excite him, my dear. It is best he should have none of his family near him,—persons with whom he has associations, you know."

Here the Doctor was heard gently tapping on the window, and Lizzie went round to the door to admit him.

She did not see Jack again all day. Two or three times she ventured into the room, but she was banished by a frown, or a finger raised to the lips. She waylaid the Doctor frequently. He was blithe and cheerful, certain of Jack's recovery. This good man used to exhibit as much moral elation at the prospect of a cure as an orthodox believer at that of a new convert: it was one more body gained from the Devil. He assured Lizzie that the change of scene and climate had already begun to tell: the fever was lessening, the worst symptoms disappearing. He answered Lizzie's reiterated desire to do something by directions to keep the house quiet and the sick-room empty.

Soon after breakfast, Miss Dawes, a neighbor, came in to relieve Miss Cooper, and this indefatigable lady transferred her attention to Mrs. Ford. Action was forbidden her. Miss Cooper was delighted for once to be able to lay down the law to her vigorous neighbor, of whose fine judgment she had always stood in awe. Having bullied Mrs. Ford into taking her breakfast in the little sitting-room, she closed the doors, and prepared for "a good long talk." Lizzie was careful not to break in upon this interview. She had bidden her patroness good morning, asked after her health, and received one of her temperate osculations. As she passed the invalid's door, Doctor Cooper came out and asked her to go and look for a certain roll of bandages, in Mr. John's trunk, which had been carried into another room. Lizzie hastened to perform this task. In fumbling through the contents of the trunk, she came across a packet of letters in a well-known feminine hand-writing. She pocketed it, and, after disposing of the bandages, went to her own room, locked the door, and sat down to examine the letters. Between reading and thinking and sighing and (in spite of herself) smiling, this process took the whole morning. As she came down to dinner, she encountered Mrs. Ford and Miss Cooper, emerging from the sitting-room, the good long talk being only just concluded.

"How do you feel, Ma'am?" she asked of the elder lady,—"rested?"

For all answer Mrs. Ford gave a look—I had almost said a scowl—so hard, so cold, so reproachful, that Lizzie was transfixed. But suddenly its sickening meaning was revealed to her. She turned to Miss Cooper, who stood pale and fluttering beside the mistress, her everlasting smile glazed over with a piteous, deprecating glance; and I fear her eyes flashed out the same message of angry scorn they had just received. These telegraphic operations are very rapid. The ladies hardly halted: the next moment found them seated at the dinner-table with Miss Cooper scrutinizing her napkin-mark and Mrs. Ford saying grace.

Dinner was eaten in silence. When it was over, Lizzie returned to her own room. Miss Cooper went home, and Mrs. Ford went to her son. Lizzie heard the firm low click of the lock as she closed the door. Why did she lock it? There was something fatal in the silence that followed. The plot of her little tragedy thickened. Be it so: she would act her part with the rest. For the second time in her experience, her mind was lightened by the intervention of Mrs. Ford. Before the scorn of her own conscience, (which never came,) before Jack's deepest reproach, she was ready to bow down,—but not before that long-faced Nemesis in black silk. The leaven of resentment began to work. She leaned back in her chair, and folded her arms, brave to await results. But before long she fell asleep. She was aroused by a knock at her chamber-door. The afternoon was far gone. Miss Dawes stood without.

"Elizabeth, Mr. John wants very much to see you, with his love. Come down very gently: his mother is lying down. Will you sit with him while I take my dinner?—Better? Yes, ever so much."

Lizzie betook herself with trembling haste to Jack's bedside.

He was propped up with pillows. His pale cheeks were slightly flushed. His eyes were bright. He raised himself, and, for such feeble arms, gave Lizzie a long, strong embrace.

"I've not seen you all day, Lizzie," said he. "Where have you been?"

"Dear Jack, they would n't let me come near you. I begged and prayed. And I wanted so to go to you in the army; but I could n't. I wish, I wish I had!"

"You would n't have liked it, Lizzie. I'm glad you did n't. It's a bad, bad place."

He lay quietly, holding her hands and gazing at her.

"Can I do anything for you, dear?" asked the young girl. "I would work my life out. I'm so glad you're better!"

It was some time before Jack answered,—

"Lizzie," said he, at last, "I sent for you to look at you.—You are more wondrously beautiful than ever. Your hair is brown,—like—like nothing; your eyes are blue; your neck is white. Well, well!"

He lay perfectly motionless, but for his eyes. They wandered over her with a kind of peaceful glee, like sunbeams playing on a statue. Poor Ford lay, indeed, not unlike an old wounded Greek, who at falling dusk has crawled into a temple to die, steeping the last dull interval in idle admiration of sculptured Artemis.

"Ah, Lizzie, this is already heaven!" he murmured.

"It will be heaven when you get well," whispered Lizzie.

He smiled into her eyes:—

"You say more than you mean. There should be perfect truth between us. Dear Lizzie, I am not going to get well. They are all very much mistaken. I am going to die. I've done my work. Death makes up for everything. My great pain is in leaving you. But you, too, will die one of these days; remember that. In all pain and sorrow, remember that."

Lizzie was able to reply only by the tightening grasp of her hands.

"But there is something more," pursued Jack. "Life *is* as good as death. Your heart has found its true keeper; so we shall all three be happy. Tell him I bless him and honor him. Tell him God, too, blesses him. Shake hands with him for me," said Jack, feebly moving his pale fingers. "My mother," he went on,—"be very kind to her. She will have great grief, but she will not die of it. She'll live to great age. Now, Lizzie, I can't talk any more; I wanted to say farewell. You'll keep me farewell,—you'll stay with me awhile,—won't you? I'll look at you till the last. For a little while you'll be mine, holding my hands—so—until death parts us."

Jack kept his promise. His eyes were fixed in a firm gaze long after the sense had left them.

In the early dawn of the next day, Elizabeth left her sleepless bed, opened the window, and looked out on the wide prospect, still cool and dim with departing night. It offered freshness and peace to her hot head and restless heart. She dressed herself hastily, crept down stairs, passed the death-chamber, and stole out of the quiet house. She turned away from the still sleeping village and walked towards the open country. She went a long way without knowing it. The sun had risen high when she bethought herself to turn. As she came back along the brightening highway, and drew near home, she saw a tall figure standing beneath the budding trees of the garden, hesitating, apparently, whether to open the gate. Lizzie came upon him almost before he had seen her. Bruce's first movement was to put out his hands, as any lover might; but as Lizzie raised her veil, he dropped them.

"Yes, Mr. Bruce," said Lizzie, "I'll give you my hand once more,—in farewell."

"Elizabeth!" cried Bruce, half stupefied, "in God's name, what do you mean by these crazy speeches?"

"I mean well. I mean kindly and humanely to you. And I mean justice to my old—old love."

She went to him, took his listless hand, without looking into his wild, smitten face, shook it passionately, and then, wrenching her own from his grasp, opened the gate and let it swing behind her.

"No! no! no!" she almost shrieked, turning about in the path. "I forbid you to follow me!"

But for all that, he went in.

Harold Frederic

from *Marsena, and Other Stories of the Wartime* (1894)

THE WAR WIDOW

I

Although we had been one man short all day, and there was a plain threat of rain in the hot air, everybody left the hay-field long before sundown. It was too much to ask of human nature to stay off up in the remote meadows, when such remarkable things were happening down around the house.

Marcellus Jones and I were in the pasture, watching the dog get the cows together for the homeward march. He did it so well and, withal, so willingly, that there was no call for us to trouble ourselves in keeping up with him. We waited instead at the open bars until the hay-wagon had passed through, rocking so heavily in the ancient pitch-hole, as it did so, that the driver was nearly thrown off his perch on the top of the high load. Then we put up the bars, and fell in close behind the hay-makers. A rich cloud of dust, far ahead on the road, suggested that the dog was doing his work even too willingly, but for the once we feared no rebuke. Almost anything might be condoned that day.

Five grown-up men walked abreast down the highway, in the shadow of the towering wagon mow, clad much alike in battered straw hats, gray woolen shirts open at the neck, and rough old trousers bulging over the swollen, creased ankles of thick boots. One had a scythe on his arm; two others bore forks over their shoulders. By request, Hi Tuckerman allowed me to carry his sickle.

Although my present visit to the farm had been of only a few days' duration—and those days of strenuous activity darkened by a terrible grief—I had come to be very friendly with Mr. Tuckerman. He took a good deal more notice of me than the others did; and, when chance and leisure afforded, addressed the bulk of his remarks to me. This favoritism, though it fascinated me, was not without its embarrassing side. Hi Tuckerman had taken part in the battle of Gaines's Mill two years before, and had been shot straight through the tongue. One could still see the deep scar on each of his cheeks, a sunken and hairless pit in among his sandy beard. His heroism in the war and his good qualities as a citizen had earned for him the esteem of his neighbors, and they saw to it that he never wanted for work. But their present respect for him stopped short of the pretence that they enjoyed hearing him talk. Whenever he attempted conversation, people moved away, or began boisterous dialogues with one another to drown him out. Being a sensitive man, he had come to prefer silence to these rebuffs among those he knew. But he still had a try at the occasional polite stranger—and I suppose it was in this capacity that I won his heart. Though I never of my own initiative understood a word he said, Marcellus sometimes interpreted a sentence or so for me, and I listened to all the rest with a fraudulently wise face. To give only a solitary illustration of the tax thus levied on our friendship, I may mention that when Hi Tuckerman said "*Aah!*-ah-*aah!*-uh," he meant "Rappahannock," and he did this rather better than a good many other words.

"Rappahannock," alas! was a word we heard often enough in those days, along with Chickahominy and Rapidan, and that odd Chattahoochee, the sound of which raised always in my boyish mind the notion that the geography-makers must have achieved it in their baby-talk period. These strange Southern river names and many more were as familiar to the ears of these four other untraveled Dearborn County farmers as the noise of their own shallow Nedahma rattling over its pebbles in the valley yonder. Only when their slow fancy fitted substance to these names they saw in mind's eye dark, sinister, swampy currents, deep and silent, and discolored with human blood.

Two of these men who strode along behind the wagon were young half-uncles of mine, Myron and Warren Turnbull, stout, thick-shouldered, honest fellows not much out of their teens, who worked hard, said little, and were always lumped together in speech, by their family, the hired help, and the neighbors, as "the boys." They asserted themselves so rarely, and took everything as it came with such docility, that I myself, being in my eleventh year, thought of them as very young indeed. Next them walked a man, hired just for the haying, named Philleo, and then, scuffling along over the uneven humps and hollows on the outer edge of the road, came Si Hummaston, with the empty ginger-beer pail knocking against his knees.

As Tuckerman's "Hi" stood for Hiram, so I assume the other's "Si" meant Silas, or possibly Cyrus. I dare say no one, not even his mother, had ever called him by his full name. I know that my companion, Marcellus Jones, who wouldn't be thirteen until after Thanksgiving, habitually addressed him as Si, and almost daily I resolved that I would do so myself. He was a man of more than fifty, I should think, tall, lean, and what Marcellus called "bible-backed." He had a short iron-gray beard and long hair. Whenever there was any very hard or steady work going, he generally gave out and went to sit in the shade, holding a hand flat over his heart, and shaking his head dolefully. This kept a good many from hiring him, and even in haying-time, when everybody on two legs is of some use, I fancy he would often have been left out if it hadn't been for my grandparents. They respected him on account of his piety and his moral character, and always had him down when extra work began. He was said to be the only hired man in the township who could not be goaded in some way into swearing. He looked at one slowly, with the mild expression of a heifer calf.

We had come to the crown of the hill, and the wagon started down the steeper incline, with a great groaning of the brake. The men, by some tacit understanding, halted and overlooked the scene.

The big old stone farm-house—part of which is said to date almost to the Revolutionary times—was just below us, so near, indeed, that Marcellus said he had once skipped a scaling-stone from where we stood to its roof. The dense, big-leafed foliage of a sap-bush, sheltered in the basin which dipped from our feet, pretty well hid this roof now from view. Farther on, heavy patches of a paler, brighter green marked the orchard, and framed one side of a cluster of barns and stables, at the end of which three or four belated cows were loitering by the trough. It was so still that we could hear the clatter of the stanchions as the rest of the herd sought their places inside the milking-barn.

The men, though, had no eyes for all this, but bent their gaze fixedly on the road, down at the bottom. For a long way this thoroughfare was bordered by a row of tall poplars, which, as we were placed, receded from the vision in so straight a line that they seemed one high, fat tree. Beyond these one saw only a line of richer green, where the vine-wrapped rail-fences cleft their way between the ripening fields.

"I'd 'a' took my oath it was them," said Philleo. "I can spot them grays as fur's I can see 'em. They turned by the school-house there, or I'll eat it, school-ma'am 'n' all. And the buggy was follerin' 'em, too."

"Yes, I thought it was them," said Myron, shading his eyes with his brown hand.

"But they ought to got past the poplars by this time, then," remarked Warren.

"Why, they'll be drivin' as slow as molasses in January," put in Si Hummaston. "When you come to think of it, it is pretty nigh the same as a regular funeral. You mark my words, your father'll have walked them grays every step of the road. I s'pose he'll drive himself— he wouldn't trust bringin' Alvy home to nobody else, would he? I know I wouldn't, if the Lord had given me such a son; but then he didn't!"

"No, He didn't!" commented the first speaker, in an unnaturally loud tone of voice, to break in upon the chance that Hi Tuckerman was going to try to talk. But Hi only stretched out his arm, pointing the forefinger toward the poplars.

Sure enough, something was in motion down at the base of the shadows on the road. Then it crept forward, out in the sunlight, and separated itself into two vehicles. A farm wagon came first, drawn by a team of gray horses. Close after it followed a buggy, with its black top raised. Both advanced so slowly that they seemed scarcely to be moving at all.

"Well, I swan!" exclaimed Si Hummaston, after a minute, "it's Dana Pillsbury drivin' the wagon after all! Well—I dunno—yes, I guess that's prob'bly what I'd 'a' done too, if I'd b'n your father. Yes, it does look more correct, his follerin' on behind, like that. I s'pose that's Alvy's widder in the buggy there with him."

"Yes, that's Serena—it looks like her little girl with her," said Myron, gravely.

"I s'pose we might's well be movin' along down," observed his brother, and at that we all started.

We walked more slowly now, matching our gait to the snail-like progress of those coming toward us. As we drew near to the gate, the three hired men instinctively fell behind the brothers, and in that position the group halted on the grass, facing our drive-way where it left the main road. Not a word was uttered by any one. When at last the wagon came up, Myron and Warren took off their hats, and the others followed suit, all holding them poised at the level of their shoulders.

Dana Pillsbury, carrying himself rigidly upright on the box-seat, drove past us with eyes fixed straight ahead, and a face as coldly expressionless as that of a wooden Indian. The wagon was covered all over with rubber blankets, so that whatever it bore was hidden. Only a few paces behind came the buggy, and my grandfather, old Arphaxed Turnbull, went by in his turn with the same averted, far-away gaze, and the same resolutely stolid countenance. He held the restive young carriage horse down to a decorous walk, a single firm hand on the tight reins, without so much as looking at it. The strong yellow light of the declining sun poured full upon his long gray beard, his shaven upper lip, his dark-skinned, lean, domineering face—and made me think of some hard and gloomy old prophet seeing a vision, in the back part of the Old Testament. If that woman beside him, swathed in heavy black raiment, and holding a child up against her arm, was my Aunt Serena, I should never have guessed it.

We put on our hats again, and walked up the drive-way with measured step behind the carriage till it stopped at the side-piazza stoop. The wagon had passed on toward the big new red barn—and crossing its course I saw my Aunt Em, bareheaded and with her sleeves rolled up, going to the cow-barn with a milking-pail in her hand. She was walking quickly, as if in a great hurry.

"There's your Ma," I whispered to Marcellus, assuming that he would share my surprise at her rushing off like this, instead of waiting to say 'How-d'-do' to Serena. He only nodded knowingly, and said nothing.

No one else said much of anything. Myron and Warren shook hands in stiff solemnity with the veiled and craped sister-in-law, when their father had helped her and her daughter from the buggy, and one of them remarked in a constrained way that the hot spell seemed to keep up right along. The new comers ascended the steps to the open door, and the woman and child went inside. Old Arphaxed turned on the threshold, and seemed to behold us for the first time.

"After you've put out the horse," he said, "I want the most of yeh to come up to the new barn. Si Hummaston and Marcellus can do the milkin.'"

"I kind o' rinched my wrist this forenoon," put in Si, with a note of entreaty in his voice. He wanted sorely to be one of the party at the red barn.

"Mebbe milkin' 'll be good for it," said Arphaxed, curtly. "You and Marcellus do what I say, and keep Sidney with you." With this he, too, went into the house.

II

It wasn't an easy matter for even a member of the family like myself to keep clearly and untangled in his head all the relationships which existed under this patriarchal Turnbull roof.

Old Arphaxed had been married twice. His first wife was the mother of two children, who grew up, and the older of these was my father, Wilbur Turnbull. He never liked farm-life, and left home early, not without some hard feeling, which neither father nor son ever quite forgot. My father made a certain success of it as a business man in Albany until, in the thirties, his health broke down. He died when I was seven and, although he left some property, my mother was forced to supplement this help by herself going to work as forewoman in a large store. She was too busy to have much time for visiting, and I don't think there was any great love lost between her and the people on the farm; but it was a good healthy place for me to be sent to when the summer vacation came, and withal inexpensive, and so the first of July each year generally found me out at the homestead, where, indeed, nobody pretended to be heatedly fond of me, but where I was still treated well and enjoyed myself. This year it was understood that my mother was coming out to bring me home later on.

The other child of that first marriage was a girl who was spoken of in youth as Emmeline, but whom I knew now as Aunt Em. She was a silent, tough-fibred, hard-working creature, not at all good-looking, but relentlessly neat, and the best cook I ever knew. Even when the house was filled with extra hired men, no one ever thought of getting in any female help, so tireless and so resourceful was Em. She did all the housework there was to do, from cellar to garret, was continually lending a hand in the men's chores, made more butter than the household could eat up, managed a large kitchen-garden, and still had a good deal of spare time, which she spent in sitting out in the piazza in a starched pink calico gown, knitting the while she watched who went up and down the road. When you knew her, you understood how it was that the original Turnbulls had come into that part of the country just after the Revolution, and in a few years chopped down all the forests, dug up all the stumps, drained the swale-lands, and turned the entire place from a wilderness into a flourishing and fertile home for civilized people. I used to feel, when I looked at her, that she would have been quite equal to doing the whole thing herself.

All at once, when she was something over thirty, Em had up and married a mowing-machine agent named Abel Jones, whom no one knew anything about, and who, indeed, had only been in the neighborhood for a week or so. The family was struck dumb with amazement. The idea of Em's dallying with the notion of matrimony had never crossed anybody's mind. As a girl she had never had any patience with husking-bees or dances or sleigh-ride parties. No young man had ever seen her home from anywhere, or had had the remotest encouragement to hang around the house. She had never been pretty—so my mother told me—and as she got along in years grew dumpy and thick in figure, with a plain, fat face, a rather scowling brow, and an abrupt, ungracious manner. She had no conversational gifts whatever, and, through years of increasing taciturnity and confirmed unsociability, built up in everybody's mind the conviction that, if there could be a man so wild and unsettled in intellect as to suggest a tender thought to Em, he would get his ears cuffed off his head for his pains.

Judge, then, how like a thunderbolt the episode of the mowing-machine agent fell upon the family. To bewildered astonishment there soon enough succeeded rage. This Jones was a curly headed man, with a crinkly black beard like those of Joseph's brethren in the Bible picture. He had no home and no property, and didn't seem to amount to much even as a salesman of other people's goods. His machine was quite the worst then in the market, and it could not be learned that he had sold a single one in the county. But he had married Em, and it was calmly proposed that he should henceforth regard the farm as his home. After this point had been sullenly conceded, it turned out that Jones was a widower, and had a boy nine or ten years old, named Marcellus, who was in a sort of orphan asylum in Vermont. There were more angry scenes between father and daughter, and a good deal more bad blood, before it was finally agreed that the boy also should come and live on the farm.

All this had happened in 1860 or 1861. Jones had somewhat improved on acquaintance. He knew about lightning-rods, and had been able to fit out all the farm buildings with them at cost price. He had turned a little money now and again in trades with hop-poles, butter-firkins, shingles, and the like, and he was very ingenious in mending and fixing up odds and ends. He made shelves and painted the woodwork, and put a tar roof on the summer kitchen. Even Martha, the second Mrs. Turnbull, came finally to admit that he was handy about a house.

This Martha became the head of the household while Em was still a little girl. She was a heavy woman, mentally as well as bodily, rather prone to a peevish view of things, and greatly given to pride in herself and her position, but honest, charitable in her way, and not unkindly at heart. On the whole she was a good stepmother, and Em probably got on quite as well with her as she would have done with her own mother—even in the matter of the mowing-machine agent.

To Martha three sons were born. The two younger ones, Myron and Warren, have already been seen. The eldest boy, Alva, was the pride of the family, and, for that matter, of the whole section.

Alva was the first Turnbull to go to college. From his smallest boyhood it had been manifest that he had great things before him, so handsome and clever and winning a lad was he. Through each of his schooling years he was the honor man of his class, and he finished in a blaze of glory by taking the Clark Prize, and practically everything else within reach in the way of academic distinctions. He studied law at Octavius, in the office of Judge Schermerhorn, and in a little time was not only that distinguished man's partner, but distinctly the more important figure in the firm. At the age of twenty-five he was sent to the Assembly. The next year they made him District Attorney, and it was quite understood that it rested with him whether he should be sent to Congress later on, or be presented by the Dearborn County bar for the next vacancy on the Supreme Court bench.

At this point in his brilliant career he married Miss Serena Wadsworth, of Wadsworth's Falls. The wedding was one of the most imposing social events the county had known, so it was said, since the visit of Lafayette. The Wadsworths were an older family, even, than the Fairchilds, and infinitely more fastidious and refined. The daughters of the household, indeed, carried their refinement to such a pitch that they lived an almost solitary life, and grew to the parlous verge of old-maidhood simply because there was nobody good enough to marry them. Alva Turnbull was, however, up to the standard. It could not be said, of course, that his home surroundings quite matched those of his bride; but, on the other hand, she was nearly two years his senior, and this was held to make matters about even.

In a year or so came the War, and nowhere in the North did patriotic excitement run higher than in this old abolition stronghold of upper Dearborn. Public meetings were held, and nearly a whole regiment was raised in Octavius and the surrounding towns alone. Alva Turnbull made the most stirring and important speech at the first big gathering, and sent a thrill through the whole country side by claiming the privilege of heading the list of volunteers. He was made a captain by general acclaim, and went off with his company in time to get chased from the field of Bull Run. When he came home on a furlough in 1863 he was a major, and later on he rose to be lieutenant-colonel. We understood vaguely that he might have climbed vastly higher in promotion but for the fact that he was too moral and conscientious to get on very well with his immediate superior, General Boyce, of Thessaly, who was notoriously a drinking man.

It was glory enough to have him at the farm, on that visit of his, even as a major. His old parents literally abased themselves at his feet, quite tremulous in their awed pride at his greatness. It made it almost too much to have Serena there also, this fair, thin-faced, prim-spoken daughter of the Wadsworths, and actually to call her by her first name. It was haying time, I remember, but the hired men that year did not eat their meals with the family, and there was even a question whether Marcellus and I were socially advanced enough to come to the table, where Serena and her husband were feeding themselves in state with a novel kind of silver implement called a four-tined fork. If Em hadn't put her foot down, out to the kitchen we should both have gone, I fancy. As it was, we sat decorously at the far end of the table, and asked with great politeness to have things passed to us, which by standing up we could have reached as well as not. It was slow, but it made us feel immensely respectable, almost as if we had been born Wadsworths ourselves.

We agreed that Serena was "stuck up," and Marcellus reported Aunt Em as feeling that her bringing along with her a nursemaid to be waited on hand and foot, just to take care of a baby, was an imposition bordering upon the intolerable. He said that that was the sort of thing the English did until George Washington rose and drove them out. But we both felt that Alva was splendid.

He was a fine creature physically—taller even than old Arphaxed, with huge square shoulders and a mighty frame. I could recall him as without whiskers, but now he had a waving lustrous brown beard, the longest and biggest I ever saw. He didn't pay much attention to us boys, it was true; but he was affable when we came in his way, and he gave Myron and Warren each a dollar bill when they went to Octavius to see the Fourth of July doings. In the evening some of the more important neighbors would drop in, and then Alva would talk about the War, and patriotism, and saving the Union, till it was like listening to Congress itself. He had a rich, big voice which filled the whole room, so that the hired men could hear every word out in the kitchen; but it was even more affecting to see him walking with his father down under the poplars, with his hands making orator's gestures as he spoke, and old Arphaxed looking at him and listening with shining eyes.

Well, then, he and his wife went away to visit her folks, and then we heard he had left to join his regiment. From time to time he wrote to his father—letters full of high and loyal sentiments, which were printed next week in the Octavius *Transcript,* and the week after in the Thessaly *Banner of Liberty.* Whenever any of us thought about the War—and who thought much of anything else?—it was always with Alva as the predominant figure in every picture.

Sometimes the arrival of a letter for Aunt Em, or a chance remark about a broken chair or a clock hopelessly out of kilter, would recall for the moment the fact that Abel Jones was also at the seat of war. He had enlisted on that very night when Alva headed the roll of honor, and he had marched away in Alva's company. Somehow he got no promotion, but remained in the ranks. Not even the members of the family were shown the letters Aunt Em received, much less the printers of the newspapers. They were indeed poor misspelled scrawls, about which no one displayed any interest or questioned Aunt Em. Even Marcellus rarely spoke of his father, and seemed to share to the full the family's concentration of thought upon Alva.

Thus matters stood when spring began to play at being summer in the year of '64. The birds came and the trees burst forth into green, the sun grew hotter and the days longer, the strawberries hidden under the big leaves in our yard started into shape, where the blossoms had been, quite in the ordinary, annual way, with us up North. But down where that dread thing they called "The War" was going on, this coming of warm weather meant more awful massacre, more tortured hearts, and desolated homes, than ever before. I can't be at all sure how much later reading and associations have helped out and patched up what seem to be my boyish recollections of this period; but it is, at all events, much clearer in my mind than are the occurrences of the week before last.

We heard a good deal about how deep the mud was in Virginia that spring. All the photographs and tin-types of officers which found their way to relatives at home, now, showed them in boots that came up to their thighs. Everybody understood that as soon as this mud dried up a little, there were to be most terrific doings. The two great lines of armies lay scowling at each other, still on that blood-soaked fighting ground between Washington and Richmond where they were three years before. Only now things were to go differently. A new general[27] was at the head of affairs, and he was going in, with jaws set and nerves of steel, to smash, kill, burn, annihilate, sparing nothing, looking not to right or left, till the red road had been hewed through to Richmond. In the first week of May this thing began—a push forward all along the line—and the North, with scared eyes and fluttering heart, held its breath.

My chief personal recollection of those historic forty days is that one morning I was awakened early by a noise in my bedroom, and saw my mother looking over the contents of the big chest of drawers which stood against the wall. She was getting out some black articles of apparel. When she discovered that I was awake, she told me in a low voice that my Uncle Alva had been killed. Then a few weeks later my school closed, and I was packed off to the farm for the vacation. It will be better to tell what had happened as I learned it there from Marcellus and the others.

Along about the middle of May, the weekly paper came up from Octavius, and old Arphaxed Turnbull, as was his wont, read it over out on the piazza before supper. Presently he called his wife to him, and showed her something in it. Martha went out into the kitchen, where Aunt Em was getting the meal ready, and told her, as gently as she could, that there was very bad news for her; in fact, her husband, Abel Jones, had been killed in the first day's battle in the Wilderness, something like a week before. Aunt Em said she didn't believe it, and Martha brought in the paper and pointed out the fatal line to her. It was not quite clear whether this convinced Aunt Em or not. She finished getting supper, and sat silently through the meal, afterwards, but she went upstairs to her room before family prayers. The next day she was about as usual, doing the work and saying nothing. Marcellus told me that to the best of his belief no one had said anything to her on the subject. The old people were a shade more ceremonious in their manner toward her, and "the boys" and the hired men were on the lookout to bring in water for her from the well, and to spare her as much as possible in the routine of chores, but no one talked about Jones. Aunt Em did not put on mourning. She made a black necktie for Marcellus to wear to church, but stayed away from meeting herself.

A little more than a fortnight afterwards, Myron was walking down the road from the meadows one afternoon, when he saw a man on horseback coming up from the poplars, galloping like mad in a cloud of dust. The two met at the gate. The man was one of the hired helps of the Wadsworths, and he had ridden as hard as he could pelt from the Falls, fifteen miles away, with a message, which now he gave Myron to read. Both man and beast dripped sweat, and trembled with fatigued excitement. The youngster eyed them, and then gazed meditatively at the sealed envelope in his hand.

"I s'pose you know what's inside?" he asked, looking up at last.

The man in the saddle nodded, with a tell-tale look on his face, and breathing heavily.

Myron handed the letter back, and pushed the gate open. "You'd better go up and give it to father yourself," he said. "I ain't got the heart to face him—jest now, at any rate."

Marcellus was fishing that afternoon, over in the creek which ran through the woods. Just as at last he was making up his mind that it must be about time to go after the cows, he saw Myron sitting on a log beside the forest path, whittling mechanically, and staring at the foliage before him, in an obvious brown study. Marcellus went up to him, and had to speak twice before Myron turned his head and looked up.

"Oh! it's you, eh, Bubb?" he remarked dreamily, and began gazing once more into the thicket.

"What's the matter?" asked the puzzled boy.

"I guess Alvy's dead," replied Myron. To the lad's comments and questions he made small answer. "No," he said at last, "I don't feel much like goin' home jest now. Lea' me alone here; I'll prob'ly turn up later on." And Marcellus went alone to the pasture, and thence, at the tail of his bovine procession, home.

When he arrived he regretted not having remained with Myron in the woods. It was like coming into something which was prison, hospital, and tomb in one. The household was paralyzed with horror and fright. Martha had gone to bed, or rather had been put there by Em, and all through the night, when he woke up, he heard her broken and hysterical voice in moans and screams. The men had hitched up the grays, and Arphaxed Turnbull was getting into the buggy to drive to Octavius for news when the boy came up. He looked twenty years older than he had at noon—all at once turned into a chalk-faced, trembling, infirm old man—and could hardly see to put his foot on the carriage-step. His son Warren had offered to go with him, and had been rebuffed almost with fierceness. Warren and the others silently bowed their heads before this mood; instinct told them that nothing but Arphaxed's show of temper held him from collapse—from falling at their feet and grovelling on the grass with cries and sobs of anguish, perhaps even dying in a fit. After he had driven off they forbore to talk to one another, but went about noiselessly with drooping chins and knotted brows.

"It jest took the tuck out of everything," said Marcellus, relating these tragic events to me. There was not much else to tell. Martha had had what they call brain fever, and had emerged from this some weeks afterward a pallid and dim-eyed ghost of her former self, sitting for hours together in her rocking-chair in the unused parlor, her hands idly in her lap, her poor thoughts glued ceaselessly to that vague, far-off Virginia which folks told about as hot and sunny, but which her mind's eye saw under the gloom of an endless and dreadful night. Arphaxed had gone South, still defiantly alone, to bring back the body of his boy. An acquaintance wrote to them of his being down sick in Washington, prostrated by the heat and strange water; but even from his sick-bed he had sent on orders to an undertaking firm out at the front, along with a hundred dollars, their price in advance for embalming. Then, recovering, he had himself pushed down to headquarters, or as near them as civilians might approach, only to learn that he had passed the precious freight on the way. He posted back again, besieging the railroad officials at every point with inquiries, scolding, arguing, beseeching in turn, until at last he overtook his quest at Juno Mills Junction, only a score of miles from home.

Then only he wrote, telling people his plans. He came first to Octavius, where a funeral service was held in the forenoon, with military honors, the Wadsworths as the principal mourners, and a memorable turnout of distinguished citizens. The town-hall was draped with mourning, and so was Alva's pew in the Episcopal Church, which he had deserted his ancestral Methodism to join after his marriage. Old Arphaxed listened to the novel burial service of his son's communion, and watched the clergyman in his curious white and black vestments, with sombre pride. He himself needed and desired only a plain and homely religion, but it was fitting that his boy should have organ music and flowers and a ritual.

Dana Pillsbury had arrived in town early in the morning with the grays, and a neighbor's boy had brought in the buggy. Immediately after dinner Arphaxed had gathered up Alva's widow and little daughter, and started the funeral cortège upon its final homeward stage.

And so I saw them arrive on that July afternoon.

III

For so good and patient a man, Si Hummaston bore himself rather vehemently during the milking. It was hotter in the barn than it was outside in the sun, and the stifling air swarmed with flies, which seemed to follow Si perversely from stall to stall and settle on his cow. One beast put her hoof square in his pail, and another refused altogether to "give down," while the rest kept up a tireless slapping and swishing of their tails very hard to bear, even if one had the help of profanity. Marcellus and I listened carefully to hear him at last provoked to an oath, but the worst thing he uttered, even when the cow stepped in the milk, was "Dum your buttons!" which Marcellus said might conceivably be investigated by a church committee, but was hardly out-and-out swearing.

I remember Si's groans and objurgations, his querulous "Hyst there, will ye!" his hypocritical "So-boss! So-boss!" his despondent "They never will give down for me!" because presently there was crossed upon this woof of peevish impatience the web of a curious conversation.

Si had been so slow in his headway against flapping tails and restive hoofs that, before he had got up to the end of the row, Aunt Em had finished her side. She brought over her stool and pail, and seated herself at the next cow to Hummaston's. For a little, one heard only the resonant din of the stout streams against the tin; then, as the bottom was covered, there came the ploughing plash of milk on milk, and Si could hear himself talk.

"S'pose you know S'reny's come, 'long with your father," he remarked, ingratiatingly.

"I saw 'em drive in," replied Em.

"*Whoa! Hyst there! Hole still, can't ye?* I didn't know if you quite made out who she was, you was scootin' 'long so fast. They ain't—*Whoa there!*—they ain't nothin' the matter 'twixt you and her, is they?"

"I don't know as there is," said Em, curtly. "The world's big enough for both of us—we ain't no call to bunk into each other."

"No, of course—*Now you stop it!*—but it looked kind o' curious to me, your pikin' off like that, without waitin' to say 'How-d'-do?' Of course, I never had no relation by marriage that was stuck-up at all, or looked down on me—*Stiddy there now!*—but I guess I can reelize [sic] pretty much how you feel about it. I'm a good deal of a hand at that. It's what they call imagination. It's a gift, you know, like good looks, or preachin', or the knack o' makin' money. But you can't help what you're born with, can you? I'd been a heap better off if my gift 'd be'n in some other direction; but, as I tell 'em, it ain't my fault. And my imagination—*Hi, there! git over, will ye?*—it's downright cur'ous sometimes, how it works. Now I could tell, you see, that you 'n S'reny didn't pull together. I s'pose she never writ a line to you, when your husband was killed?"

"Why should she?" demanded Em. "We never did correspond. What'd be the sense of beginning then? She minds her affairs, 'n I mind mine. Who wanted her to write?"

"Oh, of course not," said Si, lightly. "Prob'ly you'll get along better together, though, now that you'll see more of one another. I s'pose S'reny's figurin' on stayin' here right along now, her 'n' her little girl. Well, it'll be nice for the old folks to have somebody they're fond of. They jest worshipped the ground Alvy walked on—and I s'pose they won't be anything in this wide world too good for that little girl of his. Le's see, she must be comin' on three now, ain't she?"

"I don't know anything about her!" snapped Aunt Em, with emphasis.

"Of course, it's natural the old folks should feel so—she bein' Alvy's child. I hain't noticed anything special, but does it—*Well I swan! Hyst there!*—does it seem to you that they're as good to Marcellus, quite, as they used to be? I don't hear 'em sayin' nothin' about his goin' to school next winter."

Aunt Em said nothing, too, but milked doggedly on. Si told her about the thickness and profusion of Serena's mourning, guardedly hinted at the injustice done him by not allowing him to go to the red barn with the others, speculated on the likelihood of the Wadsworths' contributing to their daughter's support, and generally exhibited his interest in the family through a monologue which finished only with the milking; but Aunt Em made no response whatever.

When the last pails had been emptied into the big cans at the door—Marcellus and I had let the cows out one by one into the yard, as their individual share in the milking ended—Si and Em saw old Arphaxed wending his way across from the house to the red barn. He appeared more bent than ever, but he walked with a slowness which seemed born of reluctance even more than of infirmity.

"Well, now," mused Si, aloud, "Brother Turnbull an' me's be'n friends for a good long spell. I don't believe he'd be mad if I cut over now to the red barn too, seein' the milkin's all out of the way. Of course I don't want to do what ain't right—what d'you think now, Em, honest? Think it 'ud rile him?"

"I don't know anything about it!" my aunt replied, with increased vigor of emphasis. "But for the land sake go somewhere! Don't hang around botherin' me. I got enough else to think of besides your everlasting cackle."

Thus rebuffed, Si meandered sadly into the cow-yard, shaking his head as he came. Seeing us seated on an upturned plough, over by the fence, from which point we had a perfect view of the red barn, he sauntered toward us, and, halting at our side, looked to see if there was room enough for him to sit also. But Marcellus, in quite a casual way, remarked, "Oh! wheeled the milk over to the house, already, Si?" and at this the doleful man lounged off again in new despondency, got out the wheelbarrow, and, with ostentatious groans of travail hoisted a can upon it and started off.

"He's takin' advantage of Arphaxed's being so worked up to play 'ole soldier' on him," said Marcellus. "All of us have to stir him up the whole time to keep him from takin' root somewhere. I told him this afternoon 't' if there had to be any settin' around under the bushes an' cryin', the family 'ud do it."

We talked in hushed tones as we sat there watching the shut doors of the red barn, in boyish conjecture about what was going on behind them. I recall much of this talk with curious distinctness, but candidly it jars now upon my maturer nerves. The individual man looks back upon his boyhood with much the same amused amazement that the race feels in contemplating the memorials of its own cave-dwelling or bronze period. What strange savages we were! In those days Marcellus and I used to find our very highest delight in getting off on Thursdays, and going over to Dave Bushnell's slaughter-house, to witness with stony hearts, and from as close a coign of vantage as might be, the slaying of some score of barnyard animals—the very thought of which now revolts our grown-up minds. In the same way we sat there on the plough, and criticised old Arphaxed's meanness in excluding us from the red barn, where the men-folks were coming in final contact with the "pride of the family." Some of the cows wandering toward us began to "moo" with impatience for the pasture, but Marcellus said there was no hurry.

All at once we discovered that Aunt Em was standing a few yards away from us, on the other side of the fence. We could see her from where we sat by only turning a little—a motionless, stout, upright figure, with a pail in her hand, and a sternly impassive look on her face. She, too, had her gaze fixed upon the red barn, and, though the declining sun was full in her eyes, seemed incapable of blinking, but just stared coldly, straight ahead.

Suddenly an unaccustomed voice fell upon our ears. Turning, we saw that a black-robed woman, with a black wrap of some sort about her head, had come up to where Aunt Em stood, and was at her shoulder. Marcellus nudged me, and whispered, "It's S'reny. Look out for squalls!" And then we listened in silence.

"Won't you speak to me at all, Emmeline?" we heard this new voice say.

Aunt Em's face, sharply outlined in profile against the sky, never moved. Her lips were pressed into a single line, and she kept her eyes on the barn.

"If there's anything I've done, tell me," pursued the other. "In such an hour as this—when both our hearts are bleeding so, and—and every breath we draw is like a curse upon us—it doesn't seem a fit time for us—for us to—" The voice faltered and broke, leaving the speech unfinished.

Aunt Em kept silence so long that we fancied this appeal, too, had failed. Then abruptly, and without moving her head, she dropped a few ungracious words as it were over her shoulder, "If I had anything special to say, most likely I'd say it," she remarked.

We could hear the sigh that Serena drew. She lifted her shawled head, and for a moment seemed as if about to turn. Then she changed her mind, apparently, for she took a step nearer to the other.

"See here, Emmeline," she said, in a more confident tone. "Nobody in the world knows better than I do how thoroughly good a woman you are, how you have done your duty, and more than your duty, by your parents and your brothers, and your little step-son. You have never spared yourself for them, day or night. I have said often to—to him who has gone—that I didn't believe there was anywhere on earth a worthier or more devoted woman than you, his sister. And—now that he is gone—and we are both more sisters than ever in affliction—why in Heaven's name should you behave like this to me?"

Aunt Em spoke more readily this time. "I don't know as I've done anything to you," she said in defence. "I've just let you alone, that's all. An' that's doin' as I'd like to be done by." Still she did not turn her head, or lift her steady gaze from those closed doors.

"Don't let us split words!" entreated the other, venturing a thin, white hand upon Aunt Em's shoulder. "That isn't the way we two ought to stand to each other. Why, you were friendly enough when I was here before. Can't it be the same again? What has happened to change it? Only to-day, on our way up here, I was speaking to your father about you, and my deep sympathy for you, and—"

Aunt Em wheeled like a flash. "Yes, 'n' what did *he* say? Come, don't make up anything! Out with it! What did he say?" She shook off the hand on her shoulder as she spoke.

Gesture and voice and frowning vigor of mien were all so imperative and rough that they seemed to bewilder Serena. She, too, had turned now, so that I could see her wan and delicate face, framed in the laced festoons of black, like the fabulous countenance of "The Lady Iñez" in my mother's "Album of Beauty." She bent her brows in hurried thought, and began stammering, "Well, he said—Let's see—he said—"

"Oh, yes!" broke in Aunt Em, with raucous irony, "I know well enough what he said! He said I was a good worker—that they'd never had to have a hired girl since I was big enough to wag a churn dash, an' they wouldn't known [sic] what to do without me. I know all that; I've heard it on an' off for twenty years. What I'd like to hear is, did he tell you that he went down South to bring back *your* husband, an' that he never so much as give a thought to fetchin' *my* husband, who was just as good a soldier and died just as bravely as yours did? I'd like to know—did he tell you that?"

What could Serena do but shake her head, and bow it in silence before this bitter gale of words?

"An' tell me this, too," Aunt Em went on, lifting her harsh voice mercilessly, "when you was settin' there in church this forenoon, with the soldiers out, an' the bells tollin' an' all that—did he say 'This is some for Alvy, an' some for Abel, who went to the war together, an' was killed together, or within a month o' one another?' Did he say that, or look for one solitary minute as if he thought it? I'll bet he didn't!"

Serena's head sank lower still, and she put up, in a blinded sort of a way, a little white handkerchief to her eyes. "But why blame *me?*" she asked.

Aunt Em heard her own voice so seldom that the sound of it now seemed to intoxicate her. "No!" she shouted. "It's like the Bible. One was taken an' the other left. It was always Alvy this, an' Alvy that, nothin' for any one but Alvy. That was all right; nobody complained: prob'ly he deserved it all; at any rate, we didn't begrudge him any of it, while he was livin'. But there ought to be a limit somewhere. When a man's dead, he's pretty much about on an equality with other dead men, one would think. But it ain't so. One man gets hunted after when he's shot, an' there's a hundred dollars for embalmin' him an' a journey after him, an' bringin' him home, an' two big funerals, an' crape for his widow that'd stand by itself. The *other* man—he can lay where he fell! Them that's lookin' for the first one are right close by—it ain't more'n a few miles from the Wilderness to Cold Harbor, so Hi Tuckerman tells me, an' he was all over the ground two years ago—but nobody looks for this other man! Oh, no! Nobody so much as remembers to think of him! They ain't no hundred dollars, no, not so ranch as fifty cents, for embalmin' *him!* No—*he* could be shovelled in anywhere, or maybe burned up when the woods got on fire that night, the night of the sixth. They ain't no funeral for him—no bells tolled—unless it may be a cowhell up in the pasture that he hammered out himself. An' *his* widow can go around, week days [sic] an' Sundays, in her old calico dresses. Nobody ever mentions the word 'mournin' crape' to her, or asks her if she'd like to put on black. I 'spose they thought if they gave me the money for some mournin' I'd buy *candy* with it instead!"

With this climax of flaming sarcasm Aunt Em stopped, her eyes aglow, her thick breast heaving in a flurry of breathlessness. She had never talked so much or so fast before in her life. She swung the empty tin-pail now defiantly at her side to hide the fact that her arms were shaking with excitement. Every instant it looked as if she was going to begin again.

Serena had taken the handkerchief down from her eyes and held her arms stiff and straight by her side. Her chin seemed to have grown longer or to be thrust forward more. When she spoke, it was in a colder voice—almost mincing in the way it cut off the words.

"All this is not my doing," she said. "I am to blame for nothing of it. As I tried to tell you, I sympathize deeply with your grief. But grief ought to make people at least fair, even if it cannot make them gentle and soften their hearts. I shall trouble you with no more offers of friendship. I—I think I will go back to the house now—to my little girl."

Even as she spoke, there came from the direction of the red barn a shrill, creaking noise which we all knew. At the sound Marcellus and I stood up, and Serena forgot her intention to go away. The barn doors, yelping as they moved on their dry rollers, had been pushed wide open.

IV

The first one to emerge from the barn was Hi Tuckerman. He started to make for the house, but, when he caught sight of our group, came running toward us at the top of his speed, uttering incoherent shouts as he advanced, and waving his arms excitedly. It was apparent that something out of the ordinary had happened.

We were but little the wiser as to this something, when Hi had come to a halt before us, and was pouring out a volley of explanations, accompanied by earnest grimaces and strenuous gestures. Even Marcellus could make next to nothing of what he was trying to convey; but Aunt Em, strangely enough, seemed to understand him. Still slightly trembling, and with a little occasional catch in her breath, she bent an intent scrutiny upon Hi, and nodded comprehendingly from time to time, with encouraging exclamations, "He did, eh!" "Is that so?" and "I expected as much." Listening and watching, I formed the uncharitable conviction that she did not really understand Hi at all, but was only pretending to do so in order further to harrow Serena's feelings.

Doubtless I was wrong, for presently she turned, with an effort, to her sister-in-law, and remarked, "P'rhaps you don't quite follow what he's sayin'?"

"Not a word!" said Serena, eagerly. "Tell me, please, Emmeline!"

Aunt Em seemed to hesitate. "He was shot through the mouth at Gaines's Mills, you know—that's right near Cold Harbor and—the Wilderness," she said, obviously making talk.

"That isn't what he's saying," broke in Serena. "What *is* it, Emmeline?"

"Well," rejoined the other, after an instant's pause; "if you want to know—he says that it ain't Alvy at all that they've got there in the barn."

Serena turned swiftly, so that we could not see her face.

"He says it's some strange man," continued Em, "a yaller-headed man, all packed an' stuffed with charcoal, so't his own mother wouldn't know him. Who it is nobody knows, but it ain't Alvy."

"They're a pack of robbers 'n' swindlers!" cried old Arphaxed, shaking his long gray beard with wrath.

He had come up without our noticing his approach, so rapt had been our absorption in the strange discovery reported by Hi Tuckerman. Behind him straggled the boys and the hired men, whom Si Hummaston had scurried across from the house to join. No one said anything now, but tacitly deferred to the old man's principal right to speak. It was a relief to hear that terrible silence of his broken at all.

"They ought to all be hung!" he cried, in a voice to which the excess of passion over physical strength gave a melancholy quaver. "I paid 'em what they asked—they took a hundred dollars o' my money—an' they ain't sent me *him* at all! There I went, at my age, all through the Wilderness, almost clear to Cold Harbor, an' that, too, gittin up from a sick bed in Washington, and then huntin' for the box at New York an' Albany, an' all the way back, an' holdin' a funeral over it only this very day—an' here it ain't *him* at all! I'll have the law on 'em though, if it costs the last cent I've got in the world!"

Poor old man! These weeks of crushing grief and strain had fairly broken him down. We listened to his fierce outpourings with sympathetic silence, almost thankful that he had left strength and vitality enough still to get angry and shout. He had been always a hard and gusty man; we felt by instinct, I suppose, that his best chance of weathering this terrible month of calamity was to batter his way furiously through it, in a rage with everything and everybody.

"If there's any justice in the land," put in Si Hummaston, "you'd ought to get your hundred dollars back. I shouldn't wonder if you could, too, if you sued 'em afore a Jestice [sic] that was a friend of yours."

"Why, the man's a fool!" burst forth Arphaxed, turning toward him with a snort. "I don't want the hundred dollars—I wouldn't 'a' begrudged a thousand—if only they'd dealt honestly by me. I paid 'em their own figure, without beatin' ' em down a penny. If it 'd be'n double, I'd 'a' paid it. What *I* wanted was *my boy!* It ain't so much their cheatin' *me* I mind, either, if it 'd be'n about anything else. But to think of Alvy—*my boy*—after all the trouble I took, an' the journey, an' my sickness there among strangers—to think that after it all he's buried down there, no one knows where, p'raps in some trench with private soldiers, shovelled in anyhow—oh-h! they ought to be hung!"

The two women had stood motionless, with their gaze on the grass; Aunt Em lifted her head at this.

"If a place is good enough for private soldiers to be buried in," she said, vehemently, "it's good enough for the best man in the army. On Resurrection Day, do you think them with shoulder-straps 'll be called fast an' given all the front places? I reckon the men that carried a musket are every whit as good, there in the trench, as them that wore swords. They gave their lives as much as the others did, an' the best man that ever stepped couldn't do no more."

Old Arphaxed bent upon her a long look, which had in it much surprise and some elements of menace. Reflection seemed, however, to make him think better of an attack on Aunt Em. He went on, instead, with rambling exclamations to his auditors at large.

"Makin' me the butt of the whole county!" he cried. "There was that funeral to-day— with a parade an' a choir of music an' so on an' now it 'll come out in the papers that it wasn't Alvy at all I brought back with me, but only some perfect stranger—by what you can make out from his clothes, not even an officer at all. I tell you the War's a jedgment on this country for its wickedness, for its cheatin' an' robbin' of honest men! They wa'n't no sense in that battle at Cold Harbor anyway—everybody admits that! It was murder an' massacre in cold blood—fifty thousand men mowed down, an' nothin' gained by it! An' then not even to git my boy's dead body back! I say hangin's too good for 'em!"

"Yes, father," said Myron, soothingly; "but do you stick to what you said about the— the box? Wouldn't it look better—"

"*No!*" shouted Arphaxed, with emphasis. "Let Dana do what I told him—take it down this very night to the poor-master, an' let him bury it where he likes. It's no affair of mine. I wash my hands of it. There won't be no funeral held here!"

It was then that Serena spoke. Strangely enough, old Arphaxed had not seemed to notice her presence in our group, and his jaw visibly dropped as he beheld her now standing before him. He made a gesture signifying his disturbance at finding her among his hearers, and would have spoken, but she held up her hand.

"Yes, I heard it all," she said, in answer to his deprecatory movement. "I am glad I did. It has given me time to get over the shock of learning—our mistake—and it gives me the chance now to say something which I—I feel keenly. The poor man you have brought home was, you say, a private soldier. Well, isn't this a good time to remember that there was a private soldier who went out from this farm—belonging right to this family—and who, as a private, laid down his life as nobly as General Sedgwick or General Wadsworth,[28] or even our dear Alva, or any one else? I never met Emmeline's husband, but Alva liked him, and spoke to me often of him. Men who fill in the ranks don't get identified, or brought home, but they deserve funerals as much as the others—just as much. Now, this is my idea: let us feel that the mistake which has brought this poor stranger to us is God's way of giving us a chance to remember and do honor to Abel Jones. Let him be buried in the family lot up yonder, where we had thought to lay Alva, and let us do it reverently, in the name of Emmeline's husband, and of all others who have fought and died for our country, and with sympathy in our hearts for the women who, somewhere in the North, are mourning, just as we mourn here, for the stranger there in the red barn."

Arphaxed had watched her intently. He nodded now, and blinked at the moisture gathering in his old eyes. "I could e'en a'most 'a' thought it was Alvy talkin'," was what he said. Then he turned abruptly, but we all knew, without further words, that what Serena had suggested was to be done.

The men-folk, wondering doubtless much among themselves, moved slowly off toward the house or the cow-barns, leaving the two women alone. A minute of silence passed before we saw Serena creep gently up to Aunt Em's side, and lay the thin white hand again upon her shoulder. This time it was not shaken off, but stretched itself forward, little by little, until its palm rested against Aunt Em's further cheek. We heard the tin-pail fall resonantly against the stones under the rail-fence, and there was a confused movement as if the two women were somehow melting into one.

"Come on, Sid!" said Marcellus Jones to me; "let's start them cows along. If there's anything I hate to see it's women cryin' on each other's necks."

Hamlin Garland

from *Main-Travelled Roads* (1891)

THE RETURN OF A PRIVATE

I

The nearer the train drew toward La Crosse, the soberer the little group of "vets" became. On the long way from New Orleans they had beguiled tedium with jokes and friendly chaff; or with planning with elaborate detail what they were going to do now, after the war. A long journey, slowly, irregularly, yet persistently pushing northward. When they entered on Wisconsin territory they gave a cheer, and another when they reached Madison, but after that they sank into a dumb expectancy. Comrades dropped off at one or two points beyond, until there were only four or five left who were bound for La Crosse County.

Three of them were gaunt and brown, the fourth was gaunt and pale, with signs of fever and ague upon him. One had a great scar down his temple, one limped, and they all had unnaturally large, bright eyes, showing emaciation. There were no bands greeting them at the station, no banks of gayly dressed ladies waving handkerchiefs and shouting "Bravo!" as they came in on the caboose of a freight train into the towns that had cheered and blared at them on their way to war. As they looked out or stepped upon the platform for a moment, while the train stood at the station, the loafers looked at them indifferently. Their blue coats, dusty and grimy, were too familiar now to excite notice, much less a friendly word. They were the last of the army to return, and the loafers were surfeited with such sights.

The train jogged forward so slowly that it seemed likely to be midnight before they should reach La Crosse. The little squad grumbled and swore, but it was no use; the train would not hurry, and, as a matter of fact, it was nearly two o'clock when the engine whistled "down brakes."

All of the group were farmers, living in districts several miles out of the town, and all were poor.

"Now, boys," said Private Smith, he of the fever and ague, "we are landed in La Crosse in the night. We've got to stay somewhere till mornin'. Now I ain't got no two dollars to waste on a hotel. I've got a wife and children, so I'm goin' to roost on a bench and take the cost of a bed out of my hide."

"Same here," put in one of the other men. "Hide'll grow on again, dollars'll come hard. It's goin' to be mighty hot skirmishin' to find a dollar these days."

"Don't think they'll be a deputation of citizens waitin' to 'scort us to a hotel, eh?" said another. His sarcasm was too obvious to require an answer.

Smith went on, "Then at daybreak we'll start for home—at least, I will."

"Well, I'll be dummed [sic] if I'll take two dollars out o' *my* hide," one of the younger men said. "I'm goin' to a hotel, ef I don't never lay up a cent."

"That'll do f'r you," said Smith; "but if you had a wife an' three young uns dependin' on yeh—"

"Which I ain't, thank the Lord! and don't intend havin' while the court knows itself."

The station was deserted, chill, and dark, as they came into it at exactly a quarter to two in the morning. Lit by the oil lamps that flared a dull red light over the dingy benches, the waiting room was not an inviting place. The younger man went off to look up a hotel, while the rest remained and prepared to camp down on the floor and benches. Smith was attended to tenderly by the other men, who spread their blankets on the bench for him, and, by robbing themselves, made quite a comfortable bed, though the narrowness of the bench made his sleeping precarious.

It was chill, though August, and the two men, sitting with bowed heads, grew stiff with cold and weariness, and were forced to rise now and again and walk about to warm their stiffened limbs. It did not occur to them, probably, to contrast their coming home with their going forth, or with the coming home of the generals, colonels, or even captains—but to Private Smith, at any rate, there came a sickness at heart almost deadly as he lay there on his hard bed and went over his situation.

In the deep of the night, lying on a board in the town where he had enlisted three years ago, all elation and enthusiasm gone out of him, he faced the fact that with the joy of home-coming was already mingled the bitter juice of care. He saw himself sick, worn out, taking up the work on his half-cleared farm, the inevitable mortgage standing ready with open jaw to swallow half his earnings. He had given three years of his life for a mere pittance of pay, and now!—

Morning dawned at last, slowly, with a pale yellow dome of light rising silently above the bluffs, which stand like some huge storm-devastated castle, just east of the city. Out to the left the great river swept on its massive yet silent way to the south. Bluejays called across the water from hillside to hillside through the clear, beautiful air, and hawks began to skim the tops of the hills. The older men were astir early, but Private Smith had fallen at last into a sleep, and they went out without waking him. He lay on his knapsack, his gaunt face turned toward the ceiling, his hands clasped on his breast, with a curious pathetic effect of weakness and appeal.

An engine switching near woke him at last, and he slowly sat up and stared about. He looked out of the window and saw that the sun was lightening the hills across the river. He rose and brushed his hair as well as he could, folded his blankets up, and went out to find his companions. They stood gazing silently at the river and at the hills.

"Looks natcher'l, don't it?" they said, as he came out.

"That's what it does," he replied. "An' it looks good. D' yeh see that peak?" He pointed at a beautiful symmetrical peak, rising like a slightly truncated cone, so high that it seemed the very highest of them all. It was touched by the morning sun and it glowed like a beacon, and a light scarf of gray morning fog was rolling up its shadowed side.

"My farm's just beyond that. Now, if I can only ketch a ride, we'll be home by dinner-time."

"I'm talkin' about breakfast," said one of the others.

"I guess it's one more meal o' hardtack f'r me," said Smith.

They foraged around, and finally found a restaurant with a sleepy old German behind the counter, and procured some coffee, which they drank to wash down their hardtack.

"Time'll come," said Smith, holding up a piece by the corner, "when this'll be a curiosity."

"I hope to God it will! I bet I've chawed hardtack enough to shingle every house in the coolly. I've chawed it when my lampers was down, and when they wasn't. I've took it dry, soaked, and mashed. I've had it wormy, musty, sour, and blue-mouldy. I've had it in little bits and big bits; 'fore coffee an' after coffee. I'm ready f'r a change. I'd like t' git holt jest about now o' some of the hot biscuits my wife c'n make when she lays herself out f'r company."

"Well, if you set there gabblin', you'll never *see* yer wife."

"Come on," said Private Smith. "Wait a moment, boys; less take suthin'. It's on me." He led them to the rusty tin dipper which hung on a nail beside the wooden water-pail, and they grinned and drank. Then shouldering their blankets and muskets, which they were "takin' home to the boys," they struck out on their last march.

"They called that coffee Jayvy," grumbled one of them, "but it never went by the road where government Jayvy resides. I reckon I know coffee from peas."

They kept together on the road along the turnpike, and up the winding road by the river, which they followed for some miles. The river was very lovely, curving down along its sandy beds, pausing now and then under broad basswood trees, or running in dark, swift, silent currents under tangles of wild grapevines, and drooping alders, and haw trees. At one of these lovely spots the three vets sat down on the thick green sward to rest, "on Smith's account." The leaves of the trees were as fresh and green as in June, the jays called cheery greetings to them, and kingfishers darted to and fro with swooping, noise-less flight.

"I tell yeh, boys, this knocks the swamps of Loueesiana into kingdom come."

"You bet. All they c'n raise down there is snakes, niggers, and p'rticler hell."

"An' fightin' men," put in the older man.

"An' fightin' men. If I had a good hook an' line I'd sneak a pick'rel out o' that pond. Say, remember that time I shot that alligator—"

"I guess we'd better be crawlin' along," interrupted Smith, rising and shouldering his knapsack, with considerable effort, which he tried to hide.

"Say, Smith, lemme give you a lift on that."

"I guess I c'n manage," said Smith, grimly.

"Course. But, yo' see, I may not have a chance right off to pay yeh back for the times you've carried my gun and hull caboodle. Say, now, gimme that gun, anyway."

"All right, if yeh feel like it, Jim," Smith replied, and they trudged along doggedly in the sun, which was getting higher and hotter each half-mile.

"Ain't it queer there ain't no teams comin' along," said Smith, after a long silence.

"Well, no, seein's it's Sunday."

"By jinks, that's a fact. It *is* Sunday. I'll git home in time f'r dinner, sure!" he exulted. "She don't hev dinner usually till about *one* on Sundays." And he fell into a muse, in which he smiled.

"Well, I'll git home jest about six o'clock, jest about when the boys are milkin' the cows," said old Jim Cranby. "I'll step into the barn, an' then I'll say: 'H*eah*! why ain't this milkin' done before this time o' day?' An' then won't they yell!" he added, slapping his thigh in great glee.

Smith went on. "I'll jest go up the path. Old Rover'll come down the road to meet me. He won't bark; he'll know me, an' he'll come down waggin' his tail an' showin' his teeth. That's his way of laughin'. An' so I'll walk up to the kitchen door, an' I'll say, '*Dinner* f'r a hungry man!' An' then she'll jump up, an'—"

He couldn't go on. His voice choked at the thought of it. Saunders, the third man, hardly uttered a word, but walked silently behind the others. He had lost his wife the first year he was in the army. She died of pneumonia, caught in the autumn rains while working in the fields in his place.

They plodded along till at last they came to a parting of the ways. To the right the road continued up the main valley; to the left it went over the big ridge.

"Well, boys," began Smith, as they grounded their muskets and looked away up the valley, "here's where we shake hands. We've marched together a good many miles, an' now I s'pose we're done."

"Yes, I don't think we'll do any more of it f'r a while. I don't want to, I know."

"I hope I'll see yeh once in a while, boys, to talk over old times."

"Of course," said Saunders, whose voice trembled a little, too. "It ain't *exactly* like dyin'." They all found it hard to look at each other.

"But we'd ought'r go home with you," said Cranby. "You'll never climb that ridge with all them things on yer back."

"Oh, I'm all right! Don't worry about me. Every step takes me nearer home, yeh see. Well, good-by, boys.

They shook hands. "Good-by. Good luck!"

"Same to you. Lemme know how you find things at home."

"Good-by."

"Good-by."

He turned once before they passed out of sight, and waved his cap, and they did the same, and all yelled. Then all marched away with their long, steady, loping, veteran step. The solitary climber in blue walked on for a time, with his mind filled with the kindness of his comrades, and musing upon the many wonderful days they had had together in camp and field.

He thought of his chum, Billy Tripp. Poor Billy! A "minie" ball[29] fell into his breast one day, fell wailing like a cat, and tore a great ragged hole in his heart. He looked forward to a sad scene with Billy's mother and sweetheart. They would want to know all about it. He tried to recall all that Billy had said, and the particulars of it, but there was little to remember, just that wild wailing sound high in the air, a dull slap, a short, quick, expulsive groan, and the boy lay with his face in the dirt in the ploughed field they were marching across.

That was all. But all the scenes he had since been through had not dimmed the horror, the terror of that moment, when his boy comrade fell, with only a breath between a laugh and a death-groan. Poor handsome Billy! Worth millions of dollars was his young life.

These sombre recollections gave way at length to more cheerful feelings as he began to approach his home coolly. The fields and houses grew familiar, and in one or two he was greeted by people seated in the doorways. But he was in no mood to talk, and pushed on steadily, though he stopped and accepted a drink of milk once at the well-side of a neighbor.

The sun was burning hot on that slope, and his step grew slower, in spite of his iron resolution. He sat down several times to rest. Slowly he crawled up the rough, reddish-brown road, which wound along the hillside, under great trees, through dense groves of jack oaks, with tree-tops far below him on his left hand, and the hills far above him on his right. He crawled along like some minute, wingless variety of fly.

He ate some hardtack, sauced with wild berries, when he reached the summit of the ridge, and sat there for some time, looking down into his home coolly.

Sombre, pathetic figure! His wide, round, gray eyes gazing down into the beautiful valley, seeing and not seeing, the splendid cloud-shadows sweeping over the western hills and across the green and yellow wheat far below. His head drooped forward on his palm, his shoulders took on a tired stoop, his cheek-bones showed painfully. An observer might have said, "He is looking down upon his own grave."

II

Sunday comes in a Western wheat harvest with such sweet and sudden relaxation to man and beast that it would be holy for that reason, if for no other, and Sundays are usually fair in harvest-time. As one goes out into the field in the hot morning sunshine, with no sound abroad save the crickets and the indescribably pleasant silken rustling of the ripened grain, the reaper and the very sheaves in the stubble seem to be resting, dreaming.

Around the house, in the shade of the trees, the men sit, smoking, dozing, or reading the papers, while the women, never resting, move about at the housework. The men eat on Sundays about the same as on other days, and breakfast is no sooner over and out of the way than dinner begins.

But at the Smith farm there were no men dozing or reading. Mrs. Smith was alone with her three children, Mary, nine, Tommy, six, and little Ted, just past four. Her farm, rented to a neighbor, lay at the head of a coolly or narrow gully, made at some far-off post-glacial period by the vast and angry floods of water which gullied these tremendous furrows in the level prairie—furrows so deep that undisturbed portions of the original level rose like hills on either side, rose to quite considerable mountains.

The chickens wakened her as usual that Sabbath morning from dreams of her absent husband, from whom she had not heard for weeks. The shadows drifted over the hills, down the slopes, across the wheat, and up the opposite wall in leisurely way, as if, being Sunday, they could take it easy also. The fowls clustered about the housewife as she went out into the yard. Fuzzy little chickens swarmed out from the coops, where their clucking and perpetually disgruntled mothers tramped about, petulantly thrusting their heads through the spaces between the slats.

A cow called in a deep, musical bass, and a calf answered from a little pen near by, and a pig scurried guiltily out of the cabbages. Seeing all this, seeing the pig in the cabbages, the tangle of grass in the garden, the broken fence which she had mended again and again—the little woman, hardly more than a girl, sat down and cried. The bright Sabbath morning was only a mockery without him!

A few years ago they had bought this farm, paying part, mortgaging the rest in the usual way. Edward Smith was a man of terrible energy. He worked "nights and Sundays," as the saying goes, to clear the farm of its brush and of its insatiate mortgage! In the midst of his Herculean struggle came the call for volunteers, and with the grim and unselfish devotion to his country which made the Eagle Brigade[30] able to "whip its weight in wild-cats," he threw down his scythe and grub-axe, turned his cattle loose, and became a blue-coated cog in a vast machine for killing men, and not thistles. While the millionaire sent his money to England for safe-keeping, this man, with his girl-wife and three babies, left them on a mortgaged farm, and went away to fight for an idea. It was foolish, but it was sublime for all that.

That was three years before, and the young wife, sitting on the well-curb on this bright Sabbath harvest morning, was righteously rebellious. It seemed to her that she had borne her share of the country's sorrow. Two brothers had been killed, the renter in whose hands her husband had left the farm had proved a villain; one year the farm had been without crops, and now the overripe grain was waiting the tardy hand of the neighbor who had rented it, and who was cutting his own grain first.

About six weeks before, she had received a letter saying, "We'll be discharged in a little while." But no other word had come from him. She had seen by the papers that his army was being discharged, and from day to day other soldiers slowly percolated in blue streams back into the State and county, but still *her* hero did not return.

Each week she had told the children that he was coming, and she had watched the road so long that it had become unconscious; and as she stood at the well, or by the kitchen door, her eyes were fixed unthinkingly on the road that wound down the coolly.

Nothing wears on the human soul like waiting. If the stranded mariner, searching the sun-bright seas, could once give up hope of a ship, that horrible grinding on his brain would cease. It was this waiting, hoping, on the edge of despair, that gave Emma Smith no rest.

Neighbors said, with kind intentions: "He's sick, maybe, an' can't start north just yet. He'll come along one o' these days."

"Why don't he write?" was her question, which silenced them all. This Sunday morning it seemed to her as if she could not stand it longer. The house seemed intolerably lonely. So she dressed the little ones in their best calico dresses and home-made jackets, and, closing up the house, set off down the coolly to old Mother Gray's.

"Old Widder Gray" lived at the "mouth of the coolly." She was a widow woman with a large family of stalwart boys and laughing girls. She was the visible incarnation of hospitality and optimistic poverty. With Western open-heartedness she fed every mouth that asked food of her, and worked herself to death as cheerfully as her girls danced in the neighborhood harvest dances.

She waddled down the path to meet Mrs. Smith with a broad smile on her face.

"Oh, you little dears! Come right to your granny. Gimme me a kiss! Come right in, Mis' Smith. How are yeh, anyway? Nice mornin', ain't it? Come in an' set down. Everything's in a clutter, but that won't scare you any."

She led the way into the best room, a sunny, square room, carpeted with a faded and patched rag carpet, and papered with white-and-green-striped wall-paper, where a few faded effigies of dead members of the family hung in variously sized oval walnut frames. The house resounded with singing, laughter, whistling, tramping of heavy boots, and riotous scufflings. Half-grown boys came to the door and crooked their fingers at the children, who ran out, and were soon heard in the midst of the fun.

"Don't s'pose you've heard from Ed?" Mrs. Smith shook her head. "He'll turn up some day, when you ain't lookin' for 'm." The good old soul had said that so many times that poor Mrs. Smith derived no comfort from it any longer.

"Liz heard from Al the other day. He's comin' some day this week. Anyhow, they expect him."

"Did he say anything of—"

"No, he didn't," Mrs. Gray admitted. "But then it was only a short letter, anyhow. Al ain't much for writin', anyhow.—But come out and see my new cheese. I tell yeh, I don't believe I ever had better luck in my life. If Ed should come, I want you should take him up a piece of this cheese."

It was beyond human nature to resist the influence of that noisy, hearty, loving household, and in the midst of the singing and laughing the wife forgot her anxiety, for the time at least, and laughed and sang with the rest.

About eleven o'clock a wagon-load more drove up to the door, and Bill Gray, the widow's oldest son, and his whole family, from Sand Lake Coolly, piled out amid a good-natured uproar. Every one talked at once, except Bill, who sat in the wagon with his wrists on his knees, a straw in his mouth, and an amused twinkle in his blue eyes.

"Ain't heard nothin' o' Ed, I s'pose?" he asked in a kind of bellow. Mrs. Smith shook her head. Bill, with a delicacy very striking in such a great giant, rolled his quid in his mouth, and said:

"Didn't know but you had. I hear two or three of the Sand Lake boys are comin'. Left New Orleenes some time this week. Didn't write nothin' about Ed, but no news is good news in such cases, mother always says."

"Well, go put out yer team," said Mrs. Gray, "an' go 'n bring me in some taters, an', Sim, you go see if you c'n find some corn. Sadie, you put on the water to bile. Come now, hustle yer boots, all o' yeh. If I feed this yer crowd, we've got to have some raw materials. If y' think I'm goin' to feed yeh on pie—you're jest mightily mistaken."

The children went off into the fields, the girls put dinner on to boil, and then went to change their dresses and fix their hair. "Somebody might come," they said.

"Land sakes, I *hope* not! I don't know where in time I'd set 'em, 'less they'd eat at the second table," Mrs. Gray laughed, in pretended dismay.

The two older boys, who had served their time in the army, lay out on the grass before the house, and whittled and talked desultorily about the war and the crops, and planned buying a threshing-machine. The older girls and Mrs. Smith helped enlarge the table and put on the dishes, talking all the time in that cheery, incoherent, and meaningful way a group of such women have,—a conversation to be taken for its spirit rather than for its letter, though Mrs. Gray at last got the ear of them all and dissertated at length on girls.

"Girls in love ain't no use in the whole blessed week," she said. "Sundays they're a-lookin' down the road, expectin' he'll *come*. Sunday afternoons they can't think o' nothin' else, 'cause he's *here*. Monday mornin's they're sleepy and kind o' dreamy and slimpsy, and good f'r nothin' on Tuesday and Wednesday. Thursday they git absent-minded, an' begin to look off toward Sunday agin, an' mope aroun' and let the dishwater git cold, right under their noses. Friday they break dishes, an' go off in the best room an' snivel, an' look out o' the winder. Saturdays they have queer spurts o' workin' like all p'ssessed, an' spurts o' frizzin' their hair. An' Sunday they begin it all over agin."

The girls giggled and blushed, all through this tirade from their mother, their broad faces and powerful frames anything but suggestive of lackadaisical sentiment. But Mrs. Smith said:

"Now, Mrs. Gray, I hadn't ought to stay to dinner. You've got—"

"Now you set right down! If any of them girls' beaus comes, they'll have to take what's left, that's all. They ain't s'posed to have much appetite, nohow. No, you're goin' to stay if they starve, an' they ain't no danger o' that."

At one o'clock the long table was piled with boiled potatoes, cords of boiled corn on the cob, squash and pumpkin pies, hot biscuit, sweet pickles, bread and butter, and honey. Then one of the girls took down a conch-shell from a nail, and going to the door, blew a long, fine, free blast, that showed there was no weakness of lungs in her ample chest.

Then the children came out of the forest of corn, out of the creek, out of the loft of the barn, and out of the garden.

"They come to their feed f'r all the world jest like the pigs when y' holler 'poo-ee!' See 'em scoot!" laughed Mrs. Gray, every wrinkle on her face shining with delight.

The men shut up their jack-knives, and surrounded the horse-trough to souse their faces in the cold, hard water, and in a few moments the table was filled with a merry crowd, and a row of wistful-eyed youngsters circled the kitchen wall, where they stood first on one leg and then on the other, in impatient hunger.

"Now pitch in, Mrs. Smith," said Mrs. Gray, presiding over the table. "You know these men critters. They'll eat every grain of it, if yeh give 'em a chance. I swan, they're made o' India-rubber, their stomachs is, I know it."

"Haf to eat to work," said Bill, gnawing a cob with a swift, circular motion that rivalled a corn-sheller in results.

"More like workin' to eat," put in one of the girls, with a giggle. "More eat 'n work with you."

"*You* needn't say anything, Net. Any one that'll eat seven ears—"

"I didn't, no such thing. You piled your cobs on my plate."

"That'll do to tell Ed Varney. It won't go down here where we know yeh."

"Good land! Eat all yeh want! They's plenty more in the fiel's, but I can't afford to give you young uns tea. The tea is for us women-folks, and 'specially f'r Mis' Smith an' Bill's wife. We're a-goin' to tell fortunes by it."

One by one the men filled up and shoved back, and one by one the children slipped into their places, and by two o'clock the women alone remained around the débris-covered table, sipping their tea and telling fortunes.

As they got well down to the grounds in the cup, they shook them with a circular motion in the hand, and then turned them bottom-side-up quickly in the saucer, then twirled them three or four times one way, and three or four times the other, during a breathless pause. Then Mrs. Gray lifted the cup, and, gazing into it with profound gravity, pronounced the impending fate.

It must be admitted that, to a critical observer, she had abundant preparation for hitting close to the mark, as when she told the girls that "somebody was comin'." "It's a man," she went on gravely. "He is cross-eyed—"

"Oh, you hush!" cried Nettie.

"He has red hair, and is death on b'iled corn and hot biscuit."

The others shrieked with delight.

"But he's goin' to get the mitten, that red-headed feller is, for I see another feller comin' up behind him."

"Oh, lemme see, lemme see!" cried Nettie.

"Keep off," said the priestess, with a lofty gesture. "His hair is black. He don't eat so much, and he works more."

The girls exploded in a shriek of laughter, and pounded their sister on the back.

At last came Mrs. Smith's turn, and she was trembling with excitement as Mrs. Gray again composed her jolly face to what she considered a proper solemnity of expression.

"Somebody is comin' to *you*," she said, after a long pause. "He's got a musket on his back. He's a soldier. He's almost here. See?"

She pointed at two little tea-stems, which really formed a faint suggestion of a man with a musket on his back. He had climbed nearly to the edge of the cup. Mrs. Smith grew pale with excitement. She trembled so she could hardly hold the cup in her hand as she gazed into it.

"It's Ed," cried the old woman. "He's on the way home. Heavens an' earth! There he is now!" She turned and waved her hand out toward the road. They rushed to the door to look where she pointed.

A man in a blue coat, with a musket on his back, was toiling slowly up the hill on the sun-bright, dusty road, toiling slowly, with bent head half hidden by a heavy knapsack. So tired it seemed that walking was indeed a process of falling. So eager to get home he would not stop, would not look aside, but plodded on, amid the cries of the locusts, the welcome of the crickets, and the rustle of the yellow wheat. Getting back to God's country, and his wife and babies!

Laughing, crying, trying to call him and the children at the same time, the little wife, almost hysterical, snatched her hat and ran out into the yard. But the soldier had disappeared over the hill into the hollow beyond, and, by the time she had found the children, he was too far away for her voice to reach him. And, besides, she was not sure it was her husband, for he had not turned his head at their shouts. This seemed so strange. Why didn't he stop to rest at his old neighbor's house? Tortured by hope and doubt, she hurried up the coolly as fast as she could push the baby wagon, the blue-coated figure just ahead pushing steadily, silently forward up the coolly.

When the excited, panting little group came in sight of the gate they saw the blue-coated figure standing, leaning upon the rough rail fence, his chin on his palms, gazing at the empty house. His knapsack, canteen, blankets, and musket lay upon the dusty grass at his feet.

He was like a man lost in a dream. His wide, hungry eyes devoured the scene. The rough lawn, the little unpainted house, the field of clear yellow wheat behind it, down across which streamed the sun, now almost ready to touch the high hill to the west, the crickets crying merrily, a cat on the fence near by, dreaming, unmindful of the stranger in blue—

How peaceful it all was. O God! How far removed from all camps, hospitals, battle lines. A little cabin in a Wisconsin coolly, but it was majestic in its peace. How did he ever leave it for those years of tramping, thirsting, killing?

Trembling, weak with emotion, her eyes on the silent figure, Mrs. Smith hurried up to the fence. Her feet made no noise in the dust and grass, and they were close upon him before he knew of them. The oldest boy ran a little ahead. He will never forget that figure, that face. It will always remain as something epic, that return of the private. He fixed his eyes on the pale face covered with a ragged beard.

"Who *are* you, sir?" asked the wife, or, rather, started to ask, for he turned, stood a moment, and then cried:

"Emma!"

"Edward!"

The children stood in a curious row to see their mother kiss this bearded, strange man, the elder girl sobbing sympathetically with her mother. Illness had left the soldier partly deaf, and this added to the strangeness of his manner.

But the youngest child stood away, even after the girl had recognized her father and kissed him. The man turned then to the baby, and said in a curiously unpaternal tone

"Come here, my little man; don't you know me?" But the baby backed away under the fence and stood peering at him critically.

"My little man!" What meaning, in those words! This baby seemed like some other woman's child, and not the infant he had left in his wife's arms. The war had come between him and his baby—he was only a strange man to him, with big eyes; a soldier, with mother hanging to his arm, and talking in a loud voice.

"And this is Tom," the private said, drawing the oldest boy to him. "*He'll* come and see me. *He* knows his poor old pap when he comes home from the war."

The mother heard the pain and reproach in his voice and hastened to apologize.

"You've changed so, Ed. He can't know yeh. This is papa, Teddy; come and kiss him— Tom and Mary do. Come, won't you?" But Teddy still peered through the fence with solemn eyes, well out of reach. He resembled a half-wild kitten that hesitates, studying the tones of one's voice.

"I'll fix him," said the soldier, and sat down to undo his knapsack, out of which he drew three enormous and very red apples. After giving one to each of the older children, he said:

"*Now* I guess he'll come. Eh, my little man? Now come see your pap."

Teddy crept slowly under the fence, assisted by the overzealous Tommy, and a moment later was kicking and squalling in his father's arms. Then they entered the house, into the sitting room, poor, bare, art-forsaken little room, too, with its rag carpet, its square clock, and its two or three chromos[31] and pictures from *Harper's Weekly* pinned about.

"Emma, I'm all tired out," said Private Smith, as he flung himself down on the carpet as he used to do, while his wife brought a pillow to put under his head, and the children stood about munching their apples.

"Tommy, you run and get me a pan of chips, and Mary, you get the tea-kettle on, and I'll go and make some biscuit."

And the soldier talked. Question after question he poured forth about the crops, the cattle, the renter, the neighbors. He slipped his heavy government brogan shoes off his poor, tired, blistered feet, and lay out with utter, sweet relaxation. He was a free man again, no longer a soldier under command. At supper he stopped once, listened and smiled. "That's old Spot. I know her voice. I s'pose that's her calf out there in the pen. I can't milk her to-night, though. I'm too tired. But I tell you, I'd like a drink o' her milk. What's become of old Rove?"

"He died last winter. Poisoned, I guess." There was a moment of sadness for them all. It was some time before the husband spoke again, in a voice that trembled a little.

"Poor old feller! He'd 'a' known me half a mile away. I expected him to come down the hill to meet me. It 'ud 'a' been more like comin' home if I could 'a' seen him comin' down the road an' waggin' his tail, an' laughin' that way he has. I tell yeh, it kind o' took hold o' me to see the blinds down an' the house shut up."

"But, yeh see, we—we expected you'd write again 'fore you started. And then we thought we'd see you if you *did* come," she hastened to explain.

"Well, I ain't worth a cent on writin'. Besides, it's just as well yeh didn't know when I was comin'. I tell you, it sounds good to hear them chickens out there, an' turkeys, an' the crickets. Do you know they don't have just the same kind o' crickets down South? Who's Sam hired t' help cut yer grain?"

"The Ramsey boys."

"Looks like a good crop; but I'm afraid I won't do much gettin' it cut. This cussed fever an' ague has got me down pretty low. I don't know when I'll get rid of it. I'll bet I've took twenty-five pounds of quinine if I've taken a bit. Gimme another biscuit. I tell yeh, they taste good, Emma. I ain't had anything like it— Say, if you'd 'a' heard me braggin' to th' boys about your butter 'n' biscuits I'll bet your ears 'ud 'a' burnt."

The private's wife colored with pleasure. "Oh, you're always a-braggin' about your things. Everybody makes good butter."

"Yes; old lady Snyder, for instance."

"Oh, well, she ain't to be mentioned. She's Dutch."

"Or old Mis' Snively. One more cup o' tea, Mary. That's my girl! I'm feeling better already. I just b'lieve the matter with me is, I'm *starved.*"

This was a delicious hour, one long to be remembered. They were like lovers again. But their tenderness, like that of a typical American family, found utterance in tones, rather than in words. He was praising her when praising her biscuit, and she knew it. They grew soberer when he showed where he had been struck, one ball burning the back of his hand, one cutting away a lock of hair from his temple, and one passing through the calf of his leg. The wife shuddered to think how near she had come to being a soldier's widow. Her waiting no longer seemed hard. This sweet, glorious hour effaced it all.

Then they rose, and all went out into the garden and down to the barn. He stood beside her while she milked old Spot. They began to plan fields and crops for next year.

His farm was weedy and encumbered, a rascally renter had run away with his machinery (departing between two days), his children needed clothing, the years were coming upon him, he was sick and emaciated, but his heroic soul did not quail. With the same courage with which he had faced his Southern march he entered upon a still more hazardous future.

Oh, that mystic hour! The pale man with big eyes standing there by the well, with his young wife by his side. The vast moon swinging above the eastern peaks, the cattle winding down the pasture slopes with jangling bells, the crickets singing, the stars blooming out sweet and far and serene; the katydids rhythmically calling, the little turkeys crying querulously, as they settled to roost in the poplar tree near the open gate. The voices at the well drop lower, the little ones nestle in their father's arms at last, and Teddy falls asleep there.

The common soldier of the American volunteer army had returned. His war with the South was over, and his fight, his daily running fight with nature and against the injustice of his fellow-men, was begun again.

THE TEXTS

Harriet Beecher Stowe, "The Chimney-Corner." Source: *The Atlantic Monthly*, vol. 15 no. 87 (Jan. 1865), pp. 109–115.

Nathaniel Hawthorne, "Chiefly about War-Matters." Source: *The Works of Nathaniel Hawthorne*, vol. 12, ed. George Parsons Lathrop and Julian Hawthorne (Cambridge: Riverside Press, 1883). Originally published in *The Atlantic Monthly*, vol. 10, no. 57 (July 1862), pp. 43–61.

Julia Ward Howe, "Our Orders." Source: *From Sunset Ridge: Poems Old and New, by Julia Ward Howe* (Boston and New York: Houghton, Mifflin and Company; Cambridge: The Riverside Press, 1898).

Lucy Larcom, "Weaving" and "A Loyal Woman's No." Source: *The Poetical Works of Lucy Larcom. Household Edition. With Illustrations* (Boston and New York: Houghton, Mifflin and Company, 1890).

Sarah Morgan Piatt, "Giving Back the Flower." Source: *Palace-Burner: The Selected Poetry of Sarah Piatt*, ed. Paula Bernat Bennett (Urbana: University of Illinois Press, 2001). Originally published in *The Galaxy* vol. 3, no. 4 (February 15, 1867), p. 409.

Walt Whitman, "Come Up From the Fields Father." Source: *Walt Whitman's Drum-Taps* (New York, s.n., 1865). Not substantially revised when included in *Leaves of Grass*.

Kate Chopin, "A Wizard from Gettysburg." Source: *Bayou Folk* (Boston and New York: Houghton, Mifflin and Co.; Cambridge: The Riverside Press, 1894). Originally published in *Youth's Companion* (July 7, 1892).

Henry James, "The Story of a Year." Source: *The Atlantic Monthly*, vol. 15, no. 89 (Mar. 1865), pp. 257–281.

Harold Frederic, "The War Widow." Source: *Marsena, and Other Stories of the Wartime* (New York: Charles Scribner's Sons, 1894).

Hamlin Garland, "The Return of a Private." Source: *Main-Travelled Roads* (New York: Harper & Brothers, 1899). Originally published as *Main-Travelled Roads: Six Mississippi Valley Stories* (Boston: Arena, 1891; New York: Harper & Row, 1891). Title-page epigraph: "On the road leading 'back to God's country' and wife and babies."

NOTES

1. Friedrich August Gottreu Tholuck (1799–1877), Protestant theologian who emphasized the experience of faith rather than religious dogma.

2. Nicknamed the "Swedish Nightingale," the soprano Jenny Lind (1820–1887) became a celebrity after her singing tour of the United States in 1850–52.

3. Nat Turner led the 1831 slave uprising at Southampton, Virginia. See Thomas Gray's *The Confessions of Nat Turner* (1831): "I saw white spirits and black spirits engaged in battle, and the sun was darkened—the thunder rolled in the Heavens, and blood flowed in streams" (10); "and shortly afterwards, while laboring in the field, I discovered drops of blood on the corn as though it were dew from heaven" (10).

4. Fort Warren, on Georges Island in Boston Harbor, housed Confederate prisoners, including Vice President Alexander Stephens and Gen. Richard S. Ewell. As Civil War prisons went, it was not particularly unpleasant. Fort Warren is also famous as the site where Union troops, while training in 1861, sang "John Brown's Body."

5. "Quaker guns" refers to the fake cannons (painted logs) left behind by Confederate troops as they retreated from Centreville, Virginia, in October, 1861.

6. Emanuel Gottlieb Leutze (1816–1868) finished his mural "Westward the Course of Empire Takes Its Way" in 1861.

7. Benjamin Perley Poore (1820–1887) was a newspaper correspondent and editor who wrote dispatches from Washington, D.C., for a variety of newspapers. He briefly served as major in the 8th Massachusetts Infantry.

8. Edwin M. Stanton and Salmon P. Chase.

9. Fort Ellsworth, located in Alexandria, Virginia, just across the Potomac from the Capital, was named after Elmer Ellsworth. See page 591, note 40.

10. The reason this historical circumstance is "known to few" is that Hawthorne is playing fast and loose with the facts. The first importation of slaves into the British colonies in North America occurred in 1619, when a Dutch trader arrived in Jameston, Virginia, with 20 Africans captured from a Portuguese slave ship. There is no evidence that the *Mayflower*, which landed in Plymouth in 1620, carried anyone of African descent. The *Mayflower* did not make a second voyage to the New World.

11. John Greenleaf Whittier's "Brown of Osatawomie" appeared in the *New York Independent* on 22 December 1859, three weeks after Brown's execution. In this poem Whittier, an antislavery Quaker activist, celebrated "Not the raid of midnight terror, but the thought which underlies; / Not the borderer's pride of daring, but the Christian's sacrifice."

12. I.e., Gen. Benjamin Butler.

13. Baron von Steuben (1730–1794), originally a Prussian army officer, helped to train the Continental Army during the American Revolution. His influential training system emphasized regimental organization and uniformity, soldierly discipline, camp sanitation, and combat efficiency.

14. The name "Old Glory" was first given to the flag in 1831 by Captain William Diver of, fittingly enough, Salem, Massachuesetts, Hawthorne's hometown. The moniker was revived by Union soldiers in Nashville, Tennessee, whither Diver had retired before the war.
15. Commodore Joseph Smith, Chief of the Bureau of Yards and Docks.
16. The U.S.S. *Constitution*, with its iron-tough oak sides, which served in the Navy from 1798 to 1815.
17. Willard's Hotel, which is still in operation, a few blocks from the White House, was frequented by Washington's political and cultural elite.
18. Gilbert Stuart (175–1828) produced famous portraits of George Washington and other major figures of the Revolutionary era.
19. The first viable mechanized loom, named after Joseph Marie Jacquard (1752-1834) of Lyons, France.
20. See Alfred Lord Tennyson's "The Lady of Shalott."
21. "The popular song 'Hear me, Norma' was based on Vincenzo Bellini's opera *Norma* (1832). Piatt may be suggesting that like the opera's Druidic heroine, secretly involved in a liaison with the Roman proconsul of Britain, the speaker took a lover from among the enemy" (Paula Bernat Bennett, ed., *Palace-Burner*, p. 163, n.5).
22. Jane Porter's *The Scottish Chiefs* (1809), a popular novel filled with romantic violence, tells the story of William Wallace's adventures leading the Scottish rebellion against Britain at the turn of the thirteenth century.
23. Intellectual comforts.
24. The Lancers was a variation of the quadrille, a popular dance for four couples.
25. The "water-cure," or hydropathy, was a form of alternative nineteenth-century medicine, typically administered to women, involving applications of cold water in conjunction with changes in diet and exercise. Although spurned by mainstream medicine, the practice gained adherents through its spiritual and psychological potency. The water-cure, writes Susan E. Cayleff, "instilled hope, provided a moral base, offered internal logic radiating from a central truth, and proffered inclusive answers for all of life's uncertainties" (*Wash and Be Healed: The Water-Cure Movement and Women's Health* [Philadelphia: Temple University Press, 1987], p. 17).
26. First two lines of the introductory verse to Canto VI of Alfred Lord Tennyson's "The Princess: A Medley" (1847).
27. Grant.
28. Gen. James Samuel Wadsworth (1807–1864) was shot in the head and killed while leading a charge during the Battle of the Wilderness.
29. The Minié ball was a more accurate bullet, designed to expand and spin upon firing, introduced in the spring of 1863.
30. The 8th Wisconsin Infantry took its nickname from its mascot "Old Abe," a bald eagle. The regiment participated in battles and skirmishes at Corinth, Farmington, Vicksburg, and elsewhere in the Western theater.
31. Large portrait photographs.

VI

REMEMBRANCE
AND
FORGETTING

Bull Run, Va. Dedication of the battle monument, June 10, 1865. Photograph by William Morris Smith.

6

INTRODUCTION

In 1862, only a year into the conflict, the fire-breathing Richmond journalist
Edward Pollard published a work titled *Southern History of the War: The
First Year of the War*—which he later followed up with histories of the second, third, and fourth years. Pollard's choice of titles is intriguing, because it
reveals an instinctive awareness that this war would have different histories
written about it, and that he should get his into print, quickly. Pollard stands,
in this sense, at the very head of a decades-long cultural effort, involving many
actors and many agendas, to fix the place of the Civil War in American public
memory. Indeed, that effort continues to this day. The history of the war is still
being written.

On April 15, 1865, a President lay dead in the Petersen House across from Ford's
Theatre; the South lay literally in ruins; and at least 1.1 million Americans lay
dead or wounded. At no other moment in its history has the United States confronted anything close to that scale of devastation, and the country's ability to
move forward had much to do with explaining to itself the meaning of the ordeal
through which it had passed. For what purpose had so many people suffered
and died? What kind of place would the nation become, and what kind should
it become, now that the violence had ceased? How should the war dead be
remembered? Had the war fully resolved the conflicts that produced it, and if
not...?

Such questions grew insistent in the aftermath of civil war, and the writings
collected in this section suggest how the meanings of the war, still unsettled,
were interpreted and reinterpreted by people with very different ideas of American cultural identity. At the same time, they suggest that the desire for national
reconciliation, for a release from the agonies of social conflict, made it more difficult to answer those questions honestly. As with any war, the Civil War's place
in the public imagination would be determined, yet always destabilized, by the
yoked forces of memory and amnesia.

Even for individuals, memory is not a straightforward transcription of the past,
but an active process of magnifying certain experiences, distorting or suppressing others, and shaping the lot of them into some kind of coherent story. For
an entire society, with many individual memories and interests at stake, the
formation of historical memory, of a shared cultural narrative, becomes much

more difficult. Rival versions of the past have to be sorted out, prioritized, officially recognized or officially discouraged. Agents of the state must figure out how to allocate limited resources toward commemorating the past and preserving its material traces. Cultural "authorities" in universities, museums, and historical institutions must decide what to emphasize and what to de-emphasize in representing the past. And all the while, every private actor with the means to do so—from a soapbox to a laptop—can seek to influence how the public perceives its own collective history.

The controversial meanings of the Civil War, like those of any other massive social trauma, have been framed by public monuments and memorials, by the activism of private interest groups, and by a torrent of literature and commentary. The main controversy, not surprisingly, concerns the racial dimension of the conflict, and the extent to which the war entailed upon a now unified nation the obligation to secure civil rights in practice as well as in theory. The problem of race did not simply disappear with the Reconstruction amendments. "What the war did not accomplish," Paul Shackel has observed, "was to change the racial ideologies that had developed in American culture over several centuries."[1] Particularly after the end of Reconstruction in 1877, the dynamic between war remembrance and the politics of race grew more complex as the widespread desire for national harmony had to contend with widespread racial violence and the resurgence of white supremacism.

Beginning immediately after the war, battlefields, graveyards, and statues became the principal sites of Civil War commemoration and reflection. The very landscape of the country has changed because of efforts to memorialize the war dead and to preserve intact the fields where they fell. From the National Cemetery at Arlington, to the Robert Gould Shaw Memorial on Boston Common, to the Shiloh National Military Park in Tennessee, these *lieux de memoire* share certain common purposes and principles. They make memory visible, public, and grand. They serve as a link between past, present, and future, embodying the nation's sense of historical continuity. They imply permanence and coherence, in contrast to disorder and deterioration. They call upon us to invest them with emotional power, and to supply the missing context of the events they memorialize.

Similar purposes were served by the post-bellum "reminiscence industry." Well into the twentieth century, veterans' groups (principally the Grand Army of the Republic), generals' memoirs, and observances of Decoration Day and Memorial Day gave Americans a way of celebrating their common national identity despite the cataclysm of civil war.

Against that background, a number of historians have argued that the processes of memorialization and cultural reconciliation inhibited serious attention to the unfinished business of emancipation. From this perspective, the aura of heroism and sacrifice conjured up by both monuments and retrospective literature can seem like an anesthetic, serving to neutralize more critical evaluations of the war and its aftermath. The critique is not so much of nostalgia as an escape from ideology, but of nostalgia as a *form* of ideology. Other scholars, however, have emphasized the shifting, unruly meanings of memorial sites and texts, suggesting that the very act of remembering served to draw out the conflict. "To commemorate the dead," writes John R. Neff, "was to recall and honor the men themselves, the cause they championed, and especially the relationships between the dead, their cause, and the living."[2] Certainly, the highly ideological edge of both "Lost Cause" writings—offspring of Pollard's *The Lost Cause* (1867), which affirmed the principles of the defeated Confederacy—and the work of such writers as Albion Tourgée who cried out for racial justice, kept the controversy of the war ever simmering.

And finally there are the many authors who sought to explore the war in its broad social impact and its lingering power over the thoughts and lives of individuals. The literary struggle to come to terms with the Civil War meant different things to different people. At times it meant using the power of words to imagine, and help bring into being, a new social reality. At others, it provided a retreat from reality into a less difficult past, or a creative reinterpretation of the past to suit the needs of the present. Most commonly, the post-bellum literary response to the Civil War—in scores of novels and hundreds of short stories and poems—focused on the individual experience of war, and the psychological and social consequences of organized destruction. Some memories would not be buried, and they resurfaced throughout the period as claimants to the nation's attention.

NOTES

1. Paul Shackel, *Memory in Black and White: Race, Commemoration, and the Post-Bellum Landscape* (Walnut Creek, CA: AltaMira Press, 2003), p. 1.
2. John R. Neff, *Honoring the Civil War Dead: Commemoration and the Problem of Reconciliation* (Lawrence: University Press of Kansas, 2005), pp. 6–7.

SUGGESTED READING

Blair, William Alan. *Cities of the Dead: Contesting the Memory of the Civil War in the South, 1865–1914*. Chapel Hill: University of North Carolina Press, 2004.

Blight, David W. *Race and Reunion: The Civil War in American Memory*. Cambridge: The Belknap Press of Harvard University Press, 2001.

Blight, David W. *Beyond the Battlefield: Race, Memory and the American Civil War*. Amherst: University of Massachusetts Press, 2002.

Foner, Eric. *Reconstruction: America's Unfinished Revolution, 1863–1877*. New York: Harper & Row, 1988.

Foster, Gaines M. *Ghosts of the Confederacy: Defeat, the Lost Cause, and the Emergence of the New South, 1865–1913*. New York: Oxford University Press, 1987.

Hahn, Steven. *A Nation Under Our Feet : Black Political Struggles in the Rural South from Slavery to the Great Migration*. Cambridge: Belknap Press of Harvard University Press, 2003.

Leonard, Elizabeth D. *Lincoln's Avengers: Justice, Revenge, and Reunion After the Civil War*. New York: W.W. Norton, 2004.

Mills, Cynthia and Pamela H. Simpson, eds. *Monuments to the Lost Cause: Women, Art, and the Landscapes of Southern Memory*. Knoxville: University of Tennessee Press, 2003.

Neff, John R. *Honoring the Civil War Dead: Commemoration and the Problem of Reconciliation*. Lawrence: University Press of Kansas, 2005.

Shackel, Paul A. *Memory in Black and White: Race, Commemoration, and the Post-Bellum Landscape*. Walnut Creek, CA: AltaMira Press, 2003.

Silber, Nina. *The Romance of Reunion: Northerners and the South, 1865-1900*. Chapel Hill: University of North Carolina Press, 1993.

Smith, Timothy B. *This Great Battlefield of Shiloh: History, Memory, and the Establishment of a Civil War National Military Park*. Knoxville: University of Tennessee Press, 2004.

Waldrep, Christopher. *Vicksburg's Long Shadow : The Civil War Legacy of Race and Remembrance*. Lanham, MD: Rowman & Littlefield, 2005.

Weeks, Jim. *Gettysburg: Memory, Market, and an American Shrine*. Princeton, NJ: Princeton University Press, 2003.

Abraham Lincoln

SECOND INAUGURAL ADDRESS
March 4, 1865

Fellow-countrymen:

At this second appearing to take the oath of the presidential office, there is less occasion for an extended address than there was at the first. Then a statement, somewhat in detail, of a course to be pursued, seemed fitting and proper. Now, at the expiration of four years, during which public declarations have been constantly called forth on every point and phase of the great contest which still absorbs the attention and engrosses the energies of the nation, little that is new could be presented. The progress of our arms, upon which all else chiefly depends, is as well known to the public as to myself; and it is, I trust, reasonably satisfactory and encouraging to all. With high hope for the future, no prediction in regard to it is ventured.

On the occasion corresponding to this four years ago, all thoughts were anxiously directed to an impending civil war. All dreaded it—all sought to avert it. While the inaugural address was being delivered from this place, devoted altogether to saving the Union without war, insurgent agents were in the city seeking to destroy it without war—seeking to dissolve the Union, and divide effects, by negotiation. Both parties deprecated war; but one of them would make war rather than let the nation survive; and the other would accept war rather than let it perish. And the war came.

One-eighth of the whole population were colored slaves, not distributed generally over the Union, but localized in the Southern part of it. These slaves constituted a peculiar and powerful interest. All knew that this interest was, somehow, the cause of the war. To strengthen, perpetuate, and extend this interest was the object for which the insurgents would rend the Union, even by war; while the government claimed no right to do more than to restrict the territorial enlargement of it.

Neither party expected for the war the magnitude or the duration which it has already attained. Neither anticipated that the cause of the conflict might cease with, or even before, the conflict itself should cease. Each looked for an easier triumph, and a result less fundamental and astounding. Both read the same Bible, and pray to the same God; and each invokes his aid against the other. It may seem strange that any men should dare to ask a just God's assistance in wringing their bread from the sweat of other men's faces; but let us judge not, that we be not judged. The prayers of both could not be answered—that of neither has been answered fully.

The Almighty has his own purposes. "Woe unto the world because of offenses! for it must needs be that offenses come; but woe to that man by whom the offense cometh!" If we shall suppose that American slavery is one of those offenses which, in the providence of God, must needs come, but which, having continued through his appointed time, he now wills to remove, and that he gives to both North and South, this terrible war, as the woe due to those by whom the offense came, shall we discern therein any departure from those divine attributes which the believers in a living God always ascribe to him? Fondly do we hope—fervently do we pray—that this mighty scourge of war may speedily pass away. Yet, if God wills that it continue, until all the wealth piled by the bond-man's two hundred and fifty years of unrequited toil shall be sunk, and until every drop of blood drawn with the lash shall be paid by another drawn with the sword, as was said three thousand years ago, so still it must be said, "The judgments of the Lord are true and righteous altogether."

With malice toward none; with charity for all; with firmness in the right, as God gives us to see the right, let us strive on to finish the work we are in; to bind up the nation's wounds; to care for him who shall have borne the battle, and for his widow, and his orphan—to do all which may achieve and cherish a just and lasting peace among ourselves, and with all nations.

John Wilkes Booth

TO MARY ANN HOLMES BOOTH
Philadelphia, November 1864

Dearest beloved Mother

Heaven knows how dearly I love you. And may our kind Father in Heaven (if only for the sake of my love) watch over, *comfort* & protect you, in my absence. May he soften the blow of my departure, granting you peace and happiness for many, many years to come. God ever bless you.

I have always endeavored to be a good and dutiful son, And even now would wish to die sooner than give you pain. But dearest Mother, though, I owe you all, *there* is another duty. A noble duty for the sake of liberty and humanity due to my Country—For, four years I have lived (I may say) A *slave* in the north (A favored slave its true, but no less hateful to me on that account.) Not daring to express my thoughts or sentiments, even in my own home Constantly hearing every principle, dear to my heart, denounced as treasonable, And knowing the vile and savage acts committed on my countrymen their wives & helpless children, that I have cursed my wilful idleness, And begun to deem myself a coward and to despise my own existence. For four years I have borne it mostly for your dear sake, And for you alone, have I also struggled to fight off this desire to begone, but it seems that uncontrollable fate, moving me for its ends, takes me from you, dear Mother, to do what work I can for a poor oppressed downtrodden people. May that same fate cause me to do that work well. I care not for the censure of the north, so I have your forgiveness, And I feel I may hope it, even though you differ with me in opinion. I may by the grace of God, live through this war dear Mother, if so, the rest of my life shall be more devoted to you, than has been my former. For I know it will take a long lifetime of tenderness and care, to atone for the pang this parting will give you. But I cannot longer resist the inclination, to go and share the sufferings of my brave countrymen, holding an unequal strife (for every right human & divine) against the most ruthless enemy, the world has ever known. You can answer for me dearest Mother (although none of you think with me) that I have not a *single selfish motive* to spur me on to this, nothing save the sacred duty, I feel I *owe the cause I love*. The cause of the South. The cause of liberty & justice. So should I meet the *worst*, dear Mother, in struggling for such holy rights. I can say "Gods' will be done" And bless him in my heart for not permitting me, to outlive, our dear bought freedom. And for keeping me from being longer a hidden lie among my country's foes. Darling Mother I can not write you, you will understand the deep regret, the forsaking your dear side, will make me suffer, for you have been the best, the noblest, an example for all mothers. God, God bless you. As I shall ever pray him to do. And should the last bolt strike your son, dear Mother, bear it patiently And think at the best life is but short, and *not at all times happy*. My Brothers & Sisters (Heaven protect them) will add my love and duty to their own, and watch you with care and kindness, till we meet again. And if *that happiness* does not come to us on earth, then may, O May it be with God. So then dearest, *dearest* Mother, *forgive* and pray for me. I feel that I am right in the justness of my cause, And that we shall, *ere long*, meet again. Heaven grant it. Bless you, bless you. Your loving son will never cease to hope and pray for such a joy.

Come weal or woe, with never ending love and devotion you will find me ever your affectionate son

John.

John Wilkes Booth

TO THE EDITORS
OF THE *NATIONAL INTELLIGENCER*, WASHINGTON, D.C.
April 14, 1865

To My Countrymen: For years I have devoted my time, my energies, and every dollar I possessed to the furtherance of an object. I have been baffled and disappointed. The hour has come when I must change my plan. Many, I know—the vulgar herd—will blame me for what I am about to do, but posterity, I am sure, will justify me. Right or wrong, God judge me, not man. Be my motive good or bad, of one thing I am sure, the lasting condemnation of the North. I love peace more than life. Have loved the Union beyond expression. For four years have I waited, hoped and prayed for the dark clouds to break and for a restoration of our former sunshine. To wait longer is a crime. My prayers have proved as idle as my hopes. Gods [sic] will be done. I go to see and share the bitter end. This war is a war with the constitution and the reserve rights of the state. It is a war upon Southern rights and institutions. The nomination of Abraham Lincoln four years ago bespoke war. His election forced it. I have ever held the South were right. In a foreign war I too could say "country, right or wrong." But in a struggle such as ours (where the brother tries to pierce the brother's heart) for God's sake chose the right. When a country like this spurns justice from her side she forfeits the allegiance of every honest freeman, and should leave him untrammeled by any fealty soever to act as his conscience may approve.

People of the North, to hate tyranny to love liberty and justice, to strike at wrong and oppression, was the teaching of our fathers. The study of our early history will not let me forget it, and may it never.

I do not want to forget the heroic patriotism of our fathers, who rebelled against the oppression of the mother country.

This country was formed for the white, not for the black man. And, looking upon African slavery from the same standpoint as the noble framers of our constitution, I, for one, have ever considered it one of the greatest blessings, both for themselves and us, that God ever bestowed upon a favored nation. Witness, heretofore, our wealth and power; witness their elevation and enlightenment above their race elsewhere. I have lived among it most of my life, and have seen less harsh treatment from master to man than I have beheld in the North from father to son. Yet, Heaven knows no one would be willing to do more for the negro race than I, could I but see a way to still better their condition. But Lincoln's policy is only preparing the way for their total annihilation. The South are not, nor have they been, fighting for the continuation of slavery. The first battle of Bull Run did away with that idea.

Their causes for the war have been as noble and greater far than those that urged our fathers on. Even should we allow that they were wrong at the beginning of this contest, cruelty and injustice have made the wrong become the right, and they stand now before the wonder and admiration of the world as a noble band of patriot heroes. Hereafter reading of their deeds Thermopylae[1] would be forgotten.

When I aided in the capture and execution of John Brown (who was a murderer on our western border, and who was fairly tried and convicted before an impartial judge and jury of treason, and who, by the way, has since been made a God.) I was proud of my little share in the transaction, for I deemed it my duty[,] and that I was helping our common country to perform an act of justice, but what was a crime in poor John Brown is now considered (by themselves) as the greatest and only virtue of the whole Republican party.[2]

Strange transmigration! Vice to become a virtue, simply because more indulge in it. I thought then, as now, that the Abolitionists were the only traitors in the land, and that the entire party deserved the same fate as poor old Brown. Not because they wished to abolish slavery[,] but on account of the means they have ever endeavored to use to effect that abolition. If Brown were living I doubt whether he himself would set slavery against the Union. Most, or nearly all the North, do openly curse the Union if the South are to return and retain a single right guaranteed to them by every tie which we once revered as sacred. The South can make no choice. It is either extermination or slavery for themselves (worse than death) to draw from. I know my choice, and hasten to accept it. I have studied hard to discover upon what grounds the right of a State to secede has been denied, whether our very name, United States, and the Declaration of Independence both provide for secession[,] but there is now no time for words. I know how foolish I shall be deemed for undertaking such a step as this, where on the one side I have many friends and every thing to make me happy, where my profession alone has gained me an income of more than twenty thousand dollars a year, and where my great personal ambition in my profession has been a great field for labor. On the other hand, the South have never bestowed upon me one kind word; a place now where I have no friends, except beneath the sod; a place where I must either become a private soldier or a beggar. To give up all of the former for the latter, besides my mother and sisters whom I love so dearly (although they so widely differ with me in opinion), seems insane; but God is my judge. I love justice more than I do a country that disowns it; more than fame and wealth; more (heaven pardon me if wrong) more than a happy home. I have never been upon a battlefield, but oh! my countrymen, could you all but see the reality or effects of this horrid war. As I have seen them in every state save Virginia, I know you would think like me, and would pray the Almighty to create in the Northern mind a sense of right and justice (even should it possess no seasoning of mercy) and that he would dry up the sea of blood between us which is daily growing wider. Alas, I have no longer a country. She is fast approaching her threatened doom. Four years ago, I would have given a thousand lives to see her remain (as I had always known her) powerful and unbroken. And even now I would hold my life as naught, to see her what she was. Oh! my friends, if the fearful scenes of the past four years had never been enacted, or if what has been had been but a frightful dream, from which we could now awake, with what overflowing hearts could we bless our God and pray for his continued favor.

How I have loved the old flag can never now be known. A few years since and the entire world could boast of [none] so pure and spotless. But I have of late been seeing and hearing of the bloody deeds of which she has been made the emblem. And would shudder to think how changed she had grown. Oh! how I have longed to see her break from the mist of blood and death so circled around her folds, spoiling her beauty and tarnishing her honor. But no; day by day has she been dragged deeper and deeper into cruelty and oppression, till now (in my eyes) her once bright red stripes look like bloody gashes on the face of heaven. I look now upon my early admiration of her glories as a dream. My love (as things stand today) is for the South alone, and to her side I go penniless.

Her success has been near my heart, and I have labored faithfully to further an object which would more than have proved my unselfish devotion. Heartsick and disappointed I turn from the path which I have been following into a bolder and more perilous one. Without malice I make the change. I have nothing in my heart except a sense of duty to my choice. If the South is to be aided it must be done quickly. It may already be too late. When Caesar had conquered the enemies of Rome and the power that was his menaced the liberties of the people, Brutus arose and slew him. The stroke of his dagger was guided by his love of Rome. It was the spirit and ambition of Caesar that Brutus struck at.

"Oh that we could come by Caesar's spirit,
And not dismember Caesar!
But, alas!
Caesar must bleed for it."[3]

I answer with Brutus:

He who loves his country better than gold or life.

John W. Booth

John Wilkes Booth

DIARY ENTRIES
(April 17, 1865; April 22, 1865)

Zekiah Swamp and Nanjemoy Creek,
Charles County, Maryland,
17 and 22 April 1865

April 13th   14 Friday the Ides

Until to day [sic] nothing was ever thought of sacrificing to our country's wrongs. For six months we had worked to capture. But our cause being almost lost, something decisive & great must be done. But its failure is owing to others, who did not strike for their country with a heart. I struck boldly and not as the papers say. I walked with a firm step through a thousand of his friends, was stopped, but pushed on. A Col—was at his side. I shouted Sic semper *before* I fired. In jumping broke my leg.[4] I passed all his pickets, rode sixty miles that night, with the bones of my leg tearing the flesh at every jump. I can never repent it, though we hated to kill: Our country owed all her troubles to him, and God simply made me the instrument of his punishment. The country is not what it was. This forced union is not what I have loved. I care not what becomes of me. I have no desire to out-live my country. This night (before the deed), I wrote a long article and left it for one of the Editors of the National Inteligencer, [sic] in which I fully set forth our reasons for our proceedings. He or the Govmt

Friday 21—

After being hunted like a dog through swamps, woods, and last night being chased by gun boats till I was forced to return wet cold and starving, with every mans hand against me, I am here in despair.[5] And why; For doing what Brutus was honored for, what made Tell a Hero.[6] And yet I for striking down a greater tyrant than they ever knew am looked upon as a common cutthroat. My action was purer than either of theirs. One, hoped to be great himself. The other had not only his countrys but his own wrongs to avenge. I hoped for no gain. I knew no private wrong. I struck for my country and that alone. A country groaned beneath this tyranny and prayed for this end. Yet now behold the cold hand they extend to me. God *cannot* pardon me if I have done wrong. Yet I cannot see any wrong except in serving a degenerate people. The little, the very little I left behind to clear my name, the Govmt will not allow to be printed. So ends all. For my country I have given up all that makes life sweet and Holy, brought misery on my family, and am sure there is no pardon in Heaven for me since man condemns me so. I have only *heard* what has been done (except what I did myself) and it fills me with horror. God try and forgive me and bless my mother. To night I will once more try the river with the intent to cross, though I have a greater desire to return to Washington and in a measure clear my name which I feel I can do. I do not repent the blow I struck. I may before God but not to man.

I think I have done well, though I am abandoned, with the curse of Cain upon me. When if the world knew my heart, that one blow would have made me great, though I did desire no greatness.

To night I try to escape these blood hounds once more. Who can read his fate. God's will be done.

I have too great a soul to die like a criminal. Oh may he, may he spare me that and let me die bravely.

I bless the entire world. Have never hated or wronged anyone. This last was not a wrong, unless God deems it so. And its with him, to damn or bless me. And for this brave boy with me[7] who often prays (yes before and since) with a true and sincere heart, was it a crime in him, if so why can he pray the same I do not wish to shed a drop of blood, but "I must fight the course" Tis all thats left me.

Walt Whitman

from *Sequel to Drum-Taps* (1865–66)

WHEN LILACS LAST IN THE DOOR-YARD BLOOM'D

1.

When lilacs last in the dooryard bloom'd,
And the great star early droop'd in the western sky in the night,
I mourn'd . . . and yet shall mourn with ever-returning spring.

O ever-returning spring! trinity sure to me you bring;
Lilac blooming perennial, and drooping star in the west,
And thought of him I love.

2.

O powerful, western, fallen star!
O shades of night! O moody, tearful night!
O great star disappear'd! O the black murk that hides the star!
O cruel hands that hold me powerless! O helpless soul of me!
O harsh surrounding cloud that will not free my soul.

3.

In the door-yard fronting an old farm-house near the white-wash'd palings,
Stands the lilac-bush, tall-growing, with heart-shaped leaves of rich green,
With many a pointed blossom, rising, delicate, with the perfume strong I love,
With every leaf a miracle . . . . . . and from this bush in the dooryard,
With delicate-color'd blossoms, and heart-shaped leaves of rich green,
A sprig, with its flower, I break.

4.

In the swamp, in secluded recesses,
A shy and hidden bird is warbling a song.

Solitary, the thrush,
The hermit, withdrawn to himself, avoiding the settlements,
Sings by himself a song.

Song of the bleeding throat!
Death's outlet song of life—(for well, dear brother, I know,
If thou wast not granted to sing, thou would'st surely die.)

5.

Over the breast of the spring, the land, amid cities,
Amid lanes, and through old woods, (where lately the violets peep'd from the
    ground, spotting the gray debris;)
Amid the grass in the fields each side of the lanes—passing the endless grass;
Passing the yellow-spear'd wheat, every grain from its shroud in the dark-brown
    fields uprising;
Passing the apple-tree blows of white and pink in the orchards;
Carrying a corpse to where it shall rest in the grave,
Night and day journeys a coffin.

6.

Coffin that passes through lanes and streets,
Through day and night, with the great cloud darkening the land,
With the pomp of the inloop'd flags, with the cities draped in black,
With the show of the States themselves, as of crape-veil'd women, standing,
With processions long and winding, and the flambeaus of the night,
With the countless torches lit—with the silent sea of faces, and the unbared heads,
With the waiting depot, the arriving coffin, and the sombre faces,
With dirges through the night, with the thousand voices rising strong and solemn;
With all the mournful voices of the dirges, pour'd around the coffin,
The dim-lit churches and the shuddering organs—Where amid these you journey,
With the tolling, tolling bells' perpetual clang;
Here! coffin that slowly passes,
I give you my sprig of lilac.

7.

(Nor for you, for one alone;
Blossoms and branches green to coffins all I bring:
For fresh as the morning—thus would I chant a song for you, O sane and
    sacred death.

All over bouquets of roses,
O death! I cover you over with roses and early lilies;
But mostly and now the lilac that blooms the first,
Copious, I break, I break the sprigs from the bushes:
With loaded arms I come, pouring for you,
For you and the coffins all of you, O death.)

8.

O western orb, sailing the heaven!
Now I know what you must have meant, as a month since we walk'd,
As we walk'd up and down in the dark blue so mystic,
As we walk'd in silence the transparent shadowy night,
As I saw you had something to tell, as you bent to me night after night,

As you droop'd from the sky low down, as if to my side, (while the other stars all
    look'd on;)
As we wander'd together the solemn night, (for something I know not what,
    kept me from sleep;)
As the night advanced, and I saw on the rim of the west, ere you went, how full
    you were of woe;
As I stood on the rising ground in the breeze, in the cool transparent night,
As I watch'd where you pass'd and was lost in the netherward black of the night,
As my soul in its trouble, dissatisfied, sank, as where you, sad orb,
Concluded, dropt in the night, and was gone.

9.

Sing on, there in the swamp!
O singer bashful and tender! I hear your notes—I hear your call;
I hear—I come presently—I understand you;
But a moment I linger—for the lustrous star has detain'd me;
The star, my comrade, departing, holds and detains me.

10.

O how shall I warble myself for the dead one there I loved?
And how shall I deck my song for the large sweet soul that has gone?
And what shall my perfume be, for the grave of him I love?

Sea-winds blown from east and west,
Blown from the eastern sea and blown from the western sea, till there on the
    prairies meeting:
These, and with these, and the breath of my chant,
I'll perfume the grave of him I love.

11.

O what shall I hang on the chamber walls?
And what shall the pictures be that I hang on the walls,
To adorn the burial-house of him I love?

Pictures of growing spring, and farms, and homes,
With the Fourth-month eve at sundown, and the gray-smoke lucid and bright,
With floods of the yellow gold of the gorgeous, indolent, sinking sun, burning,
    expanding the air;
With the fresh sweet herbage under foot, and the pale green leaves of the trees
    prolific;
In the distance the flowing glaze, the breast of the river, with a wind-dapple here
    and there;
With ranging hills on the banks, with many a line against the sky, and shadows;
And the city at hand, with dwellings so dense, and stacks of chimneys,
And all the scenes of life, and the workshops, and the workmen homeward
    returning.

12.

Lo! body and soul! this land!
Mighty Manhattan, with spires, and the sparkling and hurrying tides, and the ships;
The varied and ample land—the South and the North in the light—Ohio's shores,
    and flashing Missouri,
And ever the far-spreading prairies, cover'd with grass and corn.

Lo! the most excellent sun, so calm and haughty;
The violet and purple morn, with just-felt breezes;
The gentle, soft-born, measureless light;
The miracle, spreading, bathing all—the fulfill'd noon;
The coming eve, delicious—the welcome night, and the stars,
Over my cities shining all, enveloping man and land.

13.

Sing on! sing on, you gray-brown bird!
Sing from the swamps, the recesses—pour your chant from the bushes;
Limitless out of the dusk, out of the cedars and pines.

Sing on, dearest brother—warble your reedy song;
Loud human song, with voice of uttermost woe.

O liquid, and free, and tender!
O wild and loose to my soul! O wondrous singer!
You only I hear . . . . . . yet the star holds me, (but will soon depart;)
Yet the lilac, with mastering odor, holds me.

14.

Now while I sat in the day, and look'd forth,
In the close of the day, with its light, and the fields of spring, and the farmer
    preparing his crops,
In the large unconscious scenery of my land, with its lakes and forests,
In the heavenly aerial beauty, (after the perturb'd winds, and the storms;)
Under the arching heavens of the afternoon swift passing, and the voices of
    children and women,
The many-moving sea-tides,—and I saw the ships how they sail'd,
And the summer approaching with richness, and the fields all busy with labor,
And the infinite separate houses, how they all went on, each with its meals and
    minutia of daily usages;
And the streets how their throbbings throbb'd, and the cities pent,—lo! then
    and there,
Falling upon them all, and among them all, enveloping me with the rest,
Appear'd the cloud, appear'd the long black trail;
And I knew Death, its thought, and the sacred knowledge of death.

15.

Then with the knowledge of death as walking one side of me,
And the thought of death close-walking the other side of me,
And I in the middle, as with companions, and as holding the hands of companions,
I fled forth to the hiding receiving night ,that talks not,
Down to the shores of the water, the path by the swamp in the dimness,
To the solemn shadowy cedars, and ghostly pines so still.

And the singer so shy to the rest receiv'd me;
The gray-brown bird I know, receiv'd us comrades three;
And he sang what seem'd the song of death, and a verse for him I love.

From deep secluded recesses,
From the fragrant cedars, and the ghostly pines so still,
Came the singing of the bird.

And the charm of the singing rapt me,
As I held, as if by their hands, my comrades in the night;
And the voice of my spirit tallied the song of the bird.

16.

Come, lovely and soothing Death,
Undulate round the world, serenely arriving, arriving,
In the day, in the night, to all, to each,
Sooner or later, delicate Death.

Prais'd be the fathomless universe,
For life and joy, and for objects and knowledge curious;
And for love, sweet love—But praise! O praise and praise,
For the sure-enwinding arms of cool-enfolding death.

Dark mother, always gliding near, with soft feet,
Have none chanted for thee a chant of fullest welcome?
Then I chant it for thee—I glorify thee above all;
I bring thee a song that when thou must indeed come, come unfalteringly.

Approach, encompassing Death—strong Deliveress!
When it is so—when thou hast taken them, I joyously sing the dead,
Lost in the loving, floating ocean of thee,
Laved in the flood of thy bliss, O Death.

From me to thee glad serenades,
Dances for thee I propose, saluting thee—adornments and feastings for thee;
And the sights of the open landscape, and the high-spread sky are fitting;
And life and the fields, and the huge and thoughtful night.

The night, in silence, under many a star;
The ocean shore, and the husky whispering wave, whose voice I know;
And the soul turning to thee, O vast and well-veil'd Death,
And the body gratefully nestling close to thee.

Over the tree-tops I float thee a song!
Over the rising and sinking waves—over the myriad fields, and the prairies wide;
Over the dense-pack'd cities all, and the teeming wharves and ways,
I float this carol with joy, with joy to thee, O death!

17.

To the tally of my soul,
Loud and strong kept up the gray-brown bird,
With pure, deliberate notes, spreading, filling the night.

Loud in the pines and cedars dim,
Clear in the freshness moist, and the swamp-perfume;
And I with my comrades there in the night.

While my sight that was bound in my eyes unclosed,
As to long panoramas of vision.

18.

I saw the vision of armies;
And I saw, as in noiseless dreams, hundreds of battle-flags;
Borne through the smoke of the battles, and pierc'd with missiles, I saw them,
And carried hither and yon through the smoke, and torn and bloody;
And at last but a few shreds left on the staffs, (and all in silence,)
And the staffs all splinter'd and broken.

I saw battle-corpses, myriads of them,
And the white skeletons of young men—I saw them;
I saw the debris and debris of all dead soldiers;
But I saw they were not as was thought;
They themselves were fully at rest—they suffer'd not;
The living remain'd and suffer'd—the mother suffer'd,
And the wife and the child, and the musing comrade suffer'd,
And the armies that remain'd suffer'd.

19.

Passing the visions, passing the night;
Passing, unloosing the hold of my comrades' hands;
Passing the song of the hermit bird, and the tallying song of my soul,
Victorious song, death's outlet song, (yet varying, ever-altering song,
As low and wailing, yet clear the notes, rising and falling, flooding the night,

Sadly sinking and fainting, as warning and warning, and yet again bursting with joy,)
Covering the earth, and filling the spread of the heaven,
As that powerful psalm in the night I heard from recesses.

Passing, I leave thee lilac with heart-shaped leaves,
I leave thee there in the door-yard, blooming, returning with spring.

20.

Must I leave thee, lilac with heart-shaped leaves?
Must I leave thee here in the door-yard, blooming, returning with spring?

Must I pass from my song for thee;
From my gaze on thee in the west, fronting the west, communing with thee,
O comrade lustrous, with silver face in the night?

I cease from my song for thee,
From my gaze on thee in the west, fronting the west, communing with thee,
O comrade lustrous with silver face in the night.

21.

Yet each I keep, and all;
The song, the wondrous chant of the gray-brown bird, I keep,
And the tallying chant, the echo arous'd in my soul, I keep,
With the lustrous and drooping star, with the countenance full of woe;
With the lilac tall, and its blossoms of mastering odor;
Comrades mine, and I in the midst, and their memory ever I keep—for the dead
    I loved so well;
For the sweetest, wisest soul of all my days and lands . . . and this for his dear sake;
Lilac and star and bird, twined with the chant of my soul,
With the holders holding my hand, nearing the call of the bird,
There in the fragrant pines, and the cedars dusk and dim.

Walt Whitman

from *Drum-Taps* (1865)

THE VETERAN'S VISION

While my wife at my side lies slumbering, and the wars are over long,
And my head on the pillow rests at home, and the mystic midnight passes,
And through the stillness, through the dark, I hear, just hear, the breath of my infant,
There in the room, as I wake from sleep, this vision presses upon me;
The engagement opens there and then, in my busy brain unreal;
The skirmishers begin—they crawl cautiously ahead—I hear the irregular snap!
    snap!
I hear the sounds of the different missiles—the short *t-h-t! t-h-t!* of the rifle-balls;
I see the shells exploding, leaving small white clouds—I hear the great shells
    shrieking as they pass;
The grape, like the hum and whirr of wind through the trees, (quick, tumultuous,
    now the contest rages!)
All the scenes at the batteries themselves rise in detail before me again,
The crashing and smoking—the pride of the men in their pieces;
The chief gunner ranges and sights his piece, and selects a fuse of the right time;
After firing, I see him lean aside, and look eagerly off to note the effect;
—Elsewhere I hear the cry of a regiment charging—(the young colonel leads himself
    this time, with brandish'd sword;)
I see the gaps cut by the enemy's volleys, (quickly fill'd up—no delay;)
I breathe the suffocating smoke—then the flat clouds hover low, concealing all;
Now a strange lull comes for a few seconds, not a shot fired on either side;
Then resumed, the chaos louder than ever, with eager calls, and orders of officers;
While from some distant part of the field the wind wafts to my ears a shout of
    applause, (some special success;)
And ever the sound of the cannon, far or near, (rousing, even in dreams, a devilish
    exultation, and all the old mad joy, in the depths of my soul;)
And ever the hastening of infantry shifting positions—batteries, cavalry, moving
    hither and thither;
The falling, dying, I heed not—the wounded, dripping and red, I heed not—some to
    the rear are hobbling;)
Grime, heat, rush—aide-de-camps galloping by, or on a full run;
With the patter of small arms, the warning *s-s-t* of the rifles, (these in my vision I
    hear or see,)
And bombs bursting in air, and at night the vari-color'd rockets.

Walt Whitman

from *Specimen Days* (1882)

THE MILLION DEAD, TOO, SUMM'D UP

The dead in this war—there they lie, strewing the fields and woods and valleys and battle-fields of the south—Virginia, the Peninsula—Malvern hill and Fair Oaks—the banks of the Chickahominy—the terraces of Fredericksburgh—Antietam bridge—the grisly ra-vines of Manassas—the bloody promenade of the Wilderness—the varieties of the strayed dead, (the estimate of the War department is 25,000 national soldiers kill'd in battle and never buried at all, 5,000 drown'd—15,000 inhumed by strangers, or on the march in haste, in hitherto unfound localities—2,000 graves cover'd by sand and mud by Mississippi freshets, 3,000 carried away by caving-in of banks, &c.,)—Gettysburgh, the West, South-west—Vicksburgh—Chattanooga—the trenches of Petersburgh—the numberless battles, camps, hospitals everywhere—the crop reap'd by the mighty reapers, typhoid, dysentery, inflammations—and blackest and loathesomest of all, the dead and living burial-pits, the prison-pens of Andersonville, Salisbury, Belle-Isle, &c., (not Dante's pictured hell and all its woes, its degradations, filthy torments, excell'd those prisons)—the dead, the dead, the dead—*our* dead—or South or North, ours all, (all, all, all, finally dear to me)—or East or West—Atlantic coast or Mississippi valley—somewhere they crawl'd to die, alone, in bush-es, low gullies, or on the sides of hills—(there, in secluded spots, their skeletons, bleach'd bones, tufts of hair, buttons, fragments of clothing, are occasionally found yet)—our young men once so handsome and so joyous, taken from us—the son from the mother, the husband from the wife, the dear friend from the dear friend—the clusters of camp graves, in Georgia, the Carolinas, and in Tennessee—the single graves left in the woods or by the road-side, (hundreds, thousands, obliterated)—the corpses floated down the rivers, and caught and lodged, (dozens, scores, floated down the upper Potomac, after the cavalry engagements, the pursuit of Lee, following Gettysburgh)—some lie at the bottom of the sea—the general million, and the special cemeteries in almost all the States—the in-finite dead—(the land entire saturated, perfumed with their impalpable ashes' exhalation in Nature's chemistry distill'd, and shall be so forever, in every future grain of wheat and ear of corn, and every flower that grows, and every breath we draw)—not only Northern dead leavening Southern soil—thousands, aye tens of thousands, of Southerners, crumble today in Northern earth.

And everywhere among these countless graves—everywhere in the many soldier Cem-eteries of the Nation, (there are now, I believe, over seventy of them)—as at the time in the vast trenches, the depositories of slain, Northern and Southern, after the great battles—not only where the scathing trail passed those years, but radiating since in all the peaceful quarters of the land—we see, and ages yet may see, on monuments and gravestones, singly or in masses, to thousands or tens of thousands, the significant word Unknown.

(In some of the cemeteries nearly *all* the dead are unknown. At Salisbury, N.C., for in-stance, the known are only 85, while the unknown are 12,027, and 11,700 of these are bur-ied in trenches. A national monument has been put up here, by order of Congress, to mark the spot—but what visible, material monument can ever fittingly commemorate that spot?)

Walt Whitman

from Specimen Days (1882)

THE REAL WAR WILL NEVER GET IN THE BOOKS

And so good-bye to the war. I know not how it may have been, or may be to others—to me the main interest I found, (and still, on recollection, find,) in the rank and file of the armies, both sides, and in those specimens amid the hospitals, and even the dead on the field. To me the points illustrating the latent personal character and eligibilities of these States, in the two or three millions of American young and middle-aged men, North and South embodied in those armies—and especially the one-third or one-fourth of their number, stricken by wounds or disease at some time in the course of the contest—were of more significance even than the political interests involved. (As so much of a race depends on how it faces death, and how it stands personal anguish and sickness. As, in the glints of emotions under emergencies, and the indirect traits and asides in Plutarch, we get far profounder clues to the antique world than all its more formal history.)

Future years will never know the seething hell and the black infernal background of countless minor scenes and interiors, (not the official surface-courteousness of the Generals, not the few great battles) of the Secession war; and it is best they should not—the real war will never get in the books. In the mushy influences of current times, too, the fervid atmosphere and typical events of those years are in danger of being totally forgotten. I have at night watch'd by the side of a sick man in the hospital, one who could not live many hours. I have seen his eyes flash and burn as he raised himself and recurr'd to the cruelties of his surrender'd brother, and mutilations of the corpse afterward. (See, in the preceding pages, the incident at Upperville—the seventeen kill'd as in the description, were left there on the ground. After they dropt dead, no one touch'd them—all were made sure of, however. The carcasses were left for the citizens to bury or not, as they chose.)

Such was the war. It was not a quadrille in a ball-room.[8] Its interior history will not only never be written—its practicality, minutiæ of deeds and passions, will never be even suggested. The actual soldier of 1862-'65, North and South, with all his ways, his incredible dauntlessness, habits, practices, tastes, language, his fierce friendship, his appetite, rankness, his superb strength and animality, lawless gait, and a hundred unnamed lights and shades of camp, I say, will never be written—perhaps must not and should not be.

The preceding notes may furnish a few stray glimpses into that life, and into those lurid interiors, never to be fully convey'd to the future. The hospital part of the drama from '61 to '65, deserves indeed to be recorded. Of that many-threaded drama, with its sudden and strange surprises, its confounding of prophecies, its moments of despair, the dread of foreign interference, the interminable campaigns, the bloody battles, the mighty and cumbrous and green armies, the drafts and bounties—the immense money expenditure, like a heavy-pouring constant rain—with, over the whole land, the last three years of the struggle, an unending, universal mourning-wail of women, parents, orphans—the marrow of the tragedy concentrated in those Army Hospitals—(it seem'd sometimes as if the whole interest of the land, North and South, was one vast central hospital, and all the rest of the affair but flanges)—those forming the untold and unwritten history of the war—infinitely greater (like life's) than the few scraps and distortions that are ever told or written. Think how much, and of importance, will be—how much, civic and military, has already been—buried in the grave, in eternal darkness.

Edward Alfred Pollard

from *The Lost Cause: A New Southern History of the War of the Confederates* (1867)

CHAPTER XLIV

The record of the war closes exactly with the laying down of the Confederate arms. We do not design to transgress this limit of our narrative. But it will not be out of place to regard generally the political consequences of the war, so far as they have been developed in a formation of parties, involving the further destinies of the country, and in the light of whose actions will probably be read many future pages of American History.

The surrender of Gen. Lee's army was not the simple act of a defeated and overpowered General; it was not the misfortune of an individual. The public mind of the South was fully represented in that surrender. The people had become convinced that the Confederate cause was lost; they saw that the exertions of four years, misdirected and abused, had not availed, and they submitted to what they conceived now to be the determined fortune of the war.

That war closed on a spectacle of ruin, the greatest of modern times. There were eleven great States lying prostrate; their capital all absorbed; their fields desolate; their towns and cities ruined; their public works torn to pieces by armies; their system of labour overturned; the fruits of the toil of generations all swept into a chaos of destruction; their slave property taken away by a stroke of the pen; a pecuniary loss of two thousand millions of dollars involved in one single measure of spoliation—a penalty embraced in one edict, in magnitude such as had seldom been exacted unless in wars synonymous with robberies.

As an evidence of the poverty of the South, produced by the war, we may cite the case of the State of South Carolina. By the census of 1860, the property of the State was value[d] at $400,000,000. Of this, it has been estimated that the injury to the banks, private securities, railroads, cities, houses, plantations, stock, etc., amounted to $100,000,000. There were, by the same census, 400,000 slaves, valued at $200,000,000. This left only $100,000,000 for the value of all the property left in the State; and the principal portion of this consisted of lands, which had fallen in value immensely.

The close of the war presented the Government at Washington with the alternative of two distinct and opposite policies, with reference to the subdued Southern States. One was the policy of the restoration of the Union with reconciliation: the other the policy of restriction. The party that favoured the latter was not long in developing the full extent of its doctrine, which involved universal confiscation at the South, a general execution of prominent men, the disfranchisement of men who acted or sympathized with the Confederates, and the granting of the right of voting to the freed blacks. This hideous programme was announced not only as a just punishment of "rebels," but as a security for the future, and the indispensable condition of the public peace.

But to men who had read the lessons of history it was clearly apparent that this policy would be destructive of the very ends it proposed; that it would increase the acerbity of feeling at the South; that it would deliver the two races over to the most violent discord;

and that it would be the occasion of immeasurable chaos and interminable anarchy. It was the immortal BURKE who uttered the great philosophical truth of history: that "liberty, and not despotism, was the cure of anarchy;" and who proposed as the speedy and sovereign remedy for the disorders of the Colonies, that they should be "admitted to a share in the British Constitution."

It was precisely this enlightened lesson which those who agreed in the sentiment of clemency, proposed to apply to the condition of the Southern States. It was this party which took its instruction from exalted schools of statesmanship; which looked at the situation from the eminence of History; and which desired to bind up with the Federal authority the rights, peace, and prosperity of all parts of the country.

Obviously the policy of this party, with reference to what was called "Reconstruction," was to consider the Southern States as in the Union, without any ceremonies or conditions other than what might be found in the common Constitution of the country. What may be designated generally as the Conservative party in the North, had long held the doctrine that, as the Union was inviolable and permanent, secession was illegal, revolutionary, null, and void; that it had no legal validity or effect; that it was the act of seditious individuals, and did not affect the *status* of the States purporting to secede. This branch of their doctrine was accepted by a large number of the Republican party; among them Mr. Seward, the Secretary of State. President Lincoln had acted upon this theory when it became necessary to reorganize States overrun by Federal armies. It was held by the Conservative party, against all rational dispute, that the business of the Federal Government, with respect to the insurgent States, was simply to quell resistance, and to execute everywhere the Constitution and laws. Its contest was not with the States, but with the illegal powers within the States engaged in resisting its authority. When the resistance of these persons ceased, the work was done; and the States were *co instante, ipso facto,* as much within the Union as ever; no act of re-admission being necessary. It only remained for the judiciary to proceed by indictment and legal trial, under the forms of law, against the individuals who had resisted the authority of the Union to test the fact of treason, and to vindicate the reputation of the Government. And this was the whole extent to which the policy of penalities [sic] could be insisted upon.

On this opinion there was soon to be a sharp and desperate array of parties at Washington. When, by the tragical death of President Lincoln, in a public theatre, at the hands of one of the most indefensible but courageous assassins that history has ever produced, the Executive office passed to the Vice-President, Andrew Johnson, the Southern people ignorantly deplored the change as one to their disadvantage, and the world indulged but small expectations from the coming man. The new President was sprung from a low order of life, and was what Southern gentlemen called a "scrub." In qualities of mind it was generally considered that he had the shallowness and fluency of the demagogue; but in this there was a mistake. At any rate, it must be confessed, Mr. Johnson had no literature and but little education of any sort; in his agrarian speeches in the Senate, he quoted "the Lays of Ancient Rome" as "*translated* by Macaulay;"[9] and he was constantly making those mistakes in historical and literary allusions which never fail to characterize and betray self-educated men. Before his elevation to the Presidency, Mr. Johnson was considered a demagogue, who seldom ventured out of common-places, or attempted anything above the coarse sense of the multitude, successful, industrious, a clod-head, a "man of the people," that peculiar product of American politics. But there are familiar instances in history where characters apparently the most common-place and trifling, have been suddenly awakened and elevated as great responsibilities have been thrust upon them, and have risen to the demands of the new occasion. An example of such change was afforded by plain Andrew Johnson, when he stepped to the dignity of President of a restored Union, with all its great historical trusts for him to administer in sight of the world. From that hour the man changed. The eminence did not confound him; he saw before him a part in American history second only to that of George Washington; he left behind him the ambitions and resentments of mere party; he rose as the man who has been secretly, almost unconsciously, great—a common-place among his neighbour, the familiar fellow of the company—suddenly, completely to the full height and dignity of the new destiny that called him. The man who had been twitted as a tailor and condemned as a demagogue, proved a statesman, measuring his actions for the future, insensible to clamour and patient for results.

President Johnson belonged to an intermediate school of politics, standing between the doctrines of Mr. Calhoun and those of Alexander Hamilton.[10] He was never an extreme State-Rights man; he had never recognized the right of nullification, or that of secession; but he was always disposed to recognize, in a liberal degree, the rights of the States, and to combat the theory that the Federal Government absorbed powers and privileges, which, from the foundation of the republic, had been conceded to the States.

It was fortunate that the Chief Magistrate of the country, who was to administer its affairs and determine its course on the close of the war, occupied this medium ground in politics—the one that suggested the practicability of compromise, and assured a conservative disposition in a time of violent and critical dispute. It was natural that on the close of hostilities the tide of public opinion should have set strongly in favour of Consolidation; and that men should apply the precedent of powers used in the war, to the condition of peace. The great question which the war had left, was as to the form and spirit of the Government that ensued upon it—in short, the determination of the question whether the experience of the past four years had been a Constitutional Revolution, or the mere decision of certain special and limited questions. This was the great historical issue. The political controversies which figured in the newspapers were only its incidents; and the questions which agitated Congress all sounded in the great dispute, whether the war had merely accomplished its express and particular objects, or given the American people a change of polity, and dated a new era in their Constitutional history.

At the time these pages are committed to the press, a series of measures has already been accomplished or introduced by the Radical party in the Congress at Washington that would accomplish a revolution in the American system of government, the most thorough and violent of modern times. Propositions have been made so to amend the Constitution as to deprive the States of the power to define the qualifications of electors; propositions to regulate representation by the number of voters, and not of population; propositions to declare what obligations assumed by the States shall be binding on them, and what shall be the purposes of their taxation. What is known as the Civil Rights Bill (passed over the President's veto) has not only established negro equality, but has practically abolished, on one subject of jurisdiction at least, State laws and State courts.[11] In short, the extreme Black Republican party at Washington has sought to disfranchise the whole Southern people, to force negro suffrage upon the South, to prevent the South from being represented in Congress so as to perpetuate the power of the Radicals, and afford them the means of governing the Southern States as conquered and subjugated territories.

The practical fault of all Despotism is that it takes too little into account the sentimentalism which opposes it, and attempts to deal with men as inanimate objects, to which the application of a certain amount of force for a desired end is decisive. It never considers feelings and prejudices. It does not understand that in the science of government there are elements to conciliate as well as forces to compel. The Northern radicals look to the dragoon with his sword, the marshal with his process of confiscation, and the negro thrust into a false position as the pacificators of the country and the appropriate sentinels of the South. They never reflect on the results of such measures upon the feelings of the Southern people; they do not estimate the loss in that estrangement which makes unprofitable companions; they do not imagine the resentments they will kindle; they do not calculate the effect of a constant irritation that at last wears into the hearts of a people, and makes them ready for all desperate enterprises.

If on this subject the Northern people are best addressed in the language of their interests, they may be reminded that the policy of the Radicals is to detain and embarrass the South, not only in the restoration of her political rights, but in her return to that material prosperity, in which the North has a partnership interest, and the Government itself its most important financial stake. The Southern people must be relieved from the apprehension of confiscation, and other kindred measures of oppression, before they can be expected to go to work and improve their condition. They must be disabused of the idea that the new system of labour is to be demoralized by political theories, before giving it their confidence, and enlarging the experiment of it. The troubled sea of politics must be composed before the industry of the South can return to its wonted channels, and reach at last some point of approximation to former prosperity.

The financiers at Washington consider it of the utmost importance that the South should be able to bear its part of the burden of the national debt, and by its products for exchange contribute to the reduction of this debt to a specie basis. The whole edifice of Northern prosperity rests on the unstable foundation of paper credit. Every man in the North is intelligibly interested in the earliest development of the material prosperity of the South. It is not by political agitation that this interest is to be promoted; not under the hand of the Fanaticism that sows the wind that there are to grow up the fruits of industry. When the Southern people obtain political reassurance, and are able to lift the shield of the Constitution over their heads, they will be prepared for the fruitful works of peace; they will be ready then for the large and steady enterprises of industry. All history shows and all reason argues that where a people are threatened with political changes, and live in uncertainty of the future, capital will be timid, enterprise will be content with make-shifts, and labour itself, give but an unsteady hand to the common implements of industry.

He must be blind who does not perceive in the indications of Northern opinion and in the series of legislative measures consequent upon the war the sweeping and alarming tendency to Consolidation. It is not only the territorial unity of the States that is endangered by the fashionable dogma of the day, but the very cause of republican government itself. A war of opinions has ensued upon that of arms, far more dangerous to the American system of liberties than all the ordinances of Secession and all the armed hosts of the Confederates.

The State Rights put in question by the propositions we have referred to in Congress, are not those involved in the issue of Secession, and, therefore, decided against the South by the arbitration of the war. The Radical programme, which we have noted above, points the illustration that the war did not sacrifice the whole body of State Rights, and that there was an important *residuum* of them outside of the issue of Secession, which the people of the South were still entitled to assert, and to erect as new standards of party. It is precisely those rights of the States which a revolutionary party in Congress would deny, namely: to have their Constitutional representation, to decide their own obligations of debt, to have their own codes of crimes and penalties, and to deal with their own domestic concerns, that the Southern States claim have survived the war and are not subjects of surrender.

And it is just here that the people of the South challenge that medium doctrine of State Rights professed by President Johnson to make the necessary explanation, and to distribute the results of the war between North and South. They do not look at the propositions in Congress as involving a mere partisan dispute; they are not disposed to encounter them in a narrow circle of disputation, and make a particular question of what is one grand issue. They regard them in the broad and serious sense of a revolution against the Constitution; a rebellion against all the written and traditionary authority of American statesmanship; a war quite as distinct as that of bayonets and more comprehensive in its results than the armed contest that has just closed.

The following remarks of the President of the United States, do not magnify the occasion. They are historical:

> "The present is regarded as a most critical juncture in the affairs of the nation, scarcely less so than when an armed and organized force sought to overthrow the Government. To attack and attempt the disruption of the Government by armed Combination and military force, is no more dangerous to the life of the nation than an attempt to revolutionize and undermine it by a disregard and destruction of the safeguards thrown around the liberties of the people in the Constitution. My stand has been taken, my course is marked; I shall stand by and defend the Constitution against all who may attack it, from whatever quarter the attack may come. I shall take no step backward in this matter."

An intelligent foreigner, making his observations at Washington at this time, would be puzzled to determine whether the Americans had a Government, or not. There are the names: The Executive, the Congress, the Judiciary; but what is the executive question, what the congressional question, what the judicial question, it appears impossible to decide. It is a remarkable fact that at Washington to-day, there is not a single well-defined department of political power! There are the paraphernalia and decorations of a government; an elaborate anarchy; but the well-defined distribution of power and the order necessary to administer public affairs appear to have been wholly lost, the charter of the government almost obliterated, and the Constitution overlaid with amendments, which, carried into effect, would hardly leave a vestige of the old instrument or a feature in which could be recognized the work of our forefathers, and the ancient creation of 1789. The controversy thus engendered is something more than a mere question of parties where there are points of coincidence between the contestants sufficient to confine opposition, and where both argue from the common premises of a written constitution. It is something more than the temporary rack and excitement of those partisan difficulties in which the American people have had so much experience of exaggerated dangers and foolish alarms that they are likely to give them attention no longer, but as ephemeral sensations. It is something vastly more than the usual vapours of the political cauldron. When a Congress, representing not much more than a moiety of the American States, and, therefore, in the condition of an unconstitutional authority and factious party, undertakes to absorb the power of the government; to determine Executive questions by its close[d] "Committee of Reconstruction;" to put down the judiciary of the Southern States and by a Freedmen's Bureau, and other devices, erect an *imperium in imperio* in one part of the Union, it is obvious that the controversy is no narrow one of party, that it involves the traditions and spirit of the government, and goes to the ultimate contest of constitutional liberty in America. Regarding these issues, the question comes fearfully to the mind: *Has the past war merely laid the foundation of another?* The pregnant lesson of human experience is that few nations have had their first civil war without having their second; and that the only guaranty against the repetition is to be found in the policy of wise and liberal concessions gracefully made by the successful party. And such reconciliations have been rarest in the republican form of government; for, while generosity often resides in the breast of individual rulers, the history of mankind unhappily shows that it is a rare quality of political parties, where men act in feverish masses and under the dominion of peculiar passions.

To the division of parties in the North—Radicals and Conservatives—there has grown up to some extent a correspondent difference of opinions among the Southern people as to the consequences of the war. But only to a certain extent; for the party in the South that, corresponding to the theory of the Northern Radicals, account themselves entirely at the mercy of a conquering power and taking everything *ex gratia*, is only the detestable faction of time-servers and the servile coterie that attends all great changes in history, and courts the new authority whatever it may be.

There is a better judgment already read by the Southern people of what the war has decided as against themselves. The last memorable remark of Ex-President Davis, when a fugitive, and before the doors of a prison closed upon him,[12] was: "The principle for which we contended is bound to reassert itself, though it may be at another time and in another form." It was a wise and noble utterance, to be placed to the credit of an unfortunate ruler. And so, too, the man, marked above all others as the orator of the South—Henry A. Wise,[13] of Virginia, standing before his countrymen, with his gray hairs and luminous eyes, has recently proclaimed with trumpet-voice that all is not lost, that a great struggle of constitutional liberty yet remains, and that there are still missions of duty and glory for the South.

The people of the South have surrendered in the war what the war has conquered; but they cannot be expected to give up what was not involved in the war, and voluntarily abandon their political schools for the dogma of Consolidation. That dogma, the result has not properly imposed upon them; it has not "conquered ideas." The issues of the war were practical: the restoration of the Union and the abolition of slavery; and only so far as political formulas were necessarily involved in these have they been affected by the conclusion. The doctrine of secession was extinguished; and yet there is something left more than the shadow of State Rights, if we may believe President Johnson, who has recently and officially used these terms, and affirmed in them at least some substantial significance. Even if the States are to be firmly held in the Union; even if the authority of the Union is to be held supreme in *that respect*, it does not follow that it is to be supreme in all other respects; it does not follow that it is to legislate for the States; it does not follow that it is "a national Government over the States and people alike." It is for the South to preserve every remnant of her rights, and even, though parting with the doctrine of secession, to beware of the extremity of surrendering State Rights in gross, and consenting to a "National Government," with an unlimited power of legislation that will consider the States as divided only by imaginary lines of geography, and see in its subjects only "the one people of all the States."

But it is urged that the South should come to this understanding, so as to consolidate the peace of the country, and provide against a "war of ideas." Now a "war of ideas" is what the South wants and insists upon perpetrating. It may be a formidable phrase—"the war of ideas"—but after all, it is a harmless figure of rhetoric, and means only that we shall have parties in the country. We would not live in a country unless there were parties in it; for where there is no such combat, there is no liberty, no animation, no topics, no interest of the twenty-four hours, no theatres of intellectual activity, no objects of ambition. We do not desire the vacant unanimity of despotism. All that is left the South is "the war of ideas." She has thrown down the sword to take up the weapons of argument, not indeed under any banner of fanaticism, or to enforce a dogma, but simply to make the honourable conquest of reason and justice. In such a war there are noble victories to be won, memorable services to performed, and grand results to be achieved. The Southern people stand by their principles. There is no occasion for dogmatic assertion, or fanatical declamation, or inflammatory discourse as long as they have a text on which they can make a sober exposition of their rights, and claim the verdict of the intelligent.

Outside the domain of party politics, the war has left another consideration for the people of the South. It is a remarkable fact that States reduced by war are apt to experience the extinction of their literature, the decay of mind, and the loss of their distinctive forms of thought. Nor is such a condition inconsistent with a gross material prosperity that often grows upon the bloody crust of war. When Greece fell under the Roman yoke, she experienced a prosperity she had never known before. It was an era rank with wealth and material improvement. But her literature became extinct or emasculated; the distinctive forms of her art disappeared; and her mind, once the peerless light of the world, waned into an obscurity from which it never emerged.

It is to be feared that in the present condition of the Southern States, losses will be experienced greater than the immediate inflictions of fire and sword. The danger is that they will lose their literature, their former habits of thought, their intellectual self-asssertion, while they are too intent upon recovering the mere *material* prosperity, ravaged and impaired by the war. There are certain coarse advisers who tell the Southern people that the great ends of their lives now are to repair their stock of national wealth; to bring in Northern capital and labour; to build mills and factories and hotels and gilded caravansaries; and to make themselves rivals in the clattering and garish enterprise of the North. This advice has its proper place. But there are higher objects than the Yankee *magna bona* of money and display, and loftier aspirations than the civilization of material things. In the life of nations, as in that of the individual, there is something better than pelf, and the coarse prosperity of dollars and cents. The lacerated, but proud and ambitious heart of the South will scarcely respond to the mean aspiration of the recusant Governor of South Carolina—Mr. Orr: "I am tired of South Carolina as she was. I court for her the material prosperity of New England. I would have her acres teem with life and vigour and intelligence, as do those of Massachusetts."[14]

There are time-servers in every cause; there are men who fill their bellies with husks, and turn on their faces and die; but there are others who, in the midst of public calamities, and in their own scanty personal fortune, leave behind them the memory of noble deeds, and a deathless heritage of glory.

Defeat has not made "all our sacred things profane." The war has left the South its own memories, its own heroes, its own tears, its own dead. Under these traditions, sons will grow to manhood, and lessons sink deep that are learned from the lips of widowed mothers.

It would be immeasurably the worst consequence of defeat in this war that the South should lose its moral and intellectual distinctiveness as a people, and cease to assert its well-known superiority in civilization, in political scholarship, and in all the standards of individual character over the people of the North. That superiority has been recognized by every foreign observer, and by the intelligent everywhere; for it is the South that in the past produced four-fifths of the political literature of America, and presented in its public men that list of American names best known in the Christian world. That superiority the war has not conquered or lowered; and the South will do right to claim and to cherish it.

The war has not swallowed up everything. There are great interests which stand out of the pale of the contest, which it is for the South still to cultivate and maintain. She must submit fairly and truthfully to *what the war has properly decided*. But the war properly decided only what was put in issue: the restoration of the Union and the excision of slavery; and to these two conditions the South submits. But the war did not decide negro equality; it did not decide negro suffrage; it did not decide State Rights, although it might have exploded their abuse; it did not decide the orthodoxy of the Democratic party; it did not decide the right of a people to show dignity in misfortune, and to maintain self-respect in the face of adversity. And, these things which the war did not decide, the Southern people will still cling to, still claim, and still assert in them their rights and views.

This is not the language of insolence and faction. It is the stark letter of right, and the plain syllogism of common sense. It is not untimely or unreasonable to tell the South to cultivate her superiority as a people; to maintain her old schools of literature and scholarship; to assert, in the forms of her thought, and in the style of her manners, her peculiar civilization, and to convince the North that, instead of subjugating an inferiour country, she has obtained the alliance of a noble and cultivated people, and secured a bond of association with those she may be proud to call brethren!

In such a condition there may possibly be a solid and honourable peace; and one in which the South may still preserve many things dear to her in the past. There may not be a political South. Yet there may be a social and intellectual South. But if, on the other hand, the South, mistaking the consequences of the war, accepts the position of the inferiour, and gives up what was never claimed or conquered in the war; surrenders her schools of intellect and thought, and is left only with the brutal desire of the conquered for "bread and games;" then indeed to her people may be applied what Tacitus wrote of those who existed under the Roman Empire: "We cannot be said to have lived, but rather to have crawled in silence, the young towards the decrepitude of age and the old to dishonourable graves."

Francis Miles Finch

THE BLUE AND THE GRAY (September 1867)

By the flow of the inland river,
    Whence the fleets of iron have fled,
Where the blades of the grave-grass quiver,
    Asleep on the ranks of the dead;—
        Under the sod and the dew,
           Waiting the judgment day;—
        Under the one, the Blue;
           Under the other, the Gray.

These in the robings of glory,
    Those in the gloom of defeat,
All with the battle-blood gory,
    In the dusk of eternity meet;—
        Under the sod and the dew,
           Waiting the judgment day;—
        Under the laurel, the Blue;
           Under the willow, the Gray.

From the silence of sorrowful hours
    The desolate mourners go,
Lovingly laden with flowers
    Alike for the friend and the foe;—
        Under the sod and the dew,
           Waiting the judgment day;—
        Under the roses, the Blue;
           Under the lilies, the Gray.

So, with an equal splendor
    The morning sun-rays fall,
With a touch impartially tender,
    On the blossoms blooming for all;
        Under the sod and the dew,
           Waiting the judgment day;—
        Broidered with gold, the Blue;
           Mellowed with gold, the Gray.

So, when the Summer calleth,
    On forest and field of grain
With an equal murmur falleth

The cooling drip of the rain;—
　　Under the sod and the dew,
　　　　Waiting the judgment day;—
　　Wet with the rain, the Blue;
　　　　Wet with the rain, the Gray.

Sadly, but not with upbraiding,
　　The generous deed was done;
In the storm of the years that are fading,
　　No braver battle was won;—
　　　　Under the sod and the dew,
　　　　　　Waiting the judgment day;—
　　　　Under the blossoms, the Blue;
　　　　　　Under the garlands, the Gray.

No more shall the war-cry sever,
　　Or the winding rivers be red;
They banish our anger forever
　　When they laurel the graves of our dead!
　　　　Under the sod and the dew,
　　　　　　Waiting the judgment day;—
　　　　Love and tears for the Blue.
　　　　　　Tears and love for the Gray.

Herman Melville

from *Battle-Pieces and Aspects of the War* (1866)

AN UNINSCRIBED MONUMENT:
ON ONE OF THE BATTLE-FIELDS OF THE WILDERNESS

Silence and Solitude may hint
    (Whose home is in yon piney wood)
What I, though tableted, could never tell—
The din which here befell,
    And striving of the multitude.
The iron cones and spheres of death
    Set round me in their rust,
        These, too, if just,
Shall speak with more than animated breath.
    Thou who beholdest, if thy thought,
Not narrowed down to personal cheer,
Take in the import of the quiet here—
    The after-quiet—the calm full fraught;
Thou too wilt silent stand—
Silent as I, and lonesome as the land.

Herman Melville

from *Battle-Pieces and Aspects of the War* (1866)

A REQUIEM:
FOR SOLDIERS LOST IN OCEAN TRANSPORTS

When, after storms that woodlands rue,
    To valleys comes atoning dawn,
The robins blithe their orchard-sports renew;
    And meadow-larks, no more withdrawn,
Caroling fly in the languid blue;
The while, from many a hid recess,
Alert to partake the blessedness,
The pouring mites their air dance pursue.
    So, after ocean's ghastly gales,
When laughing light of hoyden morning breaks,
        Every finny hider wakes—
    From vaults profound swims up with glittering scales;
    Through the delightsome sea he sails,
With shoals of shining tiny things
Frolic on every wave that flings
    Against the prow its showery spray;
All creatures joying in the morn,
Save them forever from joyance torn,
    Whose bark was lost where now the dolphins play;
Save them that by the fabled shore,
    Down the pale stream are washed away,
Far to the reef of bones are borne;
    And never revisits them the light,
Nor sight of long-sought land and pilot more;
    Nor heed they now the lone bird's flight
Round the lone spar where mid-sea surges pour.

Herman Melville

from *Battle-Pieces and Aspects of the War* (1866)

ON A NATURAL MONUMENT:
IN A FIELD OF GEORGIA

No trophy this—a Stone unhewn,
    And stands where here the field immures
The nameless brave whose palms are won.
Outcast they sleep; yet fame is nigh—
    Pure fame of deeds, not doers;
Nor deeds of men who bleeding die
    In cheer of hymns that round them float:
In happy dreams such close the eye.
But withering famine slowly wore,
    And slowly fell disease did gloat.
Even Nature's self did aid deny;
They choked in horror the pensive sigh.
    Yea, off from home sad Memory bore
(Though anguished Yearning heaved that way),
Lest wreck of reason might befall.
    As men in gales shun the lee shore,
Though there the homestead be, and call,
And thitherward winds and waters sway—
As such lorn mariners, so fared they.
But naught shall now their peace molest.
    Their fame is this: they did endure—
Endure, when fortitude was vain
To kindle any approving strain
Which they might hear. To these who rest,
    This healing sleep alone was sure.

Frederick Douglass

ADDRESS AT THE GRAVES OF THE UNKNOWN DEAD
(1871)

Arlington, Va., May 30, 1871

Friends and Fellow Citizens:

Tarry here for a moment. My words shall be few and simple. The solemn rites of this hour and place call for no lengthened speech. There is, in the very air of this resting-ground of the unknown dead, a silent, subtle, and all-pervading eloquence, far more touching, impressive, and thrilling than living lips have ever uttered. Into the measureless depths of every loyal soul it is now whispering lessons of all that is most precious and priceless; all that is holiest and most enduring, in human existence.

Dark and sad will be the hour to this nation, when it forgets to pay grateful homage to its greatest benefactors. The offering we bring today is due alike to the patriot soldiers dead and their noble comrades who still live; for, whether living or dead—whether in time or eternity—the loyal soldiers who perilled all for country and freedom, are one and inseparable.

Those unknown heroes whose whitened bones have been piously gathered here, and whose green graves we now strew with sweet and beautiful flowers, choice emblems alike of pure hearts and brave spirits, reached, in their glorious career, that last highest point of nobleness, beyond which human power cannot go. They died for their country.

No loftier tribute can be paid to the most illustrious of all the benefactors of mankind, than we pay to these unrecognized soldiers, when we write above their graves this shining epitaph.

When the dark and vengeful spirit of slavery, always ambitious, preferring to rule in hell than to serve in heaven, fired the Southern heart and stirred all the malign elements of discord; when our great Republic, the hope of freedom and self-government throughout the world, had reached the point of supreme peril; when the union of these states was torn and rent asunder at the center, and the armies of a gigantic rebellion came forth with broad blades and bloody hands to destroy the very foundation of American society, the unknown braves who slumber in these graves flung themselves into the yawning chasm where cannon roared and bullets whistled, fought and fell. They died for their country!

We are sometimes asked, in the name of patriotism, to forget the merits of this fearful struggle, and to remember with equal admiration those who struck at the nation's life, and those who struck to save it—those who fought for slavery, and those who fought for liberty and justice.

I am no minister of malice. I would not strike the fallen. I would not repel the repentant; but may my right hand forget its cunning, and my tongue cleave to the roof of my mouth, if I forget the difference between the parties to that terrible, protracted, and bloody conflict.

If we ought to forget a war which has filled our land with widows and orphans; which has made stumps of men of the very flower of our youth, and sent them on the journey of life armless, legless, maimed, and mutilated; which has piled up a debt heavier than a mountain of gold—swept uncounted thousands of men into bloody graves—and planted agony at a million hearthstones; I say, if this war is to be forgotten, I ask, in the name of all things sacred, what shall men remember?

The essence and significance of our devotions here today are not to be found in the fact that the men whose remains fill these graves were brave in battle. If we were met simply to show our sense of the worth of bravery, we should find enough to kindle admiration on both sides. In the raging storm of fire and blood, in the fierce torrent of shot and shell, of sword and bayonet, whether on foot or on horse, unflinching courage marked the rebel not less than the loyal soldier.

But we are here to applaud manly courage only as it has been displayed in a noble cause. We must never forget that victory to the rebellion meant death to the Republic. We must never forget that the loyal soldiers who rest beneath this sod flung themselves between the nation and the nation's destroyers. If today we have a country not boiling in an agony of blood, like France; if now we have a united country no longer cursed by the hell-black system of human bondage; if the American name is no longer a byword and a hissing to a mocking earth; if the star-spangled banner floats only over free American citizens in every quarter of the land, and our country has before it a long and glorious career of justice, liberty, and civilization, we are indebted to the unselfish devotion of the noble army which rests in these honored graves all around us.

Oliver Wendell Holmes, Jr.

THE SOLDIER'S FAITH
(1895)

An Address Delivered on Memorial Day, May 30, 1895, at a Meeting Called by the Graduating Class of Harvard University

Any day in Washington Street, when the throng is greatest and busiest, you may see a blind man playing a flute. I suppose that some one hears him. Perhaps also my pipe may reach the heart of some passer in the crowd.

I once heard a man say, "Where Vanderbilt[15] sits, there is the head of the table. I teach my son to be rich." He said what many think. For although the generation born about 1840, and now governing the world, has fought two at least of the greatest wars in history, and has witnessed others, war is out of fashion, and the man who commands attention of his fellows is the man of wealth. Commerce is the great power. The aspirations of the world are those of commerce. Moralists and philosophers, following its lead, declare that war is wicked, foolish, and soon to disappear.

The society for which many philanthropists, labor reformers, and men of fashion unite in longing is one in which they may be comfortable and may shine without much trouble or any danger. The unfortunately growing hatred of the poor for the rich seems to me to rest on the belief that money is the main thing (a belief in which the poor have been encouraged by the rich), more than on any other grievance. Most of my hearers would rather that their daughters or their sisters should marry a son of one of the great rich families than a regular army officer, were he as beautiful, brave, and gifted as Sir William Napier.[16] I have heard the question asked whether our war was worth fighting, after all. There are many, poor and rich, who think that love of country is an old wife's tale, to be replaced by interest in a labor union, or, under the name of cosmopolitanism, by a rootless self-seeking search for a place where the most enjoyment may be had at the least cost.

Meantime we have learned the doctrine that evil means pain, and the revolt aginst pain in all its forms has grown more and more marked. From societies for the prevention of cruelty to animals up to socialism, we express in numberless ways the notion that suffering is a wrong which can be and ought to be prevented, and a whole literature of sympathy has sprung into being which points out in story and in verse how hard it is to be wounded in the battle of life, how terrible, how unjust it is that any one should fail.

Even science has had its part in the tendencies which we observe. It has shaken established religion in the minds of very many. It has pursued analysis until at last this thrilling world of colors and passions and sounds has seemed fatally to resolve itself into one vast network of vibrations endlessly weaving an aimless web, and the rainbow flush of cathedral windows, which once to enraptured eyes appeared the very smile of God, fades slowly out into the pale irony of the void.

And yet from vast orchestras still comes the music of mighty symphonies. Our painters even now are spreading along the walls of our Library glowing symbols of mysteries still real, and the hardly silenced cannon of the East proclaim once more that combat and pain still are the portion of man. For my own part, I believe that the struggle for life is the order of the world, at which it is vain to repine. I can imagine the burden changed in the way it is to be borne, but I cannot imagine that it ever will be lifted from men's backs. I can imagine a future in which science shall have passed from the combative to the dogmatic stage, and shall have gained such catholic acceptance that it shall take control of life, and condemn at once with instant execution what now is left for nature to destroy. But we are far from such a future, and we cannot stop to amuse or to terrify ourselves with dreams. Now, at least, and perhaps as long as man dwells upon the globe, his destiny is battle, and he has to take the chances of war. If it is our business to fight, the book for the army is a war-song, not a hospital-sketch. It is not well for soldiers to think much about wounds. Sooner or later we shall fall; but meantime it is for us to fix our eyes upon the point to be stormed, and to get there if we can.

Behind every scheme to make the world over, lies the question, What kind of world do you want? The ideals of the past for men have been drawn from war, as those for women have been drawn from motherhood. For all our prophecies, I doubt if we are ready to give up our inheritance. Who is there who would not like to be thought a gentleman? Yet what has that name been built on but the soldier's choice of honor rather than life? To be a soldier or descended from soldiers, in time of peace to be ready to give one's life rather than suffer disgrace, that is what the word has meant; and if we try to claim it at less cost than a splendid carelessness for life, we are trying to steal the good will without the responsibilities of the place. We will not dispute about tastes. The man of the future may want something different. But who of us could endure a world, although cut up into five-acre lots, and having no man upon it who was not well fed and well housed, without the divine folly of honor, without the senseless passion for knowledge outreaching the flaming bounds of the possible, without ideals the essence of which is that they can never be achieved? I do not know what is true. I do not know the meaning of the universe. But in the midst of doubt, in the collapse of creeds, there is one thing I do not doubt, that no man who lives in the same world with most of us can doubt, and that is that the faith is true and adorable which leads a soldier to throw away his life in obedience to a blindly accepted duty, in a cause which he little understands, in a plan of campaign of which he has little notion, under tactics of which he does not see the use.

Most men who know battle know the cynic force with which the thoughts of common sense will assail them in times of stress; but they know that in their greatest moments faith has trampled those thoughts under foot. If you wait in line, suppose on Tremont Street Mall, ordered simply to wait and do nothing, and have watched the enemy bring their guns to bear upon you down a gentle slope like that of Beacon Street, have seen the puff of the firing, have felt the burst of the spherical case—shot as it came toward you, have heard and seen the shrieking fragments go tearing through your company, and have known that the next or the next shot carries your fate; if you have advanced in line and have seen ahead of you the spot you must pass where the rifle bullets are striking; if you have ridden at night at a walk toward the blue line of fire at the dead angle of Spottsylvania, where for twenty-four hours the soldiers were fighting on the two sides of an earthwork, and in the morning the dead and dying lay piled in a row six deep, and as you rode you heard the bullets splashing in the mud and earth about you; if you have been in the picket-line at night in a black and unknown wood, have heard the splat of the bullets upon the trees, and as you moved have felt your foot slip upon a dead man's body; if you have had a blind fierce gallop against the enemy, with your blood up and a pace that left no time for fear—if, in short, as some, I hope many, who hear me, have known, you have known the vicissitudes of terror and triumph in war; you know that there is such a thing as the faith I spoke of. You know your own weakness and are modest; but you know that man has in him that unspeakable somewhat which makes him capable of miracle, able to lift himself by the might of his own soul, unaided, able to face annihilation for a blind belief.

From the beginning, to us, children of the North, life has seemed a place hung about by dark mists, out of which comes the pale shine of dragon's scales and the cry of fighting men, and the sound of swords. Beowulf, Milton, Dürer, Rembrandt, Schopenhauer, Turner, Tennyson, from the first war song of the race to the stall-fed poetry of modern English drawing rooms, all have had the same vision, and all have had a glimpse of a light to be followed. "The end of wordly life awaits us all. Let him who may, gain honor ere death. That is best for a warrior when he is dead." So spoke Beowulf a thousand years ago.

> Not of the sunlight,
> Not of the moonlight,
> Not of the starlight!
> O Young Mariner,
> Down to the haven.
> Call your companions,
> Launch your vessel,
> And crowd your canvas,
> And, ere it vanishes
> Over the margin,
> After it, follow it,
> Follow The Gleam.

So sang Tennyson in the voice of the dying Merlin.[17]

When I went to the war I thought that soldiers were old men. I remembered a picture of the revolutionary soldier which some of you may have seen, representing a white-haired man with his flint-lock slung across his back. I remembered one or two examples of revolutionary soldiers whom I have met, and I took no account of the lapse of time. It was not long after, in winter quarters, as I was listening to some of the sentimental songs in vogue, such as—

> Farewell, Mother, you may never
> See your darling boy again,

that it came over me that the army was made up of what I should now call very young men. I dare say that my illusion has been shared by some of those now present, as they have looked at us upon whose heads the white shadows have begun to fall. But the truth is that war is the business of youth and early middle age. You who called this assemblage together, not we, would be the soldiers of another war, if we should have one, and we speak to you as the dying Merlin did in the verse which I have just quoted. Would that the blind man's pipe might be transformed by Merlin's magic, to make you hear the bugles as once we heard them beneath the morning stars! For you it is that now is sung the Song of the Sword:—

> The War-Thing, the Comrade,
> Father of Honor,
> And giver of kingship,
> The fame-smith, the song master.
>
> . . . . . .
>
> *Priest* (saith the Lord)
> *Of his marriage with victory*
>
> . . . . . .
>
> Clear singing, clean slicing;
> Sweet spoken, soft finishing;
> Making death beautiful
> Life but a coin
> To be staked in a pastime
> Whose playing is more
> Than the transfer of being;
> Arch-anarch, chief builder,
> Prince and evangelist,
> I am the Will of God:
> I am the Sword.[18]

War, when you are at it, is horrible and dull. It is only when time has passed that you see that its message was divine. I hope it may be long before we are called again to sit at that master's feet. But some teacher of the kind we all need. In this snug, over-safe corner of the world we need it, that we may realize that our comfortable routine is no eternal necessity of things, but merely a little space of calm in the midst of the tempestuous untamed streaming of the world, and in order that we may be ready for danger. We need it in this time of individualist negations, with its literature of French and American humor, revolting at discipline, loving flesh-pots, and denying that anything is worthy of reverence—in order that we may remember all that buffoons forget. We need it everywhere and at all times. For high and dangerous action teaches us to believe as right beyond dispute things for which our doubting minds are slow to find words of proof. Out of heroism grows faith in the worth of heroism. The proof comes later, and even may never come. Therefore I rejoice at every dangerous sport which I see pursued. The students at Heidelberg, with their sword-slashed faces, inspire me with sincere respect. I gaze with delight upon our polo players. If once in a while in our rough riding a neck is broken, I regard it, not as a waste, but as a price well paid for the breeding of a race fit for headship and command.

We do not save our traditions, in our country. The regiments whose battle-flags were not large enough to hold the names of the battles they had fought vanished with the surrender of Lee, although their memories inherited would have made heroes for a century. It is the more necessary to learn the lesson afresh from perils newly sought, and perhaps it is not vain for us to tell the new generation what we learned in our day, and what we still believe. That the joy of life is living, is to put out all one's powers as far as they will go; that the measure of power is obstacles overcome; to ride boldly at what is in front of you, be it fence or enemy; to pray, not for comfort, but for combat; to keep the soldier's faith against the doubts of civil life, more besetting and harder to overcome than all the misgivings of the battlefield, and to remember that duty is not to be proved in the evil day, but then to be obeyed unquestioning; to love glory more than the temptations of wallowing ease, but to know that one's final judge and only rival is oneself: with all our failures in act and thought, these things we learned from noble enemies in Virginia or Georgia or on the Mississippi, thirty years ago; these things we believe to be true.

"Life is not lost", said she, "for which is bought
Endlesse renown."[19]

We learned also, and we still believe, that love of country is not yet an idle name.

Deare countrey! O how dearly deare
Ought thy remembraunce, and perpetuall band
Be to thy foster-child, that from thy hand
Did commun breath and nouriture receave!
How brutish is it not to understand
How much to her we owe, that all us gave;
That gave unto us all, whatever good we have![20]

As for us, our days of combat are over. Our swords are rust. Our guns will thunder no more. The vultures that once wheeled over our heads must be buried with their prey. Whatever of glory must be won in the council or the closet, never again in the field. I do not repine. We have shared the incommunicable experience of war; we have felt, we still feel, the passion of life to its top.

Three years ago died the old colonel of my regiment, the Twentieth Massachusetts.[21] He gave the regiment its soul. No man could falter who heard his "Forward, Twentieth!" I went to his funeral. From a side door of the church a body of little choir-boys came in like a flight of careless doves. At the same time the doors opened at the front, and up the main aisle advanced his coffin, followed by the few grey heads who stood for the men of the Twentieth, the rank and file whom he had loved, and whom he led for the last time. The church was empty. No one remembered the old man whom we were burying, no one save those next to him, and us. And I said to myself, the Twentieth has shrunk to a skeleton, a ghost, a memory, a forgotten name which we other old men alone keep in our hearts. And then I thought: It is right. It is as the colonel would have it. This also is part of the soldier's faith: Having known great things, to be content with silence. Just then there fell into my hands a little song sung by a warlike people on the Danube, which seemed to me fit for a soldier's last word, another song of the sword, but a song of the sword in its scabbard, a song of oblivion and peace.

A soldier has been buried on the battlefield.

And when the wind in the tree-tops roared,
The soldier asked from the deep dark grave:
    "Did the banner flutter then?"
"Not so, my hero," the wind replied.

"The fight is done, but the banner won,
Thy comrades of old have borne it hence,
    Have borne it in triumph hence."
Then the soldier spake from the deep dark grave:
       "I am content."

Then he heareth the lovers laughing pass,
    And the soldier asks once more:
"Are these not the voices of them that love,
    That love—and remember me?"
"Not so, my hero," the lovers say,
"We are those that remember not;
For the spring has come and the earth has smiled,
    And the dead must be forgot."
Then the soldier spake from the deep dark grave:
       "I am content."

D. B. Lucas

IN THE LAND WHERE WE WERE DREAMING (n.d.)

Fair were our visions! Oh, they were as grand
As ever floated out of Faerie land;
        Children were we in single faith,
        But God-like children, whom, nor death,
Nor threat, nor danger drove from Honor's path,
        In the land where we were dreaming.

Proud were our men, as pride of birth could render;
As violets, our women pure and tender;
        And when they spoke, their voice did thrill
        Until at eve, the whip-poor-will,
At morn the mocking-bird, were mute and still
        In the land where we were dreaming.

And we had graves that covered more of glory
Than ever tracked tradition's ancient story;
        And in our dream we wove the thread
        Of principles for which had bled
And suffered long our own immortal dead
        In the land where we were dreaming.

Though in our land we had both bond and free,
Both were content; and so God let them be;—
        'Till envy coveted our land
        And those fair fields our valor won:
But little recked we, for we still slept on,
        In the land where we were dreaming.

Our sleep grew troubled and our dreams grew wild—
Red meteors flashed across our heaven's field;
        Crimson the moon; between the Twins
        Barbed arrows fly, and then begins
Such strife as when disorder's Chaos reigns,
        In the land where we were dreaming.

Down from her sun-lit heights smiled Liberty
And waved her cap in sign of Victory—
        The world approved, and everywhere
        Except where growled the Russian bear,
The good, the brave, the just gave us their prayer
        In the land where we were dreaming.

We fancied that a Government was ours—
We challenged place among the world's great powers;
    We talked in sleep of Rank, Commission,
    Until so life-like grew our vision,
That he who dared to doubt but met derision
    In the land where we were dreaming.

We looked on high: a banner there was seen,
Whose field was blanched and spotless in its sheen—
    Chivalry's cross its Union bears,
    And vet'rans swearing by their scars
Vowed they would bear it through a hundred wars
    In the land where we were dreaming.

A hero came amongst us as we slept;
At first he lowly knelt—then rose and wept;
    Then gathering up a thousand spears
    He swept across the field of Mars;
Then bowed farewell and walked beyond the stars—
    In the land where we were dreaming.

We looked again: another figure still
Gave hope, and nerved each individual will—
    Full of grandeur, clothed with power,
    Self-poised, erect, he ruled the hour
With stern, majestic sway—of strength a tower
    In the land where we were dreaming.

As, while great Jove, in bronze, a warder God,
Gazed eastward from the Forum where he stood,
    Rome felt herself secure and free,
    So, "Richmond's safe," we said, while we
Beheld a bronzed Hero—God-like Lee,
    In the land where we were dreaming.

As wakes the soldier when the alarum calls—
As wakes the mother when the infant falls—
    As starts the traveller when around
    His sleeping couch the fire-bells sound—
So woke our nation with a single bound
    In the land where we were dreaming.

Woe! woe is me! the startled mother cried—
While we have slept our noble sons have died!
    Woe! woe is me! how strange and sad,
    That all our glorious vision's fled

And left us nothing real but the dead
      In the land where we were dreaming.

And are they really dead, our martyred slain?
No! dreamers! morn shall bid them rise again
      From every vale—from every height
      On which they *seemed* to die for right—
Their gallant spirits shall renew the fight
      In the land where we were dreaming.

Ambrose Bierce

from *Antepenultimata* (1912)

A BIVOUAC OF THE DEAD (1903)

Away up in the heart of the Allegheny mountains, in Pocahontas county, West Virginia, is a beautiful little valley through which flows the east fork of the Greenbrier river. At a point where the valley road intersects the old Staunton and Parkersburg turnpike, a famous thoroughfare in its day, is a post office in a farm house. The name of the place is Travelers' Repose, for it was once a tavern. Crowning some low hills within a stone's throw of the house are long lines of old Confederate fortifications, skilfully designed and so well "preserved" that an hour's work by a brigade would put them into serviceable shape for the next civil war. This place had its battle—what was called a battle in the "green and salad days" of the great rebellion. A brigade of Federal troops, the writer's regiment among them, came over Cheat mountain, fifteen miles to the westward, and, stringing its lines across the little valley, felt the enemy all day; and the enemy did a little feeling, too. There was a great cannonading, which killed about a dozen on each side; then, finding the place too strong for assault, the Federals called the affair a reconnaissance in force, and burying their dead withdrew to the more comfortable place whence they had come. Those dead now lie in a beautiful national cemetery at Grafton, duly registered, so far as identified, and companioned by other Federal dead gathered from the several camps and battlefields of West Virginia.[22] The fallen soldier (the word "hero" appears to be a later invention) has such humble honors as it is possible to give.

> His part in all the pomp that fills
> The circuit of the Summer hills
> Is that his grave is green.[23]

True, more than a half of the green graves in the Grafton cemetery are marked "Unknown," and sometimes it occurs that one thinks of the contradiction involved in "honoring the memory" of him of whom no memory remains to honor; but the attempt seems to do no great harm to the living, even to the logical.

A few hundred yards to the rear of the old Confederate earthworks is a wooded hill. Years ago it was not wooded. Here, among the trees and in the undergrowth, are rows of shallow depressions, discoverable by removing the accumulated forest leaves. From some of them may be taken (and reverently replaced) small thin slabs of the split stone of the country, with rude and reticent inscriptions by comrades. I found only one with a date, only one with full names of man and regiment. The entire number found was eight.

In these forgotten graves rest the Confederate dead—between eighty and one hundred, as nearly as can be made out. Some fell in the "battle;" the majority died of disease. Two, only two, have apparently been disinterred for reburial at their homes. So neglected and obscure is this *campo santo* that only he upon whose farm it is—the aged postmaster of Travelers' Repose—appears to know about it. Men living within a mile have never heard of it. Yet other men must be still living who assisted to lay these Southern soldiers where they are, and could identify some of the graves. Is there a man, North or South, who would begrudge the expense of giving to these fallen brothers the tribute of green graves? One would rather not think so. True, there are several hundreds of such places still discoverable in the track of the great war. All the stronger is the dumb demand—the silent plea of these fallen brothers to what is "likest God within the soul."

They were honest and courageous foemen, having little in common with the political madmen who persuaded them to their doom and the literary bearers of false witness in the aftertime. They did not live through the period of honorable strife into the period of vilification—did not pass from the iron age to the brazen—from the era of the sword to that of the tongue and pen. Among them is no member of the Southern Historical Society.[24] Their valor was not the fury of the non-combatant; they have no voice in the thunder of the civilians and the shouting. Not by them are impaired the dignity and infinite pathos of the Lost Cause. Give them, these blameless gentlemen, their rightful part in all the pomp that fills the circuit of the summer hills.

Albion Tourgée

THE SOUTH AS A FIELD FOR FICTION
(December 1888)

More than twenty years ago the writer ventured the prediction that the short but eventful lifetime of the Southern Confederacy, the downfall of slavery, and the resulting conditions of Southern life would furnish to the future American novelist his richest and most striking material. At that time he was entirely unknown as a writer of fiction, and it is probable that he is now generally supposed to have turned his attention in this direction more from political bias than from any literary or artistic attraction which it offered. The exact converse was in fact true; the romantic possibility of the situation appealed to him even more vividly than its political difficulty, though, as is always the case in great national crises, the one was unavoidably colored by the other. Slavery as a condition of society has not yet become separable, in the minds of our people, North or South, from slavery as a political idea, a factor of partisan strife. They do not realize that two centuries of bondage left an ineradicable impress on master and slave alike, or that the line of separation between the races, being marked by the fact of color, is as impassable since emancipation as it was before, and perhaps even more portentous. They esteem slavery as simply a dead, unpleasant fact of which they wish to hear nothing more, and regard any disparaging allusion to its results as an attempt to revive a defunct political sentiment.

It is not surprising, therefore, that the literary men of the North should have looked upon such a forecast with contempt and impatience. It seemed to them to be not only absurd, but inspired by a malicious desire to keep alive the memory of an epoch which it was the duty of every one to help bury in impenetrable oblivion. That was a foolish notion. A nation can never bury its past. A country's history may perish with it, but it can never outlive its history. Yet such was the force of the determination in the Northern mind to taboo all allusion to that social condition which had been the occasion of strife, that the editor of a leading magazine felt called upon to make emphatic protest against the obnoxious prediction. "However much of pathos there may have been in the slave's life," he said, with the positiveness of infallibility, "its relations can never constitute the groundwork of enjoyable fiction. The colored race themselves can never regard the estate of bondage as a romantic epoch, or desire to perpetuate its memories. Slavery and rebellion, therefore," he concludes, "with the conditions attendant upon and resulting from them, can never constitute a popular field for American fiction." Time is not always prompt in its refutation of bad logic, but in this case he is not chargeable with unnecessary delay. In obedience to a pronounced and undeniable popular demand, that very magazine has given a complete reversal of its own emphatic dictum, by publishing in a recent number a dialect story of Southern life written by one of the enslaved race.[25]

Under such circumstances, however, it is hardly surprising that the writer's farther prediction should have been regarded as too absurd for refutation. He himself is almost startled, as he looks at the dingy pages, to find himself averring, in the very glare of expiring conflict, that "within thirty years after the close of the war of rebellion popular sympathy will be with those who upheld the Confederate cause rather than with those by whom it was overthrown; our popular heroes will be Confederate leaders; our fiction will be Southern in its prevailing types and distinctively Southern in its character." There are yet seven years to elapse before the prescribed limit is reached, but the prediction is already almost literally fulfilled. Not only is the epoch of the war the favorite field of American fiction to-day, but the Confederate soldier is the popular hero. Our literature has become not only Southern in type, but distinctly Confederate in sympathy. The federal or Union soldier is not exactly depreciated, but subordinated; the Northern type is not decried, but the Southern is preferred. This is not because of any essential superiority of the one or lack of heroic attributes in the other, but because sentiment does not always follow the lead of conviction, and romantic sympathy is scarcely at all dependent upon merit. The writer makes no pretension to having foreseen the events that have occurred in the interval that has elapsed. Even the results he but perfectly comprehended, having no clear anticipation of the peculiar forms which Southern fiction would assume. The one thing he did perceive, and the causes of which he clearly outlined, was the almost unparalleled richness of Southern life of that period as a field for fictitious narrative.

But whatever the cause may be, it cannot be denied that American fiction of to-day, whatever may be its origin, is predominantly Southern in type and character. The East and the West had already been in turn the seat of romantic empire. American genius has traced with care each step in the mysterious process by which the "dude" was evolved from the Puritan and "cow-boy" from the pioneer. From Cooper to Hawthorne, colonial and Revolutionary life of the East was the favorite ground of the novelist. The slavery agitation gave a glimpse of one phase of Southern life. As soon as the war was over, as if to distract attention from that unpleasant fact, we were invited to contrast American crudeness with English culture. Then the Western type came boldly to the front and the world studied the assimilations of our early occidental life; its product has not yet been portrayed. For a time each of these overshadowed in American fiction all the others. Each was in turn worked out. The public relish for that particular diet palled, and popular taste, which is the tyrant of the realm of literature, demanded something else. To-day the South has unquestionably the preference. Hardly a novelist of prominence, except Mr. Howells and Mr. James, but has found it necessary to yield to the prevailing demand and identify himself with Southern types. Southern life does not lend itself readily to the methods of the former. It is earnest, intense, full of action, and careless to a remarkable degree of the trivialities which both these authors esteem the most important features of real life. Its types neither subsist upon soliloquy nor practice irrelevancy as a fine art; they are not affected by a chronic self-distrust nor devoted to anti-climax. Yet despite these imperfections the public appetite seems to crave their delineation.

A foreigner studying our current literature, without knowledge of our history, and judging our civilization by our fiction, would undoubtedly conclude that the South was the seat of intellectual empire in America, and the African the chief romantic element of our population. As an evidence of this, it may be noted that a few months ago every one of our great popular monthlies presented a "Southern story" as one of its most prominent features; and during the past year nearly two-thirds of the stories and sketches furnished to newspapers by various syndicates have been of this character.

To the Northern man, whose belief in averages is so profound, this flood of Southern fiction seems quite unaccountable. He recurs at once to the statistics of illiteracy, with an unfaltering belief that novels, poems, and all forms of literature are a natural and spontaneous product of the common-school system. He sees that twenty-eight out of every hundred of the white people of the South cannot read or write, and at once concludes that in literary production as well as in mechanical and financial achievement the North must of necessity excel, in about the same proportion that it does in capacity to assimilate the literary product.

Yet the fact ought not to surprise any one. One of the compensations of war is a swift ensuing excitation of the mental faculties, which almost always yields remarkable results. This is especially true when fortune turns against a spirited and ambitious people. The War of Rebellion was a far more terrible experience to the people of the South than to those of the North. The humiliation resulting from defeat was intense and universal. They had and can have no tide of immigration and no rush of business life greatly to lessen the force of these impressions, while the presence of the Negro in numbers almost equal to the whites prevents the possibility of forgetting the past. The generation which has grown up since the war not only has the birthmark of the hour of defeat upon it, but has been shaped and molded quite as much by regret for the old conditions as by the difficulties of the new. To the Southern man or woman, therefore, the past, present, and future of Southern life is the most interesting and important matter about which they can possibly concern themselves. It is their world. Their hopes and aspirations are bounded by its destiny, and their thought is not diluted by cosmopolitan ideas. Whether self-absorption is an essential requisite of literary production or not, it is unquestionably true that almost all the noted writers of fiction have been singularly enthusiastic lovers of the national life of which they have been a part. In this respect the Southern novelist has a vast advantage over his Northern contemporary. He has never any doubt. He loves the life he portrays and sincerely believes in its superlative excellence. He does not study it as a curiosity, but knows it by intuition. He never sneers at its imperfections, but worships even its defects.

The Southern writer, too, has a curiously varied life from which he may select his types, and this life is absolutely *terra incognita* to the Northern mind. The "Tyrant of Broomsedge Cove" may have a parallel on every hillside; Mrs. Burnett's miraculously transformed "poor-white" Cinderellas may still use the springs for pier-glasses; Joel Chandler Harris's quaintness, Chestnut's [sic] curious realism, or the dreamy idealism that still paints the master and the slave as complements of a remembered millennial state: any of these may be a true picture of this life so far as the Northern man's knowledge or conception is concerned.[26] He has a conventional "Southern man," a conventional "poor white," with a female counterpart of each already fitted out in his fancy; and as long as the author does not seriously disturb these preconceptions, the Northern reader likes the Southern story because it is full of life and fire and real feeling. And it is no wonder that he does, for it is getting to be quite a luxury to the novel reader to find a story in which the characters have any feeling beyond a self-conscious sensibility which seems to give them a deal of trouble without ever ripening into motive or resulting in achievement.

It is noteworthy in this revival that the Negro and the poor white are taking rank as by far the more interesting elements of Southern life. True, the dashing Confederate cavalier holds his place pretty well. It is rather odd that he was always a "cavalier"; but, so far as our fiction is concerned, there does not appear to have been any Confederate infantry. Still, even the "cavalier" has come to need a foil, just as Dives required a Lazarus,[27] and with like result—the beggar has overshadowed his patron. In literature as well as in politics, the poor white is having the best of the Southern *renaissance*. The sons of schoolmasters and overseers and even "crappers" have come to the fore in the "New South," and the poor white is exalted not only in his offspring but in literature. There are infinite possibilities in the poor white of either sex; and as the supply is limited to the South, there seems to be no reason why he should not during the next half century become to the fiction of the United States what the Highlander is to Scottish literature—the only "interesting" white character in it.

But the Negro has of late developed a capacity as a stock character of fiction which no one ever dreamed that he possessed in the good old days when he was a merchantable commodity. It must be admitted, too, that the Southern writers are "working him for all he is worth," as a foil to the aristocratic types of the land of heroic possibilities. The Northern man, no matter what his prejudices, is apt to think of the Negro as having an individuality of his own. To the Southern mind, he is only a shadow—an incident of another's life. As such he is invariably assigned one of two roles. In one he figures as the devoted slave who serves and sacrifices for his master and mistress, and is content to live or die, do good or evil, for those to whom he feels himself under infinite obligation for the privilege of living and serving. There were such miracles no doubt, but they were so rare as never to have lost the miraculous character. The other favorite aspect of the Negro character from the point of view of the Southern fictionist, is that of the poor "nigger" to whom liberty has brought only misfortune, and who is relieved by the disinterested friendship of some white man whose property he once was. There are such cases, too, but they are not so numerous as to destroy the charm of novelty. About the Negro as a man, with hopes, fears, and aspirations like other men, our literature is very nearly silent. Much has been written of the slave and something of the freedman, but thus far no one has been found able to weld the new life to the old.

This indeed is the great difficulty to be overcome. As soon as the American Negro seeks to rise above the level of the former time, he finds himself confronted with the past of his race and the woes of his kindred. It is to him not only a record of subjection but of injustice and oppression. The "twice-told tales" of *his* childhood are animate with rankling memories of wrongs. Slavery colored not only the lives but the traditions of his race. With the father's and the mother's blood is transmitted the story, not merely of their individual wrongs but of a race's woe, which the impenetrable oblivion of the past makes even more terrible and which the sense of color will not permit him to forget. The white man traces his ancestry back for generations, knows whence they came, where they lived, and guesses what they did. To the American Negro the past is only darkness replete with unimaginable horrors. Ancestors he has none. Until within a quarter of a century he had no record of his kindred. He was simply one number of an infinite "no name series." He had no father, no mother; only a sire and dam. Being bred for market, he had no name, only a distinguishing appellative, like that of a horse or a dog. Even in comparison with these animals he was at a disadvantage; there was no "herdbook" of slaves. A well-bred horse may be traced back in his descent for a thousand years, and may show a hundred strains of noble blood; but even this poor consolation is denied the eight millions of slave-descended men and women in our country.

The remembrance of this condition is not pleasant and can never become so. It is exasperating, galling, degrading. Every freedman's life is colored by this shadow. The farther he gets away from slavery, the more bitter and terrible will be his memory of it. The wrong that was done to his forebears is a continuing and self-magnifying evil. This is the inevitable consequence of the conditions of the past; no kindness can undo it; no success can blot it out. It is the sole inheritance the bondman left his issue, and it must grow heavier rather than lighter until the very suggestion of inequality has disappeared—if indeed such a time shall ever come.

The life of the Negro as a slave, freedman, and racial outcast offers undoubtedly the richest mine of romantic material that has opened to the English-speaking novelist since the Wizard of the North[28] discovered and depicted the common life of Scotland. The Negro as a man has an immense advantage over the Negro as a servant, being an altogether new character in fiction. The slave's devotion to the master was trite in the remote antiquity of letters; but the slave as a man, with his hopes, his fears, his faith, has been touched, and only touched, by the pen of the novelist. The traditions of the freedman's fireside are richer and far more tragic than the folk-lore which genius has recently put into his quaint vernacular. The freedman as a man—not as a "brother in black," with the curse of Cain yet upon him, but a man with hopes and aspirations, quick to suffer, patient to endure, full of hot passion, fervid imagination, desirous of being equal to the best—is sure to be a character of enduring interest.

The mere fact of having suffered or enjoyed does not imply the power to portray; but the Negro race in America has other attributes besides mere imagination. It has absorbed the best blood of the South, and it is quite within the possibilities that it may itself become a power in literature, of which even the descendants of the old regime shall be as proud as they now are of the dwellers in "Broomsedge Cove" and on the "Great Smoky."

Pathos lies at the bottom of all enduring fiction. Agony is the key of immortality. The ills of fate, irreparable misfortune, untoward but unavoidable destiny: these are the things that make for enduring fame. The "realists" profess to be truth-tellers, but are in fact the worst of falsifiers, since they tell only the weakest and meanest part of the grand truth which makes up the continued story of every life. As a rule, humanity is in serious earnest, and loves to have its sympathy moved with woes that are heavy enough to leave an impress of actuality on the heart. Sweetmeats may afford greater scope for the skill of the *chef,* but it is "the roast beef of old England" that "sticks to the ribs" and nourishes a race of giants. Dainties—peacocks' tongues and sparrows' brains—may bring delight to the epicure who loves to close his eyes and dream that he detects the hint of a flavor; but the strong man despises neutral things and a vigorous people demand a vigorous literature.

It is the poet of action whose clutch on the human soul is eternal, not the professor of analytics or the hierophant of doubt and uncertainty. In sincerity of passion and aspiration, as well as in the woefulness and humiliation that attended its downfall, the history of the Confederacy stands pre-eminent in human epochs. Everything about it was on a grand scale. Everything was real and sincere. The soldier fought in defense of his home, in vindication of what he deemed his right. There was a proud assumption of superiority, a regal contempt of their foe, which, like Rector's boastfulness, added wonderfully to the pathos of the result. Then, too, a civilization fell with it—a civilization full of wonderful contrasts, horrible beyond the power of imagination to conceive in its injustice, cruelty, and barbarous debasement of a subject race, yet exquisitely charming in its assumption of pastoral purity and immaculate excellence. It believed that the slave loved his chains and was all the better physically and morally for wearing them.

But then came the catastrophe, and all was changed. The man who fights and wins is only common in human esteem. The downfall of empire is always the epoch of romance. The brave but unfortunate reap always the richest measure of immortality. The roundheads are accounted base and common realities, but the cavaliers are glorified by disaster. In all history, no cause had so many of the elements of pathos as that which failed at Appomattox, and no people ever presented to the novelist such a marvelous array of curiously contrasted lives. Added to the various elements of the white race are those other exceptional and unparalleled conditions of this epoch, springing from "race, color, and previous condition of servitude." The dominant class itself presents the accumulated pathos of a million abdications. "We are all poor whites now," is the touching phrase in which the results of the conflict are expressed with instinctive accuracy by those to whom it meant social as well as political disaster. It is a truth as yet but half appreciated. The level of Caucasian life at the South must hereafter be run from the bench-line of the poor white, and there cannot be any leveling upward. The distance between its upper and lower strata cannot be maintained; indeed it is rapidly disappearing. To the woefulness of the conquered is added the pathos of a myriad of deposed sovereigns. Around them will cluster the halo of romantic glory, and the epoch of their overthrow will live again in American literature.

It matters not whence the great names of the literary epoch which is soon to dawn may derive their origin. No doubt there is something of truth in Herbert Spencer's suggestion, that the poets and novelists as well as the rulers of the future will come from the great plains and dwell in the shadows of the stern and silent mountains of the West. Greatness is rarely born where humanity swarms. Individual power is the product of a wide horizon. Inspiration visits men in solitude, and the Infinite comes nearer as the finite recedes from the mental vision; only solitude must not be filled with self. No solitary, self-imprisoned for his own salvation, ever sang an immortal strain; but he that taketh the woes of a people into the desert with him, sees God in the burning bush. Method is but half of art—its meaner half. Inspiration gives the better part of immortality. Homer's heroes made his song undying, not his sonorous measures; and the glow of English manfulness spreads its glamour over Shakespeare's lines, and makes him for all ages the poet from whom brave men will draw renewed strength and the unfortunate get unfailing consolation. Scott's loving faith in a chivalry which perhaps never existed, not only made his work imperishable, but inspires with healthful aspiration every reader of his shining pages.

Because of these things it is that the South is destined to be the Hesperides Garden of American literature. We cannot foretell the form its product will wear or even guess its character. It may be sorrowful, exultant, aspiring, or perhaps terrible, but it will certainly be great—greater than we have hitherto known, because its causative forces are mightier than those which have shaped the productive energy of the past. That its period of highest excellence will soon be attained there is little room to doubt. The history of literature shows that it is those who were cradled amid the smoke of battle, the sons and daughters of heroes yet red with slaughter, the inheritors of national woe or racial degradation, who have given utterance to the loftiest strains of genius. Because of the exceeding woefulness of a not too recent past, therefore, and the abiding horror of unavoidable conditions which are the sad inheritance of the present, we may confidently look for the children of soldiers and of slaves to advance American literature to the very front rank of that immortal procession whose song is the eternal refrain of remembered agony, before the birth-hour of the twentieth century shall strike.

Jefferson Davis

SPEECH BEFORE MISSISSIPPI LEGISLATURE IN JACKSON, MISSISSIPPI
(March 10, 1884)

Friends and Brethren of Mississippi: In briefest terms, but with deepest feeling, permit me to return my thanks for the unexpected honor you have conferred on me. Away from the political sea, I have in my secluded home observed with intense interest all passing events, affecting the interest or honor of Mississippi, and have rejoiced to see in the diversification of labor and the development of new sources of prosperity and the increased facilities of public education, reason to hope for a future to our State more prosperous than any preceding era. The safety and honor of a Republic must rest upon the morality, intelligence and patriotism of the community.

We are now in a transition state, which is always a bad one, both in society and in nature. What is to be the result of the changes which may be anticipated it is not possible to forecast, but our people have shown such fortitude and have risen so grandly from the deep depression inflicted upon them, that it is fair to entertain bright hopes for the future. Sectional hate concentrating itself upon my devoted head, deprives me of the privileges accorded to others in the sweeping expression of "without distinction of race, color or previous condition,"[29] but it cannot deprive me of that which is nearest and dearest to my heart, the right to be a Mississippian, and it is with great gratification that I received this emphatic recognition of that right by the representatives of our people. Reared on the soil of Mississippi, the ambition of my boyhood was to do something which would redound to the honor and welfare of the State. The weight of many years admonishes me that my day for actual service has passed, yet the desire remains undiminished to see the people of Mississippi prosperous and happy and her fame not unlike the past, but gradually growing wider and brighter as years roll away.

'Tis been said that I should apply to the United States for a pardon, but repentance must precede the right of pardon, and I have not repented. Remembering as I must all which has been suffered, all which has been lost, disappointed hopes and crushed aspirations, yet I deliberately say, if it were to do over again, I would again do just as I did in 1861. No one is the arbiter of his own fate. The people of the Confederate States did more in proportion to their numbers and mean than was ever achieved by any in the world's history. Fate decreed that they should be unsuccessful in the effort to maintain their claim to resume the grants made to the Federal Government. Our people have accepted the decree; it therefore behooves them, as they may, to promote the general welfare of the Union, to show to the world that hereafter, as heretofore, the patriotism of our people is not measured by lines of latitude and longitude, but is as broad as the obligations they have assumed and embraces the whole of our oceanbound domain. Let them leave to their children and children's children the grand example of never swerving from the path of duty, and preferring to return good for evil rather than to cherish the unmanly feeling of revenge. But never question or teach your children to desecrate the memory of the dead by admitting that their brothers were wrong in the effort to maintain the sovereignty, freedom and independence which was their inalienable birthright—remembering that the coming generations are the children of the heroic mothers whose devotion to our cause in its darkest hour sustained the strong and strengthened the weak, I cannot believe that the cause for which our sacrifices were made can ever be lost, but rather hope that those who now deny the justice of our asserted claims will learn from experience that the fathers builded wisely and the Constitution should be constructed according to the commentaries of the men who made it.

It having been previously understood that I would not attempt to do more than to return my thanks, which are far deeper than it would be possible for me to express, I will now, Senators and Representatives, and to you ladies and gentlemen, who have honored me by your attendance, bid you an affectionate, and it may be, a last farewell.

Sidney Lanier

THE DYING WORDS OF STONEWALL JACKSON (September 1865)

"Order A. P. Hill to prepare for battle."
"Tell Major Hawks to advance the Commissary train."
"Let us cross the river and rest in the shade."[30]

The stars of Night contain the glittering Day
And rain his glory down with sweeter grace
Upon the dark World's grand, enchanted face—
    All loth to turn away.

And so the Day, about to yield his breath,
Utters the stars unto the listening Night,
To stand for burning fare-thee-wells of light
    Said on the verge of death.

O hero-life that lit us like the sun!
O hero-words that glittered like the stars
And stood and shone above the gloomy wars
    When the hero-life was done!

The phantoms of a battle came to dwell
I' the fitful vision of his dying eyes—
Yet even in battle-dreams, he sends supplies
    To those he loved so well.

His army stands in battle-line arrayed:
His couriers fly: all's done: now God decide!
—And not till then saw he the Other Side
    Or would accept the shade.

Thou Land whose sun is gone, thy stars remain!
Still shine the words that miniature his deeds.
O thrice-beloved, where'er thy great heart bleeds,
    Solace has thou for pain!

        Georgia

Sidney Lanier

LAUGHTER IN THE SENATE (1868)

In the South lies a lonesome, hungry Land;
He huddles his rags with a cripple's hand;
He mutters, prone on the barren sand,
    What time his heart is breaking.

He lifts his bare head from the ground;
He listens through the gloom around:
The winds have brought him a strange sound
    Of distant merrymaking.

Comes now the Peace so long delayed?
Is it the cheerful voice of Aid?
Begins the time his heart has prayed,
    When men may reap and sow?

Ah, God! Back to the cold earth's breast!
The sages chuckle o'er their jest;
Must they, to give a people rest,
    Their dainty wit forego?

The tyrants sit in a stately hall;
They jibe at a wretched people's fall;
The tyrants forget how fresh is the pall
    Over their dead and ours.

Look how the senators ape the clown,
And don the motley and hide the gown,
But yonder a fast-rising frown
    On the people's forehead lowers.

Sidney Lanier

RESURRECTION (1868)

Sometimes in morning sunlights by the river
    Where in the early fall long grasses wave,
Light winds from over the moorland sink and shiver
    And sighs as if just blown across a grave.

And then I pause and listen to this sighing.
    I look with strange eyes on the well-known stream.
I hear wild birth-cries uttered by the dying.
    I know men waking who appear to dream.

Then from the water-lilies slow uprises
    The still vast face of all the life I know,
Changed now, and full of wonders and surprises,
    With fire in eyes that once were glazed with snow.

Fair now the brows old Pain had erewhile wrinkled,
    And peace and strength about the calm mouth dwell.
Clean of the ashes that Repentance sprinkled,
    The meek head poises like a flower-bell.

All the old scars of wanton wars are vanished;
    And what blue bruises grappling Sense had left
And sad remains of redder stains are banished,
    And the dim blotch of heart-committed theft.

O still vast vision of transfigured features
    Unvisited by secret crimes or dooms,
Remain, remain amid these water-creatures,
    Stand, shine among yon water-lily blooms.

For eighteen centuries ripple down the river,
    And windy times the stalks of empires wave,
—Let the winds come from the moor and sigh and shiver,
    Fain, fain am I, O Christ, to pass the grave.

Sarah Morgan Bryan Piatt

ARMY OF OCCUPATION: AT ARLINGTON, 1866

The summer blew its little drifts of sound—
　　Tangled with wet leaf-shadows and the light
Small breath of scattered morning buds—around
The yellow path through which our footsteps wound.
　　Below, the Capitol rose glittering white.

There stretched a sleeping army. One by one,
　　They took their places until thousands met;
No leader's stars flashed on before, and none
Leaned on his sword or stagg[e]r'd with his gun—
　　I wonder if their feet have rested yet!

They saw the dust, they joined the moving mass,
　　They answer'd the fierce music's cry for blood,
Then straggled here and lay down in the grass:—
Wear flowers for such, shores whence their feet did pass;
　　Sing tenderly; O river's haunted flood!

They had been sick, and worn, and weary, when
　　They stopp'd on this calm hill beneath the trees:
Yet if, in some red-clouded dawn, again
The country should be calling to her men,
　　Shall the r[e]veill[e] not remember these?

Around them underneath the mid-day skies
　　The dreadful phantoms of the living walk,
And by low moons and darkness with their cries—
The mothers, sisters, wives with faded eyes,
　　Who call still names amid their broken talk.

And there is one who comes alone and stands
　　At his dim fireless hearth—chill'd and oppress'd
By Something he has summon'd to his lands,
While the weird pallor of its many hands
　　Points to his rusted sword in his own breast!

Sarah Morgan Bryan Piatt

OVER IN KENTUCKY (1872)

"This is the smokiest city in the world,"
    A slight voice, wise and weary, said, "I know.
My sash is tied, and if my hair was curled,
    I'd like to have my prettiest hat and go
There where some violets had to stay, you said,
Before your torn-up butterflies were dead—
        Over in Kentucky."

Then one, whose half-sad face still wore the hue
    The North Star loved to light and linger on,
Before the war, looked slowly at me too,
    And darkly whispered: "What is gone is gone.
Yet, though it may be better to be free,
I'd rather have things as they used to be
        Over in Kentucky."

Perhaps I thought how fierce the master's hold,
    Spite of all armies, kept the slave within;
How iron chains, when broken, turned to gold,
    In empty cabins, where glad songs had been,
Before the Southern sword knew blood and rust,
Before wild cavalry sprang from the dust,
        Over in Kentucky.

Perhaps—but, since two eyes, half-full of tears,
    Half-full of sleep, would love to keep awake
With fairy pictures from my fairy years,
    I have a phantom pencil that can make
Shadows of moons, far back and faint, to rise
On dewier grass and in diviner skies,
        Over in Kentucky.

For yonder river, wider than the sea,
    Seems sometimes in the dusk a visible moan
Between two worlds—one fair, one dear to me.
    The fair has forms of ever-glimmering stone,
Weird-whispering ruin, graves where legends hide,
And lies in mist upon the charmèd side,
        Over in Kentucky.

The dear has restless, dimpled, pretty hands,
    Yearning toward unshaped steel, unfancied wars,
Unbuilded cities, and unbroken lands,
    With something sweeter than the faded stars
And dim, dead dews of my lost romance, found
In beauty that has vanished from the ground,
      Over in Kentucky.

Cincinatti, *Ohio.*

Sarah Morgan Bryan Piatt

ANOTHER WAR (1872)

Yes, they are coming from the fort—
    Not weary they, nor dimm'd with dust;
Their march seems but a shining sport,
    Their swords too new for rust.

You think the captains look so fine,
    You like, I know, the long sharp flash,
The fair silk flags above the line,
    The pretty scarlet sash?

You like the horses when they neigh,
    You like the music most of all,
And, if they had to fight to-day,
    You'd like to see them fall.

I wisely think the uniform
    Was made for skeletons to wear,
But your young blood is quick and warm,
    And so—you do not care.

You lift your eager eyes and ask:
    "Could we not have another war?"
As I might give this fearful task
    To armies near and far.

Another war? Perhaps we could,
    Yet, child of mine with sunniest head,
I sometimes wonder if I would
    Bear then to see the dead!

But am I in a dream? For see,
    My pretty boy follows the men—
Surely he did not speak to me,
    Who could have spoken, then?

It was another child, less fair,
    Less young, less innocent, I know,
Who lost the light gold from its hair
    Most bitter years ago!

It was that restless, wavering child
    I call Myself. No other, dear.
Perhaps you knew it when you smiled
    Because none else was near.

Then not my boy, it seems, but I
    Would wage another war?—to see
The shining sights, to hear the cry
    Of ghastly victory?

No—for another war could bring
    No second bloom to wither'd flowers,
No second song to birds that sing,
    Lost tunes in other hours!

But, friend, since time is full of pain,
    Whether men fall by field or hearth,
I want the old war back again,
    And nothing new on earth!

Sarah Morgan Bryan Piatt

THE GRAVE AT FRANKFORT (1872)

I turned and threw my rose upon the mound
    Beneath whose grass my old, rude kinsman lies,
And thought had from his Dark and Bloody Ground
    The blood secured in the shape of flowers to rise.

I left his dust to dew and dimness then,
    Who did not need the glitter of mock stars
To show his homely generalship to men
    And light his shoulders through his troubled wars.

I passed his rustling wild-cane, reached the gate,
    And heard the city's noisy murmurings;
Forgot the simple hero of my State,
    Looked in the gaslight, thought of other things.

Ah, that was many withered springs ago;
    Yet once, last winter, in the whirl of snows,
A vague half-fever, or, for aught I know,
    A wish to touch the hand that gave my rose,

Showed me a hunter of the wooded West,
    With dog and gun, beside his cabin door;
And, in the strange fringed garments on his breast,
    I recognized at once the rose he wore!

Lizette Woodworth Reese

from *Spicewood* (1920)

A WAR MEMORY (1865)

God bless this house and keep us all from hurt.
  She led us gravely up the straight long stair;
We were afraid; two held her by the skirt,
  One by the hand, and so to bed and prayer.
How frail a thing the little candle shone!
  Beneath its flame looked dim and soft and high
The chair, the drawers; she like a tall flower blown
  In a great space under a shadowy sky.
God bless us all and Lee and Beauregard.—
Without, a soldier paced, in hated blue,
   The road betwixt the tents in pale array
And our gnarled gate. But in the windy yard
  White tulips raced along the drip of dew;—
   Our mother with her candle went away.

Joel Chandler Harris

from *Uncle Remus: His Songs and Sayings* (1880)

A STORY OF THE WAR (1877)

When Miss Theodosia Huntingdon, of Burlington, Vermont, concluded to come South in 1870, she was moved by three considerations. In the first place, her brother, John Huntingdon, had become a citizen of Georgia—having astonished his acquaintances by marrying a young lady, the male members of whose family had achieved considerable distinction in the Confederate army; in the second place, she was anxious to explore a region which she almost unconsciously pictured to herself as remote and semi-barbarous; and, in the third place, her friends had persuaded her that to some extent she was an invalid. It was in vain that she argued with herself as to the propriety of undertaking the journey alone and unprotected, and she finally put an end to inward and outward doubts by informing herself and her friends, including John Huntingdon, her brother, who was practicing law in Atlanta, that she had decided to visit the South.

When, therefore, on the 12th of October, 1870—the date is duly recorded in one of Miss Theodosia's letters—she alighted from the cars in Atlanta, in the midst of a great crowd, she fully expected to find her brother waiting to receive her. The bells of several locomotives were ringing, a number of trains were moving in and out, and the porters and baggage-men were screaming and bawling to such an extent that for several moments Miss Huntingdon was considerably confused; so much so that she paused in the hope that her brother would suddenly appear and rescue her from the smoke, and dust, and din. At that moment some one touched her on the arm, and she heard a strong, half-confident, half-apologetic voice exclaim:

"Ain't dish yer Miss Doshy?"

Turning, Miss Theodosia saw at her side a tall gray-haired negro. Elaborating the incident afterward to her friends, she was pleased to say that the appearance of the old man was somewhat picturesque. He stood towering above her, his hat in one hand, a carriage-whip in the other, and an expectant smile lighting up his rugged face. She remembered a name her brother had often used in his letters, and, with a woman's tact, she held out her hand, and said:

"Is this Uncle Remus?"

"Law, Miss Doshy! how you know de ole nigger? I know'd you by de faver; but how you know me?" And then, without waiting for a reply: "Miss Sally, she sick in bed, en Mars John, he bleedzd ter go in de country, en dey tuck'n sont me. I know'd you de minnit I laid eyes on you. Time I seed you, I say ter myse'f, 'I lay dar's Miss Doshy,' en, sho nuff, dar you wuz. Yon ain't gun up yo' checks, is you? Kaze I'll git de trunk sont up by de 'spress waggin."

The next moment Uncle Remus was elbowing his way unceremoniously through the crowd, and in a very short time, seated in the carriage driven by the old man, Miss Huntingdon was whirling through the streets of Atlanta in the direction of her brother's home. She took advantage of the opportunity to study the old negro's face closely, her natural curiosity considerably sharpened by a knowledge of the fact that Uncle Remus had played an important part in her brother's history. The result of her observation must have been satisfactory, for presently she laughed, and said:

"Uncle Remus, you haven't told me how you knew me in that great crowd."

The old man chuckled, and gave the horses a gentle rap with the whip.

"Who? Me! I know'd you by de faver. Dat boy er Mars John's is de ve'y spit en immij un you. I'd a know'd you in New 'Leens, let 'lone down dar in de kyar-shed."

This was Miss Theodosia's introduction to Uncle Remus. One Sunday afternoon, a few weeks after her arrival, the family were assembled in the piazza enjoying the mild weather. Huntingdon was reading a newspaper; his wife was crooning softly as she rocked the baby to sleep; and the little boy was endeavoring to show his Aunt Dosia the outlines of Kennesaw Mountain through the purple haze that hung like a wonderfully fashioned curtain in the sky and almost obliterated the horizon. While they were thus engaged, Uncle Remus came around the corner of the house, talking to himself.

"Dey er too lazy ter wuk," he was saying, "en dey specks hones' fokes fer ter stan' up en s'port um. I'm gwine down ter Putmon County whar Mars Jeems is—dat's w'at I'm agwine ter do."

"What's the matter now, Uncle Remus?" inquired Mr. Huntingdon, folding up his newspaper.

"Nuthin' 'tall, Mars John, 'ceppin deze yer sunshine niggers. Dey begs my terbacker, en borrys my tools, en steals my vittles, en hit's done come ter dat pass dat I gotter pack up en go. I'm agwine down ter Putmon, dat's w'at."

Uncle Remus was accustomed to make this threat several times a day, but upon this occasion it seemed to remind Mr. Huntingdon of something.

"Very well," he said, "I'll come around and help you pack up, but before you go I want you to tell Sister here how you went to war and fought for the Union.—Remus was a famous warrior," he continued, turning to Miss Theodosia; "he volunteered for one day, and commanded an army of one. You know the story, but you have never heard Remus's version."

Uncle Remus shuffled around in an awkward, embarrassed way, scratched his head, and looked uncomfortable.

"Miss Doshy ain't got no time fer ter set dar an year de ole nigger run on."

"Oh, yes, I have, Uncle Remus!" exclaimed the young lady; "plenty of time."

The upshot of it was that, after many ridiculous protests, Uncle Remus sat down on the steps, and proceeded to tell his story of the war. Miss Theodosia listened with great interest, but throughout it all she observed—and she was painfully conscious of the fact, as she afterward admitted—that Uncle Remus spoke from the standpoint of a Southerner, and with the air of one who expected his hearers to thoroughly sympathize with him.

"Co'se," said Uncle Remus, addressing himself to Miss Theodosia, "you ain't bin to Putmon, en you dunner whar de Brad Slaughter place en Harmony Grove is, but Mars John en Miss Sally, dey bin dar a time er two, en dey knows how de lan' lays. Well, den, it 'uz right 'long in dere whar Mars Jeems lived, en whar he live now. When de war come 'long he wuz livin' dere longer Ole Miss en Miss Sally. Ole Miss 'uz his ma, en Miss Sally dar 'uz his sister. De war come des like I tell you, en marters sorter rock along same like dey allers did. Hit didn't strike me dat dey wuz enny war gwine on, en ef I hadn't sorter miss de nabers, en seed fokes gwine outer de way for ter ax de news, I'd a 'lowed ter myse'f dat de war wuz 'way off 'mong some yuther country. But all dis time de fuss wuz gwine on, en Mars Jeems, he wuz des eatchin' fer ter put in. Ole Miss en Miss Sally, dey tuck on so he didn't git off de fus' year, but bimeby news come down dat times wuz gittin putty hot, en Mars Jeems he got up, he did, he say he gotter go, en go he did. He got a overseer for ter look atter de place, en he went en jined de army. En he 'uz a fighter, too, mon, Mars Jeems wuz. Many's en many's de time," continued the old man, reflectively, "dat I hatter take'n bresh dat boy on accounter his 'buzin' en beatin' dem yuther boys. He went off dar for ter fight, en he fit. Ole Miss useter call me up Sunday en read w'at de papers say 'bout Mars Jeems, en it hope 'er up might'ly. I kin see 'er des like it 'uz yistiddy.

"'Remus,' sez she, 'dish yer's w'at de papers say 'bout my baby,' en den she'd read out twel she couldn't read fer cryin'. Hit went on dis way year in en year out, en dem wuz lonesome times, sho's you bawn, Miss Doshy—lonesome times, sho. Hit got hotter en hotter in de war, en lonesomer en mo' lonesomer at home, en bimeby long come de conscrip' man, en he des ever-las'nly scoop up Mars Jeems's overseer. W'en dis come 'bout, ole Miss, she sont atter me en say, sez she:

"'Remus, I ain't got nobody for ter look arter de place but you,' sez she, en den I up'n say, sez I:

"'Mistiss, you kin des 'pen' on de ole nigger.'

"I wuz ole den, Miss Doshy—let 'lone w'at I is now; en you better b'leeve I bossed dem han's. I had dem niggers up en in de fiel' long 'fo' day, en de way dey did wuk wuz a caution. Ef dey didn't earnt der vittles dat season den I ain't name Remus. But dey wuz tuk keer un. Dey had plenty or cloze en plenty er grub, en dey wuz de fattes' niggers in de settlement.

"Bimeby one day, Ole Miss, she call me up en say de Yankees done gone en tuck Atlanty—dish yer ve'y town; den present'y I year dey wuz a marchin' on down todes Putmon, en, lo en beholes! one day, de fus news I know'd, Mars Jeems he rid up wid a whole gang er men. He des stop long nuff fer ter change hosses en snatch a mouffle er sump'n' ter eat, but 'fo' he rid off, he call me up en say, sez he:

"'Daddy'—all Ole Miss's chilluns call me daddy—'Daddy,' he say, 'pears like dere's gwineter be mighty rough times 'roun' yer. De Yankees, dey er done got ter Madison en Mounticellar, en 'twon't be many days 'fo' dey er down yer. 'Tain't likely dey'll pester mother ner sister; but, daddy, ef de wus come ter de wus, I speck you ter take keer un um,' sezee.

"Den I say, sez I: 'How long you bin knowin' me, Mars Jeems?' sez I.

"'Sence I wuz a baby,' sezee.

"'Well, den, Mars Jeems,' sez I, 'you know'd 'twa'nt no use for ter ax me ter take keer Ole Miss en Miss Sally.'

"Den he tuck'n squoze my ban' en jump on de filly I bin savin' fer 'im, en rid off. One time he tu'n 'roun' en look like he wanter say sump'n', but he des waf' his han'—so—en gallop on. I know'd den dat trouble wuz brewin'. Nigger dat knows he's gwineter git thumped kin sorter fix hisse'f, on I tuck'n fix up like de war wuz gwineter come right in at de front gate. I tuck'n got all de cattle en hosses tergedder en driv' um ter de fo'-mile place, en I tuck all de corn en fodder en w'eat, en put um in a crib out dar in de woods; en I bilt me a pen in de swamp, en dar I put de hogs. Den, w'en I fix all dis, I put on my Sunday close en groun' my axe. Two whole days I groun' dat axe. De grinestone wuz in sight er de gate en close ter de big 'ouse, en dar I tuck my stan'.

"Bimeby one day, yer come de Yankees. Two un um come fus, en den de whole face er de yeath swawm'd wid um. De fus glimpse I kotch un um, I tuck my axe en march inter

Ole Miss settin'-room. She done had de sidebode move in dar, en I wish I may drap ef 'twuzn't fa'rly blazin' wid silver—silver cups en silver sassers, silver plates en silver dishes, silver mugs en silver pitchers. Look like ter me dey wuz fixin' for a weddin'. Dar sot Ole Miss des ez prim en ez proud ez ef she own de whole county. Dis kinder hope me up, kaze I done seed Ole Miss look dat away once befo' w'en de overseer struck me in de face wid a w'ip. I sot down by de fier wid my axe 'tween my knees. Dar we sot w'iles de Yankees ransack de place. Miss Sally, dar, she got sorter restless, but Ole Miss didn't skasely bat 'er eyes. Bimeby, we hear steps on de peazzer, en yer come a couple er young fellers wid strops on der shoulders, en der sodes a draggin' on de flo', en der spurrers a rattlin'. I won't say I wuz skeer'd," said Uncle Remus, as though endeavoring to recall something he failed to remember, "I won't say I wuz skeer'd, kaze I wuzent; but I wuz took'n wid a mighty funny feelin' in de naberhood er de gizzard. Dey wuz mighty perlite, dem young chaps wuz; but Ole Miss, she never tu'n 'er head, en Miss Sally, she look straight at de fier. Bimeby one un um see me, en he say, sezee:

"'Hello, ole man, w'at you doin' in yer?' sezee.

"'Well, boss,' sez I, 'I bin cuttin' some wood fer Ole Miss, en I des stop for ter wom my han's a little,' sez I.

"'Hit is cole, dat's a fack,' sezee.

"Wid dat I got up en tuck my stan' behime Ole Miss en Miss Sally, en de man w'at speak, he went up en wom his han's. Fus thing you know, he raise up sudden, en say, sezee:

"'W'at dat on yo' axe?'

"'Dat's de fier shinin' on it,' sez I.

"'Hit look like blood,' sezee, en den he laft.

"'But, bless yo' soul, dat man wouldn't never laft dat day ef he'd know'd de wukkins er Remus's mine. But dey didn't bodder nobody ner tech nuthin', en bimeby dey put out. Well, de Yankees, dey kep' passin' all de mawnin' en it look like ter me dey wuz a string un um ten mile long. Den dey commence gittin' thinner en thinner, en den atter w'ile we hear skummishin' in de naberhood er Armer's fe'y, en Ole Miss 'low how dat wuz Wheeler's men makin' persoot. Mars Jeems wuz wid dem Wheeler fellers, en I know'd ef dey wuz dat close I wa'n't doin' no good settin' 'roun' de house toas'n my shins at de fier, so I des tuck Mars Jeems's rifle fum behime de do' en put out ter look atter my stock.

"Seem like I ain't never see no raw day like dat, needer befo' ner sence. Dey wa'n't no rain, but de wet des sifted down; mighty raw day. De leaves on de groun' 'uz so wet dey don't make no fuss, en I got in de woods, en w'enev er I year de Yankees gwine by, I des stop in my tracks en let um pass. I wuz stan'in' dat away in de aidge er de woods lookin' out 'cross a clearin', w'en—*piff!*—out come a little bunch er blue smoke fum de top er wunner dem big lonesome-lookin' pines, en den—*pow!*

"Sez I ter myse'f, sez I: 'Honey, youer right on my route, en I'll des see w'at kinder bird you got roostin' in you,' en w'iles I wuz a lookin' out bus' de smoke—*piff!* en den—*bang!* Wid dat I des drapt back inter de woods, en sorted skeerted 'roun' so's ter git de tree 'twix' me en de road. I slid up putty close, en wadder you speck I see? Des ez sho's youer settin' dar lissenin' dey wuz a live Yankee up dar in dat tree, en he wuz a loadin' en a shootin' at de boys dez ez cool es a cowcumber in de jew, en he had his hoss hitch out in de bushes, kaze I year de creetur tromplin' 'roun'. He had a spy-glass up dar, en w'iles I wuz a watchin' un 'im, he raise 'er up en look thoo 'er, en den he lay 'er down en fix his gun fer ter shoot. I had good eyes in dem days, ef I ain't got um now, en 'way up de big road I see Mars Jeems a comin'. Hit wuz too fur fer ter see his face, but I know'd 'im by de filly w'at I raise fer 'im, en she wuz a prancin' like a school-gal. I know'd dat man wuz gwineter shoot Mars Jeems ef he could, en dat wuz mo'n I could stan'. Manys en manys de time dat I nuss dat boy, en hilt 'im in dese arms, en toted 'im on dis back, en w'en I see dat Yankee lay dat gun 'cross a lim' en take aim at Mars Jeems I up wid my ole rifle, en shet my eyes en let de man have all she had."

"Do you mean to say," exclaimed Miss Theodosia, indignantly, "that you shot the Union soldier, when you knew he was fighting for your freedom?"

"Co'se, I know all about dat," responded Uncle Remus, "en it sorter made cole chills run up my back; but w'en I see dat man take aim, en Mars Jeems gwine home ter Ole Miss en Miss Sally, I des disremembered all 'bout freedom en lammed aloose. En den atter dat, me en Miss Sally tuck en nuss de man right straight along. He los' one arm in dat tree biz-ness, but me en Miss Sally we nuss 'im en we nuss 'im twel he done got well. Des 'bout dat time I quit nuss'n 'im, but Miss Sally she kep' on. She kep' on," continued Uncle Remus, pointing to Mr. Huntingdon, "en now dar he is."

"But you cost him an arm," exclaimed Miss Theodosia.

"I gin 'im dem," said Uncle Remus, pointing to Mrs. Huntingdon, "en I gin 'im deze"— holding up his own brawny arms. "En ef dem ain't nuff fer enny man den I done los' de way."

Samuel Watkins

from *Co. Aytch* (1882)

CHAPTER 1: RETROSPECTIVE

"We Are One and Undivided"

About twenty years ago, I think it was—I won't be certain, though—a man whose name, if I remember correctly, was Wm. L. Yancy[31]—I write only from memory, and this was a long time ago—took a strange and peculiar notion that the sun rose in the east and set in the west, and that the compass pointed north and south. Now, everybody knew at the time that it was but the idiosyncrasy of an unbalanced mind, and that the United States of America had no north, no south, no east, no west. Well, he began to preach the strange doctrine of there being such a thing. He began to have followers. As you know, it matters not how absurd, ridiculous and preposterous doctrines may be preached, there will be some followers. Well, one man by the name of (I think it was) Rhett,[32] said it out loud. He was told to "s-h-e-e." Then another fellow by the name (I remember this one because it sounded like a graveyard) Toombs[33] said so, and he was told to "sh-sh-ee-ee." Then after a while whole heaps of people began to say that they thought that there was a north and a south; and after a while hundreds and thousands and millions said that there was a south. But they were the persons who lived in the direction that the water courses run. Now, the people who lived where the water courses started from came down to see about it, and they said, "Gents, you are very much mistaken. We came over in the Mayflower, and we used to burn witches for saying that the sun rose in the east and set in the west, because the sun neither rises nor sets, the earth simply turns on its axis, and we know, cause we are Pure(i)tans." The spokesman of the party was named (I think I remember his name because it always gave me the blues when I heard it) Horrors Greeley;[34] and another person by the name of Charles Sumner,[35] said there ain't any north or south, east or west, and you shan't say so, either. Now, the other people who lived in the direction that the water courses run, just raised their bristles and continued saying that there is a north and there is a south. When those at the head of the water courses come out furiously mad, to coerce those in the direction that water courses run, and to make them take it back. Well, they went to gouging and biting, to pulling and scratching at a furious rate. One side elected a captain by the name of Jeff Davis, and known as one-eyed Jeff, and a first lieutenant by the name of Aleck Stephens, commonly styled Smart Aleck. The other side selected as captain a son of Nancy Hanks, of Bowling Green, and a son of old Bob Lincoln, the rail-splitter, and whose name was Abe. Well, after he was elected captain, they elected as first lieutenant an individual of doubtful blood by the name of Hannibal Hamlin, being a descendant of the generation of Ham, the bad son of old Noah, who meant to curse him blue, but overdid the thing, and cursed him black.[36]

Well, as I said before, they went to fighting, but old Abe's side got the best of the argument. But in getting the best of the argument they called in all the people and wise men of other nations of the earth, and they, too, said that America had no cardinal points, and that the sun did not rise in the east and set in the west, and that the compass did not point either north or south.

Well, then, Captain Jeff Davis' side gave it up and quit, and they, too, went to saying that there is no north, no south, no east, no west. Well, "us boys" all took a small part in the fracas, and Shep, the prophet, remarked that the day would come when those who once believed that the American continent had cardinal points would be ashamed to own it. That day has arrived. America has no north, no south, no east, no west; the sun rises over the hills and sets over the mountains, the compass just points up and down, and we can laugh now at the absurd notion of there being a north and a south.

Well, reader, let me whisper in your ear. I was in the row, and the following pages will tell what part I took in the little unpleasant misconception of there being such a thing as a north and south.

The Bloody Chasm

In these memoirs, after the lapse of twenty years, we propose to fight our "battles o'er again."

To do this is but a pastime and pleasure, as there is nothing that so much delights the old soldier as to revisit the scenes and battle-fields with which he was once so familiar, and to recall the incidents, though trifling they may have been at the time.

The histories of the Lost Cause are all written out by "big bugs," generals and re-nowned historians, and like the fellow who called a turtle a "cooter," being told that no such word as cooter was in Webster's dictionary, remarked that he had as much right to make a dictionary as Mr. Webster or any other man; so have I to write a history.

But in these pages I do not pretend to write the history of the war. I only give a few sketches and incidents that came under the observation of a "high private" in the rear ranks of the rebel army.[37] Of course, the histories are all correct. They tell of great achieve-ments of great men, who wear the laurels of victory; have grand presents given them; high positions in civil life; presidents of corporations; governors of states; official positions, etc., and when they die, long obituaries are published, telling their many virtues, their distin-guished victories, etc., and when they are buried, the whole country goes in mourning and is called upon to buy an elegant monument to erect over the remains of so distinguished and brave a general, etc. But in the following pages I propose to tell of the fellows who did the shooting and killing, the fortifying and ditching, the sweeping of the streets, the drilling, the standing guard, picket and videt, and who drew (or were to draw) eleven dol-lars per month and rations, and also drew the ramrod and tore the cartridge. Pardon me should I use the personal pronoun "I" too frequently, as I do not wish to be called egotisti-cal, for I only write of what I saw as an humble private in the rear rank in an infantry regi-ment, commonly called "webfoot." Neither do I propose to make this a connected journal, for I write entirely from memory, and you must remember, kind reader, that these things happened twenty years ago, and twenty years is a long time in the life of any individual.

I was twenty-one years old then, and at that time I was not married. Now I have a house full of young "rebels," clustering around my knees and bumping against my elbow, while I write these reminiscences of the war of secession, rebellion, state rights, slavery, or our rights in the territories, or by whatever other name it may be called. These are all with the past now, and the North and South have long ago "shaken hands across the bloody chasm."[38] The flag of the Southern cause has been furled never to be again unfurled; gone like a dream of yesterday, and lives only in the memory of those who lived through those bloody days and times.

Eighteen Hundred and Sixty-one

Reader mine, did you live in that stormy period? In the year of our Lord eighteen hundred and sixty-one, do you remember those stirring times? Do you recollect in that year, for the first time in your life, of hearing Dixie and the Bonnie Blue Flag? Fort Sumter was fired upon from Charleston by troops under General Beauregard, and Major Anderson, of the Federal army, surrendered. The die was cast; war was declared; Lincoln called for troops from Tennessee and all the Southern states, but Tennessee, loyal to her Southern sister states, passed the ordinance of secession, and enlisted under the Stars and Bars. From that day on, every person, almost, was eager for the war, and we were all afraid it would be over and we not be in the fight. Companies were made up, regiments organized; left, left, left, was heard from morning till night. By the right flank, file left, march, were familiar sounds. Everywhere could be seen Southern cockades made by the ladies and our sweethearts. And some who afterwards became Union men made the most fiery secession speeches. Flags made by the ladies were presented to companies, and to hear the young orators tell of how they would protect that flag, and that they would come back with the flag or come not at all, and if they fell they would fall with their backs to the field and their feet to the foe, would fairly make our hair stand on end with intense patriotism, and we wanted to march right off and whip twenty Yankees. But we soon found out that the glory of war was at home among the ladies and not upon the field of blood and carnage of death, where our comrades were mutilated and torn by shot and shell. And to see the cheek blanch and to hear the fervent prayer, aye, I might say the agony of mind were very different indeed from the patriotic times at home.

Camp Cheatham

After being drilled and disciplined at Camp Cheatham, under the administrative ability of General R. C. Foster, 3rd, for two months, we, the First, Third and Eleventh Tennessee Regiments—Maney, Brown and Rains—learned of the advance of McClelland's [sic] army into Virginia, toward Harper's Ferry and Bull Run.[39]

The Federal army was advancing all along the line. They expected to march right into the heart of the South, set the negroes free, take our property, and whip the rebels back into the Union. But they soon found that secession was a bigger mouthful than they could swallow at one gobble. They found the people of the South in earnest.

Secession may have been wrong in the abstract, and has been tried and settled by the arbitrament of the sword and bayonet, but I am as firm in my convictions today of the right of secession as I was in 1861. The South is our country, the North is the country of those who live there. We are an agricultural people; they are a manufacturing people. They are the descendants of the good old Puritan Plymouth Rock stock, and we of the South from the proud and aristocratic stock of Cavaliers. We believe in the doctrine of State rights, they in the doctrine of centralization.

John C. Calhoun, Patrick Henry, and Randolph, of Roanoke, saw the venom under their wings, and warned the North of the consequences, but they laughed at them. We only fought for our State rights, they for Union and power. The South fell battling under the banner of State rights, but yet grand and glorious even in death. Now, reader, please pardon the digression. It is every word that we will say in behalf of the rights of secession in the following pages. The question has been long ago settled and is buried forever, never in this age or generation to be resurrected.

The vote of the regiment was taken, and we all voted to go to Virginia. The Southern Confederacy had established its capital at Richmond.

A man by the name of Jackson, who kept a hotel in Maryland, had raised the Stars and Bars, and a Federal officer by the name of Ellsworth tore it down, and Jackson had riddled his body with buckshot from a double-barreled shot-gun. First blood for the South.[40]

Everywhere the enemy were advancing; the red clouds of war were booming up everywhere, but as this particular epoch, I refer you to the history of that period.

A private soldier is but an automaton, a machine that works by the command of a good, bad, or indifferent engineer, and is presumed to know nothing of all these great events. His business is to load and shoot, stand picket, videt, etc., while the officers sleep, or perhaps die on the field of battle and glory, and his obituary and epitaph but "one" remembered among the slain, but to what company, regiment, brigade or corps he belongs, there is no account; he is soon forgotten.

A long line of box cars was drawn up at Camp Cheatham one morning in July, the bugle sounded to strike tents and to place everything on board the cars. We old comrades have gotten together and laughed a hundred times at the plunder and property that we had accumulated, compared with our subsequent scanty wardrobe. Every soldier had enough blankets, shirts, pants and old boots to last a year, and the empty bottles and jugs would have set up a first-class drug store. In addition, every one of us had his gun, cartridge-box, knapsack and three days' rations, a pistol on each side and a long Bowie knife, that had been presented to us by William Wood, of Columbia, Tenn. We got in and on top of the box cars, the whistle sounded, and amid the waving of hats, handkerchiefs and flags, we bid a long farewell and forever to old Camp Cheatham.

Arriving at Nashville, the citizens turned out *en masse* to receive us, and here again we were reminded of the good old times and the "gal we left behind us." Ah, it is worth soldiering to receive such welcomes as this.

The Rev. Mr. Elliott invited us to his college grove, where had been prepared enough of the good things of earth to gratify the tastes of the most fastidious epicure. And what was most novel, we were waited on by the most beautiful young ladies (pupils of his school). It was charming, I tell you. Rev. C. D. Elliott was our Brigade Chaplain all through the war, and Dr. C. T. Quintard the Chaplain of the First Tennessee Regiment—two of the best men who ever lived. (Quintard is the present Bishop of Tennessee).[41]

On the Road

Leaving Nashville, we went bowling along twenty or thirty miles an hour, as fast as steam could carry us. At every town and station citizens and ladies were waving their handkerchiefs and hurrahing for Jeff Davis and the Southern Confederacy. Magnificent banquets were prepared for us all along the entire route. It was one magnificent festival from one end of the line to the other. At Chattanooga, Knoxville, Bristol, Farmville, Lynchburg, everywhere, the same demonstrations of joy and welcome greeted us. Ah, those were glorious times; and you, reader, see why the old soldier loves to live over again that happy period.

But the Yankees are advancing on Manassas. July 21st finds us a hundred miles from that fierce day's battle. That night, after the battle is fought and won, our train draws up at Manassas Junction.

Well, what news? Everyone was wild, nay, frenzied with the excitement of victory, and we felt very much like the "boy the calf had run over." We felt that the war was over, and we would have to return home without even seeing a Yankee soldier. Ah, how we envied those that were wounded. We thought at that time that we would have given a thousand dollars to have been in the battle, and to have had our arm shot off, so we could have returned home with an empty sleeve. But the battle was over, and we left out.

Staunton

From Manassas our train moved on to Staunton, Virginia. Here we again went into camp, overhauled kettles, pots, buckets, jugs and tents, and found everything so tangled up and mixed that we could not tell tuther from which.

We stretched our tents, and the soldiers once again felt that restraint and discipline which we had almost forgotten en route to this place. But, as the war was over now, our captains, colonels and generals were not "hard on the boys;" in fact, had begun to electioneer a little for the Legislature and for Congress. In fact, some wanted, and were looking forward to the time, to run for Governor of Tennessee.

Staunton was a big place; whisky was cheap, and good Virginia tobacco was plentiful, and the currency of the country was gold and silver.

The State Asylums for the blind and insane were here, and we visited all the places of interest.

Here is where we first saw the game called "chuck-a-luck,"[42] afterwards so popular in the army. But, I always noticed that chuck won, and luck always lost.

Faro and roulette were in full blast; in fact, the skum had begun to come to the surface, and shoddy was the gentleman. By this, I mean that civil law had been suspended; the ermine of the judges had been overridden by the sword and bayonet. In other words, the military had absorbed the civil. Hence the gambler was in his glory.

Warm Springs, Virginia

One day while we were idling around camp, June Tucker sounded the assembly, and we were ordered aboard the cars. We pulled out for Millboro; from there we had to foot it to Bath Alum and Warm Springs. We went over the Allegheny Mountains.

I was on every march that was ever made by the First Tennessee Regiment during the whole war, and at this time I cannot remember of ever experiencing a harder or more fatiguing march. It seemed that mountain was piled upon mountain. No sooner would we arrive at a place that seemed to be the top than another view of a higher, and yet higher mountain would rise before us. From the foot to the top of the mountain the soldiers lined the road, broken down and exhausted. First one blanket was thrown away, and then another; now and then a good pair of pants, old boots and shoes, Sunday hats, pistols and Bowie knives strewed the road. Old bottles and jugs and various and sundry articles were lying pell-mell everywhere. Up and up, and onward and upward we pulled and toiled, until we reached the very top, when there burst upon our view one of the grandest and most beautiful landscapes we ever beheld.

Nestled in the valley right before us is Bath Alum and Warm Springs. It seemed to me at that time, and since, a glimpse of a better and brighter world beyond, to the weary Christian pilgrim who may have been toiling on his journey for years. A glad shout arose from those who had gained the top, which cheered and encouraged the others to persevere. At last we got to Warm Springs. Here they had a nice warm dinner waiting for us. They had a large bath-house at Warm Springs. A large pool of water arranged so that a person could go in any depth he might desire. It was a free thing, and we pitched in. We had no idea of the enervating effect it would have upon our physical systems, and as the water was but little past tepid, we stayed in a good long time. But when we came out we were as limp as dishrags. About this time the assembly sounded and we were ordered to march. But we couldn't march worth a cent. There we had to stay until our systems had had sufficient recuperation. And we would wonder what all this marching was for, as the war was over anyhow.

The second day after leaving Warm Springs we came to Big Springs. It was in the month of August, and the biggest white frost fell that I ever saw in winter.

The Yankees were reported to be in close proximity to us, and Captain Field[43] with a detail of ten men was sent forward on the scout. I was on the detail, and when we left camp that evening, it was dark and dreary and drizzling rain. After a while the rain began to come down harder and harder, and every one of us was wet and drenched to the skin—guns, cartridges and powder. The next morning about daylight, while standing videt, I saw a body of twenty-five or thirty Yankees approaching, and I raised my gun for the purpose of shooting, and pulled down, but the cap popped. They discovered me and popped three or four caps at me; their powder was wet also. Before I could get on a fresh cap, Captain Field came running up with his seven-shooting rifle, and the first fire he killed a Yankee. They broke and run. Captain Field did all the firing, but every time he pulled down he brought a Yankee. I have forgotten the number that he did kill, but if I am not mistaken it was either twenty or twenty-one, for I remember the incident was in almost every Southern paper at that time, and the general comments were that one Southern man was equal to twenty Yankees. While we were in hot pursuit, one truly brave and magnanimous Yankee, who had been badly wounded, said, "Gentlemen, you have killed me, but not a hundred yards from here is the main line." We did not go any further, but halted right there, and after getting all the information that we could out of the wounded Yankee, we returned to camp.

One evening, General Robert E. Lee came to our camp. He was a fine-looking gentleman, and wore a moustache. He was dressed in blue cottonade and looked like some good boy's grandpa. I felt like going up to him and saying, good evening, Uncle Bob! I am not certain at this late day that I did not do so. I remember going up mighty close and sitting there and listening to his conversation with the officers of our regiment. He had a calm and collected air about him, his voice was kind and tender, and his eye was as gentle as a dove's. His whole make-up of form and person, looks and manner had a kind of gentle and soothing magnetism about it that drew every one to him and made them love, respect, and honor him. I fell in love with the old gentleman and felt like going home with him. I know I have never seen a finer looking man, nor one with more kind and gentle features and manners. His horse was standing nipping the grass, and when I saw that he was getting ready to start I ran and caught his horse and led him up to him. He took the reins of the bridle in his hand and said, "thank you, my son," rode off, and my heart went with him. There was none of his staff with him; he had on no sword or pistol, or anything to show his rank. The only thing that I remember he had was an opera-glass hung over his shoulder by a strap.

Leaving Big Springs, we marched on day by day, across Greenbrier and Gauley rivers to Huntersville, a little but sprightly town hid in the very fastnesses of the mountains. The people live exceedingly well in these mountains. They had plenty of honey and buckwheat cakes, and they called butter-milk "sour-milk," and sour-milk weren't fit for pigs; they couldn't see how folks drank sour-milk. But sourkraut was good. Everything seemed to grow in the mountains—potatoes, Irish and sweet; onions, snap beans, peas—though the country was very thinly populated. Deer, bear, and foxes, as well as wild turkeys, and rabbits and squirrels abounded everywhere. Apples and peaches were abundant, and everywhere the people had apple-butter for every meal; and occasionally we would come across a small-sized distillery, which we would at once start to doing duty. We drank the singlings[44] while they were hot, but like the old woman who could not eat corn bread until she heard that they made whisky out of corn, then she could manage to "worry a little of it down;" so it was with us and the singlings.

From this time forward, we were ever on the march—tramp, tramp, tramp—always on the march. Lee's corps, Stonewall Jackson's division—I refer you to the histories for the marches and tramps made by these commanders the first year of the war. Well, we followed them.

Cheat Mountain

One evening about 4 o'clock, the drummers of the regiment began to beat their drums as hard as they could stave, and I saw men running in every direction, and the camp soon became one scene of hurry and excitement. I asked some one what all this hubbub meant. He looked at me with utter astonishment. I saw soldiers running to their tents and grabbing their guns and cartridge-boxes and hurry out again, the drums still rolling and rattling. I asked several other fellows what in the dickens did all this mean? Finally one fellow, who seemed scared almost out of his wits, answered between a wail and a shriek, "Why, sir, they are beating the long roll." Says I, "What is the long roll for?" "The long roll, man, the long roll! Get your gun; they are beating the long roll!" This was all the information that I could get. It was the first, last, and only long roll that I ever heard. But, then everything was new, and Colonel Maney, ever prompt, ordered the assembly. Without any command or bugle sound, or anything, every soldier was in his place. Tents, knapsacks and everything was left indiscriminately.

We were soon on the march, and we marched on and on and on. About night it began to rain. All our blankets were back in camp, but we were expected every minute to be ordered into action. That night we came to Mingo Flats. The rain still poured. We had no rations to eat and nowhere to sleep. Some of us got some fence rails and piled them together and worried through the night as best we could. The next morning we were ordered to march again, but we soon began to get hungry, and we had about half halted and about not halted at all. Some of the boys were picking blackberries. The main body of the regiment was marching leisurely along the road, when bang, debang, debang, bang, and a volley of buck and ball came hurling right through the two advance companies of the regiment—companies H and K. We had marched into a Yankee ambuscade.

All at once everything was a scene of consternation and confusion; no one seemed equal to the emergency. We did not know whether to run or stand, when Captain Field gave the command to fire and charge the bushes. We charged the bushes and saw the Yankees running through them, and we fired on them as they retreated. I do not know how many Yankees were killed, if any. Our company (H) had one man killed, Pat Hanley, an Irishman, who had joined our company at Chattanooga. Hugh Padgett and Dr. Hooper, and perhaps one or two others, were wounded.

After the fighting was over, where, O where, was all the fine rigging heretofore on our officers? They could not be seen. Corporals, sergeants, lieutenants, captains, all had torn all the fine lace off their clothing. I noticed that at the time and was surprised and hurt. I asked several of them why they had torn off the insignia of their rank, and they always answered, "Humph, you think that I was going to be a target for the Yankees to shoot at?" You see, this was our first battle, and the officers had not found out that minnie as well as cannon balls were blind; that they had no eyes and could not see. They thought that the balls would hunt for them and not hurt the privates. I always shot at privates. It was they that did the shooting and killing, and if I could kill or wound a private, why, my chances were so much the better. I always looked upon officers as harmless personages. Colonel Field, I suppose, was about the only Colonel of the war that did as much shooting as the private soldier. If I shot at an officer, it was at long range, but when we got down to close quarters I always tried to kill those that were trying to kill me.

Sewell Mountain

From Cheat Mountain we went by forced marches day and night, over hill and everlasting mountains, and through lovely and smiling valleys, sometimes the country rich and productive, sometimes rough and broken, through towns and villages, the names of which I have forgotten, crossing streams and rivers, but continuing our never ceasing, unending march, passing through the Kanawha Valley and by the salt-works, and nearly back to the Ohio river, when we at last reached Sewell Mountain. Here we found General John B. Floyd,[45] strongly entrenched and fortified and facing the advance of the Federal army. Two days before our arrival he had charged and captured one line of the enemy's works. I know nothing of the battle. See the histories for that. I only write from memory, and that was twenty years ago, but I remember reading in the newspapers at that time of some distinguished man, whether he was captain, colonel or general, I have forgotten, but I know the papers said "he sought the bauble, reputation, at the cannon's mouth, and went to glory from the death-bed of fame." I remember it sounded gloriously in print. Now, reader, this is all I know of this grand battle. I only recollect what the newspapers said about it, and you know that a newspaper always tells the truth. I also know that beef livers sold for one dollar apiece in gold; and here is where we were first paid off in Confederate money. Remaining here a few days, we commenced our march again.

Sewell Mountain, Harrisonburg, Lewisburg, Kanawha Salt-works, first four, forward and back, seemed to be the programme of that day. Rosecrans, that wiley old fox, kept Lee and Jackson both busy trying to catch him, but Rosey would not be caught. March, march, march; tramp, tramp, tramp, back through the valley to Huntersville and Warm Springs, and up through the most beautiful valley—the Shenandoah—in the world, passing towns and elegant farms and beautiful residences, rich pastures and abundant harvests, which a Federal General (Fighting Joe Hooker), later in the war, ordered to be so sacked and destroyed that a "crow passing over this valley would have to carry his rations." Passing on, we arrived at Winchester. The first night we arrived at this place, the wind blew a perfect hurricane, and every tent and marquee in Lee's and Jackson's army was blown down. This is the first sight we had of Stonewall Jackson, riding upon his old sorrel horse, his feet drawn up as if his stirrups were much too short for him, and his old dingy military cap hanging well forward over his head, and his nose erected in the air, his old rusty sabre rattling by his side. This is the way the grand old hero of a hundred battles looked. His spirit is yonder with the blessed ones that have gone before, but his history is one that the country will ever be proud of, and his memory will be cherished and loved by the old soldiers who followed him through the war.

Romney

Our march to and from Romney was in midwinter in the month of January, 1862. It was the coldest winter known to the oldest inhabitant of these regions. Situated in the most mountainous country in Virginia, and away up near the Maryland and Pennsylvania line, the storm king seemed to rule in all of his majesty and power. Snow and rain and sleet and tempest seemed to ride and laugh and shriek and howl and moan and groan in all their fury and wrath. The soldiers on this march got very much discouraged and disheartened. As they marched along icicles hung from their clothing, guns, and knapsacks; many were badly frost bitten, and I heard of many freezing to death along the road side. My feet peeled off like a peeled onion on that march, and I have not recovered from its effects to this day. The snow and ice on the ground being packed by the soldiers tramping, the horses hitched to the artillery wagons were continually slipping and sliding and falling and wounding themselves and sometimes killing their riders. The wind whistling with a keen and piercing shriek, seemed as if they would freeze the marrow in our bones. The soldiers in the whole army got rebellious—almost mutinous—and would curse and abuse Stonewall Jackson; in fact, they called him "Fool Tom Jackson." They blamed him for the cold weather; they blamed him for everything, and when he would ride by a regiment they would take occasion, *sotto voce*, to abuse him, and call him "Fool Tom Jackson," and loud enough for him to hear. Soldiers from all commands would fall out of ranks and stop by the road side and swear that they would not follow such a leader any longer.

When Jackson got to Romney, and was ready to strike Banks and Meade in a vital point, and which would have changed, perhaps, the destiny of the war and the South, his troops refused to march any further, and he turned, marched back to Winchester and tendered his resignation to the authorities at Richmond.[46] But the great leader's resignation was not accepted. It was in store for him to do some of the hardest fighting and greatest generalship that was done during the war.

One night at this place (Romney), I was sent forward with two other soldiers across the wire bridge as picket. One of them was named Schwartz and the other Pfifer—he called it Fifer, but spelled it with a P—both full-blooded Dutchmen, and belonging to Company E, or the German Yagers, Captain Harsh, or, as he was more generally called, "God-for-dam."

When we had crossed the bridge and taken our station for the night, I saw another snow storm was coming. The zig-zag lightnings began to flare and flash, and sheet after sheet of wild flames seemed to burst right over our heads and were hissing around us. The very elements seemed to be one aurora borealis with continued lightning. Streak after streak of lightning seemed to be piercing each the other, the one from the north and the other from the south. The white clouds would roll up, looking like huge snow balls, encircled with living fires. The earth and hills and trees were covered with snow, and the lightnings seemed to be playing "King, King Canico" along its crusted surface. If it thundered at all, it seemed to be between a groaning and a rumbling sound. The trees and hills seemed white with livid fire. I can remember that storm now as the grandest picture that has ever made any impression on my memory. As soon as it quit lightning, the most blinding snow storm fell that I ever saw. It fell so thick and fast that I got hot. I felt like pulling off my coat. I was freezing. The winds sounded like sweet music. I felt grand, glorious, peculiar; beautiful things began to play and dance around my head, and I supposed I must have dropped to sleep or something, when I felt Schwartz grab me, and give me a shake, and at the same time raised his gun and fired, and yelled out at the top of his voice, "Here is your mule." The next instant a volley of minnie balls was scattering the snow all around us. I tried to walk, but my pants and boots were stiff and frozen, and the blood had ceased to circulate in my lower limbs. But Schwartz kept on firing, and at every fire he would yell out, "Yer is yer mool!" Pfifer could not speak English, and I reckon he said "Here is your mule" in Dutch. About the same time we were hailed from three Confederate officers, at full gallop right toward us, not to shoot. And as they galloped up to us and thundered right across the bridge, we discovered it was Stonewall Jackson and two of his staff. At the same time the Yankee cavalry charged us, and we, too, ran back across the bridge.

Standing Picket on the Potomac

Leaving Winchester, we continued up the valley.

The night before the attack on Bath or Berkly Springs, there fell the largest snow I ever saw.

Stonewall Jackson had seventeen thousand soldiers at his command. The Yankees were fortified at Bath. An attack was ordered, our regiment marched upon top of a mountain overlooking the movements of both armies in the valley below. About 4 o'clock one grand charge and rush was made, and the Yankees were routed and skedaddled.

By some circumstance or other, Lieutenant J. Lee Bullock came in command of the First Tennessee Regiment. But Lee was not a graduate of West Point, you see.

The Federals had left some spiked batteries on the hill side, as we were informed by an old citizen, and Lee, anxious to capture a battery, gave the new and peculiar command of, "Soldiers, you are ordered to go forward and capture a battery; just piroute up that hill; piroute, march. Forward, men; piroute carefully." The boys "pirouted" as best they could.

It may have been a new command, and not laid down in Hardee's or Scott's tactics;[47] but Lee was speaking plain English, and we understood his meaning perfectly, and even at this late day I have no doubt that every soldier who heard the command thought it a legal and technical term used by military graduates to go forward and capture a battery.

At this place (Bath), a beautiful young lady ran across the street. I have seen many beautiful and pretty women in my life, but she was the prettiest one I ever saw. Were you to ask any member of the First Tennessee Regiment who was the prettiest woman he ever saw, he would unhesitatingly answer that he saw her at Berkly Springs during the war, and he would continue the tale, and tell you of Lee Bullock's piroute and Stonewall Jackson's charge.

We rushed down to the big spring bursting out of the mountain side, and it was hot enough to cook an egg. Never did I see soldiers more surprised. The water was so hot we could not drink it.

The snow covered the ground and was still falling.

That night I stood picket on the Potomac with a detail of the Third Arkansas Regiment. I remember how sorry I felt for the poor fellows, because they had enlisted for the war, and we for only twelve months. Before nightfall I took in every object and commenced my weary vigils. I had to stand all night. I could hear the rumblings of the Federal artillery and wagons, and hear the low shuffling sound made by troops on the march. The snow came pelting down as large as goose eggs. About midnight the snow ceased to fall, and became quiet. Now and then the snow would fall off the bushes and make a terrible noise. While I was peering through the darkness, my eyes suddenly fell upon the outlines of a man. The more I looked the more I was convinced that it was a Yankee picket. I could see his hat and coat—yes, see his gun. I was sure that it was a Yankee picket. What was I to do? The relief was several hundred yards in the rear. The more I looked the more sure I was. At last a cold sweat broke out all over my body. Turkey bumps rose. I summoned all the nerves and bravery that I could command, and said: "Halt! who goes there?" There being no response, I became resolute. I did not wish to fire and arouse the camp, but I marched right up to it and stuck my bayonet through and through it. It was a stump. I tell the above, because it illustrates a part of many a private's recollections of the war; in fact, a part of the hardships and suffering that they go through.

One secret of Stonewall Jackson's success was that he was such a strict disciplinarian. He did his duty himself and was ever at his post, and he expected and demanded of everybody to do the same thing. He would have a man shot at the drop of a hat, and drop it himself. The first army order that was ever read to us after being attached to his corps, was the shooting to death by musketry of two men who had stopped on the battlefield to carry off a wounded comrade. It was read to us in line of battle at Winchester.

Schwartz and Pfifer

At Valley Mountain the finest and fattest beef I ever saw was issued to the soldiers, and it was the custom to use tallow for lard. Tallow made good shortening if the biscuits were eaten hot, but if allowed to get cold they had a strong taste of tallow in their flavor that did not taste like the flavor of vanilla or lemon in ice cream and strawberries; and biscuits fried in tallow were something upon the principle of 'possum and sweet potatoes. Well, Pfifer had got the fat from the kidneys of two hindquarters and made a cake of tallow weighing about twenty-five pounds. He wrapped it up and put it carefully away in his knapsack. When the assembly sounded for the march, Pfifer strapped on his knapsack. It was pretty heavy, but Pfifer was "well heeled." He knew the good frying he would get out of that twenty-five pounds of nice fat tallow, and he was willing to tug and toil all day over a muddy and sloppy road for his anticipated hot tallow gravy for supper. We made a long and hard march that day, and about dark went into camp. Fires were made up and water brought, and the soldiers began to get supper. Pfifer was in a good humor. He went to get that twenty-five pounds of good, nice, fat tallow out of his knapsack, and on opening it, lo and behold! it was a rock that weighed about thirty pounds. Pfifer was struck dumb with amazement. He looked bewildered, yea, even silly. I do not think he cursed, because he could not do the subject justice. He looked at that rock with the death stare of a doomed man. But he suspected Schwartz. He went to Schwartz's knapsack, and there he found his cake of tallow. He went to Schwartz and would have killed him had not soldiers interfered and pulled him off by main force. His eyes blazed and looked like those of a tiger when he has just torn his victim limb from limb. I would not have been in Schwartz's shoes for all the tallow in every beef in Virginia. Captain Harsh made Schwartz carry that rock for two days to pacify Pfifer.

The Court-Martial

One incident came under my observation while in Virginia that made a deep impression on my mind. One morning, about daybreak, the new guard was relieving the old guard. It was a bitter cold morning, and on coming to our extreme outpost, I saw a soldier—he was but a mere boy—either dead or asleep at his post. The sergeant commanding the relief went up to him and shook him. He immediately woke up and seemed very much frightened. He was fast asleep at his post. The sergeant had him arrested and carried to the guard-house.

Two days afterwards I received notice to appear before a court-martial at nine. I was summoned to appear as a witness against him for being asleep at his post in the enemy's country. An example had to be made of some one. He had to be tried for his life. The court-martial was made up of seven or eight officers of a different regiment. The witnesses all testified against him, charges and specifications were read, and by the rules of war he had to be shot to death by musketry. The Advocate-General for the prosecution made the opening speech. He read the law in a plain, straightforward manner, and said that for a soldier to go to sleep at his post of duty, while so much depended upon him, was the most culpable of all crimes, and the most inexcusable. I trembled in my boots, for on several occasions I knew I had taken a short nap, even on the very outpost. The Advocate-General went on further to say, that the picket was the sentinel that held the lives of his countrymen and the liberty of his country in his hands, and it mattered not what may have been his record in the past. At one moment he had forfeited his life to his country. For discipline's sake, if for nothing else, you gentlemen that make up this court-martial find the prisoner guilty. It is necessary for you to be firm, gentlemen, for upon your decision depends the safety of our country. When he had finished, thinks I to myself, "Gone up the spout, sure; we will have a first-class funeral here before night."

Well, as to the lawyer who defended him, I cannot now remember his speeches; but he represented a fair-haired boy leaving his home and family, telling his father and aged mother and darling little sister farewell, and spoke of his proud step, though a mere boy, going to defend his country and his loved ones; but at one weak moment, when nature, tasked and taxed beyond the bounds of human endurance, could stand no longer, and upon the still and silent picket post, when the whole army was hushed in slumber, what wonder is it that he, too, may have fallen asleep while at his post of duty.

Some of you gentlemen of this court-martial may have sons, may have brothers; yes, even fathers, in the army. Where are they tonight? You love your children, or your brother or father. This mere youth has a father and mother and sister away back in Tennessee. They are willing to give him to his country. But oh! gentlemen, let the word go back to Tennessee that he died upon the battlefield, and not by the hands of his own comrades for being asleep at his post of duty. I cannot now remember the speeches, but one thing I do know, that he was acquitted, and I was glad of it.

"The Death Watch"

One more scene I can remember. Kind friends—you that know nothing of a soldier's life— I ask you in all candor not to doubt the following lines in this sketch. You have no doubt read of the old Roman soldier found amid the ruins of Pompeii, who had stood there for sixteen hundred years, and when he was excavated was found at his post with his gun clasped in his skeleton hands. You believe this because it is written in history. I have heard politicians tell it. I have heard it told from the sacred desk. It is true; no one doubts it.

Now, were I to tell something that happened in this nineteenth century exactly similar, you would hardly believe it. But whether you believe it or not, it is for you to say. At a little village called Hampshire Crossing, our regiment was ordered to go to a little stream called St. John's Run, to relieve the 14th Georgia Regiment and the 3rd Arkansas. I cannot tell the facts as I desire to. In fact, my hand trembles so, and my feelings are so overcome, that it is hard for me to write at all. But we went to the place that we were ordered to go to, and when we arrived there we found the guard sure enough. If I remember correctly, there were just eleven of them. Some were sitting down and some were laying down; but each and every one was as cold and as hard frozen as the icicles that hung from their hands and faces and clothing—dead! They had died at their post of duty. Two of them, a little in advance of the others, were standing with their guns in their hands, as cold and as hard frozen as a monument of marble—standing sentinel with loaded guns in their frozen hands! The tale is told. Were they true men? Does He who noteth the sparrow's fall, and numbers the hairs of our heads, have any interest in one like ourselves? Yes; He doeth all things well. Not a sparrow falls to the ground without His consent.

Virginia, Farewell

After having served through all the valley campaign, and marched through all the wonders of Northwest Virginia, and being associated with the army of Virginia, it was with sorrow and regret that we bade farewell to "Old Virginia's shore," to go to other fields of blood and carnage and death. We had learned to love Virginia; we love her now. The people were kind and good to us. They divided their last crust of bread and rasher of bacon with us. We loved Lee, we loved Jackson; we loved the name, association and people of Virginia. Hatton, Forbes, Anderson, Gilliam, Govan, Loring, Ashby and Schumaker[48] were names with which we had been long associated. We hated to leave all our old comrades behind us. We felt that we were proving recreant to the instincts of our own manhood, and that we were leaving those who had stood by us on the march and battlefield when they most needed our help. We knew the 7th and 14th Tennessee regiments; we knew the 3rd Arkansas, the 14th Georgia, and 42nd Virginia regiments. Their names were as familiar as household words. We were about to leave the bones of Joe Bynum and Gus Allen and Patrick Hanly. We were about to bid farewell to every tender association that we had formed with the good people of Virginia, and to our old associates among the soldiers of the Grand Army of Virginia. *Virginia, farewell!* Away back yonder, in good old Tennessee, our homes and loved ones are being robbed and insulted, our fields laid waste, our cities sacked, and our people slain. Duty as well as patriotism calls us back to our native home, to try and defend it, as best we can, against an invading army of our then enemies; and, Virginia, once more we bid you a long farewell!

Samuel Watkins

from *Co. Aytch* (1882)

CHAPTER 8: CHATTANOOGA

Back to Chattanooga

Rosecrans' army was in motion. The Federals were advancing, but as yet they were afar off. Chattanooga must be fortified. Well do we remember the hard licks and picks that we spent on these same forts, to be occupied afterwards by Grant and his whole army, and we on Lookout Mountain and Missionary Ridge looking at them.

Am Visited by My Father

About this time my father paid me a visit. Rations were mighty scarce. I was mighty glad to see him, but ashamed to let him know how poorly off for something to eat we were. We were living on parched corn. I thought of a happy plan to get him a good dinner, so I asked him to let us go up to the colonel's tent. Says I, "Colonel Field, I desire to introduce you to my father, and as rations are a little short in my mess, I thought you might have a little better, and could give him a good dinner." "Yes," says Colonel Field, "I am glad to make the acquaintance of your father, and will be glad to divide my rations with him. Also, I would like you to stay and take dinner with me," which I assure you, O kind reader, I gladly accepted. About this time a young African, Whit, came in with a frying-pan of parched corn and dumped it on an old oil cloth, and said, "Master, dinner is ready." That was all he had. He was living like ourselves—on parched corn.

We continued to fortify and build breastworks at Chattanooga. It was the same drudge, drudge day by day. Occasionally a Sunday would come; but when it did come, there came inspection of arms, knapsacks and cartridge-boxes. Every soldier had to have his gun rubbed up as bright as a new silver dollar. W. A. Hughes had the brightest gun in the army, and always called it "Florence Fleming." The private soldier had to have on clean clothes, and if he had lost any cartridges he was charged twenty-five cents each, and had to stand extra duty for every cartridge lost. We always dreaded Sunday. The roll was called more frequently on this than any other day. Sometimes we would have preaching. I remember one text that I thought the bottom had been knocked out long before: "And Peter's wife's mother lay sick of fever."[49] That text always did make a deep impression on me. I always thought of a young divine who preached it when first entering the ministry, and in about twenty years came back, and happening to preach from the same text again, an old fellow in the congregation said, "Mr. Preacher, ain't that old woman dead yet?" Well, that was the text that was preached to us soldiers one Sunday at Chattanooga. I could not help thinking all the time, "Ain't that old woman dead yet?" But he announced that he would preach again at 3 o'clock. We went to hear him preach at 3 o'clock, as his sermon was so interesting about "Peter's wife's mother lay sick of a fever." We thought, maybe it was a sort of sickly subject, and he would liven us up a little in the afternoon service.

Well, he took his text, drawled out through his nose like "small sweetness long drawn out:" "M-a-r-t-h-a, thou art w-e-a-r-i-e-d and troubled about many things, but M-a-r-y hath chosen that good part that shall never be taken from her." Well, you see, O gentle and fair reader, that I remember the text these long gone twenty years. I do not remember what he preached about, but I remember thinking that he was a great ladies' man, at any rate, and whenever I see a man who loves and respects the ladies, I think him a good man.

The next sermon was on the same sort of a text: "And the Lord God caused a deep sleep to fall on Adam and took out of"[50]—he stopped here and said *e* meant out of, that *e*, being translated from the Latin and Greek, meant out of, and took *e*, or rather out of a rib and formed woman. I never did know why he expaciated so largely on *e*; don't understand it yet, but you see, reader mine, that I remember but the little things that happened in that stormy epoch. I remember the *e* part of the sermon more distinctly than all of his profound eruditions of theology, dogmas, creeds and evidences of Christianity, and I only write at this time from memory of things that happened twenty years ago.

"Out A Larking"

At this place, we took Walter Hood out "a larking." The way to go "a larking" is this: Get an empty meal bag and about a dozen men and go to some dark forest or open field on some cold, dark, frosty or rainy night, about five miles from camp. Get someone who does not understand the game to hold the bag in as stooping and cramped a position as is possible, to keep perfectly still and quiet, and when he has got in the right fix, the others to go off to drive in the larks. As soon as they get out of sight, they break in a run and go back to camp, and go to sleep, leaving the poor fellow all the time holding the bag.

Well, Walter was as good and as clever a fellow as you ever saw, was popular with everybody, and as brave and noble a fellow as ever tore a cartridge, or drew a ramrod, or pulled a trigger, but was the kind of a boy that was easily "roped in" to fun or fight or anything that would come up. We all loved him. Poor fellow, he is up yonder—died on the field of glory and honor. He gave his life, 'twas all he had, for his country. Peace to his memory. That night we went "a larking," and Walter held the bag. I did not see him till next morning. While I was gulping down my coffee, as well as laughter, Walter came around, looking sort of sheepish and shy like, and I was trying to look as solemn as a judge. Finally he came up to the fire and kept on eyeing me out of one corner of his eye, and I was afraid to look at him for fear of breaking out in a laugh. When I could hold in no longer, I laughed out, and said, "Well, Walter, what luck last night?" He was very much disgusted, and said, "Humph! you all think that you are smart. I can't see anything to laugh at in such foolishness as that." He said, "Here; I have brought your bag back." That conquered me. After that kind of magnanimous act in forgiving me and bringing my bag back so pleasantly and kindly, I was his friend, and would have fought for him. I felt sorry that we had taken him out "a larking."

Hanging Two Spies

I can now recall to memory but one circumstance that made a deep impression on my mind at the time. I heard that two spies were going to be hung on a certain day, and I went to the hanging. The scaffold was erected, two coffins were placed on the platform, the ropes were dangling from the cross beam above. I had seen men shot, and whipped, and shaved, and branded at Corinth and Tupelo, and one poor fellow named Wright shot at Shelbyville.[51] They had all been horrid scenes to me, but they were Rebels, and like begets like. I did not know when it would be my time to be placed in the same position, you see, and "a fellow feeling makes us wondrous kind." I did not know what was in store in the future for me. Ah, there was the rub, don't you see. This shooting business wasn't a pleasant thing to think about. But Yankees—that was different. I wanted to see a Yankee spy hung. I wouldn't mind that. I would like to see him agonize. A spy; O, yes, they had hung one of our regiment at Pulaski—Sam Davis. Yes, I would see the hanging. After a while I saw a guard approach, and saw two little boys in their midst, but did not see the Yankees that I had been looking for. The two little boys were rushed upon the platform. I saw that they were handcuffed. "Are they spies?" I was appalled; I was horrified; nay, more, I was sick at heart. One was about fourteen and the other about sixteen years old, I should judge. The ropes were promptly adjusted around their necks by the provost marshal. The youngest one began to beg and cry and plead most piteously. It was horrid. The older one kicked him, and told him to stand up and show the Rebels how a Union man could die for his country. Be a man! The charges and specifications were then read. The props were knocked out and the two boys were dangling in the air. I turned off sick at heart.

Eating Rats

While stationed at this place, Chattanooga, rations were very scarce and hard to get, and it was, perhaps, economy on the part of our generals and commissaries to issue rather scant rations.

About this time we learned that Pemberton's army, stationed at Vicksburg, were subsisting entirely on rats. Instead of the idea being horrid, we were glad to know that "necessity is the mother of invention," and that the idea had originated in the mind of genius. We at once acted upon the information, and started out rat hunting; but we couldn't find any rats. Presently we came to an old out-house that seemed to be a natural harbor for this kind of vermin. The house was quickly torn down and out jumped an old residenter, who was old and gray. I suppose that he had been chased before. But we had jumped him and were determined to catch him, or "burst a boiler." After chasing him backwards and forwards, the rat finally got tired of this foolishness and started for his hole. But a rat's tail is the last that goes in the hole, and as he went in we made a grab for his tail. Well, tail hold broke, and we held the skin of his tail in our hands. But we were determined to have that rat. After hard work we caught him. We skinned him, washed and salted him, buttered and peppered him, and fried him. He actually looked nice. The delicate aroma of the frying rat came to our hungry nostrils. We were keen to eat a piece of rat; our teeth were on edge; yea, even our mouth watered to eat a piece of rat. Well, after a while, he was said to be done. I got a piece of cold corn dodger, laid my piece of the rat on it, eat a little piece of bread, and raised the piece of rat to my mouth, when I happened to think of how that rat's tail did slip. I had lost my appetite for dead rat. I did not eat any rat. It was my first and last effort to eat dead rats.

Swimming the Tennessee with Roastingears

The Tennessee river is about a quarter of a mile wide at Chattanooga. Right across the river was an immense corn-field. The green corn was waving with every little breeze that passed; the tassels were bowing and nodding their heads; the pollen was flying across the river like little snowdrops, and everything seemed to say, "Come hither, Johnny Reb; come hither, Johnny; come hither." The river was wide, but we were hungry. The roastingears looked tempting. We pulled off our clothes and launched into the turbid stream, and were soon on the other bank. Here was the field, and here were the roastingears; but where was the raft or canoe?

We thought of old Abraham and Isaac and the sacrifice: "My son, gather the roastingears, there will be a way provided."

We gathered the roastingears; we went back and gathered more roastingears, time and again. The bank was lined with green roastingears. Well, what was to be done? We began to shuck the corn. We would pull up a few shucks on one ear, and tie it to the shucks of another—first one and then another—until we had at least a hundred tied together. We put the train of corn into the river, and as it began to float off we jumped in, and taking the foremost ear in our mouth, struck out for the other bank. Well, we made the landing all correct.

I merely mention the above incident to show to what extremity soldiers would resort. Thousands of such occurrences were performed by the private soldiers of the Rebel army.

Am Detailed to Go Foraging

One day I was detailed to go with a wagon train way down in Georgia on a foraging expedition. It was the first time since I had enlisted as a private that I had struck a good thing. No roll call, no drilling, no fatigue duties, building fortifications, standing picket, dress parade, reviews, or retreats, had to be answered to—the same old monotonous roll call that had been answered five thousand times in these three years. I felt like a free man. The shackles of discipline had for a time been unfettered. This was bliss, this was freedom, this was liberty. The sky looked brighter, the birds sang more beautiful and sweeter than I remember to have ever heard them. Even the little streamlets and branches danced and jumped along the pebbly beds, while the minnows sported and frollicked under the shining ripples. The very flocks and herds in the pasture looked happy and gay. Even the screech of the wagons, that needed greasing, seemed to, send forth a happy sound. It was fine, I tell you.

The blackberries were ripe, and the roadsides were lined with this delicious fruit. The Lord said that he would curse the ground for the disobedience of man, and henceforth it should bring forth thorns and briars; but the very briars that had been cursed were loaded with the abundance of God's goodness. I felt, then, like David in one of his psalms—"The Lord is good, the Lord is good, for his mercy endureth forever."[52]

Please Pass the Butter

For several days the wagon train continued on until we had arrived at the part of country to which we had been directed. Whether they bought or pressed the corn, I know not, but the old gentleman invited us all to take supper with him. If I had ever eaten a better supper than that I have forgotten it. They had biscuit for supper. What! flour bread? Did my eyes deceive me? Well, there were biscuit [sic]—sure enough flour bread—and sugar and coffee—genuine Rio[53]—none of your rye or potato coffee, and butter—regular butter—and ham and eggs, and turnip greens, and potatoes, and fried chicken, and nice clean plates—none of your tin affairs—and a snow-white table-cloth and napkins, and white-handled knives and silver forks. At the head of the table was the madam, having on a pair of golden spectacles, and at the foot the old gentleman. He said grace. And, to cap the climax, two handsome daughters. I know that I had never seen two more beautiful ladies. They had on little white aprons, trimmed with jaconet edging, and collars as clean and white as snow. They looked good enough to eat, and I think at that time I would have given ten years of my life to have kissed one of them. We were invited to help ourselves. Our plates were soon filled with the tempting food and our tumblers with California beer. We would have liked it better had it been twice as strong, but what it lacked in strength we made up in quantity. The old lady said, "Daughter, hand the gentleman the butter." It was the first thing that I had refused, and the reason that I did so was because my plate was full already. Now, there is nothing that will offend a lady so quick as to refuse to take butter when handed to you. If you should say, "No, madam, I never eat butter," it is a direct insult to the lady of the house. Better, far better, for you to have remained at home that day. If you don't eat butter, it is an insult; if you eat too much, she will make your ears burn after you have left. It is a regulator of society; it is a civilizer; it is a luxury and a delicacy that must be touched and handled with care and courtesy on all occasions. Should you desire to get on the good side of a lady, just give a broad, sweeping, slathering compliment to her butter. It beats kissing the dirty-faced baby; it beats anything. Too much praise cannot be bestowed upon the butter, be it good, bad, or indifferent to your notions of things, but to her, her butter is always good, superior, excellent. I did not know this characteristic of the human female at the time, or I would have taken a delicate slice of the butter. Here is a sample of the colloquy that followed:

"Mister, have some butter?"

"Not any at present, thank you, madam."

"Well, I insist upon it; our butter is nice."

"O, I know it's nice, but my plate is full, thank you."

"Well, take some anyhow."

One of the girls spoke up and said:

"Mother, the gentleman don't wish butter."

"Well, I want him to know that our butter is clean, anyhow."

"Well, madam, if you insist upon it, there is nothing that I love so well as warm biscuit and butter. I'll thank you for the butter."

I dive in. I go in a little too heavy. The old lady hints in a delicate way that they sold butter. I dive in heavier. That cake of butter was melting like snow in a red hot furnace. The old lady says, "We sell butter to the soldiers at a mighty good price."

I dive in afresh. She says, "I get a dollar a pound for that butter," and I remark with a good deal of nonchalance, "Well, madam, it is worth it," and dive in again. I did not marry one of the girls.

We Evacuate Chattanooga

One morning while sitting around our camp fires we heard a boom, and a bomb shell passed over our heads. The Yankee army was right on the other bank of the Tennessee river. Bragg did not know of their approach until the cannon fired.

Rosecrans' army is crossing the Tennessee river. A part are already on Lookout Mountain. Some of their cavalry scouts had captured some of our foraging parties in Wills valley. The air was full of flying rumors. Wagons are being packed, camps are broken up, and there is a general hubbub everywhere. But your old soldier is always ready at a moment's notice. The assembly is sounded; form companies, and we are ready for a march, or a fight, or a detail, or anything. If we are marched a thousand miles or twenty yards, it is all the same. The private soldier is a machine that has no right to know anything. He is a machine that moves without any volition of his own. If Edison could invent a wooden man that could walk and load and shoot, then you would have a good sample of the private soldier, and it would have this advantage—the private soldier eats and the wooden man would not.

We left Chattanooga, but whither bound we knew not, and cared not; but we marched toward Chickamauga and crossed at Lee & Gordon's mill.

The Bull of the Woods

On our way to Lafayette from Lee & Gordon's mill, I remember a ludicrous scene, almost bordering on sacrilege. Rosecrans' army was very near us, and we expected before three days elapsed to be engaged in battle. In fact, we knew there must be a fight or a foot race, one or the other. We could smell, as it were, "the battle afar off."

One Sabbath morning it was announced that an eloquent and able LL. D., from Nashville, was going to preach, and as the occasion was an exceedingly solemn one, we were anxious to hear this divine preach from God's Holy Word; and as he was one of the "big ones," the whole army was formed in close column and stacked their arms. The cannon were parked, all pointing back toward Chattanooga. The scene looked weird and picturesque. It was in a dark wilderness of woods and vines and overhanging limbs. In fact, it seemed but the home of the owl and the bat, and other varmints that turn night into day. Every-thing looked solemn. The trees looked solemn, the scene looked solemn, the men looked solemn, even the horses looked solemn. You may be sure, reader, that we felt solemn.

The reverend LL. D. had prepared a regular war sermon before he left home, and of course had to preach it, appropriate or not appropriate; it was in him and had to come out. He opened the service with a song. I did remember the piece that was sung, but right now I cannot recall it to memory; but as near as I can now recollect here is his prayer, *verbatim et literatim*:

"Oh, Thou immaculate, invisible, eternal and holy Being, the exudations of whose effulgence illuminates this terrestrial sphere, we approach Thy presence, being covered all over with wounds and bruises and putrifying sores, from our heads to the soles of our feet. And Thou, O Lord, art our dernier resort. The whole world is one great machine, managed by Thy puissance. The beautific splendors of Thy face irradiate the celestial region and felicitate the saints. There are the most exuberant profusions of Thy grace, and the sempiternal efflux of Thy glory. God is an abyss of light, a circle whose center is everywhere and His circumference nowhere. Hell is the dark world made up of spiritual sulphur and other ignited ingredients, disunited and unharmonized, and without that pure balsamic oil that flows from the heart of God."

When the old fellow got this far, I lost the further run of his prayer, but regret very much that I did so, because it was so grand and fine that I would have liked very much to have kept such an appropriate prayer for posterity. In fact, it lays it on heavy over any prayer I ever heard, and I think the new translators ought to get it and have it put in their book as a sample prayer. But they will have to get the balance of it from the eminent LL. D. In fact, he was so "high larnt" that I don't think anyone understood him but the generals. The colonels might every now and then have understood a word, and maybe a few of the captains and lieutenants, because Lieutenant Lansdown told me he understood every word the preacher said, and further informed me that it was none of your one-horse, old-fashioned country prayers that privates knew anything about, but was bang-up, first-rate, orthodox.

Well, after singing and praying, he took his text. I quote entirely from memory. "Blessed be the Lord God, who teaches my hands to war and my fingers to fight."[54] Now, reader, that was the very subject we boys did not want to hear preached on—on that occasion at least. We felt like some other subject would have suited us better. I forget how he commenced his sermon, but I remember that after he got warmed up a little, he began to pitch in on the Yankee nation, and gave them particular fits as to their geneology. [sic] He said that we of the South had descended from the royal and aristocratic blood of the Huguenots of France, and of the cavaliers of England, etc.; but that the Yankees were the descendants of the crop-eared Puritans and witch burners, who came over in the Mayflower, and settled at Plymouth Rock. He was warm on this subject, and waked up the echoes of the forest. He said that he and his brethren would fight the Yankees in this world, and if God permit, chase their frightened ghosts in the next, through fire and brimstone.

About this time we heard the awfullest racket, produced by some wild animal tearing through the woods toward us, and the cry, "Look out! look out! hooie! hooie! hooie! look out!" and there came running right through our midst a wild bull, mad with terror and fright, running right over and knocking down the divine, and scattering Bibles and hymn books in every direction. The services were brought to a close without the doxology.

This same brave chaplain rode along with our brigade, on an old string-haltered horse, as we advanced to the attack at Chickamauga, exhorting the boys to be brave, to aim low, and to kill the Yankees as if they were wild beasts. He was eloquent and patriotic. He stated that if he only had a gun he too would go along as a private soldier. You could hear his voice echo and re-echo over the hills. He had worked up his patriotism to a pitch of genuine bravery and daring that I had never seen exhibited, when fliff, fluff, fluff, *fluff*, FLUFF, *FLUFF*—a whir, a BOOM! and a shell screams through the air. The reverend LL. D. stops to listen, like an old sow when she hears the wind, and says, "Remember, boys, that he who is killed will sup tonight in Paradise." Some soldier hallooed at the top of his voice, "Well, parson, you come along and take supper with us." Boom! whir! a bomb burst, and the parson at that moment put spurs to his horse and was seen to limber to the rear, and almost every soldier yelled out, "The parson isn't hungry, and never eats supper." I remember this incident, and so does every member of the First Tennessee Regiment.

Presentment, or the Wing of the Angel of Death

Presentment is always a mystery. The soldier may at one moment be in good spirits, laughing and talking. The wing of the death angel touches him. He knows that his time has come. It is but a question of time with him then. He knows that his days are numbered. I cannot explain it. God has numbered the hairs of our heads, and not a sparrow falls without His knowledge. How much more valuable are we than many sparrows?

We had stopped at Lee & Gordon's mill, and gone into camp for the night. Three days' rations were being issued. When Bob Stout was given his rations he refused to take them. His face wore a serious, woe-begone expression. He was asked if he was sick, and said "No," but added, "Boys, my days are numbered, my time has come. In three days from to-day, I will be lying right yonder on that hillside a corpse. Ah, you may laugh; my time has come. I've got a twenty dollar gold piece in my pocket that I've carried through the war, and a silver watch that my father sent me through the lines. Please take them off when I am dead, and give them to Captain Irvine, to give to my father when he gets back home. Here are my clothing and blanket that any one who wishes them may have. My rations I do not wish at all. My gun and cartridge-box I expect to die with."

The next morning the assembly sounded about two o'clock. We commenced our march in the darkness, and marched twenty-five miles to a little town by the name of La-fayette, to the relief of General Pillow, whose command had been attacked at that place.[55] After accomplishing this, we marched back by another road to Chickamauga. We camped on the banks of Chickamauga on Friday night, and Saturday morning we commenced to cross over. About twelve o'clock we had crossed. No sooner had we crossed than an order came to double quick. General Forrest's cavalry had opened the battle. Even then the spent balls were falling amongst us with that peculiar thud so familiar to your old soldier.

Double quick! There seemed to be no rest for us. Forrest is needing reinforcements. Double quick, close up in the rear! siz, siz, double quick, boom, hurry up, bang, bang, a rattle de bang, bang, siz, boom, boom, boom; hurry up, double quick, boom, bang, halt, front, right dress, boom, boom, and three soldiers are killed and twenty wounded. Billy Webster's arm was torn out by the roots and he killed, and a fragment of shell buried itself in Jim McEwin's side, also killing Mr. Fain King, a conscript from Mount Pleasant. For-ward, guide center, march, charge bayonets, fire at will, commence firing. (This is where the LL. D. ran.) We debouched through the woods, firing as we marched, the Yankee line about two hundred yards off. Bang, bang, siz, siz. It was a sort of running fire. We kept up a constant fire as we advanced. In ten minutes we were face to face with the foe. It was but a question as to who could load and shoot the fastest. The army was not up. Bragg was not ready for a general battle. The big battle was fought the next day, Sunday. We held our position for two hours and ten minutes in the midst of a deadly and galling fire, being enfiladed and almost surrounded, when General Forrest galloped up and said, "Colonel Field, look out, you are almost surrounded; you had better fall back." The order was given to retreat. I ran through a solid line of blue coats. As I fell back, they were upon the right of us, they were upon the left of us, they were in front of us, they were in the rear of us. It was a perfect hornets' nest. The balls whistled around our ears like the escape valves of ten thousand engines. The woods seemed to be blazing; everywhere, at every jump, would rise a lurking foe. But to get up and dust was all we could do. I was running along by the side of Bob Stout. General Preston Smith stopped me and asked if our brigade was falling back. I told him it was. He asked me the second time if it was Maney's brigade that was falling back. I told him it was. I heard him call out, "Attention, forward!" One solid sheet of leaden hail was falling around me. I heard General Preston Smith's brigade open. It seemed to be platoons of artillery. The earth jarred and trembled like an earthquake. Deadly missiles were flying in every direction. It was the very incarnation of death itself. I could almost hear the shriek of the death angel passing over the scene. General Smith was killed in ten minutes after I saw him. Bob Stout and myself stopped. Said I, "Bob, you weren't killed, as you expected." He did not reply, for at that very moment a solid shot from the Federal guns struck him between the waist and the hip, tearing off one leg and scattering his bowels all over the ground. I heard him shriek out, "O, O, God!" His spirit had flown before his body struck the ground. Farewell, friend; we will meet over yonder.

When the cannon ball struck Billy Webster, tearing his arm out of the socket, he did not die immediately, but as we were advancing to the attack, we left him and the others lying where they fell upon the battlefield; but when we fell back to the place where we had left our knapsacks, Billy's arm had been dressed by Dr. Buist, and he seemed to be quite easy. He asked Jim Fogey to please write a letter to his parents at home. He wished to dictate the letter. He asked me to please look in his knapsack and get him a clean shirt, and said that he thought he would feel better if he could get rid of the blood that was upon him. I went to hunt for his knapsack and found it, but when I got back to where he was, poor, good Billy Webster was dead. He had given his life to his country. His spirit is with the good and brave. No better or braver man than Billy Webster ever drew the breath of life. His bones lie yonder today, upon the battlefield of Chickamauga. I loved him; he was my friend. Many and many a dark night have Billy and I stood together upon the silent picket post. Ah, reader, my heart grows sick and I feel sad while I try to write my recollections of that unholy and uncalled for war. But He that ruleth the heavens doeth all things well.

Samuel Watkins

from *Co. Aytch* (1882)

CHAPTER 17: THE SURRENDER

The Last Act of the Drama

On the 10th day of May, 1861, our regiment, the First Tennessee, left Nashville for the camp of instruction, with twelve hundred and fifty men, officers and line. Other recruits continually coming in swelled this number to fourteen hundred. In addition to this Major Fulcher's battalion of four companies, with four hundred men (originally), was afterwards attached to the regiment; and the Twenty-seventh Tennessee Regiment was afterwards consolidated with the First. And besides this, there were about two hundred conscripts added to the regiment from time to time. To recapitulate: The First Tennessee, numbering originally, 1,250; recruited from time to time, 150; Fulcher's battalion, 400; the Twenty-seventh Tennessee, 1,200; number of conscripts (at the lowest estimate), 200—making the sum total 3,200 men that belonged to our regiment during the war. The above I think a low estimate. Well, on the 26th day of April, 1865, General Joe E. Johnston surrendered his army at Greensboro, North Carolina. The day that we surrendered our regiment it was a pitiful sight to behold. If I remember correctly, there were just sixty-five men in all, including officers, that were paroled on that day. Now, what became of the original 3,200? A grand army, you may say. Three thousand two hundred men! Only sixty-five left! Now, reader, you may draw your own conclusions. It lacked just four days of four years from the day we were sworn in to the day of the surrender, and it was just four years and twenty-four days from the time that we left home for the army to the time that we got back again. It was indeed a sad sight to look at, the Old First Tennessee Regiment. A mere squad of noble and brave men, gathered around the tattered flag that they had followed in every battle through that long war. It was so bullet-riddled and torn that it was but a few blue and red shreds that hung drooping while it, too, was stacked with our guns forever.

Thermopylae[56] had one messenger of defeat, but when General Joe E. Johnston surrendered the Army of the South there were hundreds of regiments, yea, I might safely say thousands, that had not a representative on the 26th day of April, 1865.

Our cause was lost from the beginning. Our greatest victories—Chickamauga and Franklin—were our greatest defeats. Our people were divided upon the question of Union and secession. Our generals were scrambling for "*Who ranked.*" The private soldier fought and starved and died for naught. Our hospitals were crowded with sick and wounded, but half provided with food and clothing to sustain life. Our money was depreciated to naught and our cause lost. We left our homes four years previous. Amid the waving of flags and handkerchiefs and the smiles of the ladies, while the fife and drum were playing Dixie and the Bonnie Blue Flag, we bid farewell to home and friends. The.bones of our brave Southern boys lie scattered over our loved South. They fought for their "*country,*" and gave their lives freely for that country's cause; and now they who survive sit, like Marius amid the wreck of Carthage, sublime even in ruins.[57] Other pens abler than mine will have to chronicle their glorious deeds of valor and devotion. In these sketches I have named but a few persons who fought side by side with me during that long and unholy war. In looking back over these pages, I ask, Where now are many whose names have appeared in these sketches? They are up yonder, and are no doubt waiting and watching for those of us who are left behind. And, my kind reader, the time is coming when we, too, will be called, while the archangel of death is beating the long roll of eternity, and with us it will be the last reveille. God Himself will sound the "assembly" on yonder beautiful and happy shore, where we will again have a grand "reconfederation." We shed a tear over their flower-strewn graves. We live after them. We love their memory yet. But one generation passes away and another generation follows. We know our loved and brave soldiers. We love them yet.

But when we pass away, the impartial historian will render a true verdict, and a history will then be written in justification and vindication of those brave and noble boys who gave their all in fighting the battles of their homes, their country, and their God.

"The United States has no North, no South, no East, no West." "*We are one and undivided.*"

Adieu

My kind friends—soldiers, comrades, brothers, all: The curtain is rung down, the footlights are put out, the audience has all left and gone home, the seats are vacant, and the cold walls are silent. The gaudy tinsel that appears before the footlights is exchanged for the dress of the citizen. Coming generations and historians will be the critics as to how we have acted our parts. The past is buried in oblivion. The blood-red flag, with its crescent and cross, that we followed for four long, bloody, and disastrous years, has been folded never again to be unfurled. We have no regrets for what we did, but we mourn the loss of so many brave and gallant men who perished on the field of battle and honor. I now bid you an affectionate adieu.

But in closing these memoirs, the scenes of my life pass in rapid review before me. In imagination, I am young again tonight. I feel the flush and vigor of my manhood—am just twenty-one years of age. I hear the fife and drum playing Dixie and- Bonnie Blue Flag. I see and hear our fire-eating stump-orators tell of the right of secession and disunion. I see our fair and beautiful women waving their handkerchiefs and encouraging their sweethearts to go to the war. I see the marshaling of the hosts for "glorious war." I see the fine banners waving and hear the cry everywhere, "*To arms! to arms!*" And I also see our country at peace and prosperous, our fine cities look grand and gay, our fields rich in abundant harvests, our people happy and contented. All these pass in imagination before me. Then I look and see glorious war in all its splendor. I hear the shout and charge, the boom of artillery and the rattle of small arms. I see gaily-dressed officers charging backwards and forwards upon their mettled war horses, clothed in the panoply of war. I see victory and conquest upon flying banners. I see our arms triumph in every battle. And, O, my friends, I see another scene. I see broken homes and broken hearts. I see war in all of its desolation. I see a country ruined and impoverished. I see a nation disfranchised and maltreated. I see a commonwealth forced to pay dishonest and fraudulent bonds that were issued to crush that people.[58] I see sycophants licking the boots of the country's oppressor. I see other and many wrongs perpetrated upon a conquered people. But maybe it is but the ghosts and phantoms of a dreamy mind, or the wind as it whistles around our lonely cabin-home. The past is buried in oblivion. The mantle of charity has long ago fallen upon those who think differently from us. We remember no longer wrongs and injustice done us by anyone on earth. We are willing to forget and forgive those who have wronged and falsified us. We look up above and beyond all these petty groveling things and shake hands and forget the past. And while my imagination is like the weaver's shuttle, playing backward and forward through these two decades of time, I ask myself, Are these things real? did they happen? are they being enacted today? or are they the fancies of the imagination in forgetful reverie? Is it true that I have seen all these things? that they are real incidents in my life's history? Did I see those brave and noble countrymen of mine laid low in death and weltering in their blood? Did I see our country laid waste and in ruins? Did I see soldiers marching, the earth trembling and jarring beneath their measured tread? Did I see the ruins of smouldering cities and deserted homes? Did I see my comrades buried and see the violet and wild flowers bloom over their graves? Did I see the flag of my country, that I had followed so long, furled to be no more unfurled forever? Surely they are but the vagaries of mine own imagination. Surely my fancies are running wild tonight. But, hush! I now hear the approach of battle. That low, rumbling sound in the west is the roar of cannon in the distance. That rushing sound is the tread of soldiers. That quick, lurid glare is the flash that precedes the cannon's roar. And listen! that loud report that makes the earth tremble and jar and sway, is but the bursting of a shell, as it screams through the dark, tempestuous night. That black, ebon cloud, where the lurid lightning flickers and flares, that is rolling through the heavens, is the smoke of battle; beneath is being enacted a carnage of blood and death. Listen! the soldiers are charging now. The flashes and roaring now are blended with the shouts of soldiers and confusion of battle.

But, reader, time has brought his changes since I, a young, ardent, and impetuous youth, burning with a lofty patriotism first shouldered my musket to defend the rights of my country.

Lifting the veil of the past, I see many manly forms, bright in youth and hope, standing in view by my side in Company H, First Tennessee Regiment. Again I look and half those forms are gone. Again, and gray locks and wrinkled faces and clouded brows stand before me.

Before me, too, I see, not in imagination, but in reality, my own loved Jennie, the partner of my joys and the sharer of my sorrows, sustaining, comforting, and cheering my pathway by her benignant smile; pouring the sunshine of domestic comfort and happiness upon our humble home; making life more worth the living as we toil on up the hill of time together, with the bright pledges of our early and constant love by our side while the sunlight of hope ever brightens our pathway, dispelling darkness and sorrow as we hand in hand approach the valley of the great shadow.

The tale is told. The world moves on, the sun shines as brightly as before, the flowers bloom as beautifully, the birds sing their carols as sweetly, the trees nod and bow their leafy tops as if slumbering in the breeze, the gentle winds fan our brow and kiss our cheek as they pass by, the pale moon sheds her silvery sheen, the blue dome of the sky sparkles with the trembling stars that twinkle and shine and make night beautiful, and the scene melts and gradually disappears forever.

Stephen Crane

from *The Little Regiment, and Other Episodes of the American Civil War* (1896)

THE VETERAN

Out of the low window could be seen three hickory trees placed irregularly in a meadow that was resplendent in springtime green. Further away, the old, dismal belfry of the village church loomed over the pines. A horse meditating in the shade of one of the hickories lazily swished his tail. The warm sunshine made an oblong of vivid yellow on the floor of the grocery.

"Could you see the whites of their eyes?" said the man who was seated on a soap-box.

"Nothing of the kind," replied old Henry warmly. "Just a lot of flitting figures, and I let go at where they 'peared to be the thickest. Bang!"

"Mr. Fleming," said the grocer—his deferential voice expressed somehow the old man's exact social weight—"Mr. Fleming, you never was frightened much in them battles, was you?"

The veteran looked down and grinned. Observing his manner the entire group tittered. "Well, I guess I was," he answered finally. "Pretty well scared, sometimes. Why, in my first battle I thought the sky was falling down. I thought the world was coming to an end. You bet I was scared."

Every one laughed. Perhaps it seemed strange and rather wonderful to them that a man should admit the thing, and in the tone of their laughter there was probably more admiration than if old Fleming had declared that he had always been a lion. Moreover, they knew that he had ranked as an orderly sergeant, and so their opinion of his heroism was fixed. None, to be sure, knew how an orderly sergeant ranked, but then it was understood to be somewhere just shy of a major-general's stars. So when old Henry admitted that he had been frightened, there was a laugh.

"The trouble was," said the old man, "I thought they were all shooting at me. Yes, sir. I thought every man in the other army was aiming at me in particular, and only me. And it seemed so darned unreasonable, you know. I wanted to explain to 'em what an almighty good fellow I was, because I thought then they might quit all trying to hit me. But I couldn't explain, and they kept on being unreasonable—blim!—blam!—bang! So I run!"

Two little triangles of wrinkles appeared at the corners of his eyes. Evidently he appreciated some comedy in this recital. Down near his feet, however, little Jim, his grandson, was visibly horror-stricken. His hands were clasped nervously, and his eyes were wide with astonishment at this terrible scandal, his most magnificent grandfather telling such a thing.

"That was at Chancellorsville. Of course, afterward I got kind of used to it. A man does. Lots of men, though, seem to feel all right from the start. I did, as soon as I 'got on to it,' as they say now; but at first I was pretty flustered. Now, there was young Jim Conklin, old Si Conklin's son—that used to keep the tannery—you none of you recollect him—well, he went into it from the start just as if he was born to it. But with me it was different. I had to get used to it."

When little Jim walked with his grandfather he was in the habit of skipping along on the stone pavement in front of the three stores and the hotel of the town and betting that he could avoid the cracks. But upon this day he walked soberly, with his hand gripping two of his grandfather's fingers. Sometimes he kicked abstractedly at dandelions that curved over the walk. Any one could see that he was much troubled.

"There's Sickles's colt over in the medder, Jimmie," said the old man. "Don't you wish you owned one like him?"

"Um," said the boy, with a strange lack of interest. He continued his reflections. Then finally he ventured, "Grandpa—now—was that true what you was telling those men?"

"What?" asked the grandfather. "What was I telling them?"

"Oh, about your running."

"Why, yes, that was true enough, Jimmie. It was my first fight, and there was an awful lot of noise, you know."

Jimmie seemed dazed that this idol, of its own will, should so totter. His stout boyish idealism was injured.

Presently the grandfather said: "Sickles's colt is going for a drink. Don't you wish you owned Sickles's colt, Jimmie?"

The boy merely answered, "He ain't as nice as our'n." He lapsed then to another moody silence.

* * * *

One of the hired men, a Swede, desired to drive to the county seat for purposes of his own. The old man loaned a horse and an unwashed buggy. It appeared later that one of the purposes of the Swede was to get drunk.

After quelling some boisterous frolic of the farm-hands and boys in the garret, the old man had that night gone peacefully to sleep, when he was aroused by clamouring at the kitchen door. He grabbed his trousers, and they waved out behind as he dashed forward. He could hear the voice of the Swede, screaming and blubbering. He pushed the wooden button, and, as the door flew open, the Swede, a maniac, stumbled inward, chattering, weeping, still screaming: "De barn fire! Fire! Fire! De barn fire! Fire! Fire! Fire!"

There was a swift and indescribable change in the old man. His face ceased instantly to be a face; it became a mask, a gray thing, with horror written about the mouth and eyes. He hoarsely shouted at the foot of the little rickety stairs, and immediately, it seemed, there came down an avalanche of men. No one knew that during this time the old lady had been standing in her night clothes at the bed room door, yelling: "What's th' matter? What's th' matter? What's th' matter?"

When they dashed toward the barn it presented to their eyes its usual appearance, solemn, rather mystic in the black night. The Swede's lantern was overturned at a point some yards in front of the barn doors. It contained a wild little conflagration of its own, and even in their excitement some of those who ran felt a gentle secondary vibration of the thrifty part of their minds at sight of this overturned lantern. Under ordinary circumstances it would have been a calamity.

But the cattle in the barn were trampling, trampling, trampling, and above this noise could be heard a humming like the song of innumerable bees.[59] The old man hurled aside the great doors, and a yellow flame leaped out at one corner and sped and wavered frantically up the old grey wall. It was glad, terrible, this single flame, like the wild banner of deadly and triumphant foes.

The motley crowd from the garret had come with all the pails of the farm. They flung themselves upon the well. It was a leisurely old machine, long dwelling in indolence. It was in the habit of giving out water with a sort of reluctance. The men stormed at it, cursed it; but it continued to allow the buckets to be filled only after the wheezy windlass had howled many protests at the mad-handed men.

With his opened knife in his hand old Fleming himself had gone headlong into the barn, where the stifling smoke swirled with the air-currents, and where could be heard in its fulness the terrible chorus of the flames, laden with tones of hate and death, a hymn of wonderful ferocity.

He flung a blanket over an old mare's head, cut the halter close to the manger, led the mare to the door, and fairly kicked her out to safety. He returned with the same blanket, and rescued one of the work-horses. He took five horses out, and then came out himself, with his clothes bravely on fire. He had no whiskers, and very little hair on his head. They soused five pailfuls of water on him. His eldest son made a clean miss with the sixth pail-ful, because the old man had turned and was running down the decline and around to the basement of the barn, where were the stanchions of the cows. Some one noticed at the time that he ran very lamely, as if one of the frenzied horses had smashed his hip.

The cows, with their heads held in the heavy stanchions, had thrown themselves, strangled themselves, tangled themselves: done everything which the ingenuity of their exuberant fear could suggest to them.

Here, as at the well, the same thing happened to every man save one. Their hands went mad. They became incapable of everything save the power to rush into dangerous situations.

The old man released the cow nearest the door, and she, blind drunk with terror, crashed into the Swede. The Swede had been running to and fro babbling. He carried an empty milk-pail, to which he clung with an unconscious, fierce enthusiasm. He shrieked like one lost as he went under the cow's hoofs, and the milk-pail, rolling across the floor, made a flash of silver in the gloom.

Old Fleming took a fork, beat off the cow, and dragged the paralyzed Swede to the open air. When they had rescued all the cows save one, which had so fastened herself that she could not be moved an inch, they returned to the front of the barn and stood sadly, breathing like men who had reached the final point of human effort.

Many people had come running. Someone had even gone to the church, and now, from the distance, rang the tocsin note of the old bell. There was a long flare of crimson on the sky, which made remote people speculate as to the whereabouts of the fire.

The long flames sang their drumming chorus in voices of the heaviest bass. The wind whirled clouds of smoke and cinders into the faces of the spectators. The form of the old barn was outlined in black amid these masses of orange-hued flames.

And then came this Swede again, crying as one who is the weapon of the sinister fates. "De colts! De colts! You have forgot de colts!"

Old Fleming staggered. It was true; they had forgotten the two colts in the box stalls at the back of the barn. "Boys," he said, "I must try to get 'em out." They clamored about him then, afraid for him, afraid of what they should see. Then they talked wildly each to each. "Why, it's sure death!" "He would never get out!" "Why, it's suicide for a man to go in there!" Old Fleming stared absent-mindedly at the open doors. "The poor little things!" he said. He rushed into the barn.

When the roof fell in, a great funnel of smoke swarmed toward the sky, as if the old man's mighty spirit, released from its body—a little bottle—had swelled like the genie of fable. The smoke was tinted rose-hue from the flames, and perhaps the unutterable midnights of the universe will have no power to daunt the colour of this soul.

Stephen Crane

from *War Is Kind* (1896)

WAR IS KIND

Do not weep, maiden, for war is kind.
Because your lover threw wild hands toward the sky
And the affrighted steed ran on alone,
Do not weep.
War is kind.

Hoarse, booming drums of the regiment,
Little souls who thirst for fight,
These men were born to drill and die.
The unexplained glory flies above them,
Great is the battle-god, great, and his kingdom—
A field where a thousand corpses lie.

Do not weep, babe, for war is kind.
Because your father tumbled in the yellow trenches,
Raged at his breast, gulped and died,
Do not weep.
War is kind.

Swift blazing flag of the regiment,
Eagle with crest of red and gold,
These men were born to drill and die.
Point for them the virtue of slaughter,
Make plain to them the excellence of killing
And a field where a thousand corpses lie.

Mother whose heart hung humble as a button
On the bright splendid shroud of your son,
Do not weep.
War is kind.

Stephen Crane

THE BATTLE HYMN (n.d.)

All-feeling God, hear in the war-night
The rolling voices of a nation;
Through dusky billows of darkness
See the flash, the under-light, of bared swords—
—Whirling gleams like wee shells
Deep in the streams of the universe—
Bend and see a people, O, God,
A people rebuked, accursed,
By him of the many lungs
And by him of the bruised weary war-drum
(The chanting disintegrate and the two-faced eagle)
Bend and mark our steps, O, God.
Mark well, mark well, Father of the Never-Ending Circles
And if the path, the new path, lead awry
Then in the forest of the lost standards
Suffer us to grope and bleed apace
For the wisdom is Thine.
Bend and see a people, O, God,
A people applauded, acclaimed,
By him of the raw red shoulders
The manacle-marked, the thin victim
(He lies white amid the smoking cane)
—And if the path, the new path, leads straight—
Then—O, God—then bare the great bronze arm;
Swing high the blaze of the chained stars
And let them look and heed
(The chanting disintegrate and the two-faced eagle)
For we go, we go in a lunge of a long blue corps
And—to Thee we commit our lifeless sons,
The convulsed and furious dead.
(They shall be white amid the smoking cane)
For, the seas shall not bar us;
The capped mountains shall not hold us back
We shall sweep and swarm through jungle and pool,
Then let the savage one bend his high chin
To see on his breast, the sullen glow of the death-medals
For we know and we say our gift.
His prize is death, deep doom.
(He shall be white amid the smoking cane.)

Emily Dickinson

My Triumph lasted till the Drums
Had left the Dead alone
And then I dropped my Victory
And chastened stole along
To where the finished Faces
Conclusion turned on me
And then I hated Glory
And wished myself were They.

What is to be is best descried
When it has also been —
Could Prospect taste of Retrospect
The tyrannies of Men
Were Tenderer — diviner
The Transitive toward —
A Bayonet's contrition
Is nothing to the Dead —

—1871

'Tis Seasons since the Dimpled War
In which we each were Conqueror
And each of us were slain
And Centuries 'twill be and more
Another Massacre before
So modest and so vain —
Without a Formula we fought
Each was to each the Pink Redoubt —

—1881

THE TEXTS

Abraham Lincoln, Second Inaugural Address. Source: *Complete Works of Abraham Lincoln, Comprising his Speeches, Letters, State Papers, and Miscellaneous Writings*, ed. John G. Nicolay and John Hay. Vol. 2 (New York: The Century Company, 1920).

John Wilkes Booth, letters and diary entries. Source: *"Right or Wrong, God Judge Me": The Writings of John Wilkes Booth*, ed. John Rhodehamel and Louise Taper (Urbana: University of Illinois Press, 1997). Editorial note for "To Mary Ann Holmes Booth": "Autograph letter signed, National Archives." Editorial note for "To the Editors of the National Intelligencer": "Text of letter written and destroyed on 14 April 1865, reconstructed from memory by John Matthews with the help of Philadelphia journalist Frank A. Burr, and published in the *Washington Evening Star* on 7 December 1881." This letter generally follows Booth's less readable April 14 "To Whom It May Concern" letter, which was left with his sister Asia Booth Clarke and published in the 19 April 1865 edition of the Philadelphia *Inquirer*. Editorial note for Booth's diary entries: "Autograph manuscript, National Park Service, Lincoln Museum at Ford's Theatre, Washington, D.C.; transcription from William Hanchett, 'Booth's Diary,' Journal of the Illinois State Historical Society 72 (Feb. 1979): 39–56." Italics have been removed.

Walt Whitman, "When Lilacs Last in the Door-Yard Bloom'd." Source: *Sequel to Drum-Taps: When Lilacs Last in the Door-Yard Bloom'd, and Other Pieces* (Washington, s.n., 1865–66). When Whitman revised this poem for inclusion in *Leaves of Grass*, he reduced the number of exclamation points, capitalized the word "death" less frequently, made substantive additions and deletions, and renumbered the poem's sections.

Walt Whitman, "The Veteran's Vision." Source: *Walt Whitman's Drum-Taps* (New York, s.n., 1865). In *Leaves of Grass*, Whitman retitled this poem "The Artilleryman's Vision."

Walt Whitman, "The Million Dead, Too, Summ'd Up" and "The Real War Will Never Get in the Books." Source: *Specimen Days and Collect* (Philadelphia: D. McKay, 1882–83).

Edward A. Pollard, from *The Lost Cause*. Source: *The Lost Cause; A New Southern History of the War of the Confederates. Comprising a full and authhentic account of the rise and progress of the late Southern confederacy. . . .* (New York: E. B. Treat & Co., 1867).

Frances Miles Finch, "The Blue and the Gray." Source: *The Atlantic Monthly*, vol. 20, no. 119 (Sept. 1867), pp. 369–370. The *Atlantic Monthly* version is accompanied by the following text, attributed to the New York *Tribune*: "The women of Columbus, Mississippi, animated by nobler sentiments than are many of their sisters, have shown themselves impartial in their offerings made to the memory of the dead. They strewed flowers alike on the graves of the Confederate and of the National soldiers."

Herman Melville, selections from *Battle-Pieces and Aspects of the War*. Source: *The Works of Herman Melville*. Vol. 16 (London: Constable and Company Ltd., 1924). Originally published in *Battle-Pieces and Aspects of the War* (New York: Harper & Bros., 1866).

Frederick Douglass, "Address at the Graves of the Unknown Dead." Source: The Frederick Douglass Papers at the Library of Congress.

Oliver Wendell Holmes, Jr., "The Soldier's Faith." Source: *The Occasional Speeches of Justice Oliver Wendell Holmes*, ed. Mark DeWolfe Howe (Cambridge: Harvard University Press, 1962).

D. B. Lucas, "In the Land Where We Were Dreaming." Source: *War Poetry of the South*, ed. William Gilmore Simms (New York: Richardson & Company, 1866).

Ambrose Bierce, "A Bivouac of the Dead." Source: *Collected Works of Ambrose Bierce*. Vol. 11 ("Antepenultimata") (New York: Neale Publishing Co., 1912).

Albion Tourgée, "The South as a Field for Fiction." Source: *The Forum*, vol. 6 (Dec. 1888), pp. 404–413.

Jefferson Davis, "Speech before Mississippi Legislature." Source: *Jefferson Davis: The Essential Writings*, ed. William J. Cooper, Jr. (New York: The Modern Library, 2003).

Sidney Lanier, selected poems. Source: *Poems of Sidney Lanier, Edited by His Wife*, ed. Mary D. Lanier (New York: Charles Scribner's Sons, 1884). "Resurrection" and "Laughter in the Senate" were originally published in the newspaper *The Round Table* in 1868. Mary Lanier includes "Dying Words of Stonewall Jackson" under the section "Unrevised Early Poems."

Sarah Morgan Piatt, selected poems. Source: *Palace-Burner: The Selected Poetry of Sarah Piatt*, ed. Paula Bernat Bennett (Urbana: University of Illinois Press, 2001). First publications: "Army of Occupation" in *Harper's Weekly* (1866); "The Grave at Frankfort" in *The Capital* (1872); "Another War" in *The Capital* (1872); "Over in Kentucky" in *The Independent* (1872).

Lizette Woodworth Reese, "A War Memory." Source: *Spicewood* (Baltimore: The Norman, Remington Co., 1920).

Joel Chandler Harris, "A Story of the War." Source: *Uncle Remus: His Songs and Sayings*, new and rev. ed. (New York: D. Appleton & Co., 1898; orig. 1880). Originally published as "Uncle Remus as a Rebel: How He Saved His Young Master's Life" in the Atlanta *Constitution* (Oct. 14 1877).

Sam R. Watkins, from *Co. Aytch*. Source: *"Co. Aytch": A Confederate Memoir of the Civil War*, ed. Roy P. Basler (New York: Simon & Schuster, 2003; 1990, 1962). Originally serialized in the Columbia (Tenn.) *Herald*, 1881–1882.

First published as *1861 vs. 1882, "Co. Aytch," Maury Grays, First Tennessee Regiment; or, A Side Show of the Big Show* (Nashville: Cumberland Presbyterian Pub. House, 1882).

Stephen Crane, "The Veteran." Source: *The Little Regiment, and Other Episodes of the American Civil War* (New York: D. Appleton and Company, 1896). First published in *McClure's Magazine*, vol. 7 (Aug. 1896), pp. 222–224.

Stephen Crane, "War Is Kind." Source: *War Is Kind* (New York: Dodd, Mead, & Co., 1899). Written in December 1895; published in the *Bookman* in February 1896 (see Fredson Bowers, *The Works of Stephen Crane*, Vol. X, "The Text: History and Analysis," p. 208, p. 231, p. 237).

Stephen Crane, "The Battle Hymn." Source: *The Works of Stephen Crane*, Vol. X ("Poems and Literary Remains"), ed. Fredson Bowers (Charlottesville: University of Virginia Press, 1975). Unpublished manuscript.

Emily Dickinson, poems #1212, #1551. Source: *The Poems of Emily Dickinson*, ed. R. W. Franklin (Cambridge: The Belknap Press of Harvard University Press, 1999).

NOTES

1. At the battle of Thermopylae, in the fifth century B.C., the greatly outnumbered Spartans, though finally killed to the last man, managed to hold off the Persian army long enough to allow the rest of the Greek army to withdraw, setting the stage for the Greek naval victory at the Battle of Salamis.

2. A member of a militia unit called the Richmond Grays, Booth was present at Brown's execution on December 2, 1859, but had not actually "aided in the capture."

3. Imperfectly quoted from Shakespeare, *Julius Caesar*, II.i.169–171.

4. Lincoln was accompanied, at the performance of *Our American Cousin*, by Maj. Henry Rathbone and his step-sister, Clara Harris. After shooting Lincoln, Booth jumped to the stage below and reportedly shouted "Sic Semper Tyrannis" ("Thus Always to Tyrants").

5. After shooting Lincoln and jumping to the stage, Booth fled the theater, had his leg treated by a local doctor, and was later joined by his associate David Herold. After hiding for a week in the swampy Maryland woods, they crossed over into Virginia and made their way to the farm of Richard H. Garrett, where federal officers surrounded them in a barn on April 26. Herold surrendered, but the defiant Booth was shot and died a few hours later.

6. The legend of the fourteenth-century Swiss folk hero William Tell has it that Tell killed the tyrannical Austrian governor Gessler, setting the stage for Switzerland's independence.

7. David Herold, one of Booth's accomplices in the original plan to abduct Lincoln.

8. Possibly a reference to a well-known political cartoon, "The Political Quadrille, Music by Dred Scott" published in 1860 by Rickey, Mallory & Company of Cincinnati. This cartoon parodies the candidates and issues of the 1860 presidential election by portraying the popular dance's four couples as John Breckinridge and James Buchanan; Abraham Lincoln and an African American woman; John Bell and a Native American; and Stephen Douglas and a dissolute Irishman.

9. Thomas Babbington Macaulay (1800–1859) himself wrote the poems that make up the *Lays of Ancient Rome* (1842).

10. Hamilton, the first Secretary of the Treasury and co-author of the *Federalist*, was an advocate of strong centralized federal power.

11. The Civil Rights Act of 1866, introduced by Senator Lyman Trumbull, extended citizenship, with all its rights, to all persons born in the United States and gave federal authorities the final power to enforce civil rights. "In constitutional terms," writes Eric Foner, "the Civil Rights Bill represented the first attempt to give meaning to the Thirteenth Amendment, to define in legislative terms the essence of freedom" (*Reconstruction*, p. 244). The Republican-dominated Congress passed the bill over Andrew Johnson's veto in early April, 1866.

12. In the first week of April 1865, Davis and a retinue of Confederate government holdouts evacuated Richmond, then travelled southward through North Carolina and South Carolina, into Georgia. Davis and his party were tracked down and arrested by federal cavalry outside Irwinville, Georgia, on May 10, 1865. Davis was held in Fort Monroe until May 13, 1867, when he was released on bail (with the help of Horace Greeley and abolitionist Gerrit Smith); the indictment of treason against him was dismissed in February 1869, after various delays and pre-trial motions. See William C. Davis, *An Honorable Defeat: The Last Days of the Confederate Government* (New York: Harcourt, 2001), ch. 10 and p. 386.

13. Henry Alexander Wise (1806–1876) served Virginia variously as Representative, Senator, and Governor, and served the Confederacy as a competent general in the Eastern theater. Unlike many of his fellow confederates, Wise declined to request a pardon from the federal government after the war.

14. James Lawrence Orr (1822–1873) was elected the governor of South Carolina in 1865, as a Republican, and served until 1868.

15. Cornelius Vanderbilt (1794–1877), the American shipping and railroads magnate.

16. William Napier (1785–1860) was a British general and historian.

17. Ninth and final stanza of Alfred Lord Tennyson's "Merlin and the Gleam" (1889).

18. From William Ernest Henley's "The Song of the Sword" (1892).

19. Britomart in Spenser's *Faerie Queene*.

20. *Faerie Queene*, Book II, canto X, stanza 69.

21. Col. William Raymond Lee (1807–1891) commanded the famous unit sometimes called the "Harvard regiment" because of the high number of officers connected to that university.

22. The Grafton National Cemetery in West Virginia was opened in 1867, with about 1,200 interments of Union soldiers; within two years, the bodies of more than 1,200 Union and Confederate soldiers were relocated to Grafton. Many of the identities remain unknown.

23. From William Cullen Bryant's "June" (1820).

24. The Southern Historical Society was the creation of Confederate Gen. Jubal Early (1816-1894), unrepentant spokesman for the Lost Cause. The 52-volume Southern Historical Society Papers, a collection of writings by former Confederates, are a collective record of the hard-line Southern perspective on the war and its aftermath.

25. Possibly Charles Chesnutt's "The Goophered Grapevine," which was published in *The Atlantic Monthly* in 1887. The editor of the *Atlantic* at that point was Thomas Bailey Aldrich.

26. The Tennessee native Mary Noailles Murfree's novel *The Despot of Broomsedge Cove* was serialized in *The Atlantic* in 1888 under the pseudonym Charles Egbert Craddock. Frances Hodgson Burnett's novel *Sara Crewe; or, What Happened at Miss Minchin's* (1888) is a variation on the Cinderella story; the Hodgson family had moved from England to Tennessee in 1865.

27. Luke 16:19–31.

28. The nickname for Sir Walter Scott.

29. This phrase is from Sec. 4 of the 1866 Civil Rights Act. Virtually identical language was subsequently included in the Fifteenth Amendment.

30. On May 2, 1863, at the battle of Chancellorsville, Jackson was struck by friendly fire as he returned from a reconnaissance of the federal position. Despite the amputation of his left arm, Jackson developed pneumonia and died on May 10, at Guiney Station, where he reportedly said "Let us cross over the river and rest under the shade of the trees."

31. William Lowndes Yancey (1814–1863), U.S. Representative and Confederate Senator from Alabama.

32. Robert Barnwell Rhett, Sr. (1800–1876), fierce secessionist Congressman and journalist from South Carolina.

33. Robert Augustus Toombs (1810–1885), U.S. Senator from Georgia, Secretary of State and mediocre general of the Confederacy. Unrepentant to the end.

34. Horace Greeley (1811–1872), antislavery editor of the influential New York *Tribune*, and unsuccessful Presidential challenger to Ulysses S. Grant in 1872.

35. Sumner (1811–1874) was a long-serving abolitionist U.S. Senator from Massachusetts and champion of civil rights during Reconstruction.

36. Hamlin (1809–1891) was Lincoln's more radical, but not terribly influential, vice president. Watkins's reference to Noah and Ham parodies the then-common Biblical "explanation" of the origins of blackness. See Genesis 9.20–27 and Genesis 10:6–14.

37. Watkins served in the 1st Tennessee Infantry Volunteers, which was organized at Nashville in May 1861, composed of companies from Nashville and surrounding counties. Later merged with the 27th Tennessee, the regiment saw extensive service in Virginia, western Virginia, Tennessee, and Georgia. "At Perryville it lost 179 killed, wounded, or missing. The 1st/27th reported 8 killed and 75 wounded of the 457 at Murfreesboro, had 14 killed and 75 wounded at Chickamauga, and totalled 456 men and 290 arms in December, 1863. It surrendered with less than 125 effectives" (Joseph H. Crute, Jr., *Units of the Confederate States Army* [Midlothian, Va.: Derwent Books, 1987], p. 275).

38. This archetypally reconciliationist phrase is from Horace Greeley's letter accepting the Liberal Republican nomination in 1872, which Greeley concluded with a plea for the North and South "to clasp hands across the bloody chasm which has too long divided them..." Cartoonist Thomas Nast parodied the image in a series of cartoons during the summer and fall of that year.

39. Col. George Maney (1st Tennessee Infantry); Col. John Calvin Brown (3rd Tennessee Infantry); Col. James Edward Rains (11th Tennessee Infantry).

40. This incident actually took place in Virginia. Col. Elmer Ephraim Ellsworth (1837–1861) led the 44th New York regiment (the "Fire Zouaves"), which entered Alexandria on May 24, 1861. Here, after taking down a huge rebel flag flying above the Marshall House hotel, Ellsworth was shot and killed by the innkeeper, James William Jackson, who was himself then fatally shot by Corporal Francis Brownell. The episode quickly became a rallying cry in the North.

41.   Charles Todd Quintard (1824–1898) was a physician and Episcopalian priest.

42.   "A camp gambling game in which soldiers attempted to toss dice, rocks, or other small items into squares that contained different numbers" (John D. Wright, *The Language of the Civil War*).

43.   Capt. Hume R. Feild, commanding officer of Company H, was later promoted to colonel of the 1st Tennessee regiment.

44.   "The first crude spirit produced by distillation" (Wright).

45.   Gen. Floyd (1806–1863) was a not terribly effective commander who had little success halting federal advances in western Virginia. He was transferred to Kentucky later that year.

46.   Beginning in January 1862, Stonewall Jackson began a campaign against Union positions in the Shenandoah Valley. Although William Loring had occupied Romney, his complaints led Jefferson Davis to order Jackson to recall Loring to Winchester. Jackson threatened to resign in protest.

47.   *Scott's Infantry Tactics* (1835), named for Major General Winfield Scott, focused on traditional infantry lines and movements; *Hardee's Rifle and Light Infantry Tactics* (1855), named for Lt. Col. William Joseph Hardee, emphasized speed and flexibility, in response to improvements in rifle technology.

48.   Brig. Gen. Robert H. Hatton (1826–1862); Col. William A. Forbes (?–1862); Lt. Col. Paul F. Anderson; Brig. Gen. Daniel Chevilette Govan (1829–1911); William Gilliam (?); Gen. William Wing Loring (1818–1886); Col. Henry M. Ashby.

49.   Matthew 8:14.

50.   Genesis 2:21.

51.   The May 1862 siege of Corinth, Miss., and the July 1862 battle at Tupelo, Miss., were Union victories that strengthened Grant's control of the West. There were several skirmishes at Shelbyville, Tenn., during 1862 and 1863.

52.   Psalm 107:1.

53.   From Rio de Janeiro.

54.   Psalm 144:1.

55.   Gen. Gideon Johnson Pillow (1806–1878).

56.   See page 590, note 1.

57.   The Roman general and consul Caius Marius, uncle to Julius Caesar. After being arrested on orders of his rival Sulla, Marius was allowed to flee in exile to Carthage; he later returned to Rome and seized power in a violent uprising. The episode is the subject of the painting "Caius Marius Amid the Ruins of Carthage" (1807) by American painter John Vanderlyn.

58.   During Reconstruction, cash-strapped Republican governments in the South issued bonds that not only frequently lost their value, but became common fodder for graft and fraudulent speculation.

59.   Compare to Alfred Lord Tennyson, *The Princess: A Medley* (1847), Canto VII: "The moan of doves in immemorial elms, / And murmuring of innumerable bees."

GLOSSARY

Andersonville (Camp Sumter). Following the breakdown of prisoner exchanges between North and South in 1863, both sides began building facilities to house enemy combatants, many of which facilities were inadequately provisioned and poorly managed. The camp at Andersonville in southern Georgia, however, was the worst: a wretched sink of disease, malnutrition, and overcrowding. Of the 45,000 federal prisoners held there between February 1864 and May 1865, almost 13,000 died. The commander of the camp, Captain Henry Wirz, was convicted and hanged after the war, but the bitter resentment generated by Andersonville was long in abating.

Antietam (Sharpsburg). September 17, 1862. This battle, near the Antietam Creek outside Sharpsburg, Maryland, produced in excess of 22,000 casualties, more than did any other day in American history. The stakes could not have been higher. Lee had pushed north of the Potomac in the hope of reviving Southern morale, securing foreign diplomatic recognition, and putting the Union on the defensive. Lincoln, beyond the obvious need to reverse the advance, also sought a military victory that would give him political cover in issuing a proclamation of emancipation. The battle itself involved a complicated series of attacks and counter-attacks that yielded no clear advantage and that, in photographs by Alexander Gardner, produced some of the war's most startling images. Ultimately, Lee decided to withdraw his battered army across the Potomac, but the hyper-cautious McClellan refused a pursuit that could have greatly shortened the war.

Army of the Potomac. Organized, named, and commanded by George McClellan after the Union defeat at Bull Run, the Army of the Potomac would face the hardest duty of the war, along with morale problems in its early years, harassing congressional investigations, and a series of changes at the top as Lincoln tried to find the right general for the job. McClellan was replaced by Ambrose Burnside in November 1862, following Antietam; Burnside was replaced by Joseph Hooker in January 1863, following Fredericksburg; and Hooker was replaced by George Meade in June 1863, following Chancellorsville. Finally, Grant, promoted to lieutenant general in March 1864, assumed functional control of the Army while leaving Meade nominally in command, and began his long hard campaign against Lee's Army of Northern Virginia. From here to the end of the war, the Army of the Potomac fought one bloody battle after another as Grant slowly wore down Lee and eventually trapped him near the Virginia town of Appomattox Court House.

Army of Northern Virginia. Originally the Confederate Army of the Potomac, the Army of Northern Virginia was renamed by Robert E. Lee, who took command in June

1862 after Gen. Joseph Johnston was wounded at the battle of Fair Oaks. Under Lee, James Longstreet, Stonewall Jackson, and Jeb Stuart, and later Richard Ewell and A. P. Hill, the army gained fame by proving that it could win battles even when outnumbered and out-provisioned. But after clever victories at the Seven Days' battles, Second Bull Run, Fredericksburg, and Chancellorsville, the army suffered a crushing defeat at Gettysburg, and retreated back into its own state. Throughout 1864, the Army found itself on the defensive against Grant, who undertook a relentless southward campaign intended to keep the strategic initiative and inflict casualties as much as to secure territory. After a series of battles that cost him men and officers he could ill afford to lose, Lee and the depleted, cornered Army of Northern Virginia surrendered on April 9, 1865, effectively ending the Civil War.

Ball's Bluff. October 21, 1861. This early battle had a low body count but important consequences. Federal forces under Gen. Charles P. Stone, commanded by Lincoln's personal friend Col. Edward D. Baker, crossed the Potomac River into Virginia, encountered sharp resistance from the Confederates, and were driven ignominiously back into the river. The defeat electrified both North and South, for different reasons, and resulted in the creation of the Congressional Joint Committee on the Conduct of the War.

Banks, Nathaniel Prentiss (1816–1894). A self-educated lawyer, journalist, and Congressman, the moderately antislavery Banks was appointed Union major general when the war began, but showed little aptitude for military command. After early defeats in the Shenandoah, Banks was reassigned to Louisiana, where he led a costly effort to capture Port Hudson and contributed to the debacle of the Red River expedition. His controversial reconstruction efforts in Louisiana, which included the conscription of free black laborers, proved politically divisive, leading to his recall to Washington in 1865, and Banks went on to lead a varied political career.

Beauregard, Pierre Gustave Toutant (1818–1893). One of the Civil War's more colorful and complex figures, the French-speaking, self-assured Gen. Beauregard served the Confederacy well throughout the war, yet quarreled bitterly about military strategy, and never really felt that he had received his due recognition. From ordering the firing on Fort Sumter, to redesigning the Confederate flag, to overseeing the defense of coastal areas, Beauregard contributed much to the Southern cause, but generally ended up serving under superiors who preferred a more defensive strategic vision.

Belmont. November 7, 1861. The battle of Belmont, in Missouri, was part of Grant's effort to capture the nearby Confederate bastion at Columbus, Kentucky, which was part of his larger campaign to control the Mississippi River. Initially successful, the assault on Belmont fell apart as green Union soldiers broke ranks, and as the Confederates reinforced and counter-attacked.

Bragg, Braxton (1817–1876). Commanding the Confederate Army of the Tennessee, but commanding it badly, and inspiring scant loyalty from either subordinates or superiors, Gen. Bragg in 1862 led an unproductive offensive through Tennessee and into Kentucky. Easily pushed back to Chattanooga, Bragg then made a successful stand at Chickamauga, but failed to follow through. After the breaking of his siege of Chattanooga in November 1863, Bragg tendered his resignation and served out the war as military adviser to Jefferson Davis.

Brown, John (1800–1859). Along with twenty-one other zealous abolitionists, on October 16, 1859 Brown led a raid on Harper's Ferry, Virginia, intending to spark an uprising by the local slave population. Although no uprising occurred, although U.S. Marines quickly repulsed the attack, and although Brown was hanged less than two months later, his violent approach to confronting slavery became a cause célèbre among radical Northerners and signaled the approach of civil war. "He was simple, exasperatingly simply; unlettered, plain, and homely," wrote W. E. B. Du Bois fifty years later, and yet he "grasped the very pith and kernel of the evil" of slavery (*John Brown* [1909], ed. John David Smith. Armonk, NY and London: M. E. Sharpe, 1997, pp. 173, 174.)

Buchanan, James (1791–1868). Buchanan, the "Bachelor President," was nominated by the Democrats in 1856, and served as President until 1861. He was a unionist, but tilted politically toward slavery and compromise with the South.

Bull Run, First (First Manassas). July 21, 1861. The first major battle of the war, this clash near the Bull Run River in northeastern Virginia, was a harbinger of the larger engagements to come. It resulted from the over-eager Union effort, under Gen. Irvin McDowell, to grab the railway center of Manassas Junction, thereby securing territory around Washington DC, and dividing two Confederate armies under Beauregard and Joseph Johnston. A series of missteps by federal forces, however, and timely reinforcements by the rebels, turned the battle into a stinging rout (almost 3,000 U.S. casualties to the rebels' 2,000) that dispelled the hopeful illusion that the war could be won quickly and easily.

Bull Run, Second (Second Manassas). August 28–30, 1862. The second battle of Bull Run closed an already auspicious summer for the South on a high note. This latest effort to move on Richmond, following the failure of McClellan's Peninsula campaign, was badly managed by U.S. Maj. Gen. John Pope, commanding the new Army of Virginia. After some early maneuvering, Lee, to prevent the Army of the Potomac from reinforcing Pope, moved Stonewall Jackson forward to destroy federal supplies at Manassas Junction. There, Jackson's men surprised and roughed up one of the marching federal columns. Pope counterattacked the next day, but in haphazard fashion and without adequate reinforcements, and several initially successful assaults fell through. A larger attack on the third day failed badly, and after Lee ordered Longstreet to follow up, Pope was forced to retreat toward Washington, having suffered in excess of 14,000 casualties, to approximately 9,000 for the South.

Burnside, Ambrose Everett (1824–1881). A capable soldier and a decent man, Burnside's unfortunate fate is to be known less for his achievements than for his muttonchop sideburns and his military failures. After leading successful operations along the Carolina coast in 1861–1862, Burnside returned to the Washington area to reinforce McClellan in the spring. After contributing to the Union effort at Antietam, Burnside found himself given command of the Army of the Potomac, though he did not particularly want it. His first major offensive resulted in the fiasco at Fredericksburg, and Burnside was transferred to the Department of the Ohio. Here he oversaw the capture of both Knoxville and of Clement Vallandigham, a fierce Ohio Peace Democrat, in 1863. Finally, Burnside returned to the East, but found his career swallowed up by the calamitous battle of the Crater during the siege of Petersburg. He resigned in April 1865.

Butler, Benjamin Franklin (1818–1893). The South despised Butler not for his military accomplishments, which were relatively few, but for his administrative style, which was fearsome. By 1860, Butler had established himself as a successful criminal lawyer with a thriving practice and a force to be reckoned with in Massachusetts Democratic politics. Reform-minded and fiercely unionist, Butler took his first commission as a brigadier general the 8th Massachusetts Militia and began cracking down on dissent in Maryland. Transferred to Fort Monroe, Virginia, Butler took a crucial step in designating as "contraband of war" slaves who had fled to Union lines and employing these contrabands in a military capacity. Given command of New Orleans in May 1862, Butler governed that occupied city with an iron fist before complaints led to his removal to the Eastern theater. After the war, Butler led a successful career in elective politics, pursuing civil rights and workers' rights legislation.

Calhoun, John Caldwell (1782–1850). South Carolina's preeminent politician during the first half of the nineteenth century, Calhoun served variously as Representative, Senator, Secretary of War, Secretary of State, and Vice President. His political ideas centered on the distribution and balance of authority and on the importance of popular will. He became a staunch defender of the South against antislavery "interference," and yet worked to prevent tensions between North and South from spinning out of control.

Cameron, Simon (1799–1899). Cameron was Lincoln's first Secretary of War, serving from March 1861 to (January 1862). He had built his career as an opportunistic businessman and key operator in Pennsylvania politics, and at one time or another had associated himself with the Democrats, the Whigs, the American Party, and the Republicans. He negotiated a cabinet post during the 1860 Republican Convention, but was not up to the task of first overhauling and then administering the War Department as it struggled to meet the Union's military needs. After angering Lincoln by prematurely and publicly recommending the arming of slaves, Cameron was made minister to Russia, where he served for less than a year before returning to the United States to work for Lincoln's reelection and reassert himself in Pennsylvania politics.

Chancellorsville. On May 2–3, 1863, at this small hamlet near Fredericksburg, Virginia, the military genius of Robert Lee and Stonewall Jackson gave the South one of its most spine-tingling victories. Outnumbered nearly two-to-one by Joseph Hooker's bristling Army of the Potomac, and badly hampered by a lack of supplies, Lee divided his army and sent Jackson on a daring flanking attack around the Union right, confusing Hooker and setting up a more concentrated attack the next day that prompted a northward Union retreat. Yet the battle's legacy was complicated. Although inflicting more than 17,000 casualties on the North (to 13,000 of its own), the South lost one of its premier generals (Jackson was hit by friendly fire and later succumbed to pneumonia), and Lee's confidence contributed to his overreaching at Gettysburg

Chase, Salmon Portland (1808–1873). Chase served as Secretary of the Treasury from Lincoln's inauguration until June 1864. An Ohio attorney who had made his name defending fugitive slaves and had helped found the Free Soil Party, Chase was elected to the Senate in 1849 and spent the 1850s opposing slavery and trying to figure out how to become President. As Secretary of the Treasury, Chase instituted a variety of economic policies to help finance the war, principally the sale of government bonds and the levying of a federal income tax. He was ahead of the curve on issues of emancipation and civil rights, but his unsuccessful maneuvering for the Republican nomination in 1864 led to his resignation that summer. Lincoln nominated Chase for Chief Justice of the U.S. Supreme Court in December 1864, and from his seat on that court Chase fought for African American civil rights during the first years of Reconstruction.

Chickamauga. September 19–20, 1863. Fought in the dense woods around Chickamauga Creek, in northern Georgia, this bloody battle enabled the Army of the Tennessee temporarily to stop the Union's southward advance toward Georgia. Following a minor clash between federal infantry and rebel cavalry, the battle quickly mushroomed as each side sent reinforcements into the fray. On the second day, despite tactical delays, the Confederates managed to drive the Union forces back to Chattanooga. What one Confederate private described as "all this terrible thunder, blood, carnage, slaughter" produced on the order of 35,000 casualties (*The Civil War Letters of Joshua K. Callaway*, ed. Judith Lee Hallock, U of Georgia Press, 1997, p. 138).

Cold Harbor. June 3, 1864. Through May 1864, Grant had led the Army of the Potomac on a grinding campaign through Virginia in an effort to reach Richmond and defeat the wily Lee. After two days of inconclusive fighting around the Old Cold Harbor crossroads, Grant, evidently eager for a showdown, ordered an assault against well-entrenched and well-reinforced Confederate positions. The poorly coordinated attack turned into a turkey-shoot, resulting in about 7,000 Union casualties, to the Confederates' 1,500.

Contrabands. In May 1861, three escaped slaves made their way to Fortress Monroe, Virginia, where they were designated "contrabands of war" by Union Gen. Benjamin Butler and employed in construction and picking cotton. This seemingly minor incident was actually a pivotal moment in the history of the war because it focused attention on the status of African Americans in the conflict and contributed to the gradually accelerating politics of emancipation. Although the legal status of contrabands was ambiguous—not technically free (until the Emancipation Proclamation), yet no longer property—former slaves understood that reaching federal lines was a route to freedom because, in practical terms, there would be no sending them back. Although the federal government wanted to move cautiously on the issue of emancipation so as not to alienate wavering border states or Northern Democrats, the ideological meaning of the war had its own momentum, and the use of contrabands by the Union Army contributed centrally to the eventual cause of abolishing slavery.

Copperheads. This term of opprobrium was applied to Northern Democrats who criticized or worked against the Lincoln administration's conduct of the war, even if they were not in engaged in serpentine sedition. Most Copperheads—many of whom were midwesterners and many of whom were of German or Irish extraction—strongly opposed emancipation measures and feared the ascendancy of Republican economic policies. Although the administration prosecuted some Democratic dissenters, the demise of the Copperheads came about primarily through the ultimate military success of the North.

Cumberland. See *Merrimack* and *Monitor*.

Debouch. "To issue from a narrow or confined place, as a defile or a wood, into open country; hence gen. to issue or emerge from a narrower into a wider place or space" (*Oxford English Dictionary*).

Douglas, Stephen Arnold (1813–1861). Born in Vermont, Douglas's political career as a Democrat took off in Illinois, which sent him to the House in 1843 and the Senate in 1847, where he played a central role in crafting the compromises on slavery of the 1850s. Guided by the principles of Jacksonian democracy and expansionist nationalism, Douglas thought that the status of slavery should be left to the people of a given territory, and in his 1858 Senatorial campaign debates with Lincoln rejected the idea that a house divided could not stand. He ran for President as one of two unsuccessful Democrats in 1860, and after the firing on Fort Sumter, after all efforts at compromised, fiercely rejected the doctrine of secession.

Enfilade. "To subject to an enfilade; to 'rake' or to be in a position to 'rake' (a line of fortification, a line of troops, a road, etc.) from end to end with a fire in the direction of its length" (*Oxford English Dictionary*).

Fessenden, William Pitt (1806–1869). After rising through the ranks of Maine law and politics, Fessenden won a Senate seat in 1854 and emerged as an influential Republican leader. He became Secretary of the Treasury after Salmon P. Chase's resignation in July 1864, but served only for a year and then returned to the Senate, where he advocated a fairly aggressive Reconstruction policy.

First South Carolina Volunteer Infantry. The first black infantry unit of the war, the 1st South Carolina, of Hilton Head, started out inauspiciously as the "Hunter Experiment." Originally organized by General David Hunter in May 1862, in the Department of the South, the regiment ran into trouble quickly: Hunter had not obtained authorization from the War Department, and his policy of involuntary conscription worked to antagonize or alienate the very soldiers who would serve in it. Soon disbanded, the regiment was reorganized later that year by Gen. Rufus Saxton, and in November Sergeant C. T. Trowbridge was commisioned its Captain. In February 1864, the 1st South Carolina was redesignated the 33rd U.S. Colored Troops.

Forrest, Nathan Bedford (1821–1877). The great equestrian of the Confederacy, this Tennessee native and wealthy slave-owner became lieutenant colonel, then brigadier general, then major general, on the strength of his brilliant cavalry raids in the Western theater. Hot-tempered, independent-minded, and crafty, Forrest led cavalry attacks in Tennessee, Kentucky, and northern Mississippi that slowed the south-bound Grant and Sherman by disrupting supply lines and diverting federal resources. Although he cut a romantic figure, Forrest's reputation has suffered because of the 1864 Fort Pillow massacre, in which his men apparently murdered black troops who had surrendered, and because of his postwar leadership of the Ku Klux Klan.

Fort Monroe. The U.S. garrison at Fort Monroe, located at the southern end of the Chesapeake Bay near the mouth of the James River, played an important role in the Union war effort. It provided a base of operations for George McClellan during his 1862 campaign for Richmond and for Benjamin Butler during his support of Grant's 1864 campaign. It also served briefly as the prison for Jefferson Davis after the war.

Fort Pulaski. April 10–11, 1862. An island redoubt at the mouth of the Savannah River, Fort Pulaski was a state-of-the-art facility (seized by Georgia in January 1861) until it was bombarded into submission by Union forces. The bombardment, under Gen. Quincy Gillmore, demonstrated the great efficacy of rifled, as opposed to smoothbore, cannon, and the consequent vulnerability of masonry forts.

Fort Sumter. On April 12, 1861, South Carolina finally moved from rhetoric to war by firing on the federal garrison at Fort Sumter, commanded by U.S. Major Robert Anderson, and located at the entrance to Charleston Harbor. The attack, overseen by P. G. T. Beauregard, came after months of political and military maneuvering during which South Carolina Gov. Francis Pickens, the outgoing administration of James Buchanan, and the incoming administration of Lincoln struggled to resolve competing claims to the fort. As the state's siege of Fort Sumter took its toll, Anderson was prepared to surrender, but in order to prevent any possible reinforcement, the South opened fire. After a day and a half of bombardment, Anderson surrendered on April 14.

Fort Wagner. July 18, 1863. Located toward the northern end of Morris Island on the South Carolina coast, Fort Wagner figured into Union Gen. Quincy Gillmore's plans to control Charleston Harbor and besiege the city of Charleston. After a failed assault on July 11, and after an intense but fruitless morning bombardment a week later, Gillmore sent in the infantry across an unprotected stretch of beach. The lead regiment was the 54th Massachusetts Volunteers, the Union's premier African American unit. Although the attack failed badly, with over 1,500 Union casualties, it convinced many Northerners of the military prowess and determination of black troops.

Franklin. November 30, 1864. Another of the Civil War's poorly planned and disastrous frontal assaults, the battle at Franklin, Tennessee, saw John Bell Hood, commander of the Army of Tennessee, move against well-entrenched federal units commanded by John M. Schofield. Following his inability to protect Atlanta from Sherman, or to distract Sherman by harassing his supply lines, Hood reasoned that an expedition into Tennessee to capture federally occupied Nashville might shake things up. The plan went sideways at Franklin, where the Confederates' dramatic charge, intended to prevent Schofield from linking up with George Thomas in Nashville, instead resulted in about 7,300 Southern casualties in five hours.

Fredericksburg. December 13, 1862. One of the Union's most crushing defeats, the battle of Fredericksburg rocked Northern morale, derailed the career of Gen. Ambrose Burnside, and undermined Lincoln's political strength. Seeking to advance on Richmond, the Army of the Potomac faced unaccountable delays in crossing the Rappahannock River, allowing Robert E. Lee to establish a strong defensive position west of Fredericksburg, especially on the high ground of Marye's Heights. Burnside's decision to storm this position repeatedly, despite having wave after wave of men cut down in the open ground in front it, ultimately cost almost 13,000 casualties. (A second battle at Fredericksburg occurred on May 3, 1863 as part of the Chancellorsville campaign).

Frémont, John Charles (1813–1890). The brilliant yet unruly mathematician and cartographer made his name in the 1830s and 1840s as an explorer of the West. On the strength of this glamorous experience, Frémont accepted the 1856 Presidential nomination of the newly formed Republican Party, and although he lost this contest helped establish Republican political dominance in the North. During the Civil War, Gen. Frémont's commanded the Western Department poorly and angered Lincoln by issuing an unauthorized edict freeing the slaves and confiscating the property of Missouri rebels. Reassigned to West Virginia in March 1862, he found himself outmatched by Stonewall Jackson, and resigned that summer.

Gaines's Mill. June 27, 1862. Following immediately on the heels of Mechanicsville, this second, and largest, of the Seven Days' battles helped secure Lee's psychological advantage over his antagonist McClellan. After a pause following several hours of brutal but indecisive fighting, Lee ordered a full assault on Union positions and finally managed to break through against Fitz John Porter's V Corps. Although Southern casualties exceeded those of the North (about 8,700 to about 6,800), Gaines's Mill ranks as a Confederate victory because it contributed to driving the Army of the Potomac away from Richmond.

Gettysburg. If any single clash could be considered the turning point of the war, the three-day battle at Gettysburg, Pennsylvania (July 1–3, 1863), marked the moment when the South's ambitions—for foreign diplomatic recognition, for a major victory on Northern soil, and for moral recovery from the recent fall of Vicksburg—foundered and crumbled. The North, under Meade, suffered about 23,000 casualties, and the South, under Lee, about 28,000. Although Meade failed to pursue the retreating rebels and attempt a coup de grâce, and although the South would enjoy later military victories, Gettysburg galvanized the North, deterred England from recognizing the Confederacy, and became a grim omen of eventual Southern defeat.

Halleck, Henry Wager (1815–1872). Long before he became general-in-chief of Union forces in July 1862, Halleck had evidenced the academic and administrative bent that would define his Civil War leadership for good and ill. A former lawyer and the author of influential works on military science and international law, Halleck brought his scholarly and bureaucratic acumen first to the West, where he undertook a rapid reorganization of the Department of the Missouri, and then to Washington, where he helped coordinate the overall war effort. But Halleck's disinterest in field operations and his inability to manage subordinates effectively led to his reassignment to chief-of-staff in the spring of 1864, as Grant was promoted to commanding general. In the end, Halleck's primary contribution was less as a working general than as a smart desk-man who backed up Grant's offensive campaigns with good administrative support.

Harper's Ferry. This Virginia town had an importance far greater than its small size would suggest. Its strategic location at the meeting of the Potomac and Shenandoah rivers, and its national arsenal and armory, made Harper's Ferry a valuable asset to both sides. It gained notoriety in 1859 as the site of John Brown's raid, and then endured six years of back-and-forth warfare. In September 1862, the battle of Harper's Ferry, a major Confederate victory, encouraged Lee to continue his push into Maryland, and enabled the Army of Northern Virginia to reinforce once the going got rough at Antietam.

Hooker, Joseph (1814–1879). Ambitious, tough, and hard-drinking, Hooker began the war as brigadier general under George McClellan and, despite a rocky start, established himself at the battle of Antietam as a grizzled fighter. Given command of the Army of the Potomac after Burnside's defeat at Fredericksburg, Hooker worked wonders for morale by instituting an array of organizational and operational changes. But failure loomed. At Chancellorsville, Hooker was so out-generalled by Lee that his career and reputation never really recovered (he was replaced by Meade in June 1863). Despite later helping to break the siege of Chattanooga and helping Sherman push south into Georgia, a greatly diminished Hooker served out the war as commander of reserve troops in Chicago.

Hunter, David (1802–1886). From the beginning of his career, Hunter was a bit of loose cannon, and by end of his career had become the South's favorite *bête noire*. As commander of Union forces along the Southern coast, Maj. Gen. Hunter in May 1862 issued his own order freeing Southern slaves, and then undertook to organize a black regiment, the 1st South Carolina Volunteers. Neither decision was authorized from above, and both were soon reversed. Nonetheless, in his efforts at emancipation and the employment of African Americans in a military capacity, Hunter anticipated the coming year's decisive change in federal policy.

Jackson, Thomas Jonathan (1824–1863). Next to Lee, "Stonewall" Jackson emerged during the Civil War as the South's most revered general. Deeply pious yet fierce in combat; introverted and asocial yet popular with his men; hard-driven yet given to periods of strange lassitude—Jackson's austere personality proved an almost mystical asset in his war career. Seeing the Confederate cause as a kind of holy crusade, Jackson brought his faith and his formidable military skill to many of the most important battles of the war: First Manassas, Winchester, Cedar Mountain, Antietam, Fredericksburg. At Chancellorsville, as he returned to camp from a reconnaissance of Union forces, Jackson was inadvertently shot by Confederate guards. His left arm was amputated that same night, but pneumonia had set in, and Jackson died eight days later, at the Chandler plantation outside Fredericksburg.

Johnston, Joseph Eggleston (1807–1891). For a variety of reasons both personal and circumstantial, the Virginia-born Gen. Johnston never managed to thrive in the Civil War. A highly developed ego led to a pattern of contending with superiors, particularly Jefferson Davis, and a defensive strategic vision too often seemed to inhibit him from committing to a fight. After being wounded at the battle of Seven Pines, and seeing Lee thereby promoted, Johnston was transferred to the West, where his molasses-like response to the siege of Vicksburg further strained relations with Davis. During his 1864 command of the Army of the Tennessee, Johnston pursued a campaign of what might be called strategic retreat as Sherman advanced toward Atlanta. Replaced by John Bell Hood, and then in 1865 given command over the remaining Confederate forces in the Carolinas, Johnston surrendered to Sherman on April 26, 1865 in North Carolina.

Kennesaw Mountain (June 27, 1864). As Sherman pushed Joseph Johnston back through Georgia during the late spring and early summer, the fighting had been sporadic but indecisive. At Kennesaw Mountain, where Johnston had entrenched along high ground, Sherman hoped that by extending the Confederate line and then attacking at its center, he could achieve a clear victory. But the assault, hampered by poor coordination, simply provided another lesson in the folly of attacking well-entrenched fortifications. Despite the repulse, Sherman had ample recourse: he withdrew and continued his steady maneuvering toward the prize of Atlanta.

Lee, Robert Edward (1807–1870). The Confederacy invested its hope, its identity, and its pride in Lee more than in any other single individual. The son of a Virginian Revolutionary War hero, a hero himself of the Mexican War, and a former superintendent of West Point, Lee felt divided loyalties to nation and to state at the onset of civil war—but in the end, Virginia and family came first, with fateful consequences. Having resigned from the U.S. Army in April 1861 and accepted the offer of major general commanding Virginian forces, Lee got off to a slow start. But once promoted to command of the Army of Northern Virginia, on June 1, 1862, Lee quickly displayed an unequalled flair for the art of war: how to win against long odds, how to make the best of the available resources, how to seize the psychological advantage, how to keep morale high. Indeed, one of Lee's defining strengths as a general was his ability to inspire almost passionate loyalty from his men and from his society. This strength came from his qualities as a person: a sterling sense of honor and duty, and a graciousness in both victory and defeat. From his early success in keeping the Army of the Potomac away from Richmond, to his dubious forays into Maryland and Pennsylvania, to his long final defensive campaign against Grant, Lee kept the Confederacy alive beyond what could reasonably have been expected, given its relative weakness of men and materiel. When he resigned at Appomattox Court House on April 9, 1865, the South had no one else to turn to; the rebellion had faded. Unpardoned by Andrew Johnson, Lee assumed the presidency of Virginia's Washington College in August 1865, but died of a stroke five years later.

Longstreet, James (1821–1904). Though undistinguished at West Point, the Georgian Longstreet earned promotions during his service in the Mexican War and gained a reputation as a steady commander, well-liked and well-respected. His contributions at the Seven Days' battles gained him a place at Lee's side, and he went on to display his formidable tactical abilities at Second Bull Run and Fredericksburg. Gettysburg, however, remains the controversial event in Longstreet's career. Having advised Lee against an offensive campaign in Pennsylvania, and specifically against frontal assaults during Gettysburg, Longstreet performed reluctantly, delaying both a July 2 attack and the disastrous Pickett's charge on July 3. It may not have made any difference, but led to fierce criticism after the war by Jubal Early and other ex-Confederates, and second-guessing ever since.

Malvern Hill. July 1, 1862. The last of the Seven Days' Battles in Virginia, Malvern Hill was a tactical disaster for the South, but nonetheless contributed to Lee's successful effort to push McClellan back from Richmond. In a confused and controversial assault, Confederate forces stormed the heavily fortified and geographically secure Union positions around the high grounds of Malvern Hill. Although costing almost twice as many casualties as it inflicted (approx. 5,500 to 3,000), the assault prompted McClellan to withdraw—or in his view, reposition—to Harrison's Landing on the James River.

Manassas. See Bull Run.

McClellan, George Brinton (1826–1885). Seemingly destined for greatness, the Union's "Young Napoleon" found himself by the end of the war greatly decreased in stature and influence. As the commander, indeed creator, of the Army of the Potomac, McClellan showed a genius for military organization and preparation, but was cautious to a fault on the battlefield, where he preferred siege to confrontation, and conservative in his politics. After the failure of his long-delayed Peninsula campaign against Richmond in the spring of 1862, and his reluctance to pursue Lee after the battle of Antietam, McClellan was replaced by Ambrose Burnside in November 1862, amid questions about his political loyalty and his stomach for a fight. McClellan ran for President as a Democrat in 1864, losing badly to his former ally Lincoln.

Meade, George Gordon (1815–1872). A civil engineer by trade, and a veteran of both the Second Seminole War and the Mexican-American War, Meade proved himself a capable Northern general in the early battles of the Civil War. On June 28, 1863, just days before the battle of Gettysburg, Meade was given command of the Army of the Potomac. Meade's defensive strategy at Gettysburg delivered success, but he would long regret his failure to follow up with a crushing blow. Eventually overshadowed by Grant and Sherman, Meade served out his time in the military competently but without great distinction.

Merrimack **and** ***Monitor***. Hampton Roads, the main federal blockade base at the entrance to the James River in Virginia, was the site of a battle that marked a new era in naval warfare. Here, on March 8, 1862, the Confederate ironclad *Virginia* (previously the USS *Merrimack*) rammed and sank the wood-sided *Cumberland* (temporarily commanded by Lt. George U. Morris), killing 121 of its crew, and shelled the *Congress* into submission, until being driven off, with minor damage, by the Union ironclad *Monitor*, commanded by John L. Worden. Lt. Joseph B. Smith, acting commander of the *Congress*, was killed.

Missionary Ridge (November 24–25, 1863). The battle of Missionary Ridge completed the Union's successful effort to break the poorly managed siege of the Army of the Cumberland in Chattanooga by Braxton Bragg's Army of the Tennessee. Grant, recently promoted to full command of Western forces, meant to break the Confederates' line along Missionary Ridge through concerted action by Gens. Hooker, Sherman, and Thomas. After Hooker's men took Lookout Mountain on the first day, Sherman's repeated assaults the next proved unsuccessful, and Grant's plan seemed to be in trouble. Thomas's troops saved the day, however, by following up an initial advance on Missionary Ridge with an unauthorized, risky, but dramatically successful charge up the steep ridge that routed the badly positioned Confederate defenders. The "miracle" of Missionary Ridge broke the siege of Chattanooga, ruined Bragg's career, and left the path open for Sherman's advance into Georgia.

Peace Democrats. These Northern critics of the Lincoln administration formed the conservative wing of the Democratic Party and sought to bring the war to a conclusion, and thus somehow save the union, through a negotiated settlement rather than military victory. Peace Democrats accused the Republican Party of monopolizing power, of trampling civil liberties, of waging an unnecessarily cruel war, and of promoting elitist economic policies. Dubbed "Copperheads" by their detractors, these agitators occasionally faced both figurative and literal charges of treason as their dissent grew more vociferous. Their political fortunes waxed and waned with the progress of the war, however, and after Lincoln's victory in 1864 the Peace Democrats were effectively finished as a viable faction.

Petersburg. Grant's grand campaign for Petersburg, Virginia's second largest city, ran from June 1864 to April 1865, produced some of the highest body counts of the war, and eventually forced Lee to surrender. After a series of savage clashes during the Overland campaign in May and June, both armies dug in around Petersburg, a vital rail hub that linked Richmond to the rest of the Confederacy. Early direct assaults failed, so Grant moved around the city and settled in for a long siege, punctuated by a series of stabbing offensives designed to wear down the Confederates. Despite their numerically greater losses (in excess of 60,000), despite such embarrassing defeats as the battle of the Crater, and despite Lee's masterful generalling, Union forces eventually succeeded at dislodging and then pincering the Army of Northern Virginia.

Pickets. Pickets were individual soldiers, or small squads, charged with a variety of responsibilities, primarily reconnaissance, guard duty, and camp patrol. Beyond its military importance, picket duty—given its relatively unsupervised character—provided opportunities for soldiers to converse or trade with "enemy" pickets.

Rosecrans, William Starke (1819–1898). "Old Rosy," a Catholic Democrat from Ohio, participated in some of the Union's most important advances in the war, yet ultimately saw his military career fizzle out. He rose through the ranks by contributing to victories in western Virginia, Iuka and Corinth, Stones River, and—most of all—in Chattanooga, but ran into disaster at Chickamauga, where his stunned retreat stood in contrast to Gen. George Thomas's valiant stand. After Thomas replaced him as commander of the Army of the Cumberland, Rosecrans took charge of the Department of the Missouri, but had little further impact on the course of the war.

Sanitary Commission. The United States Sanitary Commission was a major charitable organization, staffed primarily by female volunteers that provided supplies, bureaucratic assistance, and medical care to thousands of Civil War soldiers at both camps and hospitals. In service of this work, it formed a slew of subsidiary relief organizations and advised the federal government on military medical policy. The Commission's approach to relief work was more pragmatic than philosophical, emphasizing workable strategies rather than lofty ideals.

Saxton, Rufus (1824–1908). After rising steadily through the military ranks, the Massachusetts-born Saxton was named brigadier general of volunteers in April 1862, and then given command of federal forces in the South Carolina Sea Islands in February 1863. His most important contribution to the Northern war effort was to organize, with authorization of the War Department, the training and deployment of freedmen and former slaves, or contrabands, whom the war had displaced. After the war, and until 1866, Saxton served as Freedmen's Bureau commissioner in South Carolina.

Scott, Winfield (1786–1866). A native of Virginia, Scott served rose to the rank of general in the War of 1812 and then served as commanding general of the U.S. Army during the Mexican-American War of 1846–48. During this latter conflict, he commanded more than 100 officers who would go on to become Civil War generals, many of them applying the military lessons learned in Mexico. During the early months of the Civil War, Scott developed a far-reaching strategy to constrict the Confederacy with naval power, but this "Anaconda Plan," as it was dubbed, seemed too slow to many Northerners. Outpaced by George McClellan, and in poor health, Scott left office on November 1, 1861.

Sedgwick, John (1813–1864). "Uncle John" Sedgwick, brigadier general and major general in the Army of the Potomac, was a skillful, intrepid, and popular commander who made significant contributions to the Union war effort, at Antietam, Rappahannock Bridge, and even Fredericksburg. Wounded several times already, Sedgwick's luck ran out at the battle of Spotsylvania, where he was shot and killed while reviewing troop positions.

Seven Days' Battles (June 25–July 1, 1862). During April, May, and June, George McClellan had been preparing (in glacially slow fashion) a major assault on Richmond. Though numerically superior, McClellan was unprepared for the inspired generalling of Lee, who had taken command of the Army of Northern Virginia after Joseph Johnston's wounding at the battle of Seven Pines. In a week-long series of battles—Oak Grove, Mechanicsville, Gaines' Mill, Savage's Station, Glendale/White Oak Swamp, Malvern Hill—Lee managed to thwart the Union advance, despite poor coordination, heavy casualties, and the repeated nonperformance of Stonewall Jackson. The battles spooked McClellan, protected Richmond, and helped to establish Lee as the South's leading military light.

Seward, William Henry (1830–1915). Ambitious, pragmatic, and complicated, Seward led one of the more colorful careers in American politics and as Secretary of State played a central role in the Civil War policies of the Lincoln administration. An antislavery Whig-turned-Republican, Seward tended to advise the moderate and publicly palatable course, in contrast to administration radicals, and he generally sought to soft-pedal the significance of emancipation and post-war reconstruction.

Sheridan, Philip Henry (1831–1888). Where some commanders had to learn aggression by experience, the North's Sheridan hit the ground running. He first proved his mettle in the West, at Perryville, Murfreesboro, Chickamauga, and Missionary Ridge, earning the opportunity to take command of cavalry in the Army of the Potomac. It was in this role that Sheridan wrote himself into history. After assisting in Grant's Overland campaign in 1864 by conducting raids around Richmond, he was sent to the fertile Shenandoah Valley to put down Jubal Early's marauding army. Here, Sheridan led his troops in a systematic scorched-earth campaign designed to deprive the Confederacy of resources and to sap its will to fight. His dramatic and unexpected victory at Cedar Creek, and then at Five Forks and Sayler's Creek in Virginia, allowed him to cut off Lee's retreat from Petersburg and thus precipitate the surrender of the Army of Northern Virginia.

Shiloh. The battle of Shiloh, in Tennessee, took place on April 6–7, 1862, and it provided a horrifying spectacle of what kind of conflict the Civil War was becoming. In military terms, the primary significance of the battle—a costly strategic Union victory, achieved after a near-breakthrough by the South—lay in the Confederacy's failure to break increasing federal control of the Mississippi Valley, which would ultimately prove decisive in the Western theater. In psychological terms, the vast numbers of dead and wounded—at least 20,000, more than twice the total of all previous Civil War battles—revealed to both sides how intense and how long-lived the war would have to be.

Spotsylvania Court House. May 9–19, 1864. Just days after the battle of the Wilderness, the Army of Northern Virginia and the Army of the Potomac met again as Grant ground on with his Overland campaign, trying to get around Lee's right flank. After an unexpected day of fighting on May 8, the Confederates continued to strengthen their already redoubtable line of fieldworks north of the town of Spotsylvania Court House. Then came day after day of seesaw attacks and counterattacks, positioning and repositioning, as the Union forces struggled to get traction. Some of the most intense fighting of the war occurred on May 12 at a line of trenches known as the Bloody Angle, where the dead piled up for almost twenty hours of unrelenting close-quarters combat. By the nineteenth, another 18,000 Union soldiers had been killed, wounded, or captured; estimated Confederate losses range from 10,000 to 12,000.

Stanton, Edwin McMasters (1814–1869). As U.S. Secretary of War from January 1862 to May 1868, the hard-nosed former lawyer from Ohio played a central role in the Union's conduct of the war and, to a lesser extent, in the formulation of postwar reconstruction policies. He advised Lincoln on military appointments and strategy, usually pushing for the more aggressive option, such as removing McClellan or emancipating slaves and enlisting African American troops. His preeminent talent was logistics; Stanton's reorganization of the War Department and his efficiency in supplying and running the Union war machine were crucial factors in the North's eventual victory.

Stuart, James Ewell Brown (1833–1864). J. E. B. ("Jeb") Stuart embodied the spirit of dashing equestrian valor on which the South prided itself. Appointed colonel of the 1st Virginia Cavalry in July 1861, and then brigadier general after his performance at Bull Run, Stuart became a master of raiding and reconnaissance, blending caution and daring in his information-gathering forays around enemy positions and his sudden strikes against Union forces. Gettysburg was the black mark on his otherwise stellar career; otherwise occupied in Pennsylvania, Stuart did not show up until late on the second day, having unintentionally deprived Lee of crucial battlefield information. Stuart was shot on May 11, 1864, during an engagement against Sheridan at Yellow Tavern, and died the next day.

Vicksburg Campaign and Siege. March–July 1863. Located on the Mississippi River about 225 north of New Orleans, Vicksburg was one of the South's major military and economic hubs, with both strategic and psychological significance. Grant had early set his sights on this "Gibraltar of the Confederacy," and after failing in direct efforts at capture, decided to circle around from the south. Landing at Bruinsburg, Mississippi, Grant's army march northeast toward Jackson, Mississippi, living off the land and confiscating what they needed—a signature development in Civil War tactics. After Sherman took Jackson, Grant moved west toward Vicksburg, pushing Confederate Gen. John C. Pemberton back into Vicksburg. Two failed assaults convinced Grant to lay siege, and his men began the process of digging trenches, firing artillery, and cutting off food and supplies to the city. By early July, with no reinforcements forthcoming from the Eastern theater, the conditions inside the city had deteriorated to the point where Pemberton saw the writing on the wall. He agreed to a surrender on July 4, turning over approximately 30,000 men and 60,000 firearms. The fall of Vicksburg was one of the major events—along with Gettysburg and the capture of Atlanta—that foretold the demise of the Confederacy.

Videts. Properly "videttes" or "vedettes," these were mounted scouts or cavalry detachments who provided advance reconnaissance for an army or larger unit.

Wilderness. The battle of the Wilderness (May 5–6, 1864) took its name from the thickly forested region of pine, scrub, and overgrowth near Chancellorsville, Virginia. It was the first confrontation between Lee and Grant, who had taken command of the Army of the Potomac in March, and had planned his Overland campaign to move south into Virginia in order to draw Lee into direct, open combat. Outnumbered nearly two to one, Lee preferred to hit the Northern army as it moved through the Wilderness, where the Union's advantage in artillery and troop strength would matter less. What followed was two days of savage but inconclusive fighting, a chaos of brushfires, blinding smoke, flying lead, hand-to-hand combat, and friendly fire. In the end, the North suffered about 18,000 casualties, the South about 11,000 (including James Longstreet) but this time, the Union commander, rather than turning back, determined to press on, toward Spotsylvania Court House.

Zouaves. Immediately before and during the Civil War, a number of military regiments, mostly Northern, adopted a colorful, exotic uniform inspired by the attire of French colonial forces in Algeria (whose Berber mercenaries were called "Zouaoua"). Zouave units enjoyed a dashing reputation probably in excess of their military performance, but they fought from start to finish in the war, and were undoubtedly good for morale.

Significant Battles, Forts, and Cities

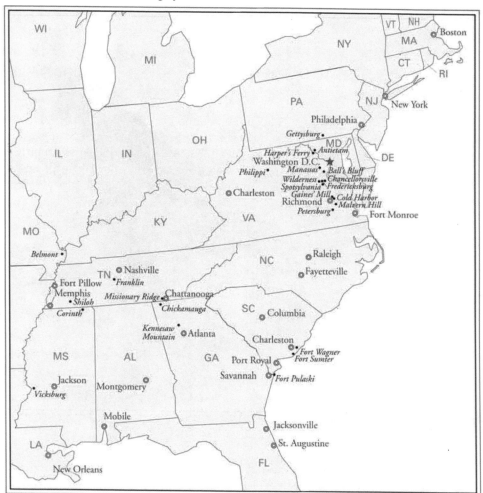

Site	Estimated casualties (killed, wounded, captured, or missing)	
	Union	Confederate
Antietam, MD	12,400	10,300
Ball's Bluff, VA	921	149
Belmont, MO	607	641
Chancellorsville, VA	18,000	12,800
Chickamauga, GA	16,170	18,454
Cold Harbor, VA	13,000	5,000
Corinth, MS	2,350	4,800
Fort Pulaski, GA	1	1
Fort Sumter, SC(first)	11	4
Fort Wagner, SC (second)	1,515	222
Franklin, TN(second)	2,633	7,300
Fredericksburg, VA (first)	12,600	5,300
Gaines' Mill, VA	6,837	8,750

Site	Estimated casualties (killed, wounded, captured, or missing)	
	Union	Confederate
Gettysburg, PA	23,000	28,000
Harper's Ferry, VA	12,719	286
Kennesaw Mountain, GA	3,000	1,000
Malvern Hill, VA	3,000	5,355
Manassas, VA (first)	2,896	1,982
Manassas, VA (second)	13,826	8,353
Missionary Ridge, TN	5,815	6,667
Petersburg, VA (campaign)	61,500	38,000
Philippi, VA	5	6
Shiloh, TN	13,047	10,699
Spotsylvania Court House, VA	18,000	12,000
Vicksburg, MS (campaign)	4,835	32,697
The Wilderness, VA	18,000	10,800

Sources: Frances H. Kennedy, ed., *The Civil War Battlefield Guide*, 2nd ed. (Boston: Houghton Mifflin, 1998);
David S. Heidler and Jeanne T. Heidler, eds., *Encyclopedia of the American Civil War: A Political, Social, and Military History* (New York: W.W. Norton, 2000)

Data Graphics: Marcia Underwood 2005

Demographic Information: 1860

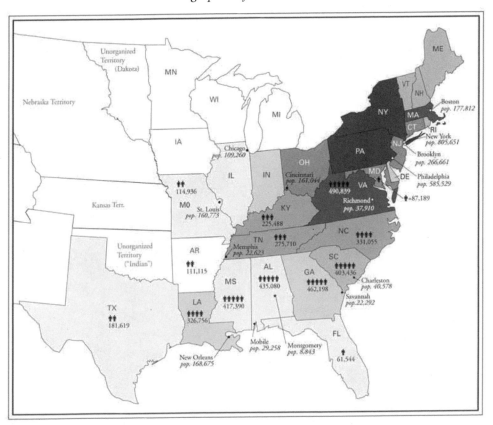

MANUFACTURING EMPLOYEES- 1860	SLAVES HELD- 1860	SOCIAL ORIGINS OF SOLDIERS		
over 60,000	††††† over 400,000		UNION	CONFEDERATE
30,000-60,000	†††† 300,001-400,000	farmers and farm laborers	47.5%	61.5%
20,001-30,000	††† 200,001-300,000	skilled laborers	25.1%	14.1%
15,001-20,000	†† 100,001-200,000	unskilled laborers	15.9%	8.5%
10,001-15,000	† below 100,000	white-collar and commercial	5.1%	7.0%
5,001-10,000		professional	3.2%	5.2%
1,001-5,000		miscellaneous and unknown	3.2%	3.7%
under 1000		native-born whites	67	90
		immigrants	24	10
		African-Americans	9	***

Source: Steven E. Woodworth and Kenneth J. Winkle, *Atlas of the Civil War* (New York: Oxford University Press, 2004)   Data Graphics: Marcia Underwood 2005

The Election of 1860

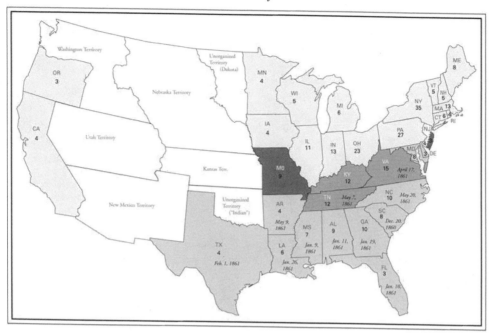

Political Parties	Electoral Vote	Popular Vote
Republican (Lincoln)	180 (59%)	1,866,452 (40%)
Southern Democratic (Breckenridge)	72 (24%)	847,953 (18%)
Constitutional Union (Bell)	39 (13%)	590,631 (13%)
Northern Democratic (Douglas)	12 (4%)	1,375,157 (29%)
	Total: 303	Total: 4,680,193

Data Graphics: Marcia Underwood 2005

THE WRITERS

Alcott, Louisa May (1832–1888). As the daughter of Amos Bronson Alcott, the eccentric educational reformer and founder of the utopian community Fruitlands, Louisa May Alcott was probably destined to see the world in unconventional terms, and her fiction seems to bear out this assessment. Beginning in mid-December 1862, Alcott volunteered as a nurse at the Union Hotel Hospital in Georgetown, but returned to Concord in January 1863 after contracting typhoid fever. Her nursing experience formed the basis for Alcott's fictional alter ego Tribulation Periwinkle in *Hospital Sketches* (1863). She returned to the war in the story collection *On Picket Duty* (1864) and, indirectly, in the novel *Little Women* (1868). Alcott's antislavery and feminist politics inform all of this fiction, but so does her essentially apolitical compassion for both civilians and soldiers caught up in the gears of war.

Bierce, Ambrose (1842–1914?). In writing of the Civil War, Bierce knew whereof he wrote. A veteran, with the Ninth Indiana Volunteers, of some of the bloodiest battles of the conflict, including Shiloh, Stones River, and Missionary Ridge, Bierce developed a grimly sardonic perspective on war and what it does to people. In the story collections *Tales of Soldiers and Civilians* (1891) and *Can Such Things Be?* (1893), and in the writings later collected as *Bits of Autobiography* (1909), Bierce returned almost obsessively to the war that had so colored his outlook on the world. Fascinated by the perceptual and experiential aspects of combat, in his fiction Bierce tends to hold at bay the broader ideological, and even military, contexts in which his characters operate, concentrating on situations and feelings that can seem abstracted from real history. Bierce disappeared during a sojourn into the state of Chihuahua to observe the Mexican Revolution.

Blackmar, Armand Edward (1826–1888). Sometimes called the "Voice of the South," the composer and music dealer Blackmar was actually born in Vermont and then lived in Ohio before heading south and setting up shop in New Orleans with his brother, Henry Clay Blackmar. There, Gen. Benjamin Butler fined him $500 for publishing pro-Confederate songs and ordered the destruction of his stores of printed music. Blackmar then headed for Georgia to resume publishing.

Booth, John Wilkes (1838–1865). We do not remember Booth for his writing, and it would be better not to have to remember him at all. But his writing sheds light on the assassination of Lincoln, and it seems to bear out the judgment that, rather than an act of insanity or deviltry, the killing was a rational "political murder," as John Rhodehamel and Louise Taper put it (*"Right or Wrong, God Judge Me"*, p. 2). Born in Baltimore as the son of Junius Brutus Booth, an accomplished tragic actor, Booth himself became a stage actor of some repute, and continued to perform during the Civil War. His identification with the

South growing more intense, Booth orchestrated an abortive plot to abduct Lincoln in the fall of 1864, but the actual assassination, on April 14, 1865, took place after Lee's surrender, and after Booth learned that Lincoln would be attending Laura Keene's performance of *Our American Cousin* at Ford's Theater. The details of the killing need not be rehearsed, but Booth's frame of mind in his final months is of documentary interest.

Bradbury, William B. (1816–1868). A native of Maine, Bradbury lived mostly in New Jersey and New York, where he started a piano manufacturing company. Better known for his religious music than his war music, Bradbury composed Sunday school songs and compiled songbooks for church choirs.

Chesnut, Mary (1823–1886). Of the many forms of autobiography to come out of the Civil War, Chesnut's diary is perhaps the most remarkable. Born into privilege in Camden, South Carolina, Chesnut received an excellent education and grew into a high-spirited, independent-minded woman. Her marriage to James Chesnut, Jr., a wealthy and well-connected politician (a moderate-turned-secessionist), gave Mary entrée to the inner circles of South Carolina and Washington DC society. In 1859 and 1860, before James resigned from the U.S. Senate, they enjoyed a vibrant time in the capitol, where she became close friends with Varina Davis, wife of Jefferson Davis. During the war, Mary Chesnut traveled between Richmond, Camden, Columbia, and the Chesnut plantation at Mulberry, and began her voluminous, rough-hewn, and riveting diary, an indispensable record of a Southern woman's perspective on the war and its participants. In the ruinous aftermath of war, Chesnut turned to other forms of writing, as she and her husband tried to rebuild their life, and began the long process of revising her diary for publication. It remained unpublished at her death, but the manuscript ended up in the hands of her friend Isabella D. Martin, who with Myrta Lockett Avary arranged for the publication of an edited version titled *A Diary from Dixie* (1905).

Chesnutt, Charles (1858–1932). During the darkest days of the post-Reconstruction South, Chesnutt sought, in three novels and two collections of short stories, to give full expression to the imaginative and cultural life of African Americans. A native of Fayetteville, North Carolina, who made his living as a legal stenographer in Cleveland, Chesnutt saw fiction as a means of shaping reality. His reimagining of plantation culture, his exploration of mixed-race experience, and his analysis of the springs of social history—all constituted a passionate rejoinder to the reduction and falsification of African American life in the literary genres of dialect fiction and local color, not to mention the popular press. Though not without later critics of a more aggressive political bent, Chesnutt's lonely battle against the literary status quo helped make their emergence more likely.

Chopin, Kate (1851–1904). Chopin's two cities were St. Louis, where she was born and raised and did almost all of her writing, and New Orleans, where she lived for ten years while married to Oscar Chopin and where she set her most famous work, *The Awakening* (1899). The stories she submitted to various magazines during the 1880s and 1890s were less scandalous than that novel, and generally reflected her liberal-minded Catholicism and sense of personal reserve. Most of Chopin's fiction has an ironic quality to it, a sensuality, a vaguely European sensibility, and a gentle touch that still allowed for flashes of outrage. She returned time and again to the theme of women's expressive potential, and in *Bayou Folk* (1894), explored the complex racial, social, and economic culture of southern Louisiana. During the Civil War, Chopin's family sided with the South, and her half-brother George O'Flaherty died from typhoid fever during his imprisonment as a Confederate soldier.

Crane, Stephen (1871–1900). Arguably the finest writer on the Civil War, or more precisely, on the individual soldier's complex experience of military service, Crane was not even born until six years after it ended. But the war gave Crane material for his signature themes: the human being under extreme pressure, the relation between the individual and the mass, the mechanization of war and society, the contrast between human ideals and universal indifference. His most important Civil War fiction includes *The Red Badge of Courage* (1895) and the stories collected in *The Little Regiment, and Other Episodes of the American Civil War* (1896). Based on his work as a war correspondent for the New York *World*, Crane also wrote a novel about the Greco-Turkish war, *Active Service* (1899), and he later drew on his reporting on the Spanish-American war for William Randolph Hearst's *Journal* for the collection *Wounds in the Rain* (1900). Crane's understanding of the Civil War, and of the society which emerged from it, cannot be separated from his experience covering these later conflicts, and his influence on the twentieth-century literary imagination is difficult to overstate. Crane died of a pulmonary hemorrhage brought on by tuberculosis.

Davis, Jefferson (1808–1889). He only reluctantly accepted the office of President of the Confederate States of America, but once the reins were in his hands, Davis saw it through to the bitter end and beyond. A Kentucky native, veteran of the annexation of Texas, and former cotton planter, Davis entered politics in the 1840s, and as a moderate states'-rights Senator from Mississippi tried to tamp down the forces of disunion—but ultimately cast his lot with his adopted state. His tactical and political leadership during the war was, and remains, controversial (could the South have won with a different President?), but his devotion to the cause is hard to question. After being imprisoned for two years, but never given the trial he would have welcomed, Davis became a popular and respected figure throughout the South, and showed no regret for his earlier course of action. In defeat, Davis found a poignant kind of personal victory.

Davis, Rebecca Harding (1831–1910). Raised in Washington, Pennsylvania, and Wheeling, Virginia, Davis gravitated toward literature at a young age, and practiced her hand at it, but it was not until she published "Life in the Iron Mills" in the *Atlantic* in 1861 that Davis put herself on the literary map. This story, an expose of industrial capitalism, bears the hallmarks of her style and ethos: a compassion for the downtrodden; an eye for detail; an interest in social and economic forces; a passionate narratorial voice; a Christian faith in the redeemability of humankind. These qualities characterize her first novel, *Margaret Howth* (1862), and her novel of the Civil War, *Waiting for the Verdict* (1867), and mark Davis as an important figure in the emergence of American realism and naturalism.

Dickinson, Emily (1830–1886). Born into a well-to-do Amherst family, Dickinson early showed an independent streak of mind, and after a brief stint at the Mount Holyoke Female Seminary, she lived quietly and privately, devoting herself to writing, but not publishing, poetry of strangely penetrating force. Since her verses tend to have an oblique, enigmatic, and enclosed quality about them, they can strike readers as disconnected from the larger political and cultural controversies of the nineteenth century. But these broader issues—from evolutionary theory to women's rights—had a powerful, fruitful impact on Dickinson's imagination. The Civil War, during which Dickinson wrote much of her best poetry, certainly informed her understanding of violence, nationalism, and religious faith. As both raw material and refractory representational challenge, the war served as a touchstone for Dickinson's incisive sketches of human fear, ambition, grief, and catharsis.

Douglass, Frederick (1818–1895). His years as an antislavery orator and his two antebellum autobiographies made Douglass the primary African American spokesman of the nineteenth century. From this position, he pushed for Northern victory in the war, which he regarded as an opportunity finally to defeat the scourge of slavery. In numerous essays and addresses, Douglass insisted that the war and its aftermath be understood as a struggle for freedom and civil rights, and sought to call his audience to a greater awareness of the racial issues at the heart of the conflict. In addition to active political employment, he devoted his post-war writing, including a third autobiography, to trying to diminish the power of American race hatred, and he "dearly hoped," writes David Blight, "that his own sense of self…would rest securely in new national traditions that he helped create" (*Frederick Douglass' Civil War*, 244)

Du Bois, William Edward Burghardt (1868–1963). Du Bois established himself as a scholar by earning a PhD in history from Harvard (the first conferred on an African American) and subsequently teaching at Wilberforce University and Atlanta University. Increasingly skeptical of academia's ability to effect major social change, however, he moved to New York and turned to political journalism, essays, and novels as his principal expressive outlets. Du Bois had long occupied the more militant wing of the African American political spectrum, and in the 1930s and 1940s deepened his involvement with communism and with the international pan-African movement. Many of his works have passed from notice, but in *The Souls of Black Folk* (1903), a rich and complex blend of sociology, art, and outrage, and a prerequisite to any adequate understanding of African American history and culture, Du Bois permanently changed the country's intellectual landscape.

Dunbar, Paul Laurence (1872–1906). His parents had been slaves in Kentucky before the war, and his father Joshua Dunbar served in the 55th Massachusetts—generating memories of violence and struggle that Dunbar absorbed as he developed his writing talents in Ohio's public schools. Like Charles Chesnutt, Dunbar struggled to give voice to African American experience while observing the rules of the late nineteenth-century American publishing industry. The result is a body of poetry and fiction expressing varying degrees of anger and accommodation. In *Oak and Ivy* (1893), *Majors and Minors* (1895), and other collections that combine dialect poetry and formal verse, Dunbar can seem ambiguously to celebrate the power of black folk traditions while pandering to the era's fascination with the antebellum plantation and its "picturesque" slaves. Other poems convey, in often subtle fashion, a stronger sense of cultural and political disfranchisement.

Emerson, Ralph Waldo (1803–1882). By the time civil war broke out, Emerson had become something of a dean of American, or at least Northern, cultural politics. After retiring from the Unitarian ministry in 1832, Emerson established himself, through his essays and lectures, as a preeminent social critic and one of the truly influential American philosophers. Increasingly committed to the antislavery cause during the 1840s and

1850s, the personally gentle Emerson welcomed the war as an opportunity to scourge the country of the blight of slavery and to align its national destiny with the will of God and Nature. As much as anything else, the realities and exigencies of full-scale war worked to temper Emerson's youthful exuberant idealism, although he never lost his lifelong belief in the power of character and the sanctity of the human spirit. Like many other abolitionists, however, Emerson's strong advocacy of emancipation and civil rights did not always comport smoothly with his condescending representation of African Americans.

Emmett, Daniel Decatur (1815–1904). The dubious American tradition of blackface minstrelsy owes much to the lyricist and composer Emmett, a founding member of the "Original Virginia Minstrels" in 1843 who continued to perform into the 1890s, with Al Field's Minstrels. The American folksong tradition also owes him for such tuneful chestnuts as "Turkey in the Straw" and "Blue Tail Fly." The peripatetic Emmett began and ended life in Mount Vernon, Ohio.

Finch, Francis Miles (1827–1907). The law came first for Finch, but literature was his mistress. A long-serving judge on the New York State Court of Appeals, Finch also developed profound connections to Cornell University, serving as trustee, counsel, lecturer in law, and then dean of the Law School. Most of his poetry was published after his death in *The Blue and the Gray, and Other Verses* (1909).

Frederic, Harold (1856–1898). For Frederic, who as an impressionable boy had witnessed with chagrin the Civil War's impact on small-town life in upstate New York, the conflict seemed neither an ordained struggle nor a glorious opportunity to destroy slavery, but an unnecessary disaster visited upon ordinary Americans. In his fiction about the war, most prominently *The Copperhead* (1893), *Marsena* (1894), and *In the Sixties* (1897) Frederic brought his journalistic eye to bear (he was London correspondent for the *New York Times*) in rendering how the war affected the rural community of Dearborn County (his fictional counterpart to Oneida County).

Garland, Hamlin (1860–1940). Another author whose star has unfortunately dimmed, Garland, for half a century, was as prolific as Henry James, in a variety of genres: the novel, the short story, the memoir, the essay. Born in Wisconsin, he lived as a young man in the "middle border" states of Iowa and South Dakota before relocating to Boston and then Chicago. This experience sensitized Garland to the social dynamic between the urban and the rural, the young and the old, and in his fiction he returns time and again to the relation between place, character, and idea. In *Crumbling Idols* (1894), his collection of essays on art and literature, Garland expressed his belief in the essential power of regional identification: "art, to be vital, must be local in its subject; its universal appeal must be in its working out,—in the way it is done."

Gilmore, Patrick Sarsfield (1829–1892). After emigrating to Boston from Ireland in 1849, Gilmore began establishing himself as one of the titans of American band music, composing, performing, and organizing festivals. Along with his band, Gilmore served in the 24th Massachusetts Infantry, and was named Bandmaster of the Union Forces in the Department of the Gulf, under Benjamin Butler's command in New Orleans. After the war, Gilmore organize several musical "peace jubilees" and served as bandmaster in the New York National Guard until his death.

Grant, Ulysses Simpson (1822–1885). Forward-leaning in war, Grant was unassuming in prose, and both qualities made him surpassingly effective as both a warrior and a writer. His *Memoirs*, written while Grant was terminally ill and heavily in debt, represent the retrospective view of a man who had led the Union to victory and served as President for eight years, but had been humbled by personal and professional setbacks. Grant's defining assets as a general were a clear grasp of the importance of logistics, a tactical and strategic flexibility, and an unflagging determination to succeed. These qualities underlay his successes in the Western theater, particularly the capture of Vicksburg, which propelled him to the top of the military hierarchy, from where he led the final long and grinding campaign against Lee in Virginia. Grant's memoirs, tracing his rise from humble origins but stopping short of his pockmarked Presidency, are remarkably free of the self-vindication, competitiveness, or revisionism that marred the accounts of many other Civil War veterans. Combined with their clarity and straightforwardness, this modesty has led the *Memoirs* to be recognized as one of the masterpieces of American autobiography.

Harris, Joel Chandler (1848 –1908). Harris bequeathed to American literature the legendary characters Uncle Remus and Brer Rabbit. He also left us a fierce debate about how his picturesque, nostalgic portrayal of life on the old plantation works both to undermine the image and interests of African Americans and to champion the weak against the powerful. A life-long resident of Georgia, a newspaperman from a young age, and a shy boy who never knew his father, Harris drew on his youthful "friendship" with two elderly slaves in writing stories that stage unexpectedly complex questions of reconciliation and violence, labor and power, comedy and tragedy, race and language.

Hawthorne, Nathaniel (1804–1864). One of the great fictional interpreters of early American history, Hawthorne met his match in the Civil War. Having returned from Europe to Concord in 1860, in ill health, Hawthorne only saw the war at a distance, but after a sojourn to Washington, DC in March 1862, he produced the anomalous "Chiefly About War Matters." Written in the tradition of the traveling observer of American ways and customs, the essay displays some of his characteristic writerly qualities: a suave mastery of the language, sharp irony, a disinclination to get political, the use of a narrator who tends to obscure the author's own thoughts. Fascinated by the relationship between moral psychology and national history, yet suspicious of "causes" and seemingly detached from the war's deeper meanings, Hawthorne may or may not have made an incisive analyst of the country's decisive cataclysm.

Higginson, Thomas Wentworth (1823–1911). Minister, poet, feminist, abolitionist, colonel, politician, author, and mentor of Emily Dickinson, Higginson lived a brimming life whose core values, he wrote in a late essay, were "the love of personal liberty, of religious freedom, and of the equality of the sexes." Having aided John Brown in planning the Harper's Ferry raid, and having raised a white Massachusetts regiment in 1862, Higginson jumped at the opportunity to organize and lead a black regiment in the Sea Islands of South Carolina. Out of this transformative experience he wrote *Army Life in a Black Regiment* (1869), a volume whose strange amalgam of personal affection, unconscious paternalism, and racial egalitarianism makes it a revealing study of radical thought at mid-century.

Holmes, Oliver Wendell, Jr. (1841–1935). As a lawyer, legal theorist, and Supreme Court Justice, Holmes had an abiding distrust of ideological abstractions. His approach to the law emphasized behavior rather than inner states of mind, the pragmatics of policy rather than legal philosophy. Louis Menand has traced this outlook to Holmes's experience in the Civil War, which "made him lose his belief in beliefs" and taught him that "certitude leads to violence" (*The Metaphysical Club*, 4, 61). Holmes served in the 20th Massachusetts Volunteers for three years, and was wounded three times, twice severely at Ball's Bluff and Antietam. In the mind of the jurist, the memory of the soldier never faded.

Horton, George Moses (1798? –c.1883). Though a slave, the self-styled "colored bard of North Carolina" made a living for himself, and a name, by selling poems in and around the college town of Chapel Hill. In his two pre-war collections, *The Hope of Liberty* (1829) and *The Poetical Works* (1845), Horton found a measure of expressive freedom (within the limits of his time and place), but legal freedom would only come with Emancipation. At the end of the Civil War, Horton traveled through North Carolina with a Capt. William Banks of the Michigan cavalry, gathering material and composing lyrics for a third volume, *Naked Genius* (1865). Only in this last collection did Horton not have to walk the razor's edge of trying to voice his discontent without alienating his white readers, and benefactors, and masters.

Howe, Julia Ward (1819–1910). The overmastering fame of "The Battle Hymn of the Republic" has somewhat obscured Howe's other activities and accomplishments, including her prolific writings in a variety of genres and her decades-long work in the abolitionist, women's suffrage, and peace movements. Along with her husband, Samuel Gridley Howe, she edited the Boston *Commonwealth*, an antislavery newspaper; directed the Perkins Institute for the Blind in New York; and was the first woman elected to the American Academy of Arts and Letters. Howe's feminism coexisted with a belief in the sacredness of domestic life, and her religiosity coexisted with a sharp sense of humor, all of which are on display in her collections *Passion Flowers* (1854), *Words for the Hour* (1857) and *Later Lyrics* (1866).

Jackson, Helen Hunt (1830–1885). In her ferocious literary and political advocacy of Native American rights, particularly in the history *A Century of Dishonor* (1881) and the novel *Ramona* (1884), Jackson turned to Harriet Beecher Stowe as a model of what a middle-aged white woman could accomplish in the cultural arena. A childhood friend of Emily Dickinson, and an adult friend of Thomas Higginson, Jackson began her literary career after the Civil War (during which her first husband, Maj. Edward B. Hunt, died in an accident on a Union submarine). But it was primarily through her later activism, including service as the first female Special Commissioner of Indian Affairs, that Jackson would make her mark on American history.

James, Henry (1843–1916). The main fact about James's relation to the Civil War was that his younger brothers enlisted while he did not, apparently disqualified from service by an "obscure hurt" (not necessarily physical) he claims having received in the spring of 1861. Unlike his brothers and many of his male peers, James turned inward, and toward the page, and began honing the writerly craft that would make him by century's end the country's most prolific, most influential, and most European novelist. In James's early fiction, including the Civil War stories "Poor Richard" (1867) and "A Most Extraordinary Case" (1868), we can see emerging his signature themes: heroic renunciation, the "life unlived," observation as experience, the delights of art and the imagination, the dangers of physicality.

Kittredge, Walter (1834–1905). A native of Merrimack, New Hampshire, Kittredge was a self-taught musician who performed both solo and with the Hutchinson Family musical troupe. For health reasons the "Minstrel of Merrimack" never served in the military, but he composed over 500 songs

Lanier, Sidney Clopton (1842–1881). A native son of Macon, Georgia, Lanier signed up enthusiastically at the beginning of war and fought for Southern independence for three years, before being captured aboard a blockade-running ship and imprisoned at Point Lookout, Maryland. After the war, he published *Tiger-Lilies* (1867), a rather labored and allegorical novel, and practiced law for several years with his father. In 1873, Lanier moved to Baltimore, where he lectured on literature at Johns Hopkins University, and began publishing poems, many of an agrarian or pastoral strain, in a variety of popular magazines. He died from tuberculosis.

Larcom, Lucy (1824–1893). Never privileged, Larcom's life was enriched by her love for nature and her sense of sisterhood with the working class. Having spent years working in the textile mills in Lowell, she attended the Monticello Female Seminary in Illinois before returning to Massachusetts and taking up work as a teacher, poet, and editor. She looked back fondly on her early life in *A New England Girlhood* (1889): "It still seems to me that in the Lowell mills, and in my log-cabin schoolhouse on the Western prairies, I received the best part of my early education." What she learned was the dignity of work and the vitality of ethics, and she put both into her studied, and steadied, poetry.

Lincoln, Abraham (1809–1865). The life and death of Lincoln are mythic to the point of opacity: his days as a lawyer in Illinois, his rise in Republican politics, his controversial leadership during the Civil War, his assassination at the hands of John Wilkes Booth. What is less well known is the impact of Lincoln's words, not just his ideas, on American political discourse. An unusually careful prose writer, simultaneously inventive and legalistically precise, Lincoln helped fashion a new kind of public language, one which eschewed ornateness, and in which metaphor worked organically with the literal meanings he wished to convey. What Whitman wrote of Lincoln's physical appearance could apply equally to his prose: "Of technical beauty it had nothing—but to the eye of a great artist it furnished a rare study, a feast and fascination."

Longfellow, Henry Wadsworth (1807–1882). Not many people read Longfellow anymore, but in the nineteenth century, the country's most famous poet—a central figure in the New England Renaissance—set the standard for what verse was supposed to do. His poems flowed easily, with natural-sounding rhythms, and presented little stylistic challenge for readers. Beneath the gracefulness of his meter, however, one can hear notes of sadness and tragedy. A professor at Bowdoin and later Harvard, Longfellow wrote on classical and mythological themes, but his most influential work—"Evangeline," "The Courtship of Miles Standish," "The Song of Hiawatha"—reflects his interest in local materials, and in helping a truly native American literature take root.

Melville, Herman (1819–1891). Melville made his reputation as the author of *Typee* (1846) and *Omoo* (1847), buoyant novels of South Sea adventure, and gradually squandered that reputation as the author of *Moby Dick* (1851), *Pierre* (1852), and other works whose stylistic and philosophical complexities confounded a reading public more accustomed to the literary sensibilities of Longfellow or Stowe. Melville's politics were unionist and antislavery, but not partisan, and he followed the Civil War from Massachusetts, and then New York, with an eye toward its poetic possibilities. His volume *Battle-Pieces and Aspects of the War* (New York, 1866) sold poorly and impressed few critics, but has gained increasing respect for its poetic originality and its willingness to explore the psychological and social subtleties of the conflict. Rebelling against his era's conventions of imagery and meter, Melville tried to convey the fractured experience of war in poems that, for the most part, are less concerned with lamentation, celebration, or moral judgment than with the impossibility of ethical and cultural certitude. They respond powerfully to specific scenes, states of mind, and philosophical ironies, but reflect Melville's misgivings about the war's meaning for American history.

Mitchell, Silas Weir (1829–1914). His pioneering clinical research on neurological disorders laid the foundation not only for Mitchell's medical fame but for his surprisingly productive literary career. As a surgeon during the Civil War at the Army's Filbert Street Hospital in Philadelphia, Mitchell witnessed a terrible variety of physical and psychic trauma, and from this experience wrote two medical treatises, *Gunshot Wounds and Other Injuries of Nerves* (1864; with George R. Morehouse and William W. Keen) and *Injuries of Nerves and Their Consequences* (1872), along with his first novel, *In War Time* (1884). The relation between mind and body, and the dependence of identity on corporeal integrity, fascinated Mitchell, and although his fiction can seem contrived, it is the richer for his medical insights—and vice versa.

Piatt, Sarah Morgan Bryan (1836–1919). Though unfairly considered a "minor" poet by her readers in the twentieth century, and by some today, Piatt was actually one of the more interesting American writers of the Victorian era. Raised in the border state of Kentucky, Piatt and her husband moved to Washington DC at the outbreak of civil war, and then to Ohio in 1867. Over a career spanning decades, Piatt wrote on family life, culture, and politics with a skeptical eye and a psychological complexity that the sentimental veneer of her poetry can sometimes obscure. Contemporary reviewers had some trouble understanding Piatt's originality of vision, but she is now beginning to receive the more serious reevaluation she deserves.

Pollard, Edward Alfred (1831–1872). Trained as a lawyer and journalist, this native son of Virginia became editor of the Richmond *Examiner* in 1861. From this post, his rabid advocacy of the Southern cause, combined with his public condemnations of Jefferson Davis, made Pollard an electrifying figure in Confederate politics. He published several books during the war, including *The Southern Spy* (1861), *The Rival Administrations* (1864), and the multi-part *Southern History of the War* (1862-66). In *The Lost Cause* (1866) and *The Lost Cause Regained* (1868), Pollard voiced an unrepentant, unreconstructed commitment to the principles of the defeated Confederacy.

Reese, Lizette Woodworth (1856–1935). A native of Waverly, Maryland, outside Baltimore, Reese was a school-teacher who wrote poetry of lasting significance. Published in a variety of journals great and small, from *Scribner's* to the *Midland*, and in a series of slender volumes including *A Branch of May* (1887), *A Handful of Lavender* (1891), *A Quiet Road* (1896), and *Spicewood* (1920), her poems celebrate nature, family life, and common things, without taking many words to do so, and without slavishly following poetic convention. In *A Victorian Village* (1929) Reese recalled her girlhood impressions of the Civil War, which divided her family as it did Maryland. "The romance and the sharper tragedy of war were everywhere about us.... Neighbor looked askance at neighbor.... Politics, which had been fearlessly public, became an entirely private affair, to be discussed behind drawn curtains and well-locked doors."

Root, George Frederick (1820–1895). After working as a composer and music teacher in New York, Europe, and his native state of Massachusetts, in 1859 Root became a partner in the successful Chicago firm of Root & Cady, publisher of sheet music for churches and schools. Root's "The First Gun Is Fired" (copyright April 18, 1861) is the first known published Civil War song.

Sawyer, Charles Carroll (1833–??). Sawyer was born in Connecticut, began writing poems at a young age, and moved to New York as a young man, where he was educated. Sawyer's songs were popular in both the North and South, and three of them, including "When This Cruel War Is Over," sold more than a million copies during the Civil War.

Sherman, William Tecumseh (1820–1891). The early indications were not promising, despite his excellence at West Point. After a series of unsuccessful business ventures and financial problems, Sherman rejoined the Army, becoming colonel in 1861, but had a mixed record in his early battles in the Western theater. Two crucial turning points were his command of Memphis, during which he began developing his concept of total war, and his effective service under Grant during the grueling Vicksburg campaign. Named commander of Western forces after Grant's promotion to Lieutenant General, Sherman began pushing into Georgia against Joseph Johnston and then John Bell Hood. After subduing Atlanta, Sherman's army cut a wide swath to Savannah, then up into South Carolina, destroying as much property as possible to in order to convince civilians of the futility of war. Having no particular animus toward Southerners, Sherman recommended lenient surrender terms and a nonvindictive Reconstruction policy. Sherman wrote his *Memoirs* while he served, rather unhappily, as commanding general of the United States Army, and they reflect the public personality of a man who had earned a profound understanding of both the details and the depths of war.

Stowe, Harriet Beecher (1811–1896). By any account, including Abraham Lincoln's, Stowe deserves some of the credit, or blame, for the outbreak of civil war. Her wildly popular abolitionist novel *Uncle Tom's Cabin* (1852) galvanized public opinion and contributed directly to the increasing animosity between North and South. Stowe's vision of the conflict over slavery was panoramic and apocalyptic, informed equally by her Christian piety, her belief in the redemptive power of domestic life, and her analytical approach toward social relations. Beginning in 1865, Stowe published a series of "Chimney-Corner" essays, some of which deal with the Civil War, but after the war she increasingly focused on religion, domesticity, and New England life rather than national politics.

Taylor, Susie King (1848–1912). Almost all of what we know about the life of Susie King Taylor—from her childhood as a slave to her work with the Woman's Relief Corps—she herself records in her autobiography, *Reminiscences of My Life in Camp* (1902). That memoir is remarkable not only in that it provides a woman's first-hand account of the business of war, but in that it creatively fuses two central genres of late nineteenth-century American literature, the slave narrative and the Civil War memoir. Doing so enabled her to focus on the war's emancipationist meaning from the perspective of direct experience rather than mere political theory.

Tourgée, Albion Winegar (1838–1905). A latecomer to antislavery who became a tireless, if rather strident, advocate of civil rights during and after Reconstruction, Tourgée was less a writer of the Civil War itself than, in his own words, of "the causes that underlay the struggle and the results that followed from it" (*An Appeal to Caesar* [New York, 1884], 44). He undertook this effort in a series of novelistic histories of the war, beginning with *A Fool's Errand* (1879) and concluding with *Bricks Without Straw* (1886), which drew on his experience both as a soldier and as a lawyer in postwar North Carolina, along with plenty of secondary reading. He regarded the conflict as one between enlightenment and barbarity, and mourned what he saw as the North's retreat from its principles as race hatred flourished in the South.

Watkins, Samuel Rush (1839–1901). A regular guy from around Columbia, Tennessee, Watkins went on to become one of the finest, most distinctive Southern writers the Civil War produced. As a private in Company H (the "Maury Greys") of the First Tennessee Infantry, Watkins served for the entire war, from the earliest skirmishes through Joseph Johnston's surrender to Sherman in April 1865. By the end of the war, both his company and regiment had suffered casualties in excess of 90 percent, but Watkins survived to return to Tennessee, earn a college degree, and start a family. What sets his memoir, *Co. Aytch*, apart from the pack of postwar retrospectives is its narrative voice: ironic, comic, outraged, modest, and perpetually fresh.

Whitman, Walt (1819–1892). His 1855 *Leaves of Grass* marks a watershed moment in American literature, when the polite verse of an age had to make room for the brash, earthy, and omnivorous poetry of a young rough from Brooklyn. Yet in Whitman's own words, the Civil War "completed" him. It gave him the raw material that, in *Drum-Taps* (1865), and in his prose works *Memoranda During the War* (1876) and *Specimen Days and Collect* (1882), he worked and reworked, reaching for an understanding of the war's commanding significance for human beings and for the country. That material, however, was bought dear. After traveling to Washington DC to find his younger brother George, who had been wounded at the battle of Fredericksburg, and seeing there the war's wounded, Whitman began working as a volunteer nurse at army hospitals in Washington. In about three years of such work, according to biographer David Reynolds, Whitman tended to between 80,000 and 100,000 soldiers (*Walt Whitman's America*, 425). The physical trauma and emotional suffering he observed changed Whitman's imagination, even as the war itself seemed to be cleansing the nation, disencumbering it of a terrible burden, and even as he appreciated something of the romance of battle. His writings on the war—sketches, snapshots, reflections, essays—show Whitman to be one of the conflict's foremost interpreters.

Winner, Septimus (1827–1902). Winner wrote some of the major musical hits of the nineteenth century, including "Ten Little Indians," the "Hawthorne Ballads" (under the pseudonym Alice Hawthorne), and a number of Civil War songs. After penning a ditty in support of the recently fired George McClellan ("Give Us Back Our Old Commander"), Winner was ordered arrested by Secretary of War Edwin Stanton, but was subsequently pardoned by Lincoln.

Work, Henry Clay (1832–1884). Over the course of his life, the printer and songwriter, Work, published upwards of seventy pieces, most of which dated from the 1860s. Born into a family with strong antislavery views in Middletown, Connecticut, Work spent much of his life in New York and Chicago—working with the musical firm Root & Cady—before returning to Hartford, Connecticut.

PERMISSIONS

"The Battle Hymn" by Stephen Crane from *The Works of Stephen Crane*, Vol. X, edited by Fredson Bowers (Charlottesville, Virginia, 1975) reprinted with permission of the University of Virginia Press.

"A Day! Help! Help!" (1859), "Success – is counted sweetest" (1859, 1862), "To fight aloud is very brave –" (1860), "The name – of it – is 'Autumn' –" (1862), "Whole Gulfs – of Red, and Fleets – of Red –" (1862), "They dropped like Flakes –" (1863), "If any sink, assure that this, now standing –" (1863), "The Battle fought between the Soul" (1862), "My Portion is Defeat – today –" (1863), "The hallowing of Pain" (1863), "My Triumph lasted till the Drums" (1871), and "'Tis Seasons since the Dimpled War" (1881) by Emily Dickinson are reprinted by permission of the publishers and the Trustees of Amherst College from *The Poems of Emily Dickinson: Reading Edition*, edited by Ralph W. Franklin, Cambridge, Massachusetts, The Belknap Press of Harvard University Press. Copyright © 1998, 1999 by the President and Fellows of Harvard College. Copyright © 1951, 1955, 1979, 1983 by the President and Fellows of Harvard College.

"The Soldier's Faith," May 30, 1895 by Justice Oliver Wendell Holmes reprinted by permission of the publisher from *The Occasional Speeches of Justice Oliver Wendell Holmes*, compiled by Mark DeWolfe Howe, pp. 78–83, Cambridge, Massachusetts, The Belknap Press of Harvard University Press. Copyright © 1962 by the President and Fellows of Harvard College, Copyright © renewed 1990.

"Retrospective," "Chattanooga," and "The Surrender" by Sam R. Watkins from *"Co. Aytch": A Confederate Memoir of the Civil War*, by Sam R. Watkins, edited by Roy P. Basler (New York: Simon & Schuster, 1962, 1990, 2003) are reprinted with permission of Scribner, an imprint of Simon & Schuster Adult Publishing Group.

INDEX

6517001

810.9358
F516

LINCOLN CHRISTIAN UNIVERSITY

121373

3 4711 00199 6729